IRELAND SINCE THE FAMINE

VOLUME II

F. S. L. Lyons

We had fed the heart on fantasies,
The heart's grown brutal from the fare;
More substance in our enmities
Than in our love . . .
      w. b. yeats, 'The Stare's Nest by
      My Window', from *The Tower*, 1928

Fontana Press

First published in Great Britain by
Weidenfeld and Nicolson 1971
First issued in 1973 by Fontana Paperbacks,
8 Grafton Street, London W1X 3LA
Eighth impression May 1982
Ninth impression, in Fontana Press, March 1985

Printed in Great Britain by
Clays Ltd, St Ives plc

FOR JOHN AND NICHOLAS

The author and publisher wish to express their thanks
to M. B. Yeats and Macmillan and Company Limited for
permission to quote from the poems of William Butler
Yeats on the title page and on pages 241 and 368.

ISBN 978-0-00-733095-9

Contents

PART IV

The Partitioned Island

A. FROM FREE STATE TO REPUBLIC

B. NORTH IRELAND UNDER HOME RULE

It is the paradox of all revolution that it paralyses the creative impulse from which it sprang. Its origin a principle, its end a formula – such is its fatal cycle. L. KOHN, *The Constitution of the Irish Free State*, p. 108

A. FROM FREE STATE TO REPUBLIC

---

1. Building the New State

(i) THE FOUNDATIONS

That the revolutionary of today is the conservative of tomorrow is a truism of politics in no way contradicted by the recent history of modern Ireland. But it is, perhaps, less often observed that the revolutionary becomes a conservative, not just because of the sobering influence of power upon responsible individuals, but also because revolutions, even when they appear to be most successful, frequently preserve as much as they destroy. The Irish revolution, though it succeeded to a far greater extent than had at one time seemed remotely possible, nevertheless ended in compromise and if the compromise seemed then, and has proved since, ephemeral, yet its very existence helped to bring into play that tension between the revolutionary and the conservative elements in Irish society which dominated the political life and institutions of the new state in its earliest years.

The most striking illustration of this is to be found in the Constitution itself. The Constitution of the Irish Free State (Saorstát Eireann) Act of 1922 embodied a highly ingenious attempt, if not to have the best of both worlds, at least to bridge those two worlds in such a way as to reconcile the ideals of the recent revolutionary past with the necessity of a continuing British connection. Thus, on the one hand, the preamble to the Act echoed the revolutionary doctrine of popular sovereignty in the phrase 'all lawful authority comes from God to the people', a doctrine restated more concretely in Article 2 of the actual Constitution, where it was laid down unequivocally that 'all powers of government and all authority legislative, executive and judicial in Ireland, are derived from the people of Ireland'. On the other hand, not only was the Crown retained at various points in the document, but the second clause of the Act made it clear that the Constitution was to be construed 'with reference to the Articles of Agreement for a Treaty between Great Britain and Ireland . . . which are hereby given the force of law, and if any provision of the said Constitution or of any amendment thereof or of any law made thereunder is in any respect repugnant to any of the provisions of the Scheduled Treaty it shall, to the extent of such repugnancy, be absolutely void and inoperative'. In short the Treaty, which was intended to hold the new dominion within the confines of the Commonwealth, was made a part of the municipal law of the state – so much so that when the new Constitution was being debated in the Dáil members were informed

471

that the articles implementing the Treaty (and also certain others designed to safeguard the rights of minorities) were regarded by ministers as so vital that their rejection would involve the resignation of the government.[1]

From the very beginning, therefore, the Constitution seemed to point in two quite different directions. But its contradictions did not end there. For not only did it seek to harmonise republican ideals with membership of the Commonwealth, it also attempted to combine the pragmatic British approach to the business of government with an attachment to those ringing declarations of human rights which were common to so many revolutionary constitutions in various parts of the world after 1918 and of which the Democratic Programme of the first Dáil had been an early example. It must be admitted, however, that the Constitution of 1922 fell a good deal short of the Democratic Programme and it was perhaps significant of the way in which the first, fine, careless rapture of revolutionary radicalism was already fading that the attempts made by some Labour members to bring the social content of the Constitution more into line with the doctrines of James Connolly came to nothing.[2] In fact, only two 'programmatic' declarations were embodied in the Constitution – one asserting the right (in practice it turned out to be a compulsion) of all citizens to free elementary education, the other providing for the legal succession of the Free State to all rights in lands, waters, mines and minerals within the territory of the Free State previously held by the Crown or a Department of State, and *also* investing the Free State with a general title to the control of all natural resources of the country and of all franchises and royalties to be derived from their exploitation. Although in practice the latter article was rarely invoked, and then on a very limited scale, it opened the way to a thorough-going policy of nationalisation of the country's resources should that ever be deemed necessary; so to this extent the old radicalism, if muted since 1919, still made itself heard.[3]

But it was not just social rights that the Constitution undertook to protect. In addition, by Articles 6 to 9, it expressly guaranteed such personal rights as *habeas corpus*, the inviolability of the citizen's dwelling, freedom to practise any religion ('subject to public order and morality'), freedom of expression and freedom of association. There was, of course, nothing particularly novel about these provisions; they were simply the embodiment in a written instrument of a familiar liberal tradition and did not involve any departure from the legal framework within which the authors of the Constitution themselves had grown up. But it was felt necessary – chiefly for the reassurance of the Protestant minority – to go rather further and to prohibit the state from endowing any religion, imposing any disability on account of religious belief or status, affecting prejudicially 'the right of any child to attend a school receiving public money without attending the religious instruction at the school', discriminating between schools managed by different denominations, or acquiring church property by compulsion except for certain clearly defined public purposes and then only after payment of compensation.[4]

This, however, was not the only protection minorities received under the Constitution. The very day the Treaty was signed Arthur Griffith had met three representative Unionists and had, it seems, given them two assurances. One was that proportional representation would be used for elections to the Dáil, and the other was that they should have due representation in the upper house, the Senate. A few weeks before his death in August 1922 Griffith met the southern Unionists again and concluded with them what were later called 'Heads of Agreement' relating more specifically to the composition and powers of the Senate, upon which many of the Protestant minority were coming to pin their chief hope for the future. Griffith's proposal that the Senate should be elected by proportional representation from a panel two-thirds nominated by the Dáil and one-third by the Senate itself was extremely cumbersome and had soon to be simplified. Of more immediate importance was the concession that in the first Senate half the sixty members would be elected by the Dáil and half would be nominated by the President of the Executive Council (Prime Minister) 'in manner calculated to represent minorities or interests not adequately represented in the Dáil'. The Unionists fought hard to secure that the Senate would have an effective power of suspending legislation, but the best they could achieve was the right to hold up bills for 270 days instead of the year they had sought for. They would have liked also, in cases of disputed legislation, to press for a joint sitting of both houses with joint voting; they were allowed the empty formula of a joint session, but the withholding of a joint vote deprived this of much of its meaning.

Although the Unionist minority professed themselves disappointed with the outcome, they recognised nevertheless that there had been a genuine effort to meet their demands 'and to integrate them into the new state. That such an effort had been made was emphasised by Kevin O'Higgins, who had shared with Griffith in the later stages of the negotiations, when he spoke in the Dáil about the minority problem shortly after Griffith's death:

> These people [he said] are part and parcel of the nation, and we being the majority and strength of the country . . . it comes well from us to make a generous adjustment to show that these people are regarded, not as alien enemies, not as planters, but that we regard them as part and parcel of this nation, and that we wish them to take their share of its responsibilities.[5]

The government was as good as its word. Of the first thirty senators to be nominated, sixteen could be said to have been broadly Unionist in their sympathies, and a seventeenth, W. B. Yeats, though certainly no Unionist, was very conscious of his Anglo-Irish heritage. The group included a number of those 'constructive Unionists' who had tried to bridge the gap between their order and the rest of the country before 1914 - for example, Sir Horace Plunkett, the Earl of Dunraven, the Earl of Mayo, the dowager Countess of Desart - and the high quality of debate in the Senate owed a great deal to them. But nothing could conceal the fact that debate did not often issue in action, and that the special position the Unionists had achieved in the Senate was not much more than a special position enabling them to watch the work of the dominant lower house from close quarters.[6]

The Dáil was deliberately intended to be dominant, not just over the Senate, but over the executive government as well. Its membership, being determined by the size of the population, was subject to periodic revision, but during the first decade of the Constitution's working was fixed at 153, including three representatives for each of the two universities then existing. The members were elected by proportional representation (the single transferable vote) on the basis of universal adult suffrage for a normal term of six years. The rules governing procedure followed British practice very closely (those governing privilege were more narrowly drawn) but although the convocation and dissolution of parliament were nominally vested in the representative of the Crown (i.e. the Governor-General), again on the British model, the exercise of those powers was expressly vested in the Dáil itself. Thus, while the Executive Council (cabinet) could advise a dissolution it could only do so when it had a majority. If it lost its majority then the Executive Council had no option but to resign and leave the task of forming a new government to its opponents.[7] This was a notable departure from English and dominion practice and was inspired at least in part by the desire to demonstrate the supremacy of the legislature over the executive.

This desire expressed itself also in other ways, some of them novel and even bizarre. The framers of the Constitution appear to have recognised that they needed cabinet government more or less after the British fashion, but at the same time to have recoiled from entrusting to ministers the degree of independence which that implied. Thus, while provision was made for the Executive Council to consist of a President and certain other ministers, not only was the President himself to be chosen by the Dáil, but his nominations for the various posts in the Executive Council had also to be approved by the lower house. This emphasis upon the authority of the Dáil was, however, only partly a tribute to the concept of popular sovereignty. It seems to have sprung also from a feeling that the effect of proportional representation would be to do away with large and strong parties on the British model. Even Kevin O'Higgins, who, as we shall see, was more closely identified with strong government than anyone else, appears to have shared this feeling. 'We will have groups here', he said in the Dáil on one occasion, 'small groups of seven or eight. We will not have parties on definite lines of political cleavage.' The moral he drew from this was that they would not have cabinet government either. Wanting, as he claimed, the maximum of individual liberty for deputies in the Dáil, he maintained that this could not be achieved 'by adhering to collective responsibility'.[8]

What this meant in practice was a strange departure from the cabinet system as ordinarily understood. In the draft Constitution submitted to the Constituent Assembly it was proposed, in addition to the 'parliamentary' type members of the Executive Council, to have certain others – 'extern' ministers – who would not be subject to collective responsibility with the rest of the Council, but would be directly and individually responsible to the Dáil. The practical reason for having them was the perfectly laudable one of bringing people with specific expertise into the work of government, but there was also a doctrinaire reason – that through such ministers it would be possible for the Dáil to exercise very direct control over the departments for which they would be responsible. Since the original draft envisaged, apart from the President, only four ministers of the normal 'parliamentary' kind and no less than eight 'extern' ministers, it can be seen how strong was the urge to turn the Executive Council away from the more conventional lines of cabinet development.

It is rather harder to see how this device can ever have been expected to work satisfactorily and it was, perhaps, the measure of the immaturity of the new government that it could have imagined it would be possible to accommodate, as it were on two separate planes, the technical ministers and those who controlled the purse-strings and the other realities of power. Not surprisingly, the scheme was modified in debate, emerging in the Constitution as a provision for a normal cabinet of not less than five and not more than seven (all members of the Dáil and collectively responsible to it), together with such other 'extern' ministers (doubly extern in that they were no longer to be members of the Executive Council) as would provide a total ministry of not more than twelve. Moreover, the appointment of the extern ministers was to be permissive only, not mandatory as had first been proposed. These extern ministers were to be chosen by the Dáil but need not be members of that body. Whether such a device as the two-tier executive could ever have been fitted into the machinery of parliamentary government, even in the most favourable circumstances, is highly problematical. As things were, the circumstances could hardly have been more unfavourable. Not only the fact that clearly-defined parties at once emerged in the Dáil (contrary to the expectations of the 'experts'), but also the need to govern strongly in a time of serious unrest, led the President of the Council, Mr Cosgrave, to rely much more upon his ordinary ministers and much less upon his extern ones. The latter did, indeed, play a considerable part in the administration of the country, and one of them, Patrick

Hogan, was an outstanding Minister of Agriculture, but the whole concept soon changed its character under the impact of experience. Not only were the extern ministers in actuality government nominees backed by the government majority in the Dáil, they were also expected to observe practical, if not theoretical, cabinet responsibility like their more conventional colleagues. It could hardly have been otherwise. The original idea behind the innovation had assumed a Dáil where there would be no rigid parties and a great deal of free voting. But once a party system of the old, familiar kind emerged the extern ministers rapidly became superfluous. The experiment was virtually abandoned after a constitutional amendment in 1927 and from 1928 onwards no more were appointed.[9]

Much the same fate befell the two other provisions of the Constitution intended to emphasise the doctrine of popular sovereignty – those relating to the referendum and the power of initiative. Both of these devices were intended to associate the people directly with the legislative process. They had a long history behind them but had suddenly become fashionable after 1918 when so many of the new constitutions then being worked out laid deliberate emphasis upon this aspect of democracy. The framers of the Constitution of the Free State were no doubt aware of, and perhaps to some extent influenced by, the experiments that were taking place more or less simultaneously in other countries, but it has been suggested by Professor Mansergh that, in spirit at least, the Irish provisions looked back to an earlier and more individualist tradition. In Ireland, as he rightly says, there was no general acceptance of an organic view of the state and the rules in the Constitution governing direct legislation by referendum and initiative were intended, as he puts it, 'to provide, not a representation of the people's will, but rather a safeguard for individual rights'.[10] Such an interpretation fits well with the Irishman's traditional attitude towards government. Like Calvin Coolidge's preacher on the subject of sin, he was, in general, 'against it'. The insertion of machinery for direct legislation with the Constitution, therefore, served two purposes. On the one hand, in theory at least, it provided a popular check on what might become an over-mighty government. And on the other it could be argued, and was argued during the constitutional debates, that 'personal actual contact between the people and the laws by which they are governed' was highly advisable in a country where the laws and those who had administered them had for so long been regarded as alien, and when, for this very reason, political education and experience were conspicuously lacking.

Alas for these great expectations. Referendum and initiative alike had a short life and a dismal one. It was indeed laid down that after a preliminary period of eight years (later extended to sixteen) no amendment of the Constitution could take place without a referendum, but on ordinary legislation the procedure was optional.[11] And even this optional procedure was limited by the two important qualifications that Money Bills were excluded from it, and also 'such Bills as shall be declared by both Houses to be necessary for the immediate preservation of the public peace, health or safety'.[12] In the early years of the Free State the government had frequent recourse to this escape clause and the elaborate machinery provided by the Constitution was left to rust. It had been intended that this machinery should allow the government's opponents in either house of the Oireachtas an opportunity of submitting any ordinary Bill of which they disapproved to the people at large. Such a Bill, even if it had been passed by the government majority, could be suspended for ninety days on the written demand (presented to the President of the Executive Council not later than seven days after the Bill had been passed) of two-fifths of the members of the Dáil or a majority of the members of the Senate. During this period of suspension the Bill might be submitted to a referendum, but only if the Senate passed a resolution demanding this and assented to by three-fifths of its members, or, alternatively, if a petition were presented signed by not less than one-twentieth of the voters. In the event, the Senate never used the power conferred on it by the Constitution – there would have been a most dangerous collision with the lower house if it had done – and although a minority in the Dáil did employ the suspensory weapon to hold up the Electoral Amendment Act of 1927 (the cause of a major party battle which will be described in the next section) it proved impossible to obtain the necessary number of signatures for a petition demanding a referendum.

The referendum has sometimes been described as the way in which the people can rectify their representatives' sins of commission. Likewise, the initiative, the power to propose new legislation, can be seen as the people's opportunity to rectify their representatives' sins of omission. But in the light of experience in many countries the tendency has been to regard such 'direct' legislation – whether by referendum or initiative – with diminishing enthusiasm. It has been criticised as crude, ill-informed, incoherent and even anarchical in its interference with the normal working of representative institutions, intolerant of racial and religious minorities and – worst of all, perhaps – as opening the way to the irresponsibility of the anonymous legislator.[13] The authors of the Free State Constitution seem to have shared these misgivings, for Article 48 of the Constitution begins with the permissive phrase – 'the Oireachtas may provide for the initiation by the people for proposals for laws or constitutional amendments'. Should it fail to do this within two years (and it did fail) then it was laid down that on a petition signed by not less than 75,000 voters – of whom not more than 15,000 were to belong to one constituency – the Oireachtas would then be obliged either to set up the necessary machinery or to submit the question to a referendum, and even this was hedged round with qualifications to make difficult the initiation of laws or amendments of the constitution.

On the other hand, Article 48 did open the way for a very small minority to raise fundamental issues and in a deeply divided country such as the Irish Free State that could have all sorts of repercussions. Realising this, a cabinet sub-committee recommended as early as 1924 that both the referendum and the initiative should be abolished. Nothing was done, however, with the result that three years later the government was confronted with a major crisis. By then Fianna Fáil had emerged as a large and potentially powerful party and after its entry into the Dáil it proceeded to carry out an intense propaganda campaign in the country, which resulted in a petition signed by 96,000 voters being presented to the Dáil in May 1928, demanding the abolition of the parliamentary oath, and so presaging a general attack upon the Treaty.* The government countered by introducing a Bill – of which, admittedly, it had given notice at the preceding general election – for the abolition of the referendum and initiative. There followed three weeks of intense and bitter debate which, though ostensibly devoted to the merits and demerits of direct legislation, was, as everyone well knew, simply a continuation of the old quarrel over the Treaty. In the end, the government, by frequent use of the guillotine, fought its measure through both houses. It was still open to the opposition to demand a referendum under Article 50 of the Constitution, but here too, Mr Cosgrave and his colleagues outflanked their opponents by declaring the Bill to be 'necessary for the immediate preservation of the public peace and safety' and as such not to be referred back to the people. The referendum (save for such constitutional amendments as might be enacted after a further period of eight years from 1929) and the initiative thereupon both disappeared from the law of the land.

It has been necessary to dwell at some length on these intricate details of the Constitution because they point to a conclusion of the highest importance for the future of the Irish Free State. It is clear that the events of the period up to 1927 had belied Kevin O'Higgins's expectation that the Dáil would be made up of small groups of deputies independent of party ties. It is hard, indeed, to see how such a prophecy could ever have been realised in the existing conditions of the time. The sort of 'deliberative assembly' that O'Higgins envisaged might conceivably have been possible, though even this is arguable, had there existed in the country a large measure of agreement about the sanctity of the Treaty and the future of the Irish Free State as a developing dominion within the framework of the British Commonwealth. But of course there was no consensus. The split that had led to the Civil War remained unhealed. All that had really happened was that the main opponents of the new regime – Mr de Valera and his friends – by refusing to take the parliamentary oath of allegiance had allowed the pro-Treaty party or parties to

* For the political background to the constitutional crisis, see below, pp. 498-9.

govern without exposing the weaknesses and deficiencies of the Constitution. When Fianna Fáil eventually did decide to enter the Dáil, it was natural that they should want to exploit these weaknesses and deficiencies, with the inevitable result that the period 1927-32 was one of almost incessant crisis.

However, from Mr de Valera's decision to participate in constitutional politics a second and even more far-reaching consequence was to flow. The very fact that after 1927 two major parties, deeply divided on fundamental issues and by passionately held principles, confronted each other in parliament could only serve to reduce the margin for constitutional experimentation. What mattered most was not that some delicately balanced lever should be pulled to elicit a free vote in the country or the Oireachtas on this issue or on that, but that a government should either rule on the basis of a well-organised majority in the Dáil, or else get out and make way for another that could. In short, a two-party dialectic became the norm of Irish politics and with it the acceptance of that fully-fledged cabinet system from which the founders of the state had been struggling to escape. As has been well said, 'the logic of the British system reasserted itself'.[14]

It was a logic that dictated continuity, not change. And if this were true of parliamentary institutions, it was even more true of other areas of government where any kind of violent break with the past was an invitation to anarchy. We find, therefore, that the same ministers who established the Constitution engaged almost simultaneously in an intensive programme of legislation to set the day-to-day administration of the country on a sound footing. By any standards this programme would have been a formidable achievement, but at a time when much of Ireland was still in the grip of Civil War or its aftermath, it was an astonishing performance. Some aspects of it will be dealt with later, but here it is necessary to single out the measures which laid the foundations for the firm and efficient government that rapidly became the hallmark of the Free State. The most important of these concerned the civil service, the police, the law courts and the whole domain of local government. It was decided by the new regime to take advantage of the transfer of power in order to make an end of the old jumble of boards and councils and put a more coherent structure in its place. This was the intention behind the Ministers and Secretaries Act of 1924 which brought all the various administrative bodies together into a system based on eleven ministerial departments – those of the President of the Executive Council, Finance, Justice, Local Government and Public Health, Lands and Agriculture, Industry and Commerce, Fisheries, Posts and Telegraphs, Education, Defence, and External Affairs. A little later (in 1928) Agriculture became a separate department and Lands and Fisheries were amalgamated, but apart from that the structure remained unchanged up to the Second World War. During and after the war other departments were added, mainly to deal with enlarged social services, but in essence the system introduced in 1924 has survived to the present, though it has latterly been subjected to criticism as being too rigid and too conservative for the rapidly changing circumstances of the modern age. Following a recent exhaustive inquiry (the Devlin Report), it is to be expected that the 'seventies will see considerable modernisation and also, no doubt, the expansion in size which always seems to follow civil service reform.

In two respects this system, while improving on the haphazard arrangements inherited from Britain, yet followed British precedent. First, the Ministry of Finance rapidly established a dominance over other departments reminiscent of the Treasury's supremacy in Whitehall. And second, the government acted quickly (by the Civil Service Regulation Act of 1923 and by other subsequent legislation) to set up Civil Service Commissioners to supervise the recruitment of candidates into the service. The establishment of this body, which has acted with great efficiency and impartiality ever since, did more than anything else to ensure that the new state would escape, at least in its central administration, the worst evils of the spoils system. It was a help, of course, that many of the senior officials appointed under British rule agreed to stay on, so that some years later a Commission of Inquiry was able to report that there had been no disturbance 'of any fundamental kind' and that 'the same main tasks of administration continued to be performed by the same staffs on the same general basis of organisation and procedure'.[15] At the time of the changeover there were 21,000 civil servants and while some of these left and others were hastily recruited under what amounted to war-time conditions, the service did not change either its character or its numbers. In the mid-thirties it was still no more than 20,000 strong and even by the mid-fifties numbered about 33,000, of whom roughly a half were in the Post Office.[16] On this stable, and by no means excessively broad base, has been reared, it is not too much to say, the entire edifice of Irish central government.*

Simultaneously with their drive to create a more coherent system of administration, ministers were turning their attention to the courts and to the police. It was a remarkable gesture of confidence in the future that in 1923, although the country was still deeply disturbed, Mr Cosgrave and his colleagues took the decision to create in the Free State an unarmed police force that would contrast favourably with the old semi-military RIC and with its lineal descendant, the RUC, which was at that time being set up in Northern Ireland.

* It has been pointed out that if those employed by local authorities and the state-sponsored bodies are included, the total in the public service rose from about 90,500 in 1940 to 134,200 in 1965; the percentage share of the total labour force absorbed by the public service went up in the same period from 6.9 to 12.1 (B. Chubb, *The Government and Politics of Ireland*, p. 222).

This force, the Garda Siochana (or Civic Guard), was at first a temporary improvisation but was given permanence by an Act of 1924 and, aimost from the start, was an unqualified success, vanquishing by its record the fears of those who had predicted that a national police force would become an instrument of government tyranny.

The Civic Guard derived originally from republican police called into being by the exigencies of the Anglo-Irish war. The same exigencies had led, as we have seen, to the emergence of so-called 'Dáil Courts' administering the law at various levels in increasingly successful competition with the established courts which still functioned under British rule. Once power had been transferred, however, the government lost no time in getting rid of the Dáil Courts and the last of them was abolished before the end of 1922. The following year parliament made provision for the formal winding-up of their proceedings and the way was clear for a thorough-going reconstruction of the ordinary courts of law. This in its turn was carried out by the Courts of Justice Act of 1924, establishing a hierarchy ranging from the District Courts at the bottom, through the Circuit Courts, the High Court, and the Court of Criminal Appeal to the Supreme Court at the top. The new hierarchy differed in some significant ways from the old. For example, the time-honoured Justice of the Peace disappeared, as did the more recent and more disliked Resident Magistrate, and the old Petty Sessions gave place to District Courts presided over by paid District Justices.[17] Again, the familiar County Court was abolished, to be replaced by Circuit Courts, each Court being assigned a circuit representing about 400,000 people and having very considerable jurisdiction in both civil and criminal matters. These two reforms between them went far to achieve the main object of government policy which was, by decentralising the administration of justice, to give the citizen quicker and less costly access to the law. At the centre also there was considerable rationalisation. Here the main innovations were the creation of the Court of Criminal Appeal; the position given to the High Court by the provision (Article 65 of the Constitution) that in all cases respecting the provisions of the Constitution it alone should have original jurisdiction; and the setting up of the Supreme Court as the final court of appeal, not only from the High Court (and in certain circumstances from the Court of Criminal Appeal as well) but also as the final arbiter in matters respecting the constitutionality of legislation.[18] The right of the individual to apply for leave to appeal to the Judicial Committee of the Privy Council was, of course, expressly safeguarded by the Constitution and nothing in the powers of the Supreme Court was to be allowed to impair this right.

It should be stressed that these changes, far-reaching though they were, were essentially changes of practice and procedure rather than of principle. The Free State still retained much in its legal system that was inherited from Britain. The tenure of judges during good behaviour, for example, was carried over into the new structure, though it was not until 1946 that this was extended to District Justices. The legal profession continued to be recruited and trained, and even to dress, much as before. Above all, the law that they professed was still essentially the common law as it had evolved over the centuries.[19]

In local government, as in the central administration, the new broom swept relentlessly clean. Over much of Ireland the local authorities, which even at the best of times had often been too small and too poor to be very effective, had been hard hit by the insecurity of life and property during the turbulent years between 1919 and 1923. What was most urgently needed was to reorganise the system brought into being by the Act of 1898 so as to create units of government which would be both competent and economically viable. At first, too, it was hoped that in this sphere, as in the law, real decentralisation would be feasible. In practice this proved to be difficult, partly because the country continued disturbed for so long, partly because local authorities came to depend increasingly upon the government in Dublin for a large part of their revenue, and partly also, it must be said, because it was not always possible to root out incompetence, corruption or simple self-interest from the local administration.

As we have already seen, the Ministers and Secretaries Act of 1924 set up the Ministry of Local Government and Public Health as a new department. Very soon it acquired a wide variety of functions, but from the outset its main concern was with the local councils and their constant struggle to deal with the often urgent problems of the poor law, public health, housing and the upkeep of roads – to name only a few of their most important responsibilities. So that these problems might be tackled with more resources and better hope of success the Local Government Act of 1925 remodelled the whole system. Negatively, it got rid of the Rural Districts, those small and generally impoverished sub-divisions of the counties which had been spawned by the Act of 1898. Positively, the new legislation provided for a different kind of administrative unit – the County Health District. In most parts of the Free State the County Health Districts coincided with the boundaries of the actual counties (though urban districts were excluded from their purview) and the County Councils (which had been in existence since 1898) were made the sanitary authorities for the County Health Districts, exercising their power through Boards of Health composed of ten members from each Council; to these Boards also, in most cases, was entrusted the business of administering public assistance to the very poor. So long as British rule had lasted, this assistance had been closely linked to the nineteenth century workhouse system and although outdoor relief had become more common as time went on, so far as the destitute were concerned (and many of the sick and mentally afflicted as well), the workhouse had continued to overshadow their penurious lives. By an Act of 1923 the new government remodelled this system also. Public assistance was organised on a county basis, most of the old Poor Law Unions were amalgamated and many of the workhouses were closed. Some were metamorphosed into the County Homes which the Act undertook to provide for the aged and infirm. In addition, County and District Hospitals were to be made available to the sick, while the able-bodied poor were to be relieved as far as possible in their own homes. To be poor in Ireland would still be a bleak enough fate after 1923 – and to be poor and ill would be still worse – but at least it could be claimed that the state was making a determined effort to break away from the Victorian conception which for so long had seemed to assume that poverty was *prima facie* evidence of some delinquency or deficiency in the pauper.

The changes brought about by the new Local Government Act produced a pattern of twenty-seven administrative counties and four county boroughs, each electing its own Council as the rate-levying authority and as the body responsible for the efficient discharge of all the multifarious duties of the local authorities; in addition, there were sixty-five urban sanitary districts charged with the care of health in their respective towns and cities.* Local government elections were, like general elections, held under a form of proportional representation, but with a property qualification which in effect limited the vote to owners or tenants (and their wives) of any land or premises with an annual rateable value of ten pounds. The effect of this was to produce an electorate which in 1929 was considerably smaller than that for the parliamentary constituencies – roughly a million as against a million and a quarter.

The local Councils were expected to raise the greater part of their revenue from the rates, but increased expenditure led to a steady growth in the contribution made by the central government. Thus, whereas in 1923-4 the revenue from rates totalled nearly 72 per cent of local government funds and the contribution from the Exchequer only 22.5 per cent, in 1931-2 the respective percentages were 52 and 42. It was not surprising, therefore, that the Act of 1925 gave the Minister of Local Government the power, not only to inquire into the conduct of a Council, but to dissolve it if such inquiry showed this to be necessary in the public interest. Out of this provision was to come what has been called 'perhaps Ireland's major invention in the field of government'.[20] The Act laid it down that where a Council was

* To these authorities must be added the borough corporations of certain specified towns, the urban district councils and the town commissioners. After various emendations of local government law and practice, the total of local authorities was officially listed in 1961 as consisting of twenty-seven councils, four county borough corporations, seven borough corporations, forty-nine urban district corporations and twenty-eight town commissioners. The seven borough corporations and the forty-nine urban district councils were linked with the county managers whose functions are described overleaf (John O'Donnell, *How Ireland Is Governed*, chap. lx; B. Chubb, *A Source-Book of Irish Government* (Dublin, 1964), p. 264).

dissolved the Minister could appoint Commissioners to exercise its duties for a period not exceeding three years when, it was hoped, a new and suitably chastened Council would be elected. This device, though intended to be punitive, turned out to be extremely popular and cases were known of the electorate refusing to choose another Council so as to force the central government into reappointing its Commissioners. This may have shown a deplorable lack of civic spirit among the inhabitants, but it accurately reflected at once the desire for greater efficiency and the serious lack of real administrative experience in most parts of Ireland.

The popularity of the Commissioners was by no means confined to the smaller and more backward Councils. In 1929 the city of Cork blazed a new trail with the appointment of a City Manager modelled to some extent on the existing Commissioners but intended to co-operate with the City Council, not to replace it. Dublin and Dun Laoghaire soon followed suit and it was probably inevitable that sooner or later the fashion would spread to the countryside as well. In 1940 provision was duly made for this by the County Management Act which laid upon all counties the obligation to have or share a manager. These officials were permanent, full-time, well-paid administrators, but the financial and legal responsibility of the Councils was carefully and elaborately preserved. In practice, of course, both because of his expertise and because he enjoyed the priceless advantage of continuity, the Manager, especially if he had the rudiments of tact, was in a position to influence very powerfully the course of local government. And if that government gained in maturity and competence over the years the 'managerial revolution' may take a large part of the credit.[21]

Thus, advancing simultaneously on many different fronts, the new and untried Ministers sought to enter into their inheritance and build upon the foundations laid by their British predecessors. At any time this task of rebuilding virtually the entire administration of the country would have been tremendous. But to begin it in the midst of a Civil War and to carry it on despite the sullen opposition of bitter, inveterate enemies was to take a fearful gamble. How nearly this gamble came to disaster we can only realise if we turn to the political history of that angry and desperate time.

(ii) THE EXERCISE OF POWER

When in the spring of 1923 Mr Cosgrave and his colleagues launched their political party – Cumann na nGaedheal – it was intended not merely to be the rallying-point for those who took the Treaty side in the Civil War, but also to bring together men of different classes, origins and creeds who were prepared to contribute to the building of the new state within the framework of the Constitution as approved in October 1922. The party did not, of course, absorb everyone who was prepared to work within the Constitution and the first general election held under the new dispensation in August 1923 produced, as might have been expected under proportional representation, a Dáil which represented a very wide spread of opinion. Apart from forty-four Sinn Féin members who had no intention of taking their seats, there were four main groups and one Independent Labour member. Of the four groups Cumann na nGaedheal, with sixty-three members, was much the largest, having in the absence of Sinn Féin a majority over all the other groups put together. The other three consisted of Independents (sixteen), Farmers (fifteen) and Labour (fourteen). The first two of these groups, while pledged to pursue and safeguard their own particular interests (extremely various in the case of the Independents) were free to give some support to the government from time to time, and the main burden of official opposition fell, therefore, upon the Labour members, led with conspicuous ability by Thomas Johnson and Cathal O'Shannon.

The new government was headed, as before, by Griffith's successor, W. T. Cosgrave, as President of the Executive Council. His Vice-President and Minister of Home Affairs was Kevin O'Higgins and his Minister of Finance was Ernest Blythe. The four other members of the Executive Council were Joseph McGrath (Industry and Commerce), Eoin MacNeill (Education), Desmond FitzGerald (External Affairs) and General Richard Mulcahy (Defence). There were, in addition, four 'extern' ministers who were not members of the Executive Council. These were Patrick Hogan (Agriculture), J. A. Burke (Local Government), J. J. Walsh (Postmaster-General), and F. Lynch (Fisheries).

Upon this small group of men rested a fearful responsibility. For although, as we saw earlier, Mr de Valera had in effect ended the Civil War some weeks before the general election with his 'proclamation' to his followers of 24 May, there was not the slightest indication that the ending of the physical struggle would lead to any easing of the tensions between the Republicans and those who had accepted the Treaty. Indeed, there was not even certainty that the Civil War itself was permanently finished, since the Irregulars had only dumped their arms, not surrendered them. Moreover, the very fact that the political exponents of republicanism, Sinn Féin, had a big enough following to win forty-four seats at the election served notice on the government that any failure of nerve on their part, any evidence that the job was too big for them, might lead, at the very least, to the destruction of the whole pro-Treaty position, at worst to a headlong plunge into anarchy.

Yet, whatever the risks, and however unpromising the circumstances, the manifold problems of reconstruction had to be faced. Four tasks in particular loomed ahead of Mr Cosgrave and his fellow-ministers. One was the reconstitution of the entire machinery of government – how this was set on foot during the Civil War and driven through to a conclusion after it was over has already been described. A second was the assertion of the status of the new dominion as a member nation of the Commonwealth, and a third was the economic regeneration of the country. Both these will be dealt with later in this book.* At this point it is the fourth objective of the government that demands our attention, since unless it had been achieved there would have been no hope of success in any of the others. This was nothing less than the restoration in the Free State of a respect for law and order, the demonstration, ruthless if need be, that here at last was a government that was prepared to govern.

Since the restoration of law and order was primarily the responsibility of the Ministry of Home Affairs it was natural that the holder of that office, Kevin O'Higgins, should seem to dominate the political stage. In fact, that remarkable man was of such a calibre that he would have played a leading role whatever post he had been assigned. In 1923 O'Higgins was still only thirty-one years old, but like many others in those revolutionary times, had matured rapidly under the responsibilities thrust upon him. Joining the Irish Volunteers while still a student, he had been swept into prison in the spring of 1918 during the government purge occasioned by the 'German plot', and later that year was elected as a Sinn Féin member for Queen's County. As such he took part in the proceedings of the first Dáil, gaining his initial experience of administration as assistant to W. T. Cosgrave when the latter was appointed Minister of Local Government in the underground movement that Sinn Féin was then developing in opposition to British rule. Later he came much under the influence of Michael Collins, an influence that was, indeed, to be the most permanent one in his life. 'I try to do what I think the Big Fellow would have done', he said once and in this sentence epitomised his whole career. O'Higgins himself was a man of contrasts. He could be gay (as a student he had been a good deal more than gay), he could be taciturn. In public he was ruthless and often careless of the enemies he made by the roughness of his tongue; in the intimacy of his family no man could be more affectionate. Deeply religious, even puritanical in some of his views, there was, however, nothing of the mystic about him and of all the heirs of Griffith and Collins he was probably the most unflinching political realist. He had great intelligence, great courage, great self-control, and powers of work which staggered his contemporaries. So much did he impress by his industry and drive that it was even the fashion, before the implications of the phrase could be fully realised, to call him 'the Irish Mussolini'. Nothing could have been further from the truth. He was inclined, certainly, to be dictatorial with his colleagues and with the Dáil, but he believed profoundly both in the parliamentary process and in the sanctity of contracts. Both beliefs led him to take his stand

* Relations with the Commonwealth are discussed in the next section; for economic policy, see chap. 4 below.

on the Treaty and perhaps no other single individual did more between 1922 and 1927 either to ensure its acceptance or to enable the country to turn its back on the rancorous past and begin a new life.[22]

But – and here we come back to the *leitmotiv* of O'Higgins's later ministerial career – that life could not begin until the ordinary conditions of civilised intercourse had been re-established. During the Civil War O'Higgins had not hesitated to accept his share of the responsibility for the extreme steps taken by the Free State government, even when these included the execution by way of reprisal of Rory O'Connor, who had been best man at his wedding but a short time before. When the war was over he did not relax his vigilance and at once took steps to obtain special powers under the Public Safety Act of 1923, enabling the government to continue the internment of such of its prisoners as it was deemed necessary to keep in jail in the public interest, and also to arrest and detain anyone suspected of being a danger to the public safety. The Minister was given wide scope under the Act – but this could be justified on two grounds. One was that the Republicans, notwithstanding the cease-fire, continued to regard themselves as *the* government and the pro-Treaty majority in the Dáil as usurpers. It was only common sense, therefore, for the government to look to its own defence. And the other was the simple fact that violence and lawlessness of all kinds continued to flourish. Between August 1923 and February 1924 there were, for example, no less than 738 cases of arson and robbery under arms, and on 21 March 1924 there occurred an incident which could easily have created (as was no doubt intended) a serious crisis in Anglo-Irish relations. A number of unarmed British soldiers, accompanied by civilians, were proceeding by boat towards the harbour of Queenstown (nowadays called Cobh) when they were fired upon by a group of men in Free State Army uniforms. The men got away in a car, leaving behind them one dead and over twenty casualties in the British party. Since Queenstown was one of the 'Treaty ports' to which Britain had right of access for defence purposes, this attack was clearly meant to embroil the two governments. Restraint on both sides ensured that this did not happen, but it was ominous that even an official reward of £10,000 did not lead to the discovery of the assassins.

Scarcely less ominous, from the point of view of the internal recovery of the country, was the difficulty that was simultaneously being experienced in the legal recovery of debts. This was partly due to the confusion bred by the Civil War, but partly also to continued intimidation after it had ended, with the result that by March 1924 there were some 7,000 decrees outstanding, representing £170,000 of debts. The figure may not seem excessive – though in a poor country like Ireland it was serious enough – but O'Higgins put his finger on its real significance when he remarked that 'the ceasing

487

of the bailiff to function is the first sign of a crumbling civilisation.'
Against this background he did not hesitate to reach for a pro-
longation and extension of his powers. The year 1924 therefore saw
a further Public Safety Act continuing the regulations for arrest
and detention, the re-enactment of the penalties (including flogging)
previously imposed for arson and armed robbery, the renewal of the
control over firearms that had been temporarily enacted in 1923,
and the passing of another measure to strengthen the powers of sheriffs
in the recovery of debts. Gradually, these draconian measures took
effect. By the end of 1924 conditions were stable enough for most
of the internees to be set free – including Mr de Valera who had
been arrested in his constituency at the time of the general election
in August 1923 but was released the following July – and in the
countryside at large commercial conditions had so far returned to
normal that by the beginning of 1926 debts outstanding had been
reduced to less than half the 1924 figure.[23]
Unfortunately, the government itself was not immune from the
confusion and passion that were the two principal legacies of the
Civil War. Mr Cosgrave's ministry, indeed his party too, was, in the
phrase Burke had used long ago about Lord Chatham's administration,
'a tessellated pavement without cement'. Or rather, the cement that
had held it together had been the pressures of the Civil War and the
necessity of standing by the Treaty. Once the immediate physical
danger was over the cement began to crack and the differences within
the Executive Council began to be more and more publicly paraded.
It was not merely that ministers were, for example, divided on
economic policy and were capable of standing up in the Dáil and
speaking one in favour of free trade, another in favour of tariffs. This,
though embarrassing, at least did not threaten the foundations of
the state. But when, quite suddenly, in March 1924 a mutiny broke
out in the Army, then truly a chasm opened at the government's very
feet. Ostensibly, the mutiny was caused by the fact that the ending
of the Civil War had led to a considerable reduction in the Free
State forces, culminating in the demobilisation of nearly 2,000 officers
at the beginning of March. This in itself would have produced some
discontent, for many of them had been bred to the gun and had little
talent for anything else. They resented the dismissals and they resented
even more the fact that several former British officers had been
recruited into the Army in recent years. But the roots of the trouble
lay deeper. Some of the soldiers and their officers had only come down
on the pro-Treaty side out of devotion to their leader, Michael Collins,
and they still believed that Collins, had he lived, would somehow or
other have gone beyond the Treaty to secure the republic. These men
had formed part of the Irish Republican Army that had fought the
Anglo-Irish war, but, since the title IRA was annexed by those who
had fought with Mr de Valera in the Civil War, the men who gave
their loyalty to the Free State went by the name of 'old IRA'. It

was, however, a very conditional loyalty, and when by 1924 it seemed clear that the Cosgrave government had no intention of going beyond the Treaty, their impatience boiled over. The result was an ultimatum (dated 6 March 1924) which was sent to Mr Cosgrave, and was signed, on behalf of these 'old IRA' veterans, by two of their officers, Liam Tobin and C. F. Dalton. It demanded the removal of the Army Council and that demobilisation should be suspended, but also, and here was the sinister note, reminded the government that the IRA had only accepted the Treaty as a stepping-stone to the republic.

What made this threat potentially so serious was that there were already serious divisions within the Executive Council about the relations between the Army and the civil power. O'Higgins, as a devoted constitutionalist, was emphatic that the military must be brought under the control of the properly constituted government of the country and he had already complained repeatedly – and emphatically – about lack of discipline. Inside the cabinet the spokesman for the Army was General Richard Mulcahy. But he, while sensitive to criticism of the armed forces, was himself in a difficult position. It appears that the doyen of all revolutionary movements in Ireland, the Irish Republican Brotherhood, was steadily establishing its influence among the Army officers. The IRB, following Collins, had accepted the Treaty, and at the time of Collins's death, General Mulcahy had been a member of the Supreme Council of that body. If, therefore, there was IRB infiltration of the Army it was not unreasonable to suppose that he might be sympathetic to it. The old IRA, on the other hand, regarded this infiltration as a threat to their own ascendancy and this explains their demand for the removal of the Army Council, on which the IRB was strongly entrenched. Where the IRB officers looked to Mulcahy as their spokesman in the government, the old IRA looked to the Minister for Industry and Commerce, Joseph McGrath, to safeguard their interests.

On receipt of the ultimatum the government acted promptly. The signatories of the document were arrested, and the Chief of Police, Eoin O'Duffy, was brought in to command the defence forces. The mutiny itself was not on a large scale, although there were some desertions, and before it had a chance to grow to dangerous proportions Mr McGrath was able to assure the mutineers that there would be an inquiry into the administration of the Army, that the Army Council would be remodelled, that there was to be no victimisation, and that deserters could return in safety to their posts. McGrath himself, however, was by that time a private individual, since he had resigned at the beginning of the affair in protest against the way in which the Ministry of Defence had, in his view, precipitated the crisis by neglecting the grievances of the old IRA, grievances which had been before the government in one form or other since the previous year and which, if promptly met, would have rendered the mutiny unnecessary.

But the incident did not end there. A few days later Free State troops surrounded a building in Dublin which contained some of the mutinous officers. The latter were armed and a grim street-battle was avoided only by the intervention of the ubiquitous McGrath. The action of the troops, it later emerged, had been ordered by the Adjutant-General who had consulted the Minister of Defence, but not his superior officer, General O'Duffy. In the absence of Cosgrave through illness, it fell to O'Higgins to resolve this latest phase of the crisis. He did so with characteristic incisiveness. Not only the Adjutant-General, but two other high-ranking officers were called on to resign, and O'Higgins was preparing to put the same pressure on the Minister of Defence when General Mulcahy forestalled him by offering his own resignation. The episode had not only cost the government two ministers, but had also shaken its authority in the Dáil. Perhaps, though, the lesson, if expensive, was cheap at the price. For what these tangled transactions had ultimately revealed was the extreme difficulty in the aftermath of a revolution of mastering the forces that have carried through that revolution. The problem had been complicated by the struggle for power within the Army, but in essence it was simple enough – could a civilian government impose its authority on those who, in effect, had brought it to power? O'Higgins had no doubt about the answer. 'Those who take the pay and wear the uniform of the state', he told the Dáil, 'be they soldiers or police, must be non-political servants of the state.' In this faith, and with equal impartiality, he stood over not only the dismissal of the generals, but also the ruling that absconding officers who had not returned to their posts were to be regarded as having 'retired' from the Army. This firm action, together with the concessions earlier made to the legitimate grievances of the mutinous troops, ended an affair which, if O'Higgins had not shown his quality at the critical moment, might well have resulted in the fall of the regime.[24]

While the government was extricating itself from this predicament another crisis was working slowly to a climax. It developed out of a subject even more explosive if possible than the relations of the Army with the civil power, the relations between the Irish Free State and Northern Ireland. It will be recalled that during the Treaty negotiations Griffith's intention 'to break on Ulster' had been thwarted by the British delegation, and by Lloyd George in particular, who persuaded him to sign the Treaty on the understanding that if the north refused to form part of a united Ireland, then a Boundary Commission would be created to determine the frontiers between the two areas of Ireland. Both Griffith and Collins, it seems, anticipated that such a Commission would recommend large transfers of territory to the Irish Free State. Article XII of the Treaty, therefore, contained the proviso that if Northern Ireland decided to opt out of the suggested union with the south, then the Boundary Commission, consisting of three persons, would be set up to 'determine, in accordance with the wishes of the inhabitants, so far as may be compatible with economic and geographic conditions, the boundaries between Northern Ireland and the rest of Ireland'.

Later, the Free State signatories to the Treaty were to come under heavy fire for agreeing to an Article cast in such vague terms and containing, in the phrase relating to economic and geographic conditions, an almost infinitely exploitable area of disagreement. At first, however, there appears to have been a general disposition only to constitute the Boundary Commission as a last resort and several attempts were made to reach agreement by direct negotiations between the parties concerned. But when by 1924 it became clear that no progress could be made along these lines Mr Cosgrave agreed with the British government not only that the Commission should be set up, but also that Britain should appoint the Northern Ireland representative which Northern Ireland itself had resolutely refused to do. As finally established, therefore, the Commission consisted of a neutral chairman, Mr Justice Feetham, of the South African Supreme Court; Mr J. R. Fisher, a prominent northern Unionist nominated by the British government to represent Northern Ireland; and finally, for the Free State, the Minister of Education, Eoin MacNeill, himself, it will be remembered, an Ulster Catholic from the Glens of Antrim.

For most of 1925 the Commission perambulated the border, taking evidence from all and sundry, but giving no inkling of how it was going to report. The Commissioners, oppressed by the gravity of their task, had agreed among themselves not to disclose their deliberations but, unhappily for his own future peace of mind, MacNeill agreed also that the Commissioners should sign a joint report and that it should not be published unless it was one which all the Commissioners could sign.[25] There can be little doubt that, like Griffith and Collins before him, he had believed that the outcome of the Commission could only be to the advantage of the Irish Free State which might, perhaps, be assigned large parts of Fermanagh and Tyrone. Then, suddenly, on 7 November the *Morning Post* published an apparently inspired statement to the effect that the Commission would leave the frontier much as before, except that an area of Donegal would go to the north and that the south would make minor gains elsewhere. Again there was a deep silence. It was broken at last on 20 November when MacNeill resigned from the Commission. Explaining his action in the Dáil a few days later, he asserted that while he had agreed in principle to sign a joint report before knowing what it was going to contain, he had come to realise that his interpretation of Article XII was quite different from Judge Feetham's and that, in consequence, he could not possibly subscribe to the report about to be issued. He had accordingly resigned from the Commission and, recognising the logic of his situation, followed this by resigning from the Executive Council a few days later.

These resignations were the acts of an honourable, but, some people could not help feeling, also a much confused and misled man. Whether they would suffice to save the government of which he had been a member was, however, another matter. Certainly, if the Commission's report was as damaging as MacNeill had indicated, and if, as was apparently the case, his resignation was no bar to the other two Commissioners publishing their findings, then the Irish Free State would be faced with the worst crisis in its short history, for its own representative would be open to the charge, however unfair, that he had spent long months *buttressing*, not diminishing, partition, and this without a word to his cabinet colleagues. The situation was made even worse by the presumption, which the Free State and the British government seemed to share, that once the Commission had presented its report, they would be bound to implement it forthwith. There was a moment in October 1925 when the British looked as if they might retreat from that position, but it is fair to say that both governments were hagridden by the fear that administrative chaos, or even bloodshed, might result from immediate implementation of the report. To prevent this happening urgent action was essential. Accordingly, on 28 November representatives of the Irish Free State government – Cosgrave, O'Higgins, Patrick McGilligan (who had succeeded McGrath as Minister for Industry and Commerce) and the Attorney-General – crossed to England and met the Prime Minister, Stanley Baldwin, at Chequers. Next day, the Northern Ireland Prime Minister, Sir James Craig, arrived and the Free State ministers met him also, finding him, it is said, as intransigent as ever where the six counties were concerned, but distinctly cool towards the British negotiators. 'Anything I can do', he said to O'Higgins, 'to help you get what you can off *those fellows*, I will.'[26]

He could, of course, afford to be generous at the expense of the British government. Had the report of the two Commissioners been promulgated and become law, Northern Ireland might have gained considerably and would not in any event have been seriously reduced. But to prevent the report being promulgated the Free State representatives consented to a tripartite agreement which was signed in London on 3 December 1925. Its purpose was in effect to amend the Treaty in respect of Article XII, but advantage was taken of the opportunity to deal at the same time with Article V, which had left the Free State liable for an unascertained share of the British public debt and also for the payment of certain war pensions. The essence of the Agreement was contained in three points. First, the existing boundary between Northern Ireland and the Irish Free State was to remain unaltered. Second, the Irish Free State was to be released from its liabilities under Article V. (By the same token, Northern Ireland was also released from its share of the British debt.) Third, the powers of the Council of Ireland relating to Northern Ireland under the Government of Ireland Act of 1920 were to be transferred to the Northern Ireland government, and the two Irish governments were to meet together in the future to settle matters of common interest. The Council of Ireland had originally been intended as a means of bringing the two parts of Ireland closer together, but it had never in fact been other than mythical. The provision for future meetings of the two governments was a much more rational approach to the problem of co-operation. Indeed, it was all too rational, since passions ran so high on both sides of the border that heads of government could not meet without committing political suicide. Forty years were to pass before the leaders of Northern Ireland and what had then become the Republic were to face each other again at a conference table.[27]

Perhaps the settlement was the best the Free State delegates could have obtained under the circumstances, but nothing could hide the fact that this agreement gave, or seemed to give, an element of permanence and stability to the border that had not been there before. The only reason Griffith and Collins had assented to the Treaty, in the last resort, had been their understanding that a door had been left open by Article XII for the reunion of the country. Now that door had been slammed in the faces of their successors the division of the country, which had been at the heart of so much of the history of the previous twenty years, seemed deeper than ever. It could be said, of course, that all that had happened was that the Irish Free State had at last been brought face to face with the ultimate reality which nationalists had always been curiously reluctant to confront – the fact that there was a solid phalanx of Ulstermen deeply and immovably attached to the Union and utterly unaffected either by threats or cajolements from the south. Southerners, very naturally obsessed by the possible fate of Ulster nationalists condemned to minority status in the six counties, could never reconcile themselves – and still cannot do so – to the notion that Northern Ireland intended to remain a separate entity. Nevertheless, in the short run, and whatever the future might hold, this was what the failure of the Boundary Commission entailed.

It was inevitable that the government which had negotiated such an agreement should be fiercely assailed at home, and it was small comfort that, had the actual report of the Commission been published then (it only appeared in 1969) the uproar might have been still worse. Even as it was, the fissiparous tendencies within Mr Cosgrave's party were intensified. Not only did he lose a prominent supporter (Professor William Magennis, one of the members for the National University), but he was faced with a rash of new parties which aimed at drawing support away from Cumann na nGaedheal. They were too small to present much of an immediate threat, but as a symptom of the loss of confidence in the government engendered by the boundary fiasco they were distinctly ominous.*

* *Report of the Irish Boundary Commission, 1925* (Dublin, 1969). See especially the introduction by G. J. Hand and also the same author's

Far more important, of course, was the reaction of Mr de Valera to this turn of events. It was a strictly predictable reaction, in that the failure of the Commission gave him an ideal opportunity at one and the same time to point to this disaster as a natural consequence of the Treaty and correspondingly to belabour the government for dismembering the country. All the same, he made less capital out of the incident than might have been expected, for the very good reason that simultaneously with the border crisis he was faced with a crisis of his own. His theoretical (or metaphysical) position during the years since 1922 had been that he was still President of the Republic. His 'government' therefore claimed to control the Irish Republican Army through the agency of the 'Minister for Defence' (Mr Sean Lemass) and the 'Chief of Staff' (Mr Frank Aiken). But the IRA had become impatient with a government that had nothing to govern and no way of making its presence felt. Consequently, at a Convention held in November 1925 it withdrew its allegiance from Mr de Valera and his colleagues, and an Army Council was set up to direct the future activities of the IRA which were more and more devoted in the future to the idea of ending partition by force.

This secession left Mr de Valera in a very exposed position. His Sinn Féin party did indeed enjoy considerable support in the country, but that could give him no political leverage so long as the party professed itself unable to enter the Dáil because of the oath of allegiance to the Crown. There soon began, therefore, the elaborate manoeuvres which were destined within a few years to bring him to power as a constitutional leader. In March 1926 the Sinn Féin party organisation met to discuss its attitude towards the oath. It had before it a motion in Mr de Valera's name to the effect that if the oath was removed it would become a matter of policy rather than principle as to whether a Republican could enter the Dáil (or for that matter the Northern Ireland parliament). This motion encountered considerable opposition and it was clear that many of those present still preferred the pure milk of revolutionary gospel – that it was incompatible with the principles of Sinn Féin to send representatives into any 'usurping' legislature. The motion was accordingly defeated by 223 votes to 218.

Regarding this, quite correctly, as in effect a vote against his policy, Mr de Valera at once broke with Sinn Féin. This marked the virtual end of what has been described as 'the third Sinn Féin party' During its brief life – it lasted only from 1923 to 1926 – it could reasonably claim to have been the logical successor to the two earlier move-

---

'Eoin MacNeill and the Boundary Commission', in F. X. Martin and F. J. Byrne (ed.), *The Scholar Revolutionary: Eoin MacNeill, 1867-1945, and the Making of The New Ireland* (Dublin, 1973). The British government's role in the crisis is in part revealed in Thomas Jones, *Whitehall Diary*, vol. iii, *Ireland, 1918-1925,* edited by Keith Middlemass (London, 1971), pp. 220-46.

ments – Griffith's original foundation, the so-called 'monarchial' party which monopolised the Sinn Féin label from 1905 until 1917, followed by the second or 'national' party resulting from the fusion with de Valera's forces in that year. This second Sinn Féin party was, as we saw, shattered by the split over the Treaty. Now in 1926 there was to be a further split. The die-hard Republicans remained outside constitutional politics to form the fourth or 'fundamentalist' Sinn Féin party which, denied all chance of power and responsibility, tended to become steadily more intransigent in its attitudes. There is a real sense in which it can be regarded as the ancestor of the present Sinn Féin organisation. At the time, however, it seemed to have no prospect but to perish in the wilderness, for Mr de Valera, having broken with the extreme men, lost no time in building an alternative power-base.[28] In May he formally launched a new party to be called Fianna Fáil – nowadays, of course, a powerful and well-organised force in Irish politics, but at the time a somewhat exotic growth whose very name – Warriors of Fál (Fál being a poetic symbol for Ireland) – seemed to look towards the mists of antiquity than towards any ascertainable future. Nevertheless, the party attracted into its ranks most of Mr de Valera's more moderate Sinn Féin adherents and its formation was seen even at the time to be the portent of a significant new departure, since it indicated that, at last the most formidable opponent of the Treaty was moving once more into the arena of practical politics.

There remained, however, the stumbling-block of the oath and as the next general election approached – it was due in 1927 – it became obvious that this would be, for Fianna Fáil at any rate, the main issue on which it would appeal to the country. Meanwhile, Mr Cosgrave's government, with that characteristic stoicism which was as morally admirable as it was politically suicidal, continued to give hostages to fortune. In March 1926 it had concluded with Britain the so-called 'Ultimate Financial Agreement' which confirmed an undertaking given in 1923 that the Irish Free State would pay to the British government the land annuities arising out of the land legislation of the late nineteenth and early twentieth centuries; in addition, the Free State accepted responsibility for the payment of certain RIC pensions, the total obligation from these two commitments being about five million pounds a year. This agreement, though regarded by Mr Cosgrave's government as an obligation of long standing, offered nevertheless a broad target for attack, partly because it had not been submitted for parliamentary approval, but even more because it could be represented as involving the Free State in payments from which, so it was argued, the previous agreement of 1925 had released her. Either way, it was an unpopular settlement and helped to weaken the government's position in the country.*

But this was not all. Towards the end of 1926 the IRA attacked twelve police barracks in various parts of the country, killing two

* For further discussion of the financial question, see chap. 2 below.

unarmed Civic Guards. The government at once reacted strongly with a new Public Safety Act, bringing back the old powers of detention and of suspending *habeas corpus*. It was intended only for use in emergency but it could very easily be attacked as a further exercise of power by tyrannical ministers. And, as if this were not enough, O'Higgins, with his fierce integrity, proceeded to alienate an extremely influential section of the electorate by passing rapidly through both houses an Intoxicating Liquor Act which aimed at limiting the number of public houses and reducing the hours of opening. As a social reform this was probably long overdue – it had been recommended by an impartial commission of inquiry – but to drive through parliament on the eve of an election a measure that was certain to infuriate the drink trade seemed, even to some of O'Higgins's faithful supporters, not so much a vindication of principle as an exercise in masochism.

O'Higgins and his fellow-ministers fought the election on their own past record. Given the kind of situation they had inherited, it was an impressive record, and they could point with justifiable pride to such achievements as the virtual completion of land purchase, the development of agriculture and the launching of the Shannon electrical project.* All this had been achieved within the framework of what was then regarded as an impeccable financial orthodoxy and if, to a later generation, Mr Cosgrave's government stands open to the charge that it spent too little on the welfare of its citizens, then it can be replied that not only is the charge anachronistic (it is unhistorical to judge the 1920s in terms of the 1960s) but that small spending was balanced, to some degree at least, by light taxation. Income tax had fallen from six shillings to three shillings in the pound, the duties on tea and coffee had been abolished, and the duty on sugar lowered. And if it be true that Cumann na nGaedheal was coming to be seen increasingly by its enemies as the party of hard-faced business men who, to adapt Stanley Baldwin's phrase about the post-1918 House of Commons, looked as if they had done well out of the Civil War, then these important reductions in the cost of the poor man's comforts have also to be remembered.[29]

It was doubtful, however, whether sober rectitude and efficient but conservative government would suffice. Passion was not yet all spent in Ireland, it had only been deflected. The many opponents of the government tried, in their different ways, to stir that passion again and to focus it on parliamentary politics. Broadly speaking, their efforts took two forms. One was to suggest that Cumann na nGaedheal had become too committed to membership of the British Commonwealth and had ceased to be – some of its extremer opponents would have said it never had been – a truly national party. The other was to assail its economic policies as inadequate to cure the two major and continuing evils of unemployment and emigration. The great panacea – held out mainly by Fianna Fáil, but attractive to some of the smaller parties

* For the government's economic achievement, see below, chap. 4.

also – was to be a programme of economic development behind high tariff barriers, a programme conveniently calculated to appeal not only to those who had genuine doubts about the continuing validity of free trade in the post-war world, but also to that very considerable section of the public which had been brought up to believe that economics was simply an extension of nationalism.

When the election came at last in June the results were intriguingly inconclusive. The government party, though still the largest individually with forty-seven seats, was closely followed by Fianna Fáil with forty-four. The Labour party came next with twenty-two seats – an upsurge in its fortunes due partly to increasing public interest in economic and social issues, but partly also, perhaps, to the reluctance of some of the electors to vote for Fianna Fáil so long as they persisted in their policy of abstention; for working class voters unsure of the future of Fianna Fáil, the natural alternative would certainly have been to go for Labour. There were in addition fourteen Independents and eleven of the Farmers' party. Apart from these, Sinn Féin had five, and the independent Republicans two, seats. One other party – the National League – returned what were likely, in the prevailing conditions of uncertainty, to be eight very important members. It had been founded the previous year by Captain William Redmond, son of the old parliamentarian John Redmond, and its programme of full co-operation with Britain and Northern Ireland appealed most to older voters who still had some nostalgia for the great days of the Home Rule movement; it had some following also amongst ex-soldiers and amongst publicans disenchanted with the reforming zeal of O'Higgins. In its social attitudes the National League leaned towards the right and only a very naïvely enthusiastic supporter could have seen in it much prospect of future growth.

Everything turned, therefore, upon Mr de Valera's reaction to the electoral stalemate. His first step was to lead his entire party to the Dáil and seek admittance. When the Clerk drew his attention to the 'little formality' of the oath which had to be 'taken and subscribed by every member of the Oireachtas before taking his seat therein', the Fianna Fáil deputies declared their intention of entering the Dáil without the oath. The doors of the chamber were then locked against them and they withdrew to their headquarters, where Mr de Valera delivered the standard philippic against the oath. 'They pledged themselves to the people', he was reported as saying, 'that as long as they were representatives of the people they would never take an oath of allegiance to a foreign king. They had been prevented because they would neither take a false oath nor prove recreant to the aspirations of the Irish people and renounce their principles.'[30] Since the second largest party was thus still immobilised, Mr Cosgrave again took office, with Kevin O'Higgins acting not only as his Vice-President, but combining also the offices of Minister for Justice and Minister for External Affairs; the remainder of the Executive Council was much as before and gave promise of a further period of stable and efficient government.

Yet in fact the situation was very serious. So long as Fianna Fáil remained outside the Dáil what went on inside the Dáil was bound to have an air of unreality. And a political situation where one large party governed because among the welter of smaller parties there was no coherent opposition to take its place was in itself unhealthy. How this situation might have developed no one can tell, for suddenly, and out of a seemingly clear sky, it was transformed by tragedy. On 10 July 1927, barely two weeks after the new government had been formed, Kevin O'Higgins was walking alone, unarmed and unguarded, to Mass at a church a short distance from his home in Blackrock, near Dublin. Three assassins, who had been lying in wait in a motor-car, opened fire on him. He ran for cover but was hit and fell, seriously wounded, to the ground. The men then stood over him, fired repeatedly into his body, and made off at high speed in their car. Their identity was unknown and has remained so (officially at least) to this day. O'Higgins was found by his old colleague, Eoin MacNeill, and taken back to his own home, where he died some hours later.[31]

This terrible stroke removed at the age of thirty-five the most brilliant and most fearless of those who had come to power after the Civil War. Had O'Higgins lived we can hardly doubt that the pattern of Irish politics would have been very different. Even his death transformed the entire balance of parties. The government at once introduced yet another Public Safety Act, giving it power to declare unlawful any association that aimed at the overthrow of the state by force and laying down severe penalties for membership of any such association; the Act gave the authorities drastic powers of search and also made provision for the setting up of a special court with power to inflict death or penal servitude for life upon those convicted of the unlawful possession of firearms. It marked, undoubtedly, a severe encroachment on the liberty of the subject and was repealed in December 1928. But the government went beyond the immediate crisis by passing two other measures which struck at the whole abstentionist policy of Fianna Fáil. The first of these, the Electoral Amendment Bill, provided that every candidate for election to either House should, when nominated, swear that if elected he would take the oath as prescribed by the Constitution. Every elected member who failed to do this within a given time would be disqualified and his seat vacated. Coupled with this was another Bill which proposed (a) to restrict the right of members to demand a referendum (under Article 47 of the Constitution) to those who had taken the oath, and (b) to abolish the initiation of laws or constitutional amendments by the people.

The Electoral Amendment Bill was clearly a deliberate attempt to oblige Mr de Valera to resolve his dilemma, and in doing so to establish in the country, virtually for the first time since the Civil War, the possibility of the peaceful evolution of a two-party system. It is hardly credible that Mr Cosgrave and his colleagues did not foresee what they were doing or did not anticipate that a direct consequence of this measure would, sooner or later, be the assumption of power by Fianna Fáil. But, as men pledged to the Free State Constitution and anxious above all to establish a working parliamentary democracy in the country, they were bound by the logic of their position to persuade Mr de Valera and his followers into accepting a full share of responsibility, even if that meant the end of Cumann na nGaedheal's ascendancy.

Whatever the motives behind the Bill it soon produced its predictable effect. Faced with the disagreeable alternative of either maintaining his aloofness on a point of principle which was beginning to strain the patience of his adherents (two of whom had in fact broken with Fianna Fáil and taken the oath and their seats), or coming to terms with political realities, he did not hesitate much longer. To get round the oath was, indeed, no insuperable obstacle to one who has some claim to be regarded as the constitutional Houdini of his generation. Mr de Valera at the time, and on many subsequent occasions, described with exquisite subtlety how he and his party reached the conclusion that the oath was simply an empty political formula which, being so regarded even by their opponents, could be taken by Fianna Fáil 'without becoming involved, or without involving their nation, in obligations of loyalty to the English Crown'.[32] He explained this in greater detail to the Dáil after he had come to power, again emphasising that because others had admitted the oath to be merely a formality he had felt justified in testing the position, by confronting the Clerk of the Dáil in a manner he described as follows:

I have here [he told the Dáil in 1932] the original document written in pencil, and in Irish, of the statement I made to the officer who was supposed to administer the oath. I said, 'I am not prepared to take an oath. I am not going to take an oath. I am prepared to put my name down in this book in order to get permission to go into the Dáil, but it has no other significance.' There was a Testament on the table and in order that it could be no misunderstanding I went and I took the Testament and put it over and said, 'You must remember I am taking no oath.'[33]

The immediate consequence of Fianna Fáil's entry into parliamentary politics was to imperil the precarious supremacy of Mr Cosgrave's party. The distinct possibility emerged that the Dáil might divide into two broad groups – on the one hand the government party plus the Farmers and most of the Independents, on the other hand Fianna Fáil in uneasy alliance with Labour and with the eight stalwarts of Captain Redmond's National League. But the latter were not quite so stalwart as they seemed. When negotiations were started to form an anti-government group in order to defeat Mr Cosgrave on a vote of no confidence, one of the eight National League members, Mr Vincent Rice, transferred his vote to the other side, on the grounds that the National League was being made the puppet of Fianna Fáil. Even so, the voting resulted in a tie and might well have gone against the government but for an incident that demonstrated the truth of the old axiom that in Ireland farce follows hard upon the heels of tragedy. Another National League member, Alderman John Jinks of Sligo, was intercepted by two Sligo friends, Major Bryan Cooper, an Independent member, and the editor of the *Irish Times*, R. M. Smyllie, who prevailed on him to absent himself from the critical division. Accounts differ as to whether they achieved this result by an excellent luncheon which the alderman was obliged to sleep off in his hotel, or whether they simply sent him home on the next train to Sligo. Either way, there was deadlock in the Dáil which was resolved by the chairman giving his casting vote in favour of the government. Mr Jinks, his moment of fame fulfilled, passed from the political stage, though not entirely from memory, since his name was carried for several years by a very successful racehorse.[34]

A Dáil so evenly divided gave no party a chance to govern and, inevitably, there had to be a second general election barely three months after the previous one. The issues were the same, but the parties were all short of funds and the smaller ones suffered as a result. Sinn Féin disappeared from view altogether, the National League was almost wiped out (it was reduced from eight to two seats), the Farmers fell from eleven to six, and, most striking of all, Labour – deeply divided between its own moderates and extremists – lost nine seats, including those of the leader, Thomas Johnson, and the influential trade unionist, William O'Brien, general secretary of the Irish Transport and General Workers' Union.[35] In contrast to the shattered fortunes of the lesser parties, the two big ones both strengthened their position – Cumann na nGaedheal winning sixty-seven seats and Fianna Fáil fifty-seven. Already, it seemed, the logic of a two-party system was beginning to assert itself, although, in order to secure himself in power, Mr Cosgrave was obliged to form an alliance with the Farmers' party. The addition of those six seats, together with the support of a number of Independents, allowed him a further lease of life for four and a half years.

Nevertheless, although the government went on much as before, and still contained most of the same able men, the gap left by Kevin O'Higgins seemed to yawn wider and wider as time went by. The administration continued to be efficient and economical, and abroad, especially in the Commonwealth, its prestige steadily increased, but it fatally lacked appeal in its own country. This was not entirely its fault, of course. It was caught, like other governments all over the world, in an economic depression so severe that copybook finance suddenly came to seem irrelevant and ministers, who knew no other kind of finance, soon found themselves in deep and stormy water. Moreover, the entry of Fianna Fáil into parliament had not solved, and could scarcely have been expected to solve, all the problems of accommodating the revolutionary spirit within the framework of constitutional politics.

In the end it was this nagging question of domestic security that did more than anything else to unseat Mr Cosgrave. The economic situation certainly became increasingly serious as the depression deepened, but we shall never know how successfully the government would have grappled with that, or how flexible it might have become in adapting traditional policies to new circumstances, because it was never able to give the matter its full attention and was overtaken by political disaster while the economic crisis was still at its height. In essence, the problem it was faced with was the problem it had been faced with ever since 1922 – how to defend the Treaty and the Constitution which was based upon the Treaty. In a sense that problem had been complicated rather than simplified by the emergence of Fianna Fáil as a constitutional party and by the split in the Republican forces which had preceded it. Formerly, it had been easy to define one's opponents and, if one had the courage, simple enough to deal with them. But now it was no longer so straightforward, for the enemy was within the gate as well as outside it.

It was true, no doubt, that the Fianna Fáil programme was perfectly explicit on the constitutional issue – they stood for the abolition of the oath. But where precisely would they go from there? How wholeheartedly constitutional had they really become? It was difficult to be clear about the answer. Difficult, for example, when Mr Lemass told the Dáil in March 1928 that Fianna Fáil was 'a slightly constitutional party'. 'We are', he continued, 'perhaps open to the definition of a constitutional party, but before anything we are a Republican party. . . . Our object is to establish a Republican government in Ireland. If that can be done by the present methods we have, we will be very pleased, but, if not, we would not confine ourselves to them.'[86] Even more difficult, when in 1929 Mr de Valera himself, while admitting that some one had to keep order in the community and that the government, by virtue of what he called its 'de facto position' was the only body that could do so, still continued to deny its legitimacy. 'You brought off a *coup d'état* in the summer of 1922', he accused them. As for himself, while he had come into the Dáil as a matter of practical policy. 'I . . . stood by the flag of the Republic, and I will do it again.' And then he added a striking remark which must have haunted him more than once in the years to come. 'Those who continued on in that organisation which we have left can claim exactly the same continuity that we claimed up to 1925.'[87]

This remark has to be seen in the context of what was actually happening in the revolutionary movement at that very time. It was suggested earlier that, with the withdrawal of Mr de Valera and his followers into constitutional politics, the IRA became to all intents and purposes a military organisation dedicated to the establishment of a republic for the whole of Ireland. But while it still contained some remarkably able men it was by no means as monolithic in its structure as apprehensive outside observers sometimes imagined. Although its objective was primarily political, it was also sensitive to economic and social problems, partly because some of its members looked back to Connolly for their inspiration, and partly for the sound revolutionary reason that unemployment and discontent were the ideal recruiting-sergeants for an underground movement. Consequently, while some of the leaders remained steadfast to the old Fenian tradition, others leaned in varying degrees to the left. One such was Peadar O'Donnell, who had been much involved in a campaign to prevent the payment of land annuities long before this became part of Fianna Fáil's official policy. O'Donnell belonged to a group with socialist leanings which in 1931 founded a new organisation, Saor Eire, whose objectives, as well as the eternal republic, were to overthrow 'Irish capitalism' and to provide 'an independent revolutionary leadership for the working class and working farmers'. Saor Eire was promptly denounced as communistic and suppressed later in 1931, but, although it is likely enough that there were some communists among its members, neither communism as such, nor, for that matter, Marxism in any shape or form, made any significant headway among the Irish workers for reasons that will be discussed later.* Institutionally, Marxism expressed itself through the Irish Workers' League, founded by James Larkin in 1923 on his return from America, and more briefly through the Communist Party of Ireland which emerged into the open ten years later, but neither of these bodies made much impact on Irish public opinion.[38]

It was otherwise with the political activists. When the Public Safety Act passed after O'Higgins's death was repealed at the end of 1928, it was noticeable that crimes of violence and intimidation – especially of juries – began to increase. This seems to have been connected with the foundation of yet another revolutionary group (the Central Council of the Republic or Comhairle na Poblachta) which in its official weekly paper, *An Phoblacht*, carried on a ceaseless campaign of vituperation against the government. To meet these threats, and especially the attacks upon jurymen, the Juries Protection Act was passed in 1929, though only under guillotine procedure in the teeth of fierce opposition from Fianna Fáil; originally limited to two years, it had later to be extended. This, however, did not prevent the situation from deteriorating still further. Illegal drilling continued in many parts of the country, and, during 1931 especially, the number of shootings became very alarming, even if some of these shootings were 'executions' by the IRA of members who had turned informers or were in other ways deemed to have betrayed the organisation. Not

* See chap. 5, section iv below.

the least disturbing feature of this grim recrudescence of violence was that in June of that year (1931) the Republicans and Fianna Fáil marched together in the annual pilgrimage to Wolfe Tone's grave at Bodenstown. Fianna Fáil, it seemed, was still only 'a slightly constitutional' party.

It was hardly surprising in the circumstances that the government should resolve to meet extremism with extreme measures. In October 1931 it introduced the Constitution (Amendment No. 17) Bill, which was really a Public Safety Bill of a most ferocious kind. The Bill set up a military tribunal of five members, empowered to deal with political crime and to punish it with the death penalty if necessary, the only appeal being to the Executive Council. The Executive Council itself was given authority to declare associations unlawful by a simple order, and wide powers of arrest and detention were conferred on the police. These regulations did, it must be admitted, mark an unprecedented limitation of the liberty of the subject and they could only be justified by the gravity of the threat to public order. The Bill was strenuously opposed by Fianna Fáil, as was only natural, but Mr de Valera was to find before long that a military tribunal had its uses; even at the time he conceded that 'if there is no authority in this House to rule, then there is no authority in any part of the country to rule'. On 17 October this exceptional measure became law, provoking, it is said, an exodus of extremists from the country that same night. Three days later the government used its powers to declare twelve organisations illegal, including Saor Eire and the IRA, thus enabling members of these organisations, if arrested, to be brought before the military tribunal.[39]

Without doubt this legislation contributed much to the government's unpopularity and it certainly helped to align the IRA behind Fianna Fáil when the election came in 1932. By that time, however, Mr Cosgrave and his colleagues were faced with a sea of troubles — mainly economic, but partly stemming from the simple fact that a party which has been ten years in office is bound to alienate some parts of the electorate and bore others. With that Roman austerity which had characterised them at so many critical moments in the past, the ministers faced the election committed to a policy of rigorous retrenchment. To a country deep in unemployment and poverty Mr Cosgrave held out the prospect of reduced pay for national school teachers and for the police. Moreover, and almost as if its aim was to produce an ecstasy of unpopularity, the government chose this moment to prosecute Mr de Valera's paper, the *Irish Press*, for seditious libel, and to prosecute it not in the ordinary courts but before the military tribunal. The result was predictable — odium for Cumann na nGaedheal and advertisement for Fianna Fáil.

Fianna Fáil's own approach to the election was exceedingly circumspect. There were many, and not only ex-Unionists, who were quite sure the heavens would fall if Mr de Valera were to obtain power.[40]

It was important to allay their fears and this the Fianna Fáil manifesto was well-calculated to do. The abolition of the oath was, of course, still in the forefront, but it may well have been the economic sections of the document that the electorate found more enticing. The land annuities and certain other charges were, it was promised, no longer to be paid to Britain (the annuities would be retained in the state treasury) and this was popular with the farmers. But even more popular – both with them and with other sections of the electorate – was the vigorous programme of economic self-sufficiency which the manifesto set out in terms alluring both to the agricultural and the industrial interests. How a mainly exporting country without adequate fuel or raw materials was to win through to such independence of the outside world was a little less than clear, but in this, as in so much else, actual experience of administration would be the great educator. The immediate effect was certainly remarkable. Fianna Fáil blossomed as a constitutional party (the republic was not mentioned in the manifesto) while Mr Cosgrave and his followers obligingly fell upon their own swords. Even so, the results of the election were by no means conclusive. Fianna Fáil, indeed, became the largest single party with seventy-two seats as against fifty-seven for Cumann na nGaedheal, but there were still eleven Independents, seven Labour, four Farmers and two Independent Labour to be taken into account. Relying upon the support of Labour Mr de Valera could reckon upon a *bloc* of seventy-nine supporters, Mr Cosgrave upon seventy-four if he could hold the other groups in line. This was certainly no landslide and he would have been a bold prophet who would have forecast for Mr de Valera sixteen uninterrupted years of office. Yet such was to be the sequel and 1932, whether contemporaries realised it or not, was to take its place as one of the great divides in Irish history.

(iii) IN PURSUIT OF STATUS

The first two articles of the Treaty, providing that 'Ireland', or 'the Irish Free State' (both terms were used, with characteristic ambiguity), should have the same constitutional status in the empire as the other dominions, and, more specifically, that her relationship to the imperial government and parliament should be that of Canada, must strike the modern historian as strangely, almost grotesquely, inadequate. The facts of the case were quite otherwise. The Irish situation could not be defined by analogy because the Irish Free State was not a dominion like the rest. This was partly because history and geography had together placed her in a far closer relationship with Britain than had ever been possible for any of the other dominions. But much more was it because she was simply a different kind of country from all the others. Where they had been countries of settlement, and, except for South Africa, countries of predominantly British settlement, Ireland was an ancient nation which was a motherland second only in the Anglo-Saxon world to England herself. Moreover, although it was true that the other dominions were at that very time moving rapidly towards wider self-government – as, for example, in their conduct of foreign policy – their progress towards dominion status had been a process of evolution, subject no doubt to setbacks and crises, but registering nevertheless a steady and peaceful advance. The Irish, by contrast, had arrived at dominion status by revolution, and thwarted revolution at that. For them such status represented not growth, but arrested development, not fulfilment but frustration. In short, to admit into the family circle an Ireland which had not only been denied its republic, but had had to submit to partition as well, was at most to reduce an impossible situation to a barely tolerable compromise. It did not, in the long run, settle anything. To its detractors the Irish Free State remained an abortion and even to its supporters it symbolised desire unappeased.

On the other hand, if, as Kevin O'Higgins pointed out, Ireland had been forced into 'this miniature League of Nations', it could be argued, as O'Higgins himself argued, that it was at any rate a League which had no fixed or rigid constitution and therefore offered the possibility of further evolution.[41] True, some of the dominions, New Zealand especially, and to a lesser extent Australia, were satiated, or very nearly satiated powers, for, as the Australian prime minister, W. M. Hughes, put it at the Imperial Conference of 1921: 'We have been accorded the status of nations . . . What greater advance is conceivable? What remains to us? We are like so many Alexanders. What other worlds have we to conquer?'[42] But there were others, notably Canada and South Africa, which shared, though less intensely, the Irish impatience with the lack of precision which seemed to prevail in all statements of what dominion status really involved. There were in fact, even in 1921, powerful pressures, of which General Smuts was the most eloquent spokesman, in favour of a clearer definition of dominion status. In a private memorandum, 'The Constitution of the British Commonwealth', which he circulated to the United Kingdom and other Commonwealth governments in 1921, and which was not published until long afterwards, he urged the necessity for rounding out dominion status and cited the Irish example as a warning that this was a question of the utmost urgency:

. . . Unless dominion status was quickly solved in a way that would satisfy the aspirations of these young nations, separatist movements were to be expected in the Commonwealth . . . The only way to meet such movements is not to wait until they are fully developed and perhaps irresistible in their impetus, but to anticipate them and make them impossible by the most generous concession of the dominion's nationhood and existence as a state. The warning against always being too late with a proper solution, of which Ireland is an example to the whole Commonwealth, is one which we can ignore only at our own peril.[43]

The essential point that Smuts was here concerned to make was that while the dominions did indeed already enjoy most of the essentials of equality with the United Kingdom, in law and constitutional form there were still elements of subordination. If the effect of definition would be to remove these elements then South Africa could certainly look to the Irish Free State as a valuable ally.

This turned out to be the case. It is probably true that in any event the decade after the Treaty would have been a period of rapid change for the empire – the dominions had grown greatly in power and self-confidence as the result of the war and this was bound to reflect itself sooner or later in constitutional advance – but there can be no doubt that this process of change was greatly assisted by the presence at Imperial Conferences of Irish delegates who were under all sorts of pressures to enlarge the freedom implied by dominion status, and who had always at their backs the unrepentant and unrelenting guardians of the republican ideal. From the very outset the presence of the new dominion began to affect the external forms, and more subtly the inward essence, of the empire. For one thing, the term 'empire' itself began to go out of fashion and its successor, 'British Commonwealth of Nations', which had been experimentally used in other contexts, made its first official appearance in Article IV of the Treaty. Further, the oath of allegiance which members of the Dáil were required to take, deeply repugnant though it was to Mr de Valera and his followers, was nevertheless significantly different from the oath which was the rule in Britain or the other dominions. The Irish parliamentarian did not in fact swear direct allegiance to the King. He swore true faith and allegiance to the constitution of the Irish Free State as by law established, and only after that did he swear to be faithful to the King and his successors 'in virtue of the common citizenship of Ireland with Great Britain and her adherence to and membership of the group of nations forming the British Commonwealth of Nations'.[44]

Even more striking than these formal changes was the fact that the Irish Free State achieved dominion status by means of the 'articles of agreement for a treaty between Great Britain and Ireland'. This had a dual significance. On the one hand, the Treaty, as a distinguished historian has remarked, 'gave to Ireland a legal guarantee' of its status of equality, thus marking 'an important step in the process by which the customary content of dominion nationhood was transformed into positive law'.[45] And on the other hand, the remarkable admission that the Treaty was between 'Great Britain and Ireland' went, from the British viewpoint, perilously close to recognising Dáil Eireann's claim to speak for the whole country. Of course, in practice provision was made for Northern Ireland to preserve its separate status, and the

British government also quickly sought, as has been said, to close 'the moment of ambiguity' about the meaning of the word 'Treaty' by passing two statutes in 1922 which, from the British viewpoint, made full provision for the new dominion. One, the Irish Free State (Agreement) Act, incorporated the Treaty as a schedule, and the other, the Irish Free State (Constitution) Act, which ratified the Treaty, also contained the Constitution as *its* schedule. Both the Treaty and the Free State Constitution were thus embodied in British statutes and in this way, it was hoped, a veil of constitutionality would be cast over the complex legal issues raised by the way in which the Anglo-Irish settlement had been reached. Discussion has continued ever since among jurists and others about the nature of the settlement, and especially about the legal basis of the Treaty. We are not here concerned with these highly technical questions, but it is necessary to stress that from the Irish point of view the Treaty was a recognition of national sovereignty and that, even among those who accepted it, and the membership of the Commonwealth which went with it, there was a determination to press the implications of this fact as far as they could be pressed. It was entirely logical, therefore, that in 1924 the Free State government should have made an issue of registering the Treaty with the League of Nations at Geneva. It was in vain that the British government protested that the Covenant of the League was not intended 'to govern relations *inter se* of various parts of the British Commonwealth'. The Irish remained adamantly of opinion that what they had signed with Britain in 1921 was an international treaty and as such came within the purview of the League. The same logic operated in 1929 when the other dominions agreed with Britain that when accepting the obligation to refer disputes to the Permanent Court of International Justice, in certain circumstances they would reserve disputes between members of the British Commonwealth. The Irish Free State made no such reservation, thus emphasising once again the fact of separate nationhood.[46] 'In the garb of "Dominion status" ', it has been well said, 'a nationally self-conscious European state was introduced into the symmetry of the Empire, a dominion neither in form nor in substance, bound indeed to transform the entire framework of dominion association by its revolutionary origin and nationalist aspiration.'[47]

The Irish Free State, admittedly, was not the only problem child with which the British government had to deal. The South Africans, too, as we have seen, were deeply concerned with questions of equality and separateness, though, in the immediate post-war years, more with equality than with separateness. At the Imperial Conference of 1921, for example, General Smuts had urged that the status of Governor-General be changed, so that in future he should only be the representative of the Crown and not an agent of the British government – a proposal which carried with it the important corollary that dominion governments should henceforth have direct access to the King.[48]

Smuts, also, had been anxious that the right of dominions to control their own foreign policy should be more precisely defined, and here too the implication was clear – definition meant, or was intended to mean, an expansion of dominion responsibility and autonomy. Smuts did not continue long in power, but his successor, General Hertzog, was even more insistent in emphasising South African nationalism. Consequently, the Imperial Conference of 1926 brought together South Africans and Irish in a common endeavour to define the nature of the Commonwealth and in so doing to place beyond argument the freedom and equality of the dominions. What emerged from that Conference is familiar history. There was heavy pressure from both delegations to produce a formula adequately descriptive of the Commonwealth as it was in 1926, and, after much discussion and many drafts and amendments, Arthur Balfour, as presiding chairman, produced the lapidary phrases which form one of the great landmarks in the constitutional history of the empire. Great Britain and the dominions alike were defined thus:

. . . autonomous communities within the British Empire, equal in status, in no way subordinate one to another in any aspect of their domestic or external affairs, though united by a common allegiance to the Crown and freely associated as members of the British Commonwealth of Nations.[49]

It is difficult even at this distance of time to be sure how to distribute the responsibility for achieving this advance, for advance it certainly was to have the equality of the dominions with Britain stated so unequivocally. Kevin O'Higgins, who was one of the leading Irish delegates to the conference, was quite clear in his own mind that the Irish contribution had been decisive. 'The onus of the "status" push . . . has fallen very largely on ourselves', he wrote from London to his wife, and afterwards, when General Hertzog returned in triumph to South Africa declaring that he had 'brought home the bacon', O'Higgins's characteristic comment was – 'Irish bacon'.[50] But Professor Mansergh, one of the most eminent historians of Commonwealth affairs, interprets the Conference rather differently. He sees the South African pressure as more significant, partly because the South Africans had been longer in the game and were therefore more experienced, and partly because, in his view, a South African secession (which was always a possibility) would, at that time, have been far more disastrous to the whole conception of the Commonwealth than an Irish secession. Professor Mansergh, indeed, would go further and assign the most influential role neither to South Africa nor to the Irish Free State, but to Canada, which he regards as having held the balance between the pro-British Pacific dominions on the one side, and nationalist South Africa and the Irish Free State on the other.[51] But this is perhaps an over-simplification, for it is known that relations between the Irish and the Canadians were very close at the Conference, and that in Dr O. D. Skelton, the secretary to the Canadian delegation, O'Higgins had an ally after his own heart. They both recognised that the Irish Free State, as a very recent member, was unlikely to win general assent for some of its more advanced proposals and it was agreed between them that the Canadians should put forward some of these as of their own initiative. 'Many of the balls fired at the Conference by the Canadians', says O'Higgins's biographer, 'were, unknown to the other delegations, manufactured by the Irish.'[52] This has been confirmed by the more recent researches of Dr D. W. Harkness whose work, incidentally, demonstrates not merely the ubiquity but also the ability of the Irish delegation.[53]

The essential achievement of the 1926 Conference had thus been to state in broad terms the concept of co-equality. What this was to mean in more specific legal senses was gradually worked out in succeeding years and after a meeting of experts in 1929 and a further Imperial Conference in 1930 (in which Irish delegations again took a prominent part) the Statute of Westminster of 1931 summed up, as it were, the accumulated changes of the previous decade and, in the light of the principles established in 1926, made clear the extent of the powers the dominion parliaments enjoyed. Starting from the assertion in the preamble that the Crown was 'the symbol of the free association of the members of the British Commonwealth of Nations', it went on to lay down that, in future, legislation by the parliament of the United Kingdom would only apply to dominions at their request and with their consent. It was also enacted that henceforward dominions would be competent to legislate in those matters affecting them which had previously been regulated by the legislation of the United Kingdom parliament and that they would have the power to repeal existing legislation by that parliament on such matters. In addition, they would have full authority to make laws having extra-territorial operation.[54] So extensive were the powers now attributed to the dominion parliaments that, in the House of Commons debate on the Statute, Winston Churchill pointed out the particular dangers this held for Anglo-Irish relations, since, he alleged, it would now be possible for the Dáil at any time legally to repudiate every provision of the Treaty. To prevent this he was prepared to move an amendment inserting a restrictive clause, but the mere threat of such a clause evoked from Mr Cosgrave a letter reminding the British government that the Treaty rested on the assent of both parties, and depended essentially upon the good faith of each towards the other. 'We have reiterated time and time again', he wrote, 'that the Treaty is an agreement which can only be altered by consent.' Any attempt to safeguard it by legislative enactment, he added, would have an effect quite opposite from that intended. The letter was actually read out in the course of the debate, but it proved to be unnecessary, since Stanley Baldwin himself urged upon the House that a restrictive clause of this kind would offend not only the Irish Free State, not only Irishmen all over the world, but other dominions as well. The Statute of Westminster had to be an act of faith or it was nothing. This was the view that prevailed and the Statute, without a restrictive clause, passed into law at the end of 1931.[55]

There was a curious irony about the timing of this event. It marked, after all, the climax of a decade of achievement in which Irishmen had taken an honourable share and for which, in a sense, Kevin O'Higgins might be said to have died. Few now would deny that the presence of the Irish representatives at the Imperial Conferences which had led up to the Statute of Westminster not only helped to shape the instrument itself, but also influenced the pace and development between 1921 and 1931. Yet the coping-stone had hardly been placed in position when Mr Cosgrave's government fell from power. With the Fianna Fáil victory in the general election of 1932, and Mr de Valera's assumption of office, the stage was set for a new phase in Ireland's relations with the Commonwealth. At the very moment when the Statute had made clear the full extent of the legislative freedom the dominions possessed, a leader had come to power who, if the past meant anything, was certain to use that legislative freedom to the full

2. The Ascendancy of de Valera

Mr de Valera was not more than a few days in office before he began his long-awaited assault upon the Treaty and all that it implied. As it developed that assault initially took two forms – the removal of the Oath of Allegiance from the Constitution and the suspension of land annuity payments to the United Kingdom Exchequer. The history of the land annuities and of the resulting 'economic war' is discussed later in this book.* Here it is enough to make the point that the coupling of the land annuities issue with the constitutional dispute had an unfortunate, but predictable, effect upon the British government, and especially upon the responsible minister, J. H. Thomas, Secretary of State for the Dominions. This, to him, sinister conjunction of an attack upon legal forms with a disavowal of financial obligations, betokened that something more than a mere readjustment of the relations between Britain and the Irish Free State was in question. He sniffed the approach of treason in every tainted breeze and saw in the return to power in 1932 of the intransigent republican of 1922 a direct threat to the whole basis of the settlement so painfully reached in the Treaty.

In this he was both right and wrong. Wrong in that he under-estimated the internal factors in Irish politics which imposed a limit upon Mr de Valera's freedom of action. Right in the sense that the arguments about the Oath and the annuities did before long broaden out to embrace other and more fundamental questions. This was apparent from the moment (22 March 1932) that the British government received its first official intimation of Mr de Valera's intentions. In the opening salvo of what became before long a general engagement the Irish leader went far beyond the technical question of whether or not the Oath was mandatory in the Treaty. He was, in fact, prepared to maintain that it was not mandatory, but what concerned him much more was to ground his attack on the basis of

* See chap. 4 below. The reactions of the British government to Mr de Valera's assault upon the Treaty position in and after 1932 have been traced by D. W. Harkness in an article, 'Mr de Valera's Dominion: Ireland's Relations with Britain and the Commonwealth, 1932-8', in *Journal of Commonwealth Political Studies* (Nov. 1970), viii, No. 3, pp. 206-28. This article, based as it is upon Cabinet papers lately made available, throws much light upon the British attitude as revealed in the proceedings of the 'Irish Situation Committee' between 1932 and 1938. I am grateful to Dr Harkness for allowing me to see his article in advance of publication.

popular sovereignty. The Constitution of the Irish Free State was the people's Constitution, he declared, and the people had a right to modify it when they chose. As for the Oath itself, it was a relic of medievalism and an intolerable burden. It had been at the root of all the civil dissension in Ireland for the past ten years and had made impossible the development of friendly relations with Britain. It had, anyway, been imposed under the threat of immediate and terrible war, and now that the people had spoken, it must go.

Not unnaturally, Mr Thomas registered shocked incredulity. He at once denied the legal argument that the Oath was not mandatory and denied even more strenuously that a general election and a change of government could cancel an agreement which Mr Cosgrave but a few months earlier had said could not be altered except by consent. But Mr de Valera swept his expostulations on one side. Replying on 5 April to the British protest, he virtually ignored the legalistic aspects of the dispute and went straight to what was, for him, the heart of the matter. 'Whether the Oath was or was not "an integral part of the Treaty made ten years ago" [he said] is not now the issue. The real issue is that the Oath is an intolerable burden to the people of this state and they have declared in the most formal manner that they desire its removal.' Such language was far removed from the diplomatic niceties that usually soften the abrasive remarks governments may feel compelled to make to each other, and it was even more alien to the careful formalism of the constitutional lawyers. Yet Mr de Valera's passionate outbursts supply the essential key to our understanding of this crucial episode. There was, indeed, to be a great deal of legal argument, for each side had an elaborate case to make. But, given the ambiguities surrounding both the Treaty and the Irish Constitution, it is not surprising that the legal argument was conducted in a fog, and though, as has been well said, 'the fog which impeded the defence was favourable to the assault', Mr de Valera showed by his actions that he was prepared to disregard the fog and drive on hard towards his objective.[1]

What exactly was his objective? When he met Mr Thomas in June in an abortive attempt to reach agreement – ostensibly over the economic dispute – Mr de Valera apparently told him that his 'ultimate' aim was the unity of the country, the recognition of Ireland as a republic, some form of association with the Commonwealth and the recognition of the King as head of the association. This was not essentially different from the programme of the famous Document No. 2 of ten years earlier, but Mr de Valera admitted that the election of 1932 had not given him this kind of mandate. For the moment, therefore, he limited his scope to achieving two main purposes – first, to remove the Oath, and second, to delete from the Constitution Act and from the Constitution itself the provisions which had made the Treaty a part of Irish municipal law. It may be contended – and the point was constantly made against him in debate – that while the first of these purposes had certainly figured in his election manifesto, the second as certainly had not. But while his opponents argued that he had no power to amend the Constitution Act, it was clear enough that his second purpose followed quite logically from the first. If he succeeded in deleting the Oath it was necessary that he should remove at the same time those parts of the Constitution Act and of the Constitution itself which might have led the Irish courts to declare the Removal of Oath Act invalid on the ground that it was repugnant to the Treaty. The second section of the Constitution Act, it has to be remembered, had contained a very specific repugnancy clause around which fierce disputes had rolled in days gone by. It ran as follows:

> The said Constitution shall be construed with reference to the Articles of Agreement for a Treaty between Great Britain and Ireland . . . which are hereby given the force of law, and if any provision of the said Constitution or of any amendment thereof or of any law made thereunder is in any respect repugnant to any of the provisions of the Scheduled Treaty, it shall, to the extent only of such repugnancy, be absolutely void and inoperative . . .

It was proposed, accordingly, to delete this section from the Constitution Act in order to remove the obstacle of repugnancy. And for the same reason Article 50 of the Constitution, which had provided for amendments of the Constitution by the Oireachtas up to a period of sixteen years 'within the terms of the Scheduled Treaty' had to be amended by the deletion of the offending phrase. Even with these precautions, it is worth adding, the Irish judges in the Supreme Court were still maintaining more than a year after the new measure had become law that the legislature had no power to amend or repeal the Constitution Act. Perhaps it was fortunate that no case directly involving the constitutionality of the Removal of Oath Act ever came before them.

What the judges might or might not do and say had no observable effect upon Mr de Valera. His Bill passed the Dáil in May 1932. It was then debated by the Senate, which returned it to the lower house with certain amendments, the most important of which was designed to prevent the measure from coming into force until agreement had been reached between the Irish Free State and the British government. The Dáil, as was to be expected, disagreed with all the Senate's amendments, but when the Bill came back to the Senate a second time, the latter insisted upon the amendments. In the normal course this deadlock would have resulted in the suspension of the Bill until November 1933, unless a general election intervened. An election did intervene (in January 1933) and resulted in a decisive victory for the government. Fiánna Fáil now numbered exactly half the House (excluding the chairman), but with the support of eight Labour members had a working majority of sixteen.* When, therefore, Mr de Valera resumed the struggle in the New Year after his position had been strengthened at the polls, he was able to press home his policy. When the Removal of Oath Bill again came before the Senate in March the upper House could do no more than retard its progress for sixty days after which, in May 1933, it became law.

The removal of the Oath was only one prong of an attack which was now developing on several fronts. This attack had two main targets – the Governor-General's position as representative of the Crown, and the citizen's right of appeal to the Judicial Committee of the Privy Council. So far as the first of these was concerned, it was understandable that a government bent upon taking the Crown out of the Constitution should wish to diminish the powers of the Crown's representative. It was less understandable that it should seek to achieve its purpose by first mounting a campaign of petty insult against the individual concerned. From 1928 onwards the post originally held by T. M. Healy had been occupied by James MacNeill who, after a distinguished career in the Indian Civil Service, had been for a time High Commissioner for the Irish Free State in London. A series of provocations in the spring of 1932 led him to publish on his own responsibility the acid correspondence he had had on the subject with Mr de Valera and not long afterwards he was dismissed, or allowed to resign. His place was taken by Domhnall Ua Buachalla. Mr Buckley (to use the English version of his name) had been a country shopkeeper and was, as may be deduced, an enthusiast for the Irish language, but he possessed no very evident qualifications for the post of Governor-General. However, it was speedily made clear that no special qualifications were required. Mr Buckley was installed, not in the Viceregal Lodge, but in a suburban villa, and his main function was to affix his signature to acts of parliament. For this it was sufficient to be, as Mr Buckley was, a faithful adherent of the party in power.[2]

Larger constitutional issues were raised when in 1933 Mr de Valera moved on to strip from the office of Governor-General the power of recommending the appropriation of money and also the power to withhold the King's assent to Bills and to reserve them pending the signification of the King's pleasure. These powers had in fact been purely formal and it could be said of the two Constitutional Amendment Bills introduced to deal with them that they were only bringing constitutional forms into accord with constitutional reality. But linked with these was a third amendment, abolishing the right of appeal to the Judicial Committee of the Privy Council. In Britain these developments were greeted with alarm as indicating a fresh assault upon the Treaty and two ministers – one of them the much-tried J. H. Thomas – even challenged the right of the Free State government to act as it had done. In this they were probably reflecting accurately

* For the circumstances of the 1933 election, see below, pp. 526-7.

enough a view that was widely prevalent in Britain at the time. This was that, notwithstanding the powers conceded to dominion legislatures by the Statute of Westminster, and notwithstanding the equality of status so memorably defined at the Imperial Conference of 1926, the parliament of the Irish Free State was debarred from the enlargements of dominion status achieved since 1922 whenever such enlargements clashed with limitations existing at the time of the Treaty and written into that document.

A crucial instance was the right of appeal to the Judicial Committee of the Privy Council. This was not mentioned directly in the Treaty at all, but since the Treaty had defined the relationship of the Free State to 'the Imperial Parliament and Government' as being that of Canada, and since Canada in 1922 did not have the right to abolish by legislation the right of appeal to the Privy Council, the presumption was that the Irish Free State did not have it either. In fact, the Free State Constitution made provision for appeal, albeit in a rather backhanded fashion. Article 66, after declaring that the decision of the Supreme Court should be 'final and conclusive' and not 'capable of being renewed by any other Court Tribunal or Authority whatsoever', then went on to add the seeming contradiction that nothing in all this was to impair 'the right of any person to petition His Majesty for special leave to appeal from the Supreme Court to His Majesty in Council or the right of His Majesty to grant such leave'. From early in the history of the Free State this provision was a source of irritation and Kevin O'Higgins made it clear in 1922 that in practice the model Ireland would follow would be that of South Africa rather than Canada, in other words that appeals would not be allowed as of right, but only in exceptional cases raising international issues.

For several years the Privy Council accepted this restriction and agreed that 'as far as possible' finality and supremacy were to be given to the Irish courts. But in 1925 it agreed to admit an appeal in a case turning on the interpretation of a Land Act – a domestic issue if ever there was one. The Free State Government was galvanised into action and rapidly passed legislation affirming its view of the law, whereupon the petition was withdrawn. That same year the Privy Council admitted another appeal (this time affecting the position of British civil servants who had retired after the change of government) and, since this related directly to Article X of the Treaty, the Privy Council felt justified in reversing the decision of the Irish Supreme Court. The Free State government met this by declining to give effect to the Privy Council's decision but, as it later turned out that the Privy Council's decision had been dubious in law anyway, it proved possible to settle the matter, not in the courts, but by agreement between the governments. A few years later, in 1930, when a third case was taken to the Privy Council, the Irish parliament again passed legislation forestalling the Privy Council's judgment.

'Only one conclusion', it has been well said, 'can be drawn from a consideration of these cases, namely the uselessness of the appeal to the Judicial Committee.' Certainly, the Irish experience had shown the machinery to be extremely ineffective and quite incapable of operating when a dominion government was determined to prevent it. The Imperial Conference of 1926 had gone some way towards anticipating this by declaring that it was no part of the British government's policy that appeals to the Judicial Committee should be determined other than in accordance with the wishes of the parts of the empire primarily affected, but it had also added a warning that any changes in the system ought only to be made after consultation and discussion. Four years later the Irish Free State delegates to the next Imperial Conference sought to obtain the right to abolish the appeal and, on failing to get this concession, seriously considered introducing unilateral legislation. It will be seen then that Mr de Valera's action in 1933 can scarcely have taken British ministers by surprise. His legislation was no more than the climax of a long history of Irish objection to a court which even Kevin O'Higgins, that devoted defender of the Treaty, had stigmatised as 'a bad court – a useless court and an unnecessary court'.[3]

Nevertheless, the reaction of the British government to the new legislation of 1933 was remarkably – indeed excessively – sharp.* This may partly have been because Mr Thomas and his advisers saw behind it what they took to be Mr de Valera's grand design for an unfolding republic, but it sprang partly also from a certain uneasiness about the extent to which the Statute of Westminster itself had opened the way for the Free State to abrogate the entire Treaty settlement. After all, both the Treaty and the Irish Constitution were, as we have seen, contained in British acts of parliament. The Statute of Westminster empowered the legislature of the Irish Free State to amend British acts of parliament. Therefore the legislature of the Irish Free State was empowered to alter the Treaty and the Constitution. Against this logic, the British sought to argue that the Statute of Westminster, so far as the Irish Free State was concerned, had been 'conditioned by the terms of the treaty under which the Irish Free State was granted the *status* which it enjoys'.[4] Apart from the exceedingly dubious question of how far a statute can be 'conditioned' by anything, this argument rested on very shaky ground when it attempted

* For Thomas's reaction in November see N. Mansergh (ed.), *Documents and Speeches on British Commonwealth Affairs, 1931-52* (London, 1953), pp. 301-3. Dr Harkness, in the article already cited, reveals further that when Mr de Valera sought an assurance that secession from the Commonwealth would not expose him to 'war or other aggressive action' from Britain, the initial British impulse was to reply simply that Ireland would become a foreign country and her citizens treated as aliens in Britain with all that that implied; in the event, fearful apparently that such an answer would merely intensify Mr de Valera's intransigence, the British government contented itself with a refusal to forecast what its action might be in hypothetical circumstances.

– as it seemed to do – to set limits to the development of the Irish Free State as a dominion on the same footing with other dominions because of what had been written into the Treaty. This was to make nonsense of everything that had happened since 1922. Either the Irish Free State was a dominion co-equal in status with the other dominions or it was not. If it was, then the Statute of Westminster applied to it in exactly the same way as to other dominions. If not, then there was little point in further association with the Commonwealth and Mr de Valera's departure from it would be, if anything, accelerated.

In the end the issue was resolved, ironically enough, by the Judicial Committee of the Privy Council itself. In 1935 it heard on appeal a test case designed to elicit whether or not the Irish legislation abolishing the appeal was valid or not.[5] The judgment then delivered made it abundantly clear that whereas before 1931 the Irish Free State parliament had not been competent to abrogate the Treaty, as a result of the Statute of Westminster it had obtained the necessary power to do so. This effectively cut the ground from under the British government's feet. It was difficult to substitute another argument which had something to be said for it – that the Treaty was an international agreement and as such ought not to be unilaterally demolished – if only because in earlier years Britain had spent a great deal of energy denying that the Treaty *was* an international agreement and asserting that it was essentially a domestic matter. The only resort left was to fall back upon international morality and to maintain, though with signs of desperation, that 'there must be some obligations that are binding other than legal obligations'.[6] But in the mid-1930s ministers had only to raise their eyes from the Anglo-Irish Treaty to the Treaty of Versailles to see how inhospitable the climate had become to that kind of plea.

More immediately to the point, the judicial decision of 1935 had left the initiative with Mr de Valera and he needed no urging to exploit it to the full. That same year, for example, he passed through the Free State parliament two measures – the Irish Nationality and Citizenship Act and the Aliens Act – which not only defined Irish nationality and made provisions for reciprocal citizenship between the Free State and other countries, but also continued still further to inflame British opinion by including British subjects in the definition of an alien as anyone who was not a citizen of the Free State. The details were technical, but the direction was unmistakable. Even though British subjects were in fact exempted from the operation of this legislation by executive order, the language used in the Acts pointed not towards membership of the Commonwealth, but towards 'external association' as Mr de Valera had sketched it long ago in Document No. 2.[7]

The very next year the abdication of King Edward VIII gave him the opportunity to make this concept much more explicit. In a sense, no doubt, the abdication crisis only precipitated what was already in train. It had been known for some time that Mr de Valera was at work on a new Constitution and it was widely assumed that this Constitution would remove the Crown, thus at long last giving a republican form to the government of the country. However, since Edward VIII had removed himself from the throne before Mr de Valera had had an opportunity of removing him from the Constitution, it was necessary to face the situation thus unexpectedly created. Mr de Valera faced it by introducing two measures. The first was designed to take the Crown out of the internal government of the Free State by abolishing virtually all the functions of the Governor-General. The second, by an apparent sleight of hand, conjured the Crown into existence again for purposes of external relations, so long as the other nations of the Commonwealth continued to recognise it as 'the symbol of their co-operation.'[8]

Of these two measures the first was not much more than the embodiment in an Act of what had been the effective practice of the government for some time past – or, more accurately, it was the culmination of a policy deliberately embarked upon when Mr MacNeill was replaced as Governor-General by Mr Buckley. The second, however, marked a genuine new departure. It had, indeed, little enough to do with the present predicament of the British monarchy, but it had a great deal to do with the past history of the Irish republic. What it did in effect was to clear the way for the Constitution of 1937, which was to be a republican Constitution in everything but name, and to retain the King merely for certain limited purposes.* These purposes were specified in Clause 3 of the Act, which used terminology of far-reaching importance. The exact wording was as follows:

It is hereby declared and enacted that so long as Saorstát Eireann is associated with the following nations, that is to say, Australia, Canada, Great Britain, New Zealand, and South Africa, and so long as the King recognised by those nations as the symbol of their co-operation continues to act on behalf of each of these nations (on the advice of the several governments thereof) for the purposes of the appointment of diplomatic and consular representatives and the conclusion of international agreements, the King so recognised may, and is hereby authorised to, act on behalf of Saorstát Eireann for the like purpose as and when advised by the Executive Council to do so.

The phrasing of this Clause indicated that the use of the Crown, even for such limited purposes, was to be both permissive and conditional. The procedure it outlined *might* be followed by the Free State government, but there was nothing to say that this would always be

* For the general significance of the Constitution of 1937 see section iii below.

the case; likewise, the procedure, if it was followed, would only be followed *so long as* the Commonwealth countries named therein continued to recognise the Crown as the symbol of their co-operation. Another way of putting this is to say that relations between the Free State and the Commonwealth had been taken out of the Constitution, where they had been a bone of contention for so many years, and had become, in effect, matters of external policy. This, as a modern authority has well said, was 'the most significant development' of the whole period since equality of status had been defined in 1926.[9]

By these manoeuvres, which to orthodox imperialists must have seemed a veritable rake's progress, Mr de Valera was not just stripping away the Treaty settlement item by item. He was doing two things of far wider significance. On the one hand, he was demonstrating the difficulty – which in the last analysis the Treaty had only papered over – of accommodating as a dominion a country which was not a 'natural dominion', in the sense of being predominantly British by settlement, but which thought of itself rather as a separate nation. And on the other hand, by bringing off these coups so successfully one after the other, he was revealing how almost infinitely elastic the Commonwealth was becoming, how far it was capable of being stretched beyond what could have been imagined twenty or even ten years earlier. Now, there were already stirring in the womb of time other territories which were clearly not 'natural dominions' and which in due course were also to regard themselves as separate nations. On them the Irish precedent had a profound influence, most marked, perhaps, in the case of India which, when deciding in 1949 to remain in the Commonwealth (as a republic), adopted a formula acknowledging the King as head of the Commonwealth virtually identical with that proposed by Mr de Valera as far back as 1922 and in essence incorporated by him in the legislation of 1936.[10]

By contrast with the hectic events of 1936, the appearance of the new Constitution in 1937 was, from the viewpoint of Commonwealth relations, almost an anti-climax. True, it contained no reference to dominion status, it dropped the names Irish Free State and Saorstát Eireann, and Article 5 declared flatly that Eire or Ireland (the two versions of the name were embodied in Article 4) was 'a sovereign, independent, democratic state'. Nevertheless, the principle of external association was carried over into the document, though it was phrased only in a very permissive fashion. The conduct of external affairs was vested in the government, but Article 29 qualified this as follows:

For the purpose of the exercise of any executive function of the State in or in connection with its external relations, the Government may to such extent and subject to such conditions, if any, as may be determined by law, avail of or adopt any organ, instrument, or method of procedure used or adopted for the like purpose by any group or league of nations with which the State is or becomes associated for the purpose of international co-operation in matters of common concern.[11]

Even this proviso, it should be stressed, was hedged round with further safeguards for the country's sovereignty. Since the Constitution could be amended by referendum there was nothing to prevent the people, if they so wished, from deleting Article 29. Moreover, the Constitution provided that every international agreement to which the state became a party should be laid before the Dáil and that war should not be declared without the assent of the Dáil. For that matter, and apart altogether from what was specifically laid down in the Constitution, it was open to the Irish parliament, as we shall presently see, to repeal the External Relations Act when circumstances appeared to demand it.

The Constitution, therefore, was emphatic in the stress it laid on sovereignty. No less emphatic, though implicit rather than explicit, was the essentially republican character of the document. But why was this character implicit rather than explicit? Why, when he had gone so far, did Mr de Valera not carry his logic to the extreme of embodying the sacred word in the written instrument? We are still too close to the event to be able to answer these questions with certainty, but one reason why the sacred word did not appear may well have been precisely because it was so sacred. Many times during his career Mr de Valera made it clear that for him the ideal was a republic of thirty-two counties, not twenty-six. To give the name to a truncated Ireland was in a sense to betray the men of 1916. But there was not only a question of doctrine, there was a question of policy. If Mr de Valera's policy was – as he and his ministers frequently affirmed – to pursue the unity of Ireland, then a republic would surely intensify rather than diminish the existing partition. And while it might be argued – and was to be argued again later – that northern Unionists had shown so little sign of wanting to join the south at any time and under any guise that the declaration of a republic was unlikely to make much difference to their attitude, those whose passion for unity blinded them to this attitude might well have felt that such a declaration in 1937, with its presumed sequel of a complete break with the Commonwealth, would only have had the effect of locking and barring a door already hard enough to open.

Further, the pursuit of unity involved not merely unity for all Ireland, but unity within the territory for which Mr de Valera was himself at that moment responsible. To a man of his antecedents – haunted as both he and his opponents were by the memory of the Civil War – it was essential to be seen to have passed as it were from the revolution to the state, to have become a national leader and to have cast off his old role as chieftain of an implacable faction.[12]

It was important for him, therefore, to steer between the Scylla of republicanism and the Charybdis of dominionism. On the one hand, he must strain to reach as many of the objectives of the republic as possible – how else could he justify his whole career? On the other hand, if he did not wish to perpetuate the divisions of the 1920s, he must do this without decisively breaking with the settlement of 1921 and so inflaming the very substantial minority which had built its whole political world upon that settlement. The Constitution of 1937 was a determined and largely successful attempt to achieve this balance. It allowed him to meet all but the diehards of the left with the plea that in its essentials the republic had been achieved. It allowed him equally to meet all but the diehards of the right with the argument that he was only using the legal forms which they themselves had bequeathed to him, to advance nearer to that ideal of sovereignty that all had held before the Treaty had been signed. They might protest, and did so most strenuously, that he was using these forms for purposes which had not been foreseen or intended, but it was difficult for them to accuse him of anything worse than consistency to his own past. No doubt they would have been ready to declare that this was accusation enough, though he, on his side, could point to the fact that in not making the republic explicit he had left himself open to the charge of *inconsistency* from his own former associates. The middle road he was taking inevitably exposed him to these fusillades from both sides but, having grasped the substance, he could afford to let his critics spend themselves on the shadow.

Internal factors such as these may have had a bearing on the decisions taken in 1936 and 1937, but it may well be that external factors were no less important. Since it was generally assumed that the declaration of the republic at that time would involve exit or expulsion from the Commonwealth, it behoved the Irish government to consider what the consequence might be. Unfortunately, this was impossible to predict. There *might* be difficulties for Irishmen living in Britain, though there was a tendency at the time to exaggerate such difficulties; there *might* be disagreeable economic results; there *might* be all sorts of legal complications; there *might* even be, in the sphere of external relations, the unpleasant necessity to walk naked and alone in a world ill-disposed towards the sovereign independence of small, unprotected states. It was impossible to tell how things would turn out, but all these considerations counselled caution.

And caution, in the end, was well rewarded. The British government's public reaction to the Constitution was phlegmatic to a degree that would have excited the envy of Phileas Fogg. In private, it is now known, the Cabinet agonised a good deal about whether the new Constitution left 'Eire' inside the Commonwealth or signalled her departure. However, it – and, after consultation, the dominions also – decided 'to treat the new Constitution as not effecting a fundamental alteration in the position of the Irish Free State . . . as a member of the British Commonwealth of Nations'.[13] This was no doubt untidy, inconsistent and perhaps even an extreme example of a deep-seated tendency in the Commonwealth to hope that awkward problems would either solve themselves or disappear if they were ignored long enough. Certainly, it created a situation which, in theory at least, was absurd enough. For the next twelve years Britain and the dominions were to go on regarding Eire (to adopt the Irish usage embodied in the Constitution) as a member of the Commonwealth. For the next twelve years Mr de Valera was to go on maintaining that, on the contrary, she was outside it and only externally associated with it for limited purposes.

But what is theoretically absurd can sometimes produce strangely practical results. So it was with the Irish imbroglio. The very tolerance with which Britain absorbed the new situation so improved relations between the two countries that the very next year it was possible to end the economic war. And not only that. By the Anglo-Irish Agreements of 1938 the British government undertook to evacuate the bases in the twenty-six counties which had been guaranteed to them by the Treaty. The motives which inspired this action of Neville Chamberlain's, and the bitter criticism it provoked from Churchill and others, do not here concern us. What is relevant is that the return of the Treaty ports enormously fortified Mr de Valera's contention that Eire was a genuinely independent state by making possible for the first time an independent Irish foreign policy. That foreign policy, as we shall presently see, was a policy of neutrality. The British concession over the ports did not in itself mean that that neutrality would be observed in the coming war, but at least it may be said to have improved the chances of such an experiment being successful.

The Agreements of 1938 did not solve everything, of course. The problem of partition still remained to bedevil Anglo-Irish relations and the fact that the south did in the end achieve its neutrality while the north became deeply involved in the war certainly made that problem, if possible, even more intractable than before. Yet there is a sense in which 1938 marks the end of a chapter not just of Commonwealth history, but of the history of the reluctant dominion itself. The dismantling of the Treaty did not end overnight the quarrel between those who had taken opposite sides in the Civil War. That quarrel, one sometimes feels, will never be ended until the last of the revolutionary generation is below ground, and perhaps not even then. Nevertheless, the progressive advance in status and the rounding out of sovereignty had removed from dispute many of the things that had divided the nation for so long. Indeed, it is permissible to go further and to ask whether one of the great ironies of Irish history was not implicit in these transactions. If in 1948-9 the political heirs of Cosgrave and O'Higgins brought themselves to make the formal and final transition to a republic in name as well as in fact, was not this only possible because the foundations had been so firmly laid between 1932 and 1938 by the political enemies of Cosgrave and O'Higgins?

If, as has been alleged, Mr de Valera and his followers entered the Dáil to take up office on 9 March 1932 with revolvers in their pockets and fearful of some counter-stroke from their opponents or the Army, then their behaviour had a symbolic significance.[14] Those who had made war upon the state now controlled the state – but could they be sure that the tide of violence which had swelled so angrily for so long would now subside? For that matter, were they correct in assuming that the main threat would come from the recently defeated protagonists of the Treaty rather than from their own irreconcilable left wing? The political history of the Irish Free State during the next six years was to revolve largely round these questions, to which the passing of the years was to provide some strange answers.

At first the assumption seems to have been that the victory of Fianna Fáil would usher in a second honeymoon between Mr de Valera and the zealots of the republic. The influence of the IRA had been thrown behind him at the election in the expectation that, if returned to power, he would 'open the jails' and release the prisoners convicted by the Military Tribunal. Sure enough, on 9 March the Minister for Defence in the new government, Mr Aiken, proceeded from the Dáil to Arbour Hill Barracks where he had an apparently cordial meeting with an imprisoned IRA leader, George Gilmore. The next day all the prisoners were released, on 12 March *An Phoblacht* (the weekly paper of the extremists) reappeared and on 18 March the government put an end to the Military Tribunal and allowed the order outlawing the IRA to lapse. Almost immediately drilling and recruiting by the physical-force men commenced again and, ominously, threats to deny to Mr Cosgrave and his friends freedom of speech and of the press became increasingly frequent. To prevent their public meetings from being broken up the former government party began to organise in their own defence. Some weeks previously a new organisation, the Army Comrades Association, had made its appearance on the scene. Springing initially (February 1932) from the energy and enthusiasm of Commandant Edmund Cronin, its first president was a distinguished soldier, Colonel Austin Brennan. Its objectives – to uphold the state and to honour Irish Volunteers who had died in the Anglo-Irish war – were unexceptionable and it seemed no more than a club or friendly society for ex-officers and men of the Free State Army. But in August the new body opened its ranks to the public and soon was claiming a membership of 30,000. Not only that, but the ailing Colonel Brennan was replaced as president by one of the leading pro-Treaty politicians, Dr T. F. O'Higgins, the brother of Kevin O'Higgins. Although still emphasising the non-political character of the Association, Dr O'Higgins made it clear that he and his friends would regard it as their prime duty to ensure freedom of speech for all and that to this end they were preparing to enrol volunteers. Thus, within a few months of Mr de Valera's coming to power two extra-parliamentary bodies – the IRA and the ACA – were already exerting a direct and potentially sinister influence upon politics.

These developments were the more disturbing because within the parliamentary system itself there was deadlock and confusion. Mr de Valera's majority, as we have seen, depended upon the support of the small group of Labour members. Their support was conditional upon Fianna Fáil adopting a vigorous programme of social reform. During the election Mr de Valera and his colleagues had made a direct and largely successful appeal to the poorer sections of the electorate. The time was coming when this image of the poor man's party would be harder to sustain, but in 1932 it had considerable validity. Broadly speaking, it was justifiable at that period to claim that Fianna Fáil drew most of its support from small farmers, shopkeepers, and sections of the artisan and labouring classes, whereas Cumann na nGaedheal represented to a much greater degree the more conservative, propertied interests in the country – the large farmers, the leaders in industry and commerce, the established professional men.[15] It may seem strange that it was Fianna Fáil rather than Labour that secured the greater part of the working-class vote, but for this there were several explanations. One was that the Labour movement suffered from deep internal divisions. Between 1918 and 1930 the Labour party and the Trade Union Congress formed a single organisation and it was unfortunate that this was a period of acute and bitter rivalries within the trade unions themselves. These will be considered later in a different context,* but to the extent that they hindered the growth of a vigorous and unified workers' movement they militated against the political effectiveness of the parliamentary Labour party. However, even when the unions and the party went their separate ways in and after 1930, the electoral showing of the Labour candidates remained unimpressive and in 1932, though they held the balance of power, their own strength had been reduced from ten effective members before the dissolution to seven in the new parliament. This failure to make headway suggests that they faced more fundamental difficulties than those caused by their own disunity. In fact, they faced three such difficulties, any one of which would have been crippling.

The first was simply that the political situation in 1932, as in all the previous elections in the history of the Free State, was inimical to the growth of a Labour party. So long as men spent their passions

* See below, chap. 5, section iv.

and their energies on the legacy of the Treaty and the Civil War—so long, that is, as the lines of division in Irish elections continued to be political rather than social, so long would Labour be doomed to sterility. But the second obstacle in their way was scarcely less immovable. Given that Ireland remained predominantly agricultural, with hardly any concentrations of industrial population, the solid proletarian basis for a Labour party was lacking. And this in turn helped to explain the third disadvantage under which the workers seemed condemned to fight their political battles – the absence of a clear, coherent ideology. Lip-service was regularly paid to James Connolly, of course, but the party never allowed its enthusiasm for the dead socialist to commit it to a living socialist faith. It was for social reform, certainly, but not apparently for the total reconstruction of society. Although it was, naturally, critical of capitalism, it rejected in 1930 a proposal to include in its constitution the objective of the ownership and control by the workers of Ireland of the whole produce of their labour. This, it must be said, was not wholly the consequence of the party's own conservatism, it was to some extent also a reflection of the conservatism of the society in which the party lived. More specifically, it was a reflection of the difficulty which many working men experienced in reconciling a deeply-felt Catholic faith with an advanced socialist programme. In 1936, for example, William Norton, who had led the party in the campaign of 1932 and was to remain at its head for many years, seemed to have succeeded in moving his colleagues to the left when he persuaded them to incorporate into their new constitution not only the 1930 resolution on public ownership, but also a demand for 'the establishment in Ireland of a Workers' Republic founded on the principles of social justice, sustained by democratic institutions and guaranteeing civil and religious liberty and equal opportunities to achieve happiness to all citizens who render service to the community'. It is true that these vaguely benevolent phrases smacked more of the Cheeryble brothers than of Karl Marx, but the use of the phrase 'Workers' Republic' was highly significant, for this, more than any other phrase that could have been used, brought the party once more close to Connolly. Uncomfortably close, as it turned out. Three years later, after a lengthy correspondence on the subject, the Roman Catholic hierarchy declared its objection to this aim of achieving a Workers' Republic and the Labour party obediently deleted it from its constitution.[16]

Even with the support of this tiny and not very effective Labour group, Mr de Valera had too small a margin for comfort if the opposition parties pulled together. At first, admittedly, there was not much evidence that they would do so. Mr Cosgrave, with his great experience and judgment, was still at the head of his party, but it was a party for the time being demoralised by defeat. History, perhaps, has not yet done justice to the man who may well ultimately stand to Irish politics in the same relation as Attlee to British politics – an astute, tenacious chairman, excellent in cabinet but lacking in charisma. Now a party in power may consent to be led by a good chairman, but a party in opposition needs a man of action. Mr Cosgrave supplied the opposition with neither the dynamism nor the colour it craved and almost immediately dissatisfaction began to show itself.

It appeared first among the farmers whose normal export market had been drastically reduced by the 'economic war' with Britain, and some of whom had a hankering to carry Mr de Valera's policy on the land annuities to what seemed to them the logical conclusion of withholding payment from the Irish, as well as from the British, government. In the autumn of 1932 they, with some other support, began to grope their way towards a new party under new leaders. One of the new leaders was Mr Frank MacDermot, a member of an old Roscommon family. He was at that time in his mid-forties, and had had a varied career. Educated in England, he had fought in the British Army during the war, and had later spent some time with a firm of New York bankers. He was highly intelligent, almost too articulate, and a firm believer in the necessity of a Commonwealth connection.* Closely associated with him was a younger man who had also entered the Dáil for the first time in 1932. This was Mr James Dillon. The son of the last chairman of the old Irish parliamentary party, he was, though still barely thirty, no stranger to politics which, from childhood up, had been part of the very atmosphere he breathed. He had important business interests (being mainly responsible for running the family firm at Ballaghaderreen, county Mayo) but by inclination and inheritance he was closely drawn to the farming community. In later years he was to become an outstanding Minister for Agriculture, but even in opposition he was a striking figure, with some claim to be considered the only real parliamentary orator produced by any party since the setting up of the Free State.

Under the guidance of these two men – both elected initially as Independents – a new political party emerged before the year was out. Originally saddled with the impossible title of the National Farmers' and Ratepayers' League, it soon became much better known as the National Centre Party. It was pledged to help the farmers recover their prosperity, to obliterate the bitterness of the Civil War, to end the Anglo-Irish dispute and to pursue a policy of friendliness towards Northern Ireland. It rapidly gathered support – to such an extent, indeed, that many well-wishers, especially among professional men, began to speak of a new party alignment which would bring under one banner all those in favour of improved relations with

* The present writer can recall, on going to live in Boyle, county Roscommon, as a child of ten just after the 1933 election, seeing on a bridge over the river the legend: 'Frank MacDermot – British spy'. It was incomprehensible to him then – and still is.

Britain. But before this movement could develop, Mr de Valera, whose sense of timing had always been one of his most remarkable attributes, suddenly dissolved parliament and plunged the country into a new election only ten months after the previous one. He had, as we have already seen, clashed with the Senate over the Removal of Oath Bill, and one object of the dissolution was to abolish the upper house 'as at present constituted'; if it was decided to retain it, he said at the outset of the campaign, its numbers would be reduced, as would also those of the Dáil. For the rest, he reiterated his previous programme for industrial development, increased tillage and the retention of the land annuities – though, as a sop to the farmers, he announced that the amount of the annuities payable to the home government would be reduced by half.[17] The labourers and small farmers were likewise wooed by promises of relief schemes and increased bounties. Against these blandishments the opposition parties offered little coherent counter-attraction and it was not surprising that Mr de Valera improved his position very considerably. The results were as follows: Fianna Fáil seventy-seven; Cumann na nGaedheal forty-eight; National Centre Party eleven; Labour eight; Independents eight; and Independent Labour one.[18]

Yet, while the election strengthened the government in parliament, it was becoming steadily clearer that the real struggle between parties was being fought out in the country at large. It was a struggle that rapidly threatened to get out of hand. After the election the IRA embarked openly on a campaign of recruitment and violent incidents began to multiply. It was at this moment that the government which, to its credit, had resisted earlier pressures to make extensive changes in the police, now decided to dismiss the Commissioner, General O'Duffy himself. O'Duffy had initially been appointed by Kevin O'Higgins in the early days of the state and to the leaders of the opposition his removal was a confirmation of their worst fears. Their reaction was to organise their own forces for a struggle that might become critical at almost any moment. Just after the election, between February and April 1933, the Army Comrades Association had been re-modelled with a view to greater discipline. The outward and visible signs of this discipline was the wearing of a blue shirt, and the be-wildered onlooker might have been forgiven if he saw in this emergence of private armies on the left and on the right an extension to Irish politics of the clash of ideologies then in full career on the continent. Such an interpretation, though too simple, would not have been entirely unfounded. There were symptoms of class war in Ireland at that time and there were men on both sides who were more or less consciously seeking to identify with one or other of the European movements. We have already seen that the IRA did contain an influential section (small in numbers, perhaps, but highly articulate), which was either communist or sympathetic to communist ideals. And even though the name communist was certainly thrown about very loosely by contemporaries, the tone of *An Phoblacht*, with its demand for war on the ranches and the banks and its condemnations of 'the economic stranglehold of imperialism', has a very familiar ring to the student of Marxist history.

But how far did this leftward tendency of the IRA call into being an equal and opposite reaction towards fascism? Some intellectuals, certainly, were obsessed by the danger of communism and one of the most outspoken of them, Professor James Hogan of University College, Cork, not only warned against the supposed impending peril in a famous pamphlet – *Could Ireland become Communist?* – but did not hesitate to draw the logical conclusion from what he saw, or seemed to see, under his very eyes. 'It was the growing menace of the Communist IRA', he declared, 'that called forth the Blueshirts as inevitably as Communist anarchy called forth the Blackshirts in Italy.' Nor did he stop there. Both Professor Hogan and Professor Michael Tierney of University College, Dublin, writing in *United Ireland* – which was the organ of the Cosgrave party – paid tribute to the corporate state in its Italian form. It was this, rather than the crude dictatorship of Mussolini, that Professor Tierney saw as the permanent legacy of fascism. The corporate state had evolved, he considered, a scheme of social and political organisation so suited to modern conditions that every civilised country would adapt it to its own needs. For him, as for Professor Hogan, the logic was clear. 'The corporate state must come in the end in Ireland, as elsewhere.'[19] In fact, as critics have since pointed out, the doctrines formulated in *United Ireland*, and even appearing in the Cosgrave party programme of 1933, owed as much to another Italian as they did to Mussolini. The teaching of Pope Pius XI in the encyclical *Quadragesimo Anno* laid heavy emphasis upon vocational organisation and representation within the state and it was this stream of thought that was likely to be more influential in Catholic Ireland. Indeed, its influence was not confined to any one party and, as we shall see, vocational ideas were to figure prominently in the Constitution of 1937.*

In the immediate future, however, it did seem for a brief moment that fascism might produce in Ireland not just abstract corporative

* For a full investigation of the attractions of fascism for some Irish intellectuals at this time, see M. Manning, *The Blueshirts* (Dublin and London, 1971), especially pp. 211-50. His summing-up of the political ideas of the Blueshirt movement as a whole cannot be improved upon: 'While the corporate ideas developed by Tierney and Hogan did give to the Blueshirt movement a distinctive ideology, it is clear that for the great majority, both of leaders and of rank-and-file supporters, this issue was largely an academic one. The issues which gave Blueshirtism its impetus, which concerned the minds and activities of its members and which determined the manner in which it developed, were far from academic. Blueshirtism was essentially the product of Civil War memories, fear and distrust, and the threat of economic collapse. Beside these, the promise of a new corporate state counted for very little.' (*The Blueshirts*, pp. 230-1).

doctrines, but a flesh and blood dictator. Once relieved of his police duties, General O'Duffy turned towards the Blueshirt movement. In July 1933 Dr O'Higgins handed over the leadership of the Army Comrades Association to him and the organisation itself was renamed the National Guard. Its supporters insisted (with a vehemence that is perhaps a little suspect) that it was unarmed, although its members were certainly proficient in the use of batons and knuckledusters.[20] The government strove to ensure that it remained without lethal weapons, by cancelling all licences to possess firearms and thus withdrawing from the former ministers, and from General O'Duffy, the right to carry revolvers, which most of the leaders had done since the assassination of Kevin O'Higgins. It is doubtful, in fact, whether the National Guard surrendered *all* their arms, but even so they were less well-equipped than the IRA, and, from the very fact that they wore uniforms of blue shirts, much more easily identifiable by the authorities.

Nevertheless, the government persisted in regarding the new movement as a menace. Almost at once an occasion arose for a trial of strength between O'Duffy and the authorities. In August 1933 (only a few days after the firearms licences had been withdrawn) the General announced a mass march to Glasnevin cemetery on a route which would pass the parliament buildings at Leinster House. The purpose of the march was to commemorate the deaths of Griffith, Collins and O'Higgins, but, with fascist analogies so much in fashion, it was not surprising that to the fevered official imagination this looked like a deliberate attempt to reproduce Mussolini's march on Rome. Hurriedly, the government brought the old emergency regulations of the Cosgrave regime into force again, thus enabling it to ban the march only a few hours before it was due to start. At the same time, it recruited into the police forces a body of auxiliaries drawn mainly from the ranks of former IRA men and equipped them with guns and armoured cars. Known from the start as the Broy Harriers (after the new Commissioner of Police, Colonel Eamonn Broy), they were formidable evidence of the lengths to which the authorities were prepared to go to prevent the *coup d'etat* that was believed to be imminent.* But O'Duffy was no Mussolini. At the last moment he cancelled the march, protesting to the end that no political stroke had been intended. All the same, the government followed up its precautionary measures by resurrecting the Military Tribunal and declaring the National Guard to be an unlawful association.

Had the fiasco of August 1933 led to the disappearance of O'Duffy from public life at that moment it might have been better for all concerned. Instead, however, it had the unexpected consequence of

* The name Broy Harriers recalled that of the famous county Wicklow hunt – the Bray Harriers. But it did not escape contemporaries that the nickname of the much hated British auxiliary force in the Anglo-Irish war – the Black and Tans – had similarly derived from the hunting-field.

causing him to deviate into precisely those party politics he had earlier condemned. The following month saw a remarkable fusion of the three main groups which felt themselves to be most threatened by the recent developments. Thus out of the junction between Cumann na nGaedheal, the National Centre party, and the National Guard arose a new body, which, characteristically, could not even agree upon a common name. In its early days it was known both as the United Ireland party and as Fine Gael (Tribe, or Family, of Gaels), though in practice the Irish title soon supplanted the English one. General O'Duffy became its leader (though he had no seat in parliament) and Mr Cosgrave, Mr MacDermot and Mr Dillon agreed to serve under him as Vice-Presidents. To comply with the law the National Guard changed its name and to some extent its character. It became the Young Ireland Association and blossomed – briefly – as a youth movement clearly owing a good deal to continental examples.

The policy of the new party was very much what that of Mr Cosgrave and his colleagues had been since their fall from power. 'United Ireland' stood for a united Ireland within the Commonwealth. It stood also for the ending of the economic war, for the abolition of proportional representation in its existing form, and, as a gesture to the prevailing fashion for corporative doctrines, it advocated the establishment of agricultural and industrial corporations with statutory powers. It must be said at once, though, that the new party began disastrously. The alliance with O'Duffy was a grave error of judgment. This was not, as some feared at the time, because he was still at heart a potential dictator. In his own mind, indeed, he may have nursed such ambitions long after they had become impracticable and it is probably true that some among his followers would have liked to see him sweep to power over the corpse of constitutionalism. But the real trouble with O'Duffy was not that he was cold-bloodedly authoritarian, but that he was warm-heartedly incompetent. A good police chief, he was a child in politics and, being a vain man with no judgment, was easily betrayed into wild language and false positions. Thus, the undoubted tendency in some quarters to see him as a 'Führer' received no encouragement from his actual performance. Whether for reasons of euphony or of irony, the chant of 'Hail O'Duffy' seemed somehow to lack the hypnotic effect of 'Heil Hitler'.

The single practical issue on which the General had a policy was, characteristically, the one most likely to separate him from his constitutional colleagues. It concerned the growing unrest among farmers whose plight was still deteriorating under the effects of the economic war. When some of these withheld payment of their local rates and of land annuities to the government, their cattle were impounded and auctioned at a fraction of their value to buyers who, naturally, were so unpopular that they had to be closely guarded by police, usually the armed Broy Harriers. O'Duffy's notion was that the new party should capitalise on this discontent and in August 1934 he presided at a convention of his movement (under government pressure, it had changed its name yet again to the League of Youth) which passed a resolution calling on farmers not to pay the land annuities and on labourers not to pay their rates. For a constitutional opposition this was, of course, a totally untenable position since, if taken seriously in the country, it could only have led to anarchy. Even as it was, some Blueshirts showed themselves more than ready to lend a hand to irate farmers in resisting cattle auctions by blocking roads and railways. As for the General himself, not content with bestowing his approval on this wrecking policy, he spoke a few days later about the possibility of a war with England over partition – into which, it appeared, he would be ready to lead his Blueshirts – and this despite the fact that he was the nominal head of a party pledged to continue within the British Commonwealth. These *gaffes* were at once followed by the resignation of Professor Hogan as a protest against O'Duffy's 'destructive and hysterical leadership' which made him 'utterly impossible' as a political colleague. 'It is about time', he said, 'the United Ireland party gave up its hopeless attempt of saving General O'Duffy from his own errors.'[21]

Apparently this was also the feeling of the other leaders of the party and on 21 September 1934 the General was obliged to resign the leadership which, after being left vacant for some months, was taken over by Mr Cosgrave the following spring. It was not clear whether or not O'Duffy had also resigned as head of the League of Youth. His opponents said he had and elected Commandant Cronin (the originator of the idea of the blue shirt) in his place. General O'Duffy denied that he had resigned both posts and some of the Blueshirts split off from the main body out of loyalty to him. He set up a rival League and followed this with a so-called National Corporative party which, however, never really struck root. There remained for him one tragi-comic episode. When in 1936 the Spanish Civil War broke out O'Duffy (who had never lacked courage or a kind of consistency of his own) led his Blueshirts to fight on Franco's side. After about a year there he returned home and to political obscurity, dying in 1944 at the early age of 52.

Meanwhile the problem that had called the Blueshirts into being was as far as ever from being settled. The years 1933 and 1934 were marked by numerous outrages and several murders or attempted murders which were unmistakably political in motive. Many of these attacks were directed either against leaders of the opposition, or against individual Blueshirts, and it became essential for the government to impose its authority upon both sides.[22] Since the Blueshirts were an open organisation it was relatively easy to keep them under supervision, but the IRA was a very different problem. Different in a technical sense because, as an underground organisation without uniform, it was hard to combat. Different in a political sense, because the ties between Fianna Fáil and the Republicans were still so close that it was difficult for Mr de Valera to bring himself to use the full force of the law against them. In fact he only did so after other methods had failed. During 1934, for example, a new Volunteer Force was created as a branch of the Army and commissions in this new body were given to ex-members of the IRA. Again, later that year, the Military Pensions Act was passed in order to provide pensions for men (and women) who had fought with the IRA in the Civil War. It is likely enough that these measures weaned some – perhaps a considerable number – away from the underground movement, but the extremists were unimpressed, denouncing the pensions as 'an attempt to buy off the hostility which exists against the rewarding and subsidising of treason'.[23] Towards the end of the year, therefore, Mr de Valera sent for one of the leaders, Sean Russell, and asked for the surrender of the IRA's weapons. This elicited the predictable reply that the arms had been retained from 1922 onwards on Mr de Valera's own order for the purposes of the republic. Would the IRA then not refrain at least from armed drilling and parading in the open? But Russell would consider nothing short of a declaration of the republic within the next five years. There was no doing business with him on such terms and he went away as secretly as he had come.[24]

The government was thus left with no option but to use the same machinery – the Broy Harriers and the Military Tribunal – against the IRA as it had done against the Blueshirts. To some extent, no doubt, its task was made easier by the splits developing among the Republicans themselves. The main division appeared to be between those who were primarily concerned with the attainment of the republic and those who wished to emphasise its character as a *workers'* republic by dwelling on the need to overthrow not just the regime in Northern Ireland, but capitalism throughout the whole country. The former section (which was the larger) was led by Maurice Twomey and Sean Mac-Bride and it retained control of the weekly newspaper *An Phoblacht* – until this ceased publication from lack of support in 1935. The dissident minority broke away to form the Republican Congress, of which the leading spirits were Michael Price, Sean McGuinness, Peadar O'Donnell, George Gilmore and James Connolly's daughter, Mrs Nora Connolly O'Brien. All but the last-named had been active in the now defunct Saor Eire* and they carried into the new body the same old disputatious fanaticism. Unedifying quarrels broke out between the two groups, resulting even in scuffles during the annual commemoration ceremonies at Wolfe Tone's grave in 1934 and again in 1935. By the latter date, however, the Republican Congress itself had split in two on the issue of whether to concentrate on the fight against imperialism or on the narrower goal of establishing a workers' republic. In practice the left-wing group found itself unable to con-

* See p. 502 above.

centrate on either since it did not receive enough support to run a newspaper or an organisation – both of which were virtually extinct by the end of 1935.

Yet, although these fissiparous tendencies may have helped the government in one way, in another way the lack of any unified control over the IRA increased the risk of serious incidents. Such incidents continued during 1935 and 1936 and three barbarous murders in particular shocked the entire country, opening the way for Mr de Valera to act more decisively than he had yet done. The first of these occurred in February 1935 at Edgeworthstown, county Longford, where Richard More O'Ferrall, the son of a local land-agent, was fatally wounded by four gunmen who had intervened in a dispute on the estate for which More O'Ferrall senior was the agent. The second (in March, 1936) was the cold-blooded murder on his own door-step of Admiral Somerville, brother of Edith Somerville, the co-authoress of *Some Experiences of an Irish R.M.* and many other books. The Admiral, seventy-two at the time of his death, had retired to Castletownshend, county Cork and his only 'crime' had been that, when asked by local youths for help in joining the Navy, he had been glad to give them references. The horror of this cowardly assassination was still fresh in the public mind when the third murder occurred a month later. This time it was the shooting down, in Dungarvan, county Waterford, of a young man, John Egan, who had been a member of the IRA and who, having incurred the displeasure of his former associates, was 'executed' by them – possibly, it has been conjectured, because he had refused to take part in the murder of Admiral Somerville. It is instructive to observe that the four men who were accused of the Edgeworthstown murder were discharged 'not guilty'; that one man was convicted of the Egan murder, but, after sentence of death had been commuted to life imprisonment, was in fact released after two years; and that the murderers of Admiral Somerville were never traced. Nevertheless, despite, or perhaps because of, the strange workings of justice, the government dared hesitate no longer. On 18 June 1936 the IRA was at last declared an illegal organisation and shortly afterwards its Chief of Staff, Maurice Twomey, previously arrested, was sentenced by the Military Tribunal to three years' hard labour.[25]

The IRA was driven below ground by this action, but it was not destroyed. Its policy, however, underwent some startling changes of direction. In the immediate sequel, the will-o'-the-wisp of the Spanish Civil War beckoned it as it had beckoned O'Duffy and, as if to perpetuate the folly and futility of their own Civil War, Irishmen fought on opposite sides in Spain – about 200 to 300 of the IRA for the republican side as against some 700 Blueshirts for Franco – in a cause that had nothing to do with any of them.

Much more significant than this was the development of a new wave of hostility towards England. The war, it seemed, was to be carried right into the enemy's own territory. The responsibility for this fresh campaign rested mainly with the new Chief of Staff of the IRA, Sean Russell, who in 1938 persuaded the remnants of the Sinn Féin representatives in the old Dáil – it was part of their mystique that they still called themselves the Second Dáil – to renew the link with the IRA which had previously existed. Thenceforward the army council of the IRA was, for Russell and his associates, the lawful government of the country. In January 1939 they dispatched an 'ultimatum' to Britain demanding her withdrawal from 'every part of Ireland', that is, from the north and from the Treaty ports. No doubt they would have been astonished if they had received an answer (they got none) for they had already decided on a plan of action which was immediately, and despite the objections of some more clear-sighted members, put into action. The plan consisted simply of arranging a series of explosions in various places in England, partly to advertise the very existence of the IRA and partly with the confused notion that this might bring home to the English people the hatred which partition kept alive in Ireland. Ostensibly it was to be a campaign of sabotage against factories, communications and power installations, but for the most part it degenerated into a series of squalid exploits that seldom rose above the planting of bombs in post-boxes and public lavatories, or in suitcases at railway luggage offices. In the first six months of 1939 over 120 such incidents had occurred at the cost of one life and fifty-five people wounded. Then came serious explosions at two railway termini and, worst of all, an outrage at Coventry where a bomb went off in a crowded street, killing five people and injuring seventy others.

What did these lethal activities achieve? The short answer is that they achieved no positive results whatever.* But on the negative side they served to inflame British public opinion as it had not been inflamed for many years. Whenever caught, IRA men received stiff prison sentences and two were hanged for their part in the Coventry explosion. Irishmen living in Britain but who had been born in Ireland were compelled to register with the police and many hundreds were sent back to their native land, where Mr de Valera was taking his own precautions. In rapid succession, in mid-summer 1939, the Dáil passed a Treason Act prescribing the death penalty for acts of treason and an Offences Against the State Act, enabling the government to reintroduce the Military Tribunal and to intern prisoners without trial. Even this did not prevent the IRA from carrying out its most remarkable coup of that year – the raid, just before Christmas, on the Army's own supply of ammunition in a heavily guarded fort at the Phoenix Park in Dublin. It was, however, a Pyrrhic victory. Most of the ammunition was recovered, many arrests were made, and the

* Unless the education of Brendan Behan be reckoned a positive result. His autobiography, *Borstal Boy*, and the play, *The Quare Fellow*, throw a curious light on the IRA mentality of the time.

government secured yet more legislation – the Emergency Powers Act – allowing it to open a special internment camp at The Curragh in county Kildare for the imprisonment of those who were in a certain sense its own spiritual and political heirs.[26]

So the wheel came full circle and the logic of the Civil War was worked out to its own grim conclusion. The men who had upheld the revolution against the state now upheld the state against the men who still believed that revolution was a sacred duty. That legacy of continuity which Mr de Valera had conceded to those who would not follow him into parliamentary politics in 1927 was now asserted against him. 'Recognition of the Free State – with or without an oath – is treason to the republic.'[27] Thus wrote one of the most fanatical republicans, Mary MacSwiney, and by that simple test she condemned not just Griffith and Collins, not just Cosgrave and O'Higgins, but de Valera and Lemass as well. To the extremists it followed that if the republic was the only lawful government in the country, then they had the right to attack – to shoot down, if need be – any traitor who claimed to be exercising authority either in the Free State or in Northern Ireland. They saw themselves, in short, as the soldiers of a perpetual revolution, or rather of a revolution which would end only when all thirty-two counties entered the republican fold.

But if the logic of principle was with them, the logic of fact was against them. Whatever they might say or do, romantic Ireland *was* dead and gone. We can see now what was hidden from them, that Mr de Valera, by dismantling the Treaty and advancing constitutionally ever nearer towards a *de facto* republic, had cut the ground from beneath their feet. The balance of forces, so evenly poised at the time of the Civil War, had been tilting against them ever since. The IRA, formerly at the centre of events, now found itself peripheral and regarded by most Irishmen as irrelevant.* No longer enjoying broad-based support in the country, no longer able to mount major campaigns in the style of the Anglo-Irish war, its members were driven inexorably back upon isolated acts of terrorism which, as in the bomb outrages of 1939, had no military objective and resulted only too often in the murder or mutilation of innocent civilians. Harried by the government, split by their own dissensions, they seemed to have come to the end of the road. Yet they were only forced underground, not completely destroyed. So long as the border existed, so long as the indivisible republic beckoned, so long would young men answer the call of their blood and their history. Neither Mr de Valera nor his opponents had heard the last of the IRA.

It has been necessary to dwell at some length on the futile violence of these years because it was an integral part of the pattern of politics between the accession to power of Fianna Fáil and the out-

* Estimates of its strength in the late 'twenties and early 'thirties vary from 15,000 to 30,000, but internal feuds and arrests and internments, especially between 1938 and 1940, reduced this figure drastically.

break of the Second World War. As one looks back upon it, it is clear that that pattern owed its distinctive character more to Irish than to European conditions. It was natural, of course, that it should take some colouration from what was happening abroad and it was certainly true, as we saw earlier, that some of the economic stresses and ideological conflicts which were tearing the continent apart made their presence felt in Ireland also. Nevertheless, they were not the preoccupations of the great majority of Irishmen. The coshes and knuckledusters, the programmes and slogans, the posturing of O'Duffy, the gang warfare between the Blueshirts and the IRA, these were not the death-agonies of a Gaelic Weimar, they were rather the last convulsive spasm of the fever that had been wasting the land since 1922 – they were the nemesis of Civil War.

(iii) THE NEW CONSTITUTION

'Ireland', it has been said, 'got a new Constitution in 1937 because Mr de Valera and the Fianna Fáil party were dissatisfied with the Constitution of the Irish Free State, but this dissatisfaction . . . was centred mainly on Commonwealth status and symbols.'[28] It is certainly true, as we saw in a previous section, that the progressive dismantling of the Treaty had left the Constitution of 1922 in a decidedly threadbare condition. However, it is equally true that internal amendments, no less than external ones, had radically changed the character of Irish government and these alterations, too, pointed to a complete re-drafting of the Constitution. This radical change of character, it needs to be stressed, had not affected the essentials of the cabinet system which, as Professor Chubb has pointed out, tended towards an even closer approximation to the British model under Mr de Valera than under his predecessors, but it had affected very drastically the structure of parliament as a representative body.[29] As his administration consolidated its position it became more and more impatient with the checks and balances that had been introduced into the Constitution mainly, though not entirely, to quieten the apprehensions of ex-Unionists in 1922. In practical terms this had meant not only that ministers came into frequent collision with the Senate, but also that they looked with a jaundiced eye upon university representation in the Dáil, and upon that peculiarity of the electoral system which ordained that there should be a fairly high percentage of constituencies with more than five members each, on the assumption (perhaps less justified in practice than its admirers imagined) that in this way proportional representation would safeguard the interests of minorities.[30]

Historically, it was the collision with the Senate that came first. We have seen already that in 1932 the upper house had blocked the

Removal of Oath Bill and that the Fianna Fáil election programme of 1933 had looked forward to a reduction in its numbers, possibly even to its complete elimination. Long before that, indeed, Mr Sean Lemass had stated his party's view of what an ideal Senate should be with a frankness that left nothing to the imagination. Speaking in 1928 in support of a motion that the Senate should be elected solely by the Dáil, he explained that the purpose of this proposal was to ensure that if there had to be a Senate it would be entirely subordinate to the lower house, 'held tight in the grip of this body and unable to wriggle unless this body so permits it'. 'We are in favour, of course', he added, 'of the abolition of the Senate, but if there is to be a Second House let it be a Second House under our thumb. Let it be a group of individuals who dare not let a squeak out of them except when we lift our fingers to give them breath to do it.'[31]

In practice, it must be said, the Senate was far from being the haven for ex-Unionists that some of its detractors alleged. It had, on the contrary, become increasingly political in its make-up and the triennial elections had come more and more to follow party lines. It was true that Fianna Fáil, though its strength in the upper house steadily increased from 1928 onwards, did not command a working majority there. On the other hand, party discipline was less rigid than in the Dáil and for non-controversial measures the government could usually get sufficient support in a Senate which took its function as a revising chamber very seriously indeed. Nevertheless, for an administration bent on rapid and revolutionary constitutional change, an upper house which still retained an independent outlook was an obvious embarrassment and it was a matter of no great surprise when in March 1934 Mr de Valera introduced a Bill for its abolition. The Senate fought vigorously against its own destruction, and even while under sentence of death fought equally vigorously during 1935 against the removal of university representation and the reduction in the number of constituencies with five members or more from eighteen out of twenty-eight to eleven out of thirty-four. This, however, as its members well knew, could be no more than a delaying action, and in May 1936 the Senate ceased to exist.

It was, therefore, under single-chamber government that Mr de Valera carried through the important legislation of 1936 defining the external association of the Free State with the British Commonwealth, and it was under single-chamber government that he added as it were the decorative frieze to this achievement by abolishing the Governor-Generalship in June 1937.[32] But by that time the draft of a new Constitution was already before the public. It was debated in the Dáil during the early summer and submitted for referendum to the people on 1 July 1937, a general election being held the same day to replace the old Dáil which had been dissolved in mid-June. The voting, both in the referendum and the election, was closer than the government would no doubt have wished, but it was decisive enough to maintain Fianna

Fáil in power, though somewhat precariously, and to bring the Constitution into force at the end of 1937.*

What was it to which the Irish people had thus lukewarmly committed themselves? The Constitution was a remarkable document – remarkable for what it contained and for what it omitted, remarkable still more because, as we now know, it was very largely the work of one man, Mr de Valera himself. It has been well described as attempting 'to reconcile the notion of inalienable popular sovereignty with the older medieval conception of a theocratic state'.[33] The notion of popular sovereignty, inherent in Irish revolutionary thought from the days of Wolfe Tone onwards, was to be balanced by the principle that in the last analysis such sovereignty could only be exercised under God. Hence the emphatic language of the preamble:

In the name of the Most Holy Trinity, from whom is all authority and to whom, as our final end, all actions both of men, and states must be referred,

We, the people of Eire,

Humbly acknowledging all our obligations to our Divine Lord, Jesus Christ, who sustained our fathers through centuries of trial,

Gratefully remembering their heroic and unremitting struggle to regain the independence of our Nation,

And seeking to promote the common good, with due observance of Prudence, Justice and Charity, so that the dignity and freedom of the individual may be assured, true social order attained, the unity of our country restored, and concord established with other nations,

Do hereby adopt, enact, and give to ourselves this Constitution.[34]

In the circumstances of 1937 and of the recent past it was inevitable that this doctrine of popular sovereignty should express itself in a deliberate turning away from the dominion type constitution under which the Free State had struggled towards the assertion of its independent status. Thus the very first Article declares that 'the Irish nation hereby affirms its inalienable, indefeasible, and sovereign right to choose its own form of Government, to determine its relations with other nations, and to develop its life, political, economic and cultural, in accordance with its own genius and traditions'. The second Article – in intention at least – is no less assertive of sovereignty, claiming as it does that 'the national territory consists of the whole island of Ireland, its islands and the territorial seas'. This, it is true, was far removed from contemporary reality – Article 3 came down to earth

* The results of the referendum were 685,105 for the Constitution, 526,945 against; it appears that some thirty-one per cent of those entitled to vote did not in fact do so. The general election gave Fianna Fáil exactly half the seats in the Dáil and left them more than ever dependent on Labour. The figures were: Fianna Fáil, sixty-nine; United Ireland (Fine Gael), forty-eight; Labour, thirteen; Independents, eight.

with the proviso that 'pending the re-integration of the national territory' the laws enacted by the parliament to be established under the
Constitution would apply only to the twenty-six counties – but to
Mr de Valera and his associates it was of the highest importance,
psychologically as well as politically, that what they conceived to be
the fundamental unity of the country should be emphasised in the
most solemn fashion. It was no less important that when the state – as
distinct from the nation – was being defined, popular sovereignty under
God should again be stressed. 'Ireland', ran Article 5, 'is a sovereign,
independent, democratic state', and the next Article expressed this, if
anything, even more forcibly. 'All powers of government, legislative,
executive and judicial', it laid down, 'derive, under God, from the
people, whose right it is to designate the rulers of the State and, in
final appeal, to decide all questions of national policy, according to the
requirements of the common good.' And, so that political independence might receive the same sort of emphasis that popular sovereignty
did, Article 7 provided for a separate Irish flag (the green, white and
orange tricolour) and Article 8 stated in its first clause that the Irish
language, 'as the national language', was *the* first official language, and
in its second clause that English was 'recognised' as *a* second official
language.*

Yet, despite all this elaboration, political independence did not
extend to calling the state by name what it quite evidently was in
fact – a republic. That this gap remained was due in a double sense
to the existence of partition. Mr de Valera himself was deeply reluctant then, as later, to identify the republic with anything less than the
thirty-two counties for which the men of 1916 had died. At the same
time, it seemed prudent (though in practice, perhaps, a little naive)
to leave open a loophole for the reunification of Ireland by deliberately
not writing into the Constitution the one word which of all others
was anathema to the men of the north. 'If the Northern problem were
not there', Mr de Valera admitted in debate, '. . . in all probability
there would be a flat, downright proclamation of a republic in this
[Constitution].'[35]

Of course the absence of the word did not impede the actuality.
This was made clear enough in the system of government embodied in
the document. And nowhere was it made plainer than in the Articles
relating to the office of President. The President was a head of state,
but he was also more than this. Elected by popular suffrage for
seven years (and eligible for re-election for a second term only), he
could not be removed from office except by impeachment and even
then the proposal to prefer a charge against him, which could be
made in either House, had to be supported by not less than two-
thirds of the members of the House in which it had been preferred.[36]
His duties were intended to be – and in practice mainly have been –
formal, but Mr de Valera himself regarded the President as the

* My italics.

guardian both of the people's rights and of the Constitution.[37] To this end he was entrusted with special, discretionary powers which differentiated him sharply from, say, the Governors-General of Commonwealth countries. Thus, first, he had the power to refer any Bill other than a Money Bill or a Bill proposing to amend the Constitution to the Supreme Court for a decision as to whether or not any part of it was repugnant to the Constitution – this procedure has been used three times.[38] Second, if asked to do so by joint petition from a majority of the Senate and not less than one-third of the Dáil, he could refuse to sign a Bill dealing with a matter 'of such national importance that the will of the people ought to be ascertained', until the will of the people had been ascertained by referendum.[39] And in the specific case of amendments of the Constitution – which could only be carried out after referendum – the President was enjoined by Article 46 only to sign the resulting law to change the Constitution after he had satisfied himself that the provisions for a referendum had been complied with. Third, the President had power at any time to convene a meeting of either or both Houses or to communicate with the Houses 'by message or address' on matters of national or public importance.[40] Finally, he had the power – which, if party strength in parliament was evenly balanced, could become important – to refuse a dissolution to a prime minister (Taoiseach) who had ceased to command a majority in the Dáil and who had asked for such a dissolution.[41] If the President did refuse a dissolution then the Taoiseach would have no option but to resign, leaving it to the Dáil to nominate his successor. Such a situation might easily lead to a serious constitutional crisis and it seems unlikely that any President would in practice make use of this particular weapon. So far, in fact, none has done so.

In this last function, and also in his supervisory role at times of referendum on amendments to the Constitution, the President was able to act on his own. But in the exercise of his other powers he was obliged to consult the Council of State, a body of notables comprising certain office-holders and such other individuals up to the number of seven as the President might think fit to appoint.[42] The Council, however, was assigned a very minor place in the scheme of things, for although it was there to advise the President, he was under no obligation to accept its advice. In the event it has met very seldom, being summoned mainly to be consulted as to whether or not certain legislation should be referred to the Supreme Court for a decision on the question of repugnancy. It will be seen, therefore, that although in normal times the President would not be expected to go outside his purely formal and ceremonial duties, yet potentially he could play a significant part in a moment of crisis. This was not so obvious in the beginning, when the first President was the aged and infirm Gaelic scholar, Dr Douglas Hyde, but in recent years Presidential elections have been fought on party lines and the fact that the President is now none other than Mr de Valera himself (at the time of writing in his second term) gives a certain piquancy to the way the office has been defined.

It would be wrong, however, to deduce from the rather elaborate mode in which the President's powers were woven into the Constitution that he was exalted at the expense of the working government, the Taoiseach and his fellow-ministers. On the contrary, particular attention was paid to the Taoiseach in the document and powers which had perhaps been implicit earlier in the office of President of the Executive Council (at least while Mr de Valera held it), were now made explicit. Thus, not only was it laid down that his advice must be sought in virtually all matters of importance, but he was also given the power of recommending in his own right that the President should dissolve parliament.[43] In addition, he could advise the President to accept the resignations of individual ministers or even to dismiss them if necessary. His powers in relation to the legislature were, if anything, even more extensive. He was to decide the date of assembly for the Dáil; he could nominate his ministers without being obliged to tell the Dáil to which departments they were being assigned – though in practice he did do so, of course; no motion or grant to appropriate funds could be considered by the Dáil except on a message from the government signed by him; it was he who presented all Bills to the President for signature; and the eleven nominated members of the Senate were in fact nominated by him.[44] Since the Constitution also provided for what is, by modern standards, a not unduly large government of not less than seven or more than fifteen members, it is clear that the Taoiseach, with no pressing necessity to delegate his very considerable powers to worry him, was well placed to dominate his colleagues. Indeed, as has been justly said, 'there can be no doubt that the intention of the 1937 Constitution was to elevate the Taoiseach formally and in practice to the position of a strong British Prime Minister'.[45] That appellation might not have pleased Mr de Valera, but it describes his own tenure of the office accurately enough. It may be a rather less exact description of his successors, with the possible exception of Mr Sean Lemass, who, despite, or perhaps because of, his readiness to act on a majority vote rather than wait for unanimity, exerted such a personal ascendancy over his own cabinet as to seem at times *plus roi que le roi*, more chief-like than de Valera himself. Nevertheless, as a modern authority (Mr Brian Farrell) has suggested, the framework within which the cabinet operates in Ireland is such as to reserve to the Taoiseach a predominant role in government. 'Given', he writes, 'parliamentary representatives whose main concerns are local, even parochial, and parties sensitive to established community interests and values, the main restraints on executive policy-making spring less from the institutions of politics than from the value systems of the community. No other body in the society can compare in potential influence and power with the state-machine; the cabinet holds within itself a near-monopoly of major public decisions and, with rare exceptions, it is clear that what it decides will be accepted by the Oireachtas [parliament] and implemented loyally by the public service. Within the cabinet no single actor – irrespective of office, personality or power base – can compare in influence with the Taoiseach; what he says, with rare exceptions, will be listened to and what he wants achieved.'*

Compared with the change of emphasis from Governor-General to President, and from President of the Executive Council to Taoiseach, the powers and functions of the Oireachtas, or parliament, were little altered in essentials from what they had been in the 1922 Constitution. True, there was provision for direct popular participation in legislation – as there had been in the earlier Constitution until it was removed in 1928 – but this was limited to referenda on constitutional amendments and to the discretionary power of the President to submit proposed legislation to the people in certain exceptional, not to say unlikely, circumstances. Nevertheless, even though limited, the power of referendum was potentially important and on two occasions – in 1959 and 1968 – has resulted in significant defeats for a government bent upon the abolition of proportional representation. More recently – in May 1972 – a referendum on the question of Irish entry into the Common Market has provided the government of the day (Mr Lynch's Fianna Fáil administration) with a majority in favour of 'going into Europe' so massive as to astonish all beholders.

The structure of parliament bears superficially more resemblance to what had been envisaged in 1922 than to the single-chamber government Mr de Valera had created by the abolition of the Senate in 1936. Though himself still apparently unconvinced of the necessity for a second chamber, he was prepared to 'give way to the people who are anxious for it'.[46] But he did not really give way very far. There was to be a Senate of sixty members consisting of eleven government nominees, six university representatives and forty-three members elected on a vocational basis from five panels of candidates 'having knowledge and practical experience of' National Language and Culture, Literature, Art, Education and certain professional interests; Agriculture and Fisheries; Labour; Industry and Commerce; Public Administration and the social services.[47] Despite its echoes of the corporative state and the papal encyclicals – or perhaps because of

* B. Farrell, *Chairman or Chief?: The Role of Taoiseach in Irish Government* (Dublin and London, 1971), pp. 82-3. This volume, the first in a series of 'Studies in Irish Political Culture', of which Mr Farrell is editor, contains a useful, and to a certain extent a comparative, account of the careers in office of the five men who have occupied the post of Taoiseach (or its equivalent) since 1922. For two views of the 'cabinet timber' available for the construction of Irish governments, see B. Chubb, *The Government and Politics of Ireland* (London and Stanford, California, 1970), pp. 171-6, and A. Cohan, *The Irish Political Elite* (Dublin and London, 1972), vol. 4 of 'Studies in Irish Political Culture', especially chaps. 1 and 2.

them – this aspect of the Senate's structure seems never to have worked nor to have been given much chance to work.[48] The upper house, it has been said, has to some extent become 'a refuge for meritorious and disappointed candidates of the Dáil'.[49] Most critics would agree with that, though some might cavil at the word 'meritorious'. The crucial question for a second chamber is of course the extent to which it can revise or hold up legislation transmitted to it by the lower house. By this acid test the Senate of the 1937 Constitution was but a shadow of its predecessor. It could suspend ordinary Bills for only ninety days, and Money Bills for no more than twenty-one days, and even these periods, as we have seen, could be 'abridged' in emergency by a certificate of the Taoiseach, a resolution of the Dáil and the concurrence of the President.[50]

The Dáil, which inevitably remained the predominant partner in the legislative process, was, as before, to be elected by proportional representation on the basis of not less than one member for each thirty thousand of the population or more than one member for each twenty thousand of the population.[51] The total number was to be revised every twelve years and the movement of population resulted in a reduction from 40 constituencies and 147 members in 1947 to 38 constituencies and 144 members in 1961.[52] Although the Constitution allowed it rather less scope than formerly for intervention in the routine business of government, the Dáil was still beyond question the chief source of legislation and it retained, naturally, its superior powers in regard to Money Bills and Bills to amend the Constitution.[53] Its procedure approximated to British practice in some, though not all, respects, even if the niceties of debate have tended – still tend occasionally, indeed – to be disturbed by bitter echoes of the Civil War. In recent years it has averaged rather more than 70 sittings, totalling over 500 hours, a year. Of this time about half has been given to financial business and only a very tiny fraction to private members' Bills.[54] Party discipline has been, on the whole, fairly rigid – no doubt because governments have usually had very small majorities – but though members can be vociferous on occasions (especially at question-time) the predominance of complicated official business has meant that relatively few back-benchers say very much. Perhaps they have not very much to say, but whether they have or not, it is difficult to avoid the conclusion that their two main functions are to vote as they are told in the House, and outside it to bring what pressure they can to bear upon ministers in the interests of their constituents. In a small, intimate country like Ireland this latter function is exceedingly important and a number of members have built their reputations less on what they do in the chamber, than on their success in obtaining jobs, pensions and so on for 'the boys' at home; in the process, it is only fair to say, the constituency as a whole often benefits as much as individuals.

All the same, one is left with an abiding impression of a parliamentary system which, however important as a forum for expressing opinions or voicing grievances, is scarcely adequate to the needs of a modern society whether in its function of criticising the government or in the sphere of creative legislation. It has, in fact, been condemned by a leading expert in this field as deficient on three counts. 'First, its procedures and techniques are archaic and ineffective; second, the staff and facilities available to members are meagre; and, third, too few of the members are equipped by education or experience to make the kinds of inquiries that are necessary or to appreciate the kind of data that ought to be made available in order to judge performance. Thus, neither the methods employed nor the personnel involved, whether representative or professional, are adequate to appraise large programmes of public expenditure upon an ever increasing range of economic and social objectives, including long-term capital programmes and extensive subsidies. Even if they were, the style and demeanour of opposition . . . and the conception members generally have of their function do not favour really effective or hard-hitting criticism.'[55]

The same conservatism which dictated that there should be little fundamental change in the legislature ensured that the law courts and the whole judicial machinery inherited from the 1922 Constitution should be carried over intact into the new dispensation. It was expressly stipulated in 1937 that 'subject to this Constitution . . . the laws in force in Saorstát Eireann immediately prior to the date of the coming into operation of this Constitution shall continue to be of full force and effect until the same or any of them shall have been repealed or amended by enactment of the Oireachtas'.[56] Similarly, it was provided by Article 58 that the pre-1937 courts were to continue in existence and with the same jurisdictions as before, 'subject to the provisions of this Constitution relating to the determination of questions as to the validity of any law'.[57] The reference here, of course, was to the power of the President to refer Bills to the Supreme Court for an opinion on the question of repugnancy. That this was something more than an interesting piece of constitutional decoration has been demonstrated by the fact that on three occasions important legislation has been so referred to the Supreme Court which in one instance (the School Attendance Bill of 1942) found parts of the measure to be unconstitutional.[58]

Mr de Valera, however, did not confine himself to questions of government and jurisdiction. He included also in his Constitution two features which then and subsequently attracted much attention both inside and outside the country. One was the declaration of certain 'fundamental rights' to which the citizen was entitled, and the other was the insertion – largely, it seems, for the guidance of the legislature – of what he called 'directive principles of social policy'. These formulations were not in themselves particularly novel. Fundamental rights are explicitly stated in many modern constitutions, and not only rights but social principles also, had appeared in one form or another in the 1916 proclamation, the Democratic Programme of 1919, and the Constitution of 1922. What gave Mr de Valera's provisions their particular interest was the way they attempted to combine the liberal, democratic mode in which such declarations were commonly expressed with a very specific Catholic content.[59]

These two aspects rubbed shoulders in the group of Articles (40 through 44) devoted to fundamental rights. Article 40, which dealt with 'personal rights', was very much in the liberal, almost one might say the egalitarian, tradition, with its opening statement that all citizens 'shall, as human persons, be held equal before the law', its explicit commitments to habeas corpus, its guarantees of freedom of speech, peaceable assembly and association, its promise that private dwellings should be inviolable and its proviso that laws regulating the rights of free assembly or of forming associations and unions should not contain any political, religious or class discrimination. It is true that these particular rights were made 'subject to public order and morality', and that this qualification was regarded by Mr de Valera's critics as characteristically devious, but in fact Article 40, together with certain other safeguards laid down in Articles 34 to 38, dealing with the law-courts, did reflect a serious concern for individual liberty. Irish lawyers, it is only fair to add, have not been slow to point out what is, technically, a greater qualification of these rights than the formula about 'public order and morality' – the ability of the government in time of war or national emergency to take powers that would nullify much of what is conceded in Article 40. On the other hand, the 'emergency' which was declared when war broke out in 1939 is still legally in existence and no law-abiding citizen seems any the worse.[60]

The other fundamental rights (Articles 41 to 44) refer successively to the family, education, private property and religion. Here if anywhere, as all accounts agree, does the Constitution take on a specifically Catholic flavour, or, as has sometimes been suggested, a Thomist and scholastic flavour. These Articles, it seems, owe much to the encyclicals of Pope Pius XI, especially *The Christian Education of Youth* (1929), *Christian Marriage* (1930) and *Quadragesimo Anno* (1931), though in all probability we should look beyond the encyclicals to that synthesis of Catholic social principles published by the International Union of Social Studies of Malines in Belgium in 1927 and known as the Social Code.[61] It is against this background that Article 41 in particular must be read. This opens with the remarkable declaration that 'the State recognizes the Family as the natural primary and fundamental unit group of society, and as a moral institution possessing inalienable and imprescriptible rights, antecedent and superior to all positive law'. From this it follows that the state guarantees to protect the family as the basis of the social order and to guard the basis of marriage. To that end it is laid down that 'no law shall be enacted providing for the grant of a dissolution of a marriage'. Furthermore, recognising that 'by her life within the home, woman gives to the State a support without which the common good cannot be achieved', the state itself was 'to endeavour to ensure that mothers shall not be obliged by economic necessity to engage in labour to the neglect of their duties in the home'.[62] These phrases, uncomfortably reminiscent of the Hitlerite formula for women of *Kinder, Küche, Kirche*, are not, however, to be seen (as feminists, understandably, might see them) simply as the expression of a paternalistic dictatorship. Not only were they in line with Catholic thinking, they corresponded to an ideal with which many Irish men and women would have been in instinctive sympathy. This is not necessarily to say that the reality approximated even remotely to the ideal. Children would still go hungry, women would still lose their youth prematurely rearing large families in the Dublin slums, marriages would still often produce more suffering than bliss – nevertheless, even though this was the burden of daily existence, the affirmation had been made, the state had committed itself publicly to upholding a pattern of life that the majority of its citizens felt to be the right pattern for them.

The emphasis on the importance of the family is carried over into Article 42, where the state acknowledges it to be 'the primary and natural educator' of the child. Parents were free to provide this education as they wished, subject to the insistence of the state on 'a certain minimum education'. To provide for this it was laid down that 'the State shall provide for free primary education and shall endeavour to supplement and give reasonable aid to private and corporate educational initiative, and, when the public good requires it, provide other educational facilities or institutions with due regard, however, for the rights of parents, especially in the matter of religious and moral information'.

When it turned (Article 43) to deal with property the Constitution trod a carefully drawn line between the rights of the person and the responsibilities of the state, though even here, as commentators have insisted, the over-riding concern was not to balance nineteenth century individualism against twentieth century collectivism, but rather to accord closely with Catholic teaching on the subject at that period. Thus, while the Article began by recognising rights to private property, it went on to declare that these ought to be regulated 'by the principles of social justice', and from this proceeded to the major qualification of what had been conceded already by enabling the state to 'delimit by law the exercise of the said rights with a view to reconciling their exercise with the exigencies of the common good'. This was not simply, however, to take back with one hand what had been given with the other. It was, on the contrary, to recognise that in such a matter hard-and-fast doctrinaire positions could not be taken up in advance, and that in its attitude towards private property a government responsive to Catholic doctrines would be guided by expedience and human welfare, conditioning factors which might easily change from time to time.[63]

It would be reasonable to suppose that a Constitution so sensitive to the social teachings of Catholicism would accord to the Catholic Church itself a specially favoured position. This it did, but only up to a point – and the reservation was deliberate and significant. The state, declared Article 44, 'recognises the special position of the Holy Catholic Apostolic and Roman Church as the guardian of the Faith professed by the great majority of the citizens', but it also recognised the Church of Ireland, the Presbyterian Church, the Methodist Church, the Society of Friends, the Jewish congregations and 'the other religious denominations existing in Ireland at the date of the coming into operation of this Constitution'. Not only this, but the next clause guaranteed freedom of conscience to every citizen and also repeated in detail the prohibitions of the 1922 Constitution against religious discrimination and interference with church property, save for 'necessary works of utility and on payment of compensation'. The broad toleration revealed by these clauses no doubt had, at least in part, a political motivation. They were as necessary in 1937 as they had been in 1922 to reassure the minority within the twenty-six counties and also to convince doubting Protestants in the six counties (if, indeed, any convincing was possible) that Home Rule had not, after all, meant Rome rule. But it is proper to add that Article 44 was not just a form of religious propaganda. It did no more than represent what had been the actual situation in the Irish Free State from the beginning, and to embody in the written document what southern Protestants had gratefully experienced in their own lives. Nor is there any reason whatever to doubt that these provisions corresponded to Mr de Valera's own deepest convictions.

It should be added that at the time of writing (1972) there is considerable pressure to change or reform the Constitution. Apart from the fact – in itself of the utmost significance – that the recent decision to join the European Economic Community will almost certainly lead to some reassessment of the concept of sovereignty, there would seem to be two other factors influencing the desire for change. One is the altered climate of religious feeling since the Second Vatican Council.* The other is the growing realisation in some quarters that if the ideal of a reconciliation between north and south is ever to be more than a pious platitude then it would sooner or later be necessary to overhaul those Articles of the Constitution which were most likely to grate upon Protestant susceptibilities. It was probably this realisation which prompted the then Taoiseach, Mr Lemass, to

* This is referred to briefly below, pp. 686-9. For a full treatment of the subject, see the admirable study by John Whyte, *Church and State in Modern Ireland, 1923-1970* (Dublin and London, 1971), especially chap. 11.

appoint an all-party committee to review the Constitution as long ago as 1966. The Committee's report was published at the end of 1967 and although the ensuing debate was at times rather desultory and inconclusive the eruption of the northern crisis has given the whole matter a fresh urgency.

The articles in this particular context which were singled out by the report were Article 41 (which prohibited divorce) and, of course, Article 44 defining the 'special position' of the Roman Catholic Church. Linked with these in public discussion – to an extent unimaginable even ten years ago – has been the Criminal Law Amendment Act of 1935 which forbade the sale and import of contraceptives. Since the issues have still to be resolved, no conclusion can yet be drawn from the ebb and flow of public argument. Two comments may, however, be made on the situation as it stands at present. First, it is evident, as was only to be expected, that the ecclesiastical reaction to proposals to relax the law relating to divorce and to contraceptives has been decidedly hostile, a reaction which, in the case of contraceptives, has been strongly reinforced by the promulgation in 1970 of the papal edict, *Humanae Vitae*. But secondly, it is equally clear that the Church has not shown itself by any means wedded to the special position guaranteed to it by Article 44. On the contrary, as recently as September 1969, Cardinal Conway openly declared that he 'would not shed a tear' if the controversial clauses disappeared and shortly afterwards this position was officially endorsed by the hierarchy as a whole.*

Although the fundamental rights provisions of the Constitution did, as already suggested, attempt to combine liberal principles with Catholic social teaching, they did so in a way which strongly suggests that what was really intended was to provide a framework within which society could evolve, without the necessity of further rapid or drastic change. To say this is to say in effect that the purpose behind these Articles was essentially conservative. No less conservative was the intention underlying the 'Directive Principles of Social Policy' embodied in Article 45. Here too a balance was delicately maintained between the rights of the individual and the needs of the community. Here too the influence of Catholic thought made its influence directly felt. Thus the state was to promote the welfare 'of the whole people' by securing and protecting 'a social order in which justice and charity shall inform all the institutions of the national life'. To achieve this the state was so to direct its policy that citizens 'may through their occupations find the means of making reasonable provision for their domestic needs'. And not only that, it was 'to safeguard with especial care the economic interests of the weaker sections of the community, and, where necessary, to contribute to the support of the infirm, the widow, the orphan and the aged'. Likewise, it was 'to endeavour to ensure that the strength and health of

* The relevant clause has now been abolished after a referendum.

workers, men and women, and the tender age of children shall not be abused and that citizens shall not be forced by economic necessity to enter avocations unsuited to their sex, age or strength'. Even in the realm of property and business enterprise the state was to enter in to prevent the exploitation of man by man – to guard against monopoly, to control credit for 'the welfare of the people as a whole', to supplement private initiative in industry and commerce wherever necessary, to settle as many families on the land as might be practicable, to ensure that the ownership and control of the material resources of the community be so distributed amongst individuals and classes 'as best to subserve the common good'.

There is a vague benevolence about some of these phrases that could easily move the critic to scepticism. And his scepticism might be fortified by the discovery that these 'principles of social policy' were intended only for the general guidance of the Oireachtas and were not cognisable by any court. Nor can it be affirmed with confidence that actual policy has to a significant degree been shaped by these principles or that the poor and the weak have become any less poor and weak because of the existence of Article 45. It is only fair, however, to make two points on the other side. One is that even though the Article is not enforceable in the courts, and even though every clause of it is so vague and imprecise as to drive a lawyer to distraction, yet it is not unfitting for a society which does broadly accept the principles embodied in the Article to display them boldly in its Constitution where they may be read and pondered not only by the legislators of the present but by the legislators of the future, who may some day come closer to translating them into reality.

And the other point that needs to be made is that these very directives, though occasionally derided by the sophisticated, were deeply admired and closely studied by some of the newly emerging nations after the Second World War, to such an extent that not only the principles of social policy, but also the fundamental rights, were incorporated in whole or in part into the Constitutions of India and Burma. Partly because of this, and partly because it provided a model for a written constitution, republican in character and containing the essentials of parliamentary democracy, the Irish Constitution of 1937 had, according to a modern authority on the subject, 'a wide significance in relation to those parts of the Commonwealth in which nationalist aspirations demanded a precise formulation of the political practices, aims and ideals they were to adopt'.[64]

Yet in the last resort the Constitution of 1937 must be judged less by what it did for an evolving Commonwealth than by what it did for Ireland. And what it did for Ireland can be summed up in a single sentence. It achieved stability. After nearly thirty years of incessant war, revolution and political change the twenty-six counties had at last reached a kind of equilibrium so profound and so firmly based that even the final step towards the formal realisation of the republic, when it came in 1948-9, could be taken by the passing of a simple act of parliament and without the necessity of far-reaching constitutional amendment. It is too soon yet to say what the verdict of history upon Mr de Valera will be. But it may well be that when the verdict has to be given the two fruits of his pre-war policy – the External Relations Act and the Constitution of 1937 – will come to be seen as the most remarkable achievement of a most remarkable man.

(iv) NEUTRALITY AND ISOLATION

It is probably inevitable that a small nation which has just achieved self-government should be preoccupied with its own affairs to the almost total exclusion of what is happening in the rest of the world. In the Irish Free State this natural preoccupation was heightened by the persistence of the deep internal divisions dating from the Civil War, but although it is no doubt true that most of the population *were* completely absorbed in their own affairs, it was never possible for the leaders of either of the two main parties to ignore for long the existence of international tensions and the effect these might have upon their country.

For Irishmen striving to assert their national identity within a Commonwealth which, however benevolently disposed, they still found restrictive, the League of Nations at Geneva was an obvious counterpoise. Even to join the League, as the Irish Free State did in 1923, was in a manner to assert separate nationhood, as was also the decision to register the Anglo-Irish Treaty at Geneva the following year in the teeth of British objections. But it was not the Irish intention simply to use the League as a convenient means of scoring points against Britain in the elaborate game of Commonwealth relations. The Free State was a member, as other small countries were members, because the League seemed – for a brief while at least – to offer some alternative to the old power-balance dominated by the great nations. Once inside the League, therefore, the Irish were prepared to take their full share of the responsibilities of membership. In 1926, for example, the Free State stood for election to the Council but, partly through lack of preparation, partly because of British opposition (on grounds of expediency, not principle, her leaders were assured), was defeated.[65] The Irish candidature was successful, however, in 1930 when it received considerable, and perhaps decisive, backing from other Commonwealth countries.[66]

Even a very brief acquaintance with what went on at Geneva was enough to induce disenchantment. Kevin O'Higgins, admittedly a man to whom scepticism came easily, expressed this disenchantment as early as 1925, in a letter to his wife written while attending an abortive disarmament conference:

On the whole [he wrote] I am, I fear, inclined to be mildly cynical about this 'League of Nations' without denying that it has certain advantages. Personal contact between representatives of Governments is good. It breaks down prejudices and insularities . . . but don't let anyone convince you that the League – whatever its germs and possibilities – is a temple of justice where great and small can meet on equal terms and only right prevails. It simply imposes the necessity for hypocrisy – vice's tribute to virtue – but once that is paid, then *sicut erat in principio*, etc.[67]

But if O'Higgins was a realist who, so far as the future of the League was concerned, took refuge in cynicism, Mr de Valera, no less a realist after his own fashion, was prepared to react very differently. His instinct was not to write off the organisation, but rather to lecture it for its own good. And by chance it happened that only a few months after coming to power he had an unrivalled opportunity to do so. In September 1932 he took office as President of the Council of the League and, discarding the well-tried platitudes offered to him by his advisers, spoke out with devastating frankness. It was a critical moment in Geneva. The Japanese aggression in China was less than a year old and everywhere men, as Mr de Valera said, were looking to the League to see how it would meet this threat to peace. He warned the astonished delegates that they were, after all, answerable at the bar of world opinion and that this opinion was becoming increasingly critical, if not hostile:

People are complaining [he said] that the League is devoting its activity to matters of secondary or very minor importance, while the vital international problems of the day, problems which touch the very existence of our peoples, are being shelved or postponed or ignored. People are saying that the equality of States does not apply here in the things that matter, that the smaller States whilst being given a voice have very little influence in the final determination of League action . . . Finally, there is a suspicion abroad that little more than lip-service is paid to the fundamental principles on which the League is founded; there is a suspicion that the action of the League in the economic sphere can be paralysed by the pressure of powerful national interests, and that if the hand that is raised against the Covenant is sufficiently strong, it can smite with impunity.[68]

That these misgivings were only too well founded the Italian invasion of Abyssinia demonstrated three years later. Here a great power, Italy, did indeed 'smite with impunity' and in doing so showed with bleak clarity just how easily the economic sanctions imposed by the League could be paralysed. For Mr de Valera (who was, incidentally, his own Minister for External Affairs) this situation posed a special difficulty. Not only was the Roman Catholic Church in Ireland uneasy about the imposition of sanctions on Italy, but the very fact the chief protagonist of a sanctions policy was Great Britain exposed him to the taunt that by supporting that policy he was kowtowing to the enemy with whom at that very moment he was engaged in an economic war. He was able to dispose of the latter argument by the famous retort that 'if your worst enemy happens to be going to Heaven by the same road you are, you don't for that reason turn around and go in the opposite direction'.[69] But the widespread anxiety in the country about getting involved in what might become an actual war with Italy was something much harder to combat.

It was, he freely admitted, a painful dilemma. Either the Free State must be 'thrown into a position of enmity with those with whom we wish to be on terms of friendship', or else it must face the terrible alternative – 'the abandonment of duty and the betrayal of our deepest convictions and of our word solemnly given'. At such a moment that rigid adherence to principle which had been the bane of his domestic opponents showed itself in its most admirable form. Convinced as he was that collective security was the only hope for the world – for great nations as well as for little ones – he realised that the League was unlikely to withstand a second crisis of confidence. What the Japanese had begun the Italians might well complete. 'The final test of the League and all that it stands for has come', he warned the Assembly in September 1935. 'Make no mistake, if on any pretext whatever we were to permit the sovereignty of even the weakest State amongst us to be unjustly taken away, the whole foundation of the League would crumble into dust.' The pledge of security, he insisted, had to be universal. 'If the Covenant is not observed as a whole for all and by all, then there is no Covenant.'

Why [he concluded passionately] can we not at least place this League of Nations on a stable foundation? Why can we not free the fundamental instrument of the League from its association with political arrangements which are universally recognised as unjust? Why can we not endeavour to forge an international instrument, not merely for settling international disputes when they arise, but for removing in advance the causes of those disputes?[70]

In the light of subsequent events, and of the suicidal stampede of Europe over the precipice of the Second World War, these read like rhetorical questions. Perhaps they seemed so even at the time, but in the evolution of an independent Irish foreign policy they have an important place. For if they could not be properly answered the moral was clear. And Mr de Valera was quick to draw it in a broadcast to his own people on his return home. If Italy succeeded like Japan in violating the Covenant, then the League of Nations would disappear as an effective safeguard. 'It becomes, in fact', he said, 'a source of danger – a trap for States trusting in it, leading them to neglect adequate measures for their own defence.'[71] This was still his view the following year and in the Dáil he actually went so far as to speculate if the time had not come to withdraw altogether from the League.[72] He was reluctant to do so, for any forum where statesmen could meet was better than no forum, but his own thoughts were turning more and more insistently towards neutrality. 'All the small States can do', he said in Geneva in 1936, 'if the statesmen of the greater States fail in their duty, is resolutely to determine that they will not become the tools of any great power, and that they will resist with whatever strength they may possess every attempt to force them into a war against their will.'[73]

It was this insistence upon neutrality that led him to resist pressure at home to recognise General Franco's regime in the Spanish Civil War. The Irish people, he freely admitted to the League in 1937, were far from indifferent to some of the issues then being fought out in Spain, but his government believed in non-intervention, both because the form of government to be adopted in Spain was a matter for Spaniards only, and even more because intervention could set off a chain-reaction leading to 'a general European disaster'.[74] But while it was relatively easy to maintain this attitude of aloofness towards a remote and obscure struggle for power in Spain, would it be possible to do so when the great storm finally broke upon Europe and all the major powers were swept into the conflict? For Mr de Valera the key to this question was the relationship of Ireland with Britain. So long as his powerful neighbour was in possession of the Treaty ports, and entitled to demand certain other facilities in time of war, there was an obvious risk that a foreign enemy might consider Irish protestations about neutrality a trifle academic, and that Ireland would find herself involved in a major struggle without having been able to exercise the smallest influence on her own fate.

That is why the return of the ports in 1938 marks so important a turning-point in the relations between the two countries. Neutrality at once became a more practicable policy and the causes of friction between Britain and Ireland were correspondingly reduced at a vital moment in history. This did not mean that Irish policy would then box the compass from isolation to involvement on Britain's side. Mr de Valera made it abundantly clear that so long as partition lasted there could be no question of Irish co-operation with Britain, or for that matter with other Commonwealth countries, in matters of defence. On the other hand, the logical corollary for him of the Agreements of 1938 was that his government would never permit any part of Ireland to be used as a base for attack against Britain. This, as has been truly said, 'assured Britain for the first time in modern history of a friendly neutral responsible for the defence of nationalist Ireland'.[75]

Mr de Valera has testified more than once to his appreciation of the part played by Neville Chamberlain in the dramatic improvement of Anglo-Irish relations during 1938 and he seems to have been no less favourably disposed towards the British Prime Minister's policy of appeasement. By a curious chance that year found the Irish leader President of the Assembly of the League of Nations (his candidature having been strongly supported by Britain) which met in September while the Munich crisis was actually unrolling. When on 30 September Chamberlain reached agreement with Hitler on the dismemberment of Czechoslovakia, it fell to Mr de Valera to announce the fact to the Assembly. 'All honour', he said, 'to those who . . . strove – as we now know, thank God, successfully – for such a solution.'[76] The 'solution', temporary as it was, had of course been reached outside the League and with absolutely no reference to it. And whatever Mr de Valera might have felt it necessary to say in public, the events of 1938 can only have confirmed him in his opinion that as a force for peace the League of Nations was finally discredited. Thenceforward the only hope for small countries – and a precarious hope at that – was neutrality. 'I have stated here in this House', he told the Dáil in April 1939, 'and I have stated in the country, that the aim of government policy is to keep this country out of war, and nobody, either here or elsewhere, has any right to assume anything else.'[77] As war came closer month by month this attitude hardened, receiving full support in parliament from all the other parties.* Indeed, the very fact that Britain now seemed certain to be drawn in strengthened the Irish determination to be neutral. For neutrality, after all, was not just the instinctive reaction of a small power to keep clear of the quarrels of big powers, it was the outward and visible sign of absolute sovereignty. To be free to choose between peace and war was the mark of independence, to be free to choose between peace and a *British* war demonstrated to all the world just how complete that independence really was.

Yet there went with it an air of unreality which the actual outbreak of war served only to intensify. Neutrality was a fine sentiment, but the harsh fact was that it could only be enjoyed on sufferance. That the twenty-six counties passed through the war – in neutral jargon it was called the 'emergency' – unviolated, was due partly to British forbearance and partly to the success of first British, and later Allied, arms. This forbearance was severely taxed several times. Even before the fighting started the British representative in Ireland, Sir John Maffey (later Lord Rugby) took private soundings from the editor of the *Irish Times* – still, at that time, reckoned to be a pro-British newspaper – to see what the Irish reaction to a landing by British troops

* It is proper to record that a leading member of Fine Gael, Mr James Dillon, took a different view and eventually (in 1941) resigned from his party on this issue, only rejoining it ten years later.

in certain circumstances might be.[78] He was left in no doubt that the reaction would be violently hostile, but the temptation to re-occupy the ports must have been very severe during the critical stages of the Battle of the Atlantic; indeed, had it not been that bases were available in Northern Ireland, and especially at Londonderry, it is hard to see how Britain could have avoided taking some desperate action to secure her western approaches.* The entry of America into the war did not ease matters, for although the United States was, almost by definition, friendly to Ireland, the American ambassador, Mr David Gray, had no hesitation in recommending the seizure of bases in the south to President Roosevelt and in 1944, with the Normandy landings imminent, it was the Americans rather than the British who wanted pressure to be brought upon Ireland, mainly with a view to preventing the leakage of vital information to the Germans. It is probably too early yet to say for certain why the Allies held their hand. No doubt they were influenced to some extent by the adverse reaction such an occupation of a small neutral country would have provoked from world opinion; though any sane calculation of risks would also have warned them that resistance would have been so fierce as to defeat the object of the manoeuvre. The regular Irish army was indeed tiny – only about 7,000 regulars with a reserve of 14,000 – and very poorly equipped, but with additional recruitment and the formation of a local defence force, there were a quarter of a million men under arms by the end of the war and capable of mounting an effective guerrilla campaign. The lessons of 1919-21 were not, after all, distant enough to have been forgotten by either side.

But if there was no Allied occupation what were the chances of a German attack? The answer appears to be that a direct invasion as a means of striking at Britain from the rear was ruled out. On the other hand, had Operation Sealion succeeded in 1940 and Britain been overrun, there can be little doubt that Ireland would have suffered the same fate. German documents captured after the war revealed

* Since the above was written the Cabinet records for 1939 have become available. These indicate that there was very strong pressure inside the government (especially from Churchill as First Lord of the Admiralty) to demand naval facilities and to take them by force if need be. In the face of Mr de Valera's adamant refusal to compromise his neutrality, the British government finally decided not to use force unless the U-boat menace became literally a matter of life and death, but it is clear from the arguments in the Cabinet that the decision might very easily have gone the other way (for a brief summary of this episode see the articles in *Irish Times*, 1 and 2 Jan. 1970). Further Cabinet papers released as this book went to press (for summary see *Irish Times*, 1 Jan. 1971) indicate that British warnings of an imminent German attack on Ireland, coupled with a rather vague promise by Britain to accept the principle of Irish unity if Eire entered the war alongside the Allies, left Mr de Valera and his policy of neutrality equally unmoved.

that plans had been laid, or at least discussed, to that end.[79] It is fair to say, therefore, that Irish neutrality depended not alone upon the Allies observing it, but upon their forces being strong enough to prevent the Germans from infringing it.

Of course, since both Germany and Britain maintained diplomatic representation in Ireland throughout the war, Dublin became, like Lisbon, one of the whispering-galleries of Europe and a natural centre for intrigue and spying of every kind. Amid all this the Irish government trod its thorny neutral path as delicately as possible and developed a remarkable capacity for not noticing disagreeable facts. Thus on the one hand it turned a blind eye to British aircraft flying over Donegal, or to the return of stranded British airmen across the border, and on the other hand it managed to ignore for a considerable time the existence of a wireless transmitter in the German embassy. The latter, admittedly, was closed down in 1944 at Allied insistence, but the rumours and the espionage continued. Even before the war the Germans were in touch with the IRA, and it has been suggested that German intelligence officers had had a hand in planning the bombing campaign in England in 1939 which, however, they would have preferred to restrain until war had actually broken out.[80] When it did break out they not only hoped to make use of two IRA leaders then in Germany – Sean Russell and Frank Ryan – but also, through an agent, Herman Goertz, to make contact with the organisation in Ireland itself.* Goertz, a brave man but not overwhelmingly competent, was taken aback by the disarray and inefficiency he found among his supposed allies. 'You know how to die for Ireland', he told them, 'but how to fight for it you have not the slightest idea.'[81] Goertz landed by parachute in May 1940 but was arrested the following February. In 1947, rather than face deportation to Germany, he committed suicide. His mission, so far as one can judge, had been entirely futile.[82]

It is doubtful whether the IRA, even if they had been more efficient or the Germans had paid them more attention, could have achieved very much. The mood of the country was set on neutrality and the harassing of control-points along the northern border, the main objective towards which the Germans sought to direct IRA efforts, commanded no widespread support in the twenty-six counties. Such raids did certainly take place, but the north was so well armed (it was, after all, on a war footing), the south was so much on the alert, and the IRA itself was so much split by internal divisions, that the

* Russell, the former Chief of Staff of the IRA, had gone to America in 1939 to raise funds. In 1940, rather than return to internment in Ireland, he went to Germany. Ryan had been imprisoned by Franco for his part in the Spanish Civil War, but his escape was engineered by the German Abwehr and by the Spanish secret police. He was then taken to Germany and he and Russell were sent together by submarine to land in Ireland. Russell died en route and Ryan, having returned without landing, died in Dresden in 1944.

effect of these attacks was simply to ruin the resources of the organisation. Apart from Russell and Ryan, twenty-six IRA men lost their lives between April 1930 and May 1946. Of these, nine were executed, five killed in gun-battles with the police on both sides of the border; six died in prison hospitals; three died on hunger-strike; two were killed in explosions and one was shot by military police at the internment camp in The Curragh.[83]

On the whole it would be a fair verdict to say that Irish neutrality, even though carried to the scrupulously correct lengths of a visit of condolence by Mr de Valera to the German embassy on the death of Hitler, favoured Britain rather than Germany. As we shall see presently the war brought the British and Irish economies even closer together than they had been before, and although Ireland's imports were hard hit by British blockade regulations (and by the desperate shortage of shipping) her own exports of cattle and meat products rose steeply. So, of course, did emigration and the amount of money sent home by the many thousands of men and women who went to work in the United Kingdom.* And not only to work, but to fight as well – during the whole period of the war some 50,000 persons from the twenty-six counties volunteered to serve in the British forces.

For those who stayed at home the war made itself felt in two main ways. One – which was more obvious at the time, but was in fact less important – was the inevitable consequence of inhabiting a small under-developed island in a hostile world. All sorts of commodities ran rapidly out of supply and various kinds of rationing had to be imposed. Private motoring virtually ceased in 1943 and long-distance travel even by public transport was not easy.[84] Gas and electricity consumption was heavily cut and coal was at times almost unobtainable There was clothes rationing, bread rationing, and a steady reduction of other foodstuffs until at one stage the weekly allowance per person was ½ oz. of tea, 6 oz. of butter and ½ lb. of sugar. There can be no doubt that this created real hardship, especially for the poor, many of whom depended very largely on bread, butter and tea and could ill-afford to buy more expensive but still available meat. Nevertheless, the great effort to achieve self-sufficiency, wasteful of natural resources and uneconomic as it may have been in the long run, did at least keep starvation at bay.

It was the other consequence of the war – psychological rather than material – that was eventually to prove far more significant for Ireland. This was, quite simply, her almost total isolation from the rest of mankind. At the very moment when she had achieved stability and full independence, and was ready to take her place in the society of nations, that society dissolved and she was thrown back upon her own meagre resources. The tensions – and the liberations – of war, the shared experience, the comradeship in suffering, the new thinking about the future, all these things had passed her by. It was as if an entire

* For the effects of the war on the Irish economy, see pp. 622-3 below.

people had been condemned to live in Plato's cave, with their backs to the fire of life and deriving their only knowledge of what went on outside from the flickering shadows thrown on the wall before their eyes by the men and women who passed to and fro behind them. When after six years they emerged, dazzled, from the cave into the light of day, it was to a new and vastly different world.

3. New Beginnings

Since, when the war ended, Mr de Valera and some of his senior colleagues had been in office for thirteen years, it would not have been surprising if the strain of carrying such a burden for so long had begun to tell. The will to rule, no doubt, was as strong as ever, but the capacity to do so was less evident. And as problems thickened round the tired and harassed government the notion that it was time for a change began to gain ground in the country.

The task of post-war adjustment in a period of continuing, or even accentuated, scarcities would have been difficult enough even under the most favourable conditions, but the conditions turned out to be as unfavourable as they well could be. Apart from the obvious problems staring everyone in the face – that industry was lacking in raw materials, fuel and capital equipment, that the consumer was hungry for manufactured goods of all kinds, and that the long wage-freeze of the 'emergency' years had built up tremendous pressures for pay-increases in all sectors of the economy, the Irish weather now added its own complications. The summer of 1946 was one of the wettest on record, so wet as to wash away all Mr de Valera's earlier appeals for increased wheat production, with the results that the meagre harvest left the government with no option but to resort once more to bread-rationing. Hard on the heels of the wretched summer came one of the hardest winters of the century. Fuel supplies, already perilously low, sank to critical depths in the early months of 1947, industry and transport were brought almost to a standstill, and the miseries of the long-suffering population were intense.

It was entirely predictable, but economically disastrous, that people, irked by these new hardships coming on top of the wartime restrictions, should have rushed to buy what little there was in the shops. Inevitably, prices rose while wages still lagged behind, and the demand for imports threatened rapidly to outpace the assets available to pay for them. Little though contemporaries may have realised it, they were already caught in the first of a recurring series of economic nightmares in which an underdeveloped economy was to be exposed to galloping inflation. The government was aware of at least some of the dangers and in an attempt to check wage advances made strenuous efforts to hold back prices; but, since the most radical of these – the introduction of subsidies to keep down the cost of essential foodstuffs – necessitated a supplementary budget in the autumn of 1947 to impose further taxes, it was obvious that, electorally speaking, Mr de Valera was giving a dangerously large number of hostages to fortune.

Almost at once fortune began to claim them. The war was not long over before scattered signs appeared in the constituencies of a kind of cumulative boredom with the old party machines, the old party slogans, even the old party leaders. The hour was ripe for a new departure in politics, and the hour duly produced the man. This was Mr Sean MacBride, son of Major John MacBride, one of the insurgents executed after 1916, and of the beautiful Maud Gonne, who had enslaved W. B. Yeats in the early years of the century. Born in 1904, Mr MacBride had grown up, naturally enough, in a republican atmosphere. Educated partly in France, he had joined the anti-Treaty side during the Civil War and never lost touch with the extreme movement thereafter. Called to the Irish bar, he became an eminent Senior Counsel, with a reputation for successfully defending IRA men who had fallen foul of the government. It was from die-hard republicans of this sort – whether survivors of the old Saor Eire movement or members of a group known as Coras na Poblachta which had split off from Fianna Fail – that the nucleus of a political party calling itself Clann na Poblachta began slowly to be formed. As the name (literally 'Republican Family') indicates, the adherents of the new party were dedicated to the establishment of an Irish republic, but to this ambition they added, with no apparent sense of incompatibility, a burning passion to end partition.

It is doubtful, however, if a new party would have had much success at that particular point in time if it had put all its eggs in the republican, anti-partition basket. Clann na Poblachta did not in fact commit that elementary error. What attracted some of the abler young men in the country towards the Clann was not just that it was republican, but that it was – or appeared to be – radical as well. Of this social radicalism Dr Noel Browne may be regarded as the leading – though not, as events were to show, the most representative – exponent. Dr Browne was totally inexperienced in politics, but his views might have been described as Christian Socialist, had not that label been annexed by the large, highly organised European parties with which his lonely individualism had little enough in common. But this very loneliness, though it left him fatally vulnerable in a parliamentary sense, was to make him in time a great symbolic figure of the Irish Left, one of the few, indeed, to have appeared since the formation of the state. Born in 1914, the son of a former policeman in the Royal Irish Constabulary, his childhood was overshadowed by the menace of tuberculosis, which carried off his father and then, after the family had moved to London, his mother and a brother and sister. Noel Browne himself attracted the favourable notice of the Jesuits, who educated him at Beaumont. Next, through the benevolence of a wealthy Dublin family, he was enabled to go to Trinity College, where he qualified as a doctor. Soon after this, he too contracted tuberculosis and on recovery made the eradication of the disease in his home country the prime business of his life. In 1947 he was introduced to MacBride – at that time framing the programme of Clann na Poblachta with Mr Noel Hartnett and Mr J. McQuillan – and from this meeting came at least a part of the welfare proposals with which the party was prepared to go to the country when the time came.[1]

That time came sooner than perhaps even the most optimistic opponents of Fianna Fáil could have expected. In the autumn of 1947 the government's always precarious control of the balance of power was suddenly endangered by the loss of two by-elections, one of them to Mr MacBride himself. Mr de Valera attempted to restore the situation, and perhaps also to nip the growing threat from the Clann in the bud, by holding a general election in February, 1948. He failed, narrowly but decisively. On a register slightly larger than at the last war-time election of 1944 which had confirmed his party in office, and with a redistribution of seats which increased the number of deputies in the Dáil from 138 to 147, the best that Fianna Fáil could muster was sixty-eight seats. To retain power Mr de Valera would have needed to share it with one or more of the other parties. They, however, were dazzled by the possibility of forming among themselves a coalition from which the veteran of so many electoral triumphs would at last be excluded, and at length, after several days of negotiation, an 'inter-party' government emerged to the astonishment of all beholders. It was a justifiable astonishment, for under the same umbrella sheltered not only Fine Gael (which, with thirty-one seats was still the second largest party in the Dáil) but also a farmers' party (Clann na Talmhan), the two groups in which the Labour party was then divided, an Independent (Mr James Dillon), and, of course, Clann na Poblachta. The Clann had won ten seats at the election and this, though far from the avalanche which some had predicted, was enough to give them two places and great influence in the cabinet that resulted from the elaborate negotiations.*

* The election resulted in the following distribution of seats: Fianna Fáil, sixty-eight; Fine Gael, thirty-one; Labour, nineteen; Clann na Talmhan, seven; Clann na Poblachta, ten; Independents, twelve. Clann na Talmhan must not be confused with the old Farmers' party which was represented in the Dáil between 1922 and 1932. The latter derived its support mainly from the larger and more prosperous farmers. It was conservative in its attitudes and a handful of its surviving members were attracted into the short-lived National Centre Party in the early 'thirties, but thereafter the wealthier members of the farming community tended to identify with Fine Gael. Clann na Talmhan, on the other hand, was launched in 1938 primarily as the vehicle for western small farmers dissatisfied with the treatment they were receiving from Fianna Fáil, the party they had consistently supported since its foundation. During the war years it was vocal and by no means ineffective, winning ten seats at the election of 1943. The unsettled climate of Irish politics in the decade after the war gave

It could hardly be called a cabinet of all the talents, for it contained too little experience (to say nothing of a modicum of incompetence), but the key posts were filled by undeniably able men eager to make the most of office after the long frustrations of opposition. The leadership, and most of the ministries, fell to Fine Gael as the strongest member of the coalition, but it was perhaps symptomatic of the difficulties lying in wait for the new government that the Taoiseach was not the man who had led the party since Mr Cosgrave's retirement in 1944. That man, General Richard Mulcahy, had been altogether too effective a leader of the Free State Forces in the Civil War for him to preside comfortably over a cabinet that contained the political heirs of the men he had fought against a generation earlier. And so, although he himself is said to have taken the initiative in the negotiations that produced the inter-party government, he emerged from those negotiations in the somewhat improbable role of Minister for Education.[2] The headship of the patchwork coalition went instead to Mr John A. Costello. Mr Costello, at that time fifty-seven years of age, was a distinguished lawyer who had served as Attorney-General during the last six years of the Cosgrave regime. Mr Costello's tenure of office was to be controversial in the extreme, but even those who differed most sharply from him admitted his skill and patience as a chairman who could, most of the time, bring order and reasonable harmony into the proceedings of his variegated and highly temperamental team.

Apart from General Mulcahy and Mr Costello, Fine Gael was powerfully represented in the cabinet by another of Cosgrave's colleagues, Mr P. McGilligan, who presided with stern austerity over the Ministry of Finance; by Dr T. F. O'Higgins, a civilian charged with Defence; by General Sean MacEoin, a soldier responsible for Justice; and by Daniel Morrissey, a refugee from Labour to whom was entrusted the important office of Minister of Industry and Commerce. The other posts were carefully distributed according to the bargaining power of the parties represented in the coalition. Mr MacBride took External Affairs, Mr Joseph Blowick (Clann na Talmhan) took Lands and Fisheries, while Mr William Norton of the Labour party took Social Welfare and acted as deputy (or Tanaiste) to Mr Costello. His Labour colleague, T. J. Murphy, went to Local Government and J. Everett (National Labour) to Posts and Telegraphs. Those appointments were all more or less predictable, but two of the most interesting were also two of the most experimental. One was that of Mr James Dillon, who had left Fine Gael in 1942 over the issue of neutrality and was not to rejoin it again until 1952; having gained a prodigious

it perhaps more importance than it deserved and it was to supply ministers to both the inter-party governments. However, with the recovery of Fianna Fáil after 1957, Clann na Talmhan dwindled and by the mid-sixties had ceased to exist.

and colourful reputation in opposition he was now, as an Independent, to have the chance (which, as we shall see, he seized with both hands) to establish himself as an imaginative and constructive Minister for Agriculture. And the other was Dr Noel Browne, whose career as a deputy and as a minister began on the same day. Assigned to the Ministry of Health, he was admirably placed to launch those schemes of social welfare which had led him in the first instance into the arms of Clann na Poblachta.

With so much ability available, and with such a wide field of initiative in reform opening out before it, the inter-party government seemed poised to give a decisive new turn to the development of modern Ireland. As we shall see presently, it did achieve in that direction more than posterity has been inclined to give it credit for, but it is one of the ironies of history that its fame – or ill-fame, according to the point of view – has come to depend less on a variety of domestic successes than on one domestic failure and on the dramatic change which it introduced into the country's relationship with the British Commonwealth.

It was this last issue that dominated the early months of the coalition's existence. Given the preoccupations of Clann na Poblachta with the republic, it was inevitable that the question of Ireland's status should have come up at the general election. Even as late as 1947 Mr de Valera was still expounding the doctrine of external association and still insisting that under his External Relations Act Ireland was to all intents and purposes a republic, in fact, if not in name.[3] During the election campaign Clann na Poblachta had of course put the repeal of that act and the declaration of the republic in the forefront of their programme. Fine Gael, on the other hand, although some of its members (including Mr Costello himself) where uneasy about the ambiguities of the existing situation, was widely regarded in Ireland as still being in some sense a 'Commonwealth' party and the election speeches of the leaders, though well-stocked, like everyone else's, with the explosive vocabulary of 'anti-partition', stopped short of the republican demand, which, indeed, was only too likely to rivet northern Unionists even more closely to the Crown and the British connection.

Nevertheless, despite this fundamental incompatibility between the achievement of a republic and the removal of the border, the government decided to repeal the External Relations Act. We are still too close to the event to be able to dogmatise about the factors which had most influence upon this decision, but three points can be made with reasonable certainty. One is that the presence of Mr MacBride in the cabinet, pledged as he was to work for a republic, was bound to bring the issue to the fore sooner or later. A second is that the balance of parties within the Dáil was so even that the inter-party coalition was highly vulnerable to an initiative from what Mr Costello (in a letter to the present writer) has called 'some person not well disposed to the government'.[4] Had such a person – say, an Independent deputy – brought forward of his own volition a proposal to modify the External Relations Act in the direction of a *de jure* rather than a *de facto* republic, the effect of this upon the coalition might well have been catastrophic.* In the absence of any agreed policy among its members, Fine Gael might well have voted one way and Clann na Poblachta another, with the result that their partnership would have ended almost before it had begun.

It may be asked why, granted that it was necessary to agree upon a policy, should that policy have been the policy of the Clann rather than the policy of the status quo? The answer may be partly in the leverage that the Clann's ten seats gave to Mr MacBride, but – and here is the third point that has to be made – it may be found also in Mr Costello's own attitude of mind. For although his main interest when taking office seems to have been in economic reform, it is undoubtedly true not only that he found the External Relations Act untidy and inadequate, but that he was deeply conscious of the way in which the idea of the republic had haunted and divided Irishmen ever since the Civil War. To take the gun out of politics by settling this problem – so far as it could be settled – was for him an act of statesmanship that would justify even the traumatic break with his own party's history which it would entail.[5]

As is well-known, he announced his intention of doing this in September 1948 while on a visit to Canada. The dramatic and seemingly sudden character of this announcement gave rise immediately to a chaos of conflicting rumours, some of which, despite frequent refutations, still circulate to this day. The most notorious of these alleges that Mr Costello – or as one version has it, Mrs Costello – was insulted by the Governor-General of Canada, who happened to be that distinguished scion of Ulster Unionist stock, Field-Marshal Earl Alexander of Tunis, and that in consequence Mr Costello stormed off in a rage to a press conference where he 'declared' the republic forthwith. Apart from the fact that this would have been constitutionally impossible, the story is completely false. The truth, however, is no less strange and absorbing.

First, it is necessary to emphasise that before Mr Costello left for Canada at all there had been a cabinet decision to repeal the External Relations Act. There is still some uncertainty about the precise date, and some confusion of ministerial recollections about the occasion (not unnatural after a lapse of twenty years), but Mr Costello himself, and his Minister for External Affairs, Mr MacBride, have both gone on record that the decision was taken that summer – in all probability in August. Not only that, but Mr MacBride and the Tanaiste (Deputy

* This is not so hypothetical as it may sound. It was believed by political commentators at the time that the cabinet had in mind specifically the possibility of intervention by the late Captain Peadar Cowan (*Irish Times*, 10 July 1962).

564

Prime Minister) Mr Norton, had made it quite clear in the Dáil that the External Relations Act would be repealed before long and had elicited indications from Fianna Fáil that on that side of the House there would be no opposition to such a move. In July, for example, Mr MacBride had remarked – and the significance of what he said had not gone unnoticed – that there was no parallel between the history of the Commonwealth countries and that of Ireland. 'The Crown and outworn forms that belong to British constitutional history', he added, 'are merely reminders of an unhappy past that we want to bury, that have no realities for us and only serve as irritants.'[6] And less than three weeks later Mr Norton roundly declared that the External Relations Act was 'a fraud on the people' and that 'it would do our national self-respect good both at home and abroad if we were to proceed without delay to abolish the External Relations Act'. To which Mr de Valera replied: 'Go ahead. You will get no opposition from us.'[7]

It seems clear, therefore, that by August 1948 the scene had been set for a radical change of policy. This still does not explain, of course, why the change was announced in Canada. It arose indirectly out of the accidental circumstance that Mr Costello had been invited as a distinguished lawyer to address the Canadian Bar Association. He arrived in Montreal on 30 August and while he was their guest (until he left for Ottawa on 4 September) he deliberately refrained from making what he has since called 'comments of a political character'. Nevertheless, the speech which he delivered to his Canadian hosts – on 'Ireland in international affairs' – had been regarded at home as sufficiently important to have been read and approved by the cabinet before his departure. For the most part it was an able and objective account of the way in which the constitutional relations of Ireland with the Commonwealth had changed since the Treaty, but Mr Costello did allow himself to refer to the 'inaccuracies and infirmities' of those sections of the External Relations Act which dealt with the position of the Crown.[8] This was in no sense a declaration of the republic, but at least it indicated to all and sundry that Mr Costello was not exactly wedded to the Act. And the very next night he himself had evidence of one of these 'infirmities'. At the Bar Association dinner, after the toast of 'The King' had been given, the Canadian Minister for External Affairs said to him, 'Doesn't that cover you?' 'I had to argue', Mr Costello subsequently recalled, 'that it did not, because we were not real members of the Commonwealth.'[9]

This was confusing enough, but worse was to come. On 4 September Mr Costello was the guest of the Canadian government at an official dinner in Ottawa. This was the famous occasion round which legend has gathered, and although the legend is far removed from the truth, during the dinner Mr Costello did have two unpleasant experiences.*

* In my account of this dinner I have drawn heavily on an essay of mine. 'The Years of Adjustment, 1945-1951', in T. Desmond Williams and

One was that at the Governor-General's table he was confronted with a replica of 'Roaring Meg', the famous cannon used in the defence of Derry in 1689 and ever since an almost sacred symbol to Ulster Unionists. This was hardly the most tactful gesture to make to a nationalist prime minister, but while it is doubtful whether the green, white and orange flower-arrangement which Earl Alexander later claimed had also been set before Mr Costello had the desired emollient effect, the incident was hardly likely to lead to the secession of Ireland from the Commonwealth. The other incident, admittedly, was more vexatious. It had been arranged by the Irish High Commissioner with the Canadian government that two toasts would be drunk – 'The King' and 'The President of Ireland'. Yet, when the time came, only 'The King' was proposed. In retrospect, so Mr Costello told the present writer, he was satisfied that this was probably no more than an error of protocol but it was a slightly ominous coincidence that a few months earlier the same thing had happened to him in Downing Street when dining with Mr Attlee. Such an omission, twice repeated, and involving in effect a denial of the existence of the republic, was yet one more illustration of the ambiguities embalmed in the External Relations Act. Even so, and although he had come believing that both toasts would be proposed, Mr Costello did not – as the story subsequently went – leave the dinner in a rage and he did not straightaway summon a press conference to make any dramatic revelations about Ireland's status in the Commonwealth.

What really precipitated his action in Canada was not these dinner irritations, but rather the appearance in next morning's *Sunday Independent* of the headlines: 'External Relations Act to go'.[10] This referred to Mr Costello's speech to the Canadian Bar Association, and also to those of Mr MacBride and Mr Norton already quoted. Whether the decision to run the story at that particular time was 'inspired' or not must remain a matter of speculation, though it is perhaps not altogether irrelevant to note that the paper was usually regarded as being particularly close to Mr Costello's own party. Reverting to the topic fourteen years later, the *Sunday Independent* itself declared that its headline had derived from 'an intelligent reading' of ministers' speeches and this judicious comment may be as near to the truth as we are likely to get.[11] Mr Costello only learnt of this development by telephone late on Sunday afternoon. He was due to give a press conference on Tuesday, 7 September, and had therefore no more than thirty-six hours in which to decide how to answer the questions he

K. B. Nowlan (ed.), *Ireland in the War Years and After* (Dublin and London, 1969). I am grateful to the editors and to Mr Michael Gill, the publisher, for permission to use this material. For the background to the whole affair see also the quotations from a memorandum by Mr Costello in B. Farrell, *Chairman or Chief?: the Role of Taoiseach in Irish Government* (Dublin and London, 1971), pp. 47-50.

would now inevitably have to face. Sheer distance made consultation with his ministers virtually impossible – at least in any satisfying depth – and in fact he appears to have come to his decision on his own, but with the memory of the cabinet discussion before he left home very much in the forefront of his mind. 'If no decision had been made before I left', he has since written, 'it would be quite improper for me to have made the statement that I did and it would have been very easy for me to deal with the matter referred to in the *Sunday Independent* of 5 September, 1948.'[12]

Knowing what he did know about the decision made before he left, he felt that he had no alternative but to speak out frankly and say, as he did say, that it was his government's intention to repeal the Act. This was the declaration which caused such a stir in Ireland, even among ministers for whom the timing of the announcement probably came as much as a surprise as for anyone else.* What gave it real significance, of course, was that it was not just a statement of intent to repeal the offending legislation, for in reply to a specific question from a foreign correspondent Mr Costello made it perfectly clear that repeal meant also secession from the Commonwealth.[13]

In accordance with his decision the Republic of Ireland Bill was introduced in the Dáil in November 1948 and had passed through all its stages by the end of the year, leaving the way clear for the republic itself to be formally inaugurated on the symbolic date of Easter Monday, 1949. In the debates Mr Costello stressed that his party had a dual intention – to put an end to ancient rancours within the country and at the same time to establish Anglo-Irish relations on a better, because a less ambiguous, basis. In reply to the obvious objection that this step would make the ending of partition even more remote than before, he contended that refraining from it in the past had not evoked a friendly gesture from Northern Ireland – why then continue to refrain from it in the hope of a reconciliation that never came?[14] This was an argument of very doubtful validity. Repeal might not make a bad situation worse, but it surely meant that it would be harder thenceforward to make that bad situation better.

* Interviewing Dr Noel Browne on 3 January 1967 I had a clear impression that the announcement had taken him by surprise. And five years earlier Lord Rugby (who, as Sir John Maffey, was the much respected British Representative to Eire in 1948) in giving his recollections of the incident had recalled that Mr MacBride also had looked surprised when receiving the news of the announcement on the evening of 7 September. Mr MacBride's comment on this, however, was that if he looked surprised, it was because he was astonished that anyone should regard the news of Ireland being ready to repeal the External Relations Act as in any way sensational (*Irish Times*, 10 July 1962). On the other hand, it is fair to add that the Irish people had a reasonable right to expect that an announcement of such momentous import might most appropriately have been made on their own soil.

And indeed, in the short run at least it must have seemed that the Irish action did make the bad situation worse, for the British riposte followed swiftly. When in 1949 the imperial parliament passed the Ireland Act with a view to regularising the position, it included in that Act a proviso that Northern Ireland would never be detached from the United Kingdom without the consent of the Northern Ireland legislature. It is true that recent events have indicated that Northern Ireland autonomy is a more precarious thing than it was then assumed to be, but this does not alter the fact that the pledge given in 1949 seemed – and was intended – to lock and bolt the door against the anti-partition movement, thus confirming the critics in all they had said about the incompatibility between the two goals of ending the border and establishing the republic.

This, however, was still in the future. So far as the Dáil was concerned, coming events cast no shadows and the government's legislation went through without let or hindrance. Fianna Fáil could scarcely oppose it, though they might have been excused for feeling that the government had caught them bathing and stolen their clothes. Moreover, the clothes did not fit very well. Mr de Valera's lifelong ideal had been an all-Ireland, not a partial, republic, and what was solemnly celebrated in April 1949 fell far short of that ideal. Perhaps, indeed, the curious sense of disenchantment that can be observed in the generation that has grown up within the boundaries of this mutilated polity is in part a consequence of the very fact that a twenty-six county republic was seen and felt to be a second-best solution – a sentiment summed up in two bitter lines of a not very popular song parodying the unofficial national anthem 'God save Ireland' inherited from the nineteenth century:

> God save the Southern part of Ireland
> Three-quarters of a nation once again.[16]

Whatever the reaction in Ireland – and there was, of course, some enthusiasm along with a good deal of indifference – the ultimate success of the government's policy depended not just on its own uni-lateral action, but upon the response of Great Britain and the other Commonwealth countries. By a curious coincidence, a conference of Commonwealth prime ministers was due to assemble at London in October 1948 – that is, between Mr Costello's Canadian announce-ment and the introduction of repeal legislation in the Dáil. Although not enough is yet known about the private reactions of the British government to the proposed Irish secession to admit of any confident generalisations, it would not have been surprising if, in the light of all that had passed between the two countries for so many centuries, some alarm and disapproval had not been voiced, or even expressed in some kind of retaliatory action. That this proved not to be the case may have been due in part at least to the good offices of the dominion members of the Commonwealth Conference. While that Conference was in progress Irish representatives met representatives of the British, Canadian, Australian and New Zealand governments at Chequers and at Paris. As a result of these meetings – at which the influence of the Australian and Canadian statesmen is believed to have been especially powerful – the view emerged, to all intents and purposes unanimously, that Ireland's withdrawal should not be allowed to affect the friendly relations existing between that country and the nations of the Commonwealth.

In practical terms this meant, and has meant ever since, that in the two areas – citizenship and trade – where the Irish were most vulnerable they had nothing to fear. So far as the former was concerned, it was mutually agreed between Britain and Ireland that the British Nationality Act of 1948 – passed, ironically enough, just before the crisis – should still apply. The effect of this was that citizens of Eire, although no longer British subjects, would, when in Britain, be treated as though they were British subjects – a fact of enormous significance for the large numbers of Irish men and women living and working in the country; by the usual device of reciprocity British subjects when in Ireland would be accorded the same treatment as Irish citizens. No less important than reciprocity for individuals was preference in trade. Here the anxious questions were whether the preferential arrangements then existing between the two countries would be annulled by the fact of Ireland's secession, and whether they would be held to clash with the General Agreement on Tariffs and Trade negotiated at Geneva in 1947. On both counts the verdict was favourable to Ireland and the special economic relationship already established between the two countries survived intact, to grow even closer as time went on.[16]

Yet, if the net result of all this furious activity, apart from reinforcing the connection between Northern Ireland and the rest of the United Kingdom, was apparently to make very little positive impact on Anglo-Irish affairs, there could be no denying that Ireland – albeit no more than 'three-quarters of a nation once again' – had, in breaking the last tenuous link that bound her to Britain, reached a turning-point in her own history. Even here, however, the spirit of paradox that had so often entered into her dealings with her powerful neighbour made one last appearance. For by a strange irony, in the very year when Ireland left the Commonwealth as a republic, India, which had also become a republic, was recognised at her own request as remaining within the association. Why then, it may be asked, if republican status was no longer to be a bar to membership, did Ireland take her final and decisive step?

It may well be that the answer to this question can only be given, not in constitutional or legal terms, but in the language of political psychology. The experiment of dominion status laboured, it has been well said, under three overwhelming liabilities. 'The first was that it came too late, the second that it came as a result of violence, and the third that as a result of partition it was deprived of strong, coherent support.'[17] Nothing, not even the labours of the pro-Treaty party, not even the sympathy of other dominions, not even the belated generosity of Britain herself, could surmount these fatal defects. Ireland remained deaf to the siren voices of the Commonwealth and in the end heard only the ghosts of Roger Casement and all those other dead men knocking on the door. Equality, it seemed, was no substitute for nationality, and in the case of Ireland too much blood had flowed too often for nationality to be satisfied by any kind of connection or tie with Britain, however widely drawn or however magnanimously conceived.

This is not to say that Ireland's brief career, whether as a dominion or in external association with the Commonwealth, was therefore entirely barren. On the contrary, it is reasonable to suggest that the history of Anglo-Irish relations in this century has burned so deep into the British official mind that the post-1945 Commonwealth has provided a much kindlier climate for emergent nations than might otherwise have prevailed. It is the fate of pioneers to be forgotten by those who come after them, but it is not altogether fanciful to see in these territories which have moved so swiftly in the last twenty years from colonial status to full independence, the chief beneficiaries of what happened in Ireland between 1916 and 1949.

If, then, Ireland has not only saved herself by her exertions, but profited others by her example, this may well turn out to be her chief positive contribution to the modern Commonwealth. Yet the lurking suspicion remains that the negative contribution may ultimately be more significant – the demonstration that not even the most imaginatively conceived association of states can fulfil the inner demands and compulsions of a passionate sense of nationality. If the Commonwealth should disappear – and recent prime ministers' conferences have brought this within the realm of possibility – it will disappear because it will have been proved that political independence is not enough. Just two months before the Easter Rising Patrick Pearse expressed this fundamental truth in words that go far beyond the immediate Irish context in which he wrote them. 'Independence', he declared, 'one must understand to include spiritual and intellectual independence as well as political independence; or rather, true political independence requires spiritual and intellectual independence as its basis, or it tends to become unstable, a thing resting merely on interests which change with time and circumstance.'[18]

(ii) POLITICS IN FLUX

Looking back nearly twenty years after the event, Mr Costello claimed the declaration of the republic as perhaps the biggest achievement of the inter-party government.[19] Certainly, it is likely to be the one for which it is most remembered. But there were others, less dramatic and less controversial, which also deserve to be recorded. Broadly, these fall into two categories – those that made an immediate impact and those that sowed a harvest others were to reap long after the coalition was no more. In the former category, four developments stand out, two of them associated with Mr James Dillon, who proved himself to be a dynamic Minister of Agriculture. The first of these was the 1948 trade agreement with Britain which obtained more favourable terms for Irish farm produce, especially by linking the price of store cattle and sheep to the guaranteed price received by British farmers for their fat cattle and sheep. The second of Mr Dillon's initiatives – and one that brought the government considerable popularity – was the launching in 1949 of the ambitious Land Rehabilitation Project, a determined enort to bring back into full production land which had remained idle through lack of capital or for other reasons. It was intended that the Project should extend to about four million acres and that the scheme, spread over about ten years, would cost the state some forty million pounds, to be met in part from United States loans under the European Recovery Programme. Even now, two decades later, it is perhaps premature to pass judgment on the economic viability of the Land Rehabilitation Project, but in terms of electoral psychology it made excellent sense, for it brought the first faint stirrings of hope to many districts long assumed to be stagnant if not dying.* As a modern economist has well said: 'Removing the rocks from Connemara may have been bad economics for Irish adherents of the Manchester school, but to many people emotionally involved in the west of Ireland and its people it was the best news since the activities of the Congested Districts Board.'[20]

If Mr Dillon's scheme for reclaiming derelict land had social as well as economic implications, the concern for welfare which the inter-party government displayed was even more evident in the other two practical reforms it managed to carry through in its three years of office. One was the remarkable improvement in the provision of houses, especially in the countryside. By the end of the war the situation in the twenty-six counties had become so bad that 110,000 new dwellings (in town and country together) were required to meet the immediate need. By 1950, largely through the enterprise of Mr T. J. Murphy as Minister for Local Government, the rate of building had reached 12,000 a year, which was far higher than anything attempted before 1939. This did not solve the problem of the Dublin slums, of course, but it began that transformation of rural housing which to the traveller revisiting the remoter parts of Ireland after a

* The difficulty of assessing the Land Rehabilitation Project is increased by the lack of reliable statistics on the subject, but for some general comments on the policy of state aid to agriculture, see below, chap. 4, section v.

lapse of ten or twenty years is one of the most exciting signs of progress.

Even more striking, and so complete that nowadays it is taken almost for granted, was the virtual eradication of tuberculosis that Dr Noel Browne succeeded in carrying through with extraordinary rapidity. This disease, which for generation after generation had eaten into the already declining population, was particularly dire in its effects because its incidence was always heaviest in the twenty to thirty-four age-group. As recently as the decade 1911-20 it had claimed 205 victims per annum for each 100,000 of the population.[21] Thereafter the situation slowly improved, though when Dr Browne came into office it was still killing between 3,000 and 4,000 people every year.[22] Although the introduction of mass radiography by his predecessors had improved diagnosis, treatment was still hampered by the lack of hospital beds. To remedy this deficiency and build enough modern sanatoria to cope with the onset of the disease even in its early stages was Dr Browne's main problem and he solved it brilliantly by a radical redeployment of his Ministry's finances. Liquidating its assets of twenty million pounds and mortgaging the next ten million pounds that could be expected to accrue, he spent the money on a vast project of supplying and staffing sanatoria throughout the country.* Admittedly, advances in medical research coincided providentially with his campaign and the introduction of BCG, together with the use of Streptomycin, brought not only cure but prevention at last within range. The combination of these four factors – mass radiography, the new sanatoria, modern methods of treatment, and vaccination, combined to produce some astonishing results. It was in 1949 that the death-rate from tuberculosis first fell below one hundred per 100,000 population and by 1952 this proportion had fallen as low as fifty-four; five years later it had been reduced to twenty-seven.[23]

Apart from these obvious and demonstrable successes, the inter-party government also set in train other reforms which, in the sphere of economics, were destined to have consequences far greater than could have been foreseen at the time. It would be a naive over-simplification to say of this patchwork coalition, composed as it was of men of widely differing ideas on almost all economic questions, that it produced anything coherent enough to be called a common view, but as some of the ideas thrown up by new men worked their way into practice it began at least to seem as if Mr Costello and his colleagues did have a recognisably different outlook from that of Fianna Fáil. This has been concisely defined by a distinguished Irish economist as a belief that the best recipe for the cure of unemployment and emigration was a rigorous application to Irish conditions of the Keynesian

* The chief source of revenue was the Hospitals' Sweepstake. For this and for the general framework of health legislation within which Dr Browne had to work, see chap. 5, section iii.

doctrines on government spending. 'State spending', he has written, 'was to become the conspicuous feature of inter-party economic policies.'[24] But if this investment were to be used to the best effect expert advice would be needed. To obtain it two new organisations were created, each of which was in due course to make a notable contribution to the growth of economic planning in Ireland. One, the Industrial Development Authority, brought together a group of influential men with wide experience of financial and industrial matters and gave them the task not only of planning and assisting industrial growth, but also of scrutinising the protectionist structure within which industry had for so long been sheltering. The other, Coras an Trachtala, was the offspring of a committee originally set up to examine ways and means of reducing the serious dollar deficit. The new organisation – a strikingly successful example of the state-sponsored bodies described below*was established primarily to promote Irish exports to the United States and Canada, but proved to be so efficient that it became a permanent institution which extended its operations all over the world.

It would be wrong, however, to equate these initiatives, valuable though they were in themselves, with anything approaching an industrial boom. There was increased activity, indeed, and there was undeniable growth. Between 1946 and 1953 industrial production increased by nearly sixty per cent and nearly 50,600 new jobs were created in industry. This was certainly an improvement on past performances, but it remained, nevertheless, subject to serious reservations. One was that the growth-rate, although superficially impressive, appeared so partly because of the low level from which development had started; if the surrounding plain is flat enough, even a mole-hill will seem imposing. A second reservation concerns the job situation. Not only was the increased industrial labour force still less than half that employed in agriculture, it represented only twenty per cent of the entire working population, a dangerously low proportion by contemporary European standards. Moreover, the continuing drain of emigration very nearly offset the new opportunities created in industry. In 1951 the total number of persons at work was only 12,000 more than in 1926. The net increase of 159,000 in industrial employment over that period had been almost wiped out by a decrease of 147,000 in agricultural employment. Even in the period of so-called expansion between 1946 and 1951, and taking the wastage from emigration into account, the Irish economy was able to create new jobs for no more than 800 people each year.[25]

Nor were these the only items on the debit side. Apart from the familiar weaknesses of the economy – the scarcity or timidity of its private capital, the conservatism of its agriculture, the poverty of its internal market, and its lack of exports – the government had to con-

* See chap. 4, section ii.

573

tend with a variety of pressures both foreign and domestic.* To the devaluation of sterling in 1949 and the inflationary effects of the Korean war were added pressures from all sides for wage-increases to chase, if not to surpass, the rising spiral of prices. The coalition had inherited from Fianna Fáil a wrangling dispute with the national school teachers (who had actually gone on strike in 1946) and growing unrest among white-collar workers which culminated in a bank strike in 1950. It was becoming clear, in short, that even among the more secure section of the community the increasing cost of living, together with the absence of social services comparable with those in Britain or Northern Ireland, was causing real hardship. The government was well aware of the problem and did what it could to solve it. In his very first budget Mr McGilligan cut expenditure in defence and other departments in order to increase the pensions payable to old people, widows and orphans. But this, though certainly overdue, was only a palliative and gradually, after much heart-searching, the government groped its way towards an elaborate and comprehensive scheme of social welfare which formed the basis of legislation introduced in the Dáil early in 1951. On 11 April this passed its second reading, but this triumph was no sooner secured than it became irrelevant, for on that very day the coalition was paralysed by the revelation of an internal crisis which was destined in the end to destroy it.

The storm had been brewing for some time. During the war years and immediately thereafter the vast and complex issues raised by the necessity to improve the health and welfare services in the twenty-six counties had been widely discussed. From the impetus provided by these discussions had sprung the legislation enacted by Fianna Fáil in 1947 which had set up separate departments of Health and Social Welfare and which had also been intended to lay the foundations for a national health service.† The health service proposals, though modest enough compared with what Britain and Northern Ireland were just then being equipped, were far-reaching enough to cause intense alarm in conservative circles and to bring about a clash between the government and its critics. This might, to some extent, have happened anyway, but two circumstances combined to make the clash unexpectedly severe. One was the fact that in the preceding twenty years Catholic thinking in Ireland had taken an increasingly 'integralist' form – that is to say, it had fallen much under the influence of continental ideas stressing Catholic concepts of the moral law and the need for thorough commitment to Catholic social teaching, and in general emphasising the special position the Catholic Church ought to occupy in the community. In the sphere of welfare, Irish Catholic writers had accorded particular weight to the papal encyclical

* For a survey of the general situation of the Irish economy at this time, see chap. 4, section v.
† For this legislation and its significance, see chap. 5, section iii.

574

of 1931, *Quadragesimo Anno* (itself an adaptation or revision of the celebrated encyclical, *Rerum Novarum*, issued by Pope Leo XIII forty years earlier). Both encyclicals were devoted to mitigating, or removing, the evils alike of unregulated capitalism and of excessive state intervention. Thus, not only did they seek instead to promote the formation of vocational groups but they also attached particular importance to the 'natural unit' of the family. In consequence, they were deeply opposed to any contemporary trends which could be interpreted as transferring responsibility for the health and welfare of children from their parents to an impersonal and external authority.

But – and this was the second circumstance liable to lead to a collision between Church and state – the long-established Fianna Fáil government seemed – perhaps because it was so long-established – to be developing an excessively paternalistic tendency. In this it may have been following rather than leading a civil service which at the time was attracting widespread criticism for its brusque and sometimes overbearing attitude towards the public, but the end result was the same. The forces of vocationalism saw themselves as leading a crusade against the bastions of bureaucracy and even before the health service provided its sensational *casus belli* the antagonists had already clashed over the decidedly short shrift given by the government to the *Report of the Commission on Vocational Organisation* (issued in August 1944) and to the Social Security Plan based on proposals for National Health Insurance published by Dr John Dignan, Bishop of Clonfert, two months later.*

It is against this background of intermittent controversy that the Fianna Fáil Health Act of 1947 has to be seen. From the outset it aroused intense opposition inside and outside the Dáil. Some of this came from the medical profession, but most of it derived from critics who insisted that the liberty and privacy of the individual would be invaded by the state to an intolerable degree if the Act became law. The storm centred round three points in particular – that in the reorganised health service free choice of doctor would not be available, as it was in the health services of most other highly developed countries; that there was a high degree of compulsion, for example in the medical inspection of schoolchildren and in the powers given to the responsible Minister to order the disinfestation – and, if need be, the detention – of persons suspected of being sources of infection; and thirdly, that the scheme, by increasing the authority vested in the

* For the intellectual and the political backgrounds to the events of 1947-1953, see J. H. Whyte, *Church and State in Modern Ireland, 1923-1970* (Dublin and London, 1971), especially chaps. 3, 4 and 5. This work, which is incomparably the best contribution to the writing of contemporary Irish history known to me, is essential to an understanding, not merely of the public role of the Catholic Church in Ireland, but also of the evolution of modern Irish Catholicism. In addition, it contains (chaps. 6, 7, 8 and 9) a masterly analysis of the 'mother and child scheme' crisis of 1951 to which my account in the following pages is greatly indebted.

Minister of Health, contributed to a further centralisation of governmental power. In addition – and, in the light of subsequent events, most important of all – the provisions relating to the establishment of a scheme for maternity and child welfare (including the education of women 'in respect of motherhood'), to be available to mothers and all children up to the age of sixteen, regardless of means, provoked from the Roman Catholic hierarchy a letter of remonstrance to Mr de Valera. This letter, private but none the less formidable for that, condemned the scheme on various grounds, but most significantly as being 'entirely and directly contrary to Catholic teaching on the rights of the family, the rights of the Church in education, the rights of the medical profession and of voluntary institutions'.

The crisis, however, did not come in 1947. Before it had had time to develop Mr James Dillon, at that time an Independent member of the Dáil, determined to test the constitutionality of the Act. It was therefore possible for Mr de Valera to temporise. This he did by informing the bishops in February 1948 that he would defer a full reply to their protest until after the courts had ruled on the validity of those sections of the Act which had been impugned. But at that very moment the electorate was ruling on the validity of his own government. In the election which had just been fought he had failed to win an overall majority and within days of his letter having been dispatched to the bishops the inter-party government had taken over the reins.

Dr Browne thus inherited a situation full of possibilities – and of dangers. His preoccupation with the campaign against tuberculosis meant that he was unable to address himself immediately to the health service problem, though soon after taking office he announced that some of the sections of the Act which had been most criticised as infringing parental rights would be repealed or amended. So far as the mother and child scheme itself was concerned, the cabinet decided in June 1948 to retain a 'free for all' scheme and not to attempt to mollify the doctors by introducing a means test. It was not in fact until June 1950 that Dr Browne began to brace himself to implement the scheme, but by that time the inter-party government had already had an ominous foretaste of the weight of 'integralist' opinion when two of its other proposals – one dealing with social insurance and one with legal adoption – encountered such opposition that the latter had to be dropped and the former had not reached the statute-book when the government fell from power in 1951.

When eventually Dr Browne was able to bring forward his draft proposals it soon appeared that the mother and child scheme in its essentials followed the precedent set by Fianna Fáil in 1947. It was ambitious by Irish standards and, since it was intended to make it available without charge to all mothers and to all children under the age of sixteen, it was certain to involve heavy expenditure. Not surprisingly it immediately came under attack from two quite different directions. The medical profession, like their colleagues in similar situations in other countries, smelled 'socialised medicine' from afar and made no secret of their distaste; they were particularly suspicious of the absence of a means test and they seem also to have feared that under a strong minister the scheme would lend itself to excessive political control. Dr Browne would certainly have had a fight on his hands to persuade his fellow-doctors into accepting the scheme, but precisely because he was a strong minister he might well have succeeded in doing so.

Unhappily, he had simultaneously to fight on a second front against a more powerful enemy. Dealing as they did with the most intimate aspects of maternity, the new proposals by their very nature impinged directly upon the family which, as we saw earlier, was enshrined in the Constitution as 'the natural primary and fundamental unit group of society', possessing 'inalienable and imprescriptible rights, antecedent and superior to all positive law'.[20] Since the family was seen as a moral as well as a social institution it could count, of course, not only upon the support of the courts but that of the Church as well. And the more the Church considered the implications of the proposed service the more uneasy it became. As far back as October 1950 the bishops had made their anxieties known to the Taoiseach. They feared that any scheme framed on the lines Dr Browne was known to be pursuing would result in an invasion of family rights and would lead to a deterioration in the confidential relations that ought to exist between doctor and patient. In addition, they were apprehensive of the results which might flow from sex education by medical officers possibly not of the same religion as their patients and they took their stand on the broad principle that provision for the health of children was an essential part of the responsibilities of parenthood. The state, they concluded, 'has the right to intervene only in a subsidiary capacity, to supplement, not to supplant'. Dr Browne attempted to meet these objections in an elaborate memorandum (he had himself taken theological advice, though it did not do him much good) and by confronting the bishops' representatives face to face. Through a series of misunderstandings that would have been farcical were not the consequences so tragic, Dr Browne believed he had satisfied the hierarchy when in fact he had done nothing of the sort.

In March 1951, when Dr Browne, having failed to reach agreement with the Irish Medical Association, published an outline of his scheme, the crisis deepened. For a few weeks there was frantic activity as ministers sought to bridge the gap between an adamant minister and a rock-like Church, but all was in vain. Once the hierarchy had made it clear that vital questions of faith and morals were involved, the resistance of the government crumbled and Dr Browne found himself increasingly isolated, even from his colleagues in Clann na Poblachta. It is fair to say that for some time past relations had been deteriorating, not merely between Dr Browne and his colleagues from other

577

parties, but also between Dr Browne and the leader of his own party, Mr MacBride. The disenchantment of his colleagues with Dr Browne may have been partly on general grounds – he was a highly-strung man under great pressure and this no doubt made him difficult to work with – but, more specifically, it seems also to have sprung from the fact that some ministers were having second thoughts about a means test, whereas he was as firmly set as ever on making his scheme free without any discrimination. The breach with Mr MacBride was by all accounts more fundamental, based as it appears to have been on Dr Browne's increasing conviction that Clann na Poblachta was being corrupted by office and was in danger of losing its radical soul. On 10 and 11 April a sharp exchange of letters took place between Dr Browne and Mr MacBride, as a result of which, and at Mr MacBride's insistence, Dr Browne sent his resignation to Mr Costello on 11 April.[27]

The most immediate casualty, apart from Dr Browne himself, was the mother and child scheme, though a little later Fianna Fáil succeeded in passing some of its provisions into law. There is clear evidence, however, that had it not been for Mr de Valera's expert guidance, Fianna Fáil, too, might have been involved in a head-on collision with the bishops.[28] But what chiefly alarmed contemporaries was less the individual fate of the minister (there were those who said he had gone the wrong way about his business, even that he was bent upon a clash) than the way in which a difficult question of principle had been resolved. It had been resolved, apparently, by the abject capitulation of the secular to the spiritual power. The *Irish Times*, pointing out the disastrous effect that this example of ecclesiastical intervention would have upon the movement to end partition, concluded bitterly that 'the Roman Catholic Church would seem to be the effective government of this country'. This, no doubt, was an exaggeration, and it would have been exceedingly naive for any layman to have expected the Church to keep silent upon such a matter, where, after all, questions of faith and morals clearly were at issue.*
But what was, and still is, alarming about the crisis was that it demonstrated the extreme difficulty in a Catholic country of drawing the line between morals and politics – the difficulty, if one follows the affair to its logical conclusion, of reconciling parliamentary democracy with ecclesiastical authority. But perhaps the very violence of the controversy had its own salutary effect. Such a collision was too dangerous to be repeated – and has not been repeated.

The inter-party government itself did not long survive Dr Browne's departure. Indeed, even before the quarrel over the mother and child scheme, Mr Costello's coalition had shown signs of breaking up. It had been exposed to ridicule – in Ireland always a deadly weapon – over the so-called 'Battle of Baltinglass', where the hapless Minister of Posts and Telegraphs was forced to withdraw his nomination to a

* The arguments on both sides are fully and fairly set out by J. H. Whyte in *Church and State in Ireland, 1923-1970*, chap. 8.

village postmastership in face of spirited, and richly comic, local resistance. More serious, the government was still baffled by the phenomenon of inflation and early in 1951 was driven to the desperate expedient of freezing prices at the level obtaining in the previous December. And if this were not enough, Clann na Poblachta, the lynch-pin of the coalition, was itself in dissolution. In February 1951, *before* the mother and child scheme had reached crisis point, one of the most influential members of the party, Mr Noel Hartnett, had resigned on the ominous grounds that the Clann had become obsessed with power and had abandoned 'any political or social philosophy'. When, on top of this, Dr Browne's resignation was followed by others – some inspired by rural dissatisfaction at the government's failure to solve its economic problems – it became clear that the coalition was fast losing its hold on power and in May Mr Costello decided to go to the country.

The ensuing election was decisive in one sense, indecisive in another. Fianna Fáil only marginally improved its position, winning sixty-nine seats as against sixty-eight three years earlier. Had the other parties been able to agree among themselves as before, a new coalition might have resulted, led once again by Fine Gael which, with forty seats, had emerged from the election nine stronger than in 1948. But the dynamism which Clann na Poblachta had provided in the previous election was sadly lacking in 1951. The party was reduced from ten seats to two and, in view of its virtual extinction, the balance of power was held momentarily by the fourteen Independents. When the Dáil assembled they used that power (Dr Browne voting with them) to replace the coalition by Fianna Fáil.*

Yet, although Mr de Valera was thus able to form a government, it was always a minority government with little real stability. True, it lasted for nearly three years and, as we shall see later, made a determined attempt to grapple with some of the problems of social reform left unsolved by its predecessor, but like that predecessor, it was dogged from start to finish by inflation and an adverse balance of payments. Domestic politics in these years of stagnation came indeed to be dominated by an unending, and often ill-informed, debate about how the economic malaise could best be cured. Some clamoured loudly for 'repatriation' of sterling assets, others blamed the rising prices on excessive capital investment by the coalition, while amid the babel of conflicting voices the government dourly addressed itself to the bleak task of restoring financial probity through high taxation and reduced expenditure. Even in this it was not very successful, for while the country groaned under a tax burden that increased from £98 million to £103 million in the year 1953-4, public spending in the same period rose from £107 to £121 million.

* The distribution of seats in 1951 was as follows: Fianna Fáil, sixty-nine; Fine Gael, forty; Labour, sixteen; Clann na Talmhan, six; Clann na Poblachta, two: Independents, fourteen.

Inevitably, by-elections began (early in 1954) to go against Fianna Fáil, but Mr de Valera's usual conditioned reflex – to call another general election – did not produce its usual results. Whereas his own party dropped to sixty-five seats (its worst showing since 1932), Fine Gael improved strikingly from forty to fifty, while Labour recovered the three seats it had lost in 1951. Between them these two parties dominated the situation and were able without too much difficulty to construct another coalition government.* But it was far from being a replica of the old, either in composition or in energy. Admittedly, Mr Costello was again at its head and Mr Norton, as Minister for Industry and Commerce, was still his deputy; Mr Dillon presided as before over Agriculture, Mr Blowick over Lands and Fisheries and General Mulcahy over Education. Moreover, although Mr McGilligan was conspicuous by his absence, there were new names and rising reputations to be accommodated – notably Gerald Sweetman (Fine Gael) who took Mr McGilligan's place as Minister of Finance, Mr B. Corish (Labour) who became Minister of Social Welfare, and Mr Liam Cosgrave (Fine Gael) who filled Mr MacBride's old berth at the Ministry of External Affairs. This last appointment – through no fault of Mr Cosgrave's, who, indeed, made an admirable debut – revealed one fundamental weakness in the coalition's situation. Mr MacBride, though pledging support to the new government, refused to join it, and since Dr Browne for obvious reasons was not available either, much of the colour and initiative which had characterised the first coalition at its best was absent from the second.

As it turned out, this reconstructed inter-party government had but a short, bleak existence. No more than Fianna Fáil was it able to damp down inflation and its efforts to do so by the old conventional methods of cutting expenditure and increasing taxation brought it the same harvest of unpopularity that Mr de Valera and his colleagues had reaped in the previous three-years. Furthermore, the new coalition had to contend with a much more critical domestic situation than the old. It had not been long in power before it was confronted by an ominous revival of IRA activities. This may in part have been a by-product of the years of economic stagnation, but it was connected both with the rise and the decline of Clann na Poblachta. During the first inter-party government, it was difficult for the police to deal as firmly as they had been in the habit of doing with the 'illegal organisation' while republicans were firmly entrenched in the citadels of power. Even the close co-operation that had grown up in the recent past between law-enforcement authorities on both sides of the border had necessarily languished when the fever of 'anti-partition' had been at its height. Under these circumstances, a new generation of extremist

* The distribution of seats in 1954 was: Fianna Fáil, sixty-five; Fine Gael, fifty; Labour, nineteen; Clann na Talmhan, five; Clann na Poblachta, three; Independents, five.

leaders found it relatively easy to regroup and rebuild. And although they might just conceivably have been prepared to hold their hand so long as Mr MacBride and his colleagues were in office, once that happy condition of affairs had ceased they were free to revert to the hallowed policy of trying by force to bring about the all-Ireland republic of their dreams. As early as 1952 arms raids on military barracks in Northern Ireland, and even England, signalled a return of violence. Not for the first time, activism, however extreme its methods and impracticable its aims, reawakened enthusiasm for the cause. Subscriptions multiplied, in America as well as in Ireland, and by 1956 the IRA felt strong enough to open a veritable campaign against police-barracks and other 'strategic' objectives. The government, though unwilling to take special, powers to deal with this fresh outbreak, had no option but to use the due process of the existing law against those who were bringing the gun back into politics. Although time was to show that more drastic methods were required, Mr Costello soon found that those he did use were too drastic to command the support he needed in the Dáil. Early in 1957, his adminis-tration was suddenly faced with a vote of no confidence moved by none other than Mr MacBride. The ostensible basis of the motion was a condemnation of the government's failure either to unify the country or to achieve an acceptable level of prosperity in that part of it for which ministers were responsible.* But Mr Costello, looking back ten years later, had little doubt that a no less significant factor influencing Mr MacBride's withdrawal of support was the attitude taken by the coalition towards the IRA.[29]

Whether this was the crucial factor, or whether, as is more likely, the government fell because of an accumulation of infirmities, it is impossible yet to decide with any real certainty. What is indisputable is that it not only fell but in doing so opened the way for a new chapter in the political dominance of Fianna Fáil. In the general election which followed in March 1957 Mr de Valera's party swept into power with a total of seats (seventy-eight) which freed it from humiliating dependence on any other party. Fine Gael sank back to its 1951 figure of forty seats, Labour was reduced from nineteen to thirteen, and Clann na Talmhan from five to three. Independent rep-resentation improved slightly from five to eight, but this modest advance was completely overshadowed by two other results. One was the virtual obliteration of Clann na Poblachta as an electoral force. It polled a beggarly 22,000 votes and though this was enough to allow it to

* It is only fair to point out that the coalition did have some success in closing the trade gap, in fact reducing the balance of payments deficit from £35 million in 1955 to £14 million in 1956. But to achieve even these results it had to resort to such draconian devices – for example, stringent import levies – that it seemed at the time only to be adding to the general sum of dreariness without offering any real hope of future improvement.

salvage one seat from the wreckage, that seat was not occupied by Mr MacBride.* His strange venture into Irish politics was to all appearances over, and before long he was to be found carving out a new career as Secretary-General of the International Commission of Jurists. The other new phenomenon which the election produced was the return of four Sinn Féin members. True to the traditional policy of their party, they refused to take their seats in the Dáil, but that they should have captured as many as four constituencies was a warning that could not much longer be ignored. Either there must be a rapid and perceptible improvement in the country's general situation, or the bankruptcy of the existing leaders, and perhaps even of the existing parties, would be manifest, with incalculable consequences for the peace and stability of the country.

In fact, as is already evident at this short distance of time, the general election of 1957 was, so far as such things can be, a turning-point in the recent history of Ireland. Admittedly, this was not immediately apparent. Mr de Valera, though then seventy-five years of age, once more took office as Taoiseach and gathered round him a team of seeming Bourbons, the very roll-call of whose names sounded as if the party had learnt nothing and forgotten nothing in the two and a half decades since it had first come to power. Yet in reality this was not so. Between 1957 and the next election in 1961 the situation was transformed in four important respects. First, the government acted promptly to deal with the activities of the IRA. The detention camp at The Curragh which had been used to detain activists during the war was reopened for the same purpose, and in July 1957 the notorious Part II of the Offences against the State Act was reintroduced, thus giving the government power to arrest and detain without trial. By the end of the year 100 people were interned in the south and perhaps twice that number in the north, where a combination of firm police action and remarkable civilian restraint gradually enabled the authorities to get the upper hand. It was a slow and painful process – the IRA did not abandon its campaign officially until 1962 – but there can be little doubt that in the Republic the evident readiness of the government to act ruthlessly whenever necessary brought the situation under control much more quickly than in the six counties.

A policy of simple repression, however, would hardly in itself have sufficed to deal with the growing unrest and discontent in the country. More constructive, and ultimately far more important, was the second major innovation of these years – the long-awaited leap forward into an era of unimagined – if, as events turned out, precarious – prosperity. Ironically enough this was in part a legacy of the second inter-party government. Preoccupied, as the earlier one had been, with the problem of how best to obtain and to deploy capital, it had

* The subsequent electoral history of Clann na Poblachta is soon told. It secured one seat at each of the elections of 1961 and 1965 and thereafter vanished from the scene.

appointed a Capital Advisory Committee which had not been long in existence before it urged that a programme for economic development should be drawn up with a view to directing investment, especially public investment, into productive channels. The coalition collapsed before any such report could be produced, but by a curious chance it bequeathed to its successors the man most capable of drafting such a document. This was a civil servant, T. K. Whitaker, who, at the early age of forty, had been selected in 1956 by the Minister of Finance, Gerald Sweetman, to fill the key post of secretary of his department. He did not begin work on the report until late in 1957 but then, with direct encouragement from his new political masters in Fianna Fáil, wrote it so rapidly that it was published in May of the following year, forming the basis for the Programme for Economic Expansion adopted by the government in November 1958. The well-nigh revolutionary implications of this new expansionist outlook will be considered later in this book.* Here it is sufficient to stress the psychological rather than the economic consequences of what was happening. In place of the old orthodoxies and the old introspection, Ireland seemed at last to be moving towards participation in the world of the mid-twentieth century. The new emphases on attracting foreign capital, developing a wider range of exports, modernising agriculture, were all designed to lift the country out of its nerveless dependence on external factors over which it had no control, and to accustom it to exercising independent judgment and initiative. Of course, there were hazards as well as advantages in this policy, and the decade of the 'sixties was to show that the economy was far from rolling forward on oiled castors. Moreover, although the Irish government did seem to speak with a more individual voice than formerly in matters of trade and finance, it could not escape the inexorable lesson of geography – that as a small and not very wealthy island it was bound to go on being deeply affected by the economic vicissitudes of its near neighbour and biggest customer, Britain, and also by the changing pattern in the larger entity of Western Europe, of which, however humble and remote, it remained inescapably a part. Yet, even though expansion for Ireland in the circumstances of the time could only mean involvement – to be expressed not just in renewed Anglo-Irish trade agreements, but in aspirations towards the Common Market – this does not alter the fact that after the Whitaker Report the former aimlessness and hopelessness had begun to give way to a drive and optimism previously unknown.

Of course, this could not have come about through the work of one man, or on the basis of a single document. It was only made possible by reason of the third of the changes we have to consider in these crowded years. This was the final replacement of the old guard by the rising generation of Fianna Fáil politicians. In 1959 Mr de Valera at last retired from the active leadership of his country, though not from

* See below, chap. 4, section v.

583

public life. The manner of his going was strange, but not uncharacter-istic. Early in the year the Senate, normally a docile enough assembly, braced itself to reject a government proposal to hold a referendum with a view to abolishing proportional representation. Since the re-jection amounted to no more than a ninety-days suspension, the Bill eventually became law and the referendum was fixed for 17 June. By a piece of rather too obvious sleight of hand the presidential election which fell that year was arranged for the same day, and to drive the point home to anyone obtuse enough not to have grasped it already, Mr de Valera stood as, in effect, the Fianna Fáil candidate. He was successful – defeating an old rival, General Sean MacEoin, by 538,000 votes to 417,536 – but the electorate refused to play politics with proportional representation and the government proposal was defeated.*

Mr de Valera's removal to Phoenix Park – where, up to the time of writing, he has filled the office of President with great dignity and dis-tinction for two full terms – left the way open for a complete re-construction of the government. The bridge with the past essential for a party with its roots deep in the conservative countryside was pro-vided by the new Taoiseach, Mr Sean Lemass. Although he had had to wait for the highest office until he was almost sixty, his political education had commenced at the age of sixteen when he was one of those who occupied the General Post Office. He fought on the anti-Treaty side in the Civil War, but had followed de Valera after the latter opted for constitutional politics in 1927. When Fianna Fáil took office five years later, Mr Lemass served as Minister for Industry and Commerce, rapidly earning a reputation for ruthless efficiency which was formidably enhanced by his performance as Minister of Supplies in the difficult years of the emergency. Scarcely less significant was the fact that he had been the principal architect, with Gerald Boland, of Fianna Fáil's constituency organisation – generally regarded as far superior to that of its rivals – and that he was personally respon-sible for the reconstruction and revival of the party after the defeat of 1948, with consequences which are still making themselves felt to this day. Intelligent, pragmatic, with an almost instinctive under-standing of economic problems (he could have made his fortune many times over in private business), the new Taoiseach was admirably equipped to preside over a period of rapid expansion. It is no mere exercise in public relations which links his name indissolubly with the forward policy of these years. To his predecessor, Dr James Ryan, and to Mr de Valera himself, may belong the credit for the initially favourable reception the government gave to the Whitaker Report, but the responsibility of implementing it fell squarely upon Mr Lemass. Characteristically, he shared it with a group of able young

* Reintroduced in 1968 by another referendum the proposal was once more rejected and it seems unlikely that proportional representation will be challenged again in the near future.

men who between them were to take over the direction of the party after his own retirement from the leadership in 1966, having fought and won two further leases of power for Fianna Fáil in 1961 and 1965.* From this group – which included his successor, Jack Lynch, his son-in-law Charles Haughey, P. J. Hillery, Brian Lenihan, George Colley and the late Donough O'Malley – were to be drawn the makers of policy in the 'sixties and, it may well be, far into the 'seventies as well.

The advent of a new generation in Fianna Fáil was matched by similar developments in the other two main parties. General Mulcahy retired from the leadership of Fine Gael within a few months of Mr de Valera leaving Fianna Fáil for the Presidency. His successor, Mr James Dillon, who had rejoined Fine Gael in 1952, served for that party the same function of bridging the present and the past as Mr Lemass did for Fianna Fáil. But whereas Mr Lemass, dominant as always over his colleagues, was able to look to the future right up to the moment of his resignation, Mr Dillon had a much more difficult task in trying to hold together a party which, while retaining its middle-class conservative bias, was under pressure from some of its younger supporters to change with the times. For a while it seemed that the mantle of power would descend on Mr Costello's son, Declan Costello, a young barrister who in the early 'sixties attempted to convert the party to a more progressive social policy. The embodiment of that policy – the programme called *The Just Society* – was, however, accepted by Fine Gael only a few weeks before the general election of 1965, and the reluctance of the electorate to swallow reforms which the protagonists themselves had quite evidently only half-digested, did much to reinforce the conservative leanings of the party. The younger Costello subsequently withdrew from politics and in 1965, when Mr James Dillon suddenly resigned the leadership, it passed to Liam Cosgrave, son of the perdurable politician who had seen the Free State through its first and stormiest decade. It should be said, though, that Fine Gael has shown greater resilience than this brief account would indicate

* In the process, however, Fianna Fáil lost its unassailable majority and held office with Independent support. At the most recent election (1969) it succeeded in the face of strong opposition and against all the odds in retrieving its independence of all other parties in the Dáil. The tenacity of its hold on power may be due partly to the very wide spectrum of support it can draw on – from a section of the farming community, from shopkeepers, from industrialists, and also from many who look to it for improved social services – but it is no doubt a product, too, of the fact that power generates its own momentum; in a country like Ireland, where patronage has always had an important function in government, to be in office is a great help towards staying in office. It would seem also that in 1969 the redrawing of constituency boundaries ensured for Fianna Fáil a 'bonus', estimated – admittedly by one of its opponents – as five or six more seats than it might otherwise have expected to win. (G. Fitz-Gerald, *Towards a New Ireland* (London, 1972), p. 43.)

and that the party has continued to attract some of the best minds in the country; an opposition front bench which includes Dr Garret FitzGerald cannot be considered less than formidable.

Almost simultaneously a change had taken place in the leadership of the Labour party when in 1961 the veteran William Norton gave place to a much younger man, Brendan Corish. It may be, though, that in the long run a much more significant event was Dr Noel Browne's decision in 1963 to throw in his lot with Labour. After his dramatic departure from the inter-party government in 1951, he, had taken temporary and somewhat uncomfortable shelter with Fianna Fáil which ended with his defeat in the election of 1954. Thereafter, he attempted to establish a party of his own, the National Progressive Democrats, but lacked the funds to build up any permanent organisation. His joining Labour in 1963 may have seemed at the time an act of political desperation, for that party was still far to the right of Dr Browne's own socialist standpoint. Three years later, however, the party formally pledged itself to 'a coherent, socialist philosophy'. In the evolution of that policy not only Dr Browne, but other intellectuals who had descried in Labour the only hope for a new radicalism — for example, Dr Conor Cruise O'Brien, Dr David Thornley and Mr Justin Keating — have played and are playing, especially since their election to the Dáil in 1969, an increasing part.* At the time of writing (summer, 1972) the Labour party appears to be in some disarray. This is partly because of differences of opinion between Dr Thornley and some of his colleagues over the crisis in Northern Ireland and, perhaps more fundamentally, because the urban radicalism of the intellectuals is rather strong medicine for a party which still draws its main support from non-industrial sources and which for that reason sometimes gives the appearance of being obliged to sail at the speed of the slowest ship in its variegated convoy.

The three developments here briefly summarised — the restoration

* This formidable accretion of intellectual strength has not yet been matched by a comparable increase in voting-power. Between 1965 and 1969 Labour representation in the Dáil declined from twenty-two to eighteen and at the general election in the latter year the Labour party could do no better than hold its figure at eighteen, compared with Fianna Fáil (seventy-five) and Fine Gael (fifty) — the remaining seat going to an Independent. This may simply mean that the electorate has not yet had time to evaluate the changed character of the Labour party, but it underlines the continuing difficulty of a workers' party in establishing itself in a country where the industrial population is still relatively small. For two interesting recent prognostications about the party's future, see M. Viney and O. Dudley Edwards 'Parties and Power', in O. Dudley Edwards (ed.), *Conor Cruise O'Brien Introduces Ireland* (London, 1969), pp. 95-103; and C. Cruise O'Brien, 'Ireland, 1969', in *Irish Times*, supplement, 21 Jan. 1969. Dr Browne's role as a socialist pioneer is perceptively analysed by M. McInerney, 'Noel Browne: Church and State', in *University Review*, vol. v, no. 2 (summer, 1968).

of public order, the new economic policy, the emergence of a new generation in politics – together pointed towards a fourth development which time may show to have been the most important of all. No one who has lived in Ireland, or studied Irish conditions, in recent decades can have failed to realise that, at least until the political explosion of 1968-9 in Northern Ireland, the Republic had begun to turn its back upon the legacy of bitterness bequeathed to it by the partition of the country and the Civil War. So far as the first of these is concerned, the exchange of visits between the two Prime Ministers of north and south (Captain Terence O'Neill and Mr Lemass) in 1965 – the first such exchange since the division of the island has become an accomplished fact – was widely seen at the time as an indication that old animosities were quietly being laid aside. And though the recent revival of sectarian and political violence in Ulster had obviously shattered the accord which seemed to have been established five years ago (the accord itself, indeed, may have contributed to Captain O'Neill's fall from power in 1969), a longer perspective may yet reveal that the precedent then established offers a foundation on which to build if, but only if, a profoundly altered regime should emerge from the present turmoil in Northern Ireland.

The crisis in the six counties – apart from the appalling dangers it holds for all those directly involved in it – carries also, of course, the risk that, if it intensifies, the hard-won stability of the other twenty-six may also be disrupted. Indeed, there have been signs that this is already happening. That the exponents of physical force, the IRA, should have been deeply stirred by what was happening in the north was only to be expected; and that their movement should rapidly have split – between the 'official' IRA who have so far tended towards caution, and the 'provisional' who have been clamant for thorough-going intervention – was also predictable. But potentially more serious are the stresses and strains which have emerged within the governing party in the Republic. Firm evidence, naturally, is still lacking, but there are strong indications of deep divisions in the cabinet over the question of whether or not the Republic should have taken more direct and positive action when the Ulster situation deteriorated so disastrously in August 1969. More recently still, in May 1970, the Taoiseach, Mr Lynch, was faced with an even graver crisis which led to the resignation of two ministers, Mr M. O'Morain and Mr K. Boland, and the dismissal of two others, Mr Charles Haughey and Mr Neil Blaney. The two dismissed ministers' names had been persistently mentioned in connection with an alleged plot – in which the IRA was rumoured to have been involved – to smuggle arms into Northern Ireland, with the obvious intention that these would find their way into nationalist hands, and one of them, Mr Haughey, was brought to trial on charges arising out of the allegations. He was subsequently acquitted, but this was far from being the end of the crisis. As the northern situation steadily worsened between 1970 and 1972 there were many occasions when it seemed that Mr Lynch must fall from power, either because of his inability to bridle the private armies of the IRA, or because the unity of his party was subjected to almost intolerable strain. In fact, despite resignations, expulsions, and the formation by Mr Boland in 1971 of a new party, Aontacht Eireann, calculated to appeal especially to Fianna Fáil dissidents, Mr Lynch has so far managed to survive. It is true that early in 1972, after the shooting of thirteen people in Derry city on 'Bloody Sunday' (30 January) as a result of action by Paratroops, and the subsequent burning of the British embassy in Dublin by an infuriated crowd, Anglo-Irish relations reached their lowest ebb for many years.* Yet within a few months of these grave events Mr Lynch registered three successes which would have been unthinkable at the beginning of the year. These were the establishment of special courts in an endeavour to deal with the gunmen; the winning at the referendum of 10 May of a crushing victory in favour of entry into the European Economic Community† and, in August 1972 the retention, again by a large majority, of a crucial seat, thus enabling Fianna Fáil to maintain a precarious lead over the combined forces of the Fine Gael and Labour.‡

The fact remains, nevertheless, that in existing circumstances Mr Lynch's options in regard to the northern crisis are distinctly limited. Given the past record of his own party (and, it would seem, the present inclinations of a section of it), together with the absence of sufficient force, or sufficiently reliable force, in the Republic to deal with the IRA, there appears to be little he can do save to maintain his contacts with the main opposition party (the Social and Democratic Labour Party) in the north, to seek to strengthen the rule of law at home, and to bring to bear in London whatever pressure is open to him for a conference aimed at producing a permanent and all-Ireland solution. But the future is so dark and uncertain that only one firm conclusion can be drawn at the present time. It is surely this – that different though the paths of north and south have been in the last fifty years, the demands of blood and history are still insistent; the island remains one island, and neither part of it can fail to be vitally affected by what happens in the other.

* For the events of 'Bloody Sunday', see below pp. 778-9.
† In a poll of about seventy per cent of the total electorate, just over a million votes were cast in favour of entry and almost 212,000 against. In each of the 42 constituencies there was a majority of over 70 per cent of those voting in favour.
‡ The traumatic experiences of the last two years have helped to whittle away the *overall* majority Mr Lynch won at the general election of 1969. In August 1972, after the Mid-Cork by-election, party strength was as follows: Fianna Fáil 70, Fine Gael 51, Labour 17, Independents (of various shades) 6.

War-time neutrality, most Irishmen would agree, had been a blessing to their country. But it was a blessing that had to be paid for, not merely in terms of a stagnant, or even retrogressive economy, but in terms of increasing psychological as well as physical isolation. Although Ireland could not be completely unaware of the new world that was coming so painfully to birth between 1939 and 1945 – Dublin, as we have seen, ranked with Lisbon as one of the key listening-posts in Europe for allied and axis powers alike – none of those who experienced what life was like in the twenty-six counties during the emergency years are ever likely to forget the intense introspection and gathering sense of unreality which geography, policy and censorship together conspired to produce.

Once hostilities had ended there was, of course, a reaction. People who had been starved for so long of contact with other countries were eager to renew their links with what had once passed for civilisation and even to play a part in building a new international polity on the ruins of the old. For individuals, it is true, the difficulties of travelling far afield, especially to the war-battered countries of Western Europe, meant that the process of emerging from isolation was a slow one, but at the government level involvement was more rapid. The reasons for this were partly political, partly economic. The economic reason was simply that, as we saw earlier, the effort to overcome the shortage of houses, fuel and manufactures caused by the war, together with the natural impulse of consumers to buy greedily whatever was available, had combined by 1947 to produce a major financial crisis. In consequence, Ireland soon found herself in the queue for Marshall Aid and, on receiving it, was inexorably caught up in the machinery of European economic reconstruction, becoming in due course a member of the Organisation for European Economic Co-operation. Participation in this sphere of post-war activity brought with it two advantages. In the short run, Ireland benefited immediately and massively from American aid which by 1950 amounted to nearly 150 million dollars in grants and loans.* But in the long run, and even more important, the country was brought into close contact with other European states, large and small, at a period when economic stringency was giving place to economic expansion and when new techniques of economic analysis and planning, as well as new extensions

* It could be argued, of course, that the injection of this amount of unearned capital into the economy not only created a false sense of security, but also, where it was not deployed on genuinely productive enterprise (and this sometimes happened) helped to intensify the inflation that became a never-ending feature of those years. But even the critics of Marshall Aid have not cared to contemplate what life would have been like without it.

of state enterprise, were being widely adopted. For the Irish economy this was both a chastening and exhilarating experience. Chastening because, as the early OEEC reports on Ireland made icily clear, standards of productivity and efficiency were among the lowest in Europe, but exhilarating also because the links with Europe, and even the opprobrious reports themselves, brought with them the possibility of change and improvement, opening the way for the genuine and sustained advance that came at the end of the 1950s.

If the economic motives for Ireland's increased participation in international affairs stemmed from her wartime experience, so also, though more obliquely, did the political ones. The neutrality of the country, as Mr de Valera had shaped and defined it even before the war had broken out, had been an expression, one might say the ultimate expression, of Irish independence. During the struggle itself, however, and especially after the entry of the United States into the war, it became necessary to find a more cogent and specific reason to explain why Ireland was not fighting by the side of the great country to which she had in the past contributed so much of her own blood. The reason which was advanced was the reason most likely to find favour with Americans in general and Irish-Americans in particular – that Ireland, as herself, a truncated state, could not join a grand alliance of which Britain, the power ostensibly responsible for the partition of the country, was a leading member.[30]

There is no reason to doubt the genuineness of this argument – however little ice it may have cut with critics like Churchill who, understandably obsessed with the strategic implications of Irish neutrality, remained obstinately blind to the connection between that neutrality and events in which he himself had played no inconsiderable part – but it had one consequence that in retrospect can only be seen as unfortunate. The linking of neutrality with partition served within Ireland to reanimate the whole issue of the border to such a degree that by 1945 the reunification of the country had come to seem for many well-intentioned people, both inside and outside official circles, the keystone of whatever tremulous arch of foreign policy the government might seek to throw across the chasm that separated a small neutral from the recently belligerent powers. And so it came about, with an irony that might have been ludicrous had it not had tragic undertones, that at the very moment when the rude surgery of partition was being used all over the world to 'solve' problems that had shown themselves insoluble, at the very moment when Europe itself was being partitioned by the Iron Curtain, the Irish signalled their return to the comity of nations by what was intended to be a powerful propaganda drive to awaken the conscience of the world to the plight of their sundered country. What began as an uproar of voluntary bodies – among which the Anti-Partition League that emerged early in 1947 was perhaps the most vociferous – became, however, much more serious when Mr de Valera fell from power in 1948 and proceeded to use his enforced leisure to conduct a tour of the United States, Australia and Britain, devoting countless speeches and the whole force of his formidable personality to 'anti-partition'.

Where Mr de Valera led, the inter-party government which had succeeded him in office could ill afford not to follow. The ending of partition was, of course, an article of faith with that government and although, as we have seen, the declaration of the republic scarcely contributed to this end, the unofficial propaganda campaign rapidly became official. Irish representatives at international gatherings were instructed to pursue what has since been aptly, if inelegantly, called 'the policy of the sore thumb' – that is, the raising of the partition issue on every conceivable occasion with the double aim of embarrassing Britain and enlisting foreign sympathy for the Irish case. But if Britain was embarrassed (which is doubtful) her embarrassment was as nothing compared with that of some of the able and intelligent Irishmen who were condemned to walk this futile treadmill.* Nor is there much evidence to show that foreign sympathy was in fact enlisted to any marked degree. At Strasbourg certainly, where Ireland became a founder member of the Council of Europe in 1949 and used the Assembly for some years thereafter as one of the main platforms for anti-partition speeches, the reaction among other delegates seems to have been one of boredom mingled with bewilderment.

But, there was one sphere in which this generally unproductive policy did directly affect – and still affects – the status of Ireland in the western world. As international tension was accentuated in the immediate aftermath of the war and the threat of a renewed communist advance across Europe seemed to become steadily more imminent, there emerged not just a local alliance of the powers that felt themselves to be in particular danger – the Brussels Pact of 1948 – but a larger grouping, the North Atlantic Treaty Organisation, which came into being the next year. There were many reasons why Ireland might have been attracted into the orbit of NATO. Geographically, she was an integral part of the Atlantic community. Ideologically, she was as deeply opposed to communism as any member of the Alliance and did not even maintain diplomatic relations with the Soviet Union. Politically, the cohesive power of NATO and its military effective-

* The chief of them, Dr Conor Cruise O'Brien, has written recently that he 'blushes to recall' the amount of his professional time that was devoted between 1947 and 1951 to 'anti-partition'. 'The only positive result of this activity, so far as I was concerned [he adds] was that it led me to discover the cavernous inanities of "anti-partition" and of government propaganda generally.' (C. Cruise O'Brien, 'The Embers of Easter', in O. Dudley Edwards and F. Pyle (ed.), 1916: The Easter Rising, p. 233.) It is fair to add, however, that once the anti-partition fever was over, Ireland became a model member of the Council of Europe, being the first country to accept the jurisdiction of the European Court of Human Rights.

ness were alike supplied by the United States, of all powers the one with which Ireland might have been expected to be most *en rapport*.

Yet, despite these inducements, Ireland declined the invitation to join the alliance. The decision not to accept was taken in the first instance by the inter-party government and it was a decision which may well have been directly influenced by the charter of that government. Had the senior partner in the coalition – Fine Gael – commanded sufficient seats in the Dáil to allow it to dispense with the inter-party arrangement and rule independently, its history and inclinations might well have taken it into NATO. But in practice Fine Gael had little freedom of manoeuvre. This was partly because it depended so heavily on the support of Clann na Poblachta, which, being almost by definition a party wedded to the concept of ending partition, would have found it difficult to sanction membership of an alliance wherein the 'author' of that partition, Britain, took a prominent part. Partly also, of course, the inter-party government as a whole, and not merely Mr MacBride's segment of it, was bound to fight shy of NATO, if only because it could not appear to be less intransigent on the subject of the border than Mr de Valera, then busily engaged in 'putting an anti-partition girdle round the earth'.[31]

Accordingly, when in February 1949 Mr MacBride, as Minister for External Affairs, was asked in the Dáil about the government's attitude to the Atlantic alliance then taking shape he was able to make this categorical reply : 'As long as partition lasts, any military alliance or commitment involving joint military action with the state responsible for partition must be quite out of the question as far as Ireland is concerned.'[32] The same answer, more impersonally worded, was returned to the formal invitation to join the alliance, with the rider that to join any military grouping of which Britain was a member would be to expose the Irish government to the risk of civil conflict within its own jurisdiction. For Ireland, it was made plain, the correct approach to North Atlantic security must involve the ending of a situation which was a standing threat to the peace of Britain and Ireland alike.[33]

The decision once made has never been reversed. Nor is this surprising. Apart from a second brief spell of inter-party government between 1954 and 1957, Fianna Fáil has remained continuously in power from 1951 until the time of writing. For much of that period the ideas of Mr de Valera remained dominant and these ideas – which in matters of foreign policy had acquired exceptional authority in the light of Ireland's wartime experience – continued to revolve round the doctrine of neutrality. But it was, nevertheless, neutrality with a difference. At the time of a great world conflict to stand aside had seemed the last, desperate resource open to a small nation, a gamble that had to be taken against the odds, and which paid off largely for reasons outside the control of the government. But in the Cold War which developed in the decade after the fighting had ended, neutrality, or neutralism as it was becoming fashionable to call it, had gained respectability as a way of life, almost a philosophy of international relations, for those countries – especially the 'emergent nations' of Asia and Africa – which had no desire to be caught up in great-power politics. Individually, their desires were doubtless of little account, but what gave them more weight than they would otherwise have had – though even that was hardly excessive – was the existence of the United Nations which, from its war-time beginnings as an attempt to give the victorious alliance some permanent status, had emerged in and after 1945 as the successor to the League of Nations.

Ireland, as a small power which had taken an honourable part in the affairs of the defunct League, might have been expected to be one of the first to apply for membership of the new organisation. And in fact such application was duly made in August 1946, to be at once vetoed by the Soviet Union on the ground that that country had no diplomatic relations with the applicant. Subsequent attempts to gain admission were regularly vetoed in the same way (though this did not apply to Irish membership of the specialised agencies of the United Nations) and it was not until after the 'package deal' of 1955 that Ireland, along with numerous other countries from both sides of the Iron Curtain, took her seat in the session of 1956, the session racked by the simultaneous Suez and Hungarian crises. The head of the Irish delegation was Mr F. H. Boland, a sagacious and experienced diplomatist who was at the time of his appointment the permanent head of the Foreign Service. That service had been much expanded over the years, notably by Mr MacBride between 1948 and 1951, and it now contained a considerable number of able young men, an astonishingly high proportion of whom were simultaneously making reputations as poets, critics and historians.

The appearance of this versatile delegation at the United Nations coincided with the brief term of office of the second inter-party government and it fell to Mr Liam Cosgrave, as Minister for External Affairs, to lay down the guiding-lines of Irish policy. The policy he enunciated – and in the formulation of which it may be conjectured his permanent officials took their share – was based upon what Dr Cruise O'Brien, at that time one of those officials, has described as the 'three principles'. Briefly, these were: first, scrupulous fidelity to the obligations of the Charter; second, that Ireland should try to maintain an independent stance, with the intention 'to avoid becoming associated with particular blocs or groups so far as possible'; but finally, and notwithstanding the second principle, Ireland was to do what she could to preserve Christian civilisation and to support wherever she could those powers primarily charged with the defence of 'the free world' against communism. 'We belong', as Mr Cosgrave observed in the Dáil, 'to the great community of states made up of the United States, Canada and Western Europe.'[84]

How far this third principle seriously compromised the second principle remained to be seen, though not to be seen by Mr Cosgrave who, with the fall of the inter-party government, gave place to Mr Frank Aiken. Mr Aiken, who became Minister of External Affairs in 1957 and retained the office until his retirement from politics in 1969, was one of Mr de Valera's oldest associates – old enough, certainly, to recall that his leader's reputation at Geneva before the war had been based on the independent attitude he had then so clearly displayed. That attitude Mr Aiken was prepared to try to reproduce in New York. For several years he did so with remarkable success and the Irish delegation – intelligent, articulate, extremely well-prepared – played a part in the world of the Assembly far out of proportion to the size or international importance of their country. One has only to read the speeches the Minister delivered between 1957 and 1961 – some of them on issues still as crucial as when he first addressed himself to them – to understand the extent to which a genuinely Irish foreign policy was beginning to emerge during those years. In some respects – as, for example, in the annual plea that Mr Aiken made for the nonproliferation of nuclear weapons – it was a policy common to all small, exposed countries. In other respects, again, in its generally anti-colonialist tone, it was a policy Ireland shared with the new Afro-Asian states and to which Mr Aiken was able to give an historical depth denied to all save, perhaps, the Americans:

We know [he said in 1960] what imperialism is and what resistance to it involves. We do not hear with indifference the voices of those spokesmen of African and Asian countries who passionately champion the right to independence of millions who are still, unfortunately, under foreign rule . . . More than eighty years ago the then leader of the Irish nation, Charles Stewart Parnell, proclaimed the principle that 'the cause of nationality is sacred, in Asia and Africa as in Ireland'. That is still a basic principle of our political thinking in Ireland today, as it was with those of my generation who felt impelled to assert in arms the right of our country to independence.[35]

But there was a sense in which Irish policy at the United Nations in those early years went beyond concern with nuclear proliferation or even with anti-colonialism. The test case was China – more precisely, whether the question of the admission of the People's Republic of China ('Red China') ought or ought not to be discussed in the Assembly. For a small neutral this was a potentially explosive issue, since American influence was totally committed to reserving the Chinese place in the Assembly and on the Security Council for the Chiang Kai Shek regime based on Formosa. As early as 1957 the Irish vote was cast with the minority which favoured such discussion, and although American pressure was at once brought to bear in a manner which

Dr Cruise O'Brien has amusingly described, Mr Aiken returned· to the charge repeatedly between then and 1961.[36]

Not surprisingly, his independence exposed him to attack from two quite different directions. Critics in America – and some in Ireland also – refused to recognise that there was an important difference between *discussing* Chinese representation and voting for the admission of 'Red China'. Yet when in 1955 Mr Aiken showed that there could be a very real difference by coupling a renewed plea for discussion with a strong condemnation of recent Chinese aggression in Tibet, he was at once assailed by the Soviet Union with the accusation that in raising the Tibetan question he was acting at the behest of another [i.e. the American] delegation. Not at all, he replied: 'We believe that whenever the rights of a small people are forcibly violated in this manner, the representatives of other small peoples in this Assembly have the duty to speak out.' And later in the same session, again referring to China's violation of human rights, he made in effect the same point that Litvinov had made long ago in the League of Nations, that peace is indivisible:

If the Assembly [he said in October 1959] demonstrates that it is prepared to condemn wholesale violations of human rights, wherever they are perpetrated, it will be maintaining intact that invisible but effective barrier against further acts of aggression which is constituted by a vigilant world public opinion. If, on the other hand, it chooses to ignore a flagrant denial of human rights to an entire people, then it weakens that barrier and must render further violations of human rights a little easier and a little more likely.[37]

In practice, it must be admitted, Irish speeches in the Assembly, however eloquent and however independent, were unlikely to have a very direct effect upon the course of world affairs. In some spheres – notably the prevention of nuclear proliferation – Mr Aiken's· initiatives were indeed made the basis for serious discussion, but this could not hide the stark and disagreeable fact that in a world of giants pigmies have only a limited role to play. And although Ireland, known to be both anti-colonialist and anti-communist, was better placed than most to follow a neutralist policy, it became increasingly difficult to do so as time went on. By 1961, certainly there were clear signs that the second and third principles of Irish policy at the United Nations were at last beginning to demonstrate their incompatibility, and this at a time when 'second principle' forces inside the Irish delegation were weakened by the resignation of Dr Cruise O'Brien, following his experiences in the Congo.* In the session of that year, faced with a situation where the China question was at last

* Dr Cruise O'Brien had been selected in 1961 by the then Secretary-General of the United Nations, Dag Hammarskjöld, to represent the organisation in Katanga with a view to ending the secession of that

on the agenda (the United States having already manoeuvred the Chinese into declaring that they did not recognise the Charter or regard previous decisions of the United Nations as binding) Mr Aiken went on record as not being prepared to support China's admission until her government gave guarantees against further aggression, withdrew from Korea and respected the rights and liberties of the Chinese people. Since the guarantees were not forthcoming there was no longer anything to prevent the Irish delegation from voting on this matter in the same lobby as the United States.

That this perceptible movement towards 'westernism' was not an isolated phenomenon was made almost brutally clear the following year when the Taoiseach, Mr Lemass, carried his party with him at its annual conference in a speech which saluted the United States as the guardian of the 'free world', while at the same time condemning the communist bloc in language that would have been music to the ears of John Foster Dulles had he lived to hear it. The American orientation which this implied was greatly reinforced by the triumphant visit of President Kennedy to Ireland in the summer of 1963, and the bond of sympathy between the two countries which he then established or renewed was not to be broken even by his assassination a few months later.

Nevertheless, despite the strong gravitational pull exerted by Washington, the limitations of the Irish role at the United Nations should not be overemphasised. Even if there had been a shift from 'second principle' to 'third principle' (and the extent of that shift may have been exaggerated) Ireland remained a conscientious and generally respected member of the organisation. She showed this most effectively not in words but in deeds, by assuming on several occasions the burdensome duty of contributing a contingent of troops to the United Nations peace-keeping forces. It is true that these excursions provided occupation for an otherwise unemployed army which the troops themselves gratefully seized upon as giving meaning to their existence, but the Congo episode of 1960 showed that something more than a military promenade could be involved. In the summer of that year an

province from the central government. The story of his mission – at first seemingly successful, but ultimately abortive – and the whole strange train of events that led to his own resignation and Hammarskjöld's death belong to international history and to the biographies of the principal figures involved. They have no place in this narrative, though it is relevant to point out that the affair had a powerful impact in Ireland, where, apart from providing a superb opportunity for Irishmen to indulge their national habit of taking sides *con brio*, it helped to bring home to a startled public both the extent of their country's involvement in world affairs and the risks inherent in playing for such large stakes. Dr Cruise O'Brien's account of the crisis is in his book, 'To *Katanga and Back*. To this fascinating, though necessarily subjective, record should be added his recently published play, *Murderous Angels* (New York and London, 1969).

Irish force was sent out to join the United Nations troops of whom General Sean MacEoin was the commander-in-chief. A few months later a party of these Irish soldiers was ambushed by Baluba tribesmen, and ten men were killed. The shock to Irish public opinion was intense, but despite a rumour (happily unfounded) nearly a year later that a much larger Irish force had been massacred at Jadotville, the country did not retreat, and has not retreated, into isolationism.* On the contrary, not only have Irish troops continued to serve overseas – in Cyprus, for example, or Kashmir – but at the United Nations itself the Irish delegation as recently as 1965 put forward drastic amendments to the existing methods of financing peace-keeping operations. These were designed to ensure that the permanent members of the Security Council who had approved of a given operation should assume responsibility for seventy per cent of the cost, the remaining thirty per cent to be provided by other member-states, in the proportion of twenty-five per cent from the wealthier, and five per cent from the poorer, countries. Predictably, this proposal fell foul of the Security Council and has not yet been found acceptable; in consequence, and as a protest against the voluntary system of financing these operations which still prevailed, Ireland decided to pay for a time the cost of its Cyprus contingent out of its own exchequer.[38]

In the last analysis, however, the chief beneficiary from the new international role of Ireland may not have been the Congolese or the Cypriots but the Irish themselves. Although no doubt there is still considerable indifference to foreign affairs in the country. There is at the same time an increasing awareness of the smallness and oneness of the world and a growing realisation that to opt out from that world, or to sit by the turf-fire crooning over ancient and still unrectified grievances, is no longer possible. Partly, no doubt, this increased awareness is a result of the tendency of people to go abroad for their holidays far more than before, but it is also an inevitable outcome of the country's heady, if sometimes chastening, experiences at the United Nations. Without these experiences it might have been much more difficult than it actually proved for the government to take a further step – perhaps the most crucial step of all – when on 1 August 1961 Mr Lemass announced that Ireland would apply for membership of the European Economic Community. The fact that she subsequently shared in the rebuffs administered to Britain by General de Gaulle may have deprived the gesture of much of its significance at the time, and may even have contributed to the air of unreality which has often since seemed to overhang such public debate as there has been on 'going into Europe'. Nevertheless, although one may suspect that for many voters the specific issues at stake may have seemed – and may still seem – too complicated to grasp, the massive vote in favour of entry registered at the 1972 referendum can neither be ignored, nor explained away as essentially a vote on domestic

* The total of Irish soldiers killed in the Congo was twenty-six.

politics – i.e. against Sinn Féin, which has always opposed the Common Market on the ground that it constitutes a threat to political independence – rather than on the larger European question.*

Despite the prognostications of stark ruin and abounding prosperity with which the opponents and supporters of the Common Market have respectively bombarded a bemused public, the consequences of joining the Community are incalculable. As with so much else that vitally affects the future of Ireland, the historian can only wait upon events and judge them in the light of what has yet to be experienced. All the same, the very fact that entry into Europe has been approved by such a vast majority does in itself suggest that Irish foreign policy may now be moving perceptibly in a direction which could scarcely have been predicted as recently as a decade ago. Up to about 1960 neutralism, combined perhaps with a discreet determination not to prejudice a future solution of partition by adopting a stance on most international questions too far removed from that of Britain, restricted Irish diplomacy to a somewhat limited range of choices. To support institutions such as the United Nations or the Council of Europe, to conform on the large issues there to be decided to an increasingly 'western' line, but at the same time to maintain a rigorous boycott of NATO – these seemed almost the only available options. But it is possible, even probable, that in an enlarged European Community Ireland will in future be considerably less under the influence of either Britain or America than hitherto and reasonably certain that if belonging to the Common Market can be shown to produce benefits, there will be no reluctance on her part to assume the corresponding responsibilities.† There are, after all, good historical grounds for arguing that to the Irish entry into Europe will be a homecoming as much as a new departure.

* For the extent of the victory, see p. 588, note above. It should be noted that although the Labour party was opposed to joining the Common Market (partly on economic grounds) the two largest parties, Fianna Fáil and Fine Gael, were both in favour of entry.

† It is also arguable that in areas such as agriculture, regional policy, or even representation in Community institutions, the effect of Irish membership of EEC may be to reveal that the common interest of Northern Ireland and the Republic will be greater than the common interest of Northern Ireland and the rest of the United Kingdom. For the development of this argument, see G. FitzGerald, *Towards a New Ireland* (London, 1972), especially chap. 6.

4. The Quest for Prosperity

We affirm the duty of every man and woman to give allegiance and service to the Commonwealth, and declare it is the duty of the Nation to assure that every citizen shall have opportunity to spend his or her strength in the service of the people. In return for willing service, we, in the name of the Republic, declare the right of every citizen to an adequate share of the produce of the Nation's labour ('Democratic Programme', *Dáil Eireann, Minutes and Proceedings*, 21 Jan. 1919, pp. 22-3).

After 35 years of native government people are asking whether we can achieve an acceptable degree of economic progress. The common talk amongst parents in the towns, as in rural Ireland, is of their children having to emigrate as soon as their education is completed, in order to be sure of a reasonable livelihood (T. K. Whitaker, *Economic Development* (1958), p. 5).

(i) ECONOMIC INTERDEPENDENCE

The years of the First World War, of the War of Independence and of the Civil War had altered so much in Ireland that it was difficult at once to realise that in economic matters continuity not change was to be the order of the day. True, the context in which economic policy had to be formulated and applied was very different from what it had been under British rule. Since Ireland was no longer a single entity, the industrial northeast – traditionally, if over-optimistically, regarded as a source of strength – was no longer available. Moreover, the disturbed condition of the rest of the country from 1919 onwards had led to much physical damage and dislocation of trade; worse still, perhaps, it had created an atmosphere of confusion and unsettlement in which business could hardly be expected to thrive. Yet the most important new development, after all, was that at last an Irish government sat in Dublin, and since it was a government reared on Griffith's economic ideas and composed of his political heirs, it was reasonable to suppose that the vigorous growth of an autonomous Irish economy would be its most urgent task.

So no doubt it was. But the Irish government, like the Irish people, was faced with certain inexorable and unpalatable facts. The first of these was that political independence, even in the sense in which that had been achieved by the Treaty, was no guarantee of economic

599

independence. On the contrary, the pattern established in the latter half of the nineteenth century proved hard to break. The Irish Free State remained part of an economic complex of which the United Kingdom was, as before, the predominant partner. The Irish monetary system was firmly tied to sterling, Irish commerce continued, for the time being at least, to be conducted within the framework of free trade, and ninety or more per cent of Irish exports still looked to Britain and Northern Ireland for their market.

Moreover, if the harsh realities of life in the great world had not been noticeably changed by the excitements of the previous decade, neither had the internal structure of the Irish economy. The new national government, like the old British one, saw in agriculture the basis of the country's existence and addressed itself at once to the problems of that key sector. This preoccupation may help to explain why Griffith's followers hesitated to follow Griffith's recipe of self-sufficiency through the development of native industries behind high tariff walls. 'The propagandist writings of one man', observed Kevin O'Higgins with characteristic bluntness, 'cannot be accepted simply as revealed truth, requiring no further investigation . . .'[1] Further investigation in fact suggested that if agriculture was the economic basis of the state, and if it depended upon exports for its well-being, then it was only common sense to seek to make Irish farmers competitive by improving the standard of their produce, if necessary by legislation aimed directly at regulating the breeding of livestock and raising the quality of dairy products. Not only that – if, as was the case, the great bulk of agricultural exports came from livestock and dairy products, then the trend must be towards encouraging this specialisation, even if that involved a growing dependence upon imported foodstuffs.

Now, since such an agricultural policy was aimed at developing the export trade, it followed that tariffs for the protection of home industries were largely inhibited by the fear of foreign retaliation. Far better, so it seemed, was it to rely upon the benefits of agricultural prosperity percolating through to other sections of the community, leading in course of time, perhaps, to a modest expansion of home industries. A few pre-existing tariffs were indeed taken over by the new government (notably those on tobacco and motor cars). Some additional ones were incorporated in the budgets of 1924, 1925 and 1926 (on such articles as boots and shoes, glass bottles, soap and candles, clothing and confectionery), but it remains true to say that up to 1926 the attitude of the Free State government was one of extreme caution towards the whole concept of industrial protection. In that year a Tariff Commission was set up to examine the case for extending duties to cover additional industries. Up to 1931 the results of its labours were scarcely impressive – a mere handful of relatively unimportant industries (with the exception of butter which received assistance actually in 1931) obtained some tariff benefits and even these only after searching inquiry. It is proper to add, however, that the few large-scale enterprises in the country – brewing, distilling and biscuit-manufacture – were themselves so dependent upon the export market that a protectionist policy would for them have been irrelevant, if not positively embarrassing.

Some expansion, no doubt, there was. Over a hundred new factories were said to have been opened in the protected industries by 1930, giving increased employment in those industries to just over 13,000 people. It can be claimed also that the Censuses of Industrial Production which began to be taken in 1926 showed an improvement for the years after the Tariff Commission had begun its work. The value of the net output in the industries covered by these Censuses (that is the gross value of output less cost of materials, fuel, light and power) went up from just over £23 million in 1926 to £25.6 million in 1931. Even these figures, not in themselves calculated to fire the blood of an economic nationalist, are too favourable, since they include a wide variety of what might more properly be classed as services. Annual inquiries into industries producing transportable goods elicited a more accurate, if bleaker, picture. The net output of those industries was valued at £16.4 million in 1916 and £18.2 million in 1931.[2] By no stretch of the imagination can this be regarded as an industrial renaissance.

Nor did it give rise to any radical redeployment of labour. The increase of the labour-force in the industries selected for annual review (in effect, the main factory-based industries) was a little under 5,000 during the five years 1926-31. In the whole range covered by the Census of Industrial Production there was an increase during the same period of from 102.5 thousand to 110.6 thousand. And if this total is swollen by the inclusion of other marginal industrial workers (as it was in the 1926 Census of Population) to 164,000, this was still only 13.5 per cent of the persons at work in the country that year. Ten years later this had gone up to 16.7 per cent, but that increase was due, as we shall presently see, to a deliberate policy of industrialisation much more forcefully pursued than any before 1932. Even within this small percentage of the total work-force, the emphasis was overwhelmingly upon production for the home market. In 1929 concerns producing goods for domestic consumption accounted for no less than eighty-five per cent of the labour employed in industry. And in that year the value of domestic manufactures exported (excluding tractors and other vehicles where imports were also involved) was only worth £1.6 million. By 1935 this figure had fallen to just over £600,000; since in the same period prices of industrial goods were estimated to have fallen by not more than seventeen per cent, there was evidence here of considerable decline in physical volume. Small wonder that the Secretary of the Department of Industry and Commerce, giving evidence to the Banking Commission, observed that there was 'no immediate propect at the present time of establishing

601

a substantial export trade in the new industries; that is, in the new industries that are established behind customs protection'.[3]

So far as Mr Cosgrave and his ministers were concerned, then, upon the well-being of agriculture rested the well-being of the country at large. They inherited an agriculture which, as we have seen, had achieved a certain stability about the turn of the century. This stability – its critics might have called it stagnation – did not change to any marked degree during the first decade of the Irish Free State, nor for that matter, for many years thereafter. The total agricultural area of the twenty-six counties (that is the area occupied by tillage and pasture) had been just over twelve million acres in 1910. Over the next twenty years it declined to about 11¾ million acres, though some, perhaps most, of this change was due to the fact that a proportion of what had formerly been reckoned as marginal pasture land had been put aside as rough grazing and so left out of calculation. The relative shares falling to tillage and pasture had not altered drastically since the great adjustment of the second half of the nineteenth century. The tendency of the area under grain to decline steadily, which had been so marked a feature of the post-Famine years, continued to be manifest under a native government. The total of just over a million acres of grain crops in 1921 (itself somewhat swollen by the recent war demand) contracted to 763,284 acres by 1931. Adding in the figures for root and green crops and flax (also declining as a group) the entire acreage of tillage may be said to have fallen from 1.8 million acres in 1921 to 1.4 million ten years later. During the same period the combined totals of hay and pasture rose roughly from 10 million acres to 10.3 million.[4] In other words, though pasture remained dominant in the agricultural economy, it had not greatly enlarged its actual area. Indeed, the full force of this central fact in the life of the country can only be realised by seeing it in a longer perspective:

Area under Crops and Pastures[5]
Percentage Distribution

	1851	1901	1931
Ploughed Land	29	14	12
Hay	9	14	20
Pasture	62	72	68
Total	100	100	100

But, while pasture was still supreme after 1921, there was no great variation in the number of animals it supported. The number of horses declined marginally between then and 1931 and so, more important, did the number of cattle – from 4.4 million in 1921 to just over 4 million in 1931. The relative decline in milch cows was slighter than in dry cattle, but the latter still accounted for three-quarters of the total.

In two instances – pigs and poultry – there was a sharp increase (poultry went up by nearly six million in the decade) and although some of this may have been due to a readiness to pay more attention to these branches of production on large farms, and to the low price of imported feeding-stuffs, poultry especially remained *par excellence* a small-farm activity.

Ireland, indeed, was still a country of small holdings, though the size of the holdings was tending to grow and the proportion of agricultural land occupied by very small farms to diminish. It is true that as late as 1931 there were still nearly 45,000 under one acre, and also true that although this was about a third less than the 1910 figure, the total was later to rise again. Such small plots of land, however, can scarcely be regarded as farms in any meaningful sense. For farms over one acre, on the other hand, the trend was undoubtedly towards consolidation. Thus, as late as 1917, holdings between one and thirty acres were about 65 per cent of the total; by 1951 they had dropped to 58 per cent and this tendency was to continue. But these small holdings under thirty acres only occupied 24 per cent of agricultural land in 1917 and 22.5 per cent in 1931. Farms between thirty and a hundred acres occupied 38.5 per cent in 1917 and 42.8 per cent in 1931. Although farms of a hundred acres and over occupied 37.4 per cent of the agricultural land in 1917, their share had fallen back to 34.7 in 1931. Over the forty years between the end of the First World War and the publication of the report on Economic Development in 1958 the most marked movements were away from farms *under* fifteen acres and *over* two hundred acres, and towards an intermediate range of between thirty and a hundred acres. By the mid-fifties farms in that range accounted for 45 per cent of the whole area under crops and pasture.[6]

But this process of consolidation has to be seen in the context of a declining rural population. Between 1926 and 1936 the total of men and women at work in agriculture fell from just over 644,000 to just over 605,000. This trend was to be greatly accelerated in succeeding years (for reasons partly connected with emigration during the Second World War), with the result that over the twenty years between 1926 and 1946 there was a total decline of 85,400; of this total no less than seventy per cent occurred on farms of less than fifteen acres.[7]

Consolidation did not necessarily mean increased efficiency, though in many cases it might be a pre-condition for it. It has been estimated, for example, that although the gross value of the output of agriculture in the Irish Free State increased from £57.8 million in 1926-7 to £61.4 million in 1929-30 (falling back thereafter under the combined effects of the depression and the Anglo-Irish economic dispute, but reviving with the onset of war), nearly all of the increase was due to the movement of prices. It has been suggested, indeed, that although the volume of agricultural output in the area of the twenty-six counties increased by perhaps twenty-five to thirty per cent between 1861 and

1909, since then (at least until the mid-fifties) there had been no significant change of volume. In fact, as the Emigration Commission Report puts it, 'during the past hundred years . . . the disappointing record of agriculture shows only a total increase of 25 per cent in the volume of output, all of which had taken place by the first decade of this century'. So small had this increase been that the Commission reckoned that despite the drift from the land the existing volume of output could have been produced by about two-thirds of the workers actually on the farms.[8] It may be argued, as a counterbalance to this rather bleak analysis, that at least it can be shown that even if volume did not rise significantly the yield of crops per acre did do so. It is certainly true that this happened between the second half of the nineteenth century and the early years of the twentieth at a rate comparable with similar developments elsewhere in Europe. But between about 1919 and the middle 'thirties there was, except for the production of potatoes, a marked slowing down. The following table will show something of this movement:[9]

Estimated Annual Average Yields Per Acre

Years	Wheat (cwt)	Oats (cwt)	Barley (cwt)	Potatoes (tons)	Hay (cwt)
1850–59	13·0	13·4	16·7	4·6	38·7
1900–09	19·1	16·7	18·3	4·2	45·2
1910–19	19·9	18·0	18·9	5·1	40·9
1932–36	20·4	19·5	20·5	7·7	41·3

We are dealing, therefore, with an agriculture which had become stabilised over a long period of years. Not only that – this stabilisation had taken place at the point in history where the tenant-farmer was at last becoming the owner of his holding as a result of the land legislation in the two generations before the First World War. The small or medium farm worked mainly as a family concern thus became the stereotype; even in the mid-1920s only nineteen per cent of the labour-force on farms in the Irish Free State consisted of paid employees. It has been suggested with some plausibility that this social pattern imposed upon Irish agriculture (or rather, reinforced) a deeply conservative approach to farming, characterised above all by a passion to acquire or to retain land almost regardless of its economic potentiality.* No doubt the farmer gained in security from becoming

* It is important to remember, however, that the conservatism of Irish agriculture was not a new phenomenon, springing solely from peasant ownership. 'Agriculture', it has been well said, 'would be plagued with the self-same problems to-day were Ireland still a tenancy at will, for these problems were inherited, not created by peasant proprietors' (Joseph

an owner; probably also, at least while agricultural prices remained buoyant, he gained in income once the land legislation began to take effect, for his judicial rents or land annuities were generally lower than the old rents in the competitive market. And although it is true that during the 1920s the cost of living index was rising faster than agricultural prices, and that those prices were severely hit at the end of the decade by the world depression, the worst effects of this were not felt in Ireland until the 1930s because, during the first decade of the Free State's existence, the prices of foodstuffs of animal origin held up rather longer than the prices of cereals.[10]

It did not follow, however, that the tenant transmogrified into owner necessarily changed his attitude towards farming – if he had more money this did not mean that he was going to invest it in improving his holding. The very stability of Irish agriculture which we have just been considering suggests, indeed, that he did not. We have seen already that in the first half of the twentieth century the area of tillage was declining, while pasture remained more or less static. It is no less significant that there was also a slowing down in the rate at which farms were being stocked with cattle and sheep. Whereas during the Famine years (1847 to 1851) livestock increased at the rate of 4 per cent per annum, the corresponding rates for 1901-21 and 1921-61 were 0.4 and 0.2 per cent respectively.[11] This is not in itself surprising; it simply means that given the kind of equilibrium between tillage, dry cattle and dairy farming that had been established, the opportunity for profitable investment was not obvious. Where such an opportunity did offer itself, as in poultry-farming, full advantage was no doubt taken of it, but there are indications that lacking any obvious outlet, and lacking also the economic spur of a rent economy, the farmer was beginning to use some at least of any increased income that might accrue to him to achieve a higher standard of living for himself and his family. That this was happening is suggested by the findings of the Commission on Derating, which reported in 1931 that there had been a marked improvement in living conditions on many Irish farms.[12] It is suggested still more by the fact that the dowry-system for farmers' daughters, though going far back into Irish social history, developed very significantly at this time. It has been observed that before about 1880 dowries were very frequently paid in kind, but that from then onwards (with the land legislation starting to take effect) sums of three or four hundred pounds began to change hands; in more recent times dowries of one thousand or even two thousand pounds have been not unknown.[13] Since in many cases the dowry of a daughter-in-law was used as a means of 'fortuning-off' the daughter of the house in her turn, it follows that this bride-price

Lee, 'Irish Agriculture', in *Agricultural History Review* (1969) xvii, part 1, p. 73). For the nineteenth century background to this subject, see Part I, chap. 2.

was not necessarily (though sometimes, no doubt, it was) an addition to the capital of the farm. Indeed, even if it did not go out again in this form, it could be, and often was, used to assist the emigration of other members of the family, in which case it was, of course, carried out of agriculture altogether.

But not only did Irish farmers cling to their land and not only were they reluctant to invest heavily in it. Their tendency towards inertia was powerfully reinforced by another factor – which was that they were growing older. In 1881, 34.7 per cent of Irish farmers were under forty-five years; 43.5 per cent were between forty-five and sixty-five, while 21.8 per cent were over sixty-five. Women farmers accounted for only 13.5 per cent of the total, and of these no more than 3.6 per cent were over sixty-five. But by 1946 a situation had been reached where a third of all farmers were over sixty-five. Women accounted for one-sixth of the total; nearly half of these were over sixty-five and three-quarters were widows.[14] It would be difficult to imagine a more infallible recipe for rural conservatism.

How far did the state in the first decade after the Treaty seek to counteract this conservatism, how far was it even felt that it needed to be counteracted? The answers to these questions cannot be simple and clear-cut, because the lines of official policy are themselves confused. Politically, the structure of Irish agriculture was sacrosanct – owner-occupancy had been the ark of the covenant for so many years that to tamper with it would have been suicide for any politician. No politician in fact showed the slightest sign of doing so. On the contrary, a continuing preoccupation of governments for at least twelve years after the Treaty was to round out the process of land purchase. The most important step towards the completion of purchase was the Land Act of 1923 (amended in 1925) under which all land where landlord and tenant still had a dual interest was ruled to pass automatically into the hands of the Land Commission, to be vested in due course in the tenants as proprietors, subject to payment of the appropriate annuities. A system of standard prices was laid down, and in addition the vendor received from the state a bonus of ten per cent of the standard price. Untenanted land in the Congested Districts was to be taken over by the Land Commission (inheriting the functions of the old Congested Districts Board) which also had power – subject to certain exceptions – compulsorily to acquire untenanted land outside this area if such land was needed either to relieve congestion or facilitate the resale of tenanted land. The problem was complex and progress slow, but the Minister for Agriculture, Mr Patrick Hogan, a man of exceptional drive and ability, achieved substantial success; nevertheless, two further acts, those of 1933 and 1934, were needed after the change of government to wind up the business and even these left some serious problems of congestion unsolved. The end result was that between 1923 and 1937 the transactions authorised by these various measures involved advances of

£27¼ million, affected the ownership of 117,000 holdings, and covered an area of 3.6 million acres.[15]

It has to be emphasised that the same government which took a fundamentally conservative view of the structure of rural society was equally orthodox in its economic attitudes. It aimed at – and largely achieved – a frugal and efficient administration. Almost Gladstonian in its approach to public finance, it exerted itself to deep taxation down to a minimum and to regulate expenditure accordingly. How far it succeeded may be judged from the fact that in 1931 exchequer receipts were, at twenty-four million pounds, only fifteen per cent of the national income, and that when Mr Cosgrave yielded office to Mr de Valera in 1932 the entire public debt of the Irish Free State was only thirty-five million pounds, which was about one-fifth of the annual national income.[16]

Against this background of impeccable financial probity has to be seen the government's campaign to improve agricultural standards. Clearly, such improvement as might be achieved would come not from any revolutionary approach – Keynesian or otherwise – to the economy as a whole, nor from any massive increase in public spending. Rather was it to be conjured out of the countryside by providing better technical education, by imposing stricter marketing regulations, and by making available to farmers the credit which in the past had either been denied them by the banks or supplied at an extortionate price by the gombeen men. The first of these policies, better education, had been the goal of all Irish agricultural reformers for many years and the new Department of Agriculture was just as much concerned as the old Department of Agriculture and Technical Instruction had been with teaching and demonstration. How effective this was has been questioned. Even as early as 1923 the Department was being criticised as unrealistic in its advice and out of touch with actual conditions on the farms, and as recently as 1958 the deficiencies of agricultural education were trenchantly exposed in the Whitaker Report. More effective, because backed by the sanctions of the law, were the series of acts passed between 1924 and 1930 regulating standards of cleanliness, purity, packaging and marketing in the branches of the industry dealing with pork, bacon, eggs and dairy produce, and also the important advance embodied in the Live Stock Breeding Act of 1925, under which every bull and boar used for breeding purposes had to be licensed by the state. Inevitably, all this cost money and even a government obsessed with the necessity of balancing budgets had to accept steadily increasing expenditure on agriculture, apart altogether from land purchase. The amount so expended rose from just under a million pounds in 1925 to £2.7 million in 1931. Much of this, it must be added, went not on directly productive work, but on expanding and continuing the old device of granting farmers relief from rates on agricultural land; the grant for this purpose was doubled in 1926 and continued to rise at intervals thereafter.[17]

The most striking new departure, however, was the decision to make available to farmers loans for productive purposes on reasonable terms. In 1927 the Agricultural Credit Act provided for the setting up of an Agricultural Credit Corporation as a limited company with a nominal share capital of £500,000, later much increased as its operations grew in scale. Its finances were guaranteed by the state and it was empowered to lend money to farmers, usually on the security of a first mortgage of their land. Up to 1936 the Corporation had advanced loans on this basis of just over a million pounds, plus a further quarter of a million on other security. Individual transactions were generally small. Of a total of 16,719 in the first nine years of operation, all but 239 were for sums under five hundred pounds and the overall average was eighty-two pounds. No doubt this reflects the scale of operations on a typical Irish farm, but perhaps it reflects also a deep-seated reluctance on the part of the farmer to cumber himself with debt charges even in the interests of efficiency. It is perhaps significant that although most of these small loans were repayable over a period of five to ten years there was evidence of a good deal of unpunctuality, leading sometimes to actual default. By 1936 almost £30,000 of bad debts had had to be written off and an additional £70,000 set aside for similar contingencies in the future. Yet despite this unpromising beginning, the Agricultural Credit Corporation had a significance that went far beyond its immediate modest operations. With the Electricity Supply Board, also established in 1927, it shared the distinction of being the first visible evidence of a trend that was to become more and more important as time went on. These two organisations were the first of a whole line of similar bodies whereby the state was increasingly drawn to intervene in various sectors of the economy into which private capital had been unable or unwilling to enter. The main development of this tendency belongs to a later period which is dealt with below, but it is strikingly indicative of the kind of pressures that were being generated in the Irish economy that even a government so little *dirigiste* as that of Mr Cosgrave should have felt it necessary to take these first faltering steps along the primrose path of state intervention.[18]

To strike a balance of profit and loss on the free trade era of the Irish Free State is not easy, the more so as policy was overtaken, not to say overwhelmed, by the onset of the world depression. And even though, as already mentioned, livestock prices held up longer than those of cereals, the crisis was only postponed. Thus, the value of agricultural exports (of which livestock and livestock products accounted for about ninety-eight per cent) fell from £35.8 million in 1929 to just under £14 million in 1935.[19] This, it is true, was not just a consequence of the depression; it was partly due also to the economic war with Britain and it is clear that the worst of the storm came after the change of government. But already by 1931 the agricultural price index number (base 1911-13 = 100) had fallen to 110 from the high point of 139.2 reached in 1929. Agricultural wages, naturally, had also declined, though this was offset by a reduction in the cost of living. Taking the country as a whole, money incomes had suffered a sharp fall between 1929 and 1931, but since the index of general prices had gone down even further the effect was to produce a slightly higher real income in 1931 than in 1929.[20]

Against this, however, must be set the fact that the number of persons receiving home assistance under the Poor Law had gone up steadily in the last years of the Cosgrave regime. In 1925-6 the total had been 47,963; in 1930-1 it was 77,474. And to this has to be added the further fact that already in the mid-twenties unemployment was running at the rate of six per cent of the total working population. The data for assessing unemployment before 1932 are inadequate and it is probable that a more accurate calculation would give a higher percentage; even as it stands, the figure of six per cent does not take into account the problem of under-employment, especially in agriculture.[21]

The indictment could be taken further. As we have seen, agriculture, despite all the efforts of an energetic Minister, had not fundamentally changed its character and still remained in many ways underdeveloped. Industry, also, though it had expanded somewhat, was still essentially small-scale and – save for a few long-established enterprises – quite unable to compete in the open market. Worst of all, the government had not succeeded in arresting the decline in population. From a total for the twenty-six counties of 3.1 million in 1911, it had fallen to 2.97 million in 1926 and this decline was to continue. What was particularly serious for a state that set so much store by agriculture was that this loss fell mainly upon the rural areas. The rural decline between 1911 and 1926 was from 2.2 million to 2.0 million and this had fallen still further to 1.9 million by 1936. Although the town population actually took an upward turn in 1926 (reaching its highest total since 1851) this was not enough to compensate for the drain from the countryside. Inevitably linked with this overall decline was emigration. The period during which the Irish Free State was founded saw a heavy outward movement. Net emigration between 1911 and 1926 (admittedly a fifteen-year period) was 405,029. That terrible momentum was indeed slowed down in the next decade to 166,751, but neither the Cosgrave nor the de Valera government could take much credit for this. Emigration fell off largely because the outlets for it diminished, but when the outlets were once more available after 1936 the old wound began to bleed again as heavily as before.[22]

On the credit side it has to be remembered that a great work of restoration and reconstruction had confronted the government after the Civil War. Understandably, its energies had been devoted primarily to creating once more in the country the conditions for economic advance in the future. By 1931 this task had been effectively carried out. The rule of law had been upheld, the Free State's international standing as a creditor nation had been maintained, budgets had been scrupulously balanced and taxation held firmly in check, administration had been frugal but competent, and if the economic ideas of ministers and their advisers savoured more of Adam Smith than of J. M. Keynes, no-one could deny that within the limits this implied, their policies had been remarkably effective.

In the last resort, Mr Cosgrave and his colleagues could with some justice have defended their decade of power on the ground that in a period of almost unprecedented difficulty they had enabled the country simply to survive. But by 1932 new pressures were demanding new responses which they were ill-fitted to provide. Their economic policy had assumed the continued existence of an international free trading system in which Ireland's principal role, as hitherto, would be to export foodstuffs and import manufactures. But that delectable, if un-sophisticated, nineteenth century world had dissolved in ruins around them. Interdependence had suddenly come to mean participation in losses as well as in profits. And, as confidence in the old economic order drained away, and protectionist policies proliferated all over the world, economic nationalism became once more respectable.

In Ireland, of course, economic nationalism had been respectable for a long time and in a world of rising tariffs Arthur Griffith's doc-trines began to seem increasingly relevant. An independent Ireland, he had claimed, must be free to impose its own tariffs and must use that power to develop, not only agriculture, but industry also so as to achieve the great end of economic nationalism, which was self-sufficiency. By one of those familiar ironies of Irish history the men who repudiated Griffith's political settlement inherited his economic ideas. Fianna Fáil, from the moment of its foundation, identified itself with the doctrine of economic nationalism and one of the first impor-tant interventions in the Dáil of Mr Sean Lemass, who in due time was to assume a large share of the responsibility for the industrial develop-ment of the country, was to enunciate this doctrine, when in 1928 he attacked the Tariff Commission for not going far or fast enough. 'We believe', he said, 'that Ireland can be made a self-contained unit, providing all the necessities of living in adequate quantities for the people residing in this island at the moment and probably for a much larger number.'[23] Here, in a sentence, was the germ of a new depar-ture, looking to the creation of an Ireland that would be both politically and economically freer of the British connection than the men of the Treaty had ever been able to make her. With the electoral victory of Mr de Valera in 1932 the way was clear for the testing of this new concept against the harsh realities of a world plunged in dire depression.

(ii) STRIVING FOR SELF-SUFFICIENCY

It is perhaps unfortunate, though inevitable, that the history of the drive towards self-sufficiency should have become inextricably inter-twined with the history of the financial dispute, or 'economic war', with Britain. Yet, since that dispute with the country's leading cus-tomer had a direct effect upon the economy at large, it cannot be ignored. Its full consequences can only be seen in the context of the general economic policy of the new government. But its history may be disposed of more briefly. Fianna Fáil came to power in March 1932. Immediately, they introduced much more extensive tariffs, the first budget (March 1932) containing no less than forty-three new duties. Simultaneously, on taking up office, Mr de Valera announced that his government would not transmit the land annuities accruing under the Irish Land Acts; later he added certain other items to this programme.

What precisely was involved? In 1923 the then government of the Irish Free State had undertaken to collect and pay to the United Kingdom the moneys due from tenant-purchasers – that is, the an-nuities in respect of holdings purchased under the Land Acts; to pay a contribution towards the interest due on additional Land Stock pre-viously issued; to pay a proportionate share of the cost of RIC pensions and those of certain other retired public servants; and to continue payments of certain annuities arising out of expenditure on public works. This 'provisional' agreement was not actually pub-lished until 1932, but in 1925 a further settlement was reached arising out of the discussions on the border questions. By its terms the United Kingdom waived any claim to an Irish Free State contribution to the public debt of the United Kingdom, as had been provided for by the Treaty, but *per contra* the Irish Free State agreed to pay £250,000 p.a. for sixty years in discharge of compensation paid out by the United Kingdom for damage to property in Ireland between 1919 and 1925. This in turn was followed by a further 'ultimate agreement' in 1926 which, like the agreement of 1923, admitted the liability to pay the land annuities.

Mr de Valera's case was that the agreements of 1923 and 1926 were invalid because they had never been ratified by the Dáil. The burden of the annuities, he constantly insisted, had never been more than a contingent liability for a share of the United Kingdom public debt from which the Free State had been specifically released by the agree-ment of 1925. Attempts to settle the dispute broke down in June, whereupon the British government rapidly imposed duties of twenty per cent *ad valorem* on Irish cattle and on the other main Irish agricul-tural exports to the United Kingdom, with the object of recovering by this means the money withheld by the Free State. These duties were later increased in severity and between July 1932 and 31 March 1935 had produced a revenue of £10.7 million against the alleged Irish de-fault of £14.5 million. Nor was this the only weapon used against the recalcitrant Irish government. Because of the dispute, the Ottawa Conference, which later that year produced a whole crop of preferential tariff agreements amongst members of the Commonwealth, could have no ameliorating effect on Anglo-Irish economic relations; on the contrary, Irish Free State goods entering the United Kingdom became subject to the general scale of import duties laid down in the British Import Duties Act of 1932. Between that date and March 1935 these duties had produced a revenue of just over a million pounds. Finally, Britain's need to protect her own agriculture led her in 1934 to restrict the import of Free State cattle by a quota system limiting fat cattle to fifty per cent of the 1933 figure, imposing a one hundred per cent restriction on store cattle and prohibiting the entry of Irish beef and veal. At the beginning of 1935 this policy was somewhat relaxed by an agreement – the so-called Coal-Cattle Pact – whereby the quotas for Irish cattle were raised by a third in return for an Irish promise to take all coal from United Kingdom sources, thus involving an increase of United Kingdom coal into the Free State of 1¼ million tions a year. The following years (1936 and 1937) these relaxations were further extended.

Against such pressures the Free State government had naturally retaliated by imposing its own duties on imports from Britain – the most important being five shillings a ton on coal and coke, and twenty per cent *ad valorem* on cement, electrical goods, machinery, iron and steel. These, in their turn, were subsequently extended to other goods as part of the general tariff policy initiated by Mr de Valera's government, for even the relaxations of 1935 and 1936 could not alter the fact that a protectionist regime was now fully entrenched in Dublin.[24]

What were the principal economic consequences of this nagging dispute between the two countries? There can be no denying that they were serious, even allowing for the complicating effects of the general collapse of world agricultural prices. We have seen already that the value of Irish agricultural exports (a great part of which went to Britain) fell from £35.8 million in 1929 to £13.9 million in 1935. The total of all Free State exports to the United Kingdom in 1929 had been worth £43.5 million – in 1935 it was worth just under £18 million. Value, admittedly, is an unsure guide at a time of rapidly falling prices. Volume is apt to be more illuminating, but volume, too, tells a sorry tale. Sorriest of all, perhaps, in the vital livestock trade, where it showed that while in 1929 775,000 cattle had been exported (the vast majority to Britain), by 1934 the figure had dropped to just over half a million.[25]

It is no exaggeration to say that the cattle industry, the very lifeblood of the country's economy, was threatened with collapse. Moreover, since there were certain commodities – for example, tea, petroleum, coal – which the Free State had still to import from Britain, there was every prospect that the adverse balance of trade, which the country had learned to live with since the Treaty, would become more serious. Whereas in 1929 imports had exceeded exports by about fourteen million pounds, this margin had increased to over twenty-one million pounds by 1934. A contemporary calculation of the real 'terms of trade' (having regard, that is, to the movement of import and export prices) suggests that up to the early months of 1932 export prices resisted the general decline a little better than import prices, but that in the latter half of that year export prices fell far below those of imports. 'This decline, which has since persisted', commented the Banking Commission report six years later, 'must largely be attributed to the imposition of the special duties and restrictions by the United Kingdom.'[26] To some extent this adverse movement was offset by invisible earnings, but even allowing for these, the deficit on current account went from £3¼ million in 1931 to £6⅓ million in 1934.[27] It recovered somewhat thereafter, but this sort of balance of payments situation, continued year after year, was bound to lead to a deterioration of the Free State's jealously guarded external assets. Precise calculations in this field are notoriously hard to come by, but perhaps it is enough to say that the best available figures indicate that there was a net decrease in the Free State's sterling holdings of just over nine million pounds in the four years ending 31 December 1935.[28]

Clearly, although even in 1935 the reserves were still substantial, alternative policies to diminish the drain were necessary. These, in fact, fitted in well enough with the programme of self-sufficiency about to be described. But before turning to that it is necessary to trace the history of the Anglo-Irish dispute to its conclusion. Although each side undoubtedly inflicted damage on the other, the effect of the quarrel seemed to be to emphasise economic interdependence rather than economic separateness. This was obviously less true of Britain than of the Free State, though Britain could ill-afford to fall from supplying the Free State with 75.8 per cent of its imports in 1932 to little more than 54 per cent in 1935. But for the Irish disputants the quarrel, bitter and prolonged as it was, could not be allowed to alter the direction of trade; indeed, there was no other direction in which trade could go. Irish exports were still utterly reliant upon the British market. In 1932 over ninety-six per cent went there and at no time up to 1938 did the percentage fall below ninety.[29]

The really serious effect of the 'economic war' upon the Free State was not just that the depression of agriculture, and of the cattle industry in particular, reduced the incomes of the farmers, but that this reduction was likely to affect other sectors of the economy as well, by reducing the demand of the agricultural population for whatever home industry might have to offer. 'Indeed', as the Banking Commission observed, 'an industrial programme has hardly had a fair chance of succeeding at a time when a large section of the market for industrial goods is severely curtailed.'[30] When, therefore, political developments at last opened the way for a settlement in 1938 the chance was firmly seized.* In their financial and economic aspects the agreements then

* For the political background, see Part IV, A, chap. 2.

reached provided that the Irish government would pay the United Kingdom ten million pounds in final settlement of all claims by either government arising out of the dispute. Mr de Valera had therefore won his battle over the land annuities. But so far as Anglo-Irish trade was concerned, the basic principle was that of a return to the pre-1932 position. The special duties imposed by each side were to be withdrawn, with the result that Irish agricultural produce was to be admitted henceforward to the United Kingdom market free of duties, while the British government obtained a virtually complete monopoly of the Irish market for British coal. Both sides accepted the Ottawa concept of equal opportunity, and preferential duties were re-established by the two governments; in effect, while each country still retained protection for certain of its own products, the agreement allowed them to develop most-favoured nation treatment on a reciprocal basis. Both, however, reserved the right to apply a quota-system to certain of the other's products should home producers be endangered by excessive competition, and in this proviso lay the real threat to Irish agriculture in the future. Initially, the agreement was to run only until August, 1940, but by then of course the whole context of the question had been drastically changed.[31]

Important though the Anglo-Irish economic war undoubtedly was, it would be wrong to allow it to loom too large in the history of the 1930s. There is, on the contrary, some truth in the contention that world conditions, apart altogether from the predilections of Fianna Fáil, were pushing Ireland along the road to protection and that the economic war itself 'was incidental to, and not a condition of, the protective policy of those years'.[32] That policy, as we have seen, started out as a policy of economic nationalism – that is to say, an attempt to break the Free State's commercial dependence upon Britain. But the conception behind the campaign for this new departure that Fianna Fáil waged ceaselessly from 1927 was broader than a mere extension of an old political quarrel into the world of business. It involved also a serious and prolonged attempt to redress the balance between the different sectors of the economy – to free the countryside from the dominance of the cattleman, to extend the area of tillage, to develop home industries and thus provide employment for those who might otherwise be obliged to emigrate.

An essential key to much of this programme is to be found in the tariff. Immediately Mr de Valera took office numerous duties at very high rates were imposed on a wide variety of goods, and this policy was continued over the years, more than 1,000 items being affected by 1936.[33] In addition, a complicated quota and licensing system was introduced to control the amounts and value of particular imports. Such steps, though they may have helped to reduce expenditure on foreign goods, were in themselves negative and in the long run could only be justified if behind this protective barrier there grew up 'infant industries' capable of holding their own in the future.

614

To help these to develop was therefore a prime object of government concern. This expressed itself in several ways. One was to ensure, by means of the Control of Manufactures Acts, 1932-4, that Irish industry should as far as possible be concentrated in the hands of Irish owners. Another was to provide, through the Industrial Credit Company, for the financing, at least in part, of such transfers of ownership to Free State nationals. Founded in 1933, the Company's capital was almost entirely subscribed by the state – a considerable expenditure since, in the first four years of its operation, it made capital issues amounting to nearly £6½ million. Yet a third device was also aimed at providing credit on reasonable terms to manufacturing enterprises which showed some promise of providing speedy employment. This was the system of trade loans provided for by the Trade Loans (Guarantee) (Amendment) Act of 1933. The system had its origins in an Act of 1924 which had empowered the government to guarantee repayment of the principal of, and payment of the interest on, certain types of loan which, it was hoped, would lead to substantial capital expenditure with consequential increases in the number of jobs available. Initial experience of this kind of encouragement had proved disappointing. Between 1925 and 1929 £317,000 had been lent to eighteen interested parties and by 1936 half of them were in default to the extent of nearly £200,000. The Act of 1933 gave further hostages to fortune by relaxing the conditions so that loans might in future be made not just for capital expenditure, but for working capital as well, which was obviously a much greater risk. When examined before the Banking Commission on this matter, the Secretary for the Department of Industry and Commerce was almost fatalistically resigned to a fresh crop of failures, leading to yet more expenditure by the state. Predictably, the Commission was considerably shocked by the story he unfolded and drew, with unwavering firmness, the classical conclusion that 'the government should not seek to deal directly with individual businesses in providing assistance for long term credit.'[34]

But the government showed itself little impressed by such doctrines. On the contrary, since it was evident that private capital was neither very extensive nor very adventurous, the state was drawn steadily further and further along the road of direct intervention in various fields of enterprise. One such field was housing. Although the primary responsibility for this belonged to the local authority, the burden of debt which this laid upon them (over £20 million by 1937) was so great that the central government had to come to the rescue. The Housing Act of 1932 provided that the state could contribute from one-third to two-thirds of housing-schemes operated by the local authorities. Up to March 1937, £3.4 million had been used for this purpose and a further £6 million was ear-marked for future expenditure along the same lines. In effect a housing subsidy, this kind of assistance really amounted to a public works policy, designed not merely to provide more houses but more employment as well.[35]

Far more important than this, however, and in the long run destined to have a much greater effect upon the social and economic life of the country, was the increasing tendency to create what have been called state-sponsored bodies for specific purposes, a tendency which, as we saw earlier, was already beginning to show itself in the 1920s, but which, after the change of government, was to be very much intensified. Almost from the earliest days of independence it had become clear that there were certain kinds of economic activity which either required too much capital or involved too much risk for private companies to venture upon. Yet often these very activities were themselves essential to further economic growth and as such the state could not ignore them. On the contrary, it became more and more deeply involved in supplying the deficiencies of the private sector.

One of the earliest and most celebrated of these state intrusions into the world of business was the development of a nationwide supply of electricity. The possibility of using the abundant water resources of Ireland as a means of providing electricity had been tentatively explored in the years immediately after the First World War, but the initiative in bringing these vague ideas to the point of practicality belonged to Dr T. A. McLaughlin, an Irish graduate of electrical engineering in the employment of the German firm of Siemens-Schuckert. His dream was of a great system of electrification based on the river Shannon. Other schemes and other interests competed with this conception, but after exhaustive inquiry the government adopted the Shannon scheme. The construction of the main power station at Ardnacrusha, near Limerick city, began in August 1925 and was completed towards the end of 1929. While it was being completed an Act of the Dáil set up the Electricity Supply Board as a statutory body with wide powers to control the generation, distribution and sale not only of Shannon electricity, but of electricity throughout the country. At that time such electrical power as the country possessed was in the hands of a number of small producers and the Act gave the Board the right to acquire either compulsorily or by agreement any electrical undertaking then in existence. In practice, compulsion was sparingly used, mainly perhaps because the superior efficiency and resources of the Board gradually drove its competitors out of the market.

In framing the Board's constitution the government was influenced to some extent by foreign, especially Swedish, experience. There was to be a full-time chairman and from two to six, later seven, ordinary members appointable for five years and eligible for renewal. The Board was responsible to the Minister for Industry and Commerce and its reports to him were to be published and laid before both Houses of the Oireachtas. From the beginning it proved to be a highly dynamic organisation. Even though demand before the Second World War roughly doubled every five years, that demand was met to such effect that by 1939-40 the Board was generating 407 million units, though the war, with its fuel shortages, led to an actual drop in consumption. After 1945 the advance was resumed and the first steps were taken to utilise turf (peat) as a fuel for generating stations, additional to coal and water-power. By March 1961 the Board's total installed capacity was 723.5 megawatts, of which steam plant (coal or oil-fired) accounted for almost forty per cent, hydro-electric plant for about a third, and steam plant using peat for the remainder. Despite the fact that industrial demand was low for most of this period and that the consuming public was not very wealthy, the Board contrived to carry out its expansion and yet keep the cost to the consumer lower than that in most European countries. In the earlier years, naturally enough, attention had been concentrated upon the towns and villages. By 1943 about ninety-five per cent of this urban and semi-urban population was being supplied, but, even with such penetration into the countryside as had then been achieved, still only about fifty per cent of the total population had electricity. It was not until after the Second World War that rural electrification began in earnest. The work was difficult and expensive, but by March 1964 out of nearly 800 areas requiring service only eight remained to be dealt with. Consumption over the country as a whole had risen to nearly 3,000 million units – almost fifty times what it had been in 1929-30.[36]

The Electricity Supply Board has been described in some detail not just because of its own achievements – though these were remarkable – but because in many ways it blazed a trail which has become a broad highway. The use of state-sponsored bodies for a variety of purposes, economic and other, has developed to such a degree that they are now so numerous, and fulfil such a variety of functions, that to generalise about them is virtually impossible, and even to define a state-sponsored body is almost beyond the wit of man. For the purposes of this study, however, it is enough to accept the recent description made by an authority on the subject – that they are 'autonomous public bodies other than universities or university colleges, which are neither temporary in character nor purely advisory in their function, most of whose staff are not civil servants, and to whose board or council the government, or ministers in the government, appoint directors, council members etc'.[37] Although this definition excludes many types of organisation in which the state takes an interest, the number coming within it is still formidable. During the period when economic self-sufficiency was being most strenuously pursued – from 1932 up to the end of the Second World War – thirteen such bodies were added to the six which had been inherited from the previous regime and five more were added during the war years. In the post-war period the pace accelerated so that by the early 'sixties there were no less than fifty-five.

Not all of these, of course, were intended to perform economic services and though there are various ways of classifying them, the most convenient for our purposes is the distinction between 'trading enterprises' and the rest. Trading enterprises may be defined as state-sponsored bodies which have significant sources of revenue other than grants-in-aid from the central government or from local authorities.[38] On this reckoning thirty-four out of the fifty-five bodies listed up to 1963 qualify as trading-enterprises, though even they, it must be added, generally derived a much larger share of their capital directly from government grants than from their own profits or from the external sources of borrowing which were occasionally open to them.

As the practice of state intervention in this way became more familiar, so did the range and scope of the state-sponsored bodies become steadily wider. Nowadays they are concerned not only with directly productive enterprises, but with radio and television, the encouragement of the arts, the prosecution of research, the control of horse-racing and betting thereon, hotel management, tourism and a wide variety of matters affecting health and the medical profession. Initially, as might be expected, the emphasis was predominantly economic, which, on the whole, it has remained. Of the nineteen bodies formed between 1927 and 1939, apart from those already referred to (the Agricultural Credit Corporation, the Industrial Credit Company and the Electricity Supply Board) the following 'trading enterprises' were created – the Industrial Alcohol Board, the Irish Sugar Company, the Dairy Disposal Company, Aer Rianta (for the management of Dublin airport), Aer Lingus (European Air Services), Milk Boards for Cork and Dublin, and the Irish Life Assurance Company. Non-trading enterprises of the same period included Bord Fáilte Eireann (tourism), the Hospitals Trust Board and the Medical Research Council. During the war years the most important of the new bodies dealing with economic matters were Irish Shipping, the Central Bank of Ireland and the Pigs and Bacon Commission. After 1945 the area of state activity continued to expand – among the most important of the new bodies then established were Coras Iompair Eireann, charged with the almost impossible task of rescuing the public transport system from bankruptcy, and Bord na Mona, which within fifteen years of its foundation in 1946 had revolutionised the production of turf or peat for both domestic and industrial purposes.

It is not necessary to seek any profound philosophy of state socialism behind the emergence of this variegated collection of organisations. They were essentially individual responses to specific situations – the intentions of the government were strictly pragmatic. This has not, of course, exempted the state-sponsored bodies from all kinds of criticism. At different times it has been said that they took too large a share of the managerial talent available in the country, that they competed too much with the private sector, that they hold the consumer to ransom, and that there is inadequate public control over their activities. Whether such charges are valid it is not for a study of this kind to determine. Just as the state bodies defy generalisation in describing them, so they defy it in judging them No doubt some of these accusations have been true some of the time; it is harder to believe that all of them have been true all of the time. But of the importance of these organisations to the economy there can be no doubt. By the early 'sixties they employed some 50,000 people (over thirty-five per cent of all the workers in state employment and some seven per cent of the total number of employees in the country), possessed assets of about £230 million and paid out over £35 million a year in wages and salaries.[39] In a sense the very criticisms that were levelled against them were a measure of their success. When they first appeared they appeared because of economic need, not as part of any deeply reasoned governmental plan. The lack of private capital, the timidity of private capitalists, the necessity to supply some public services and rescue others – these were the fundamental reasons for the formation of the state-sponsored bodies. And if latterly private capital has been critical of these public concerns, it is well to maintain historical perspective by recalling the years when the state had little alternative but to call into existence a new world of initiative to redress the deficiencies of the old.

In the period before and during the Second World War state intervention of this kind had clearly to be seen in the broader context of the pursuit of self-sufficiency. It remains to ask how far self-sufficiency was actually achieved in the two spheres which were central to the whole policy of the government – industrial development and a reorientation of agriculture by means of an intensive drive to expand the area of tillage, and especially of wheat.

In the industrial sector, certainly, both the volume and the value of production, as well as the numbers employed, increased between 1931 and 1938. The value of net industrial output rose from £25.6 million in the earlier year to £36 million in the later, while industrial employment went up from 111,000 to 166,000.[40] On the other hand, a price had to be paid for this achievement. The few large export industries which already existed were emphatically not helped by a protective tariff and the amounts earned by the export of, for example, biscuits, porter, and beer all fell sharply in the 'thirties. Indeed, there was a marked decline in the whole total of non-agricultural exports, which fell between 1932 and 1938 from £6.4 million to £4.4 million. The unpalatable fact was that the new Irish industries were unlikely to make much headway in foreign markets, for reasons which the Report of the Banking Commission makes abundantly clear. First, they were likely to be costly, since in order to attract capital at all, interest rates had to be high. Second, wages in the Irish Free State were also relatively high, high enough at all events to make it unlikely that mass-produced Irish goods would be at all competitive with those of low-wage countries such as Japan. And again, the home market was so restricted that this in itself inhibited the development of businesses large enough to trade successfully in the outside world.[41]

Not, indeed, that the creation of small, home-based industries was enough to make Ireland self-sufficient, even behind tariff barriers. Lacking most kinds of cheap fuel or raw materials, the very fact of industrialisation meant for her a larger import bill – the value of imports other than foodstuffs rose from £27.6 million in 1932 to £30 million in 1938.[42] Some of this was accounted for by the import of machinery or semi-manufactured goods to be worked up in Ireland, though some of it, it is only fair to add, may have been due to increasing sophistication among consumers as a slowly rising national income put more commodities within their reach. There was, it seems, considerable rigidity in the wage-structure which, in industry, changed very little between 1932 and 1935, even though the cost of living for most of that time had been steadily going down; the latter did, it is true, begin to rise again from 1935 onwards, but so also did industrial wages, though apparently to a lesser extent.[43]

Given the restricting conditions within which industry had to work, it was clear that any real advance in the economic life of the country would, as always, be bound up with the condition of agriculture. Only in this sector was there any real potentiality for developing the export trade, and it was only by developing that trade that purchasing ˙power within the economy could be generated.* Yet in the 1930s, in the midst of world depression complicated by the economic war with Britain, the prospects of agricultural prosperity could hardly have seemed grimmer. Irish exports (mainly agricultural) had dropped from forty-seven million pounds to thirty-six million pounds even between 1929 and 1931. Between then and 1934 they fell by a further eighteen million pounds, or by twenty-seven per cent in volume.[44] In such a situation self-sufficiency became less a policy of economic advance than a vast rescue operation. The most desperate efforts were used to re-orientate agriculture – to make the country less dependent on the badly injured cattle industry, while at the same time preventing that industry from collapsing into total ruin. All sorts of devices were used – a guaranteed price for wheat, import controls on flour and bacon, export subsidies on butter, bacon and sheep offals, compulsion to use a quantity of home-produced grain in animal feeding-stuffs, bounties on cattle exports, the development of the beet-sugar industry, the halving of land annuity charges to farmers.

Yet, despite these varied inducements, the overall volume and structure of Irish agriculture showed remarkably little change during

* It has been estimated that in 1934-5, when the national income was about £140 million, the farming community in Ireland had only about £10.5 million to spend on household necessities, a figure which improved to £20 million in 1938 and £70 million in 1950. The same authority reckons that national income, which rose from £158.2 million in 1938 to £363 million in 1950 at current prices, in real terms actually advanced by only twenty-four per cent in the period 1938-50. See the able and suggestive article by R. C. Geary, 'Irish Economic Development Since the Treaty', in *Studies* (Dec. 1951), xl, pp. 399-418.

the decade as a whole. Net agricultural output (that is, everything consumed on, or sold off, the farm less the value of feeding-stuffs, seeds and fertilizers) reached a peak in 1935-6, but was actually at a lower level in 1938-9 than in 1929-30. There had, it is true, been a substantial increase in the output of crops and the dramatic increase in the acreage of wheat is perhaps the best known fact in the economic life of the country in the pre-war years. From just under 21,000 acres in 1931 it had increased to 255,000 acres in 1936. Taking as base-year 1930=100, the index number for the acreage of wheat in 1936 was 952, falling back somewhat in the next two years and rising to 955 in 1939.[45]

But this movement is in reality misleading. More wheat was grown, certainly, and the time was fast approaching when the country would be grateful for it, but the acreage under wheat represented in the main a switch out of other crops. The overall increase in tillage had in fact been very small. Again taking the year 1930 as 100, the index number for the total area of tillage was 111 in 1936 and only 102 in 1939. What seems to have been happening was that whereas the cattle crisis, combined with government encouragement of other forms of agriculture, had caused a swing towards tillage (and to some extent dairying also) in the early part of the decade, as soon as the coal-cattle pacts gave grounds to hope for better times, farmers began thankfully to revert to their old pattern. Indeed, by 1937-8, although the value of cattle exports was still much below what it had been in 1929-30 (an annual average of £8.5 million as against £14.2 million) cattle now took 50.8 per cent of agricultural exports compared with 43.8 per cent in the earlier years; the percentage share of every other significant agricultural export except horses had declined in the interval.[46]

It is difficult, therefore, to avoid the conclusion that all the efforts of the government had done little to change the real terms of the problem. That problem has been admirably stated by a recent writer:

Manufacturing industry was geared to the small protected home market and because of this its costs were too high to warrant any hope of a substantial export trade. Agricultural exports depended to a greater extent than ever on cattle, and against an expansion of cattle production there were formidable and well-nigh impenetrable barriers. An increase in non-cattle exports implied an increase in subsidies, which in turn implied a further reduction in living standard.[47]

The consequence was that although Irish incomes were increasing slowly during the decade, the gap between those and British incomes was widening. Whereas in 1931 the average income per head in Ireland was sixty-one per cent of that in Britain, by 1939 the corresponding figure was forty-nine per cent.[48] It was hardly surprising that emigration, which had slowed down, now again accelerated, leaving two dire consequences in its train. One was that domestic demand for the products of Irish industry and agriculture was to that extent further diminished. The other, even more serious, was that while protection had created a whole complex of vested interests not necessarily compatible with present efficiency or future prosperity, emigration, by removing some of the pressures for change, contributed its share to what seemed the immutable inertia of Irish economic life.

Nor was this situation significantly altered by the war years. In a sense, indeed, they may be said to have intensified it. For the war in its turn had three principal effects upon the Irish economy. In the first place, by imposing a state of siege upon the country, it gave more emphasis than ever to the policy of self-sufficiency. Second, because of the inevitable shortages of fuel, raw material and semi-manufactured goods of all kinds, any significant industrial advance was virtually ruled out. And finally, and perhaps most important of all, the safe stagnation of Irish neutrality was more than counterbalanced in the eyes of an increasing number of young people by the swollen wage-packets of wartime Britain. In a recent, moving account of the de-population of a Mayo town, Mr John Healy recalled that his first reaction, listening as a boy to Neville Chamberlain's voice on the radio announcing the outbreak of war with Germany was: 'A war! Maybe the Germans will blow up the school above.' And he continues: 'They didn't, of course: instead the war which never touched our shores eroded our town more completely and insidiously than if it had been subjected to a one-night blitz.'[49]

To some extent this is emotional over-simplification. Emigration from Mayo was no new phenomenon, though, as Mr Healy points out, in the past it had tended to be rural rather than urban. During the war years it was both rural and urban. And the evidence of the travel documents issued during the war certainly gives point to his lament. It indicates that Mayo headed the list of counties with the greatest number of emigrants, both male and female. Between 1940 and 1951 it lost a greater total (43.4 thousand) than any other county except Dublin, while the average annual rate of 27.8 per thousand was far ahead of that of all the other counties – the nearest rivals, significantly, being those other remote and beautiful corners of the western world, Donegal and Kerry. Travel documents, obviously, are no more than a broad guide to the number actually leaving the country as permanent emigrants, but the evidence of the first two Censuses after the war suggest that net emigration for the whole of the twenty-six counties was just over 187,000 between 1936 and 1946 and 119.6 thousand in the next five years.[50]

It could be argued, almost in Malthusian terms, that, leaving aside the long-range social, economic and human problems of emigration, the exodus of so many young people helped the country in two ways to survive during the war years. On the one hand, the remittances they sent home were a much needed addition to private resources and, ultimately, to the national income. On the other hand, there were, to put the matter brutally, that many fewer mouths to feed. And feeding the existing population was, naturally, the obsessive preoccupation of the government.

To achieve this end what had to be done was to intensify the policies initiated in the pre-war years, but to do this without benefit of foreign animal feeding-stuffs, farm machinery or fertilizers. Despite these handicaps the volume of net agricultural output increased very considerably. Taking 1938-9 as 100, the index rose fairly steadily until by 1945 it had reached 116.8. There were several reasons for this. One was that output was ruthlessly maintained at the expense of the soil. Lack of fertilizers and intensive exploitation of the land meant that even during the war years the yield in starch pounds per acre fell sharply; had this been continued much longer the effects would have been ruinous. A second reason for the increase in output was the official policy of compulsory tillage. In 1940 it was made obligatory to till one-eighth of the arable land in each holding; by 1944, and until the policy was abandoned in 1948, the proportion was as high as three-eighths. A third factor affecting the volume of agricultural production was the drive to replace almost non-existent coal by turf; production of this fuel went up from just under 3.9 million tons in 1939 to 4.4 million in 1943. Finally. of course, it has to be remembered that since the main sector of Irish agriculture was and remained grass-based dairying, cattle and sheep production, the raw material, so to speak, was already there in abundance and unlikely to be too much affected by the shortage of fertilizers or machinery.[51]

In practical terms the most significant feature of the war-time years was the rise in the area of tillage and especially of that devoted to wheat. The total area of tillage (including not only grain but root and green crops and flax), which had been 1.5 million acres in 1939, had expanded five years later to 2.6 million. Wheat, which had accounted for about 250,000 acres in 1939, reached 662,000 acres in 1945 – the largest figure ever reached since agricultural statistics first began to be collected in 1847.[52] Even this vast effort did not suffice to avoid bread-rationing, which was imposed in 1942. Other commodities to be rationed were tea, sugar and butter; meat not only remained plentiful, but the export of live animals and meat products continued to be the staple of Irish trade with Britain and the principal means whereby neutral Ireland managed to build up large external assets during the war. The percentage of agricultural output exported during the war naturally declined, but the decline was not as catastrophic as might have been feared. It fell from an average of 34.3 per cent in the five years preceding the war to an average of 26.3 per cent between 1939 and 1945, reaching its lowest point, 20.6 per cent, afterwards, in the bleak year of 1947 when the British market was in various ways deeply depressed. Thereafter it revived, though even by the early 'fifties it had barely reached its immediate pre-war level.[53] But by then external conditions, and indeed internal ones also, had changed so greatly that Ireland was confronting a different world.

(iii) POST-WAR VICISSITUDES

For a time at least this different world was a world where the surpluses of the 'thirties had given place to widespread scarcity, offering a greater outlet for Irish farm produce. It was also a world where governments were deeply concerned with full employment, even if this entailed large public spending. For Ireland there was both opportunity and danger in this situation. Opportunity, in that there was now a climate of opinion very different from the rigid financial orthodoxy still prevalent in the earliest years of the Free State, and consequently an increasing pressure on governments to spend more. But danger, also, in that full employment with high wages in Britain not only continued to attract Irish men and women to the honey-pot, but created similar expectations amongst those who stayed at home.

How well equipped was Ireland to satisfy those expectations? Superficially, she was in a strong position, with large external assets (worth £270 million in 1946) and the prospect of a constant demand for her exports. On the other hand unemployment still continued at a high level and, in the immediate aftermath of the war, the natural desire of the population for an end to austerity and the pressure of long pent-up wage claims created very rapidly an inflationary situation. As early as 1947 there was a balance of payments deficit of nearly thirty million pounds and this was no isolated phenomenon. By 1956 recurrent deficits had 'more than offset the surpluses earned during the last war'.[54]

The unpleasant fact was that the economy had not fundamentally changed since the war and that its inherent weaknesses had not been eradicated. One way of illustrating this is to consider the slow growth of that entity, notoriously elusive and difficult to measure, the Gross National Product (defined as national income plus depreciation plus indirect taxes minus subsidies). Between 1949 and 1956 the *volume* of GNP grew by perhaps eight per cent, compared with twenty-one per cent for Britain and forty-two per cent for the countries grouped in the Organisation for European Economic Co-operation. But in terms of *rate of growth* the story is even more revealing. Between 1926-1938 the percentage rate of increase may have been no faster than 1.2 per cent per annum, though this can be no more than a tentative estimate. During the war, and up to 1947, it was apparently nil. Between 1947 and 1953 the rate was 1.8 per cent per annum, levelling out at about 2 per cent during the next decade.[55]

This was a perceptibly slower rate of growth than the British and quite markedly slower than those prevailing in the OEEC countries.

And even this growth owed an unhealthily large proportion to heavy state spending, directed mainly towards social welfare. What was happening in the decade after the war was that the government was making frantic attempts not merely to provide work for the population and in so doing to reduce emigration, but also to provide amenities and services of a kind that were coming to be normal elsewhere but of which Ireland was still largely innocent.

It must be said that to a certain extent, though at the cost of a mounting deficit, this policy took effect. Farm incomes improved with an expanding market, rising cattle prices, and heavy government expenditure on agriculture, and the demand for goods and services increased. Since a protectionist tariff was still jealously maintained, home industry could not but benefit. The volume of production of transportable goods in 1953 was nearly twice what it had been in the war years and the numbers employed in the industries producing such goods went up by about a third. Even so, this growth was not well sustained, at any rate beyond 1955, and it was certainly insufficient to staunch the flow of emigration. Not only was there a steady decline in the number of people working (in agriculture it dropped from 597.2 thousand in 1946 to 378.7 thousand in 1961, and in manufacturing industry from 187.6 thousand to 179.4 thousand between the same two dates) but the number leaving the country continued to be formidable. Net emigration for 1951-6 was 196,763, for 1956-61 it was 212,003.[56] These rates were nearly three times the pre-war rates and for the decade 1951-61 in particular were higher than for any other comparable period in the twentieth century.

Some at least of the current explanations for the slow growth of Irish industry are all too familiar – it still suffered from a shortage of private capital, it was still unable to develop any extensive range of competitive exports, it was still inhibited by the smallness and relative poverty of its domestic market. But in the 1950s, no more than in the 1930s, could these defects be separated from the most deep-seated problem of all – the condition of Irish agriculture. Because of her small internal market and her lack of fuel and raw materials, Ireland could not achieve Western European living standards without selling abroad. For her, to sell abroad meant in effect to sell her agricultural produce. In the last resort everything depended upon that. And it was in this sector that the government made its most determined efforts at stimulation.

In terms of policy there was no revolutionary change of direction, but there was a striking increase in the amount of money the government was prepared to spend on agriculture. This went up from about £4⅓ million in 1939 to £13¼ million in 1952; in the latter year that amounted to just over 10 per cent of total state expenditure and the proportion tended to grow as time went on, rising (with occasional set-backs) to 18.7 per cent in 1962.[57] Yet, despite this spending, the return was hardly impressive, indeed distinctly unimpressive by comparison with those Western European standards by which Ireland was beginning to measure herself. If the immediate pre-war period be taken at 100, then in 1947-8 the index number for Ireland's volume of gross agricultural production was 90, compared with a combined OEEC figure of 83. But by 1959-60, while the Irish figure had gone up only to 97, the OEEC figure stood at 139. In fact, as has often been observed, the volume of Irish agricultural output had remained virtually static since 1909, and there are grounds for believing that it was then not significantly greater than it had been in 1861.* It is true that the *net* output (that is all output consumed on, or sold off, farms less the value of feeding-stuffs, seeds and fertilisers bought by farmers) increased by about twenty per cent between 1929-30 and 1963, but a considerable part of this may well have been due to the widespread introduction of tractors (40,000 during that period) and other kinds of mechanisation.[58]

An essential feature of the 1930s had been the guaranteeing of minimum prices to the growers of particular crops. This was continued into the post-war years, though sometimes with odd results. Wheat, for example, which was *par excellence* the crop so singled out, expanded so fast that in 1957-8 there was an embarrassing surplus which had to be disposed of at an estimated loss to the exchequer of nearly £1½ million; in consequence, the government had hurriedly to revise its policy, applying the guaranteed price to a reduced tonnage and 'marrying' the price received by the growers to the total receipts for the sale of wheat. So also with sugar-beet, which in the 'fifties was approaching a position of surplus, with the result that in 1959 the Irish Sugar Company had to take steps to restrict the acreage. More significant than these variations in the yield of specific crops was the fact that because wheat and sugar-beet were economically attractive by reason of the price-supports they enjoyed, less of the available tillage was allotted to oats, potatoes and green crops. Further, with the protection of barley mainly for the benefit of the maltsters, the import of cheaper foreign barley and maize was stringently controlled. This in turn had its effect on the smaller farmer, showing itself in a marked decline of the pig industry and in the even more drastic decline of poultry.

In the broader terms this readjustment was tending to increase the country's reliance upon dairy-produce, cattle and sheep and especially the last two. Whereas in 1937-8, cattle, beef and veal had together accounted for 50.8 per cent of Irish agricultural exports, by 1960-1 this had gone up to 70.2 per cent. The rise in sheep, mutton and lamb exports was only of the order of 1 per cent, but the share of pigs, poultry and dairy-produce together had fallen from 36.3 per cent to 16.7.[59] More and more they had to find their satisfaction in the home market – the export battle on which so much depended was to be

* See above, p. 603; the estimated increase in gross volume between 1861 and 1909 was twenty-five to thirty per cent.

fought mainly by the cattle industry. What seemed to be happening was that in the old tug-of-war between intensive and extensive farming, the latter was once more gaining an ascendancy. And while this may have made sound economic sense, it was more questionable in social terms. No doubt the intention behind state aid to agriculture was to improve farm incomes, but there remains some doubt as to how far this really happened. The increase of food prices fell upon the countryman as upon the town-dweller, and so did the consequential increase in the price of consumer goods. Since Irish population was still preponderantly rural, it followed that the farmer paid heavily for his price-supports. True, there were profits to be made, but with the renewed emphasis on extensive farming, these tended to be made on the larger farms. It was not merely that the best prices were obtained for the products of the bigger grass-farms, or even that the increased price of feeding-stuffs adversely affected characteristic small-farm lines such as pigs and poultry; it has also to be remembered that technological change was at last beginning to have its impact upon Irish agriculture and that, as always, it was the larger farms that could best afford, and stood most to benefit from, mechanisation.

It would therefore be dangerous to assume that however fervently government policy may have been aimed at transferring wealth from the non-agricultural to the agricultural population, this actually happened in the way intended. We are too close to these events to be dogmatic about them, but it must be said that it is at least as possible that the real transfer of wealth may have been from small farmers to large farmers, a transfer which cannot be divorced from one of the great social problems of the post-war years – the problem of rural depopulation. It can scarcely be a coincidence that the movement towards consolidation, already well-established, continued steadily. In 1931 farms of one to thirty acres accounted for 57.9 per cent of all holdings and 22.5 per cent of farming land; by 1960 the comparable percentages were 49.6 and 17.4. Even more striking than this was the decline in the number of males engaged on small farms. Between 1931 and 1960, while the total number of males engaged in all forms of agriculture had dropped by 24 per cent, those working on farms of one to thirty acres fell by 50 per cent as compared with a 12 per cent drop on farms of a hundred acres or over.[60] Now, rural depopulation tends to be most directly influenced by the disparity of prices between rural and other incomes and by the possibility of bridging that gap through moving either to the towns or across the sea. A modern writer has put this controversial point thus: 'To the extent to which the policy of farm produce price support depressed the real income of the agricultural community, particularly of those on small farms, it must be held responsible for rural depopulation.'[61] But how far the policy of price support really has led to this result still remains a matter of debate.

The picture of a depleted countryside and of an agriculture which,

despite its considerable internal changes of structure, had not succeeded in raising its volume of output to any significant degree, must
be seen against the background, already sketched, of a national economy
that was finding it exceedingly difficult to adjust to the post-war world.
By the middle 1950s a serious crisis of confidence had developed, caused
partly by the specific and recurring nightmare of a balance of payments deficit (between 1947 and 1956 the surpluses accumulated during
the war were more than wiped out, and although a small surplus
was in fact achieved in 1957 this was only by most stringent
economies), and even more by a widespread anxiety that the general
performance of the economy was so poor that the country was
falling behind Western Europe standards, not only in productivity
but in the social benefits that productivity might be expected to
confer. In 1955, therefore, a Capital Investment Advisory Committee
was appointed to examine especially the position with regard to public
investment. It recommended, as was to be expected, that a greater
proportion of this investment should in future be directed to productive ends, and with this in view urged that a programme for economic
development be drawn up. This was entrusted to T. K. Whitaker,
the secretary of the Department of Finance, with results that historians
may yet come to describe as revolutionary.

(iv) TAKE-OFF?

After a few months of intensive work, Dr Whitaker presented his
report, entitled *Economic Development*, to the government in May
1958: on its publication at the end of that year it was at once recognised
not merely as an important contribution to the economic debate,
but as offering a way out of the economic impasse. It is hardly too
much to say, indeed, that even today it can be seen as a watershed
in the modern economic history of the country. On the one hand, it
looked forward to a prosperous future which, given certain conditions,
might be – as in many ways it has been – achieved in a relatively short
time. But on the other hand it offered a telling indictment of all the
inadequacies which the record of the previous forty years had revealed
so starkly – the backwardness of agriculture, the meagreness of industry, the decline in population, the shadow of emigration, the scarcity
and timidity of private capital, and the tendency of public capital to
be expended on projects that were without doubt socially desirable, but
were also too often economically unproductive. For the classic symptoms of low income per head combined with a consistently adverse
balance of payments, Dr Whitaker offered remedies that may at first
sight have appeared startling, but were in reality no more than the
intelligent application to the local Irish situation of doctrines that had
been current among economists elsewhere for many years.
So persuasive were his arguments that, with relatively minor excep-

tions, they were reproduced in their essential terms in the First Programme for Economic Expansion which the government laid before the Oireachtas in November 1958. It was in effect a five-year plan for expansion – expansion which was to involve many sectors of the country's economy, but principally agriculture and industry. So far as agriculture was concerned, the main effort was to go into improving grassland farming, so as to achieve an increase in output and in exports. Linked with this there was to be a campaign for the eradication of bovine tuberculosis, more efficient marketing and more intensive development of agricultural education. The amount of money spent on agriculture, which was already estimated to be nineteen million pounds for 1958-9, was to go beyond the twenty million pounds mark in succeeding years, and some price supports were still to be maintained for wheat, beet, milk and eggs.

In industry, the primary aim was seen to be the stimulation of 'a vast increase in private industrial investment while maintaining the supply of capital for productive state enterprises'. This did not mean a cessation of state intervention on the industrial front – far from it, the number of state-sponsored bodies (almost all concerned with finance, production or communications) increased by twelve between 1958 and 1961 – but it did mean that traditional policies would be re-assessed. Foreign capital, already wooed by the coalition government in 1956 and more systematically by the Industrial Development (Encouragement of External Investment) Act of 1958, would be further enticed by tax concessions and other facilities. And not only that, protection for protection's sake would no longer be tolerated. The Programme took it for granted that before long Ireland would be participating in some form of European Common Market and that to aim at self-sufficiency in the old style was simply not realistic. 'Hence', it continued, 'it must now be recognised that protection can no longer be relied upon as an automatic weapon of defence and it will be the policy in the future *in the case of new industries* to confine the grant of tariff protection to cases in which it is clear that the industry will, after a short initial period, be able to survive without protection.' There were, of course, other ways of assisting infant industries, and the government pledged itself to help in the starting of new projects, the purchase of machinery, the cost of technical assistance schemes, the siting of industry in underdeveloped areas and always and above all, in the promotion of exports.

The cost of this 'leap forward' was substantial, but, as the Programme insisted, it was a time when risks had to be taken. Adding the various kinds of promised aid together it seemed that the *new* government expenditure would amount, for the full term of the plan (from 1959-60 to 1963-4) to £53.4 million. And if this in turn were added to the cost of the existing schemes the formidable total for the five years would be £220.4 million.[62]

How far did success attend these undoubtedly strenuous efforts? It is too early to give a considered answer to this question, though some of the signs are at least encouraging.* The Gross National Product, for example, rose over the period of the plan by more than four per cent per annum instead of the modest two per cent aimed at in the Programme, though it has been pointed out that external conditions were particularly favourable at that time, that the stimulus of the prospect of entry into European Common Market may also have played a part, and that, anyway, there existed in the country unutilised capacity which only waited opportunity. Be that as it may, the fact remains that investment was almost doubled, despite an increase in savings Most remarkable of all, the long drawn-out fall in the population seemed at last to have been halted. The Census of 1966 showed an actual increase in the population of 62,411 persons, while emigration reached a new low level. The total for the five years 1961-6 was 83,855, little more than a third of the previous intercensal period, and the annual net rate per 1,000 had fallen from the disastrous 14.8 of 1956-61 to 5.7 between 1961 and 1966. It was notable also that the increase in population manifested itself most strikingly in the lower age-groups; if this were to continue it might have profound implications for the marriage rate.[63]

The new programme, however, was not free of criticism. Although it did indeed seem to have precipitated, or at least coincided with, an industrial boom of which the evidence was clearly visible in the form of new factories, increased employment and a higher standard of living, it was evidently less effective in the agricultural sector on which so much attention had been lavished. Thus, whereas net agricultural output was only one per cent higher in 1963 than in 1957, industrial output in 1963 was forty-seven per cent above its 1957 level. The relative failure in the farming sector seems to have been in part due to inadequate and rather unsophisticated planning, in part to exceptionally adverse market conditions. The agricultural expansion envisaged in the Programme laid most weight on the development of beef production, though it was also intended to shift the increasing amount of state expenditure into more constructive projects by granting subsidies rather to means of production (such as fertilizers) than to finished products (for example bacon or butter), and by gradually transferring the Agricultural Grant away from rate-relief and towards increased research, education, and advisory schemes. Hopefully, it was also suggested that the number of cows might be increased by 50,000 a year, to reach a total of 1½ million by 1964. In fact the number of cows did rise, but only from 1,235,700 in 1957 to 1,318,000 in 1963. At the same time the number of horses fell by 76,000 and the contraction of tillage, and corresponding expansion of grassland, amounted to 251,000 acres.

* The best analysis known to me is that by Garret FitzGerald, *Planning in Ireland* (London and Dublin, 1968), chap. 4; see also J. Meenan, *The Irish Economy Since 1922* (Liverpool, 1970), chap. 16.

As part of the campaign for agricultural improvement, state spending on fertilizers was raised during the five year period covered by the Programme from under £1 million to £3.6 million and the cost of these to the farmer dropped by over a third. Between 1957 and 1962 consumption of fertilizers went up by about two-thirds. If this sounds impressive it has to be remembered that the rate of increase was much the same in the bad years 1948-57, when the price of fertilizers was rising. This suggests that fertilizer use may be determined more by farm structure than by its own cost. In Ireland fertilizers have traditionally been much less used on grassland than on tillage – consequently the increase in grassland during the period of the First Economic Programme was likely to have affected adversely the consumption of fertilizer.

An integral part of the plan to develop the cattle industry still further was the scheme for the eradication of bovine tuberculosis. This was pursued with great vigour and before the Programme was completed the disease had been virtually stamped out in twenty of the twenty-six counties, though since the remaining six included some of the key dairying counties, success could hardly be called complete. Still, if the campaign had not been undertaken and carried through so swiftly, the bulk of Irish store cattle might have been banned from entering the United Kingdom. Whether the effect of such a ban might not have been to stimulate an equally lucrative trade in carcasses has been, and still is, much argued. What cannot be disputed, however, is that despite all the efforts made, the rise in the net agricultural output of the country was in reality very small. Taking as the base year 1953=100, the index of volume increased from 106.8 to 108 between 1957 and 1963. These are hardly the statistics of an agricultural revolution.[64]

Before the First Economic Programme had run its course the government was laying its plans for a Second Programme which was introduced in 1963 and intended to cover the period up to 1970. Whereas the First Programme had been deliberately flexible and reluctant, in view of the external pressures to which Ireland was exposed, to set specific targets, the Second Programme did commit itself to more precise objectives. It was intended that the Gross National Product should increase, in real terms, by fifty per cent in the decade of the 1960s – more precisely that the GNP, which in 1960 was £669 million at the prices then prevailing, should by 1970 reach £1,000 million, valued at the prices that ruled in 1960. To achieve this it was proposed that the growth rate for the economy as a whole between 1964 and 1970 should not fall below what it had been under the First Programme – i.e. 4 per cent per annum – though individual sectors were expected to grow at different annual rates, the industrial target being fixed at 7.1 per cent and that of agriculture at 3.8 per cent. It was anticipated also that exports of goods and services would rise by 75 per cent during the decade, that there would be a net increase in employment of 81,000, and that net emigration would by 1970 be reduced to 10,000 a year.[65]

These were hostages proffered to fortune, with a vengeance. And how very much Ireland was at the mercy of fortune's wheel was brought home to the country immediately after the Second Programme had got under way, when Britain, herself in the throes of economic crisis, included Ireland in the fifteen per cent levy on imports she imposed in October 1964. The Irish government protested in vain, although some of the damage was repaired by the trade agreement signed between the two countries in December 1965. By that agreement Britain undertook to remove almost all restrictions on Irish goods by July 1966 and Ireland agreed to remove hers on British imports over a period of ten years. British import quotas for Irish bacon and butter exports, which had been damaging, were to be increased and Irish exports of live animals and meat products were also to be gradually raised. In return, Ireland undertook a progressive dismantling of the special terms granted to foreign investors and management. Since at the same time Irish tariff policy was still being shaped both by the commitment to participate in the 'Kennedy round' of general tariff reductions, and by the assumption that sooner or later entry into the Common Market must come, it is obvious that her exposure to external forces, always great, was being intensified.*

Experience has shown, alas, that the high expectations of the Second Programme were somewhat over-optimistic. This was partly due to difficult economic conditions in the world at large, partly to internal strains and stresses, some of them probably inseparable from the unprecedentedly rapid economic advance the country was undergoing. Thus, while industrial development continued to make headway, unemployment (especially in agriculture) remained higher than expected, there was a heavy deficit in the balance of payments of £41.8 million in 1965 (though by 1967 this had been converted into a modest surplus of £10 million), and emigration continued at an embarrassingly high level which did not fall below 15,000 in any year between 1963 and 1967, actually rising in 1965 to over 20,000. In addition, government expenditure – partly to finance development and partly to increase social services – grew faster and consumed a greater share of resources than had been foreseen, with the result, among other things, that the tax burden on the citizen was correspondingly increased.[66] The cumulative effect of these disappointments was to produce

---

* The intimacy of the economic connection with Britain was probably inevitable in the circumstances, but it is well to remember that it could be dangerously one-sided. Irish agriculture, for example, has been vulnerable for some twenty years to the British policy of buying food in the cheapest market, a policy which could be pursued with few inhibitions once the decision had been taken – as it was after the Second World War – to cushion British farmers against its effects by compensating them with so-called 'deficiency payments'.

a major readjustment in the national plan, signalised by the ending of the Second Programme before its term and the introduction of a Third (and supposedly more realistic) Programme to cover the years 1969-72.

How this will turn out it is obviously much too soon to be able to say, though it requires no great insight to predict that it, like its predecessors, will continue to be at risk so long as there remains the present pervasive uncertainty about the kind of international frame-work to which this essentially exporting country is going to have to accommodate itself. Nevertheless, even though no quantitative test can be applied at this stage, no-one who knows the country in the mid-sixties well and compares it with what it was twenty years earlier can fail to be struck by the change. In part the change is visible and material – more factories, more office-blocks, new housing estates, better kept country cottages, an absence of barefoot children, a presence of supermarkets, television sets and family cars. But the change is more than just the emergence of a consumer society with debit as well as credit in the ledger. It is something impalpable and impossible to measure – a change of attitude, perhaps a change of heart. One can best describe it as a sense of new life and vigour, a stirring of hope, even a belief that the future will be better than the past has ever been.

Yet the last word must be one of caution. Not merely is the country faced with the great leap in the dark of entry into the Common Market, but the Third Programme has run into difficulties which, if they have little to do with the uncertainties of the European future, have a great deal to do with the realities of the Irish present. Although we are too close to events to be able to comment in any but the most tentative fashion, it is already clear that the pace of economic growth slackened between 1968, when national production rose at a record rate of 8 per cent, and 1970, when the rate of growth had declined to 2.5 per cent. The pattern for the latter year was admittedly distorted by damaging strikes in cement and banking, and there were signs of modest improvement by 1971, but how far these are the portents of a more general recovery is still (in the summer of 1972) an open question. Not only does the international economic environment remain somewhat bleak, but the continuing crisis in Northern Ireland has inevitably had an impact upon the south as well. The most obvious casualty has been the tourist industry – where, indeed, it is possible that no real growth at all will have been achieved by the end of the Third Programme in 1972 – but in general the widespread anxiety abroad as to whether violence might not spread to the Republic as well did nothing to foster foreign confidence in the Irish situation. Moreover, the country continued to be plagued by rising prices, and by the consequential wage demands, to such an extent that industry seemed to be becoming less rather than more competitive. Certainly, a comparison with certain major industrial powers for the period 1963-71 suggests that although output per man-hour had undoubtedly increased in Ireland, earnings per hour had also gone up so far and fast that Irish wage-costs per unit of output had by 1971 placed the Republic at a severe disadvantage.[67]

It was not therefore surprising that economic policy in 1971 should have had to be framed to meet a depressing combination of sluggish growth, rising prices and a large balance of payments deficit on current account. The situation might have been much worse had not agricultural exports reached a record figure of £221 million (industrial exports also rose, though not so steeply), but even so the government was obliged to resort to what looked suspiciously like an Irish version of 'stop-go', a cautious budget in the spring being followed by a dose of reflation in the autumn. It is too early yet to be able to say what the effect of these measures may be, or whether such improvisatory tactics will enable the Third Programme to get back on course, but the official forecast is not optimistic. For 1972 it anticipates a rate of increase in the volume of national production of no more than 2 to 2.5 per cent, with the implication that overall growth for the period 1969-72, instead of the 17 per cent originally projected, may be nearer to 12 per cent.[68] We can but conclude, therefore, that while entry into the Common Market may operate as a great liberating-force in succeeding years, the independently-functioning economy – so far as the Irish economy can truly be said to function independently – is still, despite the evidence of advance in many sectors, faced with large and intractable problems. The crock of gold at the foot of the rainbow remains tantalisingly elusive, and the rainbow itself seems to presage as much storm as sunshine.

5. Problems of Social Policy

(i) THE LANGUAGE QUESTION

'Ireland ... not free merely, but Gaelic as well; not Gaelic, merely, but free as well.'[1] With these words Patrick Pearse consecrated, as it were, the union of language and nationality which had been the lodestar of his life and which, largely through his own efforts, had given a new depth and intensity to the revolutionary movement that culminated in the Easter Rising. And even though at that time enthusiasts for the Irish language were, like the revolutionaries themselves, in a small minority, the swing towards Sinn Féin between 1916 and 1918 which we observed earlier necessarily involved increased emphasis upon cultural no less than political independence. It was accepted in principle, even if practice lagged far behind, that Irish was an essential element in the establishment of a separate national identity and from the moment the first Dáil assembled in January 1919 the revival of the language became a major object of policy.

For obvious reasons it was not until the Anglo-Irish war was over that the Free State government could address itself to the formidable task of translating the ideal of a Gaelic Ireland into some kind of recognisable reality. Not much investigation was required to indicate just how formidable that task was. In the primary schools, where the main hope for the future must lie, less than a quarter of the total were giving any attention to Irish at all at the time of the transfer of power in 1921–2. It is true that at the secondary level, mainly because of the decision of the National University in 1913 to make Irish a compulsory subject for matriculation, an undoubted stimulus had been given to the teaching of the language – more precisely, perhaps, to cramming it for examinations – but in the country as a whole the proportion of Irish speakers at the last Census before the war had been only 17·6 per cent of the total population.[2]

The new government did not lack advice as to how to go about the business of revival. It had before it two sets of suggestions, one emanating from the Gaelic League, the other from a conference convened by the Irish National Teachers' Organisation. The Gaelic League had not passed through the time of troubles unscathed. It had suffered a serious split in 1915 when a majority at the Dundalk Ard Fhéis (annual convention) had carried the famous resolution to include the political independence of Ireland among the League's objectives. Since it had been founded as a non-political body, Dr Douglas Hyde, its great father-figure, resigned and various other moderates followed his example.

Apart from these losses, some of the leading activists – Pearse, Mac-Donagh, Cathal Brugha – perished in or as a result of the fighting between 1916 and 1922 and the League itself, like most other nationalist institutions, was torn by the Civil War. It was, however, in 1920, with the Anglo-Irish war just beginning and the dissensions over the Treaty still far in the future, that the League issued its proposals for the future of the language, embracing all levels of education. So far as national schools were concerned it recommended that a distinction be made between three different categories – those in the Irish-speaking areas (the *Gaeltacht* properly so-called), those in partially Irish-speaking areas and those in English-speaking areas. In the first category all subjects should be taught through the medium of Irish; in the second, Irish should be regarded as the principal language of the school, and bilingual programmes should be adopted wherever possible; finally, in the English-speaking areas (which of course accounted for much the greater part of the country) Irish should still rank as the principal language and should be taught as a *spoken* language for an hour a day wherever teachers were available. It was further proposed that Irish be taught to all children in secondary schools; in the Gaeltacht it was to be the medium of instruction for other subjects and the remaining secondary schools elsewhere (again, the vast majority) were to be instructed to be in a position to do likewise at the end of five years. The universities for their part were to provide vacation courses to help teachers to reach the required level and were themselves to be prohibited from conferring degrees on students in any branch of learning who could not speak Irish fluently.[8]

This was certainly a far-reaching, not to say draconian, programme – much too much so to be practicable, given the fact that for over a hundred years the entire educational system had been exposed to pressures in favour of English less direct, perhaps, but no less effective, than those the Gaelic League would have liked to exert in favour of Irish. More significance, therefore, attached to the second set of suggestions aimed at the government in these early, formative years – the suggestions embodied in the 1921 report of the Conference organised by the Irish National Teachers' Organisation. The Conference was far from being fully representative of educational opinion in the country, but its proposals were sufficiently realistic to be taken seriously. Like the Gaelic League, the Conference was prepared to recommend compulsion, but in a modified sense. In the higher standards (classes) of the national schools Irish and English were both to be obligatory subjects, but Irish was to be the medium of instruction for the history and geography of Ireland and also for singing and drill. More radical even than this, and ultimately to be of great importance, was the recommendation that in infant classes *all* work done was to be in Irish – this despite the fact that English was the home language of ninety per cent of these small children. Since, however, at that time the country had not been

636

finally partitioned and the Dáil might, in theory at least, be supposed to be legislating for all thirty-two counties, an escape clause was added to the effect that 'in the case of schools where the majority of the parents of the children object to having either Irish or English taught as an obligatory subject, their wishes should be complied with.'[4]

It was, of course, for the government to decide how far and how fast to adopt the principle of compulsion. It began, certainly, with a number of impressive gestures. The constitution of 1922 declared that Irish was 'the national language' and steps were taken to make at least some knowledge of it compulsory for civil servants, members of the Army and the Garda Síochana as well as in the Law Courts. This policy met with greater success than has sometimes been allowed, but since the great majority of the servants of the state in the early years of independence had been recruited under an English-speaking regime, it was asking too much to expect them to become bilingual overnight. Indeed, it may be that after nearly forty years it was still asking too much. A survey in 1959 indicated that the policy of making a knowledge of Irish essential for admission to certain grades of the civil service had resulted in some 4,000 civil servants (fourteen per cent of the total) achieving fluency, and a further 14,000 (fifty per cent of the whole) attaining a 'reading and writing' knowledge of it. The disconcerting fact that a further 10,000 were returned as having little or no Irish at all may perhaps partly be explained by the fact that the qualifying examination in the language was only imposed on about a third of the personnel, but it is less easy to understand why in the Gaeltacht itself as late as 1951 the effort to ensure that all public officials would have a competent knowledge of the language was reckoned to have been 'not more than half successful'. For the civil service as a whole it would appear (according to inquiries made in 1956) that outside those departments having particular need to use Irish the proportion of official business transacted through the language scarcely amounted to as much as two per cent of the total.*

The real battle for the language, however, has not been in the service of the state, but in what successive governments have regarded as its two principal nurseries – the schools and that dwindling area of the country where Irish is the everyday language of the people. If there was ever to be a truly national solution to the problem, the revival of Irish in the schools was obviously crucial and this was realised from the very beginning. The Provisional Government of 1922 had not been more than a few weeks in office when it ordained that as from 17 March

* It has been estimated that by a curious coincidence the amount of space annually occupied by Irish in the Dáil and Senate debates was less than two per cent though the number of deputies and ministers with a good knowledge of Irish was perhaps as high as one third. (*Commission on the Restoration of the Irish Language*, English summary of Final Report, pp. 21-23.)

of that year Irish should be taught or used as a medium of instruction in all primary schools for not less than one hour a day during the ordinary school hours where there was a teacher competent to do so.[5] In this last proviso lay the rub. For a survey of schools carried out that very year revealed that of some 12,000 teachers then employed in the national schools of the Free State, only 1,107 had certificates to show that they could teach bilingually; true, nearly another 3,000 had certificates indicating they could teach Irish and a further 922 had what were mysteriously described as 'temporary' certificates in the subject, but this still left a great many teachers totally unable to meet the government's requirements. Inevitably, there was a frantic rush to achieve a basic competence through summer courses and visits to the Gaeltacht. In 1922 alone £75,000 was paid out in grants for this purpose and, after the courses had been continued for another three years, it was reckoned that by the beginning of 1926 about 6,200 out of a total of primary teachers that had grown to 13.000 had reached a satisfactory standard.[6] So that the supply of teachers well versed in Irish might not only be maintained but increased, the Department of Education established in that year the first of a series of residential preparatory colleges for teachers which eventually were sited in Galway, Dublin, Ballyvourney, Donegal, Dingle and Tourmakeady.[7] Whether as a result of this initiative, or as a simple consequence of the passage of time, it has recently (1960-1) been claimed that ninety-six per cent of primary teachers are now qualified to teach Irish and eighty-nine per cent to teach other subjects *through* Irish, though it is not made clear how many of those qualifications are at pass and how many at honours level.[8]

The massive transformation that these figures suggest was no more than was necessary if government policy in the schools was to be implemented. In 1925-6 this policy was revised in the light of a second programme put forward by a further – and much more representative – Conference organised by the Department of Education. The principal recommendations were that where a teacher was competent and where children could assimilate the instruction so given, then Irish should be extended as a medium of instruction in other subjects as far as possible, though it was not to be obligatory where these provisions did not apply. Where the full use of Irish was not feasible, then a policy of gradual introduction was to be adopted. What this appeared to mean was that in infant classes all instruction was to be given through Irish regardless of the home-language of the children, and that further up the school time spent on a variety of subjects – for example, history, geography, algebra and geometry – was to be reduced to allow more class-hours to be spent on Irish. After fifteen years of this policy the Irish National Teachers' Organisation came out strongly against it and published a report indicating widespread dissatisfaction with the practice of teaching other subjects – especially arithmetic and algebra – 'through the medium'. In practice, it must be said, the regulations actually in force were not so rigorously applied as this would seem to indicate and from the late 1940s onwards progressive relaxations could be observed.* And although the government commission on the restoration of the Irish language took its stand unequivocally on the principle of bilingualism, its own figures indicated how far that principle was from being observed in the schools. Outside the Gaeltacht (where Irish, naturally, was the medium of all instruction) there were in 1960–1 only 183 schools in the whole of the Republic where all teaching was given through Irish; of these, 47 were special infant schools and most of the remainder were in areas bordering on the Gaeltacht.[9]

But the government did not rely entirely on the stick; the carrots also provided were not inconsiderable. This was particularly true of the secondary schools. As we saw earlier, Irish, as an optional subject, was already well established before independence and this situation continued after the transfer of power to such a degree that in 1924 (the last year in which the old system operated) eighty-six per cent out of a total of nearly 10,000 candidates presented Irish at the Intermediate Examination. Official policy was directed towards sustaining and encouraging this tendency by financial inducements of various kinds. Thus 'Class A schools', where Irish was the normal medium of instruction, Class B (1) schools, where the teaching given through Irish was not less than the teaching given through English, and Class B (2) schools where at least one other subject besides was taught through that medium, were all eligible for varying increases on their capitation grants up to a maximum of twenty-five per cent.† Teachers who could give instruction through Irish received a fifty pound increment, government grants for textbooks were made available, and, as an incentive to the pupils themselves, Irish was made an essential subject to qualify for scholarships at both the Intermediate and Leaving Certificate level. A proportion of

* Latterly there have been scattered signs of further efforts towards a more flexible policy. The government has adopted a new spelling (Litriú Nua), intended to come generally into use between 1962 and 1972), with the aim of bringing the written language nearer to daily speech. On the other hand, there is still strong feeling against teaching 'through the medium', which has found vehement expression in the recently formed Language Freedom movement. In their electoral platform in 1961, Fine Gael held out hopes of a more permissive attitude in the future, but though this may have helped them to pick up votes, they are still out of office. Even among devotees, it seems, there is a less dogmatic insistence on speaking the language at all times than formerly. The sign of such intention, the gold ring or Fainne, is sometimes nowadays replaced by the Fainne Nua, which indicates that the wearer can and will speak Irish, but does not feel bound to do so on all occasions.

† For the financing of secondary education after 1922, see the following section. It should perhaps be mentioned here that in the rare cases where a child does not include Irish in his secondary-school curriculum, the parent is normally expected to pay to the school an increased fee equivalent to the capitation fee so lost.

such scholarships have been set aside for children from the Gaeltacht, where in addition the parents or guardians of children between the ages of seven and seventeen years attending as day-pupils at national, secondary or technical schools, received a grant (initially two pounds, then five, later raised to ten pounds) for each child, provided that Irish was the language of the home and that the child spoke it fluently. It was, however, ominously significant that the number of children qualifying for such grants declined from 9,844 in 1955–6 to 9,158 in 1962–3.[10]

This decline is but one small illustration of the problem that has confronted the state for nearly half a century (and the language revival movement for a generation longer than that) – the problem not merely of restoring Irish outside the Gaeltacht, but of keeping it alive within the Gaeltacht. It is a problem complicated by the fact that the native-speaking areas (nearly all concentrated along the western seaboard) were precisely the areas that were economically least viable and were therefore being emptied faster by emigration – the haemorrhage there as elsewhere being mainly of the young blood upon which the continuity of the language in the last resort depended. That the problem was at bottom economic and social as well as linguistic has been recognised in official circles for at least forty years. As long ago as 1925–6 a special commission on the Gaeltacht urgently pointed out that it was necessary not just to prop up the language along the western seaboard, but to adopt a wide-ranging policy of welfare and employment in order to ensure that native-speakers were not driven out of the area by sheer economic necessity.

For many years, however, no very positive steps were taken. The seemingly insoluble difficulties of the Gaeltacht were passed nervously from one ministry to another and it was not until 1956 that a special Department was set up to look after the area.* The following year legislation was passed through the Dáil to develop and assist local industries in the area and in 1958 a state-sponsored body, Gaeltarra Eireann, was established to act as the main channel of government assistance, though the Gaeltacht continued also to benefit from the activities of other Departments as well, especially those concerned with

* Incredibly enough, it was not until that same year, 1956, that an agreed geographical definition of the Gaeltacht was arrived at. It was then declared to cover an area of 1,860 square miles (less than six per cent of the land surface of Ireland) which, however was not a homogeneous unit, but scattered along the western seaboard (Donegal, Mayo, Galway, Kerry), Cork and a district (Ring) in county Waterford; to this should be added two tiny colonies transplanted to county Meath. The total population was then 78,524, but the number actually at work in the Gaeltacht in 1961 was only 27,282, three-quarters of them employed in agriculture. (Even after 1956, such is the ineradicable conservatism of the official mind, it seems that some government departments still continued to cling to their own cherished and diverse definitions of what actually constituted the Gaeltacht.)

the well-being of depressed areas. On its establishment, Gaeltarra Eireann took over assets valued at £700,000 and in addition received £100,000 a year, primarily to finance the production and marketing of tweed, knitwear, embroidery and toys at thirty-four centres located in or near the Gaeltacht. By the early 1960s it had 700 full-time employees and another 1,000 part-timers on its books. Sales amounted in 1963–4 to £750,000 but only the tweed industry was paying its way; the others made such heavy losses that the trading deficit for that year was just over £100,000. Part of this deficit was undoubtedly due to the absence of industrial centralisation, but, since Gaeltarra Eireann has the social function of keeping the Gaeltacht in existence, as well as the economic function of making it more prosperous, these losses have hitherto been regarded as part of the price that has to be paid if the language is to be saved from extinction. In many other ways and from many other sources, assistance has been, and still is being, poured into the area, in some instances at a higher rate than for other parts of the country. Thus under the Land Project three-quarters of the cost of reclamation is provided by the state, compared with two-thirds elsewhere; animals for breeding purposes are provided at a reduced rate; the maximum grant for a new house was a hundred pounds more than it was for small farmers in other parts of the country, and the amount advanced for the reconstruction and improvement of old houses was markedly larger in the Gaeltacht; payments for road-building, for fishing-boats, for water-supply and sewerage were all on a relatively generous scale.[11]

Still more recently (in 1969), a council – Comhairle na Gaelige – was appointed by the government to help it towards a review of policy on the language question and to advise on future implementation of such policy, particularly in regard 'to the use of Irish as a medium of general communication'. An important part of its work since then has been the investigation of what is nowadays called 'sociolinguistics', and one of its first publications was a scholarly investigation of the problems presented by bilingualism in the Irish context.* In addition, the new council itself examined the possibilities of making local government more responsive to the needs of the Irish-speaking districts, and of securing for the Gaeltacht an adequate share of the energy – and the

* M. O Murchú, *Language and Community*, Comhairle na Gaelige, 'Occasional Paper No. 1' (Dublin, 1970). The paper advocates the attainment of an Irish-English 'diglossia' – that is a linguistic situation in which two languages may be used in different but overlapping domains (or spheres) of the individual's life in society; the implication for Irish in its present circumstances would seem to be that the revival of the language does not depend upon fostering it in one particular domain, but in all, with perhaps special emphasis upon the public rather than the home-neighbourhood domains. It is worth noting that the current emphasis on bilingualism is in marked contrast with the impracticable and chauvinistic ideas of the early language enthusiasts who wanted to uproot English altogether.

cash – which in the next few years, under the impetus both of the Buchanan Report* and of entry into the Common Market, is likely to be expended on regional development. The principal specific recommendations of Comhairle na Gaelige were that in each county containing a Gaeltacht area there should be established a Gaeltacht Area Committee consisting of representatives of the local electoral districts; that the business of the Committees and their offices should be conducted in Irish; that certain functions of the county councils should be transferred to the Area Committees and that, so far as possible, the latter should be empowered to act in their own areas for the Departments of State; that a Central Council for the Gaeltacht Area Committees should be established; finally, and from the development point of view, that Gaeltarra Eireann and the Shannon Free Airport Development Company should be asked to form a working party 'to furnish an early report on the requirements, objectives and implications of development in the Gaeltacht areas, the constituents of a co-ordinated set of development policies, the organisational structure suitable for their implementation, and the new powers and additional financing required'. It is obviously too soon yet to say what may be the effect of these recommendations – which would seem to represent a rather desperate attempt to halt the juggernaut of centralisation in its tracks – but at least it should be recorded that the government, much criticised as it often is for its alleged indifference to Gaeltacht problems, has already begun to implement some of the council's recommendations. Local government organisation is in the process of being reorganised along the lines suggested and provision is being made for Gaeltacht Area Committees and for a Central Council of those Committees; the working party on the future development of the Gaeltacht has submitted its report, which is being considered by the government; and, in the meantime, apart from assistance from the Special Regional Development Fund of nearly £2 million, the resources available to the Department of the Gaeltacht and to Gaeltarra Eireann have been increased to £4 million for the year 1972–3.[12]

Yet although this is evidence of effort and concern, critics have repeatedly urged that it is not enough. The Gaeltacht, in fact, is faced with two quite different dangers. On the one hand it has continued inexorably to shrink and by 1961 had a population of less than 80,000 native Irish speakers (a 1969 estimate puts it as low as 50,000), figures which put it within measurable distance of extinction. And on the other hand, some of the very measures now being taken to revive its material prosperity – most notably the development of tourism – threaten its linguistic integrity. The pressure on the native-speaker to become bilingual is overwhelming, and since the language of commerce

* Regional Studies in Ireland. A report commissioned by the United Nations on behalf of the Government of Ireland and prepared by Colin Buchanan and Partners, in association with Economic Consultants Ltd. (Dublin, 1968).

and of intercourse with the outside world is English, the inducements to give English the major place are well-nigh irresistible. 'If the present population trends and the present rate of language change continue', a modern writer has warned, 'there will be no Gaeltacht at all – not even the present bilingual semi-Gaeltacht – in another 20 years. If these factors intensify, the final demise will be swifter still.'[13]

This brings us to the crux of the problem. 'The preservation and the strengthening of the Gaeltacht', as the recent Commission on the restoration of the Irish language observes, '. . . must not be approached as if it were an attempt to preserve the Irish language and spread it as the normal language of Ireland. . . . There can be no survival, we fear, without revival.'[14] And although no doubt it is true that government support could be much more emphatic than it has been, it would be a kind of abdication – and, indeed a recrudescence of the 'slave-mentality' of an earlier age – if the revival were simply to be left in official hands.* It is, after all, in the ordinary habit and style of life that the battle must in the end be won or lost and the issue of that battle can only be decided by people, not governments. For it is not just impersonal economic factors, but intimate social and personal ones that press inexorably against the revival. Newspapers, books, the radio, the cinema, television, the motor-car, the tourist – all combine to lure native-speaker and non-native speaker alike towards the seeming delights of a mass civilisation from which, in their naïvete, they regard it as a badge of inferiority to be excluded. And just as in the days of Douglas Hyde the Gaelic League set itself towards the de-Anglicisation of Irish life and literature, so in the past decades not only the still-surviving League. but a multiplicity of other organisations as well. have followed, faint but pursuing the same objective. Only a few of these agencies can be mentioned here, but even a selection will serve to indicate their variety.

There are, for example, several newspapers and periodicals devoted to the language – the chief of them. *Inniu* ('Today') was founded in 1943 as a monthly, but became a weekly three years later and has a circulation variously estimated at between 11,500 and 17,000. There are several publishing houses, one of them run by the government, and a book-club, *An Club Leabhar*, with about 1,500 members. And although the demand for literature in Irish is clearly limited. a school of writers has grown up whose best work has received critical acclaim. They include an outstanding playwright. Mairéad Ní Ghráda novelists and short-story writers such as Maírtin O Cadhain and Díarmaud O Súilleabhaín. together with several notable poets, among them Máire Cruise O'Brien. But it is ironic, and symbolic, that two works which in English translation had a wide circulation outside the country – *Twenty*

* The careful reader of the government White Paper of 1965 on the restoration of the language will observe that while the vast majority of the Commission's 288 recommendations are accepted in principle, the official attitude towards implementation seems decidedly cautious.

Years Agrowing by Muris O'Súileahbáin and *Peig* by Peig Sayers were both about the Blasket Islands off Kerry, which now have not only no Irish-speakers, but no inhabitants at all.

Apart from the printed word, music and sport have secured a fairly firm base in popular affection.* The Gaelic Athletic Association still continues to flourish and the All-Ireland competitions in hurling and Gaelic football attract vast crowds and enormous local patriotism.† Similarly, the music festivals (Fleadhs) organised from 1951 onwards by Comhaltas Ceoltóirí Eireann (Traditional Music Society of Ireland) have not only reawakened interest in the old songs and ballads at the parish level, but once a year bring together audiences of up to 100,000 at the All-Ireland Fleadh. More comprehensive in its appeal than either of these, and possibly the key to the whole future of the movement, is an organisation which was founded just over twenty-five years ago. This is Comhdáil Náisiúnta na Gaelige (National Gaelic Congress) created in 1943, but dominated since 1946 by a very powerful and energetic pressure-group, An Comhchaidreamh; originally composed mainly of students, several of its members have since attained to positions of considerable influence in Irish educational and intellectual circles. It was from this body that there sprang in 1953 one of the most interesting and successful initiatives in the revival movement – the organisation known as Gael Linn. Its primary purpose has been to use modern media to reach a wider public through Irish. To that end it has launched a football pool, has staged new plays, has provided gramophone records and has made two fascinating films, *Saoirse?* (Freedom?) and *Mise Eire* (I am Eire) with musical scores by the composer, Séan O'Riada, that have deservedly become famous.[15]

All this is certainly a sign of life, but the haunting question returns – how vigorous is that life and how far does this manifold activity serve to arrest the onset of ultimate extinction? No question is more bitterly debated in modern Ireland and the difficulty of arriving at a just assessment of the balance between the Irish-speaking and non-Irish-speaking sections of the population is greatly complicated by the fact that no satisfactory definition of what constitutes 'Irish-speaking' has yet been arrived at. Professor Brian O Cuiv, of the Dublin Institute of Advanced Studies, has estimated that by 1951 no more than 35,000 used Irish as their ordinary medium of speech and that no more than 3,000 people in the whole country were ignorant of English.[16] Official figures, which are sometimes criticised for being unduly over-optimistic, if not actually tendentious, do not paint so black a picture, but even so indicate a

---

* To the developments listed here should be added a new venture, Radio na Gaeltachta. This came on the air for the first time on 2 April 1972, largely because of the pressure of a group of dedicated individuals.

† The GAA continued to 'ban' its members from playing or attending foreign games on pain of expulsion from the Association, though this was only confirmed in 1965 after hot debate. Since then the ban has been removed.

grim enough situation. It has been reckoned that in 1936, of the population of three years and over, 660,601 – or 23.7 per cent of the whole – could speak Irish, but that this figure had fallen by 1946 to 588,725, or 21.2 per cent of the then population of three years and over. In 1961, on the other hand, it is claimed that the number of speakers has actually increased to 716,420 and that this amounts to 27.2 of all the people three years of age and over.[17]

It may be doubted, however, if this total is composed entirely of Irish-speakers who might by any stretch of the imagination be called fluent. On the contrary, most of the ordinary experience of life goes to suggest that not merely in Dublin, but even in Galway itself, English comes more readily to the tongue of most inhabitants.* Certainly, those who feel the language to be threatened have lost none of their sense of urgency, and schemes now being canvassed – for example, the use of language laboratories and the possibility of learning from the Israeli experiment in Hebrew – have about them an air of almost frantic enthusiasm as if their promoters knew – indeed, they must know – that time is inexorably running out. The future of the language, in short, remains as before balanced on a knife edge.[18]

(ii) EDUCATION

If the language enthusiasts sought to preserve and cherish what they had inherited from the past, the problem Irish educationists had to face presented itself in exactly opposite terms – to throw off the dead hand of history and create for their country a system of education that should be not only indigenous but modern as well. Yet for forty years after the foundation of the state, successive governments, so far from solving this problem, seemed scarcely to be aware that it even existed. And if it seems strange that Ireland, after passing through a period of intense political upheaval, should have rested content for so long with an educational structure of extreme conservativism, then one can only answer that the element of paradox in this situation was more apparent than real. As we saw earlier, almost from the moment schooling began to be organised on a national scale during the nineteenth century it took on a predominantly denominational character, both at the primary and the secondary – indeed also at the university – level. Nothing in the stormy years between 1916 and 1922 changed this situation in the slightest. True, the transfer of power resulted in a degree of centralisation, whereby the general responsibility for all kinds of education outside the universities which had been previously parcelled out

* In all fairness two points should be made here to redress the balance. One is that even if Galway city is much anglicised one does not have to go far along the coast to be in genuinely Irish-speaking country. And the other is that in Galway itself the University College has long been – and still remains – the only centre of higher education where a wide range of courses is taught and studied at degree level through the Irish language.

645

among the various Boards was vested in a Minister, operating from 1924 onwards through a newly created Department of Education. But although Professor Eoin MacNeill, who was Minister at the time of the reorganisation, spoke feelingly about the segregated and fragmented system he had inherited, that system was beyond his power to change. Neither the primary nor the secondary schools were state-owned, and although the government each year paid out considerable sums in teachers' salaries and – to the national schools – in building grants, direct control of the schools, including the appointment and removal of the teachers, remained in the hands of the managers. These, as before, were still overwhelmingly clerical, subject only to their bishops or to boards of trustees, as denominational practice might dictate.

This is not to say, of course, that the role of the state in education was restricted simply to that of milch cow. On the contrary, apart from a general responsibility for ensuring that the schools should provide adequately for the needs of society, the Minister had a primary duty to see that value was received for the money he dispensed. And although critics were in time to become vociferous about what seemed to constitute the official view of 'value', there can be no denying that, apart altogether from the financial pressures it could bring to bear, the Department's power to inspect schools and to conduct the public examinations gave it a decisive influence over the development of both the national and the secondary programmes. To understand the full extent and effect of that influence it will be necessary to look separately at the two levels, because, although it was a declared aim of policy to bring them into closer relationship with each other, they remained, and still remain, very different entities.

So far as the national schools were concerned, the government appears to have had four main objectives. The first was to revise the syllabus, partly, as we have seen, by the introduction of compulsory Irish, but partly also by the broadening of courses through the introduction of a wider range of optional subjects. After much experimentation the national school programme in the early 'sixties, on the eve, that is, of what may in time come to be called the educational revolution, was based on a five or six hour day, five days a week, for a minimum of 190 days in the year. Instruction was given in religion and in Irish, English, arithmetic, history, geography, music and (for girls) needlework; optional subjects (whose availability varied enormously, however, from school to school) included rural science or nature study, drawing, physical training, cookery or laundry or domestic economy for girls, and manual instruction for boys. Algebra and geometry were taught in some schools, but were not obligatory in the smaller ones or in classes taught by women. Of the working week about two and a half hours was spent on religion, about ten hours on vernacular languages (Irish and English in the approximate ratio of two:one), five hours on arithmetic and five hours on other subjects, with about one hour each for history and geography in the upper standards.[19] Such was the education received free of charge week by week by some 472,000 children between the ages of six and fourteen in 4,800 national schools.*

Linked with revision of the syllabus was the second objective of government policy – to facilitate movement from the primary to the secondary schools. Since the latter were fee-paying institutions (at least up to the beginning of the reform era in the mid-1960s) the most urgent need was to provide for an adequate number of scholarships to enable poor but able pupils to extend their education beyond the age of fourteen. To this end, legislation of 1921 and 1923 (the Intermediate Education Act and Local Government (Temporary Provisions) Act) empowered local authorities to levy a rate not exceeding a penny in the pound to finance such awards. The value of these scholarships was not large (varying from fifteen pounds to fifty pounds), but it underwent no significant change for forty years until the Local Authorities (Education Scholarships) Amendment Act of 1961 established the new principle whereby the state contributed an annual subvention amounting to at least half the value of the scholarships. In fact, the state tended to contribute more than the minimum amount and local authority scholarships soon rose dramatically in consequence – from 621 in 1961 to 1,775 in 1963.[20] The scholarships were of course for the exceptional minority, but for less gifted pupils the Department in the late 1920s instituted the Primary School Certificate examination, partly as a qualification to ensure admission to a secondary school, and partly in the hope that it would be of value to school-leavers seeking employment.† In practice this amiable intention resulted, as might have been anticipated, in a sacrifice of education to cramming and was condemned by the teachers themselves on more than one occasion. So long as the test was voluntary the issue was largely academic (between 1929 and 1942 only about twenty-five per cent of those eligible took it), but in 1943 the Department, in the teeth of strong criticism, made it compulsory for all who had reached the sixth standard, and by the early 'sixties some 40,000 children a year were thus committed to the examination mill.[21]

The third target at which the government aimed in these early years was one that had already attracted attention in the nineteenth century. Soon after the new Department was set up a determined attempt was made to carry forward the principle of compulsory attendance which had been half-heartedly introduced by the Irish Education Act of 1892. In 1926 the School Attendance Act only laid down that attendance should be compulsory on all school days for children between the ages

* There were in addition some 192 non-aided and fee-paying primary schools catering for about 21,000 children; these included the preparatory departments of secondary schools and were mostly in or near Dublin.

† A Primary School Certificate was not, however, essential for entry to a secondary school. Many of them held their own examinations at which the standard was notoriously low – a fact not uninfluenced, perhaps, by the system (described below) relating their government grants to the number of their pupils.

of six and fourteen, and that this should be enforced by special officers appointed by local School Attendance Committees and the police. In practice, it must be admitted, this requirement was somewhat vitiated by the right of the parent to give his child 'compulsory' education outside the state system (in his own home, if he so desired), and also by the inadequacy of the fines imposed and the slackness of the authorities themselves. Nevertheless, a perceptible improvement in average daily attendance has been registered – from 73.5 per cent in 1925-6 to 88.1 per cent in 1963.[22]

The question of school attendance was inextricably bound up with the fourth, and in some ways the most intractable, of the problems with which the new Department had to wrestle. Partly because education had developed along denominational lines, partly also because of the unavoidable effects of a declining population, a great deal of wasteful duplication had occurred over the years in the building and maintenance of the national schools. All sorts of related difficulties had arisen from this situation. Too many schools were understaffed, classes were frequently far too large, or else uneconomically small, buildings were old-fashioned and heating, lighting and sanitation were often totally inadequate. Between 1926 and 1932 efforts were made to amalgamate some of the smallest schools, but how ineffective these were may be seen from the fact that as late as 1962-3 there were still in the Republic 736 schools with one teacher each and 2,458 with two teachers each – the pupil-teacher ration being 17.9 in the first instance, and 26.3 in the second. Nor was the situation any better in the larger schools – indeed, it was actually worse, for the pressure of population was not matched by an adequate supply of teachers, with the result that the pupil-teacher ratio sometimes rose to over 40.[23] This serious imbalance – which not only affected the quality of the teaching, but also the well-being of the pupils, and in addition may often have accentuated the harshness of the discipline – was extremely difficult to rectify because of the fact that although the state paid by far the greater proportion of the cost of building (latterly its contribution compared with that of the local school authority has been in the ratio of 11 : 2), the schools nevertheless remained the property of the churches. The replacement of defective buildings, or even the provision of proper heating and water supply, rested in the last analysis with the managers, and since many of these were old and conservative clergy it frequently followed that even though aid was freely available, interminable delays interposed before anything constructive was done. In recent years, it is true, more rapid progress has been made and attractive schools are to be seen in many parts of the country, but although in the decade 1953-4 to 1962-3 grants amounting to over sixteen million pounds were sanctioned for building or improvement, about 2,400 schools – roughly half the total – still occupied accommodation that dated from the nineteenth century.[24]

Despite its archaic features, primary education in Ireland has been able to call upon the services of a body of devoted teachers (14,000 of them according to a survey for 1962-3) who have undoubtedly done a great deal, despite the difficulties just described, to lay the foundations of a sound, if somewhat old-fashioned education. But it is when we seek to peer beyond this level, into the dark and confused world of secondary schooling, that the indications of strain and stringency become more apparent. At first sight, indeed, the unsatisfactory pattern which had emerged during the nineteenth century appears to have changed remarkably little in the first half of the twentieth.* Secondary schools remained firmly in private hands, owned and run either by religious orders, or boards of governors, or in very rare instances by individuals. Nevertheless, even in this sector the state during the past fifty years has steadily become more and more intimately involved, not merely in the financial provision for these schools, but in their staffing and teaching arrangements.

The first important break in the old pattern occurred as early as 1924 when the Intermediate Education (Amendment) Act repealed the clauses in previous legislation which had tied grants to secondary schools to the results obtained by their pupils in the public examinations. Instead, the new act provided that financial assistance to the secondary schools should be given in two main ways. First, a capitation fee was to be paid in respect of each recognised pupil, a pupil being 'recognised' if he had a Primary School Certificate or had otherwise satisfied the (normally very low) entrance requirements of the school. And second, the state paid the major part of secondary teachers' salaries, with bonus payments for those who taught through the medium of Irish.[25] The appointment and dismissal of these teachers continued to rest with the school authorities, but the Department's regulations required that schools in receipt of grants should employ a certain minimum of 'registered' teachers related to the number of pupils in the school, and that they should pay these teachers, if lay, a fixed minimum basic salary. Qualifications for registration included a degree from a recognised university, a recognised graduate qualification in the theory and practice of education, evidence of a year's satisfactory experience of teaching, and oral competence in the Irish language. By 1964, of 5,000 teachers employed in state-aided secondary schools about 4,000 had achieved these qualifications and were on the register – a striking improvement on the meagre array of qualifications that category was able to offer before 1914.[26]

In addition to this basic financial assistance, the government over the years was gradually committed to giving special grants to aid in the development of science teaching, domestic economy, manual instruction and music. It was not, however, until 1964 that the far-reaching and long overdue decision was taken to make capital grants for the building of new schools and the improvement of old ones. It is too soon to say yet how radically this will change the situation in the republic, but it may have come just in time to enable the schools to

* For the nineteenth century developments, see above. Part I, chap. 3.

accommodate the steep rise in secondary schooling which has recently been projected. At the time of the 1964 decision there were 569 state-aided secondary schools catering for some 88,000 pupils, but by 1970 it was a anticipated that space would be needed for perhaps 114,000 pupils.* If this estimate is correct, the building programme will indeed have been a race against time.

Scarcely less important than the schools we have been considering, which represent the Irish equivalent of a grammar-school, was the other branch of secondary education concerned with vocational training. As we saw earlier, this kind of training – then called 'technical education' – had only reached a very rudimentary stage by the time of the transfer of power.† Such as it was, the Department of Education took it over in 1924 and two years later set up a commission to investigate the whole field. From its recommendations, which were largely implemented by the government in the Vocational Education Act of 1930, have stemmed most subsequent developments. Under the general control of the Minister, Vocational Education Committees were to be selected by the local rating authorities; the Committees were to be representative of educational, cultural, commercial and industrial interests in the area, but the local authorities themselves were limited to not more than eight seats out of a minimum total strength of fourteen. These new bodies were to be given wide powers of initiation and control over the courses offered, subject to the Minister's approval. The all-important finance was to be provided partly from local rates, partly from government subventions which were intended to be on a *pro rata* basis, but have in fact often outpaced the local contribution. Fees were payable by the students participating, but they were deliberately fixed at a very low level and accounted probably for not more than ten per cent of income.

Under this stimulus there emerged thirty-eight Vocational Education Committees which between them covered the whole country. Their main responsibility was – and still is – to provide two quite different kinds of education – 'continuation' and 'technical'. 'Continuation' education was defined in the act as 'education to continue and supplement education provided in elementary schools, and [it] includes general and practical training in preparation for employment'. This was in effect full-time education for boys and girls, beginning usually at fourteen years and lasting for two or three years – the emphasis being on woodwork, metalwork, mechanical drawing and mathematics for the boys, domestic economy and commercial subjects for the girls. Irish and

* Non-aided secondary schools (apart from a handful of specialised institutions) were only three in number in 1964 and catered for no more than 250 pupils. If the specialised schools were added the total of pupils accommodated would amount to 2,600; it was not anticipated that there would be any significant increase in this figure by 1970 (*Investment in Education*, pp. 4, 36 and 58).

† See Part I, chap. 3.

English were taught in all the schools, art and science in some, and other options according to the resources at the Committee's disposal. The numbers attracted by this kind of opportunity have steadily grown and in 1964 there were nearly 250 schools catering for some 29,000 students; attendance was voluntary, save in the county boroughs of Cork, Limerick and Waterford.[27]

Side by side with 'continuation' education, 'technical' education has simultaneously been developed. Defined as 'education in or pertaining to trades, manufactures, commerce and other industrial pursuits', it has come to embrace a wide variety of activities, from training for apprentices to courses leading to professional qualifications; inevitably, as most of those coming to the schools were already in employment, the great bulk of the teaching was done through evening classes. It has to be said, however, that outside Dublin, Cork, Limerick and Waterford, facilities were limited and advanced technological training over a wide field was really only possible in Dublin and to a lesser extent in Cork. The discrepancy between the demand and the supply was to lead, as we shall see in a moment, to radical rethinking of this whole subject.

Radical rethinking, indeed, was to be the keynote of the 1960s in almost every field of Irish education, but before turning to these revolutionary new developments, one fundamental change, almost coeval with the creation of the Department of Education itself, remains to be mentioned. In 1924 the old Junior, Middle and Senior Grade examinations were swept away, to be replaced by the Intermediate Certificate (usually taken by pupils leaving school at about sixteen) and by the Leaving Certificate, which was intended to be the culmination of the pupil's secondary education and to fit him for admission to a university. In preparing for these examinations all students were required to undergo a curriculum which must include Irish, English, history and geography, mathematics, another language or science or commerce, domestic science (for girls). It soon became the general tendency at both examinations to present five or six subjects and in the Leaving Certificate separate papers are set at the pass and honours levels. The most striking conclusion to be drawn from a study of the papers actually taken by the students at the Leaving Certificate – the more important of the two examinations from the career point of view – is that secondary education in Ireland retains to the present day a strong literary bias. A survey based on the 1962–3 examination, which is presumably not untypical, indicates that apart from Irish (the only 'essential' subject for the examination), boys almost all took English and mathematics and eighty-eight per cent of them took Latin. Physics and chemistry on the other hand were taken by about thirty per cent of candidates from boys' schools and French by only twenty-one per cent. Among girls a similar pattern declared itself, except that more of them (sixty-four per cent) took French and even fewer of them took any scientific subject – the percentages being 4·8 per cent for chemistry, 4·7 per cent for physics and 4·7 per cent for the combined physics and chemistry paper.

Only one per cent of all girls taking mathematics in that year obtained honours in the subject.[28]

There are of course obvious explanations for this bias. Partly, no doubt, it was due to the prohibitive financial cost of providing adequately for science teaching, partly to the shortage of good teachers, and partly also, perhaps, to the tendency of Church-run schools to favour the old and well-tried subjects. It is at any rate significant that Latin stands so high on the list and that modern languages are by comparison neglected. To some extent this latter phenomenon reflects the difficulty of obtaining modern language teachers who also fulfil the requirement to have a competent knowledge of Irish, but it may also be a consequence of the natural tendency of pupils, confronted by strong pressures to take Irish and Latin, to limit their commitments to those two languages. For a country that is committed to the European Community this would seem to be an unfortunate development, which has been accentuated both by the failure to develop any marked skill in speaking languages, and by the relapse – after fifteen years of free experimentation between 1925 and 1940 – into the system of set-texts which Patrick Pearse long ago denounced in *The Murder Machine* as one of the worst features of the old examination system.[29]

It is against this background of a school system that had struggled for forty years to produce an acceptable minimum of education for its children in the teeth of poverty, public indifference and official complacency that the exciting new developments of the last decade have to be seen. Without doubt the changes that have been set in motion are part and parcel of the expansionist mood through which the country has been passing. Certainly, they could not have been envisaged without the notable upsurge in the Irish economy which followed – or, as some would say, coincided with – the adoption of the Whitaker Report. But no less important than the readiness of the government to pour money into education has been the psychological impulse towards reform which derives from the increasing tendency of Irishmen to measure their achievements by the standards of Western Europe. There was a curiously apt symbolism in the fact that the first scientific study in depth of the educational situation in Ireland – *Investment in Education* – should have been produced under the joint sponsorship of OECD and the Department of Education. Appointed in 1962 and reporting some three years later, the survey team provided at long last the statistical and factual basis for the schemes of practical improvement which have proliferated since the publication of their findings.*

The impact of this report – at least upon informed opinion – was in many respects shattering. It was difficult to decide which of its reve-

* The group responsible for this epoch-making document were Mr Patrick Lynch, Director (University College, Dublin); Mr W. J. Hyland (Statistics Office of the United Nations, formerly of the Central Statistics Office. Dublin); Dr Martin O'Donoghue (Trinity College, Dublin); Mr P. U. O'Nualláin (Inspector of Secondary Schools).

lations was the more alarming – the extent to which the needs of the present had not been fulfilled, or the extent to which the needs of the future had not been anticipated. Central to both these deficiencies was the fact, which the survey demonstrated with crushing finality, that the 'flow' into secondary education was far below what was either desirable or needful. On the basis of its findings it has been estimated that of the 57,000 children who left primary schools in 1957, only about 40,000 went on to some form of post-primary education. Of these, only some 10,000 would sit for the Leaving Certificate and fewer than 2,000 would end in the universities.[30] Not only that, but the report also uncovered important regional and social distinctions, though in this it did no more than give substantial foundation to what might in any event have been supposed. Post-primary education, it pointed out, was more readily available in the prosperous and populous parts of the country which, naturally, had more and better equipped schools. Similarly, the professional and white-collar workers, who were twenty per cent of the working population in 1961, were shown to have obtained sixty-five per cent of the university places awarded on the result of the Leaving Certificate examination of that year, whereas the manual workers, accounting for twenty-five per cent of the working population, gained only two per cent of university places.[31]

For these phenomena – not all of them peculiar to Ireland by any means – there are various, as yet insufficiently investigated, explanations. The fact that Irish secondary education – and still more, university education – traditionally rested partially on a fee-paying basis is no doubt one reason for the imbalance which has resulted, but it is not a completely convincing one, since Irish school fees are in general very low. University costs are, of course, heavier and the lack of adequate state or local government aid must certainly have had an inhibiting effect upon university applications.* Nevertheless, other reasons for the 'wastage' among school-leavers have to be found and they are not obscure. The lure of paid employment, geographical remoteness from centres of good teaching, the liability of school careers to be interrupted by family emigration, an inherited suspicion in certain classes of the community that secondary or higher education is at worst useless, at best for 'them' and not for 'us' – all these have played, and still play, their part in preventing the country from tapping all the resources of talent at its disposal.[32]

To evoke this talent and to give it the opportunity it needs has become the dominant concern of the Department of Education, which has been fortunate in attracting for this very reason some of the best of the

* In secondary day-schools in the early 1960s they ranged from as little as £10 per annum to £100; in boarding-schools the range was from about £75 to £150 per annum and upwards. At universities tuition fees in most subjects worked out at between £50 and £65 for arts, £80 for applied sciences, and around £100 for medicine and allied subjects. But to these would have to be added the cost of subsistence in and out of term.

younger politicians to have achieved office during the past decade. These new developments are so very recent that it is quite impossible at the time of writing to assess them in terms of results, but the mere list of the major schemes emanating from successive ministers from about 1963 onwards conveys something of the atmosphere of urgency that has suddenly pervaded this hitherto quiescent area of Irish life. The list, then, includes a much more determined drive than hitherto to consolidate and amalgamate the small or rural schools; the building of comprehensive schools designed to combine both grammar-school and vocational courses for scattered communities; a massive development of vocational education in general, with particular emphasis upon the establishment of regional Colleges of Technology; the provision of free secondary education, though on terms that make the participation of Protestant schools difficult, and also of free transportation; the allocation of much larger funds for scholarships, especially to the universities; the revision of the Leaving Certificate syllabus to allow of greater specialisation.

Not all of these proposals, of course, have met with unqualified approval. Local patriotism has put up a sturdy rearguard defence against the suppression of the smaller schools; secondary school authorities (especially those which run the more expensive schools) have anticipated serious difficulties in implementing free education; and educationists generally have looked askance at the Department's lurch towards specialisation at a time when elsewhere the tendency has been in the opposite direction. More recently, in 1971, considerable friction was aroused by the proposal of the Minister for Education to rationalise post-primary instruction in twenty-five centres throughout the country by merging publicly-owned (and multi-denominational) vocational schools with private schools run by Catholic religious orders. The new schools were to be vested in trustees to be appointed by the Catholic bishops in whose dioceses they were located, and on their managing committees the private school owners were to have two thirds of the representation. Despite these supposed concessions, the private schools remained unappeased by a scheme which so obviously struck at their autonomy, while Protestants were not unnaturally uneasy at the prospect of their children being placed under predominantly Catholic management. While the issues were still being debated, the Minister acted in the spirit of his proposals by creating in two rapidly-expanding Dublin suburbs what were called 'community schools', but which in effect involved the submersion of the existing public vocational schools in new units to be created with the co-operation of the religious orders, and to be, in the main, under Catholic ownership and control. After pressure in the Dáil from both Fine Gael and Labour, the Minister modified his plan to admit a broader base both for the trustees and the board of management, but the episode had given a painful shock to Protestant susceptibilities at the precise moment when it seemed more urgent than ever to convince northern

Unionists that the Republic was not a theocratic state and that their co-religionists were not exposed to sectarian pressures.[33]

But all these controversies have been over-shadowed by the high drama which since 1967 has surrounded the question of future university development. The 'solution' of the university question that had been reached in 1908 had proved much more enduring than it looked at the time. As we saw earlier, this had created a National University, consisting of the three University Colleges at Dublin, Cork and Galway, while leaving the independent status of Dublin University intact. The three University Colleges, after a period of slow growth and financial stringency, began to expand very rapidly from about the time of the Second World War, but while they were rooting themselves more and more deeply in the life of the country, the position of Trinity College remained embarrassingly anomalous. The end of British rule had left that ancient foundation impoverished and exposed, yet although it remained firmly embedded in the popular mind as an 'anti-national' institution, successive governments, genuinely anxious to promote good relations with the Protestant minority, had almost ostentatiously refrained from any interference with the College. The same, however, could scarcely be said of the Roman Catholic hierarchy, which at frequent intervals reminded the faithful that they were forbidden, without a special dispensation, to attend the university With or without a dispensation, some did in fact continue to come to Trinity, but never in sufficient numbers to enable the university to fill all its available places, and the authorities were increasingly drawn to rely upon the foreign – more specifically, British – connection that had always been important to them. Even with this reinforcement, however, the College remained poor, isolated and in a state of apparent decline until the end of the Second World War. Thereafter, the influx of students from outside grew much greater. By 1952–3, out of a student population of 2,000, slightly more than a third came from outside Ireland. Ten years later, in a student population of 3,000, the foreign proportion had gone up to nearly fifty per cent.

It began to seem in fact as if one of the two fully autonomous universities in the republic was becoming little more than an annexe of the English educational system. This was never the university's own intention and from 1962 onwards the most strenuous efforts were made to reduce the non-Irish element.* There was a sound prudential reason

* Commentators from outside Trinity College seem to find difficulty in accepting this. The present writer, who became Senior Tutor responsible for admissions at this very time, can testify that a rapid reduction in foreign numbers was the prime objective; this policy has since been carried much further. It is also important to remember in the context of partition that of all the universities in the Republic, Trinity has much the closest connection with Northern Ireland. In 1952-3 students from the six counties numbered 386 (as against a total of 111 for the three Colleges of the National University combined); in 1962-3 the respective totals were 472 for Trinity, 128 for the National University.

for doing so, for almost simultaneously with the rise in foreign students had come an important new development in government policy. Until just after the Second World War, whereas the three Colleges of the National University had been heavily financed by the government, the grants paid to Trinity had been negligible. In 1947, recognising that the old foundation was, or could become, a national asset, the then government began to put its payments to Trinity on a different basis. By 1952–3 the university was receiving £100,000 a year and ten years later this annual grant had gone up to £250,000. This put it above University College, Galway, roughly on a par with University College, Cork but still decidedly below University College, Dublin. At the latter date (1962–3), student numbers were 1,785 for University College, Cork, 1,471 for University College, Galway, 3,188 for Trinity College, Dublin and 6,272 for University College, Dublin.*

With the demand for university places rising and government expenditure increasing, it was perhaps inevitable that the long and calm autonomy the universities had enjoyed should sooner or later be broken into by a commission of inquiry. Such a commission – a very powerful one – was appointed in 1960 to investigate not merely the universities, but the whole field of higher education. It worked long and laboriously, eventually in 1967 producing an admirable and far-reaching report. It recommended among other things that the federal structure of 1908 should be dissolved and that UCC, UCG and UCD should be established as independent universities; that the constitution of Trinity College, should be 're-stated' – with the implication that it should remain a separate entity; that no new university should be established, but that 'New Colleges' should be established in various centres, commencing with Dublin and Limerick; that increased financial aid be provided to open the universities 'as fully and freely as possible' to all qualified students; that a Technological Authority be established to promote and assist technological training and research and that a permanent Commission for Higher Education should be set up to keep the problems of university finance and expansion under constant review.[34]

Almost at the very moment when this long-considered document was being made public the then Minister for Education – the late Mr Donogh O'Malley – made his own independent foray into the field. In an announcement that immediately became famous, and which has dominated discussion of the whole question of higher education ever since, he declared that the time had come to end the isolation of Trinity from the mainstream of national life, and that he proposed to achieve this by promoting a merger of the two Dublin colleges – Trinity

* The totals include part-time and full-time students for all save Trinity, which lists only the full-time students. The actual grants in 1962–3 were: £193,380 for Galway, £209,000 for Cork, £275,250 for Trinity and £942,500 for University College, Dublin. This last figure is swollen by a capital grant of £424,000, and the Trinity figure included a capital grant of £50,000 for repair of historic buildings.

College and University College – to form a new University of Dublin.*
Many explanations have been advanced to explain the Minister's
dramatic and unilateral intervention, and as he died suddenly the following year it may be that we shall never know the whole truth. He
himself presented it as a determination, not only to give Trinity the
opportunity of 'taking the final step across the threshold of the mansion to which it properly belongs, the Irish nation', but also to ensure
that the universities used money provided by the state to the best advantage, by avoiding wasteful duplication and achieving those economies of scale which always haunt ministerial thinking but which
higher institutions of learning mysteriously find it so difficult to achieve
by themselves. No-one doubts the sincerity of these motives, but there
may also have been another one less easy to proclaim from the roof-
tops. It has been suggested – and the suggestion persists despite official
denials – that to make TCD and UCD one flesh would be to circumvent
the ecclesiastical ban against the former. If this were indeed an object
of policy it would be open to the criticism that to disrupt the entire
structure of two important institutions with the aim (admittedly, among
other aims) of finding a devious way round a prohibition which ought
to be fought in the open, would be to betray a curious sense of values.
Since the ban was removed in 1970 by the Catholic hierarchy, the question as to whether or not it influenced the government initiative is less
important than the fact that as the official plan for a merger subsequently grew and changed, the rude surgery whereby it was proposed
to 'distribute' subjects arbitrarily between the two Colleges has not only
run into administrative difficulties but has aroused intense academic hostility. The situation remains fluid and all prognostications are hazard-
ous. It begins to seem, however, as if there may be growing support for
the notion that Dublin should be allowed to keep two separate universities but that co-operation between them, and avoidance of duplication, should be achieved through the Higher Education Authority
which the Commission recommended and which was in fact brought
into being in September 1968. It may be that here lies the germ of progress for the future.

It will be obvious that with so much in ferment at every level in the
country's educational system, no easy generalisations are possible. Indeed, with the action still developing, any kind of summing up is quite
out of the question. But it may be possible to make two points in conclusion. One is that whatever the issue of the various controversies now
at boiling point, there can be no going back to the old stagnation. For
good or ill, Irish education finds itself at last in the mid-twentieth

* He made his announcement on 18 April 1967 when the Commission
on Higher Education had just issued a summary of its report and recommendations; the Commission's main report appeared later that year. The
Minister's statement and the immediate academic reactions to it can be
followed in *Studies* (Summer, 1967) which devoted virtually the whole
issue to the university question.

century world. Yet – and here is the second point that needs to be made – the fact that this happened because an economic expansion has enabled it to happen, has occurred, one might say, largely in response to the needs created by that expansion, brings its own dangers. In other countries where rapid educational advance has been carried out under government initiative, it has not been uncommon for a conflict to develop between those who champion what they conceive to be the values of a liberal education – the freedom to question, to teach, to learn, and to engage in independent research without pressure from external forces – and those who see in the whole machinery of school and university a means of fulfilling specific objectives dictated by the state or other agencies to supply the needs, real or supposed, of the community. That a country's educational system has a resopnsibility to meet the reasonable demands of society few would nowadays dispute, but that this responsibility should be balanced by the kind of freedom under which alone universities have been able to flourish in the past, is surely no less essential. To reconcile freedom and responsibility has always been the classic dilemma and it does not get any easier. In Ireland now, politicians, administrators, managers of all kinds, speak with clamant and insistent voices, but perhaps it is not altogether idle to suppose that the words uttered by John Newman in Dublin in the summer of 1852 may still waken a sympathetic echo. Anticipating the demands of those who make 'utility' their touchstone in judging a university training and who ask 'what is the real worth in the market of the article called "a liberal education" on the supposition that it does not teach us definitely how to advance our manufactures, or to improve our lands, or to better our civil economy', his reply is still not without contemporary relevance:

This process of training by which the intellect, instead of being formed or sacrificed to some particular or accidental purpose, some specific trade or profession, or study or science, is disciplined for its own sake, for the perception of its own proper object, and for its own highest culture, is called liberal education; and though there is no one in whom it is carried as far as is conceivable . . . yet there is scarcely anyone but may gain an idea of what real training is, and at least look towards it, and make its true scope and result, not something else, his standard of excellence. . . . And to set forth the right standard, and to train according to it, and to help forward all students towards it according to their various capacities, this I conceive to be the business of a university.[35]

(iii) WELFARE

It is a natural though melancholy consequence of the way an independent Ireland came into being that its history should have been written primarily in terms of political and ideological strife with, latterly, some attention being directed also to the economic factors which are inextricably bound up with that strife. But if the inquirer turns away from the high drama of this familiar and overlit stage, and seeks to find how far revolutions, wars and changes of government have benefited the ordinary citizen in his daily life, the answer is often difficult to elicit. Recently, however, partly as the result of work done in the universities, partly because of the emergence of new centres of research – most notably the Economic and Social Research Institute and the Institute of Public Administration – it has begun to be possible to fill some of the gaps, even though the material for a definitive study is still not as detailed or as plentiful as could be wished. What follows here is an attempt, necessarily brief, to use some of the material these bodies have provided in order to illustrate how, during nearly fifty years of self-government, the twenty-six counties have been drawn gradually but inexorably into the twentieth century world of social welfare. Three main themes have been selected for treatment – health, social insurance and social assistance – but linked with these will be a fourth, the steady adaptation of the structure of Irish local government to meet all sorts of requirements its British originators had never contemplated.

In nothing was this administrative revolution so apparent as in the domain of health and public assistance. We saw earlier that legislation of 1923–5 had swept away some of the more archaic and less efficient machinery – the boards of guardians and the rural district councils – and had vested their functions in the county councils, or more strictly in the boards of health and assistance which were in effect sub-committees of those councils; and since the councils retained the control of the mental health service, the tuberculosis service and the school medical service – all initiated before the transfer of power – it is obvious that the process of concentration of power was already well advanced.* Yet there still remained considerable differentiation of actual

* For the administrative changes wrought by the Local Government Act of 1925, see above pp. 482-4. It should be added here that the sanitary and preventive health services operated by the councils through their new boards applied only to the countryside; the town authorities remained responsible for these services in their areas. The tuberculosis service dated from the Tuberculosis Prevention (Ireland) Act of 1908 which gave power to county councils and county borough corporations to provide sanatoria and clinics for the treatment of this disease, at that time regarded as perhaps the deadliest of all diseases prevalent in Ireland. Shortage of money combined with apathy to prevent anything like an adequate programme of building until, as we saw earlier (p. 572), Dr Noel Browne transformed the situation almost overnight. The medical inspection and treatment of children attending national schools had been provided for by the Public Health (Medical Treatment of Children (Ireland) Act of 1919) legislation of the British parliament passed, by one of those familiar ironies of Irish history, at the very moment when the King's writ was ceasing to run over a large part of the country. The basis for,

executive responsibility. Thus, while the Local Government Act of 1925 provided for the appointment of county medical officers who would be responsible not only for the tuberculosis and school medical services, but also for the various preventive services in both town and country, these new officials were excluded alike from the dispensaries, the general hospitals, and the treatment of mental diseases.[36]

Clearly, there was still a good deal to be done by way of rationalisation. At the higher administrative level this was carried further during the years of the Second World War when the emergence of the county managers led to further unified control, signalised by the disappearance of the boards of health and assistance and the transfer of their functions to the managers.* But the consolidation of the services themselves had to wait until after 'the emergency' was over. By then the climate of opinion in the country had greatly changed. There was mounting dissatisfaction with the existing services, partly because, as we shall see in a moment, they had been demonstrably inadequate ever since independence and in some of their most important aspects were still associated in the popular mind with the hated Poor Law; partly because the middle classes, driven by inflationary pressures to use such facilities as were provided, were now learning for the first time what the poor had to put up with and were becoming correspondingly vociferous in their criticisms; but most of all, no doubt, because the welfare state then being established in Britain cast a long shadow across the Irish Sea. Out of the ferment of discussion – official, medical, even episcopal† – there came a major reorganisation of the whole health administration. The war was scarcely over when the Ministers and Secretaries (Amendment) Act of 1946 at last separated Health from Local Government and brought virtually the whole array of services under the control of one responsible Minister. The new Department, which actually began to function in 1947, was charged with the prevention and cure of disease, and with the treatment and care of the mentally ill or the physically handicapped; with the training and registration of personnel and the control over the appointment of the appropriate local officers; with the initiation and direction of research; with the enforcement of pure food regulations and control of proprietary medical and toilet preparations; with the registration of births, deaths and marriages and also with the collection, preparation and dissemination of

---

a somewhat rudimentary Maternity and Child Welfare Service, to be developed both by local authorities and voluntary agencies, was also established by a British Act of Parliament (Notification of Births (Extension) Act, 1915) at a time when most Irishmen had other things on their minds.

* For the county managers, see above, p. 484.

† The most striking contribution to the debate was made by the then Bishop of Clonfert, Dr Dignan, who proposed a thoroughly comprehensive scheme of social security in 1944 – much too comprehensive, it was soon made plain, for the official mind to digest or the official purse to afford.

health statistics of all kinds.[87]

Side by side with this growth in the power of the central authority marched, almost inevitably, a simplification of local health administration. The Health Act of 1947 concentrated an increasing amount of responsibility into the hands of the county Councils – in effect into those of the county managers – and by taking away from the urban districts (other than the county boroughs) their supervision of preventive services, succeeded in reducing the number of authorities charged with this function from about ninety to thirty-one, composed of the twenty-seven county councils and the four county boroughs of Cork, Dublin, Limerick, and Waterford.* The ancient distinction between 'health' and 'public assistance' authorities remained for a little longer, but it too was swept away when the Health Act of 1953 transferred all services remotely connected with medical care, cure or prevention to the health authorities. The most important effect of .this, though it appeared on the surface to be little more than a change of nomenclature, was that the general hospitals previously under the public assistance authorities were placed firmly under the health authorities, thus at last removing from those institutions the stigma of the Poor Law which had been attached to them for over a hundred years. In more general terms, the end result of these various legislative reforms was that the county councils as health authorities thenceforward administered all the health services of the country (Dublin, Cork, Limerick and Waterford being, as we have seen, special cases), except for mental health; this in most instances was the responsibility of joint boards on which neighbouring counties were represented.

It is time now to turn from the machinery to the product and to ask what sort of health service actually emerged from all this juggling of administrative agencies. No single generalisation is possible, except perhaps to stress the importance of the Second World War as a watershed. Up to 1939, indeed even up to 1945, the provision of health services for people who could not afford to pay for private treatment changed little, either in scope or in character, from what it had been in the last years of British rule. It was scanty, old-fashioned and frequently humiliating to those whose poverty left them with no other alternative. It is true that the county medical officers were able to make considerable if unspectacular progress in the curbing of outbreaks of infectious diseases, and in prophylactic measures of which diphtheria immunisation was probably the most important. But in the day to day care of the sick poor, the resources of the local authorities remained very much what they had been – dispensaries and general hospitals, both frequently old, uncomfortable and inadequate, and both administered on the basis of a stringent means test. Things could hardly have been otherwise so long as the services had to be paid for mainly

* The four county boroughs were subsequently fused with the counties of the same name for health purposes giving a total of twenty-seven health authorities.

out of local rates, and we need scarcely look further than the total cost of local authority health services in 1937–8 – amounting only to £2·75 million – to find the most fundamental explanation for the meagreness of what they had to offer. Even ten years later, when expenditure had about doubled to reach £5·7 million (due mainly to inflation) the local authorities were still supplying over eighty per cent of the cost of their services, while the state contribution as recently as 1947–8 was no more than £830,000.

Thereafter the picture changed swiftly and radically. Not only was the burden of expenditure adjusted so that it came to be shared in roughly equal proportions by state and local authorities, but the actual amount of that expenditure climbed steeply. In a single decade it mounted from the £5·7 million of 1947–8 already mentioned (the year in which the local authorities met eighty per cent of the cost) to £16·4 million in 1958–9. Admittedly, this seemingly striking advance occurred – like the smaller one during the Second World War – at a time of rapid inflation; if this is taken into account and the expenditure of 1958–9 restated in 1947–8 terms (the Consumer Price Index in the meantime having risen from 100 to 147) the true figure would be about twelve million pounds.* Even so, this represents a doubling of the outlay corresponding, as we shall see in a moment, to a very real improvement in the services themselves, a fact reflected in the percentage of the country's Gross National Product that was devoted to current public expenditure on the country's health services. This rose from 1·72 in 1947 to 2·74 in 1958, an increase which, remarkable as it is, would without question be even more remarkable if private and capital expenditure were also to be taken into account.[38]

Private expenditure is for obvious reasons impossible to estimate with any accuracy, but capital costs are more easily traced. These – arising principally from the building of new hospitals – have for much of the past forty years been met in the first instance by the brilliantly successful expedient of the Hospital Sweepstakes. Begun in 1930 as a tentative experiment, they were put on a more permanent footing by the Public Hospitals Act of 1933. This set up a statutory body, the Hospitals Trust Board, to administer moneys raised by sweepstakes on the principal horse-races of each year. The money realised by the sweepstakes was lodged in a hospital fund from which the responsible Minister, advised by another body, the Hospitals Commission, was empowered to make grants, not only to the state institutions, but to the voluntary hospitals as well, nearly all of which had deficits and nearly all of which (the Adelaide Hospital was for long a notable exception on grounds of principle) were ready and eager to receive assistance. Up to 1958 the total amount accruing to the fund from the sweepstakes was

* A recent estimate of expenditure suggests that in 1963-4 it was running at £22.5 million (in current, not 1947 values) and that this represented 2.7 per cent of the GNP (P.R. Kaim-Caudle, *Social Policy in the Irish Republic* (London, 1967), p. 29).

£44·5 million. Of this, £11 million was paid out in stamp duty, leaving £33·5 million for health purposes. The voluntary hospitals absorbed nearly a third of this amount between 1933 and 1958, but there still remained some £23 million for capital expenditure. Up to the Second World War advances for this purpose were distinctly meagre, amounting only to £1·8 million, in addition to £3 million handed over before the fund had been established. Between 1934 and 1948 a further £1·6 million was made available, but at that point the situation was transformed, as we saw earlier, by Dr Browne's onslaught on the problem of tuberculosis, and between 1948 and 1958 nearly £24 million was expended on the building programme, in addition to another £3·6 million deriving from the local authorities themselves or from other sources. So great was the outflow, indeed, that for the latter part of that period (1953-7) the state actually had to supplement the fund by nearly £7 million more. To sum up, therefore, between 1948 and 1958, spending on the construction or reconstruction of hospitals amounted to £27·4 million, of which £17 million came from the sweepstakes, £6·8 million from the state subvention and £3·6 million from the local authorities. Of this total, tuberculosis hospitals accounted for £9·3 million, and maternity and children's hospitals absorbed £2·5 million, this last figure being just short of the £2·6 million spent on mental hospitals and homes.[39]

If we now turn to ask what sort of benefits did all this expenditure confer upon the citizen we shall find the key to the answer in what are nowadays called the General Medical Services, but which are in reality the modern version of the old dispensary system. The persons entitled to use these services were defined in the Health Act of 1953 as those 'unable to provide by their own industry or other lawful means the medical or surgical appliances necessary for themselves and for their dependants'. To become eligible every applicant had to be considered individually in relation to his means or lack of means. If he satisfied the means test, his name was then placed on the General Medical Register and he was issued with a blue card, annually renewable. On presentation of this card he was then entitled to the services of the District Medical Officer (the equivalent of the old dispensary doctor) and to medicines and appliances free of charge. It is a striking commentary on the standard of living in the country that in 1958 some 28·5 per cent of the population was recorded as being eligible for this free attention.[40] The remainder of the population had to pay for any general services it made use of, but a very large proportion – between eighty and ninety per cent of the whole – was entitled to use at low cost the Hospital and Specialist Services provided under the 1953 Health Act. This not only included the lower income group already on the register as being in possession of a blue card, but also applied to anyone (and his dependants) who was employed on manual labour and insured under the Social Welfare Acts, and to other employed and insured persons (with their dependants) who were paid less than £1,200 a year (originally £800 but changed in 1965). In addition, the services were open to all whose family income was less than £1,200 a year and their dependants; to agricultural workers whose holdings did not exceed £50 valuation and their dependants – over eighty per cent of all farming families; to children attending the national schools who received hospital treatment for ailments discovered at school medical examinations; and to anyone else who could not without undue hardship provide such services from his own resources.

The benefits thus available to these large classes of the population were considerable – considerable, at least in relation to the Irish past if not in relation to what the contemporary world outside had to offer. For those on the General Register all specialist and hospital treatment was free of charge. All others treated under the Health Act paid very small amounts per day for hospital care and for specialist consultation, fixed initially at ten shillings a day for the former and 2/6 per consultation for the latter. Apart from these basic services the Act provided for a number of other facilities, though their availability depended very much on the economic status of the patient. In the so-called 'higher income group' (over £1,200 a year) which in 1959 was about fifteen per cent of the population, the only free services were those relating to infectious diseases, child welfare clinics, and health examination in the national schools or medical treatment arising therefrom; since many of these families did not use either national schools or welfare clinics they were to all intents and purposes outside the system.[41] The 'middle income group' – that is the group above those who were on the General Register and accounting for fifty-five per cent of the population – could use not only the General Hospital and Specialist Services, but also the services relating to Maternity and Infant Care and those concerned with mental illness. For the lower income-group – consisting of all those who were on the General Register – there were, free and in addition to the facilities already mentioned, dental and eye and ear services, free milk, maternity cash grants, disablement allowances and access to county homes in case of dire need and destitution.

It would be naïve to suppose that because these various kinds of assistance have become available on a larger scale than before that all is for the best in the best of all possible worlds. Even in far more affluent countries with far longer traditions of welfare, islands of hardship and neglect are constantly being discovered, and it was not to be expected that Ireland could wipe out overnight the effects of generations of parsimony and indifference. An example – probably the most extreme example and certainly the one which is attracting most attention today – is the treatment of mental illness. To provide such treatment for those classes of the population that were eligible for it – i.e. those who were also eligible for the Hospital and Specialist Services – a series of acts of the Oireachtas had laid upon the mental health authorities the obligation to supply proper and sufficient accommodation for patients in need of it, whether in a district mental hospital, a county home, or a variety of other institutions. Elaborate regulations surrounded the committal of any individual to these centres and the Inspector of Mental Hospitals was expected to ensure that improper detentions did not occur. No doubt these duties were faithfully carried out, but illicit detention did not exhaust the ills to which the system was prone and in recent years there has been a mounting volume of criticism against the way in which the mentally ill (and indeed the aged also) are cared for. If there have been deficiencies, there have been many well-identified causes for these deficiencies. Not the least of these has been the rise in the number of the mentally ill – more accurately, perhaps, in the number of those who are diagnosed nowadays as mentally ill. At the end of 1957 there were in the Republic nearly 22,000 people officially classed as being in that category, of whom almost 20,000 were in the mental health authorities' institutions. A decade later a government report indicated that mental illness might be more prevalent in Ireland than in any other country and that the rate of beds provided for the mentally ill 'appears to be the highest in the world'. At any one time, it was reckoned, one in every seventy people in the country over the age of twenty-four was in a mental hospital. When to these figures is added another estimated 24,000 mentally handicapped of whom only a fraction ever received institutional treatment, and to these again the 10,000 old people in county homes many of whom suffered from some degree of mental disability, it is clear that there exists a problem whose surface has barely been scratched.[42] Many things have combined to make it a complex and peculiarly intractable problem – the large number of elderly people in the population, the low marriage rate, the burden on some women of bringing up large families in adverse conditions, alcoholism, inbreeding in the remoter parts of the country, the pressures of rural isolation, and, above all perhaps, the selective effects of the emigration which for many years has tended to take the young and vigorous and to leave behind those less well fitted to make their way in the world. But whatever the hierarchy of causes, the facts of the situation have become so starkly self-evident that advance in this sector is now widely recognised to be among the most urgent priorities in any future reform of the health services.

That such reform is already overdue – not just in mental treatment, but over a wide front – was a major contention of the principal opposition parties at the general election of 1965. Both the Fine Gael and Labour parties criticised the means test and the indignities to which it still often exposed the poorer sections of the population, and Fine Gael in particular denounced the system as administratively cumbersome and of varying effectiveness in different parts of the country. Moreover, the fact that the existing structure made no provision for free services for the bulk of the population led the two parties to advocate a comprehensive service based on a free choice of family doctor, embracing hospital and specialist services, and financed in large measure by compulsory social insurance contributions. The principal difference between the programmes was that whereas Labour came out in favour of a universal service covering everyone, the Fine Gael proposals would have extended the free services to eighty-five per cent of the people, while at the same time abolishing the hated means test for all sections of that eighty-five per cent.[48]

Against this philosophy of a greatly expanded scheme of welfare there has been ranged the opposition of a government still, in this sphere at least, apparently wedded to a tradition of laissez-faire, backed by a medical profession which, as in many other parts of the world, sees in the means test an essential instrument for the preservation of private practice and a differential fee-structure, and which also, to put the argument on a broader basis, resents the diminution of the doctor's independence which it feels would result from increased intervention by the state. Nevertheless, the tide appears to be flowing irresistibly in the direction of 'socialised' medicine and a government White Paper, issued in 1966 as a basis for further discussion, envisaged a considerable expansion of the services and a certain degree of liberalisation in the way in which they were administered. But even these proposals did not include the abolition of the means test and they made it plain that a comprehensive and free service for the middle and higher income groups was not immediately in prospect. It was hardly likely, therefore, that they would satisfy the protagonists of reform and, in fact, the debate continues. At the time of writing (1972) there are indications that the pace of change has once more begun to quicken. A new Health Act, passed in 1970, has led to substantial reorganisation of the hospital services, a compulsory health contribution scheme was introduced in 1971 for the middle income group, and in the general medical services a choice of doctor began to be introduced during 1972.

It would, of course, be unreal to assess this debate simply in terms of the health services alone. Other manifestations of the welfare state have also to be taken into account and especially those relating to what is broadly, and sometimes loosely, described as social security.* In the Irish context three separate kinds of benefit are in question – family allowances, social insurance and social assistance. The first of these may be described as 'public service welfare' granted indiscriminately irrespective of contributions of need – and in Ireland it is a type of welfare

* Some definitions of social security include expenditure by the state on education, housing and health, as well as cash payments to individuals for social purposes, but for the purpose of the present discussion I have followed the definition adopted in the International Labour Office paper 'The Cost of Social Security, 1949-57', cited by R. P. Kaim-Caudle in 'Social Security in Ireland and Western Europe', Economic Research Institute, Paper No. 20 (Dublin, June 1964), pp. 9-10. This identifies as social security services those services 'the object of which is (a) to grant curative or preventive medical care or (b) to maintain income in case of involuntary loss of earnings or of an important part of earnings or (c) to grant supplementary incomes to persons having family responsibilities'.

represented only by children's allowances. Introduced as far back as 1944, these were then payable for third and subsequent children in a family. In 1952 they were extended to second children and in 1963 to first children – the allowances being paid out of general taxation and to all parents irrespective of their employment status, without a means test. In 1969–70 the annual payment was £6 for the first child, £9 for the second and £16 for each subsequent child. In addition to these universal allowances there were also certain other, roughly analogous, payments on a selective basis – for example, maternity grants and allowances linked to social insurance, supplemental family allowances paid to certain state employees (school teachers, members of the Defence Forces and some civil servants), as well as remissions of income tax where applicable.*

If children's allowances were a creation of the comparatively recent past, the same cannot be said of either social insurance or of social assistance, both of which were inherited in a rudimentary form from

* Any overall assessment of state benefits to the family would of course have to include the medical and educational facilities discussed earlier in this book. It would also have to take account of subsidised housing. In Ireland this dated from the late nineteenth century, local authorities having provided cottages for agricultural labourers since 1883 and town dwellings since 1890. Between those dates and the early 1960s the local authorities had built about 180,000 houses, roughly a quarter of all the dwellings in the state. In this enterprise they were stimulated from time to time by contributions from central funds, amounting latterly to about two-thirds of the loan charges incurred by the local authorities up to a certain price limit per house or apartment. So large have the subsidies been, in fact, that it is arguable that many rents have been fixed, or held, so low as to be hopelessly uneconomic. The rate of building in recent years has not been rapid, certainly not rapid enough to replace the 50,000 local authority houses – outside Cork and Dublin – which as long ago as 1960 were described as unfit for human habitation. If the two big cities were included this situation would be revealed as being even worse than appears on the surface; indeed, it is now so bad that any perceptible increase in population would precipitate a crisis. To avoid such a crisis 12,000 – 14,000 houses a year needed to be built between 1960 and 1970 – twice the rate actually attained in 1964, but still one of the lowest in Europe (R. P. Kaim-Caudle, *Social Policy in the Irish Republic*, chap. vii). A more recent official estimate reckons that the number of houses needed for the period 1966 to 1971 was 9,000 a year, but that from then on the rate would rise (partly because of expanding demand, partly because of obsolescence of existing houses) until in the mid-seventies 15,000 to 17,000 houses would be needed each year. Very considerable expansion has already taken place and capital expenditure on housing rose from £65 million in 1970-71 to about £87 million in 1971-2. In the latter year a record total of 15,500 were completed, suggesting that the target for the mid-seventies might be achieved ahead of schedule; it is noteworthy that of 15,500 houses built in 1971-2 private enterprise accounted for about two-thirds (*Housing in the Seventies*, 1969 (Prl. 658), p. 9; *Review of 1971 and Outlook for 1972*, p. 73).

the old regime. These derived in their original, narrow sense, from the acts of parliament which had marked Britain's own first hesitant steps along the road to the welfare state. The first of these, the Old Age Pensions Act of 1908, had provided non-contributory pensions for old people over seventy at the initial rate of five shillings, or twenty-five new pence, a week (raised in 1919 to ten shillings, or fifty new pence) subject to a severe means test and certain other restrictions; in 1920 this legislation was supplemented by an equivalent pension to every blind person of not less than fifty years of age who was incapacitated for any work for which eyesight was essential. The second part of the inheritance from Britain, the National Insurance Act of 1911, instituted a compulsory insurance scheme whereby virtually all manual workers and non-manual workers earning less than £160 a year (£250 after 1919) were to be insured by contributions from the state, the employers and the workers themselves, to a scheme which was intended to provide sickness benefit for those eligible at the rate of 10 shillings (50 p.) a week for a man and 7/6 (37.5 p.) for a woman (15 shillings (75 p.) and 12 shillings (60 p.) respectively after 1920); full benefit was to be paid for the first half-year, reduced benefit thereafter without limitation of time.* This same legislation also provided a minimal scheme of unemployment insurance, but this was radically amended by the Unemployment Insurance Act of 1920. That Act applied unemployment insurance to almost all industries except agriculture, covering manual workers and also non-manual workers earning less than £250 a year. Unemployed people who were able and willing to work but could find no one to use their labour were to receive fifteen shillings (75 p.) a week for a man and twelve shillings (60 p.) a week for a woman, up to a period of fifteen, later twenty-six, weeks; after 1921, originally as a temporary measure, these amounts were supplemented for married men by five shillings (25 p.) a week for a wife and one shilling (5 p.) a week for each child. Even by the standards of the time these payments were meagre enough and the expectation seems to have been that they would be supplemented – as in many cases, of course, they were – by savings, charity or other kinds of assistance.

Such, then, were the foundations on which an Irish social insurance system was to be built. At first, admittedly, the native government showed little inclination to do more than keep the existing system in being. Indeed, in 1924 the old age pension was actually cut for some categories by a shilling (5 p.) a week and not restored until 1928. It was only after Fianna Fáil came to power in 1932 that a slightly more humane approach began to be apparent with the reduction of the age for blind pensions to thirty and the decision to assess applications for old age pensions without reference to the means possessed by other members of the family. Thereafter, there were frequent changes in the

* This legislation also included a rudimentary scheme for the provision of medical care for employees, but largely because of the opposition of the medical profession, Ireland was excluded from that section of the Act.

amount of both blind and old-age pensions in a vain attempt to keep pace with the rising cost of living, while the Social Welfare Act of 1948 further reduced the age-qualification for blind pensions to twenty-one and eased the conditions under which such pensions would be granted. Nevertheless, despite the passing of no less than nine further Social Welfare Acts between 1951 and 1963, the age at which old people could qualify for a pension remained at seventy and the means test still limited the applicant to an independent income of not more than about £2 15s. od. (£2.75 p.) a week; moreover, the amount paid out was on a graduated basis, the maximum for a pensioner whose means did not exceed roughly a pound a week being 35 shillings (£1.75 p.) a week in 1964, falling to as little as 5 shillings (25 p.) a week where his own means amounted to approximately £2 15s. od. (£2.75 p.) a week. Even with such stringent and not over-generous provisions, the annual cost to the state of these non-contributory pensions amounted to between £10 and £11 million between 1959 and 1964. Another way of putting this, and of emphasising the critical age-structure of the population, is to point out that at that time out of every 1,000 persons in the total population thirty-nine (or forty-one if the blind are included) were in receipt of old-age or equivalent pensions.[45]

In the broader area of contributory insurance there has been, admittedly, more experimentation and a greater readiness to extend the range of benefits available. Thus, before the Second World War, marriage benefits and widows' and orphans' pensions had been added to the existing payments, while during the war itself – apart from the introduction of the children's allowances already mentioned – an interesting innovation, 'wet-time insurance', was adopted in order to protect manual workers in certain trades against loss of wages due to bad weather. But in this sphere, as in so many others, it was the ferment of ideas during and after 'the emergency' that produced the most important changes. As a result of the governmental reconstructions of 1947 a separate Deparment of Social Welfare was created which immediately set about the task of unifying the various kinds of social benefit that had evolved almost haphazardly in the previous quarter-century. As a result, the Social Welfare Act of 1952 (Fianna Fáil's substitute for the ill-fated inter-party scheme aborted by the 'mother and child' crisis) brought together into a single unified conception national health insurance, unemployment insurance and the widows' and orphans' schemes. The principal provisions of this comprehensive scheme were: equal benefits for men and women; identical benefits for unemployment, sickness and widowhood; increases of all benefits in respect of dependants; a new disability benefit without time limit in place of the old restricted provisions governing sickness and disablement. It was particularly significant that it extended unemployment insurance to employees in agriculture (at a lower rate of contribution) and that it substituted new conditions under which the duration of the benefit was not limited to the number of contributions paid.

In short, from 1952 onwards the state was committed to operating a compulsory insurance system of which it paid approximately two-fifths of the cost and to which employers and employees contributed weekly at flat rates, with benefits, also at flat rates, covering unemployment, disability, marriage, maternity, widows' pensions, orphans' allowances, and various kinds of treatment, mainly dental and optical. As originally envisaged the scheme had made no provision for contributory old age pensions, but this omission was rectified in 1961 when legislation provided that old people over seventy might qualify for contributory pension of £3 a week for a single person and £5 7s. 6d. (£5.37½) for a married couple as from 1 January 1966.[46]

The level of social insurance, sickness and unemployment benefit at that date was to be 52/6 (£2.62½) a week per person, 92/6 (£4.62½) for a married couple, plus 13 shillings (65p.) a week each for two children and 8 shillings (40p.) for subsequent children. This was certainly a considerable advance on the conditions obtaining before the Second World War, but it was less than some reformers had hoped for and less in every respect than the comparable benefits in Northern Ireland.[47] Or, to take another example, in the republic in the early 1960s, a married man with three children who was dependent on social insurance benefits might have expected to receive approximately forty per cent of the earnings of a male industrial worker in the transportable goods industries, a proportion which was markedly lower than that prevailing even in the poorer countries of the European Economic Community. Comparisons with Britain are perhaps more relevant, but even they redound to the disadvantage of the republic. At face-value, the benefits available in the early 'sixties were at about two-thirds the level of those available in the United Kingdom, but in reality, since Irish prices were no lower than British ones, and possibly even higher, the actual benefits accruing were almost certainly less than two-thirds.[48] Moreover, it has to be remembered that large categories of the Irish population were excluded, partially or wholly, from the operation of the scheme. Some of these – for example, female domestic servants, fishermen or out-workers – were excluded from unemployment benefit; others – such as civil servants, teachers, local government officials, officers in the Defence Force and employees of statutory transport undertakings – were insured for widows' and orphans' pensions only. In addition, persons whose employment was non-manual and at a rate of salary exceeding £800 (originally £600) a year, or whose work was family employment, were not covered at all by compulsory insurance; subsequent legislation periodically raised the remuneration limit for compulsory social insurance until in 1971 it stood at £1,600 for a non-manual worker.[49]

From time to time efforts have been made to win government sanction for much more wide-reaching suggestions. One of the most famous of these, the scheme put forward by Dr Dignan as long ago as 1944, advocated that all employed persons should be compulsorily and comprehensively insured and that all who did not come within this category should have the right to become voluntary contributors. Somewhat on the same lines, but going in certain respects even further, the White Paper of 1949 had proposed that social insurance should be extended to every person over sixteen who worked for an employer, that there should be a retirement pension for men at sixty-five and for women at sixty, and that there should be a death benefit. All these schemes, and even one put forward by the Labour party in 1965 for graduated social insurance contributions, were resisted by the party (Fianna Fáil) then in power. Partly, no doubt, this was on grounds of financial caution, but partly also this resistance may have reflected two deep-rooted characteristics of Irish society. One is the tradition whereby the unfortunate have been able to call on the resources of various kinds of private or institutional charity; the modern view that such transactions are humiliating for the recipient and a source of spiritual pride in the donor seems not to have penetrated very far as yet in Ireland. If this is so, perhaps it is because of the second characteristic, one which Dr Dignan warned against – the Irish dislike of regimentation and the feeling, still strongly represented inside and outside official circles, that the individual ought, in some way not always clearly specified, to take arms himself against his own particular sea of troubles.

But suppose there were individuals and families, as there always are, who, if no lifebelt was thrown to them, would infallibly go under in their own seas of troubles? For them contributory insurance schemes were not, and could not be, the answer. To meet this problem, and to deal with the different kinds of hardship by which these unfortunates were threatened, the state assumed the burden of assistance – to such a degree, that in the mid-1960s the amount paid out in this way was over one third of expenditure on all social security cash payments.[50] Most of this went on non-contributory pensions for old people over seventy, for widows, for orphans and for blind persons, but some went also on unemployment assistance, home assistance, disability allowances and certain payments for medical treatment. A detailed analysis of a single year, 1962, indicated that of a total of about £13.5 million spent in these various kinds of relief £8.5 million went to old people and their dependants, nearly £2 million to widows and their families and about £500,000 to the blind. Unemployment assistance and health allowances each accounted for about £1 million. A more recent estimate suggests that the total amount spent on these services may have risen to about £90 million.[51] A great part of the explanation both of the extent of this burden and of its distribution is to be found, yet again, in the structure of Irish society. At the time of the 1961 Census some two-fifths of gainfully employed men were self-employed – many of them small farmers. These stood outside the contributory insurance schemes and might have found it hard enough to sustain their contributions even if they had been included. Such people were of course entitled, subject

671

to the usual test, to old age pensions when they reached seventy, but before that their main resource equally subject to the means test, was unemployment assistance. That this was a problem with roots deep in the countryside is suggested by the fact that as recently as 1965 the five counties of Connacht and the three Ulster counties in the republic, which together accounted for twenty-two per cent of the population, supplied no less than sixty per cent of the persons receiving unemployment assistance.[52] Even though the rates actually paid out, not just for unemployment assistance but for other kinds as well, have tended to rise steadily in recent years, they have remained low in relation to the level of prices, low in relation to earnings and low also in relation to the comparable benefits offered in Northern Ireland. In 1966, for example, old age pensions were 47/6 (£2.37½) a week in the republic compared with 76 shillings (£3.80) in Northern Ireland (where the pensionable age was sixty-five for men and sixty for women); for widows the comparable figures were 46 shillings (£2.30) in the republic, 76 shillings (£3.80) in the north; for unemployment, 34 shillings (£1.70) in the republic and 76 shillings (£3.80) in the north.[53]

But not only was assistance in the south less generous than in the north, it was available to fewer categories of people. In the republic, deserted wives and families, and mothers of illegitimate children, did not qualify. Neither did men suffering from short or long term illness, nor persons permanently handicapped by mental or physical disabilities. This last group were, indeed, allowed meagre grants of not more than two pounds a week irrespective of the number of dependants and in 1966 some 17,000 were receiving such aid, together with a further 2,000 tuberculosis patients who got similar payments. But all other necessitous persons had still in effect to rely upon poor relief – or home assistance as it has come to be called. This, which was paid for out of local rates, was provided generally by the county councils or in the larger centres of population by the health authorities. Sometimes these grants were used to supplement payments from social insurance benefits, or other forms of assistance, but often enough they represented all that the recipient could count on receiving from any source except charity. There was no national scale according to which this dole was meted out, but in the most extreme cases these poor people had to be given institutional aid, either in county homes or, in the case of children, by boarding-out with families or by residence in approved schools. Within the homes themselves, which have attracted much adverse comment, some of it official, a commission of inquiry found in 1951 an intermingling of sick, aged, blind, deaf, mentally defective, unmarried mothers and casual vagrants reminiscent of the eighteenth century. The aim of subsequent policy has been to house only the sick and aged in these homes, but ten years after the commission's report had appeared little progress had been made and the sum of human flotsam washed up on those bleak shores had not significantly diminished.[54]

(iv) THE ORGANISATION OF LABOUR

One of the most striking aspects of the slow and uneven progress towards a greater degree of social security for the underprivileged which we have just been discussing was the extent to which that progress, such as it was, was made without the strong and sustained pressures of a vigorous labour movement. This is not to say that individual labour leaders were not in favour of welfare, nor that the Labour party and the trade unions were not committed to fight for better conditions for the workers. Of course they were in favour of welfare, and of course they fought for better conditions. Nevertheless, the fact remains that their influence on the course of events, their ability to shape the development of Irish society in any fashion that would have been remotely acceptable to, say, James Connolly, seemed almost in inverse ratio to the vehemence of their protestations. _

For this yawning gap between what the Labour movement ostensibly stood for and what it actually achieved there are many explanations. Some of these we glanced at earlier when tracing the political ineffectiveness of Labour between the two world wars.* But although the reasons there suggested – the poisoning of the national life by the Civil War, the continuing predominance of political over social issues, the unwillingness of working-class leaders to fall foul of the Church by openly espousing socialist doctrines, the sheer difficulty of winning support in a country where rural and small-town conservatism easily outweighed urban radicalism – all doubtless contributed to the feebleness of the workers' attempts to form a large and efficient pressure-group, other factors, which relate more directly to the industrial side of the movement, have also to be taken into account. If, that is to say, we wish to understand the partial paralysis of organised Labour for much of the period since 1922, we shall have to reckon with the infirmities of the trade unions as well as with those of the political party.

On a superficial view, but on a superficial view only, the Irish trade union movement was well placed in 1922 to play an important role on both sides of the border. Indeed, for it the border could scarcely be said to have existed, since unions in north and south continued for the most part to be linked with the Irish Trades Union Congress formed nearly thirty years before. The total membership affiliated to the ITUC in that year of the great divide was not far short of 200,000.[55] Many of these members belonged to small craft unions which were still, as they had been since their inception, branches of larger organisations with their headquarters in Britain. But the dominant feature of the Irish movement, giving it an appearance of strength and unity that time was to prove deceptive, was the central position occupied by the Irish

* See above, pp. 524-5.

Transport and General Workers' Union. This, as we saw earlier, though badly battered in the fight with the employers in 1913, had survived not only that ordeal, but also the departure to America of its General Secretary, Jim Larkin, the following year. Although Larkin retained his title during the eight and a half years he was away, the very length of his absence and the fact that during it he became involved in American affairs to the virtual exclusion of everything else, meant that the ITGWU fell into other hands. It fell, in fact, largely into the capable hands of its President, Thomas Foran, and its General Treasurer, William O'Brien. Within a few years they had completely transformed the situation, and when Larkin returned at the end of April 1923 he found his union financially solvent and approximately 100,000 strong in numbers.

The importance of this development cannot be overstated. From it there sprang almost at once a deep division within the ranks of Labour which was to last for nearly forty years and to damage severely its industrial effectiveness. The root of the trouble was that Larkin had come back apparently believing that he had only to take up the threads where he had dropped them in 1914, whereas the new leaders, not unnaturally, regarded the revivified ITGWU as their own creation and, being ambitious as well as efficient men, were reluctant to share the power they had gathered into their own grasp. Even before Larkin's return there had been friction between these *apparatchiks* and an opposition composed mainly of former intimates of 'Big Jim' who still persisted in regarding him as the ultimate court of appeal. They were no match, however, for the union's officers who, just at the very moment that Larkin reappeared in Dublin, succeeded in revising the rules in such a manner as to give increased power to the Executive Committee on which they had an assured majority.

The primary responsibility for carrying through this *coup de main* rested with William O'Brien – a man of great ability, but also dour, suspicious, unyielding and, once involved in a quarrel, capable of carrying it on with extreme tenacity for a lifetime if need be.[56] The contrast between this superb, coldly-efficient organiser and the flamboyant and impulsive Larkin could not have been more extreme, and historians ever since have seen in it a main reason for the quarrel that now broke out. Although it is not the whole explanation of what followed, there is no doubt whatever that a formidable clash of personalities occurred within weeks, almost days, of Larkin's return. The details of the quarrel need not concern us here – they revolved round the control of the union, even the physical control of its premises – but the results were of the utmost significance. Larkin was expelled from the union he had himself originally created (the formal breach occurred in March 1924, but it had been preceded by months of recrimination) and while the former leader was absent in Russia, throwing himself with characteristic zest into the affairs of international communism, his brother, Peter Larkin, in June 1924 formed a break-away organisation, the Workers' Union of Ireland. But this, though it initially succeeded in attracting into its rank about two-thirds of the Dublin membership of the ITGWU (roughly 16,000 men), made little headway in the rest of the country, only twenty out of some 300 branches transferring their allegiance.[57]

The split could scarcely have come at a worse time. The year 1923, which saw the quarrel become virtually irreconcilable, was not only the time chosen by the employers to carry out extensive wage-cuts during a period of economic depression, but it was also the year of a general election at which the Labour party had hoped to establish its image as a large and coherent opposition party. To that end it put up fifty-three candidates, only to find when all was over that its representation in the Dáil had actually fallen from seventeen to fourteen. No doubt this eclipse was partially to be explained by lack of funds, and of political organisation and experience, as well as by the continued preoccupation of the electors with the aftermath of the Civil War, but it is not unreasonable to suppose that the Labour showing at the polls was also directly affected by the uninhibited rancour with which it was washing its dirty linen in public. A movement that could not even govern itself scarcely inspired confidence as to its capacity to govern the country.

Yet, if the Larkin-O'Brien split did undeniably contribute to the eclipse of Labour at a crucial moment in Irish history, it is not enough to explain that split solely in terms of an ugly dispute between two totally incompatible individuals. The fact is that Larkin and O'Brien represented fundamentally different conceptions of what the role of the Irish trade union movement should be. The predominance of Larkin and Connolly in union affairs before the First World War has sometimes led observers to take an exaggerated view of the extent to which that movement was as extreme as its leaders. It is, in reality, very doubtful if their Marxism was shared by more than a small minority of the rank-and-file. Most Irish working-men remained as before – undeviatingly Catholic in their personal beliefs and incorrigibly opportunist in their economic demands. Indeed, the 'Trade Union Congress and Labour Party' which had come into being in 1912 shared, as a modern commentator has pointed out, 'neither Connolly's Marxism nor his militant and explicit nationalist republicanism'.[58] And although the Citizen Army of 1913 might be claimed as the spearhead of that militancy it was, as we saw earlier, always a very small body and not in any true sense the striking-force of a large and committed trade union movement. For most trade unionists after 1916 – and this holds good especially for the ITGWU as it was refashioned by Foran and O'Brien – the safeguarding of their wages and the improvement of their working-conditions continued to be their primary concern.

We are confronted here, of course, with a phenomenon by no means peculiar to Ireland. What was being fought out in the Irish labour movement during those confused and angry months of 1923 and 1924 was the battle that had been fought in many countries, and even in the Second International itself, beiore 1914 – the battle between revolution and reformism. For Larkin a trade union was still an instrument to be used for an end far greater than the short-term advantage of its members – tne overturning of capitalism and the creation oɪ a totally new kind of society.* For O'Brien, on the other hand, a trade union remained what it had habitually been, a bargaining mechanism whereby the workers could achieve material betterment within the existing framework of state and economy.

The real significance, then, of the dispute which racked the Labour movement in those years, and which left O'Brien dominant in the ITGWU, was that it marked a decisive turn to the right. This had two important consequences – one doctrinal, the other practical. In doctrinal terms the turn to the right meant that despite annual lip-service to the memory of Connolly, which year by year came to seem more and more unreal, there would not in the foreseeable future be a place in the movement for anything that could be recognised as a full socialist programme, with the result that men of the more extreme left were increasingly deflected into splinter-groups or even into organisations, like the IRA for example, which were dedicated to political objectives that might or might not be compatible with social radicalism.†

The practical consequence of the turn to the right was that the labour movement as a whole failed to offer a credible alternative to the middle-class, conservative regime inaugurated by Mr Cosgrave and his colleagues. And although it is true that the chief burden of opposition in the Dáil during the 'twenties did fall upon the Labour group – a burden carried conscientiously if not always very effectively – the return of Mr de Valera and his followers to constitutional politics in 1927, not merely deprived Labour of a good part of its role, but also brought back into the foreground all those political issues arising out of the Treaty and the Commonwealth connection which succeeded only too well after 1932 in deafening the ears of the electorate to social and economic abuses that clamoured in vain for redress.

It has to be admitted, however, that external circumstances, quite apart from internal divisions, militated against any strong labour pressure for reform. The power of trade unions to protect their members, let alone secure large improvements, is notoriously weak in times of economic stringency and the Irish unions, still deeply divided by the Larkin-O'Brien dispute, were in no position to resist the onset of depression in and after 1929. Moreover, although north and south were

* Larkin's espousal of communism (albeit of a very individual brand) in America and after his return home can only have added to his difficulties in a country where even 'liberalism' was sometimes used as a term of abuse.

† It was a process that could cut both ways. As we saw earlier, the IRA itself was socially as well as politically to the left in the inter-war years, and shows signs of being so again at the present time.

both affected by the depression, and though the bulk of unions on either side of the border were still affiliated to the same Congress, the very fact of political separation brought with it different preoccupations which impeded concerted action on economic problems that were often at bottom very similar. The northern unions, which might reasonably have been expected to provide a secure industrial base for the promotion of an all-Ireland movement, were if anything in even greater disarray than their southern counterparts, since the collapse of the General Strike in 1926 had left them with a legacy of depleted membership and, as a result of the Trade Disputes and Trade Union Act of 1927, diminished freedom of action.*

Disunity and depression together cast a gloom over the whole movement which expressed itself in a steady decline of numbers and resources. By 1929 affiliated membership of Congress for the whole country had dropped to under 100,000 while members' contributions had fallen from £184,000 in 1923 to £78,000 in 1929.[59] Nor was there much sign of recovery in the years that followed. The formal connection between the political party and the union movement was severed in 1930, but the ostensible purpose of this manoeuvre, which was to allow the party to develop its organisation in the constituencies, did not in fact lead to any marked extension of Labour support in the countryside. The party remained predominantly rural – only within the past few years has it seemed that expanding industrialism may enable it to broaden its industrial base – and although it might have been expected to appeal strongly to the rural and small-town proletariat which undoubtedly existed, it found difficulty in competing either with the extremism of the IRA or the reformism of Fianna Fáil. Once the latter achieved power its attractiveness to the working-class voter increased – at least in the earlier years of Mr de Valera's long tenure of office – and there is good reason to believe, in the words of a recent writer, that 'Labour's failure to win any real measure of popular support was due to the fact that it was forced to compete, on very unequal terms, for the same votes as Fianna Fáil.'[60] Individual unions – especially the ITGWU – did certainly maintain close ties with the Labour representatives in the Dáil, but, because of the relatively small numbers of the industrial working-class, this did not in itself guarantee any growth of political effectiveness. On the contrary, Labour's share of seats after the general election of 1932 sank to seven (improving slightly to eight at the election of the following year), and although the even balance of the other parties made Mr de Valera dependent for a time on Labour support, this was not a situation that was likely to endure indefinitely. True, as we saw earlier, the Labour party under its new leader, William Norton, a shrewd and able bargainer, did its best to push Fianna Fáil to the left, or rather to compel it to honour its election promises of social reform, but although in the early 'thirties these efforts had some moderate success, they were constantly frus-

* See Part IV B, chap. 5.

trated by the intrusion of other issues, and especially of course by the dispute with Britain.

In the years immediately before the Second World War, however, the situation seemed at last to be improving. The new industries established behind tariff barriers had given some additional employment and trade union numbers in the twenty-six counties responded to this stimulus, rising by 1939 to about 150,000.[61] But at this point the war called an abrupt halt to progress. Not only was industry crippled by shortages of fuel, raw materials and equipment – with obvious repercussions on the level of employment – but since the shortages themselves drove prices steadily upwards, wages and social benefits alike were quite unable to keep pace with the resulting inflation. There was in all this the material for an explosion of working-class discontent of which, it might be assumed, the labour movement would be the obvious spokesman. The discontent and unrest were certainly there, but events were soon to show how powerless either the political party or the trade unions were to exploit them.

Two developments in 1941 demonstrated this with painful clarity. First of all, in May the government introduced a Wages Standstill Order which in effect prevented any union from striking for higher wages by removing the legal protection for strike action afforded by previous legislation. Although a partial concession was made the following year – relating only, however, to increases in the cost of living from 1942 onwards – the Wages Standstill Order remained substantially intact until September 1946. How effective it was in depressing the standard of living may be judged from the fact that whereas the cost of living index had risen by about two-thirds between 1939 and 1946, the average weekly wage in industry went up by no more than one-third during the same period.

No less direct an interference with the bargaining power of the workers was the second development of that year – the passing of a Trade Union Act designed to achieve two objects. First, it laid down that while only government licensed trade unions could carry on collective bargaining, to obtain a licence it was first necessary for a union to lodge a substantial sum of money with the High Court. This, though bearing heavily on very small unions, was at least defensible as a safeguard against wild-cat or unofficial strikes. But the second feature of the Act was more ominous. With the intention of avoiding inter-union disputes, it was proposed to set up a tribunal which should have the power of determining that one union alone should be entitled to organise a particular class of workers if that union could show that it already had the allegiance of a majority of the workers in the class in question. Additionally – though this was later ruled as unconstitutional by the Supreme Court – it was intended that only an Irish-based union should be given sole negotiating rights by the tribunal.

This far-reaching proposal evoked very different reactions within the Irish Labour movement. The biggest union, the ITGWU, recognised the need for rationalisation – naturally, since it stood to gain from the dis-appearance of what William O'Brien called with remarkable frankness 'the superfluous unions which we all want to see eliminated – or, to use an expression in fashion in some quarters "liquidated".'[62] Many others, however, combined to form a Council of Action to oppose the measure and in the campaign which followed James Larkin once more regained something of his old authority. His Workers' Union of Ireland was still excluded from the Irish TUC – O'Brien's influence had seen to that from the beginning – but he himself had sufficient following in the capital to have sat for a while on the City Council and even to have represented northeast Dublin briefly in the Dáil just before the war.* In 1941, spurred on by the belief that the workers must make a united stand against the Trade Union Act, he applied to join the Labour party and he and his son James were admitted in December. The next year he was elected as an official Labour candidate to the City Council and followed this by recapturing northeast Dublin at the general election of 1943. But in doing so he precipitated a fresh quarrel with O'Brien and the ITGWU. Worsted in his attempt to prevent Larkin from receiving official backing for his candidature, O'Brien then led his union into the very serious step of withdrawing their affiliation from the Labour party which thus found itself deprived not only of valuable financial support, but also of some of its parliamentary representatives, five out of eight of whom (as members of the ITGWU) broke away from the main body to form their own group, the National Labour Party. Not surprisingly, the Labour vote, which in 1943 had topped 200,000 for the first time (and in doing so had captured seventeen seats) fell sharply when Mr de Valera called another election the following year; indeed, the Labour performance in 1944 was so lack-lustre that the party might almost be said to have abstained from participating. Only after both sections had agreed to join the inter-party government in 1948 was the way opened for the reconciliation which took place two years later.

It proved, unhappily, less easy to heal the deep wounds in the trade union movement. These, indeed, were if anything aggravated by the course of events in the latter part of the war. As we have seen, the Irish TUC, since its first small beginnings in 1894, had catered for the whole country and for all kinds of unions regardless of whether these were based in either part of Ireland or in England. In practice the Irish-based unions had operated mainly in the south, while the British-based unions were strongest in the north. But over the years the feeling had grown, especially among the Irish-based unions – and among these, especially inside the ITGWU – that Irish workers ought to be or-ganised in Irish unions, a xenophobic view to which the wartime Irish government was not unsympathetic. It was indicative of the prevailing mood that when in 1943 the Irish TUC was invited by the British TUC to attend a world conference of trade unionists to be held in

* Elected in 1937 he lost his seat at the general election the following year.

London in 1945, the National Executive of the Irish Congress, though sharply divided on the matter, should in the end have declined the invitation on the ground, which at this distance seems a shade metaphysical, that acceptance would involve a breach of Irish neutrality. The following year, at the annual meeting of the Irish TUC, the British-based unions launched their counter-attack and succeeded in passing a resolution reversing the previous decision, thus enabling representatives to attend the conference, which they duly did in February 1945. This action provoked – more accurately, perhaps, brought to a head – yet one more dispute within the movement in which the Transport and General Workers Union was intimately involved. Shortly after the London conference was held, the ITGWU, together with a number of other Irish based unions, withdrew from Congress and established their own organisation, the Congress of Irish Trade Unions, dedicated to the principle that Irish workers must free themselves from the domination of British-based unions.[63]

For the next fifteen years this division within the ranks of the Irish movement continued. At the time of the split the ITUC had an affiliation of about 145,000 members; those belonged to both British and Irish-based unions, among the latter being Larkin's Workers' Union which, true to form, entered at one door as O'Brien's ITGWU left by another. The Congress of Irish Unions was, and remained, smaller, having at the outset an affiliation of about 77,500.[64] But both organisations stood to gain from the rise in trade union membership which came with increasing industrial activity, north and south, after the war. In 1958, for example, the ITUC had a quarter of a million members in sixty-four unions, while the Congress of Irish Unions had 188,000 in twenty-one unions.[65] By then, however, the long dispute was drawing to a close, partly because, of the two ancient protagonists, Larkin was dead and O'Brien had retired, but also perhaps because the idea of the solidarity of labour, which had been at the root of the original TUC conception, had come again to appear more attractive and more feasible at a time when the emphasis in both parts of the divided island seemed to be directed more towards stimulating economic growth than towards reopening political animosities. At any rate, after long and arduous negotiation, the two organisations reunited in 1959 to form the Irish Congress of Trade Unions, membership of which was open to unions with headquarters in any part of Ireland, and to unions based outside Ireland provided the latter safeguarded the autonomy of their Irish members.

But not only were the unions larger in numbers and more united in purpose than they had been for a long time, they were also moving steadily towards a better bargaining position. In the south this had been foreshadowed as far back as 1946 when the Industrial Relations Act of that year had established an independent tribunal, the Labour Court, on which employers and employees had equal representation. True, the recommendations of the Court as to the settlement of industrial disputes were not mandatory, but as its first chairman observed, it 'helps to create a kind of voluntary law or common rule' by a process of inquiry or conciliation.[66] It could not prevent strike action, nor was it designed to do so, but it did markedly reduce tension and it did succeed in gaining acceptance for a large proportion – possibly as high as four-fifths – of its suggestions.[67] Moreover, apart from its action in specific cases, the Labour Court was instrumental in negotiating the first National Wage Agreement in 1948, a precedent that was to be followed later on numerous occasions and which undoubtedly helped to reduce the amount of direct industrial action taken by workers in support of their claims, though not, of course, to eliminate it entirely.

In the north, the development of bargaining power took a rather different direction, being directed mainly towards the removal of two deeply-felt grievances. One of these was the reluctance of the Northern Ireland government to follow the lead of Westminster in repealing the Trade Disputes Act of 1927. It was not in fact until 1959, thirteen years after the decisive step had been taken in Britain, that the Act, with its vexatious restraints upon union activity, at last disappeared in the six counties.* But it was not for another four years after that the second grievance was remedied. When the Irish movement had split in 1945, the affairs of the northern unions which had remained affiliated to the ITUC were entrusted to a 'Northern Committee' of trade unionists elected each year by their fellow-members of the ITUC unions in Northern Ireland. The official, governmental line in the north (though not in practice followed with equal rigidity by all departments) was that this Committee, being subordinate to a Congress which had its headquarters outside the state, could not be formally recognised. In 1964, however, the Irish Congress of Trade Unions amended its constitution so as to make it clear that the Northern Committee did enjoy real autonomy, whereupon the Northern Ireland government took steps to establish an Economic Council on which the unions were represented.[68]

There remained, however, and must still remain, an unanswered question about the future growth of trade unionism in Northern Ireland – the fundamental question of whether or not union solidarity is a strong enough force to overcome religio-political sectarianism. As recently as 1962 two perceptive and sympathetic observers of the Ulster scene concluded that it was. Citing the action of northern trade unionists in condemning discrimination of all kinds, they commented that it 'seems reasonable therefore, to regard the signs of religious difference within the trade union movement as secondary, the natural result of other divisions in the province, and to consider the movement as being an important uniting influence'.[69] Who now could echo the confidence

* Among other things, the Act had placed difficulties in the way of sympathetic strikes, had declared certain forms of industrial action illegal as 'intimidation', and had introduced a 'contracting-in' system for the payment of the political levy to the Labour party.

of that assertion?*

In all that has been said in the preceding sections about policy even the non-Irish reader will have found a good deal that is familiar. Irish governments in the last few decades – their preoccupation with the language revival apart – have shared the general concern of governments in most parts of the world to open to their citizens the possibility of a decent existence and to save them from the worst abysses of poverty by hanging beneath them a safety-net of social security. But although the 'minimum standard' which society nowadays takes for granted may not in Ireland be very imposing, at least compared with that of the European Community to which she aspires, the same impatience with welfare, the same distrust of bureaucracy, the same instinctive urge for the individual to assert himself against the impersonal complexities of the modern world, that have become so characteristic of the age in so many places, have begun to manifest themselves in the republic also.

Yet, while the problem of reconciling private liberty with the demands of society may be a universal one, the form it takes in a particular country will obviously depend upon the situation in that country at any given time. In Ireland it is clear that past history and present circumstances both play an important part in generating the tensions that are now so conspicuous. It would be easy, but extremely misleading, to say that these tensions result from the interplay between an old, deep-seated conservatism and a new liberalism still seeking a direction and a goal. It would be misleading to say this because although there are senses in which it is certainly true that Irish society has been profoundly conservative ever since independence, to confuse this conservatism with simple reaction would be to misunderstand the whole drift of history in the last fifty years. On the contrary, it was of the highest importance to the men who took power in 1922, and no less so to the men who replaced them in 1932, that the part of Ireland over which they ruled should be seen to be a successful experiment in building a modern state. This was necessary, not only to establish the regime in the eyes of the outside world as eligible to be admitted to the

* It is fair to add that since this was written evidence has come to light of the constructive and moderating influence exercised by the northern trade unionists in Belfast during the disturbances of August 1969; since northern trade unionists numbered 215,000 out of a total membership for all Ireland of more than half a million, their role clearly was, and could be again, important. See *Irish Times*, 29, 30 and 31 Dec. 1969. It should be noted also that the labour movements in both parts of the island have a common meeting-place in the National Council of Labour proposed by the Irish Labour Party Conference of 1966.

comity of nations, but also as a standing demonstration to the minority inside the twenty-six counties, and to those who were watching critically from across the border, that revolution would not be the prelude to sectarian tyranny – in short that Home Rule would not mean Rome Rule. Nor, despite certain manifestations of clerical influence mentioned earlier in this book – notably the Browne affair and the ecclesiastical ban on Trinity – has Home Rule in fact meant Rome Rule.* The new creation, through all its constitutional mutations from Free State to Republic, has remained a parliamentary democracy of a classically simple kind, in which freedom of speech, of worship and of political association have in all essentials been preserved intact. True, the state, like most other states, has from time to time taken special powers against those who would destroy it, but one has only to point to the way in which the path was made clear for Mr de Valera to return to constitutional politics in 1927, to the secure – not to say privileged – position of southern Protestants, and to the fact that twice in a decade the electorate has resisted proposals for the abolition of proportional representation, to realise something of the stability and maturity which have come with the years.

However, even if all this be conceded, certain dark shadows fall across the scene and will not easily fade. No one can study the history of Irish politics in the last forty years, no one can read what Irish writers have written about their country's condition (especially the numerous and recurrent variations on the theme of alienation), no one can look at the evolution of Irish society, without becoming aware of an undercurrent of frustration and cynicism thrusting its way steadily to the surface. For this there would appear to be four principal explanations – the feeling, until recently almost inarticulate, that much that has happened since 1916 has in some sense been a betrayal of the rebellion; the deep, perhaps permanent wounds left by the Civil War; the traumatic effects of the realisation that political independence of England did not mean the end of English influence in Ireland; and finally, the internal stresses that have resulted from the exposure of a deeply Catholic country to a modern world itself changing with unparalleled

* Apart from the instances mentioned in the text, the principal grievances of Protestants relate chiefly to the exclusion of divorce from the law of the land, the prohibition against birth control (which, however, can be surmounted without much difficulty), and the operation of the Ne Temere decree, which entails that the children of a mixed marriage should be brought up as Catholics. Protestant opinion was particularly alarmed by the Tilson case, when the Supreme Court ruled in 1951 that a promise to do this given in writing by a Protestant husband was enforceable in law despite his subsequent wish to revoke the promise. Such instances are exceptional, however, and I have tried elsewhere to do justice to the generally favourable position of Protestants in the community (see my essay, 'The Minority in the 26 Counties', in F. MacManus (ed.), *The Years of the Great Test*, 1926-39, pp. 92-103). For the more generalised influence of the Church on Irish society at large, see below, pp. 688-90.

speed and completeness. Each of these important elements in the present mood of restlessness needs some further consideration.

We may start with the obvious proposition that the spick-and-span republic of 1970 is not the republic of 1916. It remains only a part of what the dead men died for. Not just a geographical part, but even within its own truncated frontiers something less than the society which Connolly and Pearse had sought to bring to birth. Not united, not Gaelic, not 'cherishing all the children of the nation equally', not even a republic at all until the hurried *accouchement* of 1948, it is not really surprising if it has seemed to a disenchanted generation a crude parody of everything they have been taught to believe.

But linked with this – and a second element in the climate of dis-illusionment – is the way in which the state actually came into being. That revolutions devour their children is a trite enough observation, but it is necessary to insist that when they devour them as a result of civil war the consequences are more than usually dire and far-reaching. Time and again in these pages we have had occasion to trace the distorting effects of that central and crucial disaster upon subsequent events and policies in Ireland. Only two points need to be made here by way of recapitulation. The first is that from 1922 to the present the real has been haunted by the ideal – or, to put it another way, that sober calculation has been at endless war with irrepressible fantasy. In practical terms, this has meant that on the one hand the gun has always been liable to re-enter politics and, on the other, that those in power at any given moment have been led by the inexorable logic of their situation to use force against those who claimed that their sole allegiance was to that indivisible republic to which all had at one time subscribed – hence the Civil War reprisals, hence the special powers taken first by Cosgrave's government and then by de Valera's, hence the Curragh detention-camp and the long running fight between the IRA and the police, hence also (to some extent) the recent fissures within Fianna Fáil. That governments so placed could not have done other than they did most Irishmen would probably agree – at least, they have been slow to overthrow governments that acted thus – yet the compulsion to behave in this way has been precisely the tragedy of those governments. Caught in the collision between the unattainable absolute and the realisable compromise, they have opted for the latter and, given that their aim has been to create an orderly society, they could have made no other choice. But still 'those dead men are loitering there to stir the boiling pot'.

The second point that needs to be made about the regime that emerged from the Civil War is the superficially obvious one that it was a regime wedded to the economic ideas of Griffith rather than to those of Connolly. The programme of intensive industrial development behind a tariff wall, which Griffith had laid down in those early, idyllic years of the new century when the most doctrinaire theories could be formulated in the blissful certainty that they would not be put to the rest in the foreseeable future, became in the course of time the foundation of a policy which, it is scarcely too much to say, has influenced, where it has not dictated, the evolution of the entire economy. But because it was at bottom a business policy and not a social policy, it conflicted from the very beginning with those ringing declarations of the Proclamation of Independence and of the First Dáil which promised a new world for the poor and downtrodden. It was, however, the function of the Civil War to make that new world safe, not for Wolfe Tone's men of no property, but rather for business, for the shopocracy, and for the farmer-owners of the rising generations. From that single fact a long, sad history of disillusionment was to follow.

We saw earlier, of course, that to think of economic policy as if it were something consciously framed in Dublin and carried out by Irishmen under laboratory conditions and free of all extraneous influences, was always an illusion. It was an illusion for the sufficient reason that in the years after 1922, as for many centuries before that date, what men made or grew or bought or sold in Ireland depended in the last resort upon the state of the larger economy of the British Isles, to which the country continued to belong regardless of treaties signed in London or of lines drawn upon the map. The lesson of interdependence has been etched deeply into the national consciousness by a continuing process in which, at different times and in different ways, emigration, economic war, trade agreements and currency crises have all played their part. And although one of the attractions to many people of entry into the Common Market is precisely that it may diminish the closeness of the connection with Britain, ordinary commonsense suggests that what will in fact happen will be the replacement of one form of interdependence by another.

But while this kind of interdependence is tolerable, because unavoidable, there exists simultaneously a different kind of interdependence which has seemed to some people not unavoidable and therefore intolerable. It is the interdependence that comes from sharing a common language – English – with a powerful neighbour, and from being exposed to all sorts of contacts and pressures which a small country is ill-equipped to resist.* There is at stake here – and it is the third element in the contemporary unease – not merely the problem of how to preserve and revive the Irish language, but the much larger question of how, if at all, to maintain intact the values that are felt both to be characteristic of a separate Irish culture and essential to its continued existence. The fact that these values have proved notoriously difficult to define and, when defined, have often proved to be strangely

---

* To speak of the common language as English is perhaps an over-simplification, since the pressures have come from across the Atlantic as well as from across the Irish Sea. But it remains true that the constant traffic between England and Ireland, the intermingling of peoples and the influence of the mass media based on Britain have all combined to make the threat seem in Irish eyes a distinctively English threat.

at odds with contemporary reality, is perhaps less important for the historian than the fact that many people have been content to sum them up as Catholic and Gaelic. What do these large and vague terms mean in the Irish context? They mean simply that there has existed, and still exists, a substantial body of opinion which holds that Irish society should be governed by Catholic principles of morality and also that it should strive to preserve whatever of speech, or music, or literature, or customs and pastimes, still links the present to an antiquity passionately invoked, if imperfectly comprehended.

The attempt to keep these values inviolate has produced over the years a vast amount of honest (if misdirected) effort, a good deal of more or less conscious hypocrisy, and one specific experiment which has possibly done more to damage the reputation of Ireland abroad than anything that has happened outside Londonderry or West Belfast. This has been the attempt by censorship to preserve the Irish public from noxious and corrupting influences from elsewhere. In 1926 the Cosgrave administration set up a committee of investigation into 'evil literature' with a view to excluding from the country the steady stream of English newspapers and magazines which trafficked chiefly in the more lurid aspects of sex.* But when, three years later, the Censorship of Publications Act was passed, it went much further than striking at the gutter press and at salacious paperbacks. Not only did the Act contain a section designed to banish from Ireland any publication advocating birth control, but it also set up a Censorship Board with the responsibility of recommending to the Ministers of Justice the banning of books which they considered to be indecent or obscene. The censorship thus imposed was, it must be emphasised, motivated neither by political nor religious intolerance. It was, indeed, reinforced by the argument that neither art nor literature had any rights against God and the censorship at its inception and afterwards certainly had strong clerical approval. Equally, many politicians supported it at the time and would, presumably, support it at the present day. But churchmen and politicians did not welcome it because it protected specific creeds or parties. Their attitude may rather be seen as an extreme example of the maxim that the worst is sometimes the corruption of the best. For them the censorship in its pristine form was at least in part an attempt to translate into reality the puritanism that often goes with revolution – to establish, so far as laws could establish it, that the new Ireland should shine like a good deed in a naughty world. But it is essential to an understanding of modern Ireland (north and south) to realise that

* In the early days of the Free State the old British machinery of police seizure of obscene articles and subsequent trial of the offender before a magistrate's court was all that was available to the government, but these prosecutions could not touch the publisher, who was usually outside Irish jurisdiction. See M. Adams, *Censorship: the Irish Experience* (Dublin, 1968), pp. 14-15. This book is much the most complete account of the Irish censorship in operation.

this puritanism – especially in regard to obscenity and pornography –
is an important element in the Irish character and more enduring than
the products of more permissive societies elsewhere can easily grasp.
There is, in fact, a case for arguing that, at least at the outset, the
policy of the government reflected rather than distorted the idealism
of the people.

Of course in practice it did not work out like that for long. The
Censorship Board, composed of five people (intended originally to consist of a representative of the Catholic Church, a lawyer, a medical man
and one representative from each of the two universities), was set up
in 1930 and went to work with a will. Before long it had begun to make
not only itself, but the whole country, ridiculous as its probing finger
moved on from the pornography which had set the whole strange mechanism in motion to the works of eminent contemporary authors, and
even to those of other authors long since dead. Nevertheless, despite
the outraged protests of Irish intellectuals – and scarcely any Irish writer
of note in the last fifty years has escaped condemnation – the principle
of censorship was written into the Constitution of 1937 and the Censorship Act itself amended in 1946.* Ostensibly a relaxation of the system in the sense that it provided for appeal machinery (though too
cumbersome and expensive to be very helpful), the amended law formally empowered the Board itself to ban books – which, in effect, it
had been doing from the outset – and also gave authority to the customs
officials to seize any literature which in their opinion ought to be
brought to the Board's attention.† In practice, the way the censorship
had functioned has been that anyone who considers a book in any way
objectionable can send it, with the offending passage clearly indicated,
to the Censorship Board. If the complaint is accepted as serious by
the secretary, the book is then circulated to the five members of the
Board who meet once a fortnight to discuss the books they have been
sent. If three out of five favour a ban and there is no more than one
dissentient, the book is then automatically banned. Since in the mid-
sixties the censors were receiving about 500 books a year it does not
seem as if the attention individual books received could have been very
great. Nevertheless, between January 1960 and January 1965 – and
this was a period of relative relaxation compared with the 1950s – some
1,900 books were banned, an average of about thirty a month.[70] Since
then there has been a marked reduction and in 1967 it was decided to
'release' from banning many books previously condemned, and to

* Mention should be made here of the courageous fight against the
censorship led by the distinguished Irish writer, Mr Sean O'Faolain,
especially when he was editor of *The Bell* magazine. He fought this battle
mainly in the 1940s but it is plain from the recently revised edition
(1969) of his famous book, *The Irish*, that his attitude has not changed; see
pp. 161-2.

† For the official role of the Customs officials, see Adams, op. cit., pp.
171-6.

amend the law so that newly banned books could not be prohibited for more than twelve years, though they could of course be banned again thereafter.

The cynic may say, perhaps, that one reason why book censorship has lasted so long is because so few people in Ireland read or buy books. If the mass of the population was to be protected against indecency and obscenity, then foreign periodicals and films were arguably a more important target. Periodicals were dealt with (and ruthlessly) by the ordinary machinery, but films required special treatment. In fact, they have had it from as far back as 1925 when a Film Censor was first appointed. This was a paid government appointment (unlike the literary censors who were part-time and unpaid) and it carried with it very considerable power, since no film could be shown in the country without a certificate from the Censor. There developed, indeed, a hierarchy of certificates, as elsewhere, but the much cruder method of simply cutting out passages deemed to be objectionable has always been extensively used. Aimed ostensibly at preventing what has been called 'Californication', the censorship has not in practice been restricted to the cruder fantasies of Hollywood, but has also been used, often with devastating effect, upon some of the masterpieces of the modern cinema. Here too, however, there has latterly been a shift towards a more liberal policy, with the appointment in 1964 of a Film Appeal Board which has undoubtedly introduced an element of discrimination into a process that was frequently ludicrous and always vexatious.

The attempt to maintain 'values' against corrupting influences from outside which lies at the very heart and core of the censorship is in essence the attempt to maintain Christian – more specifically Catholic – values, and it leads us straight to the fourth strand in the current restlessness – the tensions inevitably experienced by a long-sheltered Catholic community abruptly confronted with the need to come to terms with a largely pagan world. From what has already been said earlier in this book it will be apparent that no easy generalisations are possible about the influence of the Church upon Irish society. Even in the nineteenth century, as we saw, although the bishops were frequently a conservative force in politics, this was not invariably the case, and even when it was the case – as, for example, in the Fenian period – there were still to be found parochial clergy who were prepared to disregard episcopal thunders and minister to men whom their superiors had excommunicated. Much the same was true of the troubled years from 1916 onwards, and although the Church was uncompromising in its denunciation of republicans who refused to accept the Treaty, at the parish level some of the old flexibility still remained.

Just because the Church was not in reality so monolithic as it seemed on the surface, it was relatively easy for Irishmen to display that curious dualism so often seen in Catholic countries – combining devotion to their faith with frequently outspoken anti-clericalism. The devotion is real enough, though it would perhaps be excessively naïve to judge it by external manifestations, frequent and striking as these may be. Thus, the fact that of a population which is ninety-five per cent Catholic, something like ninety per cent go to Mass on Sunday, though a remarkable phenomenon, might on investigation turn out to be as much a sociological as a religious one; the high ranking of the Cardinal (directly after the President) in the Irish order of precedence does not exempt the bishops, individually or collectively, from frequent and searching criticism; and the insertion of a clause in the Constitution (Article 44), recognising the 'special position' of the Church as 'guardian of the Faith professed by the great majority of the citizens', has not in practice affected the broad toleration to which the state is committed, and in any event is unlikely to survive much longer.* The convincing proofs of Irish devotion lie less in these outward evidences than in the underlying reality of a simple faith early inculcated but tenaciously retained, and in the special position which the parish priest still holds in his community. The peculiar authority, and often affection, the priest enjoys, derives of course partly from the nature of his office, but also from his historical role. Given the penal discrimination against Irish Catholicism in the eighteenth century, and the absence of a Catholic ruling class for most, if not all, of the nineteenth century, the priest found himself in the position where he and he alone supplied the necessary local leadership, not just in matters of religion, but in all sorts of other matters as well, a leadership which, as we have seen, gained added force once the national school system had planted him, as the school manager, at the very heart of the country's educational network. His influence, then, was paramount, but although in political questions it might in certain circumstances take a radical form, in questions of faith and morals it was, with very few exceptions, conservative. Conservative, not just because the priest was the humble instrument of an international Church dedicated to the preservation of standards and attitudes which the world at large was prepared to ignore, but also because his own training in the seminary, and the fact that full control of a parish might often not come to him until he was near sixty, combined to make him, as an individual, resistant to change.

Yet change there has been and change there is likely to be in the future. Whether elderly bishops were prepared to recognise it or not, a new era began with the short but revolutionary reign of Pope John XXIII and with the deliberations of the Second Vatican Council. The discussion of ideas previously stifled, the questioning of authority hither-

* Note that although the clergy in Ireland are numerous, the ratio of priests to population is not quite so high as is sometimes supposed. In 1958 there were 3,833 secular clergy and 1,776 regular clergy, giving a ratio of 585 Catholics to one priest (secular and regular). A further calculation of 1965 suggested a ratio of one priest (secular and regular) to 553 Catholic laity, as compared with a world ratio of 1:1,270; the English ratio, however, was 1:500. See K. Connell, *Irish Peasant Society*, pp. 160-1; T. Gray (citing D. A. Thornley), *The Irish Answer*, pp. 280-1.

to taken for granted, the reconsideration of questions, like the celibacy of the clergy or the Church's attitude to birth control, have sent shock-wave after shock-wave through Catholicism all over the world. If Ireland has been rather more insulated against these shock-waves than many other countries, this is no doubt due mainly to the deep-seated conservatism already mentioned. It may also, however, have been due to the presence within the hierarchy of strong personalities disinclined for change. Of these the most eminent was certainly the Archbishop of Dublin, Dr John Charles McQuaid, a devoted ecclesiastic who over many years worked to better the conditions of the poor in his diocese, but at the same time sought so to shelter them from the winds blowing from without that, returning from the Vatican Council, he was able to tell them that they need not heed the talk of changes to come. 'Allow me to reassure you. No change will worry the tranquillity of your Christian lives.'[71]

Even so, although this tranquillity may to a considerable extent still be unimpaired, initiatives which have already been taken suggest that no archbishop, however authoritative or authoritarian, can long arrest the movement towards change, and indeed Dr McQuaid himself has not been immune to the process. At the beginning of 1972 he resigned the see to which he had been appointed in 1940 at the age of forty-five. It is too soon yet to say what the effects of this epochal event may be, but already there are indications that his successor, Dr Dermot Ryan, a distinguished Jesuit scholar who was long a professor at University College, Dublin, has begun to establish a reputation for greater humanity and accessibility. Change can be traced in many different directions – in the co-operative venture of Father James McDyer at Glencolumcille, an effort by one man to restore life and soul to a dwindling community in a remote part of Donegal; in the growing interest of the Church in sociology, evidenced among other things by the influential periodical, *Christus Rex*;* in the ferment of ideas inside the seminaries, and especially in Maynooth itself, where a new periodical, *The Furrow*, has become an important channel for communicating to Irish readers the trend of ideas and events outside Ireland; in the recent adoption of the vernacular for the service of the Mass and the new emphasis on liturgical reform; in an increasing discussion of ecumenism and an increasing preoccupation with the mission of the Church in a secular world. The results that flow from all this debate and reappraisal may not as yet appear very impressive – it would be premature to expect that they would be – and the forces that favour the maintenance of the status quo are by no means routed. Indeed, it may even be that *Humanae Vitae* has given them a new lease of life, and not only on the central issue of resisting birth control. Nevertheless, the evidence ad-

* It is proper to add that this interest was shared by Archbishop McQuaid himself who founded not only the Dublin Institute of Catholic Sociology, but also the Catholic Social Service Conference and the Catholic Social Welfare Bureau.

duced by Catholic writers themselves that there can be no return to the old quiescence is, to an outsider, cumulatively convincing.[72]

There can be no return because no man is an island and no island is – any longer – an entity. The twentieth century cannot be kept out of Ireland because it is already and inexpugnably there through the simple fact of physical and cultural permeation. Latterly, this has taken two specific forms whose ultimate importance has hardly yet begun to be understood. The first of these derives from the much greater direct contact Irish men and women now have, not merely with their English neighbours, but with people from other countries as well. To the traditional intermingling that emigration has always brought in its train has been added both the visible presence of foreign firms employing Irish labour in Ireland, and the even more potent influence of tourism. This last has cut two ways. On the one hand, the Irish themselves now travel abroad for their holidays much more than previously, and on the other hand their own country has become a highly attractive magnet to visitors from other lands. The Irish tourist industry, at least on an economically significant scale, is very much a creation of Bord Fáilte, the organisation set up in 1957 as a state-sponsored body with the function of co-ordinating the work of the various tourist interests in the country. It has itself undertaken numerous initiatives, chiefly in the improvement and extension of hotel accommodation and in mounting an exceedingly effective campaign of advertising. The results are writ large in the trade returns, which indicate that the gross receipts from tourism rose from about forty-six million pounds in 1962 to eighty million pounds in 1967, with every expectation – until the northern crisis intervened – that they would rise still higher in time to come.[73]

But while this kind of contact with visitors has no doubt had a liberating effect, there is another kind of contact – ethereal rather than corporal – which has beyond question made an even more dramatic impact upon popular attitudes. This is, of course, television. Ireland had developed its own wireless service – Radio Eireann – as early as 1925, in effect as a branch of the civil service under the control of the Department of Posts and Telegraphs. It derived its revenue mainly from licence fees and from sponsored programmes, but despite this slender foundation soon became something of a national institution, attracting a number of very able men into its service. In the post-war years, however, it fell inevitably under the shadow of its natural competitor, television. When in 1960 the government decided to provide the new medium in Ireland, it created a state-sponsored body to administer both kinds of broadcasting. A special authority was set up to launch the new service, which was to be financed mainly on the basis of licence fees and receipts from commercial advertising. Telefís Eireann went on the air for the first time on New Year's Eve, 1962, and was, predictably, assailed from all points of the compass before it was very much older. It was said to devote too little time – or too much – to the Irish language; it was either dominated by the Church or did not spend enough time on religion; it was too parochial, but it also relied too heavily on American material; it was either under the thumb of the government, or else it was dangerously outspoken. Nevertheless, despite these and many other accusations, it matured remarkably quickly, breaking through taboos of all kinds to discuss before a startled public such issues as birth control, drugs, premarital relations, pornography, and the place of the Church in the modern world. By the mid-1960s it was reckoned that about 348,000 out of 680,000 homes in the country had television sets; the total impact of television, however, has to be measured not just by this figure but by the estimated number of homes – 137,000 – which were able to receive the BBC and Independent Television programmes as well.* The fact that such a considerable proportion of Irish families could see on their hearthrugs all the manifestations of the permissive society which British television relays with such unflagging zeal, not only made nonsense of the censorship of books and films, but threw many stones, or rather bombshells, into the quiet waters of Irish domesticity.

These diverse pressures, combined with the economic and social changes described earlier, have wrought such a transformation that the traveller returning after ten, or even five, years' absence finds himself almost a Rip Van Winkle in this pushing and restless society. The mood that now possesses the country is one of impatience and of criticism, but also one of excitement, which seems indeed to have been checked by a sense of horrified impotence in the face of events in the north, but which may before long be rekindled by the challenge of entry into Europe. It is, naturally, a mood that is expressed with least inhibition by the young and among them it has taken forms familiar elsewhere, including a measure of student unrest, a revival of interest in politics and a growing preoccupation with social justice.† But also, and in the long run, this may prove to be of crucial importance, the new generation is to be distinguished from its predecessors by its changed attitude to the past. It is not the case, as some have said, that young people in Ireland have become indifferent to, or ignorant of, their history. On the contrary, there has never been a time when the past was more accessible to them, by reason of the quiet revolution which has taken history out of the realm of myth and passion and into that of reason and ascertainable fact. The first steps in this revolution

* A survey made in 1967 showed that 77 per cent of households in Dublin City and County owned television sets; for the rest of Leinster the percentage was 55. Munster registered 54 per cent, but in Connacht and the three Ulster counties only 31 per cent of households owned sets. In all regions the proportion of urban owners was, predictably, much higher than that of rural owners. For a valuable account of the impact of television on the electorate, see B. Chubb, *The Government and Politics of Ireland*, pp. 134-44.

† Student unrest in the Republic, it should be said, has hitherto been more pragmatic than ideological, concerned essentially with real grievances about accommodation, library facilities, contact with teachers, and the like.

were taken just over thirty years ago by two scholars, T. W. Moody and R. Dudley Edwards, when, with the encouragement in his old age of no less a figure than Eoin MacNeill, they founded the journal, *Irish Historical Studies,* which at once became, and has since remained, the vehicle for accurate, informed and judicious historical research, not just in the twenty-six counties but in the whole of Ireland. This venture has been followed by others in which the same two pioneers, with the aid of such colleagues as D. B. Quin, J. C. Beckett, T. Desmond Williams and F. X. Martin, have repeatedly taken a leading part, and of which the cumulative effect has been to change the historical outlook of a whole generation.*

It is true, of course, that the new Irish historiography has scarcely yet graduated from fundamental research to synthesis, and that therefore its ability to penetrate into the schools has so far been limited. But it is not too much to claim for it that it has had a very direct effect upon the ideas of an intellectual elite both inside and outside the universities. And since it is this elite which is making its way into politics and into the public service, the fact that its attitude towards the past should have become less romantic, less distorted by prejudice and by patriotic over-simplification, than that of its predecessors may yet prove to be one of the great formative influences upon the future. Some change of attitude there would have been in any event because of the mere passage of time, but the historiographical revolution has helped to ensure that it would be a change in the direction of understanding, not indifference. In this there is a germ of liberation, for to understand the past fully is to cease to live in it, and to cease to live in it is to take the earliest steps towards shaping what is to come from the materials of the present. For the first time in fifty years it is legitimate to believe that those steps are at last being taken.

* Among these ventures may be numbered two series of historical monographs; the establishment of the Thomas Davis lectures broadcast every winter on a wide variety of historical themes extending even to events so near in time as 1951; the launching of a television series of lectures which, when published as *The Course of Irish History,* at once established itself as the balanced yet readable general work the country had been lacking since Edmund Curtis had produced his *History of Ireland* thirty years earlier; and, now in prospect, a multi-volume *New History of Ireland* which will bring together the work of a whole generation of historians who, like the present writer, have had the great good fortune to be trained in this famous school. It would be invidious to name names here, but in the preface will be found listed those among them who, either by their research or their personal assistance, helped in the preparation of this book.

I am not saying that they did not do right in starting their government, they were compelled to do it because they had yelled about 'No Home Rule' for a generation and then they were compelled to take a form of Home Rule that the Devil himself could never have imagined.

Rev. J. B. Armour, cited in W. S. Armour, *Armour of Ballymoney*, p. 332

B. NORTHERN IRELAND UNDER HOME RULE

---

1. Growing-pains of Devolution

The history of Northern Ireland has been dominated by three principal problems which have changed extraordinarily little throughout the entire period of its existence. These are, first, the problem of the triangular relationship with the rest of the United Kingdom and the rest of Ireland; second, the problem of the deep and continuing internal division of the population between, in the main, Unionists and Protestants on the one hand, and Nationalists and Catholics on the other; finally, the problem not only of developing a viable economy in such a small area, but of securing for the people public services and standards of welfare comparable with those in Britain. It would be difficult to determine any order of importance for these problems; indeed, they were all interconnected in one way or another, since each was powerfully influenced by the form of government which the six counties found themselves saddled with in and after 1920. The logical starting point, therefore, for any survey of the province in the early years of partition is to examine the curious experiment in devolution which started it on its course and remained virtually intact until the crisis began in 1968.

The constitutional basis of the experiment is to be found in the Government of Ireland Act of 1920. Originally, as we saw earlier, that Act had been intended to confer Home Rule upon the whole of Ireland. It had recognised, of course, that the deep divisions between north and south could not be ignored and it had provided for separate parliaments and separate executives in the six counties and in the twenty-six counties. But at the same time it had envisaged a single Lord Lieutenant to represent the King in both areas and it had proposed a Council of Ireland consisting of twenty representatives from each parliament through which, it was fondly hoped, better relations between the sundered portions of the country would be established, leading in the end to the peaceful evolution of a single parliament for all Ireland.

This conception has never yet emerged from the realms of fantasy.*

* We may not have heard the last of it, however. At the time of writing

695

The course of events in the south between 1920 and 1922 made it plain that the kind of Home Rule embodied in the Government of Ireland Act would meet with no acceptance there and that the Act, if it was to work at all, would be worked only within the area of the six counties, though even this area was a subject of argument and uncertainty until the collapse in 1925 of the Boundary Commission appointed to adjust the division of territory between north and south. In December of that year it was agreed 'in a spirit of neighbourly comradeship' that the extent of Northern Ireland should continue to be the six counties designated in the Government of Ireland Act – that is, Antrim, Armagh, Down, Fermanagh, Londonderry and Tyrone.

Long before then, however, Northern Ireland had begun to function as a separate entity, accepting that status reluctantly and as a sacrifice, but accepting it because that was the only way in which Ulster Unionists could be sure of staying within the United Kingdom until, of their own volition, they joined the rest of Ireland.[1] It followed, therefore, that since they had no real wish for self-government, the actual form of that self-government reflected, not the striving for autonomy usual in a newly-emerging state, but rather a deep-seated desire to disturb the close relationship with Britain as little as possible. Their leader, and Northern Ireland's first Prime Minister, Sir James Craig, summed up this attitude best in a letter to Lloyd George in 1921: 'As a final settlement and supreme sacrifice in the interests of peace the Government of Ireland Act was accepted by Northern Ireland, although not asked for by her representatives.'[2]

The basis of Northern Ireland's limited self-government is a parliament consisting of the Sovereign, the Senate and the House of Commons. The Sovereign is represented by the Governor (until 1922 by the Lord Lieutenant) who summons, prorogues and dissolves parliament in the Queen's name and gives the royal assent to bills. Although technically the Governor must comply with any instructions issued by the Crown (i.e. Whitehall) in respect of any bill, and must, if so directed, reserve the royal assent, this has only been done once – in 1922 – when it provoked a very sharp reaction in the Northern Ireland parliament. Normally, his functions are mainly ceremonial, though the first Governor, the Duke of Abercorn, probably exerted considerable indirect influence upon ministers partly because he was personally respected, and partly because, as the head of a great Ulster family, he had an intimate knowledge of the province. Of the two Houses, the Senate, as usual in modern bicameral legislatures, is much the less important. It is composed of only twenty-six members. Of these, two – the Lord Mayor of Belfast and the Mayor of Londonderry – are members *ex officio*, the remainder being elected by the House of Commons by proportional representation. Senators hold office for eight years, half re-

---

it still figures occasionally among the mechanisms by which men of good will hope to foster better relations between the two parts of the country.

tiring, every four years, and although their power of amending legislation (except, of course, financial legislation) could theoretically lead to a conflict between the two Houses and thence to a joint sitting as laid down in the Government of Ireland Act, that has never happened. This is scarcely surprising. Since all but two of the Senators are elected by the House of Commons, for them not to echo the opinions of that House would be as much against nature as for a ventriloquist to be contradicted by his dummy.

The House of Commons itself consists of fifty-two members, elected for five years, forty-eight of whom represent territorial constituencies and (until 1969) four the Queen's University, Belfast. The latter were elected by proportional representation, but this method, which applied initially to all constituencies, was replaced in 1929 by a system of simple majorities in single-member constituencies for elections outside the university. The franchise, though based on universal suffrage and broadly similar to that in Britain, had two peculiarities. One was that an elector had to have been born in Northern Ireland or resident in the United Kingdom for seven years. The other was that plural voting was retained, though an elector could only vote once in one constituency. The territorial constituencies underwent no general adjustment of their boundaries between 1929 and 1969, though four new ones replaced the university seats in the latter year. In addition, Northern Ireland sends twelve members to the British House of Commons, the majority of whom over the years have been in effect members of the British Conservative and Unionist party.*

The executive power technically vested in the Sovereign, and on her behalf by the Governor, was in fact exercised by the Executive Committee, commonly called the Cabinet, which normally consisted of nine members – the Prime Minister, a Minister in the Senate, and Ministers responsible respectively for Finance, Home Affairs, Health and Social Services, Education, Agriculture, Commerce and Development. In 1969 a Ministry of Community Relations was added in circumstances later to be described. These ministries have tended over the years to bring within their own control an increasing range of activities which elsewhere in the United Kingdom were still, partially at least, under the control of the local authorities – thus police, fire service, electricity, housing, health and public transport have all been heavily centralised. Local government itself had changed little in structure from that established for all of Ireland by the Act of 1898. Northern Ireland still had, up to 1969, two county boroughs (Belfast and Londonderry), six administrative counties (i.e. the six designated in the Government of Ireland Act), ten boroughs, twenty-four urban districts and thirty-one rural districts. Each of these bodies had an elected council with functions,

* Initially, a university seat was included in the Ulster representation at Westminster, but this was abolished in 1948. Note that the above description of the Stormont parliament applies only to the period before the imposition of direct rule in 1972.

697

composition and sources of revenue broadly similar to the English pattern, but the most significant departure from that pattern lay in the fact that the local government franchise was largely restricted to ratepayers and weighted in favour of property. As a result of this it has turned out that perhaps as many as a quarter of those who were on the parliamentary register had no vote in local elections. We shall have to return to this subject – one of the most explosive in Northern Ireland politics – when we come to deal with the theme of discrimination in northern society.*

The legal system, as one would expect, is similar in its essentials to that of England, since it has changed little in the years after 1920. There is a Supreme Court (as there was in Dublin in the days before partition), there are county courts (as there had been in Ireland for many generations) and there are magisterial courts. The latter were created for all Ireland in the nineteenth century because, with a landed class that tended to be absentee, the English system of justices of the peace had proved ineffective. Consequently resident salaried magistrates were appointed – the 'Irish RMs' described in a previous chapter.† This practice was taken over by Northern Ireland, or rather, taken further, since an act of the local parliament in 1935 discontinued the old method whereby lay justices sat with the resident magistrates and put the latter in sole control of summary jurisdiction.

But to this pattern of an old-established legal system based on a long-accepted English model there is one outstanding exception, the Civil Authorities (Special Powers) Act. In assessing the institutions and practices of government in Northern Ireland it is never possible to move very far from the tumultuous origins of the state. The Government of Ireland Act came into operation in May 1921 and both then and for many months afterwards there was much violence and disorder inside the six counties and along their borders – and this at a time when control of the police was still vested in the British government.‡ In the face of this, and of a campaign of what amounted almost to civil disobedience by many Nationalists, the newly-fledged government in 1922 passed rapidly through the Northern Ireland parliament a bill which, as one member remarked, really only needed to have one clause : 'The Home Secretary shall have powers to do what he likes, or else let somebody else do what he likes for him.' What the Act, when passed, did was to give the Minister power 'to take all such steps and issue all such orders as may be necessary for preserving the peace' according to the regulations laid down, regulations which he could add to from time to time. Originally intended as an annual Act, and as such renewed from year to year from 1922 to 1928, in 1928 it was renewed for five years

* There is a useful account of the evolution of local government in M. Wallace, *Northern Ireland: 50 Years of Self-Government* (Newton Abbott, 1971), pp. 44-56; for recent developments, see below, chap. 6.

† See above, part I, chap. 3.

‡ For this situation, see Part II, chap. 6.

and in 1933 was made permanent. The regulations to which the Act opened the way certainly covered a wide field. There could, if and when required, be regulations imposing a curfew and against the possession of firearms and explosives; there could be others against unlawful drilling and illegal uniforms, or against membership of illegal organisations; there could even be regulations empowering the arrest and detention of persons suspected of having acted or being about to act in a manner prejudicial to peace and order, or regulations enabling the authorities to exclude a person from entering Northern Ireland or confining him to a specific area of the province. And not only this – these regulations were reinforced by the Public Order Act of 1951 imposing controls on disorderly meetings and processions, and by the Flags and Emblems Act of 1954 giving the police powers to seize provocative emblems. In 1970, following the disturbances to be described later, a Public Order (Amendment) Act was passed in the teeth of bitter opposition at Stormont, with the dual object of giving better protection to lawful processions and of enabling the government to deal more effectively with counter-demonstrations.[3]

It has to be said in fairness that while the mainspring of all these special regulations – the so-called Special Powers Act itself – is permanent, the regulations are not, and many of them from time to time have been revoked. Nevertheless, two comments need to be made. One is that so long as the internal tensions within Northern Ireland persist, the government is unlikely to abandon the measures it originally took as necessary to its survival and which, to the extent that its survival is still in question, it may need to revive again at any moment. And the other comment is that an unfortunate consequence of the semi-anarchical circumstances in which the Special Powers Act emerged was that, lacking at first full control of the Royal Ulster Constabulary (replacing the Royal Irish Constabulary), the government took steps to strengthen its position by relying upon a special constabulary created in 1920. It is true that from 1925 this ceased to be a full-time force, but one class, the 'B specials', was retained on a part time basis subject to full-time duty if the need arose.* It has also to be remembered in this context that when control over the Royal Ulster Constabulary did pass to Northern Ireland that force continued to carry arms, as the old Royal Irish Constabulary had done in the days of the Union. Few outward features of life in Northern Ireland have attracted so much adverse comment as the presence in the streets of armed police, and even though critics are often ignorant of the historical reasons for the existence of such a force, the simple fact that it did exist was a perpetual irritant.

It would, however, be unjust to lay too much emphasis upon the special powers that the Northern Ireland government has from time to time made use of. What is most likely to strike the dispassionate ob-

* For the circumstances leading to the decision to disband them in 1969, see below, chap. 5.

server is not the magnitude of the government's powers but rather the curious gaps in its armoury. Unlike, say, the dominion parliaments, or the imperial parliament itself at Westminster, it is in general unable to make laws having extra-territorial effect – its basic function is to legislate on matters relating only to Northern Ireland. But it is far from having a monopoly of these. The Government of Ireland Act set out a list of 'excepted' matters over which the Northern Ireland parliament had no powers of legislation. These were matters concerning the Crown, peace and war, the armed forces, treaties with foreign states, dignities and titles, treason, naturalisation, domicile, trade with any place outside Northern Ireland, cables and wireless, air navigation, lighthouses, coinage and negotiable instruments, weights and measures, trade marks, copyright and patents.

This is a formidable list, but it can be justified on the ground of the need for uniformity within that United Kingdom of which the majority in Northern Ireland so passionately claimed to be a part. But that is not the end of the story. There were three further kinds of limitation on the powers of the Northern Ireland parliament – one negative, the others positive. Negatively, there was a prohibition of laws aimed at religious discrimination, and there was a prohibition against the state taking property without compensation. More positively, there were, in addition to the 'excepted' matters already mentioned, certain other 'reserved' matters on which also the Northern Ireland parliament had not power to legislate. These included the Supreme Court, the postal service, the imposition and collection of customs duties, excise duties on articles manufactured or produced, income tax and surtax, purchase tax and any tax on profits. Further, and as a kind of blanket proviso, the Government of Ireland Act had laid it down that the supreme authority of the United Kingdom parliament at Westminster remained undiminished, that the local parliament could not repeal or alter either the constituent Act (the Government of Ireland Act) or any United Kingdom statute passed after 3 May 1921 and extending to Northern Ireland, and that Northern Ireland statutes would themselves be void to the extent that they were repugnant to the United Kingdom statutes passed after 3 May 1921 and extending to Northern Ireland.[4]

Clearly we have here a complicated situation, arising from the fact that the government of this small area was deliberately divided between two different parliaments and two different administrations. Perhaps it would be more correct to say that it was divided between the Northern Ireland government and legislature on the one hand and Whitehall on the other. Although in theory the shadow of Westminster legislation loomed over Northern Ireland from the beginning in practice the mother parliament has devoted very little time to the affairs of the six counties – in one period of just over a year in 1934-5 the time spent was one hour and fifty minutes, and that seems, until very recently, to have been about the average.[5] The real crux of relations between the authorities in Belfast and the authorities in London has been the question of services – which services shall be administered by which authority and how the cost of these services shall be met. Since, as we have already seen, most kinds of major taxation were among the matters 'reserved' to the parliament at Westminster, it follows that those which were transferred to the Northern Ireland government were few and unimportant – they consisted, in the main, of motor-vehicle and stamp duties, death duties and a few minor excise duties. Altogether, these produced about one-tenth of the revenue raised in the province. Most of the rest came from the 'reserved' taxes, the chief of these being customs duties, the greater part of the excise duties, and taxes on incomes – all of them, of course, being imposed and collected at uniform rates throughout the United Kingdom. The amount of this revenue to be handed over to Northern Ireland was calculated by the Joint Exchequer Board, consisting of a chairman appointed by the Crown and one member each from the Treasury and the Ministry of Finance in Belfast. From Northern Ireland's share of this revenue were, however, deducted, first, the cost of the reserved services (for example the Supreme Court), and second, the contribution to be made by the six counties to the imperial services – such as defence or diplomatic and consular representation – from which Northern Ireland benefited in the same way as other parts of the United Kingdom. The logic of this 'imperial contribution' seemed impeccable – that to the extent that Northern Ireland gained from being an integral part of the empire, so she should be prepared to pay a proportionate amount to the expense of running that empire – but almost from the beginning it was a source of passionate, though frequently ill-conceived, argument. Even more productive of possible friction was the strange arrangement whereby the Northern Ireland government, though charged with the responsibility of administering the wide area of services assigned to it, was utterly unable to control, or even to anticipate in advance, what money (other than the share represented by the transferred taxes) would be available for this purpose. Not only had the imperial contribution to be met each year, and the full cost of the reserved services, but since the actual rate at which taxes would be collected in Northern Ireland was fixed at Westminster, the local Minister for Finance was faced with a revenue that would expand or contract entirely without regard to whatever policies he might be planning to pursue. It was true that the Government of Ireland Act empowered the local parliament to grant relief from income tax, but this was of little real help since this relief could be met only from the six counties' own resources and not at the expense of the United Kingdom.

It was not long before this complex plan began to show itself to be unworkable. Under the Government of Ireland Act the imperial contribution was initially fixed at £7·9 million and the cost of reserved services at £2·2 million. Since the estimated reserved revenue for the province was £14·7 million and the estimated transferred revenue was £1·8 million, this meant that what would be left to Northern Ireland would in fact be £6·4 million. Out of this sum all the domestic services would have to be financed. To the new government, anxious to sweep away the consequences of many years of neglect and to develop schemes of housing, public health and education, this was a very narrow margin within which to have to operate. Too narrow, as it turned out. It was quite true that at the moment when Northern Ireland was being created revenue was buoyant – the total was £16·5 million and expenditure on services (i.e. excluding the imperial contribution) was only £6·3 million. But by 1923, the first full financial year, revenue was down to £13·8 million and from this was deducted an imperial contribution of £6·7 million and payments for reserved services of £1·9 million, leaving little more than £5 million for the province's own expenditure. Thus by 1923, even with an imperial contribution that had not reached the amount originally fixed, the Northern Ireland government was already in difficulties. Indeed, had the full amount of the imperial contribution been insisted upon, either then or in the immediately succeeding years, Northern Ireland would straightway have begun to run at a deficit. What had been left out of account was the way in which the economic circumstances of the whole of the United Kingdom had altered in the years after the war. The six counties suffered their share of the industrial depression of the early twenties – as we shall see presently, unemployment in north-east Ulster was exceptionally high – while at the same time they had to accept the consequences of tax cuts introduced in Britain in 1924.

It is not surprising that this situation resulted in what the Northern Ireland Minister of Finance described as 'long and irritating controversies with the Treasury', which ceased only when an arbitration committee under Lord Colwyn was appointed in 1923 to consider whether any alteration in the imperial contribution was needed. After two years of arduous negotiation, this committee produced an acceptable formula which was partly obtained by standing the Government of Ireland Act on its head. It was recognised that to make the imperial contribution a first charge on the revenue of the province was no longer feasible. Therefore logic dictated that the imperial contribution must be the residue left over *after* domestic expenditure had been met. But what was to prevent an ingenious Minister of Finance in Belfast ensuring that there never was any residue of this kind? Even in 1924, the then Minister of Finance had delivered himself of the, from the British point of view, slightly sinister remark that 'in all matters of social welfare we should be entitled to the same benefits as in Great Britain . . . local autonomy did not necessarily imply any lower social status.'[6]

But did it not? The Colwyn committee was not so sure. True, it accepted the argument that as taxation fell with equal severity upon the Ulsterman as upon the Englishman, Scotsman or Welshman, so, from 1924 onwards, expenditure per head of the population should increase at the same rate as in Britain. But, while this seemed to concede parity of a kind, it was in fact qualified by the way in which the committee defined the *necessary* domestic expenditure of Northern Ireland. That key word 'necessary' was hedged round by three qualifications. First, it must not be taken as allowing Northern Ireland a higher average standard of service than existed in Britain. Second, because the social structure of Northern Ireland was different from that of Britain, expenditure on services was to have regard to 'any lower general level of prices, of wages, or of standards of comfort or general amenity which may exist in Northern Ireland as compared with Great Britain'. Finally, and almost too obvious to be stressed, Northern Ireland would not be allowed to spend money on services which did not exist in Britain.[7] In short, Northern Ireland's permissible expenditure would be limited in two ways – by the fact that spending per head must keep pace with the rate set by Britain, and by the fact, given her social and economic *disparity*, she ought not to expect to be able to finance services of the same scale and scope as those across the water.

There can be little doubt that this arrangement represented clear gain for Northern Ireland, since it ensured that if revenue continued to fall, then so would the imperial contribution to the extent that it might even disappear altogether. Moreover, although the Colwyn committee might frown on the Ulsterman's ambition to have the same social services as his fellow-citizens in Britain, he had no intention of abandoning that ambition. Provided he did not seek to exploit his British connection, either by keeping his own transferred taxes below the levels obtaining in the rest of the United Kingdom, or by pushing his expenditure above that prevailing elsewhere, he could easily convince himself that parity in taxation meant parity in the public services.

But although this may have been the activating principle in Belfast it proved very difficult to put into practice, especially during the depression years of the 1930s, as revenue continued to fall and expenditure continued (with a vengeance) to rise. And even though one consequence of this was that by 1933 the imperial contribution had dwindled almost to vanishing point, the Northern Ireland Minister of Finance was still desperately hard put to it to balance his budget. He was in difficulties, ironically enough, precisely because the increased expenditure on these basic services was necessitated by the principle of parity, and parity was fast becoming a test of the viability of the whole devolutionary experiment. Northern Ireland had to offer its citizens not less than what they would achieve elsewhere in the United Kingdom or it would stand condemned in the eyes of its numerous and implacable critics.

It was unemployment that provided the most extreme test of the principle of parity. Northern Ireland had an insurance scheme identical with that of Britain, the Unemployment Fund being financed by contributions from employers, employees and the state. The trouble was that the amount of unemployment was proportionately much greater in northeast Ulster than in most (though not all) parts of Britain. By 1925 almost a quarter of the insured population in the six counties was out of work and the *deficit* in the Unemployment Fund was £3·6 million. The

Northern Ireland government was caught in a terrible dilemma. On the one hand, it could not hope to exert more than a marginal influence on economic policies which were determined in London for the United Kingdom as a whole. On the other hand, it could not increase its contribution to the Unemployment Fund, partly because the Colwyn formula bound it to observe the same rate as prevailed in Britain, but also because, if it had had liberty to enlarge its contribution, this would only have been liberty to plunge deeper into debt. The orthodox remedies would have been either to increase employers' and workers' contributions, or to cut benefits, or both. But any of these remedies would have been political suicide, since they would at once have been taken to mean that Northern Ireland was no longer able to carry on as a separate entity.

The only course that remained was to plead in London that because Northern Ireland was, after all, not just a separate entity, but also an integral part of the United Kingdom, she deserved to be helped. Up to a point this plea was successful. By the Unemployment Insurance Agreement of 1926 it was settled that the Unemployment Funds of the two parts of the United Kingdom might be kept in a state of parity on the basis of insured populations by making grants to the poorer fund. Ostensibly reciprocal, the Agreement in fact resulted in grants being made by the United Kingdom to Northern Ireland, though this was – it was hoped – to be kept within bounds by the proviso that if in any year the Northern Ireland government paid out more per head of the *total* population than did the British government, then Britain would only meet three-quarters of this excess expenditure.

Even with this limitation it seemed for a time as if the arrangement might work. In 1926–7 the British government paid over to the Northern Ireland government nearly £900,000 in 'equalisation' grants and though in succeeding years the figure never approached that level, it remained substantial up to 1931. But then in 1932 it suddenly ceased altogether. The explanation was simple – though devastating in its effect. Because equalisation payments were made on the basis of total population, and because after 1929 unemployment in Britain was so heavy, she was actually making a heavier payment per head than Northern Ireland was. Consequently no more grants were made and for the next three years Northern Ireland had to try to keep her Unemployment Fund in parity with that of Britain from current revenue alone. It was an impossible task and between 1932 and 1935 the Minister for Finance balanced his budget – if balanced is the right word – by a series of expedients that, had he been there to see them, might have served to convert even Gladstone himself from Home Rule. Indeed, so far from receiving assistance from a hard-pressed Treasury in London, Northern Ireland was required to take two further steps – to revalue the province so as to produce a larger yield in taxes, and to impose an education rate – which were, indeed, long overdue, but which could hardly have come at a worse time.

However, virtue, even if enforced, proved its own reward. In 1936 the Unemployment Insurance Agreement was amended so that equalisation payments should thenceforth be calculated on the basis not of total, but of insured, populations. Since the proportion of the population in Ulster in insurable employment was much smaller than in Britain, the former's *per capita* payments were inflated. It followed, therefore, that manna not only again began to fall from Whitehall, but that it did so more abundantly. And there was even better to come. In May 1938 the Minister of Finance extracted from the British Chancellor of the Exchequer a promise that in the event of a deficit in the Northern Ireland budget money should be found to make it good, *provided* that the deficit was not the result of a standard of social expenditure higher than, or of a standard of taxation lower than, that of Britain. Whether or not it was a coincidence that this announcement was made only a matter of days after Britain had agreed to the return of the treaty ports to the Irish Free State it is impossible to say, but that decision had at one stroke enormously increased the importance of northeast Ulster to British naval strategy. Northern Ireland was no longer just an embarrassingly demanding poor relation, she had become a vital link in the defences of the United Kingdom.

The internal consequences for the province of this change of status, as it might almost be described, will be discussed later.* Here it is sufficient to draw three conclusions from these intricate but crucial transactions of the inter-war years. First, it is evident that the financial provisions of the Government of Ireland Act, even though amended in the ways that we have seen, condemned Northern Ireland to much uncertainty and difficulty in her day-to-day administration. It is true that in the key areas of pensions and unemployment insurance the great objective of parity was achieved, but it was achieved at a price. And this leads us to the second conclusion – that so much effort and so much money went into the frantic race to keep up with Britain in the scale of social benefits paid out, that there were no resources left to put through those essential long-term reforms that ministers had set their hearts on in the first flush of enthusiasm. So in 1939, as in 1922, the province was still plagued by ill-health, poor housing, bad roads, and inadequate schools.

To say all this is to point to the final inescapable conclusion – that whatever hope Ulstermen might have had of turning the unwanted gift of self-government to constructive ends through developing the powers of their own legislature, it was thwarted by the bitter experience of life as part of the United Kingdom in the depression years. A recent verdict on the achievement of Lord Craigavon (as Sir James Craig had become in 1927) sums up that experience harshly but not unfairly: 'On the ramshackle foundations of the Act of 1920 he and his colleagues had built, not a half-way house, but a lean-to whose stability depended on ties that bound it to Britain.'[8]

* See chap. 5 below.

2. The Depression Years

In economics, as in politics, the aim of Northern Ireland in the inter-war years might be summed up by the single word – survival. Yet the very nature of devolution complicated the task of economic adjustment. In one sense, of course, it was true that the continuance of close political ties with Britain only reflected the economic realities of the situation. Even in the nineteenth century northeast Ulster had been much more closely integrated with the economy of the rest of the United Kingdom than with the economy of the rest of Ireland. That integration was bound to continue, perhaps even to grow, given the fact that from 1921 onwards the six counties remained part of a free trade area in which men, capital and goods could move easily to and fro, which shared the same monetary and financial system, and which, without significant differentiation, participated in the same economic institutions and social services.

However, although Northern Ireland seemed inescapably a part of the British economy, it was, like some of the distressed areas across the water, a part which, being highly specialised, had its own particular problems that required local knowledge if they were to be successfully dealt with. And this was where the political settlement created a difficulty. Because, although the Government of Ireland Act did entrust considerable powers of economic regulation to the region, those powers had to be exercised within a broader framework of policy that was laid down at Westminster for the United Kingdom as a whole and over which Belfast had little enough influence. Thus, devolution in effect restricted Northern Ireland not only, as we have seen already, in matters of taxation, but in the power to achieve any measure of real economic independence. It could not set up its own tariffs, or interfere in other ways with external trade, it could not have a separate fiscal policy, and it had to accept whatever monetary policy happened to be in vogue in London. Any survey of the economy of the province, therefore, has to strike a balance of profit and loss between the effects of integration on the one hand and of decentralisation on the other.

An orphan of the political storm, almost, one might say, a *faute de mieux* creation, the six counties hardly seemed a rational, let alone an ideal, economic unit. Even its borders seemed to militate against it. On the landward side, a straggling frontier which owed more to religious than to economic geography, and cut off one of its two large towns, Londonderry, from its natural hinterland; to the east, the inhospitable sea, adding to the cost of its imports and subtracting from the value of its exports. Within these boundaries was a small and fairly thinly populated area. The province consisted of 5,238 square miles – about one-sixth of the land area of all Ireland – supporting a population which, though it fell in the later nineteenth century like that of other parts of Ireland, had tended to increase from the turn of the century onwards. In 1911 it was 1¼ million. When the next census was taken in 1926 it had increased by 7,000 and in 1937 it had gone up to 1,280,000. Emigration had taken its toll in the earlier years, here as elsewhere in the country, but during the inter-war years it had slowed down. Between 1926 and 1937, for example, the net loss seems only to have been about 20,000 altogether; although this is difficult to measure precisely as there is evidence of a considerable mobile element in the population which moved, and still moves, to and fro between Northern Ireland and Great Britain according to the state of the labour market.[1]

The most striking feature of this population was its distribution. By 1937 about sixty-three per cent of the whole population lived either in Belfast or in towns and villages within a thirty mile radius of the city.[2] It was this which gave the demographic structure of Northern Ireland its curiously lopsided appearance and, as we shall see, it was this which made the problem of industrial employment so crucial to the welfare of the province as a whole.

The growth of the Belfast conurbation was no doubt at the expense of the countryside and even though it sometimes happened that in years of acute industrial depression the flow of migrant labour would be from the urban to the rural areas, on balance it was the farm-worker who was attracted to the town rather than the other way about; between 1926 and 1937, it has been calculated, the net outflow from agriculture was about 5,000, and this would probably have been considerably larger but for a transfer of nearly 4,000 in the other direction in 1931–2.[3] Nevertheless, the extent of this agrarian depopulation should not be exaggerated. Both in appearance and in economic reality the northeast remained strongly agricultural. In 1926 farming accounted for about a quarter of all occupied persons and this proportion was to remain remarkably stable over the years – as late as 1945 the percentage was almost exactly the same, the actual number then employed being the equivalent of about 140,000 full-time workers.[4]

Agriculture was thus, in terms of the amount of labour employed, the largest single industry in Northern Ireland, but, paradoxically, it was also an industry which was organised on a very small scale. The typical unit was the family farm making little use, and that generally on a seasonal basis, of outside agricultural labour. The tendency towards consolidation of holdings which we have noticed elsewhere in Ireland, was evident in the six counties also, though up to the time of the 1937 census, and indeed beyond it, the emphasis was still overwhelmingly on farms of between one and thirty acres which – in that year – accounted for nearly 60 per cent of the total. Farms of over one hundred acres were relatively few and totalled only 4.1 per cent of all holdings, compared with nearly 9 per cent in the Irish Free State.[5]

As might be expected from such a structure – though influenced also, it must be said, by soil and climate – there was little attempt between the wars to grow wheat on any extended scale and crops in general were much less important than livestock. It was characteristic of this intensive, small-scale farming that while livestock of all kinds figured largely, the trend was somewhat away from cattle (declining from 173,000 in 1930–1 to 156,000 in 1938–9) and towards sheep, pigs and poultry. Sheep went up in the same period from 261,000 to 397,000, pigs from 250,000 to 844,000 and poultry from almost 5½ million to almost 6¼ million. To a limited extent this emphasis may have been influenced by subsidies (which went mainly to beef producers) but it is more likely that the real salvation of agriculture in the six counties during the 1930s was that it continued to enjoy access to the British market.[6]

The pattern of production which these figures reflect, while no doubt dictated by the environment and the market, was sedulously fostered by the government through an agricultural policy which might almost have been said to march step by step with that of the Irish Free State in the first decade of its existence. Thus in the north, as in the south, the process of land purchase was rounded out by further legislation (in the case of Northern Ireland by an act of the imperial parliament in 1925) applying the principle of compulsion and creating in the course of time 40,000 more farmer-owners; it is perhaps worth adding, in view of Mr de Valera's policy after 1932, that when Northern Ireland was set up it was conceded that the land annuities worth about £658,000 in the mid-thirties, arising out of agreements to purchase *before* 1920, should be transferred to the new government as a 'free gift'.[7] Apart from this legislation, reinforcing, if reinforcement were needed, the dominance of the small family farm, the local parliament passed its own measures designed primarily to improve agricultural education and to increase the value of the product. Into the former category fell the creation of a Faculty of Agriculture in the Queen's University, Belfast, which had from the beginning a strong bias towards research and, at a humbler level, the provision of winter classes throughout the province and the establishment of residential schools in selected places. Side by side with these projects went a series of enactments between 1924 and 1933, prescribing minimum standards of quality and packing to be observed by exporters of eggs, fruit, meat and dairy products at the same time, and again reminiscent of the Free State, the Livestock Breeding Act of 1922 required the registration of all bulls and thus enabled the Ministry of Agriculture to supervise the transition to a better quality of cattle. In the realm of marketing, also, the government was ready to intervene: the Agricultural Marketing Acts of 1931 and 1933 set up marketing boards, composed of representatives of producers and of the Ministry of Agriculture, which had power not only to compel registered producers to sell direct to the Board, or through its agency, but also to fix prices and determine the conditions of sale.

These various measures, combined with the native shrewdness and industry of the Ulster farmer, helped to produce an increase in the gross agricultural output of Northern Ireland from about £11 million in 1926 to an average of £16·4 million for the years 1936-7 to 1938-9 inclusive. Although modest in scope, this increase, it has to be remembered, was made at a time of worldwide depression and is evidence of perhaps greater vitality than the bare figures would suggest.[8]

Yet, although the state of Ulster agriculture would doubtless have been worse if there had been no governmental initiatives of this kind, that is not to say that all was well during the inter-war years. On the contrary, small farmers in the six counties were much like small farmers elsewhere. They lived a hand-to-mouth existence with little or no capital to spare for improving their buildings, or buying fertilizers and machinery. Even as late as 1947, an inquiry revealed that in many parts of the province, farmers and labourers were working with implements little different from those used a hundred years earlier.[9] Moreover, the wages of agricultural labourers before the war were substantially lower than those of their British counterparts (22/3 a week in 1936 on average, compared with 32/6 in England and Wales) while the working week was longer.[10] No doubt this was an important factor in the drift from the land even before the Second World War, just as the prominence of agriculture itself in the whole economy had the effect of depressing income in total and per head.[11]

But agriculture, significant though it might be, was not what made the province unique in Ireland. In the first half of the twentieth century, as in the second half of the nineteenth, its economic welfare was inextricably bound up with the fate of its industries. Even before 1914 these industries had begun to reveal serious deficiencies, some at least of which seemed beyond the power of man to remove. Thus it was a geological, and not a human fault, for example, that the northeast, like the rest of Ireland, lacked mineral resources, especially coal, and that fuel, iron and steel had to be imported from the mainland. This had a doubly damaging effect. On the one hand, the cost of bringing the fuel to the industrialist added to the cost of the product. And on the other hand, precisely because the supply and cost of fuel was a critical factor, industry tended to be concentrated into a few highly specialised lines. This tendency in its turn was reinforced both by the smallness of the domestic market and by the consequent necessity of exporting overseas a large part of what was manufactured in the province.

We find, therefore, that in the first half of the twentieth century specialisation continued in much the same direction as before, with two main groups of industries absorbing between them about fifty per cent of the labour force. One of these was textiles – where linen was still predominant, though increasingly under strain – and the other was shipbuilding, engineering, vehicle building and repairing. These two groups were complementary rather than competitive, for whereas the first employed mainly women, the second relied almost entirely upon male workers. Unhappily, both groups proved to be extremely vulnerable in the situation that developed after 1918. Being so heavily dependent upon their ability to export, they suffered naturally from every deterioration of trading conditions. Thus they were hit by the postwar slump which set in about 1921 and in the first full year of the new Ministry of Labour's administration eighteen per cent of insured workers were unemployed. Next, they were put at a heavy disadvantage by the return to the gold standard in 1925 and the consequent overvaluation of sterling, with the result that both in that year and in 1926 about a quarter of the insured labour force was out of work. Things improved somewhat during what came to be regarded as the 'boom years' of 1927–9, but as the level of unemployment continued to average about fifteen per cent it will be seen that the definition of a boom is rather elastic. Even this improvement was speedily halted by the world depression and by 1932 the percentage of unemployed was over twenty-seven. Throughout the decade 1930–9 it never fell below twenty per cent and averaged about twenty-five per cent. In 1938, indeed, nearly 85,000, or 28·3 per cent of the insured population, had no jobs.[12]

Within individual industries there were, of course, different problems, but most of them had this in common – that not only were they export industries adrift in an increasingly protectionist world. but they were also industries for whose products there was likely to be a diminishing demand even in reasonably prosperous times. Linen was perhaps a supreme example of this. losing ground. as it did. first to cotton, then to man-made fibres. And the decline in linen affected also the highly specialised engineering industry which had developed great expertise in the manufacture of textile machinery, not only for the mills and factories of the Lagan valley, but for buyers overseas. The shipping industry, and with it the closely associated rope-making industry, was likewise faced with a shrinking market. As world trade dwindled, so the need for ships to carry goods or passengers also declined, until in the Belfast shipyards employment shrank from about 20,000 in 1924 to scarcely more than 2,000 in 1933. In that grim year Harland and Wolff launched no ships at all, the first time a year had passed without a launching from their slipways for over a century. And when in 1934 the other large firm, Workman and Clark, went out of business, the industry seemed to be within sight of the end.[13]

Was it not possible to arrest this decay, if necessary by government action? To a generation well accustomed to the intervention of the state in all sorts of economic matters the urgent need of some kind of official initiative will seem self-evident. It was not so self-evident in the 1930s, partly because the Keynesian revolution in economic thinking had not yet taken its effect in government circles, and partly because, in the absence of any commitment to the idea of deficit finance, ministers and parliaments were mesmerised by what seemed the inescapable duty of facing a wholly unorthodox situation by the orthodox methods of unemployment assistance and relief. It is, however, only fair to add that the Northern Ireland government did seek legislation empowering it to assist, financially or by other means, firms wishing to start new enterprises or to extend existing businesses. These powers were embodied in the Loan Guarantee Acts passed between 1922 and 1938, and in the New Industries (Development) Acts of 1932 and 1937. The Loan Guarantees were of only very limited scope and were aimed mainly at the rescue of the shipping industry. Up to the time when the Acts ceased to operate (1940) a total of £22½ million had been advanced to firms in need of support and by 1950 nearly all of this had been repaid. The New Industries (Development) Acts, on the other hand, were more directly designed to attract new business to the area, since they contained a proviso that the government could make grants to undertakings established in order to produce goods not available in Northern Ireland – the grants being equivalent to about twenty years' rent of premises and supplemented sometimes by exemption from rates. The 1937 Act went even further by making interest-free loans available for building or adapting factories or works. But it cannot be said that the response was overwhelming. There was certainly some evidence of differentiation in the engineering industry – a switch, in some cases, from textile machinery to heating equipment, industrial fans, electric motors and so on – while the establishment of an aircraft factory by Short and Harland in Belfast in 1937 was a new portent. However, the total number of firms taking advantage of the new facilities was only fifty-four, and even by 1955 they were providing employment for not much more than 6,000 workers.[14]

This bleak picture of the situation in Belfast is to some extent offset by the growth in the so-called 'service industries' – in the distributive trades, the professions, education and administration. Because, despite unemployment, the city continued to grow in population, the need for such services increased, as indeed it did also, though to a lesser degree, throughout the province. In the whole of Northern Ireland the number of insured workers in the service industries in 1926 was 70,000 and by 1939 this had grown to 102,000. Even here, however, there were 20,000 out of work in the latter year.[15] It is, in short, impossible to escape for long from the overwhelming problem of economic life in the six provinces between the wars – the persistence at all times and in every sector of massive unemployment.

The government response to this challenge was scarcely impressive. True, within the framework of devolution and of the financial orthodoxies of the time, there may not have seemed to be over-much room for manoeuvre, although it is hard to resist the impression that some of the inadequacies of these years may also have been due to lethargy, or even complacency, especially among local authorities. Housing is a case in point. Even though the first census (in 1926) showed that eighteen per cent of the population lived at a density of more than two persons to a room, no housing survey was undertaken until the middle of the war, when it was found that 100,000 new dwellings were urgently

711

needed. Yet between 1919 and 1936 the *total* of all types of dwellings built in Northern Ireland was only 50,000 and of these the vast majority were built by private enterprise. Lack of money, no doubt, is part of the explanation but not all, since at least for rural housing, generous exchequer assistance was available in the early years of the state. Even so, by 1939 less than 4,000 labourers' cottages were built by local authorities under legislation passed by the Northern Ireland government and of these Antrim, Down and Londonderry accounted for most. Not a single cottage was built in Fermanagh by a rural district council in the whole of that time. Such cottages as were built elsewhere were for the most part of a very low standard, frequently lacking gas or electricity or reasonable sanitation; on the eve of the war eighty-seven per cent of rural dwellings had no running water.[16]

Nor were conditions any better in the towns – if possible, they were worse. Under the various Northern Ireland Housing Acts passed in the inter-war period a total of 34,312 houses was built in Ulster towns and of this total the local authorities provided precisely 2,166. It was not all, of course, the fault of the local authorities. Many of them were too small to conduct such operations and they were not helped by the fever chart of government subsidies which shot up and down with bewildering rapidity, vanishing altogether in 1937. The result was that although the bad times drove down the rents of houses that were built, even these houses were beyond the reach of the very poor, who still often lived in dwellings officially regarded as uninhabitable, but which could not be destroyed because there was no money (and indeed no coherent plan) for slum-clearance and nowhere for the occupants to go if their tenements were pulled down.[17]

The imprint of the grim years of depression was felt in other spheres also. Public health, for instance, which should have been a matter of the highest urgency, was seriously neglected throughout this period. Ministers who would have liked to have cut a path through the administrative jungle inherited from Dublin Castle were inhibited from doing so time and time again by lack of finance. Thus, although at the outset of the new regime Northern Ireland actually had the worst death rate in the British Isles (in the years 1922–4 it averaged 15.5 per 1,000 of the population) its position on the eve of the war had scarcely improved at all. The death-rate was then 14.4 per 1,000 and it was a poor consolation to know that although Northern Ireland was still at the bottom of the list, it now shared that place with the Irish Free State. The contributory factors to this sorry situation were many – they included a serious scarcity of hospitals; grossly inadequate pay for dispensary doctors, and for nurses and midwives; sanitary conditions throughout the province of an almost medieval primitiveness; little effective check on the purity of food and milk; above all, perhaps, no serious effort to deal with the ravages of tuberculosis, which in 1938 reached such an appalling degree of intensity that it carried off forty-six per cent of all those who had died between the ages of fifteen and twenty-five, and thirty-eight per cent of those between twenty-five and thirty-five. This fearsome wastage of young life was further compounded by extremely high rates of both maternal and infant mortality. More mothers died in childbirth at the end of the inter-war period than they did at the beginning (5.5 per 1,000 births in 1936-8 compared with 4.7 in 1922-4), and although the number of infants dying did decrease slightly (from seventy-nine per 1,000 in the earlier years to seventy-six in the later), the Northern Ireland rate was considerably above that prevailing in the twenty-six counties. No doubt the concentration of population in Belfast had a good deal to do with this, but a committee reporting on the problem in 1939 commented that 'for the whole of the population above the status of pauper, midwifery provision in the broader sense is a private matter'. Paupers, however, were not so privileged as this might seem to indicate, for despite the sweated labour of over-worked midwives, perhaps a quarter of all children dying under the age of one year in 1937-8 died in a workhouse.[18]

The shadow of the workhouse, indeed, hung over all categories of the very poor, for although in practice outdoor relief had been becoming steadily more usual over the whole of Ireland in the second half of the nineteenth century, the Irish poor law still placed institutional relief at the centre of the system. Increasingly, however, 'the house' had become the refuge not of the able-bodied poor, but of the sick, the aged, infirm, and insane; as well as of illegitimate children and their mothers. The new brooms at Stormont had hoped to abolish this ancient system with its apparatus of unions and boards of guardians, but they were hamstrung by lack of resources and until after the Second World War the poor of the six counties continued to depend either on the shelter of the workhouse or on a meagre pittance of relief if they managed to stay outside. It is true, of course, that Northern Ireland followed the United Kingdom's lead in extending the scope of unemployment insurance and in introducing unemployment assistance in 1934 (not fully operative until 1937) for those who had no right to insurance benefit. But these innovations did not exempt the local authorities from having to shoulder the main part of the burden of poor relief which, at a time of heavy unemployment, could reach astronomical proportions. In Belfast alone expenditure under this head rose from £98,265 in 1923-4 to over £330,000 in 1933-4, by which time it was absorbing more than a third of all the revenue from the rates.

Vast though such expenditure seemed to contemporaries, it trickled through to the individual recipients as the bitter dregs of official charity grudgingly conceded after a searching means test. In some country districts it was apparently deemed possible to support life on as little as 2/6 a week for a single person, and in Belfast in 1932 a married man with one child could expect only 12 shillings a week. It is hardly surprising that that very year saw a remarkable demonstration in the city's streets in which both Protestant and Catholic workers joined together — hunger and degradation obscuring for a brief moment the deeply etched lines of religious and political division.[19] Nor was it surprising that the children of the Belfast unemployed in the 'thirties were reported to be two or three inches shorter and ten pounds lighter than their middle-class contemporaries, or that a survey of working-class conditions in the city in 1938-9 showed that thirty-six per cent of those investigated were living in absolute poverty – unable to buy enough food, clothing or fuel to maintain health and working capacity.[20] It was the final ironic comment on the Prime Minister's clarion call of 23 June 1921, the very day after the formal opening of the new parliament: 'We have nothing in our view except the welfare of the people. Our duty and our privilege are from now onwards to have our parliament probe to the bottom those problems that have retarded progress in the past, to do everything that lies in our power to help forward developments in the town and country. . . .'[21]

3. The Politics of Siege

The defence of Derry against the investing forces of James II ranks with the battle of the Boyne in the mythology of Ulster Protestantism. Indeed, even more than the Boyne, Derry is an exact and enduring symbol of the siege mentality – outwardly aggressive, but masking a deep sense of insecurity – which has distinguished the northern Protestant for most of his history. Admittedly, the Act of Union with Britain, by binding the two islands closer together politically and economically, ended the isolation which lay at the root of Protestant anxiety, and also helped to make possible the remarkable industrial expansion of the northeast in the latter part of the nineteenth century. But when that Union began to be threatened and was eventually broken then the old fears came flooding back and the siege mentality reasserted itself. For the first twenty years of Northern Ireland's existence this mentality dominated the politics of the six counties. Indeed, even the very acceptance of the fact that 'Ulster' was to consist of six counties, rather than of the traditional nine, reflected the siege mentality, indicating as it did that, given the heavy preponderance of Unionists over Nationalists in the area marked out for Home Rule, the Unionist leaders had finally accepted that six would be easier to control than nine.

'What we have now we hold', Sir James Craig had said in 1922, when refusing to co-operate with the Boundary Commission, and in this single phrase he summed up the central creed of Ulster Unionism, which ever since has been dedicated to the proposition that the status of Northern Ireland as a self-governing entity within the United Kingdom must at all costs be preserved. And since he himself remained in power uninterruptedly until his death in 1940, it followed that continuity, both of leadership and of belief, was preserved intact for the first crucial generation of the experiment in devolution. A man of undoubted courage and ability, though of limited intellectual horizons, he had begun to make a name for himself before the First World War as one of the more intransigent Ulster Unionists in the British House of Commons. At that time somewhat overshadowed by Carson, he differed from his leader in two important respects. One was in the matter of temperament. Carson, though dogged by ill-health and a prey to hypochondria, was intensely dramatic, almost flamboyant, in his approach to politics, bringing to his role not only the forensic skill of a great advocate, but also a genuine, if sometimes theatrical, passion. Craig on the other hand, as befitted a northern Presbyterian who was also the son of a wealthy distiller, was more cautious, more dour, but also – and in the long run – more tenacious.

The other difference between them went much deeper. Carson, though he had led *Ulster* Unionism brilliantly, was at heart an *Irish* Unionist, and for him – just as much as for any Nationalist, though, of course, for quite opposite reasons – partition was a tragedy. It was a tragedy because it left the southern Unionists, to whom he belonged and whom he understood so well, isolated in what seemed in 1921 circumstances of deadly danger. It is legitimate to doubt whether Craig's heart was wrung to any overwhelming degree by the loss of his colleagues in the south. He was an Ulsterman through and through, and once it became apparent that the Union, and with it the unity of Ireland, was doomed, his business was to do the best he could for his own people.

At first it hardly seemed that that best could be good enough. Not only did the actual area of the six counties remain in doubt until the collapse of the Boundary Commission in 1925, but at the very moment the new government was set up in the north its physical existence was threatened by violence from the IRA along its borders as well as by the internal religio-political frictions between Protestant Unionists on the one hand and Catholic Nationalists on the other.* So bad did the situation become that in 1922 no fewer than 232 people were killed in the north and nearly 1,000 were wounded, while more than three million pounds' worth of property was destroyed.[1]

The danger from without was overcome, partly with the help of the British army, partly by the use of emergency powers and the creation of the special constabulary, and most of all, perhaps, because the outbreak of the Civil War in the south relieved the pressure on the north. But the internal division within the province remained, heavy with menace and apparently insoluble. Put in its starkest terms, it was the division between those who were committed to upholding the new state and those who regarded it as an intolerable tyranny to be torn down as soon as possible. The polarisation of politics around this single issue, which derived additional bitterness from the inescapable fact that it was a religious as well as a constitutional issue, condemned public life to what, on the face of it, seemed perpetual paralysis.

This superficial impression is misleading. Tension, not stasis, has been the normal condition of politics in Northern Ireland. But it is true that the tension, at any rate between the wars, arose mainly out of the constitutional question and that, by comparison, important aspects of the economic or social well-being of the community tended either to be neglected altogether or to be treated within the framework of the abiding political and religious rivalries of majority and minority. For that generation there could be no real work of reconciliation – all at-

* The identification of a particular creed with a particular political attitude is not absolute. There have of course been exceptions on both sides, but most commentators agree that, unhappily, a man's politics in Northern Ireland can generally be deduced from his religion.

titudes had to be related to the central problem of whether or not the state was to continue in being.

For the Unionist majority, therefore, politics reduced itself to two main preoccupations: first, to develop the concept of devolution (as we have already seen them developing it) in such a way as to make the British connection more indissoluble, while at the same time making it financially more beneficial to the six counties; and secondly, to maintain the status quo at home. That status quo may in fact have been safer than they believed, or affected to believe. Later we shall examine some of the internal weaknesses in the Nationalist position, but first it is necessary to insist upon the strength of the Unionists. If, as is unfortunately to a large extent the case, religious persuasion is an index of political affiliation, then census of population will help us towards at least an approximate estimate of the relative proportions of the two opposing groups. During the inter-war period (and the pattern did not alter greatly after 1945), Catholics amounted to about a third of the population. To be more precise, in 1926, the first census of the new regime showed the Catholic proportion to be 33·5 per cent. Presbyterians came next with 31·3 per cent, followed by the Church of Ireland with 27 per cent. The remainder consisted of Methodists (3·9 per cent) and others (4·3 per cent).[2]

How, it may be asked, were these groupings reflected in the results of general elections? In 1921 the Unionist party gained forty seats, the Nationalists six and the Republicans six. In 1925 the comparable figures were Unionists thirty-seven (but including four Independents of various kinds), Nationalists ten, Labour three and Republicans two. Subsequent elections continued to produce broadly similar results, the dominant parties being the Unionists and, to a markedly lesser degree, the Nationalists. The cry has repeatedly been raised that the boundaries of constituencies were drawn in such a way as to discriminate against Nationalists. If this were true on the massive scale that is sometimes alleged one would expect to see that constituencies held by Nationalists had larger populations than those held by Unionists; in fact they tended on the average to have smaller populations. Alternatively, one would expect to see small Unionist majorities in some areas, with large Nationalist majorities in adjoining areas. Something of this kind has happened in Fermanagh and in Londonderry, though in the former case geography may have had as much to do with the result as conscious manipulation. The subject has long been, and still is, extremely controversial, but the charge of extensive gerrymandering for elections to the Northern Ireland parliament is difficult to prove conclusively. Perhaps the fairest comment is that made in a recent and admirably detached survey: 'Our inquiries do not, however, support the view that "gerrymandering" has any large influence on parliamentary (as opposed to local) elections.'[3] Local elections are, indeed, a very different matter and will be considered later in the broad context of discrimination in general.* But so far as elections to the parliament at Stormont are concerned, the fact seems to be that, as one would expect, the election results follow very closely the geographical distribution of the different religious groupings; but since Nationalist support is drawn mainly from the rural areas it is more widely dispersed and therefore often unable to bring its weight to bear very effectively. It is, however, true that Unionists have had two built-in advantages – three out of the four university seats went regularly to swell their strength, and the plural vote for business premises also worked in their favour. On the other hand it is surely significant that in the election for seats in the imperial parliament at Westminster, for which the constituencies were drawn up by independent Boundary Commissions, the usual pattern has been for Unionists to win from eight to ten out of twelve seats.

It seems then that Unionist fears of being out-voted were from the beginning ill-founded. This, however, did not prevent them from making assurance doubly sure. The abolition of proportional representation for local elections as early as 1922 was bitterly criticised on this ground, and though other forms of discrimination (for example, qualifications regarding property and residence) may have been just as damaging, there can be little doubt that when proportional representation was withdrawn from parliamentary elections also in 1929, the motivation was directly political. The immediately preceding years had seen the return to Stormont of a sprinkling of Independent Unionists claiming to represent either specific interests – ratepayers, for instance, or temperance enthusiasts – or else a more generalised desire to move the government forward along the path of social and economic reform. Lord Craigavon had no doubts at all about the possible effects of such deviationism. Proportional representation, he made it clear, 'submerges and clouds the issue. At election times, the people do not really understand what danger may result if they make a mistake when it comes to third, fourth, fifth or sixth preferences. By an actual mistake they might wake up to find Northern Ireland in the perilous position of being submerged in a Dublin parliament.'[4] In practice, however, it seems to have been the peripheral parties that suffered most and the two elections that followed the abolition of proportional representation reproduced the old pattern in all essentials. In 1929 Unionists, including Independents, had forty-one seats, Nationalists ten, and Labour and Republicans one each. In 1933, the grouping was little different – Unionists of various shades won thirty-nine seats, Nationalists nine, Labour and Republicans two each.[5]

From this electoral pattern two consequences followed – each with an important bearing on the character of northern politics. One was that the opposition throughout this period was painfully weak. Indeed, in the technical sense of the term, there was no *official opposition*, since the Nationalists refused to play that role and did not even take their seats at all until 1925. This led directly to the second consequence im-

* See chap. 5 below.

posed by the electoral pattern – that because there was no possibility of government alternating between rival parties, the Unionist bloc remained virtually unchanged year after year. Even the intermittent (though persistent) eruptions of Independent Unionists failed to fracture this monolithic structure, which was characterised not only by the regular return of a large number of Unionists without a contest, but also by the fact that many of the same people sat for long periods without replacement. Of the fifty-two members sitting in 1927, fifty-four per cent were still members in 1936, and forty per cent of *them* had sat in the Northern Ireland parliament since 1921.[6] The same tendency was repeated within the government itself. Not only did Lord Craigavon die in office (in November 1940), but no fewer than four of his six cabinet colleagues had held government posts continuously from 1921 onwards.[7] It is true that this state of affairs was eventually to produce a demand for change, and even something approaching a palace revolution, but the fact remains that in the innermost citadel of Unionist power there has been unbroken continuity since the foundation of the state.

Yet although this points towards an old, stale oligarchy, it would be wrong to underestimate the extent to which official Unionism appealed to a wide variety of classes and interests. Admittedly, the representation of the party in the Northern Ireland House of Commons was mainly confined to industrialists, lawyers and other professional men, with a handful of the landed-gentry. But outside Stormont its roots went much deeper. The essence of its strength, as has been well said, was that it was 'a party of the Protestant people'. As such it had to contain not only the old, and by no means dormant, radicalism of the Presbyterians, but also the Anglican conservatism of the landed gentry, while taking account at the same time of the needs and prejudices of a largely urban working class which, in the dockyards or on the factory floors, was deeply sensitive to economic as well as religious rivalries with its Catholic counterpart.[8]

In the more distant past there had been deep divisions between the non-conforming churches and the Anglicans. These, however, had tended to disappear during the nineteenth century. On the one hand, the disestablishment of the Church of Ireland and the land legislation enabling farmers to buy out their landlords had together undermined the position of the traditional leaders of society. On the other hand, the growth of industrialism and the obvious benefits accruing from membership of the British free trade system had helped to convince both manufacturers and workers that the Union was essential to their well-being. This is not to deny that social divisions remained in the six counties – they did and do. But it is indisputable that the things which divided Protestants from each other had come to be much less important than the things which united them against Catholics.

One of the things uniting them most was undoubtedly the Loyal Orange Order. We have seen already how during the Home Rule crisis it served as a focus of political and religious sentiment. It continued to fulfil that function after 1921 and although it may be true that among the middle-class some of its rituals began to be regarded as archaic, if not laughable, its influence should not be under-estimated. Even now, for a Protestant to seek a career in politics without joining the Order would be foolhardy and almost certainly futile.* No details of membership are published, but it has been estimated that two-thirds or more of the adult male population may belong to it.[9] For them it has traditionally fulfilled two essential functions. First, with its marches, its sashes and banners, its bands (and above all those thudding, evocative drums), it has provided the Ulster Unionist with much of the colour and drama of his creed. Each year the twelfth of July is a gigantic exercise in catharsis which serves to give a kind of identity to what otherwise would be a variegated and much fragmented Protestantism. The Order's other function is, if anything, even more important. It serves as a link between different sections of society – small farmers, aristocratic landlords, linen magnates, shipyard workers – all can enter it on the same basis of equality. As a social emollient, therefore, no less than as a stimulus to patriotic emotions, the Orange Order has been essential to the structure of Unionism.

The very fact that it spread its net so wide may help to explain one feature of politics in the six counties which is apt to puzzle the outside observer – the absence of any strongly developed Labour party. Such development as there has been belongs mainly to the years after 1945, and although two or three seats at Stormont were won from time to time in the inter-war period by Labour candidates, there was little indication of anything resembling a modern Labour party emerging at that time. There were, of course, other reasons for this besides the attractions of the Orange Order. One was the fact that although there was a trade union movement in Northern Ireland it lacked any real centre of authority. Northern trade unionists were either affiliated to British unions with headquarters across the Irish Sea, or else they hankered after affiliation with southern Irish unions with headquarters across the border.† In the first case they could exercise little influence upon policy, and in the second case they were baulked by the refusal of the Northern Ireland government to recognise either the Irish Congress of Trade Unions or its Northern Ireland Committee.[10] In any event, the numbers involved were very small. In 1935 only twenty-six per cent of the total of insured workers (excluding agriculture) belonged to a trade union, which, in numerical terms, would give a membership of about 72,000, in that year.[11]

* There were indications in the late 1960s that membership of the Order was ceasing to be a *sine qua non* for a political career in the Unionist party. On the other hand, the Orange lodges are heavily represented on the Ulster Unionist Council and, perhaps more important, also play a part on its standing and executive committees.
† See above, Part IV A, chap. 5, section iv.

Apart from this, it cannot be too heavily stressed that while individual Ulster labour leaders might claim an apostolic descent from James Connolly, the rank and file were generally either too absorbed in the main constitutional and religious issues, or too cowed by unemployment, to be ready to absorb socialist doctrines of the inevitable class war. It was unlikely, indeed, that class conflict would be very clearly defined in a community such as that of the six counties, where nearly half the population lived on the land, where the size of the average business was small and where the possibility of self-employment was greater than in many other industrial regions. Amongst the workers, therefore, as elsewhere in northern society, the line of fracture was not economic, it was based on religion and on the great debate over the legality of the government. Northeast Ulster, stubbornly resistant to most kinds of schematic analysis, did not readily fall into any of the more conventional Marxist categories. Perhaps it was symptomatic of this obstinate illogicality that not long before he succeeded Lord Craigavon as Prime Minister, Mr J. M. Andrews was in the same year Minister of Labour, Chairman of the Belfast Chamber of Commerce and President of the Unionist Labour organisation.

We are driven back then, as in Northern Ireland one is always driven back, to the fundamental divisions – Catholic versus Protestant, Nationalist versus Unionist. As we have seen, it was the threat from the large Catholic-Nationalist minority that caused the majority most anxiety and it was this threat that was used with monotonous regularity by the Unionist leaders to maintain conformity and discipline within their own ranks. Yet how far were these fears really justified? How great a threat to the status quo did the minority actually constitute? In the sense that they repudiated the whole concept of a separate parliament in the six counties and looked longingly southward towards reintegration with the rest of Ireland they were, of course, to use a term that belongs to the 'thirties rather than the 'twenties, a permanent fifth column. But their immediate reaction to the setting-up of the new regime was one of stunned disbelief, mingled with acute fear for their own future safety. Their instinct was to hold themselves absolutely apart. Thus, not only did their elected representatives refuse to take their seats, but Catholics refused to sit on the Lynn committee to examine the whole structure of education, Catholic school managers refused to accept grants and some school-teachers even – for a while – declined their salaries.

These gestures reflected an attitude of mind which was natural enough in 1921, but which the passage of time was soon to make irrelevant. In 1921 it was possible to believe, as many of the minority evidently did believe, that the regime would not last, that the government would be brought down, either by pressure from outside or by non-cooperation from within – even, in the last resort, that the Boundary Commission would put paid to the whole sorry farce. But when none of these things happened some urgent rethinking became necessary. If the new government were once to establish itself, then it would be certain to take decisions directly affecting the welfare of Catholic families. Could Nationalists continue to stand on one side and let these decisions be taken without seeking to influence them?

This was not a hypothetical question. Almost at once a major issue arose which revealed with cruel clarity the nature of the Nationalist dilemma. In 1923, after receiving the report of the Lynn committee, the Northern Ireland parliament passed an Education Act, designed to remodel the primary – or public elementary – school system. There were to be three types of school in the future – schools wholly maintained or 'provided' by the local authorities, including any former private or denominational schools that were transferred to 'wholly maintained' status; voluntary schools under 'four and two committees'; and other voluntary schools. The 'four and two committees' consisted of four representatives of the body providing the school (usually a church) and two representatives of the school authority. Such schools would qualify for grants in payment of teachers' salaries, for help with maintenance and even, in certain circumstances, for capital grants. The pure voluntary schools, on the other hand, would qualify only for the payment of teachers' salaries and of half the cost of heating, cleaning and lighting. But the Act went much further than that. It stipulated that every public school should be open to children of all denominations and that religious instruction should not be given within the hours of compulsory attendance. In those schools that were wholly financed by public money the local education authorities were forbidden to require teachers to belong to any particular church or to provide religious instruction – though the local authorities could provide for any religious teaching outside the hours of compulsory attendance to which parents did not object.

Education, then, was to be essentially secular. The laudable intention behind the Act was no doubt to try to break down sectarian barriers by providing mixed schools in which Catholic and Protestant children could mingle without affront to their separate religions. But religious education was something about which many people of many different persuasions felt passionately. The Catholic bishops condemned the Act and very few Catholic clergy allowed their schools to pass under the control of the 'four and two committees'. Protestants, too, were deeply displeased and in 1925 they secured an Amending Act which was negotiated by the Prime Minister over the head of his Minister of Education. This Act restored Bible teaching to schools under the control of local education authorities, who were now allowed to require teachers in provided and transferred schools to give such instruction as part of the ordinary school course. Even this concession, however, was soon felt to be inadequate. Simple Bible teaching was all very well, but the highly self-conscious and articulate denominations of Northern Ireland began to ask why they should not prescribe more exactly what religious teaching was to be given to their children, and why they should not have a greater say in the appointment of teachers. They had only to press hard enough for the government to yield, and a further Amending Act in 1930 conceded in effect what they demanded. In addition, it was laid down that in all provided and transferred schools it was the duty of the education authority to provide Bible instruction if the parents of not less than ten children asked for it. Thus, in the Prime Minister's words, were the schools made 'safe for Protestant children'.

This in itself was hardly likely to recommend them to Catholics. Bible teaching was not what they wanted. They wanted quite simply the Catholic teaching of Catholic children in Catholic schools under their own managers. And they viewed with intense distrust a system which, given the way in which local elections were, in their eyes, rigged, might put their children at the mercy of education authorities in which Protestants had a majority. The issue was too explosive to be allowed to rest in this unsatisfactory state and in the end a compromise of a kind was reached. The government refused to accept the Catholic suggestion that in the four and two committees Catholics should be allowed to control religious teaching and the selection of the teachers responsible for it. But, since it was realised that the effect of this refusal would be that Catholics would continue to boycott the four and two arrangement, it was agreed instead that the government would pay half the cost of building or reconstructing voluntary schools and would lend the other half, irrespective of whether the schools had a four and two committee or not. So, from 1930 onwards, in the provided and transferred schools (overwhelmingly Protestant) Bible instruction carried out by teachers approved by the denominations was the normal practice, while in the voluntary schools (overwhelmingly Catholic) distintive religious education was assured, but the state assumed a share of the responsibility for their cost.[12]

It has been necessary to treat this episode in some detail, since it brought into the open so many of the points at issue between the minority and the majority. It touched so intimately the lives of the people that the political representatives of nationalism could scarcely hold aloof even when they resented – as Joseph Devlin, the most eminent of them did resent – being caught up in what appeared to be a sectarian quarrel. And in fact, while the controversy was at its height, Devlin had made up his mind to enter the northern parliament. After 1921 he had taken the view that he would not do so until he had seen what the Boundary Commission might propose. When the Commission ended in fiasco, he and another Nationalist MP duly took their seats; others followed gradually and by 1927 he was leading a group of ten in the northern House of Commons. The following year (1928) he took a main part in founding the National League which, while aiming at the unity of Ireland, was more conciliatory than Nationalists had previously been towards the existing regime. Devlin himself, indeed, declared that there was no conspiracy to force northerners into a Dublin parliament and he and his colleagues tried hard to work constructively for social amelioration; it is doubtful, however, whether he ever fully realised how far Northern Ireland was restricted by the finances of devolution and the last years of his public life were a sad anti-climax to the notable reputation he had won at Westminster in the generation before 1918.

He, and others like him, laboured under a double difficulty, which curiously repeated in microcosm the difficulty of the old Irish parliamentary party during the later stages of its career in the British House of Commons. The constitutional Nationalists who sat in Belfast, like the constitutional Nationalists who had sat in London, were in the assembly but not of it. They were there only for the purpose of breaking the system that had brought them there. Being a minority, they could never hope to be other than an opposition. But they could not become an *official* opposition since, by definition, they could not form a government. Their participation in local parliamentary politics was always bedevilled by this dilemma and it is not surprising that, so far from forming an official opposition, they pursued a wavering course even towards actual participation in the proceedings of the Northern Ireland House of Commons, and were still apt to withdraw from time to time under the pressure of other forces.

The chief of these forces was republicanism. And this was where Devlin encountered his second difficulty. He and his colleagues were competing, just as the old parliamentary party had had to do, against a more extreme form of nationalism. The old party had been wiped out in 1918 by the victory of Sinn Féin, identified at that time with the triumph of the republican ideal. From the point of view of constitutional politics, therefore, it was distinctly sinister that in the first Northern Ireland election of 1921 the six Nationalist seats were exactly balanced by six Republican seats. The Republicans, of course, followed the classical Sinn Féin tactic of total abstention, but it was not easy then, and it is not easy now, to be sure how much those six seats were a product of the general upsurge of revolutionary nationalism throughout Ireland, or how much they represented a substantial amount of separatist feeling in the north. It has to be remembered that the Nationalist population in the six counties consisted chiefly of small farmers, shopkeepers, publicans and unskilled labourers, with some reinforcement from the professions, especially law and medicine. Many of these people were self-employed, and in social and political matters were conservatively inclined. Moreover, they were nearly all Catholic and as such amenable to the leadership of bishops and priests, leadership which the Church was not backward in providing. This was the environment Devlin had grown up in, which he understood intimately, and where he enjoyed enormous influence and respect, intensified no doubt by his long-standing connection with the Ancient Order of Hibernians, providing for Catholics, though on a smaller scale, the same kind of rallying-point as the Orange Order did for Protestants. It has to be admitted, however, that this kind of social structure and this kind of organisation had not been enough to halt the growth of Sinn Féin in the rest of Ireland in the decade before 1921 and it was, if anything, less likely that it would do so in the north where the minority, surrounded – as they felt – by the bigoted intolerance of the majority, might well be pushed towards their own extremists by the extremism of their neighbours. There are signs that this was in fact an attitude held by many of the younger people. Certainly, between 1916 and 1921 Sinn Féin made the same sort of headway in the north as it had done elsewhere and Ulster Nationalists contributed their share of the republican leadership.

But this movement towards the left was checked by the course of events after the Treaty. The split in the revolutionary forces in the south, the toughness and resilience of the new regime in the north, the growing suspicion that perhaps Sinn Féin did not really know a great deal about the special problems of northern Nationalism – all this served to diminish the attractions of republicanism. And when the dust had settled after the Civil War in the south, and the Irish Free State stood revealed as a correct, if restive, member of the Commonwealth, the impetus towards violent change slackened. The way was clear, therefore, for Devlin and his friends to take their seats in the northern parliament and to begin that frail and tenuous experiment in co-operation of which we have already spoken.

It was an experiment destined to be shattered when the coming of Fianna Fáil to power in the south in 1932 promised a resumption of more vigorous policies. The release of republican prisoners, the beginnings of the dispute with Britain, the fact that de Valera himself contested and won the northern seat of South Down in the election of 1933 on an 'abstentionist' platform – these were straws in the wind eagerly grasped by the more extreme Nationalists in the north.* But as the Fianna Fáil campaign to loosen the ties binding the Free State to the Commonwealth developed year by year this action called into being an equal and opposite reaction from Northern Ireland Unionism. The more de Valera seemed bent on destroying the imperial connection in the south, the more Craigavon and other Unionists insisted upon it in the north. These years, therefore, saw an intensification of the familiar stresses in the six counties and a renewal of sectarian bitterness of which the Twelfth of July orations of 1933 may serve as a lamentable example. It was on this occasion that Sir Basil Brooke (Minister of Agriculture at the time and later Prime Minister) made his famous declaration that he had not one Catholic in his employment. 'Catholics', he was reported as saying, 'were out to destroy Ulster with all their might and power. They wanted to nullify the Protestant vote and take

* Mr de Valera's electoral success, and that of another abstentionist in West Tyrone, led the government in 1934 to pass an act providing that unless a candidate declared his intention to take his seat if elected his nomination would be refused.

all they could out of Ulster and then see it go to hell.' And it was on this occasion also that J. M. Andrews, the Minister of Labour (and destined to succeed Craigavon as Prime Minister), solemnly declared that after investigating the thirty-one porters employed at the newly opened parliament buildings at Stormont 'I have found that there are thirty Protestants and only one Roman Catholic – there temporarily.'[13]

It would be easy to point to other similar instances of bigotry, and indeed to match them with utterances from the other side, for example Cardinal MacRory's provocative remark, also dating from this decade of bitterness, that the Protestant churches did not form part of the true Church of Christ.[14] It would be easy, but it would be pointless. It is enough to record that in the years between 1932 and the outbreak of the Second World War religious and political frictions, which had never at any time disappeared, were intensified. And it is important to realise that this occurred not only during a period of worsening relations between north and south, but during a period of dire distress when competition for jobs was added to inherited prejudices. It was characteristic of Ulster society that economic pressure should produce not a class war, but a religio-political explosion. There is some evidence, indeed, that one wing of the IRA which had communist sympathies attempted to collaborate with some of the more militant trade unionists, and certain Roman Catholic bishops took this seriously enough to warn their flocks against such manoeuvres. But this alliance, such as it was, sank into insignificance in the face of the bitter, long-drawn-out and bloody riots which disgraced Belfast in the summer of 1935. As a result of this religious war – which was what, in effect, it was – 11 people were killed and nearly 600 injured, while cases of arson amounted to 133 and of malicious damage to 367. Catholics demanded a commission of inquiry, but this was refused. Instead, in 1936, a report issued by a private body, the Council of Civil Liberties, charged the government with using the Special Powers Act in such a fashion as to drive its opponents 'into the way of extremism'. It is true that this report has subsequently been assailed as suspect, on the ground that some members of the Council were allegedly communists or fellow-travellers, but the observer of Northern Ireland in the mid-thirties did not have to stand very far to the left to see how deep were the divisions in the province and how vulnerable was the minority, alike to the unbridled violence of private individuals and to the special powers of the government.[15]

For the majority such considerations were of only secondary importance. To them the safety of the state was the supreme law and in the late 'thirties the safety of the state seemed more than ever at risk. To safeguard the British connection was, as always, the overriding aim of policy, and with the return of the treaty ports to the Irish Free State that connection had come to be even more precious, not just to Northern Ireland, but to the rest of the United Kingdom as well. There were, it is true, flashes of enlightenment and gestures of mutual goodwill. In 1936, for example, two bishops, the Catholic Dr Mageean and the Anglican Dr MacNiece, called upon their flocks to live together in Christian unity. Two years later Major-General Hugh Montgomery founded the Irish Association for Cultural, Economic and Social Relations, to encourage respect for the convictions of others and 'to foster . . . more neighbourly relations between those Irish people who differ from each other in politics and religion'.[16] These, however, were portents for the future; they could do little in the short run to mitigate the harshness with which the two communities confronted each other. And in 1938, Dr Mageean, despite his earlier appeals for tolerance, was driven to denounce the history of the Northern Ireland parliament as 'one long record of partisan and bigoted discrimination'.[17] But this was a vain outburst. As the international horizon darkened and war approached the old siege mentality began to assert itself amongst the majority once more. That mentality was described, simply and concisely, by the *Belfast Newsletter* in the same year, 1938, on the eve of an election which gave Lord Craigavon his customary assured majority:

Lord Craigavon's purpose in this election is to show that Ulster stands precisely where it did in relation to the Free State, or rather that its attachment to Great Britain and the Empire is as strong as ever and that in no circumstances will they give up their place in the United Kingdom.[18]

It was the old philosophy of 'not an inch' restated in language that had altered hardly a syllable in a generation. Upon this beleaguered garrison the Bishop's denunciations would have no effect whatever. It would be a long time yet before the walls of Derry would crumble at the blast of an ecclesiastical, or any other, trumpet.

4. War as a Catalyst

When Lord Craigavon hailed the result of the general election of 1938 as a vindication of the Unionist resolve 'that come what may our position within the United Kingdom and the Empire must remain unchanged', he could not have known that the war which was already looming was going to affect Northern Ireland's position dramatically – not, indeed, by changing it, but by reinforcing it beyond his wildest hopes. His own instinctive reaction when war actually broke out – and in this he spoke for Ulster Unionism in general – was 'to place the whole of our resources at the command of the government in Britain'. 'We are King's men', he said in a famous broadcast, and he and his followers never wavered from that stance. Admittedly, the existence of a large Nationalist minority in the province made it inexpedient to apply conscription, as many Ulstermen would have wished, but, this apart, the involvement of Northern Ireland was as near total as it was possible to be. Ulster men and women served and died all over the world and Ulster men and women served at home, and died in the severe air-raids on Belfast in the spring of 1941. All told, war casualties amongst persons born in the province totalled more than five and a half thousand, of whom nearly 900 were civilians.[1]

But the contribution of this small fragment of the United Kingdom to the Allied cause was far greater than either its casualties or its resources would lead one to expect. With Mr de Valera's resolute adoption of a policy of neutrality for the south, the geographical situation of Northern Ireland in relation to the sea-lanes connecting Britain with North America at once became exceedingly important. This importance was immeasurably heightened after the fall of France in 1940, when German submarines and aircraft were in a position to range far out into the Atlantic in pursuit of Allied shipping. To combat them naval bases were necessary and Belfast, Londonderry and Larne supplied this vital need. From these ports went out many of the escort vessels used in the early stages of the war at sea to bring in the convoys heading for the Mersey and the Clyde by the only avenue left to them – the northwest approaches where Ulster, as Churchill later wrote, 'stood a faithful sentinel'. And even while the war still raged he paid this tribute to Northern Ireland:

> We were alone and had to face single-handed the full fury of the German attack, raining down death and destruction on our cities and, still more deadly, seeking to strangle our life by cutting off the entry to our ports of the ships which brought us food and the weapons we so sorely needed. Only one great channel remained open.

That channel remained open because loyal Ulster gave us the full use of the Northern Irish ports and waters, and thus ensured the free working of the Clyde and the Mersey.[2]

So long as the battle of the Atlantic continued, so long did the Ulster bases remain essential to the Allied cause. But as time went on those bases were put to other uses besides the sheltering of British naval units. As early as March 1941 – nine months *before* Pearl Habour – Londonderry had been selected as a depot for American destroyers should need arise, and when the need did arise the port became a 'US naval operating base' for the American Atlantic fleet within three months of the United States entering the war. Moreover, as the character of the Atlantic battle changed – especially during 1943 – Northern Ireland became almost as important as an aircraft carrier as it had been in the role of naval fortress. Simultaneously, it provided one of the main training-grounds for American forces preparing to invade Axis territory. The first American troops arrived there in January 1942 and large forces were stationed in the six counties for nearly a year before the Normandy invasion.[3]

To the comradeship Northern Ireland could claim with the Allies through her key function as a base of operations could be added also a community of suffering. True, the ordeal of the civilian population was not so prolonged as that endured by the citizens of, say, London or Liverpool. Nevertheless, the four air raids on Belfast in April and May 1941 were a grievous blow and brought home to the inhabitants, not only of the city but of the whole province, the realities of total war. Inadequately provided with air protection, short of anti-aircraft guns and fire-fighting equipment, with a programme of evacuation only sketchily carried out, Belfast was fearfully vulnerable. Two of the raids – on Easter Tuesday (15-16 April) and on 4-5 May – were exceptionally severe. In the first of these attacks large areas of the city were demolished either by direct hits or by fire, over 700 people killed and some 1,500 injured, a third of them seriously. 'No other city in the United Kingdom save London', the official historian has written, 'had lost so many of her citizens in one night's raid. No other city, except possibly Liverpool, ever did.'[4] The defence services, depleted though they were, responded gallantly to the challenge, but it was understandable that the terrible experience of a major air raid should have caused some panic, especially as many had convinced themselves that Northern Ireland was beyond the range of enemy bombers. In consequence, at least a hundred thousand people, it was officially estimated, left the city to try to find homes in the country.

Yet when the second serious raid came three weeks later – this time largely an ordeal by fire – Belfast was again inadequately protected and, although there was less loss of life, there was enormous damage to property, while production at Harland and Wolff's works and other important factories was brought almost to a halt. And since, to quote the official war historian again, 'the degree of shelter protection available to the citizens of Belfast was probably lower than that in any other British city of comparable size and vulnerability', it was not surprising that what he calls 'a powerful surge' developed to get away from the city at all costs.[5] Unhappily, there was all too little accommodation to spare in the surrounding countryside; even more unhappily, many of the refugees were among the poorest of the poor, who had now been blasted or burnt out of slums the authorities had been neglecting for twenty years. They brought with them standards of hygiene and problems of public health that were a revelation to the comfortable bourgeoisie. 'I have been working nineteen years in Belfast', said a leading Presbyterian clergyman of his newly discovered fellow-citizens, 'and I never saw the like of them before. If something is not done now to remedy this rank inequality there will be a revolution after the war.'[6]

This belated recognition of social evils that needed a radical cure was one positive result to flow from the bombing. Another was the spontaneous coming together of Catholic and Protestant in their hour of crisis when death fell on them impartially from the sky.

More than all else [Professor Blake has written] it was this tragic aspect of the raid which left indelible memories: of the queue at the mortuary in St George's market where men and women tried to identify their missing; and of the public funeral . . . when Protestants and Roman Catholics joined in prayer, and, as the cortege of five covered waggons moved slowly through the scarred city streets paid their last respects to over 150 of the victims.[7]

This softening of ancient asperities was helped also by the fact that even the border, so implacably defended over the years, ceased miraculously to exist when, during each of the heavy raids, fire-brigades hastened northwards from as far away as Dublin to do what they could to help.

Time alone would tell whether these spontaneous gestures of goodwill could be translated into something permanent. What was permanent, and seen even at the time to be permanent, was that the connection with the United Kingdom had been formidably strengthened by the fact that Northern Ireland had made good in blood its pledge to stand by Britain 'come what might'. And even though for the time being politics had been thrust into the background, when they came to the fore again, as they inevitably would, that blood would not be denied. The six counties, by the magnitude and devotion of their war effort, had done more to perpetuate the partition of Ireland than a whole generation of Twelfth of July demonstrations.

But the war had two additional and no less far-reaching consequences. At one and the same time it raised the Ulsterman's standard of living in the present and aroused his expectations for the future. Although the six counties shared with the rest of the United Kingdom in the rationing and other austerities of those years, the immediate economic effects of the war were dramatically beneficial. Almost overnight Northern Ireland was wafted from chronic depression to bustling prosperity.

730

This prosperity was experienced in many sectors of the economy, but it was most marked, as might be expected, in the shipbuilding and engineering industries. Harland and Wolff, and the associated firm of Short and Harland, were transformed into a veritable arsenal. The shipyards had almost more work than they could cope with, launching more than 150 vessels, totalling over half a million tons, during the war years In addition, 550 tanks of various kinds were produced between 1939 and 1943, while the war-time output of bombers alone was 1,500.* Such feverish activity (which extended also into other kinds of war production) resulted in a steady flow of manpower into the various industries concerned. This caused various problems of adaptation, and it has even been suggested that if there had been military conscription, the use of civilian labour might have been more efficient. But however this may be, to an area that had known two decades of dire unemployment the creation of so many jobs seemed the beginning of a new era. In shipbuilding, for example, the numbers employed went up from 7·3 thousand in 1938 to 20·6 thousand in 1945. In engineering the increase during the same years was from 14·0 thousand to 26·1 thousand. Most remarkable of all, the aircraft industry, which before the war had been struggling to establish itself, rose from a mere 5·8 thousand in 1938 to 23·5 thousand in 1945.[9]

The contribution of the other main branch of Ulster industry – textiles – was more limited but still considerable. The great Belfast ropeworks, for example, was fully extended by War Office and Admiralty contracts. The shirt-making industry based on Londonderry also woke to new life, producing not only shirts for military use, but battle-dress and denim overalls as well. Production of shirts was about fifteen million a year (double the peacetime figure) and employment rose by twenty-five per cent to a total of nine thousand. It was, however, in the linen industry – which, after all, was and remained the predominant element in the textile group – that the problems of adaptation were most severe. There were problems of supply, of machinery, even problems of marketing. Shortages of flax were to some extent remedied by intensive cultivation on home farms, the acreage under this crop rising from 21,000 in 1939 to 124,000 in 1944. At the same time the most stringent rationing of flax and linen stocks was imposed, and efforts were made to divert highly specialised linen machinery to work on other fabrics. Even so, the industry was in a critical condition by September 1940 with 23,000 operatives out of work and another 20,000 threatened with the loss of their jobs. Gradually, thanks to war contracts, efficient management and experimentation with new fabrics – notably rayon – the linen manufacturers began to surmount the worst of their difficulties and although under-employment persisted, they were able to contribute to the supply not only of uniforms, but of a host of other articles, including wing fabrics, parachutes, flying-suits, sailcloth and various kinds of tenting. There is no disguising the fact, however, that progress was decidedly uneven. The peak year for production came as early as 1940 when 125 million lineal yards of cloth were produced, but nearly two-thirds of this was for civilian use or export. Thereafter, government contracts took the larger share of an output which could go as high as 106 million lineal yards in 1941 or sink as low as 64·5 million in the wartime months of 1945.[10]

Problems of unemployment, though more serious in the linen industry than in most others, persisted at various levels throughout the war. Even during the years of maximum mobilisation of labour, 1942 – 44, there were always some who could not get work, though it is probably true to say that most of these were unskilled workers for whom appropriate jobs could not easily be found. The dates of maximum mobilisation suggest that the deployment of labour was a rather more leisurely process than it might have been. Indeed, so slowly did the pace gather way that in January 1941 the total of unemployed, 68·7 thousand, was 4,000 more than it had been at the outbreak of war. This, admittedly, was due mainly to the crisis in the linen industry, and once the great construction boom began, with the building not only of ships and planes and weapons, but also of aerodromes, barracks, factories and other adjuncts to the war effort, the amount of unemployment dropped very strikingly. For most of the period 1942–4 it fluctuated between 15,000 and 20,000, occasionally falling to around 10,000 in the peak summer months. This was still, of course, a considerable figure in relation to the labour force as a whole – as late as June 1943 one in every twenty insured persons was unemployed in Northern Ireland compared with one in two hundred in Britain – and the situation would have been even worse if there had not been an outflow of some 60,000 persons to work in England, Scotland and Wales during the war. The difference in the speed and thoroughness with which the labour force was mobilised in Britain and in Northern Ireland was no doubt partly due to the specialised character of many of the latter's industries which made them specially vulnerable to war conditions, but a more important factor was that Britain was able to apply industrial conscription, whereas Northern Ireland, though possessing the power to do so, was reluctant to use it in the absence of conscription for the armed forces. Movement out of certain key industries – agriculture or engineering, for instance – was from time to time restricted, but for the most part the government relied on inducement and persuasion rather than coercion.[11]

Almost more than any other industry, agriculture was fully stretched by the war and, although there was no dramatic change in the structure of farming, there was a remarkable improvement in its productivity. This was in part a response to firm leadership by the Northern Ireland government, even more perhaps it was the farmer's natural reaction to the British government's decision to buy the main products of agriculture at uniform prices throughout the United Kingdom, thus removing at a stroke the Ulsterman's long-standing disadvantage of having to accept as his net price the British market price less the cost of transporting his products. The effect of this is to be seen in the steep rise in the value of net as contrasted with gross agricultural output. The value of gross agricultural output in Northern Ireland in 1945 was 122 per cent of the average for the years 1936–7 to 1938–9, which differs little from the comparable British figure of 116 per cent. But whereas in Britain the value of net output (that is gross output less purchases of feeding-stuffs, stores and seeds from abroad) in 1945 was 176 per cent of what it had been in the pre-war years, in Northern Ireland this was 205 per cent.[12]

To the Ulster farmer the system of uniform prices brought two major benefits. First, it reduced the normal uncertainties of farming, since prices were fixed in advance each year. And second, the price structure was so devised as to ensure that in normal circumstances farmers would earn a reasonable profit. However, even these inducements would hardly have sufficed to produce the great expansion in northern farming, had the government not taken steps to guide agriculture along the lines of maximum advantage to the community as a whole. A primary aim, of course, was to increase tillage up to the furthest possible limits, bearing in mind that those limits were fixed not only by the physical area of the six counties, but also by the inevitable shortages of fertilizers, seeds and farm machinery. To bring about this increase the Northern Ireland government, like that of Eire, resorted to compulsory tillage orders, requiring first twenty per cent and later forty-five per cent of all arable land to be put under the plough. By 1943 this process had gone about as far as it could and from then on increased productivity had to be won by raising the yield per acre. In that year the total acreage of tillage was 851,000 – almost double what it had been in 1939.

This great drive towards higher production was not directed primarily towards wheat. Wheat production did indeed increase, rising from 3,000 tons in 1939 to 18,000 in 1941, but falling thereafter until in the last year of the war a diminishing acreage produced only 2,000 tons. Barley and mixed corn also rose, in acreage and in volume, but the most important and sustained growth was in flax, oats and potatoes. We have already seen something of the effort farmers made to meet at least some of the flax needs of the linen industry, but it was in oats and potatoes that they really excelled themselves. Where in 1939 the six counties produced 270,000 tons of oats, two years later they produced 432,000 tons and although this tapered off to 383,000 in 1945, the total remained extraordinarily high. So also with potatoes, where a 1939 production of 864,000 tons was raised to about 1¼ million for each of the years 1941, 1942, and 1943, and was still over a million in 1944 and 1945.

By no means all of this increased production was intended for human consumption. On the contrary, it was an essential part of policy to nurture the livestock and dairying industries which had been the strongest sectors of northern agriculture before the war. The shortage of feeding-stuffs had its effect, of course – chiefly in the sharp decline of sheep and pigs. But the number of cattle in the province was driven steadily upwards from 753,000 in 1939 to 919,000 in 1945, while poultry increased from 10·2 million to 17·5 million during the same period. The raising of these levels of output was no doubt achieved partly at the expense of sheep and pigs, since the precious feeding-stuffs were diverted from them to cattle, but it was made' possible also by the massive growth in the tonnage of oats and in the amount of root crops produced. The results of this very considerable achievement were of importance not only for the domestic supplies of Northern Ireland but for the rest of the United Kingdom, whither the surplus was regularly exported under the all-pervading authority of the local Ministry of Agriculture. It was no insignificant matter, for example, that Northern Ireland supplied about one-fifth of all the eggs produced in the United Kingdom during the war, or that Ulster farmers, at last weaned from milk produced mainly for manufacture to the production of liquid milk, were not only able to meet the increased needs of their own province but to send some three million gallons to Britain in the last year of the war.[13]

It was extraordinary, but true, that this prolonged effort did not result in serious deterioration of the soil. Some deterioration there was, no doubt, but although for most crops the yield per acre did decline in the later years of the war, this was in no case catastrophic. That the damage was not worse was primarily due to intelligent planning from the centre. Conservative farmers were given constant advice and assistance with crop rotation; the import of fertilizers, though hard hit in the early stages, never altogether ceased and in fact developed considerably from 1943 onwards, by which time Ulster agriculture had trebled its pre-war consumption of these artificial aids to agriculture. Intensive cultivation also demanded the employment of a large labour force and that this labour force should be supplemented by mechanisation. Both these demands were met in all essentials. Despite enlistments in the forces and the lure of highly paid jobs in industry, the total number of workers on the land (most of them full-time) rose from 154 thousand in 1939 to 184 thousand in 1945. Even more striking was the growth in mechanisation. In 1939 there were, to take the extreme example, only 858 tractors in the whole province; by 1945 this figure had been multiplied nearly nine times to reach a total of 7.240.[14] The contrast in all this with the slow development of agriculture in Eire was very marked. So marked indeed that the historian of wartime Northern Ireland was moved to comment, in a moment of patriotic exuberance, that to go south across the border 'was to be transported in a matter of minutes from the twentieth to the seventeenth century'.[15] This was, perhaps, a little harsh; the southern observer who wrote more sedately that 'while the twenty-six counties repeated the experience of the First World War, Northern Ireland was able to follow a new and more profitable course', was rather nearer the mark.[16]

It was scarcely surprising in these conditions of strenuous agricultural and industrial endeavour that the material well-being, not just of the farmer, but of the urban worker as well, was greatly improved during the war. Wages went up sharply and, since there was little enough to spend them on, savings also increased, to the extent that during the war years £152 million was invested, nearly half of which was in small individual savings.[17] Real wages in a situation where there is a shortage of consumer goods are difficult to compute and not entirely reliable, but two significant pointers to the wartime prosperity of Northern Ireland may be mentioned. One was that income per head, which had been less than three-fifths of that in Britain, before the war, rose in Northern Ireland between 1939 and 1945 until it was three-quarters of the British figure.[18] The other pointer is that although the government was necessarily involved in all sorts of additional expenditure, revenue (mainly from taxation) was so buoyant that the amount of the 'imperial contribution' rose to what only a few years earlier would have been regarded as fantastic heights. From a total of three million pounds in 1939–40 it climbed more and more steeply until in each of the last two years of the war it was thirty-six million pounds. Another way of putting this is to say that whereas the total payment for the entire period from 1921 to 1939 had been twenty-nine million pounds, the amount paid over during the six war years came to no less than £131 million.[19]

All this was evidence of a state of affairs very far removed from the dire stringencies which had been the lot of the six counties in the inter-war period. Yet there was another side to the story. Total war brought with it a readiness to look freshly at old institutions, to look critically at old men who had been in power too long. The very fact that Northern Ireland moved onto a war footing more slowly than the rest of the United Kingdom exposed the government to criticism and even Lord Craigavon himself, only two months before his death, had to face a vote of censure. His successor, J. M. Andrews, had been as long in office as his former chief and was no more prepared than he had been to make sweeping changes. Consequently, between 1941 and 1943 the murmurings of complaints grew steadily louder. Two normally safe seats at Stormont were lost – one to an Independent Unionist and the other to Labour – and in addition a Labour candidate captured one of the Westminster seats. Early in 1943 matters came to a crisis. In January the back-benchers revolted, demanding more new faces in the cabinet, and in May Mr Andrews resigned to make room for Sir Basil Brooke (later Lord Brookeborough). There is a certain irony in the fact that Sir Basil was himself destined to hold office as Prime Minister for over twenty years – longer even than Craigavon – but at the time, and in the midst of a great war, he seemed to be the new broom that the situation demanded. He got rid of practically all the older men, replacing them by a new generation which was ready and willing to direct the war effort more vigorously, and, perhaps most important of all, he and his cabinet began to lay plans for the development of Northern Ireland after the war.

Here, indeed, lay the crux of the matter. What was to be the future of Northern Ireland after the war? It was this nagging preoccupation with what might be in store that lay behind a good deal of the restlessness which even the Unionist rank-and-file manifested from time to time. And as men's horizons began to widen, as they saw more of the world themselves and acted as hosts to hundreds of thousands of servicemen stationed in the six counties, so the old isolation, and with it the old complacency, began to break down. The shabbiness, the poverty, the lack of adequate schools, houses, hospitals or roads, the ill-health, the squalor of the slums – all these things, which had to be put up with at a time when there seemed no way to do anything about them, became all at once an intolerable affront, to be wiped out as quickly as possible in the new world that men began to look for with growing impatience as the war drew near its close.

Moral indignation and high ideals were, however, equally impotent without money. And money, in the quantity that would be needed, could only be obtained with the help and favour of Britain. True, the case for parity in the social services had been argued over and over again before the war, but could this be maintained in the light of the enormous expansion of welfare envisaged in the Beveridge Report? For Northern Ireland this new trend involved the addition of a second concept to the original and well-worn formula about advancing 'step by step' with Britain. Now, it was argued, the province must not only march 'step by step' in the existing services, but must also be enabled to make up the 'leeway' that separated her from her more prosperous neighbour in a whole range of amenities hitherto either rudimentary or even non-existent in the pre-war years. It was a large claim, but the north would never be in a better position to press it than in the midst of the war which had so triumphantly demonstrated her value to the whole Allied cause. And in 1942 that claim was conceded in principle, when the British Chancellor of the Exchequer assured Mr Andrews that he recognised that in certain spheres Northern Ireland had 'considerable leeway' to make up if she were to attain equality with the United Kingdom as a whole. 'You can confidently rely', he added, 'on the Treasury always considering such a case sympathetically, as indeed the principle of parity requires us to do.'[20]

What this might involve for the future it was impossible to forecast in wartime. But it is evidence of the catalytic effect the war itself was having on Northern Ireland that long before the fighting was over severe and searching scrutinies had begun to be made into the various services that would need overhauling if 'leeway' was to be overcome. Health, housing, education, roads, the reconstruction of Belfast – one after another each was investigated and for each a plan was devised in readiness for the day when it might be possible to translate these dreams into reality. By the spring of 1945 it was clear that that day was close at hand. In May it was announced that the province would enjoy the full range of the social security schemes that would be introduced in Britain and that, where necessary, finance would be available to raise the standard of the social services to the level achieved in other parts of the United Kingdom. For a moment at least it was possible to believe that the past had been left behind for ever.

5. The Politics of Welfare

The past had not gone for ever, of course. On the contrary, politics in Northern Ireland still continued to revolve round the three great issues that had filled all horizons in the inter-war period – the maintenance of the British connection, the fate of the economy, the internal tensions generated by a deeply divided society. Nevertheless, the war had changed the context in which these problems were discussed and the events of the immediate post-war years were to change that context even further.

The most striking illustration of this is the way in which the constitutional position of the six provinces was reinforced not only, as was suggested in the previous section, by the claims the Northern Irish war effort established on British gratitude, but also, ironically enough, by Britain's own reaction to the establishment of the Republic in the twenty-six counties. In the Ireland Act of 1949, regulating the relations between the United Kingdom and the Republic, it was laid down in the most explicit fashion that the existing status of Northern Ireland would be maintained:

It is hereby declared that Northern Ireland remains part of His Majesty's dominions and of the United Kingdom and it is hereby affirmed that in no event will Northern Ireland or any part thereof cease to be a part of His Majesty's dominions and of the United Kingdom, without the consent of the parliament of Northern Ireland.

This seemed as watertight a pledge as any die-hard Unionist could desire and it was certainly a remarkable concession from a British Labour government, some of whose supporters had long looked with a very cold eye on what they regarded as the reactionary character of Northern Ireland politics. But the pledge was not as absolute as appeared on the surface. The legislative supremacy of the Westminster parliament was left intact and what one statute of that parliament could ordain another statute could repeal. To say this is merely to emphasise what has been from the beginning a constant element in the link between the two areas – which is that the supremacy of the Westminster parliament carried with it the implication that any radical shift of political attitudes in Britain could have direct and drastic effects upon Northern Ireland.

But the strength of the British connection did not rest solely on a legalistic basis. We have seen already how closely intertwined were the finances of Northern Ireland and the rest of the United Kingdom before the war, and that during the war the province received a clear promise of assistance from Britain in bringing its social services up to the standards established in England, Scotland and Wales. The return of Labour to power in 1945 was a traumatic experience for Ulster Unionists, so long and so deeply embedded in the fabric of British conservatism, but they managed to keep their balance and to dispose their forces in a manner that did credit to their heads, if not perhaps entirely to their principles. What happened was that at Westminster the Unionist representatives joined with the Conservative opposition in resisting the socialist legislation which established the welfare state, while at Stormont the Unionist party solemnly resolved to annex as much of this legislation as possible to its own purposes. To be able to do this satisfactorily, however, the Belfast government needed to revise its financial relations with Whitehall. Between 1945 and 1951 that revision was successfully carried out by a series of agreements relating to financial and insurance problems. These had two principal effects. One was to reduce the financial autonomy previously enjoyed by the Northern Ireland government. In the depression years, indeed, that autonomy may often have seemed somewhat unreal already, but after 1945 it was made clear that if the six counties were to receive more money from Britain then there would have to be closer Treasury control. It was decided, therefore, in 1946 that the Northern Ireland budget would be agreed each year between the Treasury and the Ministry of Finance for submission to the Joint Exchequer Board; that Northern Ireland Supplementary Estimates would also be put before the Treasury for information and agreement; and finally, that the Ministry of Finance would consult with the Treasury in advance about any new items of expenditure of over £50,000 in Northern Ireland, other than expenditure incurred on services that were being kept in parity with those in Britain.

The logic behind this arrangement was still the old logic – that parity of services *and* of taxation must be the guiding principle in the financial relations of the two areas. But the other two agreements that were reached in these crucial years were, so to speak, the sugar that coated the pill of increased Treasury supervision. And from them flowed the second consequence of importance to Northern Ireland – that provided parity was maintained, Britain would in effect finance the increased expenditure that the enlarged social services would entail. One of these agreements (actually signed in 1951, but taking effect from 1948) concerned national insurance covering payments for unemployment, sickness, maternity, widowhood, orphanhood, retirement and death. As a result of the agreement the two National Insurance Funds (originally separate) were virtually amalgamated and the principle established that in case of need money could be transferred from one to the other on a basis of reciprocity. Since Northern Ireland was the poorer area with the higher rate of unemployment, the transfer principle worked consistently in her favour. Similarly with the Social Services Agreement (signed in 1949, but again taking effect from 1948). This applied to the four main services of national assistance, family allowance, noncontributory pensions and health. It laid down that if the cost of these four services in Northern Ireland was proportionately higher than in the rest of the United Kingdom, Britain would pay eighty per cent of the cost of the excess. Technically, this too was a reciprocal agreement, but once again the movement of funds was one way only – towards Northern Ireland.

The expansion of the social services which these agreements took for granted inevitably involved the Northern Ireland government in heavy expenditure of its own. It was able to meet this, partly because it was bound by the rules of the game to impose the same heavy taxes as in Britain, and partly because (again by the rules of the game) it was able *pari passu* to reduce the amount of the imperial contribution. That annual contribution which, as we saw, had reached thirty-six million pounds at the end of the war, might, it has been calculated, have reached about sixty million pounds fifteen years later – if the cost of common services had been shared out solely on a basis of relative populations. In fact, of course, this criterion was not used. On the contrary, not only was the imperial contribution allowed to fall (in 1962–3 it was only £7.5 million) but in addition Britain paid over every year large amounts to the National Insurance Fund, large amounts under the Social Services Agreement, and even larger amounts in the form of subsidies, mainly to agriculture. During the three years 1961–3 these payments, with some other minor ones, averaged no less than forty-five million pounds a year, and this did not include special measures to encourage industry in the province, costing the British taxpayer about fifteen million pounds a year, even if some of this fifteen million pounds represented a reduction of the increasingly mythical imperial contribution he might otherwise have received.*

* Since this was written two calculations have been made as to the extent of inter-regional transfers from Britain to Northern Ireland, one for 1967-8 and one for 1971-2. For 1967-8 the direct transfers are reckoned at £51 million and the 'shortfall' of the imperial contribution (i.e. the amount that would have been due *from* Northern Ireland if this contribution had been paid at full rate instead of being left at a nominal £1 million) at £70 million. The total of £121 million thus reached has to be further corrected to take account of an additional £16 million paid by Britain under Reinsurance Agreement and also, on the other side, of an estimated shortfall of £11 million in capital receipts which could have been borrowed by the Northern Ireland government if it had not been restricted by its financial links with Britain. For 1967-8, therefore, the final total would appear to be of the order of £126 million. By 1971-2, however, the direct transfers are calculated at £135 million and the shortfall in the imperial contribution at £85 million, to which should be added payments under the Reinsurance Agreement of £15 million. Together these produce the staggering total of £235 million. It may be objected that the allowance for the shortfall in the imperial contribution is unrealistic, though in a UDI situation this would not necessarily be so, for an independent Northern Ireland government would almost certainly be faced with heavy defence expenditure. Even if it were to form part of an all-Ireland regime its pro rata defence bill would amount to approximately

Despite these contributions, there was so much 'leeway' to be made up in the building of houses, schools and hospitals, and in staffing the health and educational services, that Northern Ireland expenditure was bound to be heavy. A large part of this expenditure was met out of the proceeds of taxation. The 'transferred' taxes which Northern Ireland herself could impose were, as always, relatively insignificant. In the last decade before the war they had averaged only £1·7 million a year and in the first decade after the war they averaged £4·2 million. But in the same two periods the yields from the major 'reserved' taxes went up from £7·8 million a year to £52·4 million. And this figure continued to rise dramatically – by 1963 it had been more than doubled to reach nearly £109 million, which was not far from the amount spent in 1962–3 on transferred services, the chief of these being education, health and development. With remarkable ingenuity, the Northern Ireland government managed not only to meet a large part of the running cost of these services, but also to undertake very considerable capital expenditure, especially in the building of houses. It was this achievement, combined with the effect of the special agreements already mentioned, that provided the main justification for the decline of the imperial contribution, which by the early 'sixties stood at what must be reckoned in modern terms a purely nominal figure. 'Lord Craigavon's prophecy', it has been well said, 'to the effect that in the long run a contribution would be paid to, and not by, Northern Ireland has been borne out in full measure.'[1]

The consequence of this transformation can be summed up in a single sentence. Within a decade Northern Ireland passed from the status of an exceptionally backward area to full membership of the welfare state. The picture was not without its dark shadows, as we shall see, but it is necessary to insist on the extent of the improvement, since this improvement opened a wide gap between the social services in the two parts of Ireland and in doing so did more to reinforce the partition of the country than perhaps any other single factor. If the figures recently cited are correct – and comparisons between different systems are apt to be misleading – then the contrast between north and south has become formidable. A few examples of this trend must suffice. Thus in education, Northern Ireland, with a population less than half of that of the Republic, had 95,000 children in secondary schools in 1964 compared with 85,000 in the south, while expenditure on university education in 1963 was 17 shillings (85p.) per head in the Republic and 48/9d (2.44) in the six counties. And as recently as 1969 unemployment benefit for a single man was £3.25 per week in the

£11 million. On this (probably over-generous) basis the total to be found if British resources were cut off and if existing standards were to be maintained would still be in the neighbourhood of £160 million. For these calculations, see J. Simpson, 'Regional analysis: the Northern Ireland experience', in *Economic and Social Review*, vol. 2, No. 4 (July, 1971) and G. FitzGerald, *Towards a New Ireland*, pp. 54-7, 180-7.

Republic as against £4.50 in Northern Ireland. An unemployed man with two children drew £7.42½ per week in the south as compared with £9.20 in the north. Similarly, a widow's weekly pension in the Republic is £3.25; in Northern Ireland it was £4.50. In the south again children's allowance and maternity benefits were considerably lower, while between the health services the differences were so great that little comparison was possible.[2] Even if it be conceded that much of this contrast reflected higher taxation in the north than in the south, and that in any event Northern Ireland could not have afforded her benefits without the massive financial contribution from Britain, the fact remains that the differential exists and that until the Republic is able to overcome it, the hard-headed northerner is unlikely to see much inducement to abolish the border.

Attempts have been made from time to time to estimate how much it would cost the Republic to bring its social services into line with those of Northern Ireland and thus to remove, or lessen, one of the chief disincentives to reunion. Calculations cannot be absolutely exact because in certain respects the two systems are not comparable, but a recent and detailed analysis by the principal opposition spokesman for Finance in the Dáil, Dr FitzGerald, suggests that if northern eligibility provisions and benefit rates were to have been applied in the Republic in the year 1969/70, the existing expenditure of almost £143 million would have had to be increased by about a further £150 million, in other words by *one hundred and five per cent*. The same authority calculates that if, in addition to raising its own standards by this amount, the Republic had also to shoulder the cost of the inter-regional transfers from Britain to Northern Ireland – when mentioned earlier (p. 740n above) these were reckoned at upwards of £130 million – the effect would be to raise the level of taxation by nearly sixty per cent. This would, in practice, be an impossible burden and would in itself seem to suggest that until the Republic can increase its rate of economic growth sufficiently to narrow the gap between the two regions, any conceivable scheme of reunification would have to be underpinned for perhaps a generation by outside assistance – either from Britain, or from the European Economic Community, or both – if it were to have any prospect of being financially viable.[3]

It would be fairer perhaps to compare, not the Northern Ireland and the Republic of the 'sixties, but rather the Northern Ireland of the 'sixties with the Northern Ireland of the pre-war generation. The change is certainly very remarkable, whether one looks at the remodelling of the educational system, the creation of the Health Service, or the great expansion in state-subsidised housing. In the area of schooling alone, the seventeen years after the new Education Act of 1947 was passed showed an increase in pupils in grant-aided schools from 213,211 to 295,855, an increase paralleled in the building and extension of many new schools, especially at the secondary level which had been so much neglected before 1939. The structure of education followed the changes already brought about in England – primary education ending at the age of eleven plus, and all children thereafter receiving secondary education until the age of fifteen in grammar schools, secondary intermediate schools or technical intermediate schools. In addition, such generous provision was made for grants enabling students to go to the university that it might be said without too much exaggeration that the door to higher education was open to any child of sufficient ability to qualify for admission, regardless of what his social or economic background might be. Against this progress has to be set the fact that the Northern Ireland government's aim of overcoming denominational separation was not fulfilled. The voluntary schools – the great majority Catholic – remained obstinately under their own, mainly clerical, management and even won a great victory when they succeeded in extracting from the government the concession that the grants which they received under the Act of 1930 for fifty per cent of running costs, new building and reconstruction would be raised to sixty-five per cent. It was, however, symptomatic of how deep-rooted sectarian sentiment continued to be in the province that the courageous Minister who carried through this amendment with the interests of the children at heart was bitterly assailed by Nationalists for not offering grants of a hundred per cent, and by Unionists for yielding as much to the Catholics as he had done; eventually, in 1949, unable to make headway against persistent opposition from within his own party and from the Orange Order, he resigned.*

Just as education benefited from what was happening in Britain, so also the rapid development of the Health Service across the water had its repercussions in Northern Ireland. The old dispensary system went by the board, as did the other survivals of the poor law, and in 1944 a new Ministry of Health and Local Government was created. Within three years of the end of the war the north had its own General Health Services Board, its Hospitals Authority and – an innovation peculiar to Northern Ireland – its own Tuberculosis Authority. Thus the principle of parity was again demonstrated in action and, with very little ad-

* Education continued – and still continues – to be a source of controversy. Thus, the Education Act of 1968, while increasing building grants to voluntary schools from sixty-five to eighty per cent of the total, linked this with the proviso that such schools must become 'maintained' schools and as such come under the management of 'four and two' committees, i.e. committees on which the managers and the education authority should be respectively represented in those proportions. It was only after prolonged negotiation and the working out of the most elaborate rules for the constitution and conduct of such committees that the Catholic Church agreed, with reservations, to give the new system a fair trial. It is not surprising that liberal voices – including that of Captain O'Neill as he then was – should from time to time have been raised in criticism of segregated education. But such criticism, however muted, has always rebounded from the iron front presented by the Catholic bishops and, to a lesser extent, by other religious leaders as well.

743

ditional cost to themselves, Ulstermen were able to enjoy a comprehensive medical service on all fours with that of Britain. No doubt other factors – better medical knowledge, better housing and food, less unemployment – would have led to an improvement in the health of the community anyway, but the change would hardly have been so dramatic had the state not intervened to the extent it did. The end result was a striking decline in mortality (amongst mothers and infants, as well as in the population at large), a successful onslaught on tuberculosis, a remarkable advance in dealing with mental health, an extensive programme of water and sewerage schemes, and a spate of hospital building which, it was estimated, would have cost £66·5 million by the time it was completed in the early 'seventies.[4]

In all these aspects of social improvement Northern Ireland was being drawn into the contemporary pattern of increasing state intervention. Even before the war, indeed, this had begun to happen, when the road transport board had taken over large sections of road services formerly in private hands. After 1945 the pace was much accelerated and the scope greatly widened. This was true not only of transport – in 1948 the Ulster Transport Authority was formed to bring rail as well as road transport under public control – but also in a sphere where formerly the central and local authorities had been conspicuously inadequate. Long before the bombs had done their worst, Ulster housing had been sadly dilapidated. The housing survey carried out in 1943 showed that most of the houses in the entire province would have had to be condemned if the best modern criteria were to be strictly applied; and even if they were not, as nobody seriously suggested they could be, the minimum required in the immediate future would be 100,000 – twice that number if any real progress was to be made with slum clearance. The response to this challenge was at first sluggish, but within a few years the pace began to quicken.* This was partly due to an exceptionally generous policy of state subsidies for house-building in both the private and the public sectors, and partly due to the creation in 1945 of a special government agency, the Northern Ireland Housing Trust, which had the duty of providing and managing houses built at the Exchequer's expense. Admittedly, it took nearly twenty years before the 'immediate' target of 100,000 houses was reached – slightly over 112,000 had been built by 1963. But this progress, even though sedate enough in relation to the needs of the community, would probably have been much slower but for the initiative taken by local and central authorities. Thus of the total number built by 1963, local authorities provided about a third and the Housing Trust about a quarter. Private builders accounted for just over 40,000 new houses and all but about 5,000 of these had the benefit of a government subsidy.[5]

This growing activity by a seemingly benevolent state, impinging upon so many aspects of the lives of its citizens, has however to be seen against the background of a community where many old problems –

* For the darker side of the housing policy, see the next chapter.

744

economic, political and religious – still remained unsolved. It is, of course, true that the economic outlook was by no means as grim as it had been before the war and that this very fact at least helped to remove one complicating factor from the political and religious rivalries that continued to obsess so many Ulstermen. But the economic performance of the six counties, though improved, was so far from being completely satisfactory that any serious trade recession would be only too likely to bring back the competition for jobs and thus, with the help of all the other frictions, to recreate, especially in Belfast, the pre-war paradox of a society that contrived to be both inert and explosive.

In most sectors of the economy some at least of the impetus gained during the war was carried over into the peace. The modernisation of agriculture, in particular, continued to yield results in the shape of steadily expanding production of which a large share went, as before, to Britain. The privileged position the Ulster farmer enjoyed as the recipient of British agricultural bounties, and with access to the British market on terms not quite so favourable as in war-time, but still more than adequate, allowed him to benefit from steadily rising prices, especially of the livestock on which he most relied.[6] Indeed, it could be said that the war, while providing him with an assured market, had in a sense distorted his agriculture because of the insistence upon tillage beyond what in other circumstances would have been an economically acceptable limit. Once the need to produce crops was over, land reverted fast to its more normal uses and this in its turn was soon reflected in output. The volume of net agricultural output in 1946 was actually only five per cent greater than in 1937; in 1951 it was seventeen per cent higher than it had been in 1946. In terms of 1948–9 prices, the money value of net agricultural output reached its wartime peak in 1940–1 with a total of £43·7 million. In 1946–7 the comparable figure was £41 million. But by 1951–2 it had gone up to £46·8 million. Gross output in 1964–5 was estimated at just under £117 million. An estimate for the previous year, 1963–4, suggested that in comparative terms (1924–5 = base 100) gross agricultural output for cattle stood at 188, for pigs at 1,142, for milk at 156, but for crops and garden produce at 95.[7] It was not surprising, in this context, that exports of certain key commodities should have risen very sharply. Thus, whereas in 1940 66,000 cattle were sent out of Northern Ireland, in 1952 the total was 90,000, rising to 216,000 in 1965. In 1940, 92,000 tons of potatoes were exported; by 1952 this had become 211,000 tons, though by 1965 that figure had declined to 116,000. And between 1940 and 1952 the outflow of fresh milk climbed from 9,000 cwt to 684,000 and of processed milk from 45,000 cwt to 674,000; in 1965 the combined amount of milk products was 1½ million cwt.[8]

This, certainly, was a remarkable transformation, but northern agriculture had always been a sturdy plant, needing only adequate opportunity to grow and flourish. Northern industry, however, was another matter. The hectic conditions of the war years could not be expected to continue. And indeed the old spectre of unemployment, not by any means exorcised between 1939 and 1945, soon again began to haunt the mills and dockyards. During the two decades after the war it fluctuated between five and ten per cent, and was consistently well above the overall British figure. This was bad, but it might have been much worse had the government not taken vigorous action to prevent it. That action was mainly embodied in a series of acts of parliament designed to attract new industry to the province by offering various inducements. This legislation took several forms. First in point of time was the series of Industries Development Acts passed between 1945 and 1953 and designed to give financial assistance to firms starting new industries or extending old ones; grants or loans could be made especially for the purchase of new plant, machinery and buildings. Next came the Capital Grants to Industry Acts (1954-62) providing government grants of a proportion (usually a third) of the expenses incurred by firms in new buildings or new installations. This was followed by the Aid to Industry Acts (1961-4) by which the government undertook to pay further grants to industry to help with the cost of fuel (always a hampering factor where northern industry is concerned) and, finally, by the Industrial Advice and Enterprise Acts of 1964 and 1967 providing yet more money for replacement of obsolete plant and buildings as well as special payments to firms employing consultants with a view to improving their efficiency.* Left-wing critics, who see in the economic plight of Northern Ireland an inevitable outcome of 'monopoly capitalism', contend that the influx of foreign capital is at best a temporary palliative, not a permanent cure. Not only, they argue, is new industry labour intensive and therefore incapable of taking up the slack left by the old declining staple industries, but its economic surplus is exported and it will in any event move out again if and when government aid begins to dry up. On the other side it is worth pointing out that although fly-by-night firms may indeed be tempted to take what quick pickings they can get, the whole policy of introducing new business is too recent for the long-term results to be assessed. In the short term, it is hard to see how Northern Ireland could otherwise have found the new industrial concerns (over 160 of them) and the 55,000 new jobs

* Other inducements included a generous de-rating policy and a large coal subsidy; for full details, see Report of the Joint Working Party on the Economy of Northern Ireland (Cmd. 1835), 1962, Appendix ix, pp. 75-7. Another Industrial Development Act in 1966 increased the government grants to industry and this was further augmented for a three-year period following the disturbances of 1969. In addition, key industries, notably shipbuilding and aircraft, have received individual treatment, for instance the £3½ million lent to Harland and Wolff under special legislation of 1966, the £8 million lent towards the construction of a new shipbuilding dock in 1970 and the grants and loans, totalling some £16 million, to the aircraft industry between 1963 and 1969. The assistance given to these heavy industries has generally been shared by the British and Northern Ireland governments.

which, it is estimated, had been created by the mid-1960s.[9] Furthermore, the post-war development was not intended to be a mere flash in the pan. The *Report of the Joint Working Party* (the Hall Report cited in the footnote on the previous page set out starkly enough the problems with which the government and the province were confronted in their quest for further expansion. Yet the response to this challenge was anything but defeatist. The immediate sequel to the Hall Report was the scheme propounded by Sir Robert Matthew. His main proposal, embodied in the *Belfast Regional Survey and Plan* (1963), was to 'demagnetize' Belfast as the centre of the region and to link Portadown and Lurgan in a new city, subsequently called Craigavon. It is true that both the name of the city and its situation – it was of little relevance to the underdeveloped west of the province – aroused Nationalist criticism. but in other ways the conception was imaginative and, above all, it portended further growth. This also was the theme of another document, 'Economic Development in Northern Ireland', drawn up by Professor T. H. Wilson and published in 1965. This set targets for house-building and for employment which called for the construction of 12,000 new houses a year by 1970 and for 30,000 new jobs to be created in manufacturing, 5,000 in the building industry and a further 30,000 in the service industries.[10]

This sounded impressive, and to a certain extent it was impressive, but it was not in itself enough to banish unemployment. True, the target in housing (both for actual houses and for jobs) was reached in 1968, but it was not reached in the service industries and the very real achievement in manufacturing was to a considerable extent off-set by the contraction and closure of existing firms. The growth rate, particularly in male employment, was not unimpressive. But the pious hope expressed in the *Northern Ireland Development Programme* for 1970-5, that 'if Northern Ireland can maintain these faster growth rates in the years ahead, and if major adjustments such as the decline in shipbuilding employment are no longer required on the same scale, then faster employment growth will be possible in the future', was already being jeopardised by events. The consultants who drew up the *Development Programme* themselves pointed out that in mid-1969 unemployment stood at 6·8 per cent compared with 2·2 per cent for the United Kingdom as a whole, and that output per head of the working population was then running at about three-quarters of the national average. They recognised even then the danger that the province would be caught 'in a vicious circle of political instability and industrial decline'. The forecast of 40,000 new jobs to be provided between 1970 and 1975, at first regarded as the minimum desirable now, in their view, 'has . . . the appearance of presenting a formidable task'.[11] By no means all of the trouble was due to a political disturbance, of course. Despite all the efforts of the government – and further steps were and are being taken to implement the *Development Programme* – Northern Ireland cannot escape its economic heritage overnight. A good part of the explanation for the sluggishness of the economy to respond rapidly to all these well-intentioned initiatives is to be found in the fact that many of the new enterprises are light industries or else variants of the textile industry – either consumer-goods such as processed foods and electrical equipment, or the manufacture of man-made fibres such as Acrilan, Terylene or Ulstrom. What this means in effect is that new industries can prosper if they can minimise the traditional defects of the economic structure of the region. But for the industries which, so to speak, have been bred in the bone in the six counties, those traditional defects still remain – the difficulty of maintaining themselves in a world which no longer needed so much of their products (this applied to both linen and shipbuilding), the absence of minerals and fuel, the smallness of the domestic market, the cost of reaching the all-important export market, the difficulty of finding work for men rather than for women, and the lack of capital at home. While the bringing in of new industries no doubt helped to solve some of these problems in this sector or in that, it could not give rapid relief to those who still depended on the old, specialised, highly vulnerable industries. There, the outlook remained gloomy and because this was so there still remained the possibility – latent but nevertheless real – that competition for jobs could once again aggravate an already tense situation as it had done in the thirties.*

How far was this tense situation reflected in the political life of the province? The answer depends upon how deep one digs. On the surface, what mostly strikes the observer is the apparent immobility of politics and society in Northern Ireland during the first forty-five years of its existence. The same party was still in power that was in power at the beginning of the state and although the men may have changed within the last few years the policies – at least until very recently – were much as they had always been. It is not the purpose of this survey to carry the history of Northern Ireland in any detail beyond the early 1960s and at that time, certainly, with Sir Basil Brooke still in the saddle, continuity with the past of Ulster Unionism seemed almost unbroken. Even the population the politicians were there to represent, though growing slightly, was not very different from what it had been before the war. From a total of 1,256,561 in 1926 it had moved only to 1,425,042 in 1961. The number of members representing that population in the Northern Ireland House of Commons remained at fifty-two (or fifty-one if we exclude the Speaker) and the Unionist dominance in that House was still much the same as ever. In the years before the war the various opposition parties could seldom hope to win more than ten or a dozen seats; in 1958 the total 'anti-partition' representation was ten,

* The overall unemployment level has stayed obstinately high. Since 1951 the average has never remained below 30,000 for a full year; in the mid-1960s it hovered about the six per cent mark in an insured population of roughly half a million (*Report of the Joint Working-Party*, pp. 18-9; *Ulster Yearbook*, 1966-68, pp. 188-9).

in 1962 it was twelve, and in 1965 eleven. Political parties, as we have seen, tended to follow very closely the lines of religious affiliation and here, too, there had been no very marked shift in the distribution of the population. In 1926 Catholics had accounted for 33·5 per cent, in 1961 they accounted for roughly 35 per cent. The remainder were almost entirely Protestant of one denomination or another. Presbyterians remained the largest of the Protestant groups – 29 per cent in 1961, against 31·3 per cent in 1926. The Church of Ireland share also fell slightly, from 27 to 24·2 per cent; among other denominations Methodists remained the most numerous, though small in relation to the three major gaps.*

Given this kind of stability, it was not to be expected that the Northern Ireland parliament would be the scene of any very exciting new development. In fact, it remained much what it had always been – a chamber where ministers explained their policies to the faithful (who, however, could be critical), and endured with equanimity protests from the minority which both protesters and protested against knew to be chiefly for the record and without much likelihood of influencing the course of government action. In short, those who might in ordinary circumstances have done most to challenge the existing scheme of things and even in time produce alternative governments – either the Nationalists or the Labour representatives – were debarred from doing so by the operation of the same factor that had deprived them of their usefulness before the war – the overwhelming importance of the constitutional issue and the seemingly inescapable need to discuss everything else in the light of that issue.

Both these potential centres of opposition had, therefore, very dispiriting records in the years after 1945. It might have been expected, in view of the industrial revival during the war and of the attempts to develop industry after it was over that a strong Labour party would emerge as the principal alternative to Unionism. It is true that the membership of the trade union movement did increase very considerably. By the early 'sixties there were about 200,000 trade unionists, about ninety per cent of whom belonged to unions which had their headquarters in Britain. Since some of these unions also had members in the Republic there was here, one would have thought, a nucleus around which might have developed that working-class solidarity which James Connolly had striven for in the past and which, correctly, he had anticipated would be one of the first casualties of partition. But such solidarity proved hard to achieve. This was partly, as we saw earlier, because of divisions within the Irish movement as a whole, but partly also because the stature of the northern unions was diminished by the reluctance of the Northern Ireland government either to repeal the obnoxious Trade Union Act of 1927, or to recognise the Northern Committee of the Irish Congress of Trade Unions. With the advent to power of Captain O'Neill, these obstacles were at

* Religious groupings are listed in *Ulster Yearbook, 1966-68*, pp. 8-10.

last removed and the way was cleared for somewhat easier relations between organised labour and the authorities.*

Nevertheless, this improved status of the trade unions was not reflected in the improved status of Labour as a political force. On the contrary, the electoral showing of Labour candidates for the local parliament continued to be extremely poor. The reason for this was essentially the same as the reason for their poor showing before the war. In a society where the fundamental cleavage was religious and political, the concept of a workers' party dedicated to the overthrow of capitalism still seemed to many workingmen to be peripheral, even irrelevant.† Consequently, after the war as before it, Labour candidates were apt to come forward with qualifying epithets – 'Commonwealth' Labour, 'Republican' Labour, 'Eire' Labour and so on – which pointed firmly to their attitude towards partition, the presumption being that this was what really interested the electors. In an effort to counteract this fissiparous tendency the Northern Ireland Labour party took two important steps in 1949. On the one hand, it made it clear that it wished to be a party on the lines of the British Labour party and to be associated with that party. And on the other hand, it put all its eggs in the basket of constitutionalism. Following the declaration of the Republic in the south (April 1949), a Labour conference in the six counties passed the following resolution: 'That the Northern Ireland Labour party believes that the best interests of Northern Ireland lie in maintaining the constitutional links with the United Kingdom.' But the chill wind that blew across northern politics in that bleak year was unkind to the delicate plant of Labour orthodoxy. In the general election which was Stormont's immediate reaction to Mr Costello's Republic, all nine Labour candidates were defeated. They did no better in 1953, but in 1958 and 1962 managed to secure four seats, though even these were likely to remain precarious so long as the central preoccupation of northern politics continued to be with issues that had little to do with the role of Labour in modern society. The fact that other 'unofficial' Labour candidates, with prefixes of various kinds, managed to win two or three seats in those same elections does not affect the generalisation – on the contrary, the very paucity of their representation reinforces it.

* For the all-Ireland context of these developments, see Part IV A, chap. 5, section iv.

† This is confirmed by the researches of Professor Richard Rose during the late 'sixties. Of the trade unionists, he writes: 'The absence of a strong relationship between union membership and political outlooks is surprising and significant. It is surprising because of the extent to which union membership is strongly associated with political attitudes elsewhere. It is significant because the failure of unions to encourage a more secular approach to politics is not a function of weak union organisation, but in spite of the well-established position of unions in Northern Ireland'. And he adds: 'Religion more than economics determines who the enemies of the workers are thought to be'. (*Governing Without Consensus* (London, 1971), pp. 261, 284.)

If, then, Labour suffered because in the last resort it was crowded out by the all-devouring issue of partition, did this not mean that the Nationalist party, which by definition was totally concerned with that issue, had a golden opportunity to assume the main role in opposition? In a sense it did assume that role, since it was the second largest party in the Northern Ireland parliament, but it was still inhibited from becoming an *official* opposition because this would imply more recognition of the existing regime than it was prepared to concede.* The very fact that it was bound by its history and situation to remain obsessed by the border had several consequences which seriously affected its ability to win more votes and move nearer to power. One was that, so long as the constitutional issue remained in effect the only issue, its policy on other matters appeared to be unconstructive, or even nonexistent. Nationalists were certainly prompt to expose and to denounce instances of what seemed to them unfair discrimination against their fellow citizens and co-religionists, but this, though a necessary function, was also a negative one. Again, it has to be remembered also that although there have always been important Nationalist enclaves in Belfast, Londonderry, and other towns (Newry, indeed, being predominantly Nationalist), the main electoral support for the party has come from the rural areas where the opinion they had to represent is the opinion of mainly conservative farmers and shopkeepers. When to that is added the further fact that Nationalist members at Stormont were the spokesmen for the Catholic Church on such matters as education, health and the social services, it will be seen that the opportunities open to them for taking a radical line were severely limited. The epithet derisively applied to them by some workingmen – 'Green Tories' – indicates sufficiently where their sympathies were believed to lie.

Unfortunately these have not been the only weaknesses in their position. They have inherited from their predecessors of the 1920s that nervous paralysis which comes from awareness of another and more extreme form of nationalism at their elbow with which at any time they might expect to be in competition. This has led them at times into irresolution and inconsistency. Lacking the will or the wish to join the Republicans, they have also lacked the nerve to fight them tooth and nail. Accordingly, under stress, they have tended to compromise. The most striking political example of this was the tacit agreement in the late 'fifties to leave electioneering for the Westminster seats to Sinn Féin, while the constitutional Nationalists concentrated on the elections to the local parliament at Stormont.

But to sup with Sinn Féin needed a longer spoon than the constitutional Nationalists possessed. For militant republicanism had more than one weapon in its armoury. To mark one's disapproval of the

* It became the official opposition in 1965, but subsequently (autumn 1968) withdrew again in protest against police action in breaking up the Civil Rights demonstration in Londonderry.

British connection by winning seats in the Westminster parliament one never meant to occupy was too negative to appeal for long to the more hot-headed young men in the movement. When the military wing of that movement – the Irish Republican Army – was reorganised in the mid-fifties it soon became clear that the use of force to overthrow 'British rule in occupied Ireland' had by no means been abandoned. The campaign of violence which then developed was confused and largely ineffective – chiefly because of the tendency of the extremists to split into splinter groups owing little or no obedience to the Army Council of the IRA. Nevertheless, the campaign, whether 'official' or 'unofficial', produced some very ugly incidents along the border, where several policemen were killed in circumstances that deeply shocked public opinion – one constable, for example, being riddled with bullets as he was returning from a visit to his fiancée, and a sergeant being blown to pieces by a booby-trap in a deserted farm-house. Altogether, the 'offensive' waged by the IRA and other groups cost nineteen lives between 1956 and 1961, caused considerable material damage, and led to heavy expenditure in north and south on increased security precautions. Indeed, the governments of Northern Ireland and of the Republic both reacted with similar firmness to the threat posed by these new outbreaks. There appears to have been considerable exchange of information between their police forces and, although there were no extradition arrangements between the two parts of Ireland, each government used its powers to intern the members of these 'illegal organisations'. In Northern Ireland, the peak period of attack was between 1957 and 1959, and in those years an average of 150 IRA members or sympathisers were detained in the six counties under the special regulations. It was, however, impressive evidence of the then stability and strength of the Stormont government that not only was it able to restrain its own partisans from massive reprisals (a very real danger in the light of previous history) but it also felt able to release all the internees in 1961 – a year before the campaign was called off by the Army Council of the IRA.[12]

Although both governments had behaved responsibly and with restraint during the episode there can be little doubt that among ordinary men and women in the north this recrudescence of violence simply tended to reinforce traditional attitudes. Unionists, certainly, were much inflamed not simply by the violence, but by the fact that in some quarters in the south its perpetrators were apparently regarded as heroes in the Fenian tradition. For constitutional and conservative-minded Nationalists this hardening of tempers could only spell further damage. Many of them, anyway, were totally alienated by a campaign which was at variance with everything constitutional Nationalism stood for and which, moreover, had repeatedly been condemned by the leaders of their Church. It was not surprising, therefore, that in 1959-60, when the threat from the IRA was still very much of a reality, more moderate Nationalists began to draw together into a new organisation,

National Unity, pledged to work for the unification of the island by the consent of the people of Northern Ireland. A few years later this was transformed into the Nationalist Political Front, to bring together all those Nationalists who were repelled by violence and were at the same time impatient with the lack of progress of the older generation of parliamentarians.

To look back at such developments across the chasm which now separates Northern Ireland from even its recent past is to peer dimly into a world so different from the present as to be almost incomprehensible. With hindsight we can see – contemporaries themselves, indeed, can never really have forgotten it – that political, like religious, ecumenism is at best a struggling plant where the soil remains so bleakly inhospitable. What most affects the man in the street, after all, is what happens in his own locality or in his own personal experience. It is at this level that the burden of discrimination makes itself felt most heavily and it has usually been at this level that the most grating frictions have occurred. What constitutes discrimination is, of course, a vexed question. No doubt much that seems to the minority to be diabolically deliberate discrimination may in reality be the results of the geographical and economic configuration of the country. The fact that Catholics, for example, are thickest on the ground in the south and west of the province is a partial consequence of the Plantation of three hundred years ago, just as the industrialisation of the east is the product of the technological revolution of a hundred years ago. But to argue that because the east figures largely in the development plans of the government and the west does not, this is part of a general scheme of discrimination, is to fall into the all-too common error of oversimplification by foreshortening history.

Nevertheless, if some of the economic and social discrimination against Catholics can be explained away as the historical consequence of their having been for many years a poor and exploited section of the population this is no argument either for condoning or for continuing the exploitation. Nor is it any justification for the other kinds of discrimination that have arisen directly from the siege mentality of the majority – from their fierce determination, that is, to maintain their Protestant and Unionist faith and institutions against all comers. These have generally been seen by the minority as a deliberate attempt to 'hold the pass', so to speak, against Catholic infiltration. Many and various have been the allegations made in support of this contention – ranging from the siting of the projected new town (to be called, provocatively enough, Craigavon) and the placing of the new university in Coleraine in preference to Londonderry, to the general and never-ending complaint about a religious test being applied in a wide variety of employments. Such a test certainly is applied (it may not be unknown in Catholic areas, either, but since Protestants dominate most councils their actions are more conspicuous) and no doubt the intention is often to preserve the status quo intact. It is, however, only fair to add two comments. One is that many of the better-paid and more senior posts, for example in the civil service, require a standard of education to which relatively few Catholics have in the past been able to aspire. There is a vicious circle here. They have not been able to aspire because so many are in the poorer-paid occupations. Because they are in the poorer-paid occupations they have to leave school as early as possible. Because they leave school as early as possible they cannot aspire to the quality of education which would admit them to the more prestigious jobs. No doubt over the years more Catholic children have been benefiting from a longer and better education, but it is significant that in the early 'sixties the proportion attending the Queen's University was still only twenty-two per cent of the total student population in the university.[18]

The second comment to be made is this. Each side has its own reasons for regarding certain kinds of employment as unsuitable. Many Nationalists have been reluctant to enter the service of a state whose legality they refuse to recognise. This has, of course, been pre-eminently true of the Royal Ulster Constabulary, where, despite efforts from the earliest days to make the force non-political and inter-denominational, in 1961 only twelve per cent of the police were Catholic, as against thirty-seven per cent Church of Ireland and forty per cent Presbyterians.* These proportions, however, suggest another consideration of wider relevance – which is that if Catholics themselves would regard acceptance of certain kinds of employment as a betrayal of their principles, some Protestants would hesitate to employ them anyway lest they should prove untrustworthy or even engage in what, from a Unionist viewpoint, might be regarded as treasonable activities. This, incidentally, is an argument that has been used not only about employment, but also to justify the exclusion of Catholics from their due share in local government.

Much of all this, however objectionable, can be seen as a natural outcome of the unhappy but inescapable fact that over many generations (this is true in the south as well as in the north) the different religious denominations have tended to keep very much to themselves. We have seen how this has affected the pattern of education; it has affected similarly not only the pattern of employment but even the use of leisure and the social groupings in which people live. There are exceptions to this, of course. The trade unions have to a considerable extent, though not entirely, cut across the frontiers of religion and politics; the professions, notably the law, have enabled considerable mixing to take place; most of all, perhaps, the Queen's University has played a conspicuously successful part in breaking down among its students barriers which their home environment had often enough raised against common understanding.

But such shafts of light are rare enough in a situation which has

* The part-time B Specials were, for obvious historical reasons, exclusively Protestant.

been gloomy ever since the foundation of the state and in the last few years has become steadily gloomier. Over the years, the key to advance has generally been seen not so much in some magical formula for apportioning jobs in an equitable fashion between the various denominations, but in applying democratic concepts to local government, which impinges so directly and in so many ways upon the lives of men, women and children. Naturally, therefore, since the effective working of the social services depends in such large measure upon fair and efficient administration by the local councils, the battle for representation on them has grown steadily more bitter in the last twenty years.

The most frequent accusation levelled against the Unionist majority has been that they have retained control of the local councils in certain areas by shameless gerrymandering – that is, by so drawing the boundaries of the various districts and wards that even where Nationalists have been in a majority, that majority has not been reflected in the composition of the councils. This is still the subject of the most acute and violent controversy and the historian can do little more at this point in time than illustrate the nature of the controversy by referring to what is generally regarded as a crucial instance.

The *locus classicus* of this dispute about local representation is the city of Londonderry, where the issues involved were not only religious, political and economic, but also social, since, as seems to be clear beyond all reasonable doubt, a deliberate policy had there been followed of manipulating council housing policy so that Catholic voting power would not increase to such an extent as to endanger the Unionist supremacy on the city council. In general, in Londonderry as in other local government areas, the vote was given to 'resident occupiers' and to 'general occupiers'. The first category consisted of persons residing in dwelling-houses as owners or tenants. In such cases the resident occupier's wife could also vote, but others living under the same roof would normally be excluded, even if they were of voting age.* To vote as a 'general occupier' a person had to be the occupier of land or premises (other than a dwelling-house) of annual valuation of not less than ten pounds; no more than two joint-occupiers could qualify for the franchise unless they were engaged in business as partners. Limited companies were entitled to appoint one nominee for every ten pounds' valuation of their premises up to a maximum of six nominees. This system, weighted in favour of property as it obviously was, has been defended on the grounds that since the essential function of a local council is to fix and to spend rates then those who are to pay the piper should choose the tune, but the 'business vote' always attracted great hostility

* Legislation of 1946, 1948 and 1962 did, however, extend the definitions of 'resident occupier' to include certain other categories of persons, including married couples who, living in part of a dwelling-house let to them furnished or unfurnished, had qualified hitherto as parliamentary electors but not as local government electors. See *Ulster Yearbook, 1966-68*, pp. 37-8.

and, like so much else in the province, has disappeared in the turmoil of the last four years.*

Over the province as a whole these regulations resulted in a striking difference between the number of electors for the parliament at Stormont and for the local councils; according to the register of February 1964 there were 911,940 of the former, but only 658,778 of the latter.† In Londonderry itself the system worked as follows. The city was divided into three wards, containing in all a population which in 1961 amounted to 53,762. In that year (the last, incidentally, when religious affiliation was listed), there were 36,073 Catholics and 17,689 others; roughly half the Catholics and forty per cent of the others were under the voting age of 21. By 1967, the last year for which reliable figures are available at the time of writing, the number of Catholics entitled to vote was 14,429 and the number of others similarly qualified was 8,781. The fact the Catholic majority among voters was so small in relation to their overall majority of the population reflected of course their economically inferior status, but it was also directly related to their lack of houses since, as we have just seen, to be a resident occupier was one of the principal qualifications for the franchise. But this Catholic majority, such as it was, did not produce a majority in the city council, where the normal division of parties had long been twelve Unionists against eight non-Unionists. This result was achieved by the curious fashion in which the population was grouped within the three wards. In 1967 the North Ward, with 2,530 Catholic voters and 3,946 others, returned eight Unionists. The Waterside Ward had just over 5,500 voters divided between 1,852 Catholics and 3,697 Unionists – it returned four Unionists. The South Ward, with slightly more than 11,000 voters, of whom 10,000 were Catholics, accounted for the entire non-Unionist representation of eight seats.[14]

Thus, by a heavy concentration of Catholics into one ward, was the Unionist majority obtained, even though over sixty per cent of the adult population was Catholic. To some extent, it is fair to say, a concentration of Catholic Nationalists into one area, and of Protestant Unionists into others, might have happened anyway, since that is part and parcel of the segregation of the two communities to be found all over the province, but the fact remains that the particular form this segregation took in Londonderry city resulted in a pattern of Unionist control which was too consistent too long to be anything other than deliberately contrived.

The crux of this unhappy situation was the housing problem – both because houses meant votes and because lack of houses meant miserably cramped conditions for those who felt they were being dis-

* This was written shortly before the reforms of November 1968 announced its impending abolition.

† More recent figures (for 1967) give the Stormont electorate in that year as 933,724, the Westminster electorate as 909,841, and the local government electorate as 694,483.

criminated against on religious and political grounds. Much play, it is true, has been made with the argument that in the twenty years after the war Catholics have received more than twice the number of houses allotted to Protestants. But against this have to be set three other considerations – that the Catholic population was larger, that the Catholic need was greater, and that many of the houses, those built by the Housing Trust for example, represented replacements of houses condemned or demolished. Moreover, so long as political considerations were deemed to require the containment of Catholics mainly within the South Ward, then the sheer physical facts of the situation were bound sooner or later to confront the Unionist-dominated council with a terrifying dilemma. Eventually it would be impossible to put any more houses in the Catholic ward. Would Catholics then be allowed to spill over into the other wards with all that that implied or would there be some other, more explosive outcome? The whole world now knows the answer to that question even if it remains as much in the dark as ever about the ultimate solution to the problems of discrimination and segregation of which Londonderry has become, in a sense, the symbol.*

Londonderry may be a symbol, and no doubt it is an extreme case, but it is by no means unique. The manipulation of local government boundaries, it now seems abundantly plain, had created in other centres also large pockets of under-represented and deeply resentful Catholics.[15] This in turn produced a dangerous situation which could at any time be precipitated into crisis by an increase in the number of Catholics above the opportunities of employment or housing available to them. Until the early 1960s, it has been suggested, the safety-valve of emigration operated to reduce the tension to some extent, since in the six counties between 1937 and 1961 Catholics, who were consistently about a third of the population, accounted for fifty-five to fifty-eight per cent of all Ulstermen leaving the province.[16] Apart from the fact that the vicissitudes of the British economy render this a safety-valve of dubious value, the very fact that it was Catholics who had, proportionately, to make most use of it, in itself constituted a grievance, reinforcing both their sense of an imposed inferiority and the bitter resentment which that sense of inferiority evoked.

The problem of Northern Ireland has been complicated by the rise of the welfare state, but it is at heart the old problem. When most people were poor and the whole province was backward inequalities seemed less blatant. But now, when spending is so much greater, and the expectations of the people have risen so much higher, it is inevitable that the local councils should be seen to be important centres of influence and power. In a small area such as Northern Ireland the politics of welfare are necessarily and properly local politics. But the tragedy of the six counties is that it has not been possible to disentangle

* The answer, and the problem to which it in turn gave rise, are discussed in the next chapter.

the politics of welfare from the politics of siege. The work of local councils, valuable and constructive as it often is, cannot simply be judged, as it might be elsewhere, from the way these bodies deal with drainage, health, education or the social services. Always overshadowing these preoccupations is the larger question – is local government to remain in the hands of those who uphold the political settlement as it is now or of those who wish to destroy it? Is it, to put the matter more brutally, designed to intensify the existing segregation or to alleviate it? Up to the mid-sixties, certainly, the aim of policy seemed to go no further than the maintenance of the status quo. But there was always the possibility that, as so often before, any action to change the status quo in a sense favourable even to moderate Catholic or Nationalist aspirations would call into being an ardent Protestant and Unionist reaction.

Already, by the mid-sixties, there were signs that exactly this might be about to happen. Ironically, it was the accession to power in 1963 of a Prime Minister, Captain Terence O'Neill, who appeared to turn his face firmly against sectarian bigotry, that may eventually be seen as the catalyst that set sectarian bigotry in motion once more. Born in 1914, of an ancient, landed family, educated at Eton, and Anglican by religion, Captain O'Neill set himself not only to divert domestic energies away from internecine quarrels and towards constructive policies, but also to cultivate more amicable relations with the south, a new departure dramatised, as we have seen, by his exchange of visits with Mr Sean Lemass in 1965. This change of style in government did not mean that Captain O'Neill had ceased to be a Unionist, and it emphatically did not imply any weakening of official determination to maintain the sanctity and integrity of the border, but precisely because his regime had broken – or, more accurately, was believed to have broken – so radically with tradition, it brought out again into the open all the deeply-felt fears and antagonisms of old-style Unionism. Of this Unionism, which still remained extremely strong in the constituencies, representatives were to be found even in Captain O'Neill's own cabinet and, as we shall see, they were eventually to topple him from power. Yet, although Captain O'Neill was clearly pursuing a course which was likely to alienate many Unionists it seemed for his first five years of office that he was strong enough to withstand reactionary pressures. Indeed, if there was a threat to his position in those relatively untroubled years, it appeared to come less from the politicians than from embattled Protestantism in the formidable shape of the Reverend Ian Paisley, the dominating figure, one might say the Alpha and Omega, of the militant Free Presbyterian Church. Mr Paisley, still in his early forties, but with a decade of strenuous activity behind him, is a very large man with a very loud voice which has been raised at all times and seasons to warn his fellow-citizens against the perils of Popery and the dangers of tampering with entrenched Protestant and Unionist positions. His protests against 'Romanism' had begun to take on a political tinge in the (Westminster) general election of 1964 when he organised demonstrations against a Republican candidate in Belfast, but it was in 1966 that his Protestantism and his Unionism really combined to make him a powerful, if somewhat unpredictable, figure. His own emphasis was then – as it probably still is, at bottom – primarily upon the threat to the Protestant position poised by the fast-growing ecumenical movement, but the very year in which he chose to launch his anti-ecumenical thunders was also the year in which Unionist sensibilities were ruffled by the celebrations attending the fiftieth anniversary of the 1916 Rising. Mr Paisley's activities that summer earned him a prison sentence and also laid the foundation for the fierce hostility between himself and Captain O'Neill which, before long, was to have dire consequences for the latter. Nevertheless, although a preacher and orator of undeniable power and magnetism, and later to be the driving-force behind the extreme right-wing Ulster Constitution Defence Committee and its Ulster Protestant Volunteers, Mr Paisley, in the middle 1960s, might still perhaps have been dismissed as *vox et praeterea nihil*. Whether the future belonged to his brand of Unionism or to Captain O'Neill's was then impossible to predict, though onlookers who did not know the north too well would probably have been disposed to plump for the Prime Minister. But all guesses and calculations as to how the delicate balance of power within the Unionist party might turn were soon to seem crudely inadequate when in 1968 the long-stifled resentment of the deprived sections of the population began to force its way inexorably to the surface. For upholders of the status quo, whether moderate or extreme, time was beginning to run out.

6. The Continuing Crisis

It is extraordinary to reflect in 1972 that as recently as six years ago the state of Northern Ireland appeared even to well-informed observers to be quiescent and the omens for a brighter and more harmonious future decidedly propitious. The advent to power of Captain Terence O'Neill as a more 'liberal' Unionist than any of his predecessors, the *rapprochement* between north and south, the initially favourable effect of development policies on the northern economy, the decision of the Nationalist party to accept the role of official Opposition at Stormont – all these pointed, or seemed to point, to the success of the Prime Minister's avowed intention to build bridges between the rival communities and, by emphasising the need for the common pursuit of prosperity, to obtain Catholic as well as Protestant support for his programme.[1]

Yet, despite these hopeful signs, very little hindsight is needed to see that the anticipated golden age was largely the product of wishful thinking. No-one acquainted with the history of the province could rationally have supposed that the memory of centuries of conflict and tension could be forgotten overnight or that the realities of discrimination and alienation could be dispelled by a wave of Captain O'Neill's wand. But even if we were to think the unthinkable and leave Ulster history for the moment out of Ulster politics, it would still be clear that Captain O'Neill's initiative was threatened at the very moment he made it by both external and internal factors over neither of which did he have much, if any, control. The most important external factors were the rise of religious ecumenism in the outside world and the revival of interest in republicanism in nationalist Ireland following the fiftieth anniversary of the 1916 Rising. The first of these aroused the anger and apprehension of the extremer Protestant elements in Northern Ireland and, as we have seen, the Reverend Ian Paisley first achieved extensive notoriety by his attacks upon what he conceived to be the 'Romeward' tendencies of the Presbyterian Church. Although these may not have been very apparent to less prejudiced observers, there was enough Protestant fundamentalism in the province for this accusation to carry with it an element of political danger for a prime minister who was deliberately seeking to cultivate better relations with Catholics. And few antagonisms in the next few years were to be so bitter or so personal as those which developed between Captain O'Neill and Mr Paisley.

The republican revival in the south was, in 1966, perhaps a less obvious fact than ecumenism, but its importance for the future was to be far greater. Although the Easter celebrations produced the usual surplus of frothy rhetoric they also provoked a reassessment of the Rising which the rhetoricians themselves had been shirking for most of the previous fifty years. From this reassessment flowed three consequences, each of them directly relevant to both parts of the island. One was a tendency to contrast the ideals of 1916 with the realities of partition and thus to reawaken, especially in the young, an interest in, even a sympathy with, the IRA, which still continued to claim continuity of tradition with the men who had made the Easter rebellion. A second consequence was that increased attention was paid to James Connolly, with the inevitable corollary that the abortive social programme of the original revolution came to be critically contrasted with the existing condition of affairs in both north and south. Finally, the 1916 anniversary convinced staunch Ulster Unionists, if they needed any convincing, that the leopard had not changed his spots and that inside every nationalist there was a ravening republican waiting to get out.

By any reckoning this was an absurd over-simplification which took no account of the changes wrought on either side of the border by fifty years of partition. But it was especially an over-simplification when applied to the Catholic third of the population of Northern Ireland. No doubt that population did contain a militantly republican minority, and no doubt also a larger number were capable of an emotional response to the songs and symbols of extreme nationalism, but it is worth remarking that a survey carried out as recently as 1968 indicates that while about two-thirds of the Catholics questioned were in favour of abolishing the border, few of them regarded the issue as one of immediate importance.[2] More to the point, perhaps, is the evidence of the IRA itself which, when it called off its previous campaign in 1962, publicly admitted that lack of Catholic support in Northern Ireland was 'foremost' among the reasons for this defeat.[3]

In 1966, however, these external factors menaced Captain O'Neill's peace of mind less than the internal pressures which were already building up against him. These came both from within his own party and from outside it. His emergence as Prime Minister in 1963 (prime ministers in Northern Ireland were not at that time elected by their colleagues) had been a source of some uneasiness to the right-wing members of his party and as his policies unfolded in the succeeding years this uneasiness increased. It was accentuated when, following Mr Paisley's religious demonstrations, that forceful cleric was jailed for three months, and when the government showed a mounting disposition to deal harshly with Protestant gunmen who had begun to attack and kill Catholics in Belfast. The secret or semi-secret Protestant extremist organisation, the Ulster Volunteer Force, was declared illegal under the Special Powers Act in June 1966 and it was not, perhaps, entirely coincidental that O'Neill's first leadership crisis occurred that autumn when he faced and overcame what he himself described as a 'conspiracy' against him. The vote of confidence he then received was substantial, but more significant was the fact that the Unionist back-benchers set up a '66 Committee' to scrutinise more closely the actions of their leader. It was believed at the time that three ministers, Mr Brian Faulkner (then Minister of Commerce), Mr Harry West (Minister of Agriculture) and Mr William Morgan (Minister of Health and Social Services) would even then have welcomed a change of leadership.[4]

Seemingly unperturbed by these criticisms Captain O'Neill continued to shape his course towards reform – outlining a programme whereby the business vote in Stormont elections would be abolished, the four Queen's University seats would be suppressed and redistributed, and a boundary commission would re-draw the constituencies, first in Belfast and then for the province as a whole. These however, did not touch the roots of Catholic resentment of discrimination and there were in-dications that even to moderate nationalists Captain O'Neill's liberal protestations were beginning to ring rather hollow, partly because it was dubious whether he would survive the impending conflict with his own right wing, and still more because his reforms were projected within a framework of uncompromising Unionism which did not hold out to Catholics much, if any, hope of real participation in govern-ment. Moreover, even though it could be demonstrated that genuine economic progress was being made in the mid-sixties, this did not lead to a significant reduction in the rate of unemployment and com-petition between Catholics and Protestants for jobs as well as for houses remained acute.

Historically, it was the competition for houses which provided the spark that was to set the whole province alight. As far back as 1963, Mrs Patricia McCluskey, wife of a doctor in the town of Dungannon, was provoked by the failure of the Protestant-dominated council to provide adequate accommodation for Catholics into establishing a Homeless Citizens League which, by adroit publicity and direct action in the form of 'squatting', secured its desired objective. Recognising this as merely a local manifestation of a much wider problem, Mrs Mc-Cluskey and her husband went on to found the Campaign for Social Justice in January 1964 to collect and publicise information about cases of discrimination in Northern Ireland. This body, though itself non-political in origin and intention, speedily established contacts with critics of the Unionist regime inside and outside Ulster. In 1965 it affiliated with the National Conference of Civil Liberties in London and it may be regarded as the forerunner of the Northern Ireland Civil Rights Association which was formed two years later. It was not, how-ever, until the summer of 1968 that the latter organisation found its opportunity and its role. Once again, the flash-point was housing. A Nationalist MP for county Tyrone, Austin Currie, failed to secure a council house in the village of Caledon for a Catholic family because the local council intended to let it to an unmarried nineteen-year-old Protestant girl who happened to be the secretary of a Unionist politician. Mr Currie responded by organising a 'squat in' at the house and fol-lowed this up by a Civil Rights march at the neighbouring town of

Dungannon. The march received wide coverage from the mass media, it was attended by leading non-Unionist politicians and it was peaceful and well-conducted. Its real importance, however, had little to do with the rectification of the housing situation in Caledon, or even in Tyrone. The Dungannon march was both a symbol and a portent. It was a symbol because it demonstrated that opponents of the regime could combine against it, however diverse their own backgrounds and interests. It was a portent because its success was eagerly watched elsewhere and nowhere more than in the city of Londonderry where the Civil Rights Association planned to widen their protest on a much larger scale and in a much more explosive situation.

Their attempt to do so on 5 October 1968 has already passed into history. That public marches and parades should lead to violence was nothing new in the experience of that bitterly divided city, but two factors ensured that the Civil Rights demonstration, though intended to be peaceful, would in reality be highly dangerous. One was the growing interest in the Civil Rights movement of various left-wing bodies for whom a confrontation with the police in full view of the television cameras would be the kind of publicity on which they throve. And the other was the intervention of the Minister for Home Affairs, Mr William Craig, who, two days before the march was due to take place, had prohibited it from following part of its advertised route. Almost inevitably confusion resulted and a section of the march collided with the police who, in their turn, used excessive and indiscriminate violence.[5]

The immediate and predictable outcome of the affair was an intensification of protest and a growth of organisation among both moderates and extremists. In Londonderry itself a number of the groups involved in the demonstration of 5 October met four days later in that city and elected the Derry Citizens Action Committee, pledged to non-violent pursuit of the same kind of aims as those enunciated by the Civil Rights Association. It soon became an effective exponent of Civil Rights ideas and its spokesmen, Mr John Hume and Mr Ivan Cooper, emerged as among the most capable, articulate and responsible of the leaders.[6] The same day which saw the formation of the Derry Citizens Action Committee saw also the creation in the Queen's University of a new and potentially more extreme protest group. This, which became known a little later as the People's Democracy, contained from the outset a number of Young Socialists and others whose politics inclined, in varying degrees, to the left. Miss Bernadette Devlin was one of the students prominent in the earliest days of this organisation, but control soon passed to former members of the university, when Mr Michael Farrell and Mr Eamonn McCann became the effective leaders.[7] Their aims, while embracing the anti-discriminatory ideas of the Civil Rights Association, in fact went far beyond the redress of immediate grievances, envisaging as they did the eventual creation of a 'workers' and small farmers' republic' for the whole of Ireland.[8] Although it too professed non-violence, the People's Democracy was not averse to confrontations with the police and in the course of time developed the techniques of 'defensive' violence with considerable expertise.

During the two months after the Londonderry demonstration intermittent protest marching continued there and in Belfast, carried out by the Civil Rights Association and the People's Democracy on the one hand, and by the militant Protestant followers of Mr Paisley and one of his associates, Major R. Bunting, on the other. In an effort to end what was rapidly becoming an intolerable situation the Northern Ireland government, after consultation with the British government, announced a series of reforms. These included promises to ensure that housing authorities 'placed need in the forefront in the allocation of houses' and made their future allocations on the basis of published and 'readily-understood' schemes; to appoint a Parliamentary Commissioner (or 'Ombudsman') to investigate citizens' grievances; to press on with the appointment of a Development Commission for the city of Londonderry; to reform local government comprehensively within three years; and finally, to withdraw their special powers as soon as they considered that this could be done without hazard.

Such concessions represented a very considerable advance on anything that had previously been offered, but because some of them were intended to be spread over a period of years, and particularly because the local government proposals did not include the immediate grant of 'one man, one vote', the tension in the province remained unabated. Indeed, it was further accentuated by an exceedingly ugly incident at Armagh on 30 November when a Civil Rights march in that city was rendered impossible through the virtual occupation of the centre of the town by followers of Mr Paisley. A momentary lull followed after Captain O'Neill had made a moving television appeal for support and had followed this up with the dismissal of his Minister for Home Affairs, Mr Craig, whose handling of the demonstrations was shortly to be severely criticised by the Cameron Commission and whose relations with his prime minister on the broad issue of the future of the province were distinctly cool. The Civil Rights Association responded to Captain O'Neill's appeal by a month's moratorium on demonstrations. But the People's Democracy, which at this point seemed to be steadily diverging from the Civil Rights movement, persisted with its provocative scheme for a march from Belfast to Londonderry, which duly took place between 1 and 4 January 1969. The marchers were seriously harassed during their journey, especially by a savage attack from militant Protestants at Burntollet, and their appearance in Londonderry itself was the signal for a further clash with the police.

More violence followed at Newry a few days later and it was against this sombre background that Captain O'Neill announced that a general election would be held on 24 February. His intention presumably was to establish such an ascendancy within his own party as to be able to carry through the November reforms with the minimum of delay. But his plan miscarried and the election was notable for the appearance in the field of a number of Unionist candidates openly hostile to the Prime Minister. These divisions did not of course disturb the usual overall Unionist majority, but they did open the door for the election of a number of Independents (including Mr Hume and Mr Cooper) and, even more ominously, they left Captain O'Neill in a fatally exposed position. Nevertheless, despite the fact that his control over his own party was growing weaker almost day by day, he attempted as before to combine firmness with moderation. Thus the month of March saw the imprisonment of Mr Paisley and Major Bunting for their part in the Armagh disturbances of the previous November, and the month of April brought the key decision to concede the Civil Rights demand of 'one man, one vote' at local elections, while at the same time postponing the elections due in 1970 until the new register could come into full operation.[9]

Unhappily for Captain O'Neill this concession came too late. It was, in fact, a classical example of the inadequacy of reform conceded under duress. Had it come earlier it might have obviated crisis, but to those whom it was designed to placate, it clearly had come only as a result of crisis. And so the situation continued, almost of its own momentum, to deteriorate – on the one hand, sporadic outbursts of violence, on the other hand growing dismay among Unionists at the speed and completeness with which their 'heritage' was being dismantled. It was this latter factor which was immediately decisive for Captain O'Neill's career. The party vote of 23 April in favour of universal adult suffrage for local elections was only twenty-eight in favour to twenty-one against and for the Prime Minister this was virtually the signal to go. On 28 April he finally relinquished office.

His successor was Major J. D. Chichester-Clark, a distant cousin of O'Neill's and, like him, sprung from an ancient Ulster landed family. But there the resemblance ended. O'Neill, though he had incurred the bitter enmity of his own right-wing both by his aloof style of government and by his reform initiatives, had at least left the Unionist party in no doubt that he intended to be a governing Prime Minister so long as he could outface and outmanoeuvre his critics. But Major Chichester-Clark, apart from his habitual air of shambling bewilderment, as of an amateur fallen among professionals, never had the remotest chance of dominating his party. He was in fact elected as leader and Prime Minister by a solitary vote, seventeen to sixteen. And time was to show that this margin was to be more significant as indicating the strength of the support for the runner-up than as evidence of the party's confidence in its new head. The runner-up was Mr Brian Faulkner and his emergence so near the top of the greasy pole was a portent in several different ways. First, he represented a different social order from that typified by the Brookes, the O'Neills and the Chichester-Clarks. The son of a shirt manufacturer and himself a business-man of no mean capacity, his growing importance in Ulster politics reflected the impatience of the commercial middle-class with half a century of semi-oligarchical rule by the landed gentry. Second, although his ability in a Stormont which was never over-stocked with that commodity ensured him a rapid advance in the party hierarchy, his differences with Captain O'Neill had been both widely-publicised and almost unbridgeable even before the Civil Rights agitation had begun to shake Unionism to its foundations.[10] He had been absent in America – and noncommittal in his comments – when O'Neill had been fighting for his political life in 1966; and in 1967, when the Prime Minister had dismissed Mr Harry West, his Minister for Agriculture, for failing to live up to the code of conduct he expected his cabinet to observe whenever a possible conflict arose between private interests and public duties, it was observable that Mr Faulkner had declared the dismissed Minister to be 'absolutely blameless'. Moreover, it was Mr Faulkner's resignation in January 1969 in protest against Captain O'Neill's insistence on setting up the Cameron Commission that had helped to push the Prime Minister into the election which, as we have seen, decisively registered his impotence.* But this past history of conflict between Mr Faulkner and Captain O'Neill itself indicates a final reason why the former's challenge to O'Neill's successor should have been so significant. It is difficult to avoid the conclusion that Mr Faulkner came so near to defeating Major Chichester-Clark because he was thought to be – and at that time was, whatever flexibility he may later have revealed – to be the man whom the right-wing of the party instinctively felt would do what had to be done to maintain the Unionist stranglehold on power.

This, however, could hardly be said with equal confidence of Major Chichester-Clark. Taking up O'Neill's commitment to reform, he did his best to prepare the way for peaceful change by declaring an amnesty soon after he became Prime Minister. But in fact the tension in the province was already too great for olive-branches of this kind to have any hope of success. Perhaps, if the government had felt able to ban the Protestant marches customary in July and August, some degree of relaxation might have been achieved, though even this is doubtful. As things were, however, the marches assumed in Protestant eyes even greater significance than usual, since they represented a reaffirmation of the Unionist ascendancy which had been threatened or 'betrayed' by Captain O'Neill's policies of the previous twelve months. Predictably, there were serious riots in various parts of the province on 12 and 13 July, but these paled into insignificance beside the naked and unbridled

* Yet, such were the complexities of Ulster politics even in that relatively uncomplicated phase, it has also to be recorded that Major Chichester-Clark himself had resigned from Captain O'Neill's administration on 23 April 1969, the last straw which preceded the Prime Minister's own departure. There remained, however, one further irony. The issue on which Major Chichester-Clark resigned was O'Neill's promise to institute 'one man, one vote' in local elections, the very policy which the Major had himself to accept after he became Prime Minister.

sectarian warfare that broke out in Londonderry during the Apprentice Boys' march on 12 August and spread soon afterwards to Belfast. Naturally the police – the Royal Ulster Constabulary – were heavily involved, but it soon became apparent that they were neither numerous nor strong enough either to hold the combatants apart or to reimpose peace and order in Londonderry and Belfast. In the former city, indeed, they were unable even to enter the Catholic stronghold of the Bogside and part of that district – known to its defenders as 'Free Derry' – was to continue for another three years to be what later became known as a 'no-go' area, that is an area into which the police, and subsequently the army, could not enter without grave risk of provoking large-scale hostilities and which, consequently, they tended to leave severely alone.

The riots of July and August caused, directly or indirectly, the deaths of ten people, eight Catholics and two Protestants. But in addition to that tragic outcome, and over above the numerous cases of bodily injury and the damage to property amounting to several million pounds, the eruption of those months had other far-reaching consequences. The inadequacy of the police, and the fact that their actions finally confirmed the Catholic population in their already ingrained distrust of the force, led to the intervention of the British Army. Without that intervention it is very possible that a sectarian civil war might have developed in Belfast, or even in the province as a whole, and in the light of what was to come it is important to be clear that to the Catholic minority the soldiers were regarded at the time as all that stood between them and a merciless pogrom. But the Army could not be committed without the British government being led to concern themselves directly with what was happening in this remote and incomprehensible province which was nevertheless a part of the United Kingdom.

The responsibility for translating this concern into action was entrusted to the Home Secretary, Mr James Callaghan. After the ground had been prepared by a joint communiqué issued by the two governments on 19 August – the Downing Street Declaration – disclaiming any intention to alter Northern Ireland's constitutional status but stressing the need to maintain the momentum of internal reform, Mr Callaghan visited the province later that month and elicited from Major Chichester-Clark and his colleagues the promise that further rapid progress would be made in a programme designed to achieve equality of opportunity in employment and in housing; to prevent religious discrimination and incitement to religious hatred; to develop the Northern Ireland economy; to foster better community relations; and to examine the role and function of the police.[11]

These initiatives did not in themselves constitute a solution of the Ulster problem but they did at least offer a breathing-space in which the effectiveness of the promises made in August might be assessed. This, however, did not mean that the Catholics were ready to abandon the barricades they had built for their protection in Belfast and London-

767

derry, nor did it mean that the Protestant majority had relaxed its sus-
picions that it had been, or was about to be, sold down the river. Each
side regarded the breathing-space as no more than a truce, and an im-
perfect truce at that broken almost from day to day by sporadic outbursts of violence. The government's attempt to walk a tight-rope between the two angry communities was made first difficult and then
almost impossible by the publication of the Cameron Report in September and of the Hunt Report on the police in October. The Cameron
Report, with its direct criticism of Unionist attitudes and policies, was
a bitter enough pill to swallow, but it was as nothing compared with
the Hunt Report, which recommended unequivocally the disbandment
of the 'B' specials and the disarming and reorganisation of the main
body of the RUC.[12] The Northern Ireland government, under pressure
from London, had little option but to accept the report in its essentials.
But when these became known the Protestant Shankill Road erupted
in a riot of which the first victim, by a cruel irony, was an RUC constable shot by a mob protesting against the disarming of the force of
which he was a member. Once more the Army had to intervene, killing two Protestants, wounding many more, and using, it has been
alleged, a degree of force considerably in excess of that which the RUC
had been accustomed to employ in like circumstances.[13]

On the short-term view it was still, by the end of 1969, possible to
hope that the military intervention, however brutal, had achieved its
primary purpose of keeping the peace. Unfortunately, however, this
achievement, such as it was, was not matched by any corresponding
political advance. People's expectations – hopeful on the one side, dire
on the other – had been aroused, but there was no clear way either to
gratify or to allay them. Reforms had indeed been agreed – and at the
Ministry of Development Mr Faulkner was deploying his administrative
talent in implementing some of them as quickly as possible – but of
their very nature their impact upon Ulster society was bound to be
gradual. Nevertheless, a large part of the tension which persisted in
Northern Ireland during the winter of 1969–70 sprang from the Catholic
frustration that the changes did not occur overnight and the Protestant
fear that they might.

Something else, however, had begun to happen behind the scenes
which before long was to make all talk of phased reforms largely
irrelevant. We are still too near the events of these last few years to
achieve a proper perspective, but it may confidently be predicted that
future historians of the Ulster crisis will recognise as one of the crucial
turning-points in the drama the moment when the IRA began to emerge
from the shadows. This, despite the deeply ingrained tendency of many
Unionists to attribute the worsening situation to the Machiavellian tactics of the Republicans, came at a much later stage in the crisis than
might have been expected. Even during the disturbances of August 1969,
although the Tribunal of Inquiry appointed to investigate that episode
found traces of IRA activity, the verdict then and since has been that

the organisation was taken by surprise and did less for the Catholics than the latter thought they had a right to expect.* This relative inactivity (such activity as there was before the August débâcle may indeed have been devoted to staving off rather than provoking sectarian clashes) reflected the deep internal stresses which by the middle 'sixties had reduced the IRA to a condition of paralysis. The whole militant movement had been disrupted by the failure of the 1956-62 campaign and especially by the double traumatic experience of its members having been interned by both Irish governments and rejected by northern Catholics. When it began painfully to regroup the new leaders – Cathal Goulding (Chief of Staff) and Tomás Mac Giolla (President of Sinn Féin, the 'political wing' of the IRA) – sought to turn the movement towards a less physical approach to the problem of Irish unity. The emphasis was increasingly on economic analysis along Marxist lines (provided partly, it would appear, by a Dublin intellectual, Dr Roy Johnston who later resigned, seemingly in protest against violence) with the implication that the masses should be educated to see that their common interest was to forget their sectarian rivalries and combine to end the colonial relationship which still bound Northern Ireland to Britain.

Not unnaturally this more sophisticated trend held little appeal for the traditionalists of the northern IRA. They were, after all, traditionalists precisely because they recognised the ever-present danger of a Protestant pogrom against the Catholic minority and because they regarded it as their function both to protect that minority in the short term and to rescue it permanently by achieving the thirty-two county republic which was, or had been, the *raison d'être* of the IRA throughout its history. There was in fact nothing new about an internal conflict between the ideologues and the traditionalists – a similar conflict had developed in the 'thirties – but it was given a sharper edge by the recrudescence of crisis in the north. The details of how the northern wing now began to diverge from their leaders in the south may never be known in their entirety, but enough has emerged to indicate that as early as February 1969 – that is to say, little more than a month after the Protestant attack upon the People's Democracy march at Burntollet – the Derry section of the IRA was approached by an emissary from the south, allegedly with Fianna Fáil contacts, promising them financial aid if they organised themselves for self-defence. By self-defence was meant the creation of a northern command quite separate from the headquarters of the IRA based, as always, on Dublin. Four months later the offer was repeated but, although it was then neither accepted nor rejected, it gave rise to fierce argument within the IRA. The northern leaders were naturally apprehensive about the continued

* This was the finding of the Scarman Tribunal itself. See *Violence and Civil Disturbances in Northern Ireland in 1969: Report of Tribunal of Inquiry* (Cmd. 566), Apr. 1972, vol. i, pp. 11-12. The opinion of some of the local inhabitants can be gathered from the graffiti on the walls of Derry and Belfast, 'IRA. I Ran Away'.

isolation of the Catholic community and, lacking guns or money, were in no position to defend them. Moreover, they were distrustful of the new ideology and particularly critical of the way in which IRA support had been thrown behind Miss Bernadette Devlin to secure her election to Westminster as member for Mid-Ulster in April 1969. This seemed to traditionalists not merely an unwarrantable recognition of an alien institution, but also irrelevant to the serious business in hand.

It seemed more than ever irrelevant in the aftermath of the violence of July and August when the impotence of the IRA had been made pitilessly clear. This in itself would probably have precipitated the final split in the movement, but when the break eventually came it may have had something to do with the internal stresses in Mr Lynch's government in the Republic as well as with the organisation's own internal stresses. It was Mr Lynch's misfortune that his cabinet contained a strong representation of 'northerners', of whom the chief were Mr Charles Haughey (Minister of Finance), Mr Neil Blaney (Minister of Agriculture) and Mr Kevin Boland (Minister of Local Government). When the street-battles began in Belfast and Londonderry this group pressed for strong action – apparently for actual armed intervention – but although Mr Lynch was able to prevent the disintegration of his government on this issue and also to avoid any formal involvement in the crisis, the solution he actually adopted, the creation of a Northern Sub-Committee of the cabinet, was potentially a dangerous one for a leader who wished to keep his options open, since the Sub-Committee was dominated from the outset by Messers Haughey and Blaney.*

Meanwhile, in the north the local IRA leaders were still desperate for arms and still contemplating a breach with the rest of the organisation. Early in September 1969, after a conclave held at Moville in county Donegal, they decided in principle to accept the offer of financial aid from the south, now for the third time made to them on the familiar condition that they should set up their own command. They appear to have been led to believe that the offer came not only from businessmen but also from politicians – an assumption that raises all sorts of questions to which no clear answers have emerged at the time of writing. How 'official' was the approach from the south? Were ministers implicated, and if so, which? How much did Mr Lynch know at

* Mr Lynch's public stance, as enunciated in his speech of 12 August 1969, was that his government could no longer stand by (or 'idly by' in some versions) and see innocent people injured 'or perhaps worse'. The use of British troops in the north was not acceptable 'certainly not in the long term'. He announced the establishment of Irish Army field hospitals along the border and called for the dispatch of a United Nations peace-keeping force to Northern Ireland. He also added this pregnant sentence: 'Recognising, however, that the re-unification of the national territory can provide the only permanent solution of the problem, it is our intention to request the British Government to enter into early negotiations with the Irish Government to review the present constitutional position of the Six Counties of Northern Ireland.'

the time of what was going on? And if these negotiations had a political motivation, was this no more than a simple desire to help, or was it rather a Machiavellian scheme to allow the IRA in the north to bear the brunt of the fighting, to split the organisation in two and thus ease the task of government in the south?

Set out thus starkly the questions seem to raise so many embarrassing issues that it is not in the least surprising that no-one has yet been able to give a satisfactory reply to any of them. But one or two details have since emerged which throw a wavering light on an admittedly confused and murky scene. It is known, for example, that an officer of the Irish Army, Captain James Kelly, was, in the course of duty, in regular contact with the northern IRA leaders before and after the 1969 disturbances and that he kept his superiors informed of their needs and their attitudes. It is also known – in fact a matter of public record – that the government set aside £100,000 for the relief of suffering and distress in the north. It would appear, further, that a training scheme for northern Catholics was to be instituted under cover of their being sworn into the Local Defence Force (the Irish equivalent of the Territorial Army). That particular scheme, it would appear, had been launched without Mr Lynch's knowledge and, on learning of it, he halted it at once. The destination and function of the money voted for relief is, however, a more obscure subject and up to the time of writing it is impossible to be sure how much reached the northern Catholics by various routes and how precisely they spent whatever did succeed in reaching them.*

More important than such speculations is the fact – and it at least does seem to be a fact – that the northern IRA leaders were convinced that the south was on their side and that help of one kind or another was

* The Dublin Arms Trials of September and October 1970 (see p. 587 above) threw only a few fugitive gleams of light on these obscure matters. In December 1970 the Dáil ordered that the Committee of Public Accounts should examine the Grant-in-Aid for Northern Ireland Relief (which the Dáil had accepted without debate in the supplementary estimates of March 1970) but it was not until August 1972 that the Committee of Public Accounts was in a position to report. Its investigation had been severely hampered by the absence of certain key documents and by the refusal of various witnesses to co-operate; legal action to compel the appearance of certain individuals was ruled unconstitutional by the Supreme Court. Nevertheless, the Committee found that of £110,000 intended to be spent on Northern Ireland Relief (consisting of the Dáil grant of £100,000 together with additional payments from elsewhere), just under £30,000 could be identified as having been so spent. A further sum of almost £35,000 was possibly spent in Belfast on undetermined purposes, but there still remained £41,000 which was not spent on relief. Another way of putting this is that a total of just over £76,500 was unaccounted for, though it appeared that there had been withdrawn from this part of the fund an amount totalling £32,000 which was used for the arms purchases that precipitated the 1970 trials. For text of the Committee's report, see *Irish Times*, 23 Aug. 1972.

about to reach them. Conscious of sympathy, expectant of aid, their desire to form a separate command could no longer be withstood, though the actual break did not come until an IRA conference in Dublin during November 1969 delivered the final insult by agreeing to recognise *de facto* the two Irish governments and the Westminster parliament. It was significant that this conference was boycotted by the Belfast dissidents; even more significant for the future was that one of the leading Dublin officers, John Stephenson – or Sean Mac Stiofáin as he preferred to be called – walked out of the conference with some of his colleagues announcing the establishment of the 'Provisional Army Council', dedicated to the traditional fight for the traditional goal of the thirty-two county Republic. When, shortly afterwards, the political wing of the movement, Sinn Féin, also split in two – with Rory O'Brady as head of the 'Provisional Sinn Féin' – the fissure in the movement was now complete. North and south, 'Officials' and 'Provisionals' faced each other in an uneasy hostility which sometimes seemed hardly less than that with which both regarded their hereditary foes, the Unionists.[14]

These complicated transactions partly explain the relative calm of Northern Ireland during the winter of 1969-70. But it was an illusory calm which was soon to be broken when the dreaded 'marching season' began again. Punctually, as if on cue, Easter provided the first premonitions of what was to come. Sporadic scuffles between Protestants and Catholics found the soldiers, as in 1969, interposed between the rival mobs. But this time there was a difference. The stones and bottles began to come from the Catholic side – the Catholics were resentful of the Army's show of force *inside* a Catholic area – and the military retorted with CS gas. This did not provoke an IRA intervention – the Provisionals were still only a handful at that stage, but it has its own historical significance in that it registered the first clash between the Catholics and the Army they had welcomed with open arms the year before. From the distrust implanted on this occasion the Provisionals were to reap a formidable harvest in the future.

April, as so often, was merely a dress-rehearsal for the summer. Just conceivably, trouble might have been avoided if the traditional Orange parades had been banned. But this presupposes that the Orangemen would have obeyed the ban which was by no means certain. It also presupposes that it would have been politically possible for Major Chichester-Clark to impose the ban and to remain Prime Minister; this was, if anything, still more doubtful. By an unfortunate coincidence pressure which might have been applied from London in favour of defusing the situation was not forthcoming for the simple but sufficient reason that the transfer of power from Labour to Conservatives left the latter with no time to get their bearings. So, when the usual provocative marches produced the usual response and the shooting began in east and west Belfast, the Army was hopelessly overstretched and quite unable to prevent the serious riots which then developed. But worse was to come. Following a successful search for arms in the Falls Road area on July 3 the troops were stoned by indignant Catholics and only extricated themselves with difficulty. Later that evening they went in again in an attempt to bring the district under control and came under fire from the IRA. They returned the fire, and used CS gas; to prevent large-scale bloodshed the Army Commander, General Freeland, imposed a thirty-five hour curfew. During that curfew a house-to-house search for arms was carried out. Some were found, but the political price paid for them was enormous. The inhabitants of the Falls Road saw the troops as invaders and no longer as protectors.* They drew their own conclusions and IRA recruiting, particularly into the Provisionals, went up so fast that their strength increased from about a hundred in the early summer to nearly 800 by the end of the year.[15]

It was hardly surprising, therefore, that friction should have persisted or that a fresh outburst of rioting should soon have occurred. What *was* new, and ominous, was that it should have begun in the New Year of 1971, outside the usual 'season'. On the Catholic side this was evidence both of increasing hostility towards the Army and of a more generalised frustration. But to Unionists it betokened gross ingratitude for the reforms already passed and this in turn strengthened the determination of the right wing – always buoyant and vocal in the rare intervals of calm – that there should be no more pandering to the minority. It was understandable that each side should feel a sense of grievance. The Unionists could point to a whole series of enactments and while these had, as it seemed to them, dismantled a large part of their ascendancy, the violence in the streets showed no sign of ceasing It was certainly true that since the resignation of Captain O'Neill much indeed had changed. The police had been disarmed and civilianised (though they had not been able to resume patrolling in the Catholic ghettoes); an Ombudsman had been established to investigate grievances against the central government and a similar official appointed to do the same in local affairs; electoral changes had brought the franchise at last into line with that of Britain; a points system related to need had been adopted for the allocation of houses (a Housing Executive Act to carry this policy still further became law at the end of February); a Ministry of Community Relations had been created and a Community Relations Commission set in motion. On the other hand, these changes

* This disenchantment was undoubtedly hastened by the Criminal Justice (Temporary Provisions) Act which the Northern Ireland government rushed through Stormont at the end of June 1970. This made mandatory a sentence of six months' imprisonment for anyone convicted of 'riotous behaviour', 'disorderly behaviour', or 'behaviour likely to cause a breach of the peace'. Upon the Army fell the brunt of the arrests to be made under the act and since these were very numerous during the six months before the Act was partially repealed in December, this further worsened the relations of the troops with the civilian population and especially the Catholics, by whom the new measure came to be regarded as almost as objectionable as the Special Powers Act itself.

took time to implement and there were other areas where there had been little or no movement — for example, in the appointment of a public prosecutor distinct from the police, the introduction of anti-discrimination clauses into government contracts and, of course, the notorious Special Powers Act itself. Consequently, the Catholic community, impatient at the lack of visible progress and deeply confused about the direction in which it ought to be going, inclined more and more to the view that reforms handed down from on high in response to the threat or the actuality of violence were in themselves an insufficient substitute for the recognition they sought of their right to play their part as full and equal citizens in the life of the province.*

But as the disturbances continued Unionist thoughts ran not unnaturally upon the suppression of violence rather than upon the extension of concessions. The Prime Minister appealed repeatedly to London for more troops and firmer action from those already on the ground. For a time he got neither and there are indications that early in 1971 the Army and the Provisionals were precariously co-operating in an effort to keep the ghetto mobs under control.[16] But this could scarcely be expected to last — for the Provisionals, who were bound by their history to regard the British as an army of occupation, it can never have been more than a temporary, tactical expedient — and, in fact, at the beginning of Februry, an Army search in a Catholic area brought on renewed fighting which resulted in the death of the first soldier since the troops had intervened the previous August. Thereafter the situation worsened rapidly, reaching a pitch of horror then unprecedented (but later often to be equalled, if not surpassed) in the cold-blooded murder of three Scottish soldiers on the outskirts of Belfast. Major Chichester-Clark flew to London to seek further reinforcements. He got some, but by no means all he reckoned he needed. Worse, he failed to convince the British government of the urgency of the situation and on 20 March, to underline that urgency, he resigned.

His logical, almost inevitable, successor was Mr Faulkner who, despite his earlier criticisms of the reformist tendencies of Captain O'Neill, had himself been actively concerned in implementing the reforms introduced by the Chichester-Clark régime. At first it seemed as if he would continue on this course and in June he offered not only to create three new committees at Stormont, to consider and advise on government policy in regard to the social services, industrial development and environmental matters, but also to entrust the chairmanship of at least two of these committees to opposition MPs.[17] It is true that

* Later in 1971 the government published details of its performance, *A Record of Constructive Change* (Cmd. 558), August 1971. It is however symptomatic of the general deterioration in the situation by then that some of the most pungent criticism of that document should have come not from IRA militants but from Catholic moderates in a pamphlet, *Commentary upon the White Paper entitled A Record of Constructive Change*, Sept. 1971. It should be noted, however, that this publication followed hard on the heels of internment.

the committees were to be devoid of executive or legislative powers, and also that they would have permanent Unionist majorities, since membership was to be proportional to existing party strength at Stormont, but this should not detract from the importance of the gesture, particularly since it was made at a time when all the indications were that the Provisionals had abandoned the tactic of gun-battles with the Army in favour of a massive campaign of bombing which, producing as it did 37 explosions in April, 47 in May and 50 in June was calculated to exacerbate Unionist opinion still further.

The first impulse of the leading opposition party was, if not to grasp the olive-branch, at least to examine it closely and not unsympathetically. This in itself was a major development since that party, the Social and Democratic Labour Party, represented most sections of what might reasonably be called moderate and Catholic opinion. It had only been formed the previous August and it brought together six members of the Northern Ireland House of Commons and one Senator. Its leader was Mr Gerry Fitt (Republican Labour) who sat at Westminster as well as at Stormont, and the remaining five Stormont MPs included John Hume and Ivan Cooper (Independents), Austin Currie (Nationalist), Patrick O'Hanlon (Independent Nationalist) and Paddy Devlin (Northern Ireland Labour Party). The policies of the new party were stated at the outset to be based on 'radical left of centre principles' and its first public statement certainly laid much emphasis on the redistribution of wealth. But in the circumstances of the time it was inevitable that the question most people asked was where it stood on the fundamental question of the future of Northern Ireland. It expressed itself as avowedly non-sectarian, but since at the time it announced its intention 'to promote co-operation, friendship and understanding between north and south with a view to the eventual reunification of Ireland through the consent of the majority of the people in the North and in the South', its chances of making any immediate appeal to northern Protestants did not seem bright [18]

Although it was difficult at first to determine whether the new party was a vehicle for reform or merely a tessellated pavement without cement, it embraced such a diversity of talent and outlook (as well as of temperament) that it was clearly a great potential source of constructive effort. It was therefore a major tragedy that within days of Mr Faulkner's initiative in June 1971, the cautiously approving reception the SDLP gave to the committee scheme should have vanished in the face of further catastrophe on the streets. This time it was in Londonderry where the Army had been under strain for many weeks and where eventually, as was almost bound to happen, two men were shot dead whom the Army judged to be gunmen but whom local opinion passionately insisted were harmless civilians. A hurriedly assembled meeting of such of the SDLP as were available was summoned by Mr Hume – in the absence of the party leader, Mr Fitt – and this meeting approved an ultimatum to the British government, demanding an independent inquiry into the two deaths within a matter of days, 'failing which the SDLP would leave Stormont and set up an alternative parliament.' The British government, not unnaturally, refused to accept this ultimatum and though it appears that Mr Fitt risked the wrath of his more impulsive colleagues by seeking some compromise solution in London this proved impossible and on 16 July he had no option but to announce his party's withdrawal from Stormont the previous day.[19]

This decision by the SDLP marked a further serious deterioration in the general situation. At one stroke Stormont was deprived of the steadying influence of a constitutional opposition and that constitutional opposition itself, in its anxiety not to be outbid from the left, had ended by creating a vacuum that was soon to be filled by what was to all intents and purposes a large-scale conflict between the Army and the Provisionals. Incidents, and deaths multiplied so rapidly that the government, apparently believing a major assault to be imminent, resolved at last to use the weapon which right-wing Unionists had long insisted should be brought into play. In the early hours of 9 August the machinery of internment was set in motion and by the evening of that day nearly 350 people had been arrested and lodged in three detention centres. The operation, however, appears to have been mishandled. The key figures among the Provisionals escaped arrest and the months after the crucial decision to intern had been taken witnessed a crescendo of violence. In the seven months before internment ten soldiers were killed, two policemen and fifteen civilians. In the four months after internment, thirty-two soldiers were killed, nine policemen, ninety-eight civilians, and five members of the Ulster Defence Regiment which had been formed to take over some of the duties of the defunct 'B' specials.[20]

Against this horrendous background has to be placed a political fact of the first magnitude – the total alienation of the Catholic community (or a very large part of it) from the regime. The very fact that internment appeared to operate almost entirely, if not wholly, against Catholics (up to December 1,576 arrests had been made though nearly 1000 of these were released by the end of the year) would in itself have created a wave of indignation. But when to the facts about internment were added rumours, and later well-authenticated stories, about the ill-treatment of the internees when undergoing interrogation by the Army, the fury of the Catholic minority knew no limits, with the natural result that moderates were increasingly driven into the arms of the IRA.* The government, on the other hand, seemed to have miscal-

* The persistent critical reports of Army methods during the arrest and detention of internees led the British government on 31 August to appoint a committee of inquiry headed by Sir Edmund Compton, the Ombudsman for Britain and for Northern Ireland. Despite the fact that it operated under such severe difficulties that its report was in various ways unsatisfactory the committee did adduce sufficient evidence of ill-treatment under 'deep interrogation' as to cause the government to order the methods used by the Army to be modified forthwith. These criticisms,

culated, perhaps because Mr Faulkner put too much reliance on the false analogy of previous experience. Internment could not work in 1971 as it had worked a dozen years earlier, partly because there was no corresponding will in the south to proceed simultaneously against the IRA, partly because the new IRA were urban guerrillas fighting in streets where they had overwhelming advantage of local knowledge, and most of all because the Catholic population, previously inert, had in the past two years been wrought to such a high pitch of anger and frustration that for the time being at least it was willing to provide the safe cover which the guerrillas needed. Not until nearly a year after internment did ground support for the IRA begin to waver in face of the ferocity and indiscriminateness of the Provisionals' bombing campaign, but even then Catholic opinion remained, and remains, extremely volatile, liable to desert the middle ground at the slightest indication of military toughness or Protestant backlash.

As the months passed without any sign of a way out of the vicious circle of outrage and arrest the province moved steadily closer to anarchy. Whatever faint hope there may once have been of bridging the gulf between the two communities vanished in the angry aftermath of internment. Catholics boycotted not only Stormont but also local councils and other bodies. The dissident MPs set up their own assembly at Dungiven which, though apparently not much more than a talking-shop, awakened uneasy echoes of the establishment of Dáil Eireann in 1919. Ordinary citizens, perhaps 20,000 of them, participated in a campaign of disobedience by withholding their rents and rates. Against this evidence of massive estrangement Unionists could only point indignantly to the reforms already conceded and demand, still more indignantly, that law and order be restored. But while the Army battled with the IRA on the streets Mr Faulkner moved cautiously towards a further instalment of change. In October he published proposals for proportional representation and for a larger House of Commons and Senate at Stormont. He also appointed to a cabinet post Dr Gerard Newe, the first Catholic to hold such a post in the fifty year history of the state. But the effect of both these gestures was somewhat blunted by the fact that, in putting forward his suggestions, Mr Faulkner made it absolutely clear that his administration was still committed to the maintenance of Northern Ireland as an integral part of the United Kingdom and also that it regarded as 'fundamentally unrealistic' the idea of a 'mixed' government of Catholics and Protestants which was being much touted at that time.[21]

---

however, should be seen in the context of the claim repeatedly made by the British authorities that the Army's discipline and morale remained high and that, considering the provocation under which it was operating, its restraint was most of the time remarkable. The crucial objection to its actions ought, one feels, to be based on the fact that it was constantly being used for duties for which it was not really fitted.

Although these initiatives were a world away from the Unionist stance of only three years previously they were already outmoded at the moment when Mr Faulkner made them. He was in fact imprisoned in a dilemma from which there seemed no possible escape. On the one hand, partial concessions were regarded as irrelevant by extremists who wanted only the end of Stormont and the reunification of Ireland and, although his new proposals might at one time have appealed to moderate Catholics, it was doubtful if this was any longer the case, while the possibility of discussing the matter with their representatives, the SDLP, was inhibited by the latter's unbending insistence that internment must be ended before they could come to any conference-table. On the other hand, Mr Faulkner could not but be aware of a rising tide of Unionist bitterness and resentment. This made the abolition of internment unthinkable – though there is no evidence to indicate that Mr Faulkner was thinking of it – and it also put a large question-mark opposite the future of any Prime Minister who jeopardised the Unionist position by going further along the road of reform. This, indeed, was the real core of the dilemma. Given that the state had been built around the concept of Protestant ascendancy, to dismantle that ascendancy piece-meal, however severe the pressure to do so, was to weaken the credibility of the whole regime and to weaken it, not merely in the eyes of its declared enemies, but in those of its supposed friends – the Conservative government in Britain – who in the last resort carried the responsibility for propping it up.

There were in fact indications, as well as many rumours, that in both main British parties the belief was growing that Stormont was becoming too costly a luxury. For the Opposition, Mr Wilson, in September and again in November, made detailed proposals for modifying the structure of Northern Ireland government very substantially, and there were persistent stories – one of which was given currency by Mr Paisley, and another of which emanated from a highly responsible journalist, Mr James Downey, London editor of the *Irish Times* – that direct rule was on the way. The British government hesitated, however, perhaps because the nettle was so difficult to grasp, probably also because of the pressure of other events. But while they hesitated the situation in Northern Ireland deteriorated still further. On January 30, despite an official prohibition, a Civil Rights march took place in Londonderry. The authorities decided not only to contain it within the Bogside but also to combine this with one of the 'snatching', or arresting operations they mounted from time to time. The troops employed were from the Parachute Regiment and when, on going in among the crowd they came under fire – or believed they came under fire – they retaliated, with the result that thirteen civilians were shot dead and others wounded. An inquiry under Lord Widgery was at once set up. His tribunal was faced with the usual difficulty of obtaining reliable evidence and his report, like other investigations into earlier disasters, was predictably written off by the opponents of the regime as just one more exercise in whitewashing. He found that the troops had in fact been fired on *before* they fired back, but he also found – and it was on this that the Catholic community naturally fastened – that 'none of the deceased or wounded is proved to have been shot whilst handling a firearm or bomb' though there was a strong suspicion that some of them had been so engaged in the course of the afternoon.[22]

This deplorable affair was at once recognised on all sides to be a major catastrophe and many consequences, direct or indirect, were to flow from it. One of the most direct was the burning of the British Embassy in Dublin on 2 February in the presence of a huge crowd which, though probably manipulated by the IRA, was animated by a hatred and revulsion which to some observers recalled the mood which had spread through Dublin in the aftermath of the executions of 1916. This passion subsided rather sooner than might have been expected but it contributed to a marked worsening of Anglo-Irish relations at a critical moment. In Northern Ireland itself 'Bloody Sunday', as it was almost immediately called, had the predictable effect of polarising the conflict still further. Although another Civil Rights march in Newry the following Sunday passed off peacefully, the tempo of violence increased. This in turn stimulated the Protestants into activity and led directly to the formation of the Vanguard movement in February 1972. This, which had been foreshadowed since the previous autumn, was intended as a kind of 'umbrella' under which might shelter a variety of militant Unionist organisations.* It was pledged to maintain the constitution, but it was widely believed that, if pushed to the brink, it would not stop short of unilateral independence. Led by Mr William Craig, its real strength lay in the support it received from Protestant workers, whose organisation, the Loyalist Association of Workers, had it in its power to disrupt the entire life of the province if it so chose.[23]

Although the extremism of Vanguard was no doubt the obverse of the extremism of the IRA, it owed something also to a well-founded suspicion that Mr Faulkner was running out of time. Indeed, he was also running out of support. The previous autumn Mr Paisley and Mr Desmond Boal had formed their own Democratic Unionist party and soon constituted themselves an effective opposition party. And in February 1972 a former minister, Mr Phelim O'Neill, left the Unionist party and, with two other MPs, joined the moderate, non-sectarian Alliance Party which, though formed as far back as 1970, had hitherto lacked representation in Stormont. All these signs and portents, together with the manifest inability of the Northern Ireland government to restore peace to the province, led inexorably to the decision announced by Mr Heath on 24 March to suspend Stormont and to institute direct rule from Westminster. True, this decision was accompanied by

* Subsequently, the role of 'umbrella' was taken over by the Ulster Loyalist Council, on which were represented all the leading militant organisations, including what is probably the most effective striking force of all, the Ulster Defence Association, allegedly 50,000 strong.

the promise of periodic plebiscites on the border issue and by a pledge
to 'phase out' internment, but nothing could disguise the brute fact that
the British government had at last recognised the necessity of itself
taking responsibility for law and order and in doing so had drawn the
further conclusion that to 'suspend' Stormont for a year would give the
best opportunity for a new initiative towards a permanent settlement.
Responsibility was therefore entrusted to a member of the British
government and Mr William Whitelaw, as Secretary of State for Northern Ireland, stepped into the vacuum left by the ending of the fifty
years' experiment in devolution.

    It is at that point that this brief survey must cease, for the situation
created by direct rule is still evolving and remains so unstable that no
assessment of its effects can yet be attempted. It is sufficient to point
out that direct rule itself cannot be – nor was it intended to be – a
solution. Its purpose was to secure a breathing-space so that a fresh
approach to a solution might be made. But this has always depended
upon the British government's ability to contain and suppress violence
– Protestant no less than Catholic – and to bring the conflicting parties
to the conference-table. The first attempt to achieve the latter aim –
the Darlington Conference of September 1972 – was little more than a
travesty since it was boycotted both by the SDLP and by Mr Paisley's
Democratic Unionist party. And although on all sides Mr Whitelaw's
next step, the issuing of a 'Green Paper' surveying the possible forms a
new regional administration might take, is awaited with painful expect-
ancy, the very fact that two of his most cherished expedients – the holding of local government elections under the reformed franchise and of a
referendum on the border issue – are, at the time of writing, shrouded
in uncertainty, indicates the extreme difficulty he is encountering in
undertaking any constructive policy whatever. Meanwhile violence has
continued unabated and by the autumn of 1972 the total of deaths in
Northern Ireland resulting from the troubles has passed the appalling
figure of 600. The continuing hostility between the troops and the Provisionals has begun to be matched by a corresponding hostility between
the troops and the striking-force of Protestant militancy, the Ulster
Defence Association, and it is hardly surprising that in Britain there
should have begun to emerge a movement of opinion in favour of
withdrawing the Army whatever the cost might be. So the historian
can only draw his bleak tale to a close by recording that the fate of the
province is still, as it has been for so long, poised on a knife-edge between a slow climb back to some form of ordered existence, or a swift
plunge into unimaginable anarchy and civil war.

Notes

Part I

1. CHANGING THE QUESTION? (pp. 15-33)

1 R. Dudley Edwards and T. Desmond Williams (ed.), *The Great Famine* (Dublin, 1956), p. 1.
2 Arnold Schrier, *Ireland and the American Emigration, 1850-1900* (Minneapolis, 1958), especially chap. i and appendix table 4.
3 See the admirable study by D. W. Harkness, *The Restless Dominion* (London, 1968) which deals mainly with the decade after the Treaty. For Ireland as a factor in Anglo-American relations, see A. J. Ward, *Ireland and Anglo-American Relations, 1899-1921* (London, 1969).
4 For the size of the various denominations see *Census of Ireland, 1911*, General Report, pp. xlvi-vii.
5 J. C. Beckett, *The Making of Modern Ireland* (London, 1966), p. 285.
6 E. Larkin, 'Economic Growth, Capital Investment and the Roman Catholic Church in Nineteenth Century Ireland', in *American Historical Review* (Apr. 1967), lxxii, pp. 856-8.
7 Ibid., pp. 864-5.
8 Cited in E. R. Norman, *The Catholic Church and Ireland in the Age of Rebellion* (London, 1965), pp. 18-19.
9 On this general theme, see J. H. Whyte, 'Revolution and Religion', in F. X. Martin (ed.), *Leaders and Men of the Easter Rising: Dublin, 1916* (London, 1967), pp. 215-26; also R. McHugh, 'The Catholic Church and the Rising', in O. Dudley Edwards and F. Pyle (ed.), *1916: The Easter Rising* (London, 1968), pp. 196-201. Dr Whyte estimates that whereas one bishop, Dr O'Dwyer of Limerick, in effect condoned the Rising, seven published emphatic condemnations and one a somewhat equivocal condemnation. No less than twenty-three, however, remained silent.
10 *Census of Ireland, 1911*, pp. xlvii-viii; M. O'Riordan, *Catholicity and Progress in Ireland* (Dublin, 1906), pp. 315-16.
11 For these developments see J. C. Beckett, 'Ulster Protestantism', in T. W. Moody and J. C. Beckett (ed.), *Ulster Since 1800: A Social Survey*, pp. 159-69.

2. THE ECONOMIC ENVIRONMENT (pp. 34-70)

1 For a recent discussion of these developments see R. D. Crotty, *Irish Agricultural Production: Its Volume and Structure* (Cork, 1966), chap. i. For Irish agricultural exports in the eighteenth century see Tables 2 and 3 on pp. 19-20 of his book.
2 See especially, R. N. Salaman, *The History and Social Influence of the Potato* (Cambridge, 1949) and K. H. Connell, *The Population of Ireland*,

781

1750-1845 (Oxford, 1950). For a criticism of Professor Connell's seminal work, see M. Drake, 'Marriage and Population Growth in Ireland', in *Economic History Review*, second series (1963), xvi, 301-13.

3 R. D. Crotty, *Irish Agricultural Production*, Appendix Note II, pp. 294-307, examines pre-Famine rents in detail, and suggests that landlords' rents may have quadrupled between 1760 and 1815. For the function of the potato in eighteenth century Ireland, see M. Drake, 'The Irish Demographic Crisis of 1740-41', in T. W. Moody (ed.), *Historical Studies* (London, 1968), vi, 101-24.

4 K. H. Connell, *The Population of Ireland*, especially chap. iii, but Professor Connell's views have been to some extent modified since he wrote his book.

5 R. D. Crotty, op. cit., p. 32.

6 Ibid., p. 35.

7 Ibid., pp. 38-9. See also M. Drake, op. cit., pp. 312-13.

8 R. D. Crotty, op. cit., p. 39; also K. H. Connell, *The Population of Ireland*, pp. 27-9. See also the criticisms of Joseph Lee, reviewing Mr Crotty's book in *Agricultural History Review* (1969), xvii, part 1, pp. 64-76.

9 R. N. Salaman, *The History and Social Influence of the Potato*, pp. 603-8.

10 R. D. Crotty, op. cit., and sources quoted, p. 40.

11 E. R. R. Green, 'Agriculture', in R. Dudley Edwards and T. Desmond Williams, *The Great Famine* (Dublin, 1956), p. 99; K. H. Connell, 'The Colonization of Waste Land in Ireland, 1780-1845', in *Econ. Hist Rev.*, 2nd series (1950), iii, 44-7; J. Lee, 'Irish Agriculture', in *Agricultural History Review* (1969), xvii, part 1, pp. 64-76.

12 For analyses (sometimes differing in detail) of the division of holdings see K. H. Connell, 'Marriage in Ireland after the Famine: the Diffusion of the Match', in *JSSISI*, xix (1955-6), 82-103; E. R. R. Green, op. cit., p. 89; T. W. Freeman, *Pre-Famine Ireland* (London, 1957), pp. 54-8.

13 L. M. Cullen, *An Economic History of Ireland since 1660* (London, 1972), pp. 114-15.

14 *Return of Evictions Known to the Constabulary in Each Year from 1849 to 1880*, P.P. (1881), lxxvii, 725. For the administrative problems presented by the Famine, see T. P. O'Neill, 'The Administration of Relief', in Edwards and Williams (ed.), *The Great Famine*, pp. 207-59.

15 Cited by O. MacDonagh, 'Emigration During the Famine', in Edwards and Williams, op. cit., p. 321.

16 Ibid., pp. 324-9.

17 S. H. Cousens, 'Emigration and Demographic Change in Ireland, 1851-61', in *Economic History Review*, 2nd series (1961-2), xiv, 275-88.

18 *Report of the commission on emigration and other population problems, 1948-54* (Dublin, 1954), Pr. 2541. See especially chap. vii.

19 Ibid., p. 63.

20 Ibid., pp. 73-8.

21 K. H. Connell, 'Catholicism and Marriage in the Century after the Famine', in *Irish Peasant Society* (London, 1968), p. 113.

22 *Report of Emigration Commission*, chap. v.

23 Ibid., chap. vi. As late as the 1940s the figure for the twenty-six counties was sixty-six per thousand.

24 Ibid., pp 9-13.

25 R. D. Crotty, *Irish Agricultural Production*, pp. 351, 353; P. M. A. Bourke, 'The Agricultural Statistics of the 1841 Census of Ireland: A Critical

Review', in *Econ. Hist. Rev.*, 2nd series (1965), xviii, 376-91.

26 L. M. Cullen, *An Economic History of Ireland since 1660*, pp. 138-40, 150-51; B. Solow, *The Land Question and the Irish Economy, 1870-1903* (Cambridge, Mass., and London, 1972), pp. 72-4.

27 The price statistics in this and the succeeding paragraph are based on Thomas Barrington, 'A Review of Irish Agricultural Prices', in *JSSISI* (1926-7), xv, 249-80.

28 For the export trade, see J. O'Donovan, *The Economic History of Live-stock In Ireland* (Dublin and London, 1940), chap. xi; Crotty, op. cit., p. 72.

29 See T. Grimshaw, 'A Statistical Survey of Ireland from 1840 to 1888', in *JSSISI* (1889), ix, 321-61; W. P. Coyne (ed.), *Ireland: Industrial and Agricultural* (Dublin, 1901), pp. 191-2; P. M. A. Bourke, op. cit.

30 The point has been developed by K. H. Connell in three articles — 'Marriage in Ireland after the Famine: The Diffusion of the Match', in *JSSISI* (1955-6), xix, 82-103; 'Peasant Marriage in Ireland after the Great Famine', in *Past and Present* (1957), pp. 76-91; 'Peasant Marriage in Ireland: Its Structure and Development Since the Famine', in *Econ. Hist. Rev.* (1961-2), 2nd series, xiv, 502-23.

31 W. P. Coyne (ed.), *Ireland Industrial and Agricultural*, pp. 60-1; *Census of Ireland for the Year 1911: General Report*, H.C. (Cd. 5691), 1911, pp. 10, 15.

32 R. E. Matheson, 'The Housing of the People of Ireland, during 1841-1901', in *JSSISI* (1904), xi, 196-213; N. J. Synnott, 'Housing of the Rural Population in Ireland,' in *JSSISI* (1904), ix, 215-301.

33 For the two economies, see especially, P. Lynch and J. Vaizey, *Guinness's Brewery in the Irish Economy, 1759-1876* (Cambridge, 1960), chap. i; also E. Larkin, 'Economic Growth, Capital Investment and the Roman Catholic Church in Ireland', in *American Historical Review* (April, 1967), lxxii, 852-84.

34 The stages by which currency assimilation was achieved are well set out in the introduction to F. W. Fetter, *The Irish Pound, 1797-1826* (London, 1955).

35 W. P. Coyne (ed.), *Ireland: Industrial and Agricultural*, pp. 72-83; E. J. Riordan, *Modern Irish Trade and Industry*, chap. xiii; F. G. Hall, *History of the Bank of Ireland* (Dublin and Oxford, 1949), pp. 172-86; K. Milne, *A History of the Royal Bank of Ireland* (Dublin, 1964), chaps. iii and iv.

36 Cited by E. R. R. Green, 'Early Industrial Belfast', in J. C. Beckett and R. E. Glasscock (ed.), *Belfast* (London, 1967), p. 85. For these developments see also the same author's articles 'The Beginnings of Industrial Revolution', and 'Business Organization and the Business Class', T. W. Moody (ed.), *Ulster Since 1800*, vols i and ii (London, 1954 and 1957). The growth of the city of Belfast is best followed in E. Jones, *A Social Geography of Belfast*, part ii (London, 1960).

37 W. E. Coe, *The Engineering Industry of the North of Ireland* (Newton Abbot 1969), chap. v.

38 E. J. Riordan, *Modern Irish Trade and Industry*, p. 111. See also D. L. Armstrong, 'Social and Economic Conditions in the Belfast Linen Industry, 1850-1900', in *IHS* (1950-51), vii, 235-69.

39 *Final Report of the First Census of Production of the United Kingdom* (1907), P.P. [Cd. 6320] 1912, pp. 352-7. The figures given in E. Riordan, op. cit., pp. 112-13 are in some instances wrongly transcribed.

40 E. J. Riordan, op. cit., pp. 122-3, L. M. Cullen, op. cit., p. 160.
41 *Census of Production* (1907), p. 346.
42 E. J. Riordan, op. cit., p. 126; *Census of Production* (1907), p. 346.
43 For the history of shipbuilding in Belfast, see C. H. Oldham, 'The History of Belfast Shipbuilding', in *JSSISI*, xii, 417-43; E. J. Riordan, *Modern Irish Trade and Industry*, pp. 227-36; E. Jones, *A Social Geography of Belfast*, pp. 46-50; J. C. Beckett and R. E. Glasscock (ed.), *Belfast*, chaps. vii-x. Most modern accounts of the genesis of nineteenth century ship-building lean heavily on the unpublished doctoral thesis of a former managing director of Harland and Wolff, D. Rebbeck, 'The History of Iron Shipbuilding on the Queen's Island up to July, 1874', completed 1950.
44 *Census of Production* (1907), p. 19.
45 E. J. Riordan, op. cit., pp. 92-4.
46 P. Lynch and J. Vaizey, *Guinness's Brewery in the Irish Economy, 1759-1876*, p. 260; E. J. Riordan, op. cit., pp. 156-7.
47 *Census of Production* (1907), p. 524.
48 Ibid., pp. 527-8; E. J. Riordan, op. cit., pp. 160-4.
49 Scattered evidence of wage-rates is to be found in E. J. Riordan, *Modern Irish Trade and Industry*, pp. 46-7; J. W. Boyle, 'Industrial Conditions in the Twentieth Century', in T. W. Moody and J. C. Beckett (ed.), *Ulster Since 1800* (second series), pp. 130-1; D. L. Armstrong, 'Social and Economic Conditions in the Belfast Linen Industry, 1850-1960', in *IHS* (Sept. 1951), vii, 263-7; P. Lynch and John Vaizey, *Guinness's Brewery in the Irish Economy, 1759-1876*, p. 146; E. Larkin, *James Larkin, 1876-1947*, pp. 45-6; L. M. Cullen, *Life in Ireland*, pp. 167-8; W. E. Coe, *The Engineering Industry of the North of Ireland*, pp. 177-8.
50 *Census of Production* (1907), p. 19.
51 A. W. Semmels, 'The External Commerce of Ireland', in *JSSISI* (1909), xii, 193-218. Slightly different figures (but pointing towards the same conclusion) are given in E. J. Riordan, op. cit., p. 228.
52 C. H. Oldham, 'Economics of Industrial Revival in Ireland', in *JSSISI* (1909), xii, 175-89. See also his two articles, 'Changes in Irish Exports During Twelve Years', and 'Changes in Irish Exports', both in *JSSISI* (1919), xiii, 541-53 and 629-37.

3. GOVERNMENT AND SOCIETY (pp. 71-103)

1 Cited in R. B. McDowell, *The Irish Administration* (London, 1964), p. 51.
2 For an excellent outline of the Irish departmental system see R. B. McDowell, op. cit., chap. i.
3 Ibid., p. 28. The official was Sir Algernon West Ridgeway, but at the time of his comment, 1889, the Irish government generally had been under several years of heavy strain.
4 The phrase was first used by W. L. Burn about the British readiness to uproot accepted notions of property when legislating about Irish land, but it has a much wider application. See his article, 'Free Trade in Land: An Aspect of the Irish Question', in *Transactions of the Royal Historical Society*, 4th Series, vol. xxxi. For the development of this idea in depth, see also O. MacDonagh, *Ireland*, chap. ii.

5 R. B. McDowell, op. cit., pp. 114-16; V. T. H. Delany, *The Administration of Justice in Ireland* (Dublin, 1965), p. 31.

6 R. B. McDowell, op. cit., pp. 135-45; see also R. Hawkins, 'Dublin Castle and the Royal Irish Constabulary, 1916-1922', in T. Desmond Williams (ed.), *The Irish Struggle, 1916-1926* (London, 1966), pp. 167-81.

7 R. B. McDowell, op. cit., chap. vi; see also B. Hensey, 'The *Health Services of Ireland* (Dublin, 1959), chap. i.

8 O. MacDonagh, *Ireland*, p. 27.

9 T. W. Grimshaw, 'A Statistical Survey of Ireland from 1840 to 1888', in *JSSISI* (1889), iv, 321-61.

10 *Census of Ireland, 1911*, p. lxiv.

11 For the working of the Local Government Board, see McDowell, op. cit., chap. vi.

12 Ibid., pp. 203-14.

13 G. Balfour, *The Educational Systems of England and Wales* (London, 1898), pp. 82-3; D. H. Akenson, *The Irish Education Experiment* (London, 1970), chaps. i and ii.

14 For these developments, see N. Atkinson, *Irish Education* (Dublin, 1969), chap. 5; also J. Murphy, 'Primary Education', in P. J. Corish (ed.), *A History of Irish Catholicism* (Dublin, 1971), vol. 5, fascicule vi, *Catholic Education*, pp. 5-47.

15 T. J. McElligott, *Education in Ireland* (Dublin, 1966), pp. 4-5.

16 G. Balfour, op. cit., pp. 91-2; R. B. McDowell, *The Irish Administration*, pp. 244-5.

17 T. J. McElligott, op. cit., p. 6.

18 Ibid., p. 7.

19 G. Balfour, op. cit., pp. 115-16; R. B. McDowell, op. cit., pp. 252-3; T. J. McElligott, op. cit., pp. 100-2.

20 G. Balfour, op. cit., pp. 112-13; *Census of Ireland, 1911*, pp. 84-5; T. J. McElligott, op. cit., pp. 13, 15-16.

21 P. H. Pearse, 'The Murder Machine', in *Political Writings and Speeches* (Dublin, n.d.), pp. 39-40.

22 G. Balfour, op. cit., p. 203.

23 Ibid., p. 204.

24 W. B. Kelly, *Intermediate and University Education in Ireland* (London and Dublin, 1872), *passim*; M. O'Riordan, *Catholicity and Progress in Ireland* (London, 1906), pp. 460-1.

25 *Census of Ireland, 1911*, p. 256, Table 133.

26 T. J. McElligott, *Education in Ireland*, p. 62.

27 For a very fair and thorough account of the development of the intermediate system, see S. V. O'Sulleabhain, 'Secondary Education', in P. J. Corish (ed.), op. cit., pp. 53-81.

28 For the history of the Catholic University, see *A Page of Irish History*, by the Jesuit Fathers (Dublin, 1930); F. McGrath, *Newman's University: Idea and Reality* (Dublin, 1951); M. Tierney (ed.), *Struggle with Fortune: A Miscellany for the Centenary of the Catholic University of Ireland, 1854-1954* (Dublin, n.d.); K. Sullivan, *Joyce among the Jesuits* (New York and London, 1957).

29 T. J. McElligott, *Education in Ireland*, p. 138.

30 These developments are well treated in F. McGrath, 'The University Question', in P. J. Corish (ed.), op. cit., pp. 84-142.

31 Ibid., p. 139.
32 *Census of Ireland, 1911*, p. liii; T. J. McElligott, op. cit., p. 140. The Census gives the figures for 1901 and 1911, but those for the latter year, which are nearly a thousand *lower*, are completely unreliable because of the failure of both Trinity College and University College, Dublin, to make any return.
33 T. W. Moody, 'The Irish University Question of the Nineteenth Century', in *History* (1958), xlii, 90-109. See also the detailed investigation of the whole subject in T. W. Moody and J. C. Beckett, *Queen's Belfast, 1845-1949: The History of a University* (London, 1959), 2 vols.
34 L. Paul-Dubois, *Contemporary Ireland* (Translated by T. M. Kettle, Dublin, 1908), p. 335.
35 For their numbers in Dublin, see E. Larkin, *James Larkin* (London, 1965), pp. 43-4.

4. VARIATIONS ON THE THEME OF NATIONALITY (pp. 104-38)

1 For this aspect of his career, see Angus Macintyre, *The Liberator* (London, 1965), *passim*.
2 The best recent account of Thomas Davis and of his relations with his friends is in T. W. Moody, 'Thomas Davis and the Irish Nation', in *Hermathena* (Dublin, 1966), ciii, 5-31. See also the valuable bibliography appended to this article.
3 These phrases are taken from the prospectus Davis himself wrote for the new paper; it is reprinted in *Thomas Davis: Essays and Poems, with a Centenary Memoir* (Dublin, 1945), p. 13.
4 For the extraordinary activity of the immediate post-Clontarf years, see R. Kee, *The Green Flag* (London, 1972), pp. 232-41.
5 For a summary of the problem see T. W. Moody, 'The Irish University Question of the Nineteenth Century', in *History*, xliii, 90-109. The matter is authoritatively discussed in a wider context by T. W. Moody and J. C. Beckett, *Queen's Belfast, 1845-1909: The History of a University* (London, 1959), i, 1-103.
6 L. Fogerty (ed.), *James Fintan Lalor: Patriot and Political Essayist, 1807-1849* (Dublin and London, 1918), p. 10.
7 Ibid., p. 21.
8 K. B. Nowlan, *The Politics of Repeal*, chap. viii.
9 Ibid., chap. x.
10 O. Dudley Edwards, 'Ireland', in O. Dudley Edwards, Gwynfor Evans, Joan Rhys, and Hugh MacDiarmid, *Celtic Nationalism* (London, 1968), p. 142.
11 P. H. Pearse, *Political Writings and Speeches* (Dublin, n.d.), 'The Sovereign People', p. 369.
12 L. Fogerty, op. cit., pp. 60-1.
13 O. Dudley Edwards, op. cit., p. 141.
14 *Return . . . of Cases of Evictions which have Come to the Knowledge of the Constabulary in Each of the Years from 1849 to 1880*, H.C. (1881) (185), lxxvii.
15 J. H. Whyte, *The Independent Irish Party, 1850-9* (London, 1958), pp. 5-6.

16 Ibid., pp. 7-8; see also B. Kennedy (ed.), 'Sharman Crawford on Ulster Tenant Right, 1846', in *IHS* (Mar. 1963), viii, 246-53.

17 C. Gavan Duffy, *The League of North and South* (London, 1886). Like all of Gavan Duffy's works, this history tends to exaggerate the importance of the part played by Gavan Duffy.

18 M. G. Moore, *An Irish Gentleman – George Henry Moore* (London, 1913).

19 J. H. Whyte, 'Political Problems, 1850-1860', in P. J. Corish (ed.), *A History of Irish Catholicism* (Dublin, 1967), vol. iii, fascicule 2, p. 23. See also the same author's *The Independent Irish Party*, chap. ix.

20 J. H. Whyte, *The Tenant League and Irish Politics in the Eighteen-Fifties* (Dundalk, 1966), p. 22.

21 For a reconstruction of his early career, see D. Ryan, *The Fenian Chief* (Dublin, 1967), chap. i.

22 See Michael Doheny, *The Felon's Track* (Dublin, 1914 ed., reprinted 1951).

23 For Luby's career see D. Ryan, 'James Stephens and Thomas Clarke Luby', in T. W. Moody (ed.), *The Fenian Movement* (Cork, 1968), pp. 49-61.

24 E. R. R. Green, 'The Beginnings of Fenianism', in T. W. Moody, op. cit., pp. 17-18; also D. Ryan, *The Fenian Chief*, chap. xiv. For the other side of the question see A. M. Sullivan's own account in *New Ireland* (London, 1877), chap. xvii. This work went through many editions and became almost the political testament of the new generation of constitutional nationalists.

25 E. R. R. Green, 'Charles Joseph Kickham and John O'Leary', in T. W. Moody, op. cit., pp. 77-88. See also the recent biography, *John O'Leary*, by Marcus Bourke (Tralee, 1968). The influence of O'Leary upon Yeats is manifest in the latter's *Autobiographies* (see especially pp. 209-13) and in much of the poetry he wrote between 1900 and 1913. O'Leary's own *Recollections of Fenians and Fenianism* (London, 1896) is a rambling and sadly disappointing mélange of frequently inaccurate recollections.

26 P. J. Corish, 'Political Problems, 1860-1878', in *A History of Irish Catholicism*, vol. v, fascicule iii, p. 7.

27 *Freeman's Journal*, 10 March 1867.

28 *Irish People*, 9 Apr. 1864. For the context of this article, see Donal Macartney, 'The Church and Fenianism', in *University Review* (Dublin, 1967), iv, 203-15. For more detailed investigation of the problem, see E. R. Norman, *The Catholic Church and Ireland in the Age of Rebellion, 1859-1873* (London, 1965), especially chap. iii; also P. J. Corish, op. cit.

29 See, for example, the kind of changes envisaged in the *Irish People*, 7 May 1864.

30 D. Macartney, op. cit., p. 208.

31 Ibid., p. 215.

32 The most interesting study of his career remains that by Desmond Ryan, *The Phoenix Flame* (London, 1937). Devoy's own *Recollections of an Irish Rebel* (New York, 1929), are, like the memoirs of most other Fenians, unreliable and much given to special pleading. These faults can, however, be corrected to some extent from his published correspondence; see D. Ryan and W. O'Brien (ed.), *Devoy's Post Bag, 1871-1928*, 2 vols. (Dublin, 1948 and 1953).

Part II

1. GENESIS OF HOME RULE (pp. 141-59)

1 For the context of this speech, see R. Blake, *Disraeli* (London, 1966), pp. 178-9.
2 J. L. Hammond, *Gladstone and the Irish Nation* (London, new impr. 1964), p. 51.
3 Ibid., p. 80.
4 E. R. Norman, *The Catholic Church and Irish Politics in the Eighteen-Sixties* (Dundalk, 1965), pp. 16-17. For an admirable but detailed treatment of the same theme see E. R. Norman, *The Catholic Church and Ireland in the Age of Rebellion, 1859-1873* (London, 1965), chap. vii.
5 E. R. Norman, *The Catholic Church and Ireland in the Age of Rebellion*, chap. viii; J. C. Beckett, 'Gladstone, Queen Victoria and the Disestablishment of the Irish Church, 1868-9', in *IHS*, xiii (Mar. 1962); J. C. Beckett, *The Making of Modern Ireland, 1603-1922* pp. 367-9; P. J. Corish, *A History of Irish Catholicism: Political Problems, 1860-78* (Dublin, 1967), vol. v, fascicule 3, pp. 23-36; P. M. H. Bell, *Disestablishment in Ireland and Wales* (London, 1967); H. Shearman, *How the Church of Ireland was Disestablished* (Dublin, 1970), a distillation of his important doc-toral thesis (Trinity College, Dublin), 'The Economic Results of the Disestablishment of the Irish Church'; M. Hurley (ed.), *Irish Anglicanism, 1869-1969* (Dublin, 1970); D. H. Akenson, *The Church of Ireland: Ecclesiastical Reform and Revolution, 1800-1885* (New Haven and London, 1971).
6 H. Shearman, 'State-Aided Land Purchase under the Disestablishment Act of 1869', in *IHS*, iv (Mar. 1944), 58-80.
7 E. R. Norman, *The Catholic Church and Ireland in the Age of Rebellion*, p. 382.
8 The comparable Conservative figures were thirty-six from the landed in-terest, one from the professions and three from commerce. Neither party possessed a tenant-farmer representative. For details, see D. Thornley, *Isaac Butt and Home Rule* (London, 1964), chap. vi.
9 See the list in A. M. Sullivan, *New Ireland* (London, 16th ed., n.d.), pp. 339-41; it is somewhat amended in Thornley, op. cit., pp. 92-3.
10 For the growth of the movement, see L. J. McCaffrey, 'Irish Federalism in the 1870s: A Study in Conservative Nationalism', in *Transactions of the American Philosophical Society* (Philadelphia, 1962), new series, vol. lii, pp. 10-12 (cited hereafter as 'Irish Federalism').
11 D. Thornley, *Isaac Butt and Home Rule*, pp. 90-1.
12 Butt's own exposition of his ideas is still the best. See his pamphlet, of which the full title is: *Home Government for Ireland, Irish Federalism: Its Meaning, Its Objects and Its Hopes* (Dublin, 1870).
13 P. J. Corish, 'Political Problems, 1860-1878', pp. 55-7.
14 D. Thornley, *Isaac Butt and Home Rule*, p. 167.
15 Ibid., chap. v, for the political affiliations of the newly returned members. See also L. J. McCaffrey, 'Home Rule and the General Election of 1874', in *IHS* (Sept. 1954), ix, 190-212, and the same author's 'Irish Federalism

788

in the 1870s', pp. 16-21. Professor McCaffrey differs from Professor Thornley in allotting twelve seats to the Liberals instead of ten, and thirty-two to the Conservatives instead of thirty-three. In fact, the number of *individuals* elected in 1874 was 102; two boroughs (Cashel and Sligo) had been disfranchised and one member, Philip Callan, held two seats.

16 D. Thornley, *Isaac Butt and Home Rule*, chap. vi.
17 Ibid., p. 213.
18 For Parnell's early career see R. B. O'Brien, *The Life of Charles Stewart Parnell* (London, 3rd ed., 1899), i, chaps. ii and iii; also F. S. L. Lyons, *Parnell* (Dundalk, 1963), pp. 3-5. There is an interesting 'revisionist' essay by Michael Hurst, *Parnell and Irish Nationalism* (London, 1968), chaps. ii and iii.

2. LAND AND POLITICS (pp. 160-77)

1 Cited in T. N. Brown, *Irish-American Nationalism* (Philadelphia and New York, 1966), p. 24. Professor Brown's admirable study is essential to an understanding of the Irish-American contribution to the Irish cause and indeed lifts the whole discussion of this question onto a new plane.
2 For the 'New Departure', see T. W. Moody, 'The New Departure in Irish Politics, 1878-9', in *Essays in British and Irish History in Honour of James Eadie Todd*, ed. H. A. Cronne, T. W. Moody and D. B. Quinn (London, 1949). See also T. N. Brown, *Irish-American Nationalism*, chap. v. and T. W. Moody's review of that book in *IHS*, xv, no. 60 (Sept. 1967).
3 R. B. O'Brien, *Parnell*, i, 177.
4 *Return of Evictions Known to the Constabulary in Each Year, 1849 to 1880*, P.P. (1881), vol. lxxvii, p. 725. The total number of families evicted in 1879 was 1,238, involving 6,239 persons; but of these, 140 families (663 persons) were subsequently reinstated.
5 *Preliminary Report on the Returns of Agricultural Produce in Ireland*, P.P. (1880) [c. 2495], table v, p. 899; N. D. Palmer, *The Irish Land League Crisis* (New Haven and London, 1940), p. 64.
6 F. S. L., Lyons, 'The Economic Ideas of Parnell', in M. Roberts (ed.), *Historical Studies*, ii (London, 1959), p. 64.
7 R. B. O'Brien, *Parnell*, i, 240.
8 *Nation*, 11 Oct. 1879.
9 R. B. O'Brien, *Parnell*, i, 247, n 1; J. L. Hammond, *Gladstone and the Irish Nation*, p. 155.
10 J. L. Hammond, op. cit., pp. 196-7.
11 C. Cruise O'Brien, *Parnell and His Party* (London, 1957), chap. i. The most striking 'militarists' were Lysaght Finigan (Foreign Legion), J. J. O'Kelly (war correspondent and duellist), and The O'Gorman Mahon, who had been not only a duellist and soldier of fortune, but an admiral in one country and a general in another. It is fair to set against this the fact that the party also contained one well-known novelist (Justin McCarthy) and several prosperous business men.
12 J. L. Hammond, *Gladstone and the Irish Nation*, pp. 192-3. See F. S. L. Lyons, *John Dillon*, pp. 37-40 for the leading part taken by Dillon in the agitation at this time. His speech at Kildare in August was one of the most extreme he ever made and led to an angry scene in parlia-

ment. In that speech he urged the farmers to bring pressure on their neighbours to join the League, hinted at a policy of a general strike against the payment of rent, and talked darkly about the possibility of seeing 'that every man had a right to have a rifle if he liked'. This went a good deal further than either Parnell or Davitt would have deemed politic and indicated that this new and passionate recruit to the cause might be difficult to control.

13 B. Solow, *The Land Question and the Irish Economy, 1870-1903*, p. 155. See chap. 6 of this book for a penetrating criticism of the presuppositions and the actual terms of the Land Act of 1881.

14 *Freeman's Journal*, 8 and 10 Oct. 1881.

15 K. O'Shea, *Charles Stewart Parnell: His Love Story and Political Life* (London, 1914), i, 207.

16 For a consideration of the forces affecting the fate of the land agitation at this time, see C. Cruise O'Brien, *Parnell and His Party*, pp. 65-72; M. Hurst, *Parnell and Irish Nationalism*, chap. iv; F. S. L. Lyons, *John Dillon*, chap. ii.

17 J. L. Hammond, *Gladstone and the Irish Nation*, pp. 266-7; more extended details are in R. B. O'Brien, *Parnell*, i, 329-30.

18 For the question of Parnell's supposed swing towards constitutionalism, see C. Cruise O'Brien, op. cit., pp. 72-9; F. S. L. Lyons, *Parnell* (Dundalk, 1963), pp. 12-13; M. Hurst, *Parnell and Irish Nationalism*, pp. 73-8.

3. PARNELL: ZENITH AND NADIR (pp. 178-201)

1 For the working of the League and the general question of finance see C. Cruise O'Brien, *Parnell and His Party*, chap. iv. The surplus of the Land League funds – estimated variously at between £30,000 and £40,000 – were not handed over to the Land League, but lodged in Paris under the control of Parnell and two of his colleagues. This 'Paris fund' was later to be the subject of angry dispute between them.

2 Ibid., p. 152.

3 C. H. D. Howard (ed.), 'Documents Relating to the Irish "Central Board" Scheme, 1884-5', in *IHS* (March, 1953), vii, 237-63; C. H. D. Howard, 'Joseph Chamberlain, Parnell and the Irish "Central Board" Scheme, 1884-5', in *IHS* (Sept. 1953), viii, 324-61. As to the fall of the Liberal government, contemporaries were hard put to it to decide whether ministers were more relieved, or their opponents more delighted, at the result.

4 The Churchill-Parnell meeting is described in L. P. Curtis, *Coercion and Conciliation in Ireland, 1880-1892* (Princeton, 1963), p. 36.

5 S. J. Lynch, 'Land Purchase in Ireland', in *JSSISI*, xiii, 1-16; B. Solow, op. cit., pp. 188-9, 193.

6 The electoral situation is discussed in C. Cruise O'Brien, op. cit., pp. 105-118. See also C. H. D. Howard, 'The Parnell Manifesto of 21 November 1885 and the Schools Question', in *EHR* (Jan. 1947), lxii, and the criticisms of that article in V. A. McClelland, *Cardinal Manning, His Public Life and Influence, 1865-92* (London, 1962), pp. 83-5, 187-9, and in Michael Hurst, *Parnell and Irish Nationalism*, pp. 104-7.

7 E. Strauss, *Irish Nationalism and British Democracy* (London, 1951), pp.

168-80; C. Cruise O'Brien, op. cit., pp. 109-14; F. S. L. Lyons, 'The Economic Ideas of Parnell', in *Historical Studies*, ii, 70-2.

8 J. L. Garvin, *Joseph Chamberlain* (London, 1932), ii, 12.
9 D. C. Savage, 'The Origins of the Ulster Unionist Party, 1885-6', in *IHS* (March 1961), xii, 185-208.
10 R. B. O'Brien, *Parnell*, ii, 38-9.
11 L. P. Curtis, *Anglo-Saxons and Celts* (New York, 1968), p. 100.
12 Professor Curtis discusses the general problem of anti-Irish feeling in his interesting and original essay; for its particular bearing on the Home Rule debate see chap. viii.
13 *United Ireland*, 23 Oct. 1886.
14 I have described the working of the Plan of Campaign in detail in *John Dillon*, chap. iv.
15 For the syndicate, see L. P. Curtis, *Coercion and Conciliation in Ireland*, pp. 248-52.
16 Cited in F. S. L. Lyons, op. cit., pp. 94, 97.
17 The best account of the special commission is in J. L. Hammond, *Gladstone and the Irish Nation*, chap. xxix.
18 F. S. L. Lyons, op. cit., pp. 106-7.
19 C. Cruise O'Brien, *Parnell and His Party*, pp. 233-4.
20 M. Hurst, *Parnell and Irish Nationalism*, p. 96. For the background to Parnell's more extreme speeches, see F. S. L. Lyons, *The Fall of Parnell* (London, 1960), chap. vi.

4. CONSTRUCTIVE UNIONISM (pp. 202-23)

1 I have tried to indicate the issues involved in two books: *The Irish Parliamentary Party* (London, 1951), chaps. i and v; *John Dillon*, chap. vi.
2 L. P. Curtis, *Coercion and Conciliation in Ireland*, p. 344.
3 S. J. Lynch, 'Land Purchase in Ireland', *JSSISI*, xiii, 1-16; L. P. Curtis, op. cit., pp. 350-55; B. Solow (op. cit., p. 193) gives a figure of 35,000 which includes some additional sales under variants of the acts.
4 The history of the Board has been written – largely from the inside – by W. L. Micks, *An Account . . . of the Congested Districts Board for Ireland from 1891 to 1923* (London, 1925).
5 For Plunkett's career, see Margaret Digby, *Horace Plunkett* (Oxford, 1949); also J. J. Byrne, 'AE and Sir Horace Plunkett', in C. Cruise O'Brien (ed.), *The Shaping of Modern Ireland* (London, 1960), pp. 152-63.
6 Sir H. Plunkett, *Ireland in the New Century* (London, 1904), p. 82.
7 Ibid., p. 68.
8 Ibid., pp. 80-1.
9 Ibid., chap. iv.
10 J. G. Knapp, *An Appraisement of Agricultural Co-operation in Ireland* (Dublin, 1964, Pr. 7464), pp. 9-50.
11 R. B. McDowell, *The Irish Administration, 1801-1914*, pp. 224-9.
12 R. D. Crotty, *Irish Agricultural Production: Its Volume and Structure* (Cork, 1966), pp. 117-19.
13 Margaret Digby, *Horace Plunkett*, chaps. v and vii; J. G. Knapp, *An Appraisement of Agricultural Co-operation in Ireland*, pp. 25-38.
14 J. J. Byrne, op. cit., p. 162.

15 William O'Brien, *An Olive Branch in Ireland* (London, 1910), chaps. vi. viii and ix; the report is printed in an appendix, pp. 475-9.
16 For details of these two Acts see F. S. L. Lyons, *John Dillon*, pp. 229-35, 307-8; under the Wyndham Act alone some 200,000 tenants purchased their holdings (B. Solow, op. cit., p. 193).
17 Earl of Dunraven, *Past Times and Pastimes* (London, 1922), ii, 25.
18 The politics of the devolution crisis are sketched in F. S. L. Lyons, 'The Irish Unionist Party and the Devolution Crisis of 1904-5', in *IHS* (Mar. 1948), vi, 1-21.
19 *National Review*, Oct. 1904, p. 368.

5. THE BATTLE OF TWO CIVILISATIONS (pp. 224-46)

1 There is an excellent sketch of the growth of these Irish studies in W.I. Thompson, *The Imagination of an Insurrection* (New York, 1967), chap. i.
2 For Cusack's career see David Greene, 'Michael Cusack and the Rise of the G.A.A.', in C. Cruise O'Brien (ed.), *The Shaping of Modern Ireland*, pp. 74-84.
3 T. F. O'Sullivan, *The Story of the G.A.A.* (Dublin, 1916), pp. 9-10.
4 The two Literary Societies are described in Ernest Boyd, *Ireland's Literary Rennaissance* (Dublin, 1916; new ed., 1968), pp. 84-93.
5 Douglas Hyde, 'The Necessity for De-Anglicising Ireland', in *The Revival of Irish Literature* (London, 1894), p. 119.
6 Ibid., p. 160.
7 William Rooney, *Prose Writings* (Dublin, 1909), pp. 244, 250. For the history of the language revival, see especially B. O. Cuiv, 'The Gaelic Cultural Movements and the New Nationalism', in K. Nowlan (ed.), *The Making of 1916*, pp. 1-27.
8 Ibid., pp. 230, 231-2.
9 *Leader*, 1 Sept. 1900.
10 D. P. Moran, *The Philosophy of Irish Ireland* (Dublin, 1905), p. 34. The essays in this book were all written between 1893 and the first appearance of the *Leader* in Sept. 1900.
11 Ibid., pp. 40, 43.
12 D. Macartney, 'Hyde, D. P. Moran and Irish Ireland', in F. X. Martin (ed.), *Leaders and Men of the Easter Rising*, p. 49.
13 D. P. Moran, *The Philosophy of Irish Ireland*, p. 37.
14 Ibid., p. 96.
15 M. Digby, *Horace Plunkett*, p. 152.
16 For these preoccupations, see Ernest Boyd, *Ireland's Literary Renaissance*, pp. 213-15; John Eglinton, *A Memoir of AE* (London, 1937), pp. 11-12; J. M. Hone, *W. B. Yeats, 1865-1939* (London, second ed., 1962), chaps iii and v; A. N. Jeffares, *W. B. Yeats, Man and Poet* (London, 1949), chaps. iii, iv and v; Richard Ellman, *Yeats, the Man and the Masks* (revised ed., London, 1960), chaps. iv to vii; H. Howarth, *The Irish Writers, 1880-1940* (London, 1958), *passim*.
17 See especially, H. Howarth, op. cit., chaps. i and v; also R. J. Loftus, *Nationalism in Modern Anglo-Irish Poetry* (Madison and Milwaukee, 1964), chaps. 3, 4 and 5.
18 AE, 'The Dramatic Treatment of Heroic Literature', in *United Irishman*, 3 May 1902.

19 Yeats's own later account of this clash is illuminating. See especially *Autobiographies* (London, 1955), pp. 224-8.
20 D. P. Moran, *The Philosophy of Irish Ireland*, p. 22.
21 John Eglinton, 'The Island of Saints', in *United Irishman*, 8 Feb. 1902.
22 *United Irishman*, 22 Feb. 1902.
23 John Eglinton, 'A Word for Anglo-Irish Literature', in *United Irishman*, 22 Mar. 1902.
24 *United Irishman*, 31 Mar. 1902.
25 *The Leader*, 11 Jan. 1902.
26 A. N. Jeffares, *W. B. Yeats: Man and Poet*, pp. 137-8.
27 For Synge's career, see David H. Greene and Edward M. Stephens, *J. M. Synge, 1871-1909* (New York, paperback ed. 1961); also R. Skelton, *The Writings of J. M. Synge* (London, 1971).
28 *United Irishman*, 10, 17 and 31 Oct. 1903.
29 Ibid., 24 Oct. 1903; F. S. L. Lyons, 'James Joyce's Dublin', in *Twentieth Century Studies* (1970).
30 C. Cruise O'Brien, 'Passion and Cunning', in A. N. Jeffares and K. G. W. Cross (ed.), *In Excited Reverie* (London, 1965), pp. 212-16.
31 *Samhain*, Oct. 1901.
32 W. B. Yeats, 'The Cutting of an Agate' (written in 1907), in *Essays and Introductions* (London, 1961), p. 259.
33 *United Irishman*, 10 Oct. 1903; *Samhain*, 1903.
34 *United Irishman*, 17 Oct. 1903.
35 Ibid., 24 Oct. 1903.

6. THE RISE OF SINN FEIN (pp. 247-59)

1 William Rooney, *Prose Writings* (Dublin, 1909), pp. 73-5.
2 R. M. Henry, *The Evolution of Sinn Féin* (Dublin, 1920), p. 63.
3 P. S. O'Hegarty, *A History of Ireland Under the Union* (London, 1952), p. 639.
4 Ibid., p. 640; but drink was discouraged, says O'Hegarty, 'because it ruined the character'.
5 *United Irishman*, 1 Nov. 1902.
6 Arthur Griffith, *The Resurrection of Hungary*, first preface to the third (Dublin, 1918) edition.
7 *United Irishman*, 23 July 1904.
8 Cited in Griffith's pamphlet, 'The Sinn Féin Policy', and reprinted in 1918 with *The Resurrection of Hungary*. See especially p. 143. Griffith was also to some extent influenced by the American protectionist, Henry Carey, but List's work, which he read in translation, was much the most important formative element in his economic policy.
9 Ibid., p. 144.
10 P. S. O'Hegarty, *A History of Ireland Under the Union*, p. 643.
11 Ibid., p. 652. These words he actually spoke to P. S. O'Hegarty. The discussions behind the scenes which eventually produced the ambivalent constitution are described on pp. 651-3.
12 D. Macartney, 'The Sinn Féin Movement', in K. B. Nowlan (ed.), *The Making of 1916* (Dublin, 1969), p. 38.
13 Ibid., p. 39.
14 R. M. Henry, *The Evolution of Sinn Féin*, p. 87.

7. HOME RULE REVIVED (pp. 260-69)

1 The standard biography is D. R. Gwynn, *The Life of John Redmond* (London, 1932). See also the illuminating essay by N. S. Mansergh, 'John Redmond', in C. Cruise O'Brien (ed.), *The Shaping of Modern Ireland*, pp. 38-49.

2 The circumstances and aftermath of reunion are described in F. S. L., Lyons, *The Irish Parliamentary Party*, chap. iii and the same author's *John Dillon*, chaps. vii and viii. For the Hibernians see J. J. Bergin, 'History of the Ancient Order of Hibernians' (Dublin, 1910).

3 H. W. McCready, 'Home Rule and the Liberal Party', in *IHS*, xiii (Sept. 1963), 316-48.

4 F. S. L. Lyons, *John Dillon*, pp. 292-8; A. C. Hepburn, 'The Irish Council Bill and the fall of Sir Antony MacDonnell in 1906-7', in *IHS*, xvii (Sept. 1971).

5 F. S. L. Lyons, op. cit., pp. 308-11.

6 J. R. Fanning, 'The Unionist' Party and Ireland, 1906-10', in *IHS*, xv (Sept. 1966), 147-71. For another attempt to popularise the idea of federalism as a solution of the Irish question, see A. J. Ward, 'Frewen's Anglo-American Campaign for Federalism, 1910-21', in *IHS*, xv (Mar. 1967), 256-75.

8. LABOUR IN FERMENT (pp. 270-86)

1 J. D. Clarkson, *Labour and Nationalism in Ireland* (New York, 1925), p. 167.

2 Ibid., p. 183.

3 Ibid., chap. vii.

4 For Connolly's early life, see D. Ryan, *James Connolly* (Dublin and London, 1924); see also Ryan's essay – the last he ever wrote on this subject – in J. W. Boyle (ed.), *Leaders and Workers* (Cork, n.d.), pp. 67-75.

5 Cited in C. D. Greaves, *The Life and Times of James Connolly* (London, 1961), pp. 60-2.

6 J. D. Clarkson, op. cit., p. 252.

7 For his career see the essay 'William Walker' by J. W. Boyle in *Leaders and Workers*, pp. 57-65. Walker was not, as has sometimes been stated, the first labour candidate to contest an election. In 1885 Alexander Bowman contested North Belfast and was soundly beaten; he stood ostensibly as a Liberal, but was closer to what in England would have been called a 'Lib-Lab' candidate. Dr Boyle has dealt with Walker's career in greater detail in chap. viii of his unpublished doctoral thesis. 'The Rise of the Irish Labour Movement'.

8 E. Larkin, *James Larkin* (London, 1965), pp. 25-40.

9 Ibid., pp. 41-8.

10 *Sinn Féin*, 9 Sept. 1911; see also the articles on the Cork dispute in the same paper, 3 and 24 July 1909.

11 Cited in C. D. Greaves, op. cit., pp. 176-7.

12 James Connolly, *Labour in Irish History* (original ed., 1910, revised ed.,

Dublin, n.d.), pp. 167-8.
13 C. D. Greaves, op. cit., p. 203.
14 J. D. Clarkson, *Labour and Nationalism in Ireland*, pp. 292, 295-7.
15 E. Larkin, *James Larkin*, pp. 108-9. Contemporary estimates, friendly and unfriendly alike, went nearly as high as 25,000 but these were exaggerated.
16 For his two verdicts, see *Forward*, 7 Feb. 1914 and *Irish Worker*, 28 Nov. 1914. The best account of this whole episode is in E. Larkin, *James Larkin*, chaps. vi and viii.
17 J. W. Boyle, 'Connolly, the Citizen Army and the Rising', in K. Nowlan (ed.), *The Making of 1916*, pp. 53-7.
18 A considerable literature has grown up around the Countess. The most valuable studies are: S. O'Faoláin, *Constance Markievicz* (London, 1938; new paperback edition, 1967); E. Coxhead, *Daughters of Erin* (London, 1965); Anne Marreco, *The Rebel Countess* (London, 1967); Jacqueline Van Voris, *Constance de Markievicz in the Service of Ireland* (Massachusetts, 1967).

9. ULSTER BLOCKS THE WAY (pp. 287-311)

1 For its previous history, see H. Senior, *Orangeism in Ireland and Britain, 1795-1836* (London, 1966).
2 The organisation of Irish and Ulster Unionism is the subject of two recent studies: D. C. Savage, 'The Origins of the Ulster Unionist Party, 1885-6', in *IHS*, xii (Mar. 1961), 185-208; and P. J. Buckland, 'The Southern Irish Unionists and British Politics, 1906-14', in *IHS*, xv (Mar. 1967), 228-55.
3 R. Lucas, *Colonel Saunderson, MP: A Memoir* (London, 1908), *passim*.
4 Cited in D. C. Savage, op. cit., p. 196.
5 *Belfast Newsletter*, 22 and 23 Feb. 1886 for Churchill's visit.
6 The quotation is from 'Belfast' by Louis MacNeice in his *Collected Poems, 1925-1948* (London, 1949), p. 73.
7 For this incident, see R. Lucas, *Colonel Saunderson*, pp. 318-23.
8 For these developments, see F. S. L. Lyons, *The Irish Parliamentary Party*, pp. 134-6; also J. W. Boyle, 'Belfast and the Origins of Northern Ireland', in J. C. Beckett and R. E. Glasscock (ed.), *Belfast: The Origin and Growth of an Industrial City* (London, 1967), pp. 133-7. The origins of the Independent Orange Institution are explored in E. Larkin, *James Larkin, 1876-1947*, appendix D; see also J. W. Boyle, 'The Belfast Protestant Association and the Independent Orange Order', in *IHS*, xiii (Sept. 1962), pp. 117-52.
9 P. J. Buckland, 'The Southern Irish Unionists and British Politics, 1906-14', in *IHS*, xv, 228-55.
10 H. M. Hyde, *Carson* (London, 1953), p. 291. For the background to the meeting, see also A. T. Q. Stewart, 'Craig and the Ulster Volunteer Force', in F. X. Martin (ed.), *Leaders and Men of the Easter Rising: Dublin, 1916*, pp. 701-1, and the same author's *The Ulster Crisis* (London, 1967), pp. 47-8.
11 R. Blake, *The Unknown Prime Minister* (London, 1955), p. 129.
12 The arguments can be followed through many pages of Hansard, in H.C. Debates, 5th series, vol. 46. See also the introduction to, and

appendix I of, R. J. Lawrence, *The Government of Northern Ireland* (London, 1965).

13 R. Blake, *The Unknown Prime Minister*, p. 130.

14 R. Jenkins, *Asquith* (London, 1964), p. 279.

15 For these exchanges, see F. S. L. Lyons, *John Dillon*, pp. 332-4.

16 The Ulster gun-running is briefly described by A. T. Q. Stewart, 'Craig and the Ulster Volunteer Force', in *Leaders and Men of the Easter Rising*, pp. 74-6, and at more length in the same author's *The Ulster Crisis*, chaps viii to x, and xiv to xvi. See also Crawford's own account, *Guns for Ulster* (Belfast, 1947).

Part III

I. PHOENIX RESURGENT (pp. 315-28)

1 See the amended Constitution, Article 3, in Bulmer Hobson, *Ireland Yesterday and To-morrow* (Tralee, 1968), p. 103.

2 Ibid., p. 28.

3 F. X. Martin, 'McCullough, Hobson and Republican Ulster', in F. X. Martin (ed.), *Leaders and Men of the Easter Rising: Dublin 1916* (London, 1967), p. 98.

4 Bulmer Hobson's recollections (1947), in F. X. Martin (ed.), *The Irish Volunteers, 1913-1915*, pp. 19-20.

5 B. Hobson, *Ireland Yesterday and To-morrow*, p. 104.

6 For these incidents see D. Ryan and William O'Brien, *Devoy's Post Bag* (Dublin, 1953), ii, 401, 570.

7 B. Hobson, *Ireland Yesterday and To-morrow*, pp. 38-9. The nominal editor was Patrick MacCartan, who, after leaving school, had gone to America. There he joined Clan na Gael and on his return to Ireland was transferred to the IRB. He then began to study medicine (qualifying in 1910) but combined this with extensive work for Sinn Féin. He was co-opted to the Supreme Council in 1914-15.

8 B. Hobson, op. cit., p. 36; see also S. Cronin, 'The Fenian Tradition', in *Irish Times*, 9 Apr., 1969.

9 Ibid., p. 43.

10. For details of The O'Rahilly's early career, see Marcus Bourke, *The O'Rahilly* (Tralee, 1967), chaps. 3 and 4; for the writing of 'The North Began', see MacNeill's own account, dictated in 1932 and published in F. X. Martin (ed.), *The Irish Volunteer, 1913-1915*, pp. 71-2.

11 *An Claidheamh Soluis*, 1 Nov. 1913.

12 Events moved so rapidly in November 1913 that even the principals most heavily involved have differences of recollection. Thus Hobson states that he asked The O'Rahilly to see MacNeill, whereas MacNeill conveys the impression that The O'Rahilly was accompanied by Hobson. The O'Rahilly's biographer accepts Hobson's version, but it is possible of course that several interviews took place within the same few days and that in retrospect it became impossible to tell who was present at which. See F. X. Martin (ed.), *The Irish Volunteers, 1913-15* (Dublin,

1963), pp. 24-5, 71-2; also M. Bourke, *The O'Rahilly*, p. 71.

13 For the membership see F. X. Martin (ed.), *The Irish Volunteers*, pp. 95-6. Originally, twelve names were selected: Eoin MacNeill, Bulmer Hobson, The O'Rahilly, P. H. Pearse, Sean MacDermott, W. J. Ryan, Eamonn Ceannt, Sean Fitzgibbon, J. A. Deakin, Piaras Béaslaí, Joseph Campbell, D. P. Moran. Of these Moran declined and Hobson, as already stated, absented himself: Deakin, Campbell and Ryan withdrew after the first meeting.

14 Ibid., pp. 98-101.

15 D. Ryan and W. O'Brien (ed.), *Devoy's Post Bag*, ii, 426.

16 See R. B. McDowell, *Alice Stopford Green: A Passionate Historian* (Dublin, 1967).

17 It is reprinted in B. Hobson, *Ireland Yesterday and To-morrow*, pp. 99-102.

18 Casement's career has produced an enormous, and frequently controversial, literature. The following works are useful guides to the career and the controversies: C. E. Curry, *The Casement Diaries and the Findlay Affair* (Munich, 1922); D. R. Gwynn, *The Life and Death of Roger Casement* (London, 1931); G. de C. Parmiter, *Roger Casement* (London, 1936); W. Moloney, *The Forged Casement Diaries* (Dublin, 1936); R. Monteith, *Casement's Last Adventure* (Dublin, 1953); H. O. Mackey, *The Life and Times of Roger Casement* (Dublin, 1954); R. MacColl, *Roger Casement* (London, 1956); Alfred Noyes, *The Accusing Ghost: Or Justice for Casement* (London, 1957). In 1959 there appeared *The Black Diaries*, edited by P. Singleton-Gates and Maurice Girodias and published originally in Paris by the Olympia Press. The editorship of this volume leaves something to be desired and some mysteries remain unsolved, but the book contains what are described as 'faithful reproductions' of the typewritten copies of Casement's alleged diaries for 1903 and 1910 made in Scotland Yard at the time of his trial in August 1916. Recently the British government has made the diaries available for inspection by *bona fide* scholars, but a definitive judgment as to their authenticity has not yet emerged.

19 The personalities and the plotting in this extraordinary incident are admirably brought to life in F. X. Martin (ed.), *The Howth Gun-Running, 1914* (Dublin, 1964). See also, for Mrs Green's anxieties lest MacNeill be exploited by extremists, R. B. McDowell, *Alice Stopford Green: A Passionate Historian*, pp. 100-1.

20 F. X. Martin (ed.), *The Irish Volunteers*, p. 47.

21 For this crisis, see D. R. Gwynn, *The Life of John Redmond*, pp. 307-22; F. X. Martin, *The Irish Volunteers*, pp. 43-53, 141-4; B. Hobson, *Ireland Yesterday and To-morrow*, pp. 48-56; F. S. L. Lyons, *John Dillon*, pp. 350-2.

22 The effect of the Howth gun-running on recruiting was frequently commented on by the police. See B. MacGiolla Choille (ed.), *Intelligence Notes, 1913-16* (Dublin, 1966), pp. 81, 83, 85.

2. THE ROAD TO REVOLUTION (pp. 329-58)

1 For these events see D. R. Gwynn, *Life of John Redmond*, pp. 384-92, and F. X. Martin (ed.), *The Irish Volunteers*, pp. 144-55.

2 F. X. Martin (ed.), *The Irish Volunteers*, pp. 194-5.

3 F. X. Martin (ed.), 'Eoin MacNeill on the 1916 Rising', in *IHS* (March 1961), xii, 228. For a penetrating analysis of the recent literature on the rising and its antecedents, see F. X. Martin, '1916 – Myth, Fact, and Mystery', in *Studia Hibernica* (Dublin, 1967), no. 7, pp. 7-24. See also the same author's further study of the same subject, 'The 1916 Rising – *Coup d'Etat* or a "Bloody Protest"?' in *Studia Hibernica* (1968), no. 8, 106-37 and the two excellent essays by Maureen Wall in K. B. Nowlan (ed.), *The Making of 1916* (Dublin, 1969), pp. 157-97; they are entitled 'The Background to the Rising from 1914 Until the Issue of the Countermanding Order on Easter Saturday, 1916', and 'The Plans and the Countermand'.

4 M. Bourke, *The O'Rahilly*, p. 94. For Plunkett's background see the essay by his godson, Donagh MacDonagh, 'Plunkett and MacDonagh', in F. X. Martin (ed.), *Leaders and Men of the Easter Rising*, pp. 165-76.

5 For MacDonagh see Donagh MacDonagh (his son) 'Plunkett and MacDonagh' in *Leaders and Men of the Easter Rising*, pp. 165-76, also Michael Hayes, 'Thomas MacDonagh and the Rising', in F. X. Martin (ed.), *1916 and University College, Dublin* (Dublin, 1966), pp. 35-49.

6 Pearse has not, on the whole, been fortunate in his biographers. For long the 'standard' life of him was a somewhat cloying book, *Patrick N. Pearse* by L. N. Leroux (Dublin, 1932); more recently there has been a slender volume by H. McCay, *Padraic Pearse* (Cork, 1966), which does not add a great deal to our knowledge. There are two interesting articles by D. A. Thornley, 'Patrick Pearse – the evolution of a republican', in F. X. Martin (ed.), *Leaders and Men of the Easter Rising: Dublin 1916* (London, 1967), pp. 151-63, and 'Patrick Pearse and the Pearse Family' in *Studies* (Nos. 239-40, autumn-winter, 1971) xl, 332-46. See also the important revisionist essay by Father F. Shaw, S.J., 'The Canon of Irish History – a Challenge', in *Studies* (no. 242, summer, 1972) xli, 115-53, and my comment upon it in *Irish Times*, 11 Sept. 1972.

7 D. Macardle, *The Irish Republic* (American ed., New York, 1965), pp. 81-2.

8 P. H. Pearse, *Political Writings and Speeches*, pp. 58-9.

9 Ibid., pp. 176-7, 179, 185, 194-5.

10 Two recent investigations of this subject are especially to be noted – R. J. Loftus, *Nationalism in Modern Anglo-Irish Poetry* (Madison and Milwaukee, 1964), chap. vi, and W. I. Thompson, *The Imagination of an Insurrection: Dublin, Easter 1916* (New York, 1967), pp. 113-39.

11 P.H. Pearse, *Political Writings and Speeches*, p. 226, from 'Ghosts', written late in 1915.

12 T. MacDonagh, *Poetical Works: Lyrical Poems* (Dublin, 1916), p. 48. This particular poem was written in 1912.

13 Joseph Plunkett, *Poems* (Dublin, 1916), pp. 59-60.

14 P. H. Pearse, *Political Writings and Speeches*, pp. 91-9.

15 W. I. Thompson, *The Imagination of an Insurrection*, p. 77.

16 P. H. Pearse, *Political Writings and Speeches*, pp. 133-7.

17 Ibid., pp. 215-18.

18 P. H. Pearse, *Plays, Stories, Poems* (Dublin, 1924), pp. 324-5.

19 Ibid., p. 333. The prison poem to his mother is printed for the first time by Leon O Broin, *Dublin Castle and the 1916 Rising* (Dublin, 1966), p.

137. It ends thus:

> I would have brought royal gifts, and
> I have brought you
> Sorrow and tears: and yet, it may be
> That I have brought you something else beside –
> A splendid thing which shall not pass away.
> When men speak of me, in praise or dispraise,
> You will not heed, but treasure your own memory
> Of your first son.

20 P. H. Pearse, Plays, Stories and Poems, p. 44.
21 Ibid., pp. 335-6.
22 For these events see S. T. O'Kelly in An Phoblacht 30 Apr. 1926; W. O'Brien, introduction to James Connolly, Labour and Easter Week (Dublin, 1949); D. Lynch, The I.R.B. and the 1916 Insurrection (Cork, 1957); F. X. Martin (ed.), 'Eoin MacNeill on the 1916 Rising', in IHS (Mar. 1961), no. 47, xii, 226-71.
23 For Casement in Germany, see D. Ryan, The Rising (Dublin, 3rd ed., 1957), chaps. ii and iii; also R. MacColl, Roger Casement, chap. viii. A sympathetic view of his mission is given in Roger McHugh, 'Casement and German Help', in F. X. Martin (ed.), Leaders and Men of the Easter Rising, pp. 177-87.
24 F. X. Martin (ed.), 'Eoin MacNeill on the Rising', p. 243, n. 15.
25 For the Volunteer strategy see Bulmer Hobson, Ireland To-day and To-morrow, pp. 69-71; see also M. Bourke, The O'Rahilly, pp. 87-8.
26 M. Bourke, op. cit., pp. 94-5.
27 D. Lynch, The I.R.B. and the 1916 Insurrection, passim; F. X. Martin (ed.), 'Eoin MacNeill on the Rising' – see especially the informative notes to MacNeill's two memoranda.
28 Cited by William O'Brien, introduction to James Connolly, Labour and Easter Week (ed. D. Ryan), pp. 1-2.
29 Worker's Republic, 18 Dec. 1915.
30 Worker's Republic, 15 Jan. 1916.
31 This passage is cited in Pearse's pamphlet. The whole article can be read in L. Fogarty (ed.), James Fintan Lalor: Patriot and Political Essayist (Dublin, 1918), pp. 52-66.
32 P. H. Pearse, 'The Sovereign People', in Political Writings and Speeches, especially pp. 335-40.
33 Worker's Republic, 30 Oct. 1915.
34 F. X. Martin (ed.), 'Eoin MacNeill on the 1914 Rising', IHS, xii, 246, 'Memorandum II'. Professor Martin would place this interview as taking place about 16 Jan. 1916.
35 Ibid., p. 253, n. 6, drawing especially upon the new evidence supplied by P. Béaslaí in Irish Independent, 29-31 May 1957 and in C. O'Shannon (ed.) Fifty Years of Liberty Hall (Dublin, 1959).
36 F. X. Martin (ed.), 'Eoin MacNeill on the 1916 Rising', p. 247 and n. 14 and 15. For the network radiating outwards from Dublin see D. Ryan, The Rising, pp. 78-89. There is interesting confirmation of IRB activity in the Volunteers in D. FitzGerald, Memoirs (London, 1968), chaps. iv and v.
37 F. X. Martin (ed.), 'Eoin MacNeill on the 1916 Rising', p. 246 and p. 254, n. 11.

38 Ibid., pp. 246-7 and pp. 254-5, n. 12 and 13.

39 Ibid., p. 242, n. 8; p. 243, n. 15; pp. 243-4. n.~16. Police estimates for mid-April 1916 give the number of Volunteers loyal to Redmond as about 105,000 and those adhering to MacNeill as 15,000. The Citizen Army is given as 100, but this seems a notional figure which had remained unchanged since the previous August (B. MacGiolla Choille (ed.), *Intelligence Notes, 1913-16*, p. 176). The most recent estimates of Citizen Army men (and women) participating in the rising are about 210 (D. Nevin, 'The Irish Citizen Army', in O. Dudley Edwards and F. Pyle (ed.), *1916: The Easter Rising* (London, 1968), p. 130), or 218 (F. X. Martin '1916 – Myth, Fact and Mystery', in *Studia Hibernica* (1967), no. 7, p. 19).

40 For the arms landing D. Ryan, *The Rising* is still indispensable, especially chap. vii. See also tne two essays in F. X. Martin (ed.), *Leaders and Men of the Easter Rising* and the bibliographies attached thereto: (1) R. McHugh, 'Casement and German Help', and (2) F. O Donoghue, 'Ceannt, Devoy, O'Rahilly and the Military Plan'.

41 F. O'Donoghue, op. cit.

42 F. X. Martin (ed.), 'Eoin MacNeill on the 1916 Rising', p. 247 and pp. 255-6, n. 18. The reference here is to MacNeill's Memorandum II which was written in the latter half of 1917. Thanks to Professor Martin's careful scholarship it is now possible to check the statements in this document against many other sources.

43 For the 'Castle Document', see D. Ryan, op. cit., chap. vi; also F. X. Martin, op. cit., pp. 247-8 and pp. 257-8, n. 23-6.

44 Bulmer Hobson's statement of 1 May 1916 in F. X. Martin, op. cit., p. 261; also B. Hobson, *Ireland Yesterday To-morrow*, pp. 76-7. It appears to be a by-product of this meeting on Friday morning that Sean MacDermott, who reached MacNeill's house ahead of the others, subsequently spread abroad the quite unfounded rumour that MacNeill had resigned as Chief of Staff. In the same way, earlier that week, he had told Tom Clarke, among others, that MacNeill knew of the plan for an Easter Sunday rising and had agreed to it. Both of these statements were untrue and were used deliberately as *ruses de guerre* – in the former instance to eliminate MacNeill from the situation and in the latter case to quieten the misgivings of those who took their cue from him.

45 F. X. Martin, op. cit., 'Memorandum II', p. 249. In a note written earlier than this Memorandum (in fact on 9 May 1916) MacNeill commented that he had tried to dissuade both his visitors from going on with the hopeless venture, 'They were a bit shaken but not convinced.' For Pearse's movements on the night of Good Friday see D. Ryan, *The Rising*, p. 94.

46 Ibid., pp. 249-50, pp. 264-5, n. 45-7. Casement had tried to get a message to MacNeill from Kerry and John Devoy later believed that it was this, together with the sinking of the *Aud*, which impelled him to call off the rising. It is doubtful if MacNeill ever received this message and possible that it got as far as Connolly who did not forward it (ibid., p. 264, n. 43).

47 Ibid., pp. 265-6, n. 48.

48 F. X. Martin, 'Eoin MacNeill and the Easter Rising: Preparation', in F. X. Martin (ed.), *1916 and University College, Dublin*, pp. 30-1.

49 F. X. Martin (ed.), 'Eoin MacNeill on the 1916 Rising', p. 268, n. 53.

3. THE RISING (pp. 359-80)

1 F. X. Martin (ed.), 'Eoin MacNeill on the 1916 Rising', in *IHS* (Mar. 1961), xii, 240.

2 B. MacGiolla Choille (ed.), *Intelligence Notes*, 1913-16, pp. 201, 202, 205, 209, 211. The information to be gathered from these police reports needs to be used with the caution indicated by the editor in his admirable introduction. It has to be remembered especially that the *Intelligence Notes* are only a précis of general reports which themselves were compiled from a multitude of local reports, and also that the police, though knowledgeable, did not know everything and were often, indeed, much isolated from the communities among which they lived. Nevertheless, the cumulative evidence of agricultural prosperity is very strong.

3 C. H. Oldham, 'Changes in Irish Exports', in *JSSISI* (Feb. 1919), xiii, 629-37, especially the tables in pp. 631 and 637.

4 E. Holt, *Protest in Arms* (London, 1960), p. 68.

5 L. O Broin, *Dublin Castle and the 1916 Rising*, p. 73. The government apparently hoped to reduce tension by deporting two of the most ubiquitous agitators – Ernest Blythe and Liam Mellows. These two 'Banishees' (to use the irrepressible Birrell's term for them) were seized on 25 March and sent to England shortly afterwards. Mr O Broin surveys the tangled problem of the intelligence reports in chap. x and xv of his excellent book.

6 Ibid., p. 85.

7 James Connolly, *Labour and Easter Week* (ed. D. Ryan, Dublin, 1949), p. 21; the most complete summary of the numbers involved on the insurgents' side is in D. Lynch, *The I.R.B. and the 1916 Resurrection*, edited by F. O'Donoghue (Cork, 1957), pp. 105, 143-4.

8 W. B. Yeats. 'The O'Rahilly', in *Collected Poems* (London, 2nd ed., 1950), p. 354. Desmond FitzGerald, one of his closest friends, wrote this about him long afterwards: 'He had shown his readiness to give his life for Ireland as anyone who knew him as I did knew he would do. But the joy of that sacrifice had been marred by the knowledge that those with whom he worked and with whom he shared his hopes thought that a consideration of his personal safety would influence his decision. I felt that he was the most tragic figure in that tragic gathering of men. He was devoted to his wife and family with a rare devotion, but he had decided to leave them to serve Ireland even when the call to service came from men who were revealed as not having realised how ready he was to give all for his country.' (*Memoirs of Desmond FitzGerald, 1913-1916* (London, 1968), p. 155).

9 *Irish Times*, 7 and 15 Apr. 1966; *Memoirs of Desmond FitzGerald*, pp. 140-1.

10 The best of the accounts by contemporaries, though written long after the event, is Desmond Ryan, *The Rising* (Dublin, 3rd ed., 1957). Of recent narratives by outsiders the best are E. Holt, *Protest in Arms*, chaps. viii and ix; M. Caulfield, *The Easter Rebellion* (London, 1965) and C. Younger, *Ireland's Civil War* (London, 1968), chap. ii. For a critical survey of the recent literature, see F. X. Martin, '1916, Myth, Fact and

Mystery', in *Studia Hibernica* (Dublin, 1967), no. 7. An indispensable contemporary source remains the *Royal Commission on the Rebellion in Ireland: Minutes of Evidence and Appendix of Documents* (London, 1916).

11 For Sheehy-Skeffington, see the narrative by his son Owen, in O. Dudley Edwards and F. Pyle, *1916: The Easter Rising*, pp. 135-48. Sheehy-Skeffington's views on the Volunteers and the dangers of militarism are in his 'Open Letter to Thomas MacDonagh', printed in the same volume, pp. 149-52.

12 B. MacGiolla Choille (ed.), *Intelligence Notes, 1913-16*, pp. 240-1. One estimate (E. Holt, *Protest in Arms*, p. 117), places the damage at 2.5 million pounds.

13 Ibid., p. 238.

14 Ibid., pp. 238-9.

15 For an interesting survey of press reactions, see the two appendices in F. Pyle and O. Dudley Edwards (ed.), *1916: The Easter Rising*, pp. 241-71. Of the other three daily newspapers published in the capital, the *Irish Times* and the *Daily Express*, being Unionist, were predictable in their attitude to the rising, though this did not prevent the *Irish Times* from producing a highly professional *Sinn Féin Rebellion Handbook*, which is still a source of valuable material. The *Freeman's Journal*, the organ of the parliamentary party, was handicapped by the destruction of its premises but when it did begin to appear again, on 5 May, it was of course hostile to the rising. It was, however, closely under the eye of John Dillon and reflected his view that what the situation now needed was leniency not severity.

16 The speech is in Hansard, H.C. Debates, 5th series, vol. 82, cols. 935-51. It has lately been reprinted in F. Pyle and O. Dudley Edwards (ed.), *1916: The Easter Rising*, pp. 62-78. For the background see my essay, 'Dillon, Redmond and the Irish Home Rulers', in F. X. Martin (ed.), *Leaders and Men of the Easter Rising*, pp. 29-41; also the more extended treatment in chap. xiii of my biography of John Dillon.

17 B. MacGiolla Choille (ed.), *Intelligence Notes, 1913-16*, pp. 199-220 *passim*.

18 For a detailed examination of this crisis, see my *John Dillon*, pp. 387-403.

4. SINN FEIN TRANSFORMED (pp. 381-99)

1 S. O Luing, 'Arthur Griffith and Sinn Féin', in F. X. Martin (ed.), *Leaders and Men of the Easter Rising*, pp. 62-3.

2 F. S. L. Lyons, *John Dillon*, p. 391.

3 Ibid., p. 395.

4 Ibid., pp. 410-11.

5 D. Macardle, *The Irish Republic* (American ed., New York, 1965), pp. 223-4.

6 Ibid., p. 222. For the American background see Charles A. Tansill, *America and the Fight for Irish Freedom, 1866-1922* (New York, 1957), especially chaps. vii and viii. This is a highly controversial work which needs to be used with caution. It should be supplemented by Owen Dudley Edwards's essay 'American Aspects of the Rising', in F. Pyle and O. Dudley Edwards, *1916: The Easter Rising*, and by Alan J. Ward, 'America and the Irish Problem', in *IHS* (March, 1968), xvi, 64-90;

see also Dr Ward's book, *Ireland and Anglo-American Relations, 1899-1921* (London, 1969), chap. vi.

7 P. Béaslaí, *Michael Collins and the Making of a New Ireland* (London, 1926), i, 166.

8 D. Ryan, *Remembering Sion* (London, 1934), pp. 229-38 still remains the best description. For his early career, see P. Béaslaí, op. cit., i, chaps. v to x; also R. Taylor, *Michael Collins* (London, paperback edition, 1961), chaps. i to vi, and *Memoirs of Desmond FitzGerald*, p. 14;.

9 The cabinet dilemma is well described, on the basis of recently available documents, by C. Younger, *Ireland's Civil War* (London, 1968), chaps. iii and iv.

10 D. Macardle, *The Irish Republic*, p. 251.

11 Ibid., pp. 249-52.

12 F. S. L. Lyons, *John Dillon*, p. 435.

13 Ibid., pp. 437-40 for the election and its significance.

14 P. S. O'Hegarty, *A History of Ireland Under the Union* (London, 1952), pp. 721-2.

15 D. Macardle, *The Irish Republic*, pp. 253-5. For the meagre evidence made public see 'Minutes of Meeting of War Cabinet, 23 May 1918' (PRO, War Cabinet Papers, Cab. 23/6, 416 and appendix). The background material, which for obvious reasons could not be published at the time is in PRO, Cabinet Paper CP 2392 of 31 Dec. 1920 and is summarised in C. Younger, *Ireland's Civil War*, pp. 65-6.

16 R. Taylor, *Michael Collins*, p. 71 and note.

17 F. S. L. Lyons, op. cit., p. 441.

18 P. Béaslaí, *Michael Collins and the Making of a New Ireland*, i, chap. x; R. Taylor, op. cit., pp. 71-2; E. Holt, *Protest in Arms*, pp. 163-5.

19 P. Béaslaí, op. cit., pp. 208-9, 211-12.

20 The censored and uncensored versions of the manifesto are in Macardle. op. cit., pp. 919-22.

21 B. Farrell, *The Founding of Dáil Eireann* (Dublin and London, 1971), chaps. 3 and 4.

22 J. L. McCracken, *Representative Government in Ireland* (London, 1958), pp. 20-1; F. S. L. Lyons, op. cit., pp. 451-3.

5. THE STRUGGLE FOR INDEPENDENCE (pp. 400-38)

1 For the attendance see the roll-call, in *Dáil Eireann: Minutes of Proceedings*, 21 Jan. 1919, pp. 10-12; also J. L. McCracken, *Representative Government in Ireland*, p. 22. The figure of thirty-six imprisoned members given in D. Macardle, *The Irish Republic*, p. 272 is incorrect, perhaps because two members elected for two constituencies each have been counted twice.

2 For the English version, see Macardle, op. cit., pp. 923-4.

3 The Declaration appears in Irish, French and English in *Dáil Eireann: Minutes of Proceedings*, pp. 14-16.

4 Ibid., pp. 17-20.

5 Ibid., pp. 21-3.

6 P. S. O'Hegarty, *A History of Ireland Under the Union*, p. 727. O'Hegarty was at this time a member of the IRB and stood very close to Michael Collins.

7 B. Farrell, *The Founding of Dáil Eireann*, p. 54; see also M. Comerford, *The First Dáil* (Dublin, 1971).

8 Ibid. See also Patrick Lynch, 'The Social Revolution that Never Was', in T. Desmond Williams (ed.), *The Irish Struggle, 1916-1926*, pp. 41-54. Collins though officially recorded as present at the inaugural meeting of the Dáil, was in fact absent on a secret mission which will be described presently. The most convincing summary of the argument is in B. Farrell, op. cit., pp. 56-61.

9 For a corrosive statement of the disillusionment of a subsequent generation at this and other failures to live up to the ideals of 1916, see Conor Cruise O'Brien, 'The Embers of Easter', in O. Dudley Edwards and F. Pyle (ed.), *1916: The Easter Rising*, pp. 225-40.

10 For Irish-American opinion and the presentation of the Irish case see the account, hostile to Devoy and Cohalan, by the then Irish envoy to the USA, Dr Patrick McCartan, *With de Valera to America* (Dublin, 1932). This hostility is repaid with interest (and combined with a bitter attack on Wilson) by Charles C. Transill, *America and the Fight for Irish Freedom*, chaps. viii, ix and x. There is a more recent and more balanced account by Alan J. Ward, 'America and the Irish Problem, 1899-1921', in *IHS* xvi, 83-6.

11 J. L. McCracken, *Representative Government in Ireland*, pp. 29-34.

12 Ibid., pp. 23-4.

13 R. Taylor, *Michael Collins*, Appendix C., pp. 245-6. The figure of £379,000, which is sometimes given, appears to be an overestimate.

14 D. Macardle, *The Irish Republic*, p. 981.

15 *Dáil Eireann: Minutes of Proceedings, 1919-1921*, pp. 178-80; *The Constructive Work of Dáil Eireann, No. 1: The National Police and Courts of Justice* (Dublin, 1921). See also the comments of V. T. H. Delany, *The Administration of Justice in Ireland* (Dublin, 2nd ed., 1965), pp. 38-9.

16 *Dáil Eireann: Minutes of Proceedings* (10 Apr. 1919), pp. 67-9.

17 For the decline of the RIC see the scholarly article by Richard Hawkins, 'Dublin Castle and the Royal Irish Constabulary, 1916-1922', in T. Desmond Williams (ed.), *The Irish Struggle*, pp. 167-81. For a more indulgent view of the force, see G. C. Duggan, 'The Royal Irish Constabulary', in O. Dudley Edwards and F. Pyle (ed.), *1916: The Easter Rising*, pp. 91-9.

18 *Dáil Eireann: Minutes of Proceedings* (10 Apr. 1919), p. 47.

19 Ibid. (20 Aug. 1919), pp. 151-3.

20 P. Béaslaí, *Michael Collins and the Making of Modern Ireland*, i, 377-8.

21 B. Taylor, *Michael Collins*, p. 12.

22 K. B. Nowlan, 'Dáil Eireann and the Army: Unity and Division', in T. Desmond Williams (ed.), *The Irish Struggle*, pp. 67-77. This is a very fair and perceptive survey of an extremely complex problem.

23 There is already a large literature on the Anglo-Irish war. A helpful summary of the earlier work on the subject – and the struggle itself – is to be found in C. L. Mowat, *Britain Between the Wars, 1918-1940* (London, 1955), chap. i, sections 15 and 16 and chap. ii, sections 1-8; see especially the *Note on Authorities on the Irish War* at the foot of p. 72. Two recent accounts contain in their bibliographies further guidance to the main printed sources. These are E. Holt, *Protest in Arms*, chap. xxv, and C. Younger, *Ireland's Civil War*, passim. Much work, however, remains to be done on the whole subject and this will not be possible

until the Irish archives – especially those of the Bureau of Military History – are made available to students.

24 *Constabulary Gazette*, 6 Sept. 1919, p. 90.

25 For English reactions see C. L. Mowat, 'The Irish Question in British Politics, 1916-1922', in T. Desmond Williams (ed.), *The Irish Struggle*, pp. 141-52. Since the first edition of this book appeared the whole subject of British opinion about Ireland in these critical years has been thoroughly investigated in D. G. Boyce, *Englishmen and Irish Troubles* (London, 1972).

26 It is fair to say that Crozier had a reputation for unreliability among some who knew him well; all the same, his resignation was decidedly inconvenient for the government (D. G. Boyce, op. cit., pp. 96-7.).

27 See the figures quoted in C. L. Mowat, *Britain Between the Wars*; also R. Hawkins, 'Dublin Castle and the Royal Irish Constabulary', in T. Desmond Williams (ed.), *The Irish Struggle*, pp. 178-9 and notes; G. C. Duggan, 'The Royal Irish Constabulary', in O. Dudley Edwards and F. Pyle (ed.), *1916: The Easter Rising*, pp. 96-9; E. Holt, *Protest in Arms*, p. 252, accepts Collins's figure of 3,000 but suggests that the total strength of the IRA was 112,000. It had indeed stood at or about this figure in the closing months of 1918, but it was a largely nominal figure thereafter, partly because of resignations and partly because of the sheer inertia in some areas of which Collins violently and repeatedly complained.

28 C. L. Mowat, *Britain Between the Wars*, p. 69; E. Holt, op. cit., p. 210.

29 C. Younger, *Ireland's Civil War*, pp. 116-17.

30 The best description of these events is James Gleeson, *Bloody Sunday* (London, 1962).

31 C. Younger, op. cit., p. 119.

32 Macardle, op. cit., p. 368; K. O'Doherty, *Assignment – America* (New York, 1957), pp. 132-4.

33 For the American visit, apart from the works by Macardle and O'Doherty already cited, see also D. R. Gwynn, *Eamon de Valera* (London, 1933) and Charles C. Tansell, *America and the Fight for Irish Freedom*. Details of finance are in Alan J. Ward, 'America and the Irish Problem, 1899-1921', in *IHS*, xvi, 88-9.

34 *Dáil Eireann: Minutes of Proceedings*, 25 Jan. 1921, pp. 240-1.

35 These preliminaries are clearly set out by T. P. O'Neill in his introduction to Frank Gallagher, *The Anglo-Irish Treaty* (London, 1965). For the British attitude at this crucial stage in the Anglo-Irish war, see D. G. Boyce, op. cit., chap. 4.

36 *Dáil Eireann: Minutes of Proceedings*, 25 Jan. 1921, pp. 240-1.

37 J. L. McCracken, *Representative Government in Ireland*, pp. 30-4.

38 For the speech, see Harold Nicolson, *King George V* (London, 1952), chap. xxi.

39 A. J. P. Taylor, *English History, 1914-1945* (Oxford, 1965), p. 157.

40 L. S. Amery, *My Political Life* (London, 1954), ii, 230. It has been also suggested that one of the guerrilla leaders in the south, Liam Lynch, had told Collins a month earlier that the war would have to end soon because of the shortage of arms, but this has been emphatically denied by other IRA officers (E. Holt, *Protest in Arms*, p. 255). Collins himself, on the other hand, was under no illusions. 'Once a truce is agreed and we come out into the open, it is extermination for us if the truce should fail . . . we shall be, in the event of a truce, like rabbits coming out

from their holes . . . (R. Taylor, *Michael Collins*, p. 110).

41 Lord Beaverbrook, *The Decline and Fall of Lloyd George* (London, 1963), p. 84.

42 These developments are chronicled in *Dáil Eireann: Official Report*, 16, 17 and 26 Aug. 1921, pp. 1-87.

43 D. Macardle, *The Irish Republic*, p. 491.

44 *Dáil Eireann: Official Report*, 16 Aug. 1921, pp. 7-8.

45 Ibid., 17 Aug. 1921, p. 15.

46 The correspondence is printed at length in Macardle, op. cit., chaps. xlix-lii.

47 F. Pakenham, *Peace by Ordeal*, pp. 177-9 for the session of October 24; also T. Jones, *Whitehall Diary, vol. iii, Ireland, 1918-1925*, ed. K. Middlemass (London, 1972), pp. 141-4.

48 Thomas Jones, *Whitehall Diary*, iii, 155-6.

49 For these discussions, and the notes made of them at the time, see R. Taylor, *Michael Collins*, pp. 144-6.

50 M. Forester, *Michael Collins: The Lost Leader* (London, 1971), pp. 248-50.

51 These crucial exchanges are set out in F. Pakenham, *Peace by Ordeal*, pp. 206-302 and in R. Taylor, *Michael Collins*, Appendix D, pp. 247-52.

6. THE GREAT DIVIDE (pp. 439-68)

1 Michael Collins writing to a friend on 6 Dec. 1921, cited in R. Taylor, *Michael Collins*, p. 152.

2 For these exchanges see D. Macardle, *The Irish Republic*, p. 596; also Earl of Longford and T. P. O'Neill, *Eamon de Valera* (London, 1970), pp. 166-70.

3 *Private Sessions of Second Dáil* (Dublin, n.d. [1972]), pp. 141-218.

4 *Official Report: Debate on the Treaty between Great Britain and Ireland Signed in London on 6 December 1921* (Dublin, n.d., hereafter cited as *Treaty Debates*), 19 Dec. 1921; pp. 20-3.

4 Ibid., pp. 24-7.

6 Ibid., pp. 27-8.

7 See above, p. 437.

8 P. S. O'Hegarty, *Ireland Since the Union*, p. 754.

9 *Treaty Debates*, pp. 36-42.

10 Ibid., pp. 42-8. See also T. de V. White, *Kevin O'Higgins* (Tralee, paperback edition, 1966), chap. vi.

11 Both versions are printed in *Private Sessions of Second Dáil*, pp. 317-24. The clauses omitted from the second version all dealt with Northern Ireland and in effect accepted the Treaty position on that subject.

12 *Treaty Debates*, 6 Jan. 1922, p. 274.

13 For examples of joint meetings see Ernest Blythe, 'Birth Pangs of a Nation', *Irish Times*, 19 and 20 Nov. 1968. This article a (review of Calton Younger's *Ireland's Civil War*) is a striking example of how even the most meticulous and recent research can still be supplemented by the recollections of men still living.

14 For this see R. Taylor, *Michael Collins*, pp. 174-5.

15 S. O Luing, *Art O Griofa* (Dublin, 1963), p. 395, based on information supplied by Ernest Blythe. Mr Blythe has confirmed this interpretation in 'Birth Pangs of a Nation', *Irish Times*, 19 Nov. 1968.

16 See *Irish Independent*, 17, 18 and 20 March 1922, for speeches at Dungarvan, Carrick-on-Suir, Thurles and Killarney.

17 The question of nomenclature presents a problem. Each side was reluctant to abandon the title, Irish Republican Army, though in practice this came in time to be identified more with the anti-Treaty forces. For the purposes of this study the pro-Treaty men will be called 'government forces' and their opponents anti-Treaty forces or 'Irregulars'. The origin of the latter term has been the subject of some dispute but it may first have been coined by Piaras Béaslaí.

18 For this interesting memorandum, see C. Younger, *Ireland's Civil War*, pp. 256-8.

19 P. Béaslaí, *Michael Collins and the Making of a New Ireland*, ii, 385-90.

20 Ibid., ii, 393-4.

21 Ernest Blythe, 'Birth Pangs of a Nation', *Irish Times*, 19 Nov. 1968. For Collins's own defence see his *The Path to Freedom* (Dublin, 1922), pp. 15-17. This follows the line already indicated – that the pact was 'a last effort on our part to avoid strife'. Blythe's recollections are also in S. O Luing, *Art O Griofa*, p. 396.

22 Cited in C. Younger, op. cit., pp. 285-6.

22 D. Macardle, *The Irish Republic*, p. 982, gives figures slightly more favourable to the republican side, but the difference amounts only to the transfer of one Independent to the republican total. The guerrilla leader, Dan Breen, appeared on both panels, but belongs more properly to the anti-Treaty side.

24 Ernest Blythe, 'Birth Pangs of a Nation', *Irish Times*, 19 Nov. 1968.

25 The evidence, which no historian could regard as completely conclusive, is gathered together in R. Taylor, *Assassination* (London, 1961). See especially chaps. iv and ix and the documents printed on pp. 207-19. It should be noted also, as Mr Taylor demonstrates, that Collins concerned himself closely with abortive plans for the rescue of Dunne and O'Sullivan. This in itself does not of course prove complicity; he would have done as much for any IRA men under sentence of death.

26 E. Neeson, *The Civil War in Ireland, 1922-1923* (Cork, revised paperback ed., 1969), p. 152.

27 For the circumstances surrounding the death of Collins – some of them strange enough to have led to the wildest rumours – see P. Béaslaí, *Michael Collins and the Making of a New Ireland*, ii, 418-42; R. Taylor, *Michael Collins*, pp. 197-211, 270-3; C. Younger, *Ireland's Civil War*, chap. xx; E. Neeson, *The Life and Death of Michael Collins* (Cork, 1968), pp. 98-142; M. Forester, *Michael Collins: the Lost Leader*, chap. 20.

29 For the policy of reprisals, see especially T. de V. White, *Kevin O'Higgins*, chap. viii and the articles already cited by Ernest Blythe in *Irish Times*, 19 and 20 Nov. 1968. The prison atmosphere at the time of the executions has been powerfully caught in Peadar O'Donnell, *The Gates Flew Open* (London, 1932; paperback ed., Cork, 1965).

28 Earl of Longford and T. P. O'Neill, *Eamon de Valera*, chap. 18. The phrase is taken from a letter de Valera wrote to a friend and colleague, P. J. Ruttledge, on 11 April 1923.

Part IV

1. BUILDING THE NEW STATE (pp. 471-510)

1 N. S. Mansergh, *The Irish Free State: Its Government and Politics* (London, 1934), p. 45. In practice, as Professor Mansergh points out (pp. 47-8), there were several instances in which the provisions of the Treaty conflicted with those of the Constitution.

2 L. Kohn, *The Constitution of the Irish Free State* (London, 1932), p. 172.

3 Articles 10 and 11 of the Constitution.

4 Article 8.

5 For this episode, see D. O'Sullivan, *The Irish Free State and its Senate* (London, 1940), pp. 75-82.

6 F. S. L. Lyons, 'The Minority Problem in the Twenty-six Counties', in F. J. Macmanus (ed.), *The Years of the Great Test, 1926-39* (Cork, 1967), pp. 92-103. Dr O'Sullivan, it is fair to add, has attached greater importance to the work of the Senate in its early years, particularly the contribution made by Lord Glenavy and Senator J. G. Douglas in upholding the Senate's position in relation to the Dáil – see especially *The Irish Free State and its Senate*, chaps. vi, viii and ix.

7 Articles 28 and 53.

8 Cited in B. Chubb, *The Government: An Introduction to the Cabinet System* (Dublin, 1968), p. 29. Professor Chubb's pamphlet is an admirable brief exposition of the evolution of the cabinet system in Ireland.

9 The status and powers of ministers are defined in Articles 51 and 59 of the Constitution; see also L. Kohn, op. cit., pp. 271-83, and N. S. Mansergh, op. cit., chap. ix.

10 Mansergh, op. cit., pp. 137-8; for the opposite view, that it was the post-1918 fashion which chiefly influenced the framers of the Free State Constitution, see Kohn, op. cit., p. 238.

11 Article 50 deals with constitutional amendments.

12 Article 47.

13 Kohn, op. cit., pp. 244-5.

14 B. Chubb, *The Government: An Introduction to the Cabinet System in Ireland*, p 29.

15 *Final Report of the Commission of Inquiry into the Civil Service* (1932-5), cited in B. Chubb (ed.), *A Source Book of Irish Government* (Dublin, 1964), p. 117.

16 Ibid., p. 118. In 1965 the total was just short of 32,000 (S. Finlay, *The Civil Service* (Dublin, 1966), p. 12).

17 In place of the Justice of the Peace, a new office, that of Peace Commissioner, was created for the performance of the non-judicial functions of the former JPs.

18 Article 66.

19 For the legal and judicial reforms see L. Kohn, *The Constitution of the Irish Free State*, pp. 336-63; N. S. Mansergh, *The Irish Free State: Its Government and Policies*, chap. xvii; V. T. H. Delany, *The Administration*

of *Justice in Ireland* (Dublin, 2nd revised ed., 1965), chaps. v and ix; B. Chubb (ed.), *A Source Book of Irish Government*, chap. xi.

20. B. Chubb (ed.), *A Source Book of Irish Government*, p. 261.

21 For local government in general, see N. S. Mansergh, op. cit., chap. xiii; also J. Collins (2nd ed. by D. Roche, Dublin, 1963), *Local Government*. There is a brief description in J. O'Donnell, *How Ireland Is Governed* (Dublin, 1965), chap. ix. For the principal provisions of the County Management Act of 1940 which made provision for every county to have or share a manager, see B. Chubb (ed.), *A Source Book of Irish Government*, pp. 282-7. It should perhaps be mentioned here that the trend towards centralisation, and perhaps also purification, of local government was reinforced by the establishment of the Local Appointments Commission in 1926 and by the development of bulk purchasing arrangements.

22 For his career see the sympathetic but penetrating biography by T. de V. White, *Kevin O'Higgins* (paperback ed., Dublin, 1966).

23 D. O'Sullivan, *The Irish Free State and its Senate*, pp. 138-41.

24 T. de V. White, *Kevin O'Higgins*, chap. x; T. P. Coogan, *Ireland Since the Rising*, pp. 56-60, supplies some new facts. It is proper to add that General Mulcahy remained entirely loyal to Mr Cosgrave and in fact re-entered the government in 1927. Mr McGrath attempted, with some other dissident members of Cumann na nGaedheal to form a new party, the National Party, and they resigned in a body from the Dáil. However, on offering themselves for re-election they were heavily defeated, the only mandate their party received from the electorate being, it has been said, 'a mandate to efface itself' (O'Sullivan, op. cit., p. 142). Mr McGrath, who was a man of great wealth and strong personality, became in 1930 the chief organiser of the Irish Hospitals Sweepstake and was largely responsible for its phenomenal success over the next thirty years.

25 It appears, however, that Mr Fisher did write quite freely to the wife of an Ulster Unionist MP about the progress of the Commission (St J. Ervine, *Craigavon: Ulsterman*, pp. 498-500). MacNeill, on the other hand, carried his scrupulous reticence so far as to keep his own cabinet colleagues completely in the dark; for his resignation speech see *Dáil Debates*, xii, 796-804.

26 T. de V. White, *Kevin O'Higgins*, p. 210.

27 The history of the Boundary Commission can be followed in T. de V. White, op. cit., chap. xii; D. O'Sullivan. *The Irish Free State and its Senate*, chap. xi; D. R. Gwynn, *The History of Partition, 1912-1925* (Dublin, (1950), chaps. vii-ix; Maureen Wall, 'Partition: The Ulster Question (1916-1926)', in T. D. Williams (ed.) *The Irish Struggle*, pp. 79-93.

28 For an account of the evolution of Sinn Féin, see P. Pyne, 'The third Sinn Féin party, 1923-26', in *Economic and Social Review*, vol. 1, Nos. 2 and 3 (1969-70).

29 For the budgetary problems of the government at this time, see D. R. Gwynn, *The Irish Free State, 1922-27*, (London, 1928), chap. xvii.

30 *Irish Independent*, 24 June 1927, cited in D. O'Sullivan, op. cit., p. 194.

31 T. de V. White, *Kevin O'Higgins*, pp. 240-2.

32 Statement to the press on behalf of the Fianna Fáil party, *Irish Times*, 11 Aug. 1927.

33 *Dáil Debates*, xii, 1101-2. For a slightly different wording based on Mr

de Valera's own written record, see Earl of Longford and T. P. O'Neill, *Eamon de Valera*, p. 256. On entering the Dáil Fianna Fáil promptly combined with Labour to obtain the necessary signatures for a 90-day suspension of the Electoral Amendment Bill to enable it to be submitted to a referendum. This should have been followed up by a petition signed by not less than one-twentieth of the voters, but this did not materialise and on 9 November 1927 the Bill became law. It had, however, been rendered virtually obsolete from the moment Fianna Fáil had taken its decision.

34 O'Sullivan, op. cit., pp. 219-20; T. P. Coogan, *Ireland Since the Rising*, pp. 65-6.
35 D. Nevin in *The Years of the Great Test*, pp. 56-7.
36 Cited in O'Sullivan, op. cit., p. 224.
37 For the speech at length see *Dáil Debates*, xxviii, 1398-1405.
38 E. Larkin, *James Larkin*, p. 288; T. P. Coogan, op. cit., pp. 256-9.
39 D. O'Sullivan, op. cit., pp. 255-65.
40 F. S. L. Lyons, 'The Minority Problem in the Twenty-six Counties', in F. MacManus (ed.), *The Years of the Great Test*, p. 102.
41 Cited by N. Mansergh, 'Ireland and the British Commonwealth of Nations', in T. Desmond Williams (ed.), *The Irish Struggle, 1916-1926*, p. 136; see also T. de V. White, *Kevin O'Higgins*, pp. 71-4.
42 Mansergh, op. cit., p. 135.
43 N. Mansergh, *Survey of British Commonwealth Affairs: Problems of External Policy, 1931-39* (London, 1952), pp. 10-11; the memorandum was originally published in C. M. van der Heever, *General J. B. M. Hertzog* (Johannesburg, 1946), p. 232
44 W. K. Hancock, *Survey of British Commonwealth Affairs, 1918-1939* (London, 1937), i, 147.
45 Ibid., i, 146.
46 Other examples of the same tendency were the appointment of diplomatic and consular representatives by the Irish Free State in various parts of the world and also the insistence of the Free State government on using its own Seal rather than the Great Seal of the Realm.
47 L. Kohn, *The Constitution of the Irish Free State*, pp. 71-2. The position was, however, more complex than this forthright statement would lead one to believe. For an indication of its ramifications see N. Mansergh, *The Irish Free State*, chaps. ii, iii and xv; also W. K. Hancock, op. cit., chap. iii, sections 1, 3 and 4.
48 In effect this became the situation in Ireland from the moment the first Governor-General (the indestructible T. M. Healy) was appointed. Not only did the Constitution succeed in eliminating the discretionary authority of the holder of the office, but the Free State government persistently maintained, long before this view was accepted by the Imperial Conference of 1930, that a Governor-General should not merely be acceptable to the government concerned but should only be appointed on the advice of that government. From 1930 onwards the dominions in general secured direct access to the King for this purpose (Mansergh, *The Irish Free State*, pp. 147-52).
49 *Report of the Inter-Imperial Relations Committee* (Cmd. 2768), p. 14.
50 T. de V. White, *Kevin O'Higgins*, pp. 222-3.
51 N. Mansergh, *Survey of British Commonwealth Affairs*, pp. 14-15.
52 T. de V. White, *Kevin O'Higgins*, p. 223.

53 D. W. Harkness, *The Restless Dominion* (London, 1969), chap. vi.
54 See generally K. C. Wheare, *The Statute of Westminster and Dominion Status* (London, 4th ed. 1949).
55 D. O'Sullivan, *The Irish Free State and its Senate*, pp. 253-4. It does not seem that Churchill had the best legal authorities on his side (Hancock, op. cit., i, 330-1).

2. THE ASCENDANCY OF DE VALERA (pp. 511-58)

1 For these exchanges, see W. K. Hancock, *Survey of British Commonwealth Affairs*, i, 320-50.
2 D. O'Sullivan, *The Irish Free State and its Senate*, pp. 291-4.
3 For the history of the right of appeal to the Judicial Committee of the Privy Council, see N. Mansergh, *The Irish Free State*, pp. 320-7; J. G. Latham, 'The Law and the Commonwealth', in Hancock, op. cit., i, 546-60. The irritation felt by O'Higgins and others on this subject is well described in D. W. Harkness, *The Restless Dominion* (London, 1969), chap. vi, and (in relation to the Imperial Conference of 1930), pp. 204-7.
4 Lord Hailsham in the House of Lords (25 July 1934), cited in Hancock, op. cit., i, 372.
5 *Moore and others v. Attorney-General for the Irish Free State*, 1935 A.C. 434, 51, T.L.R.
6 Hancock, op. cit., i, 373, citing the Attorney-General, Sir Thomas Inskip.
7 Ibid., i, 378-9.
8 They were entitled the Constitution (Amendment No. 27) Act and the Executive Authority (External Relations) Act respectively.
9 N. Mansergh, 'Ireland: External Relations 1926-1939, in *The Years of The Great Test*, p. 134.
10 N. Mansergh, 'Ireland and the British Commonwealth of Nations', in T. Desmond Williams (ed.), *The Irish Struggle, 1916-1926*, p. 139.
11 *Bunreacht na h Eireann*, Article 29, sections 2 and 5.
12 Hancock, op. cit., i, 327.
13 Cited in N. Mansergh, *Survey of British Commonwealth Affairs*, p. 305.
14 For this incident see T. Desmond Williams, 'De Valera in Power', in F. MacManus (ed.), *The Years of the Great Test*, pp. 30-1.
15 J. L. McCracken, *Representative Government in Ireland* (London, 1958), pp. 114-16. Professor McCracken has assembled evidence to show that once Fianna Fáil had consolidated its position, the lines of social cleavage between the two main parties tended to become blurred, though in his view Fine Gael (the later name of the Cosgrove party) 'is still in the main, the party of wealth, property and position'. See also B. Chubb, *The Government and Politics of Ireland* (London and Stanford, Cal., 1970), chap. 3; also M. Manning, *Irish Political Parties* (Dublin and London, 1972), chaps. 2 and 3.
16 D. Nevin, 'Labour and the Political Revolution', in F. MacManus (ed.) *The Years of the Great Test*, pp. 55-68. Mr Nevin, who is a Research Officer of the Irish Congress of Trade Unions, makes the point (p. 67) that even in Dublin, where trade unionists were heavily concentrated, the Labour party had negligible support. 'Loyalties born of the Civil War divisions', he writes, 'proved stronger than any class consciousness or any disposition to follow the political promptings of the trade union movement.'

17 *Irish Press*, 21 Jan. 1933.

18 While these figures indicate the extent to which Fianna Fáil had improved its position in the Dáil, the first preference votes showed that
Mr de Valera's party had won less than the other parties put together
– 689,043 against 697,326.

19 Quoted by D. Thornley, 'The Blueshirts' in *The Years of the Great Test*,
pp. 45, 49.

20 Statements on the National Guard by General O'Duffy, cited in M.
Manning, *The Blueshirts* (Dublin and London, 1971), chap. 3.

21 D. O'Sullivan, *The Irish Free State and its Senate*, pp. 407-8.

22 For a first-hand account of some of these incidents, see S. O'Callaghan,
The Easter Lily (London, revised ed., 1966), chap. xi; he maintains that
the Blueshirts retaliated in kind, whereas Dr O'Sullivan (op. cit., chap.
xix) emphasises their restraint under provocation; being less well-
armed than their opponents they probably were more restrained, but it
would be strange if sometimes their reactions had not been violent.

23 Cited in O'Sullivan, op. cit., p. 404.

24 M. C. Bromage, *De Valera and the March of a Nation* (London, paperback ed., 1967), pp. 129-30.

25 For these events, see D. O'Sullivan, op. cit., chap. xxv.

26 See T. P. Coogan, *The I.R.A.* (London, 1970), chaps. v to vii; also S.
O'Callaghan, *The Easter Lily* (revised, paperback ed., London, 1967),
chaps. xiii, xiv; and L. B. Bell, 'Ireland and the Spanish Civil War, 1936-
1939, in *Studia Hibernica*, No. 9 (1969), pp. 137-63.

27 M. MacSwiney, *The Republic of Ireland* (Cork n.d.), p. 34.

28 B. Chubb, *The Constitution of Ireland* (Dublin, 1966), p. 25.

29 For cabinet government see B. Chubb, *The Government: An Introduction
to the Cabinet System in Ireland* (Dublin, 2nd ed., 1968), chap. vii.

30 Under the Electoral Act of 1923 there were only ten constituencies with
less than five members out of a total of twenty-eight.

31 Cited in O'Sullivan, op. cit., p. 234.

32 Ibid., pp. 489-90. This involved special legislation – the Executive Powers
(Consequential Provisions) Act.

33 N. Mansergh, *Survey of British Commonwealth Affairs*, p. 297.

34 *Bunreacht na h Eireann*, preamble.

35 *Dáil Debates*, 14 June 1937, col. 430.

36 Article 12.

37 *Dáil Debates*, 11 May 1937, col. 51.

38 Article 26. Article 24, which provided for abridging the time allowed to
the Senate for consideration of Bills judged by the government to be
urgently and immediately necessary for the preservation of peace or in
case of emergency, could only be brought into operation by resolution of the Dáil or 'if the President, after consultation with the Council
of State, concurs'. Moreover, if dispute arose between the two Houses as
to whether a given Bill was or was not a Money Bill (the Dáil of
course had primary responsibility for, and control of, Money Bills) then
the Senate, by Article 22, could request the President to refer the
disputed Bill to a Committee of Privileges. The President, however,
after consultation with the Council of State, had the power to decide
whether to accede or not to accede to this request.

39 Article 27.

40 Article 13.

41 Article 13 (2) and 28 (10).
42 Articles 31 and 32.
43 Article 28 (10).
44 For his powers see Article 28; also B. Chubb (ed.), *A Source-book of Irish Government*, pp. 100-1.
45 B. Chubb, *The Government: An Introduction to the Cabinet System in Ireland*, p. 37.
46 *Dáil Debates*, vol. lxvii, col. 56.
47 Article 18 (7.1).
48 For stringent criticism, see B. Chubb, 'Vocational Represenation and the Irish Senate', in *Political Studies* (1954), ii, 97-111.
49 V. T. H. Delany, 'The Constitution of Ireland: Its Origins and Development' in *University of Toronto Law Journal* (1957), xii, 1-26.
50 Article 23 (1) (ii); Article 24 (1).
51 Article 16 (2).
52 J. C. Smyth, *The Houses of the Oireachtas* (Dublin, 1964), p. 9. For the delimitation of powers between the two houses, see chaps. vi to ix of Mr Smyth's pamphlet; also J. L. McCracken, *Representative Government in Ireland*, especially chaps. x to xii.
53 J. C. Smyth, op. cit., chap. ix.
54 Ibid., p. 50, referring to the period, 1958-62.
55 B. Chubb, *The Government and Politics of Ireland*, p. 195.
56 Article 50 (1).
57 See V. T. H. Delany, op. cit., pp. 13-14. As Professor Chubb has pointed out, there resulted from the fact that Article 58 was one of the 'transitory provisions' of the Constitution doomed to disappear after a certain lapse of time, the curious situation that the whole court system depended on an Article which was not to be found in copies of the Constitution printed between 1941 and 1961. In the latter year this anomaly was rectified by the enactment of the Courts (Establishment and Constitution) Act (B. Chubb, *The Constitution of Ireland*, pp. 30-1.)
58 V. T. H. Delany, op. cit., pp. 21-2.
59 The best analysis is in J. M. Kelly, *Fundamental Rights in the Irish Law and Constitution* (Dublin 1961). But see also B. Chubb, *The Constitution of Ireland*, chap. vii; D. Barrington, 'The Irish Constitution', in *Irish Monthly* (1952-3), vols. lxxxi and lxxxii; D. Costello, 'The Natural Law and the Constitution', in *Studies* (1956), xlv, 403-14; V. T. H. Delany, 'Fundamental Rights in the Constitution of Ireland', in *University of Malaya Law Review* (1960), ii, 17-18; V. Grogan, 'The Constitution and the Natural Law', in *Christus Rex* (Dublin, 1954), viii, 201-18.
60 See D. Barrington, 'The Irish Constitution', in *Irish Monthly*, vol. 80, pp. 133-4, 226-30, 268-72; J. M. Kelly, *Fundamental Rights*, especially pp. 25-30.
61 J. M. Kelly, op. cit., p. 33 and V. Grogan, 'Towards the New Constitution', in F. MacManus (ed.) *The Years of the Great Test*, pp. 170-1.
62 Articles 41 (2) (i and ii).
63 B. Chubb, *The Constitution of Ireland*, pp. 35-6.
64 N. Mansergh, *Survey of Commonwealth Affairs*, p. 302.
65 D. W. Harkness, *The Restless Dominion*, pp. 74-7.
66 Ibid., pp. 174-6.
67 T. de V. White, *Kevin O'Higgins*, p. 193.

68 *Peace and War: Speeches by Mr de Valera on International Affairs*, (Dublin, 1944), p. 10.
69 M. J. MacManus, *Eamon de Valera* (Dublin, 1944), p. 324.
70 *Peace and War*, pp. 45-6, 47-8.
71 Ibid., p. 50.
72 N. Mansergh, *Survey of Commonwealth Affairs*, p. 325.
73 *Peace and War*, p. 59.
74 Ibid., p. 62.
75 N. Mansergh, op. cit., p. 329.
76 *Peace and War*, p. 76.
77 Cited in Mansergh, op. cit., p. 332.
78 T. P. Coogan, *Ireland Since the Rising*, pp. 119-20.
79 J. W. Blake, *Northern Ireland in the Second World War* (Belfast, 1956), pp. 154-7; G. A. Hayes-McCoy, 'Irish Defence Policy, 1938-51, in K. B. Nowlan and T. Desmond Williams (ed.), *Ireland in the War Years and After* (London, 1969), pp. 39-51.
80 T. P. Coogan, op. cit., p. 119 *n*.
81 S. O'Callaghan, *The Easter Lily*, p. 168. During 1939 a German intelligence agent, Oskar Pfaus visited Ireland and J. O'Donovan, an IRA explosives expert, visited Germany.
82 Ibid., p. 173. There is an excellent account of the whole subject in E. Stephan, *Spies in Ireland* (London, 1963).
83 T. P. Coogan, op. cit., p. 274 *n*.
84 Part of the difficulty was to keep rolling-stock in repair. When the situation was reviewed after the war, it was found that the average age of the steam locomotives then in use was fifty-one years and that of passenger-coaches forty-eight years. (*Report of Committee of Inquiry into Internal Transport*, 1957 (Dublin), Pr. 4091, pp. 11-17.)

3. NEW BEGINNINGS (pp. 559-98)

1 Dr Browne's early career is sympathetically sketched in T. P. Coogan, *Ireland Since the Rising*, pp. 101-2; see also M. McInerney, 'Noel Browne: Church and State', in *University Review*, vol. v, no. 2 (Summer, 1968).
2 For General Mulcahy's part in these negotiations, see the remarks of Mr Costello in an interview with Michael McInerney, 'Mr John A. Costello Remembers', part 4, *Irish Times*, 7 Sept. 1967.
3 *Dáil Debates*, vol. 107, cols. 86-7.
4 J. A. Costello to F. S. L. Lyons, 6 Jan. 1967. This letter followed an interview Mr Costello was kind enough to give me on 2 Jan. 1967, at which we discussed this and other matters at considerable length.
5 Mr Costello made this point most emphatically to me in the interview mentioned in the previous footnote. See also his speech of 24 Nov. 1948 in *Dáil Debates*, vol. 113, cols. 347-87.
6 *Dáil Debates*, 20 July 1948, cited in *Irish Times*, 10 July, 1962.
7 *Dáil Debates*, 6 Aug. 1948, cited in *Irish Times*, 10 July, 1962.
8 J. A. Costello, *Ireland in International Affairs* (Dublin, n.d.), p. 27.
9 J. A. Costello to F. S. L. Lyons, 6 Jan. 1967.
10 *Sunday Independent*, 5 Sept. 1948.
11 *Sunday Independent*, 15 July, 1962; see also *Sunday Independent*, 1 Nov. 1970.

12 J. A. Costello to F. S. L. Lyons, 6 Jan. 1967.
13 On this point, see Nicholas Mansergh, 'Irish Foreign Policy, 1945-1951', in K. B. Nowlan and T. D. Williams (ed.), *Ireland in the War Years and After, 1938-51* (Dublin and London, 1969), p. 140.
14 *Dáil Debates*, vol. 113, cols. 347-87.
15 Cited by C. Cruise O'Brien, 'The Embers of Easter', in O. Dudley Edwards and F. Pyle (ed.), *1916: The Easter Rising*, p. 230.
16 Nicholas Mansergh, op. cit., pp. 142-3.
17 Nicholas Mansergh, *Survey of British Commonwealth Affairs: Problems of Imperial Policy, 1931-39* (London, 1952), p. 272.
18 Patrick Pearse, 'The Spiritual Nation', in *The Complete Works of P. H. Pearse: Political Writings and Speeches*, p. 299.
19 'Mr John A. Costello Remembers', in *Irish Times*, 7 Sept. 1967.
20 P. Lynch, 'The Irish Economy in the Post-war Era', in K. B. Nowlan and T. Desmond Williams (ed.), *Ireland in the War Years and After*, p. 198. Mr Dillon's energy overflowed in many other directions also, including a new drive to promote agricultural education at the parish level and an imaginative attempt to co-operate with the Northern Ireland government in the development of the Foyle fisheries which lay on both sides of the border.
21 *Report of the Commission on Emigration and Other Problems* (Dublin, 1954), Pr. 2541, chap. vi.
22 T. Gray, *Ireland's Answer* (London, 1966), p. 330.
23 *Report of the Commission on Emigration*, chap. vi; B. Hensey, *The Health Services of Ireland* (Dublin, 1959), pp. 105, 134.
24 P. Lynch, op. cit., p. 187.
25 Ibid., p. 194.
26 *Bunreacht na h Eireann*, Article 41. See also pp. 539-41 above.
27 The essential documents are printed in *Irish Times*, 12 Apr. 1951; see also the *Dáil Debates* for the whole of that month. This, and much more relevant information, is brought together in J. H. Whyte, *Church and State in Modern Ireland, 1923-1970* (Dublin and London, 1971), chap. 7.
28 J. H. Whyte, op. cit., chap. 9.
29 'Mr John A. Costello Remembers', in *Irish Times*, 7 Sept. 1967.
30 See the valuable articles by T. Desmond Williams in the *Leader* 31 Jan. to 25 Apr. 1953 and in the *Irish Press*, 27 June to 17 July, 1953. There is a more extended analysis in V. P. Hogan, *The Neutrality of Ireland in World War II* (Michigan, 1953).
31 A contemporary description of his activities by the *Leader*, cited by C. Cruise O'Brien, 'Ireland in International Affairs', in O. Dudley Edwards (ed.), *Conor Cruise O'Brien Introduces Ireland*, p. 123.
32 *Dáil Debates*, vol. cxiv, cols 323-6.
33 Nicholas Mansergh, 'Irish Foreign Policy, 1945-1951', in K. B. Nowlan and T. Desmond Williams (ed.), *Ireland in the War Years and After, 1938-1951*, p. 137.
37 *Dáil Debates*, vol. clix, cols 127-226. For a critical analysis of the 'Three Principles', see C. Cruise O'Brien, 'Ireland in International Affairs', pp. 127-34. This essay, though written some years after the events it describes, deserves to be regarded as in some sense a primary source.
35 *Ireland at the United Nations: Speeches by Mr Frank Aiken* (Dublin,

1960), pp. 3-5.
36 C. Cruise O'Brien, *To Katanga and Back* (London, 1962), chap. i.
37 *Ireland at the United Nations: Speeches by Mr Frank Aiken* (Dublin, 1959), pp. 29 et. seq.
38 Tony Gray, *The Irish Answer* (London, 1966), p. 366.

4. THE QUEST FOR PROSPERITY (pp. 599-634)

1 Cited by James Meenan, 'From Free Trade to Self-Sufficiency', in F. MacManus (ed.), *The Years of the Great Test* (Cork, 1967), p. 70.
2 For the effects of the tariff upon industry, see George O'Brien, 'Industries', in *Sáorstat Eireann: Official Handbook* (Dublin, 1932), chap. xv; also *Report of the Commission of Inquiry into Banking, Currency and Credit*, 1938 (P. no. 2628), pp. 58-64; and J. Meenan, *The Irish Economy Since 1922* (Liverpool, 1970), p. 132.
3 *Report of the Banking, Currency and Credit Commission*, pp. 25, 58-68; *Reports of the Commission on Emigration and other Population Problems, 1948-1954* (Pr. 2541), p. 31.
4 R. D. Crotty, *Irish Agricultural Production: Its Volume and Structure* (Cork, 1966), Appendix II, p. 353.
5 Derived from *Reports of Emigration Commission*, Table 23, p. 38.
6 Ibid., p. 43; T. K. Whitaker, *Economic Development*, p. 55.
7 *Reports of Emigration Commission*, pp. 34-5; J. Meenan, op. cit., p. 41, has slightly different figures.
8 *Reports of Emigration Commission*, p. 42. The nineteenth century calculations were made by H. Stäehle, 'Statistical Notes on the Economic History of Irish Agriculture, 1847-1913', in *Journal of the Statistical and Social Inquiry Society of Ireland* (May, 1951), xviii, 444-71.
9 Derived from *Report of Commission on Banking and Credit*, pp. 37-8, 107, 109-10.
11 Crotty, *Irish Agricultural Production*, p. 90. For a detailed analysis of the economic effects of owner-occupancy upon Irish agriculture, see chap. iv of that book. Two other aspects of farming that suggest reluctance to invest are machinery and fertilizers. Up to 1929, at least, the evidence points to an overwhelming reliance upon draught animals on farms; in that year 436,000 horses and 202,000 mules, jennets and asses were in use. Thirty-five years later these had declined to 190,000 and 82,000 respectively, the change being mainly due to the introduction of 40,000 tractors (Crotty, op. cit., p. 161). As for fertilizers, though they had been used in one form or another from the mid-nineteenth century, the amount spent on them was certainly inadequate, especially in the vital areas of pasture. Even as late as 1948 a foreign observer commented that 'in any attempt to estimate the fertilizer requirements of Irish grasslands one is dumbfounded by the magnitude of the problem' (T. K. Whitaker, *Economic Development*, p. 65).
12 Crotty, op. cit., p. 91.
13 K. H. Connell, 'Peasant-Marriage in Ireland: Its Structure and Development Since the Famine', in *Econ. Hist. Rev.*, 2nd series (1961-2), xiv, 503-23; also Crotty, op. cit., pp. 91-2, who makes the point that since the farm itself would descend to only one child, there was an element

of equity in using the dowry of benefit others if possible. The same argument would apply to any means taken to improve living standards, whether through more varied diet, the purchase of a car, or a wireless-set. Such improvement would be shared among the whole family.

14 Reports of the Emigration Commission, pp. 84-5; Crotty, op. cit., pp. 104-5.
15 Report of Banking, Currency and Credit Commission, p. 14.
16 Sáorstát Eiieann: Official Handbook, p. 95; Crotty, op. cit., p. 113.
17 T. K. Whitaker, Economic Development, chap. xii; Sáorstát Eireann: Official Handbook, pp 119-27; Crotty, op. cit., p. 120. A more favourable view of the Department of Agriculture's record is given by one of its late officials, D. Hoctor, The Depa:tment: a History of the Department of Agriculture (Dublin, 1971), especially chaps. 5 and 6.
18 The working of the Agricultural Credit Corporation in its early years is detailed in Report of the Commission on Banking, Currency and Credit, pp. 251-63.
19 Ibid., p. 35.
20 Ibid., pp. 62-4, 109-110. It appears that industrial wages in a number of trades in Dublin held up exceptionally well; between 1929 and 1936 they may have even have been better maintained than comparable wages in London.
21 Ibid., p. 640; Reports of the Emigration Commission, pp. 33-4.
22 Reports of the Emigration Commission, p. 10, Table 3 and p. 20, Table 11; see also Census of Population, 1961 and D. O'Mahony, The Irish Economy (Cork, 2nd ed., 1967), p. 4.
23 Cited by James Meenan, 'From Free Trade to Self-Sufficiency', in F. MacManus (ed.), The Years of the Great. Test (Cork, 1967), p. 74.
24 For this account I have drawn upon a summary of the dispute made for the use of the British cabinet in July 1935 by the Dominions Secretary, Malcolm MacDonald, and also upon Mr MacDonald's memorandum, 'Relations with the Irish Free State', drafted for the cabinet in May 1936 (PRO 1517, Cabinet Papers 24/262). I am indebted to Dr D. Harkness for drawing my attention to these documents. For the general history of the dispute, see the admirable analysis by W. K. Hancock, Survey of British Commonwealth Affairs, 1918-1939 (London, 1937), vol. 1, chap. vi; also Report of the Banking, Currency and Credit Commission, pp. 89-91, and N. Mansergh, Survey of British Commonwealth Affairs (London, 1952), pp. 307-12.
25 Hancock, Survey of Commonwealth Affairs, i, 356.
26 Report of Banking, Currency and Credit Commission, pp. 91-2; see especially the graph of price movements on p. 91.
27 Ibid., p. 89.
28 Ibid., p. 84. A more tentative estimate by Hancock (Survey of Commonwealth Affairs, i, 358) reckoned that the Free State's excess of external assets over debits sank from £88 million to £74 million during the same period.
29 Hancock, op. cit., pp. 364, 367 n. 2; Mansergh,·op. cit., p. 308.
30 Report of the Banking, Currency and Credit Commission, p. 53.
31 The agreements are printed in N. Mansergh (ed.), Documents and Speeches on British Commonwealth Affairs, 1931-1952 (London, 1953), pp. 367-76.

32 Crotty, *Irish Agricultural Production*, p. 134.
33 Hancock, *Survey of Commonwealth Affairs*, i, 359. It has been estimated that in 1937 Ireland stood fourth in a list of the relative tariff levels in twenty countries. Only Spain, Turkey, Germany and Brazil had higher tariffs (W. J. L. Ryan, 'Measurement of Tariff Levels for Ireland', *JSSISI* (1948-9), xviii, 130).
34 For details of these credit operations, see *Report of the Banking, Currency and Credit Commission*, pp. 56, 267-80. In a different direction, the government also sought to develop industry by making it more attractive to those who worked in it. Thus the Conditions of Employment Act (1936) sought to fix maximum working hours per week and also provided for holidays with pay for certain categories of employee. In the same way, the Control of Prices Act (1957) attempted, though with questionable success, to mitigate for the consumer some of the more unpleasant effects of tariffs on home prices.
35 Ibid., 319-20, 350-52.
36 *Sáorstát Eireann: Official Handbook*, pp. 157-62; also the unpublished thesis by Miss U. Munikanon, 'The Use of State-Sponsored Bodies in the Exploitation of the Natural Resources in Ireland', pp. 61-8, 105-30.
37 Garret FitzGerald, *State-Sponsored Bodies* (Dublin, second ed., 1963), p. 5.
38 Ibid., p. 7.
39 Ibid., pp. 2-3.
40 *Report of the Banking, Currency and Credit Commission*, pp. 58-60; Crotty, *Irish Agricultural Production*, pp. 135-6, citing the *Statistical Abstracts* (1935), p. 70 and (1940), p. 83; J. Meenan, op. cit., p. 57.
41 *Report of the Banking, Currency and Credit Commission*, pp. 66-7; Crotty, op. cit., p. 137.
42 Crotty, op. cit., p. 137.
43 *Report of the Banking, Currency and Credit Commission*, pp. 109-10.
44 Crotty, op. cit., pp. 137-8.
45 Ibid., pp. 141-2; Hancock, op. cit., pp. 360-1; J. Meenan, 'From Free Trade to Self-Sufficiency', in *The Years of the Great Test*, p. 78, where by a misprint the wheat acreage for 1931 appears as 2,000.
46 Crotty, *Irish Agricultural Production*, pp. 141-55.
47 Ibid., p. 156. The chief barrier against a major increase in cattle exports was that, given the extensive methods of cattle production used in Ireland, it could only be achieved by a contradiction of the area devoted to other forms of agriculture – in short by upsetting the equilibrium which had established itself in Irish farming over many years. In war conditions, with renewed emphasis on tillage, this barrier to increased cattle production was of course still further heightened. For the achievement of equilibrium, or 'stability' in Irish farming, see Crotty, chap. iv.
48 Ibid., pp. 131, 156.
49 John Healy, *The Death of an Irish Town* (Cork, 1968), p. 17.
50 *Reports of the Emigration Commission*, p. 115; also the summary in D. O'Mahony, *The Irish Economy*, p. 4.
51 Crotty, op. cit., pp. 158-9.
52 *Reports of the Emigration Commission*, pp. 38-9; Crotty, op. cit., p. 353.
53 *Reports of the Emigration Commission*, p. 42.

54 T. K. *Whitaker, Economic Development*, p. 15; J. Meenan, *The Irish Economy Since 1922*, p. 84. P. Lynch, in *Ireland in the War Years and After* (ed. K. B. Nowlan and T. Desmond Williams), p. 196, reckoned gross Irish sterling assets at 'around £430 million'; for the figure in the text, see Crotty, op. cit., p. 166.

55 Whitaker, op. cit., pp. 10-20; Crotty, op. cit., pp. 163-4.

56 *Census of Population, 1961* (Pr. 6991), vol. i, Table 1; Crotty, op. cit., pp. 165-6.

57 Crotty, op. cit., p. 160.

58 *Reports of the Emigration Commission*, pp. 41-2; Crotty, op. cit., p. 160. The estimates relating to the nineteenth and early twentieth centuries are by H. Stäehle, 'Statistical Notes on the Economic History of Irish Agriculture, 1847-1913', in *JSSISI* (May, 1951), xviii, 444-71.

59 Whitaker, *Economic Development*, pp. 101-3; Crotty, op. cit., pp. 167-78.

60 Crotty, op. cit., pp. 187-8.

61 Ibid., p. 187. The involved technical argument underlying this assertion will be found in chap. vii of Mr Crotty's book.

62 *Programme for Economic Expansion* (Pr. 4796), especially pp. 26-7, 35-45.

63 D. O'Mahony, *The Irish Economy*, pp. 4. 182-3; O. MacDonagh, *Ireland* (New Jersey), (1968), p. 133; J. Meenan, *The Irish Economy Since 1922*, p. 206.

64 Crotty, *Irish Agricultural Production*, chap. viii; see also G. FitzGerald, *Planning in Ireland* (London and Dublin, 1968), p. 45.

65 See the summary of objectives in *Second Programme for Economic Expansion*, Part I (Pr. 7239), p. 17 and also the estimate of future exports on p. 57. The figures for industrial and agricultural growth for the period 1964-70 are taken from the revised tables in *Second Programme for Economic Expansion*, Part II (Pr. 7670), Appendix I, p. 298. See also the criticisms by G. FitzGerald, *Planning in Ireland*, chap. 8.

66 See *Second Programme for Economic Expansion: Review of Progress, 1964-7* (Pr. 9949), especially the first three chapters.

67 *Review of 1971 and Outlook for 1972* (1972) (Pr. 2357), Table 7, p. 86.

68 Ibid., pp. 27, 33.

5. PROBLEMS OF SOCIAL POLICY (pp. 635-93)

1 P. H. Pearse, 'O'Donovan Rossa: Graveside Oration', in *Collected Works: Political Writings and Speeches*, p. 135.

2 *Census of Population of Ireland, 1961*, vol. ix, Table 2; *An Coimisiun um Atribheochan na Gaelige* (Commission on the restoration of the Irish language), Summary, in English, of Final Report, July 1963 (Pr. 7256), p. 10.

3 B. O Cuiv, 'Education and Language', in T. Desmond Williams (ed.), *The Irish Struggle, 1916-1926*, pp. 160-1.

4 Ibid., pp. 162-3.

5 Ibid., p. 163. As Professor O Cuiv points out this programme was even more ambitious than the Gaelic League proposals of 1920.

6 T. J. McElligott, *Education in Ireland*, pp. 30-1.

7 Ibid., p. 19.

8 *Commission on the Restoration of the Irish Language*, Final Report (English summary), pp. 11-12; T. P. Coogan, *Ireland Since the Rising*, p. 194.

,9 *Commission on the Restoration of the Irish Language*, Final Report, pp. 11-12; T. J. McElligott, op. cit., pp. 34-5. The high-water mark for primary schools teaching through Irish was about 1939, when the number was 704. Thereafter it fell steeply and by 1951 had dropped to 523; the figure for 1960-1 therefore represents an accentuation of a long-continuing trend.

10 *Athbeochan na Gaelige* (government white paper on the restoration of the Irish Language), 1965 (Pr. 8061), p. 56; T. J. McElligott, op. cit., pp. 33-4.

11 *Athbeochan na Gaelige*, Appendix, pp. 172-81. But note on the other side the criticism that of moneys made available for capital investment in the Republic (4½ million by March 1961), the Gaeltacht received only £33,000.

12 *Comhairle na Gaelige, Local Government and Development Institutions for the Gaeltacht* (Dublin, 1971); *Review of 1971 and Outlook for 1972*, p. 58-9.

13 Desmond Fennell, 'Language Revival: Is It Already a Lost Cause?', in *Irish Times* (supplement), 27 Jan. 1969. The distinguished folklorist, Kevin Danaher, put the number as low as 50,000 in 1969. See his article 'The Gaeltacht' in B. O Cuiv (ed.), *A View of the Irish Language* (Dublin, 1969), especially pp. 118-19.

14 *Commission on the Restoration of the Irish Language*. Final Report, p. 38.

15 For a brief survey of these new developments, see T. P. Coogan, *Ireland Since the Rising*, pp. 198-205.

16 B. O Cuiv, *Irish Dialects and Irish-Speaking Districts* (Dublin, 1951), pp. 31-2.

17 *Census of Population of Ireland, 1961*, vol. ix, Tables 1 and 2.

18 For the contemporary situation, see Tony Gray, *The Irish Answer*, chap. x; T. P. Coogan, op. cit., chap. ix; Donald S. Connery (London, 1968), pp. 154-9; Máire Cruise O'Brien, 'The Two Languages', in O. Dudley Edwards (ed.), *Conor Cruise O'Brien Introduces Ireland*, pp. 43-60; Desmond Fennell, article already cited in *Irish Times* supplement, 27 Jan. 1969.

19 *Investment in Education: Report of the Survey Team Appointed by the Minister for Education in October, 1962* (Pr. 8311), pp. 6-7, 246-7. The figures are as at 1 Feb. 1964.

20 Ibid., pp. 88, 91-2; T. J. McElligott, *Education in Ireland*, pp. 24-5, 153-4.

21 T. J. McElligott, op. cit., pp. 24-9.

22 Ibid., pp. 20-1.

23 *Investment in Education*, p. 226, Table 9.2.

24 T. J. McElligott, op. cit., pp. 38, 50; see also *Investment in Education*, p. 247, for slightly more recent, and slightly more favourable, figures.

25 *Council of Education Report*, 1960, p. 64.

26 *Investment in Education*, pp. 10-11.

27 Ibid., chap. iii, Table 1.1 on p. 4, and pp. 11-15; T. J. McElligott, op. cit., chap. iii.

28 *Investment in Education*, pp. 276-80.

29 T. J. McElligott, *Education in Ireland*, pp. 68-9, 76-82, 96-7. Spanish,

Italian and German are exempt from this generalisation, but they are taken by only a tiny handful of students.

30 These are the calculations of Dr Valentine Rice, Professor of Education in the University of Dublin. See his article, 'Education in Ireland', in O. Dudley Edwards (ed.), *Conor Cruise O'Brien Introduces Ireland*, pp. 170-8. The fate of the different categories of school-leavers is minutely examined in *Investment in Education*, pp. 111-47.

31 V. Rice, op. cit., p. 173. The situation regarding university entrants is also analysed in depth in *Commission on Higher Education, 1960-67 Report*, 11, p. 760-4.

32 See on this, *Investment in Education*, pp. 148-76; *Commission on Higher Education, Report*, 11, pp. 725-8 and 760-4.

33 For criticisms of the various new proposals, see N. Atkinson, *Irish Education*, chap. 7, and G. FitzGerald, *Towards a New Ireland* (London, 1972), pp. 49-50.

34 *Commission on Higher Education, Report*, 11, pp. 855-60 ('Conclusion'); for university statistics, see also T. J. McElligott, op. cit., chap. iv.

35 J. H. Newman, *The Idea of a University* (Image Books Edition, New York, 1959), pp. 171-2.

36 For these developments see B. Hensey, *The Health Services of Ireland* (Dublin, 1959), chap. i; also *The Child Health Services: Report of a Study Group appointed by the Minister for Health*, 1967 (Pr. 171), chaps. 1 and 2.

37 B. Hensey, op. cit., p. 17.

38 Ibid., pp. 44-7.

39 Ibid., pp. 49-50.

40 Ibid., pp. 60-1; R. P. Kaim-Caudle, *Social Policy in the Irish Republic*, pp. 26-7, reckons the average percentage receiving free medical treatment at the time of his study (1967) to have been thirty.

41 B. Hensey, op. cit., p. 24.

42 See especially the informative articles, 'Mental Illness', by Michael Viney, originally printed in the *Irish Times*, 1963, and later published separately (Dublin, 1964); also the brief account in Donald Connery, *The Irish*, pp. 146-8; and *Report of Commission of Inquiry on Mental Illness*, 1966 (Pr. 9181), passim. It should be added that a subsequent inquiry found that the provision of beds for psychiatric patients was 'generally considered excessive' and explained this mainly in terms of the necessity for providing for senile patients with nowhere else to go (*Report of the Consultative Council on the Health Services*, 1968 (Pr. 154), p. 72). The numbers in health board psychiatric hospitals have recently declined quite sharply, from just over 19,000 at the end of 1960 to just under 15,000 at the end of 1971 (*Review of 1971 and Outlook for 1972*, pp. 70-2).

43 R. P. Kaim-Caudle, *Social Policy in the Irish Republic*, pp. 29-35.

45 D. Farley, *Social Insurance and Social Assistance in Ireland* (Dublin, 1964), passim and Appendix II. By 1966 the top-rate for old-age pensions had risen from 35 shillings (£1.75) to 47/6 (£2.37½).

46 Ibid., chap. xi.

47 See the revealing table of comparisons in R. P. Kaim-Caudle, *Social Policy in the Irish Republic*, pp. 114-15.

48 Ibid., pp. 47-8; see also the elaborate tables in the same author's paper, 'Social Security in Ireland and in Western Europe', Economic and Social

Research Institute (Dublin, 1964), p. 15.

49 For the various categories, see D. Farley, op. cit., pp. 84-7; *Review of 1971 and Outlook for 1972*, p. 76.

50 R. P. Kaim-Caudle, *Social Policy in the Irish Republic*, p. 61.

51 R. P. Kaim-Caudle, 'Social Security in Ireland and in Western Europe', p. 17; G. FitzGerald, *Towards a New Ireland*, p. 186.

52 R. P. Kaim-Caudle, *Social Policy in the Irish Republic*, p. 64.

53 Ibid., pp. 114-15.

54 D. Farley, op. cit., pp. 5-7; B. Hensey, *The Health Services of Ireland*, chap. ix.

55 The exact figure appears to have been 189,000. See R. Roberts, 'Trade Union Organisation in Ireland', *JSSISI* (1958-9), xx, part ii, pp. 93-111.

56 For a recent assessment, see Arthur Mitchell, 'William O'Brien, 1881-1968, and the Irish Labour movement', in *Studies* (Nos. 239-40, autumn-winter, 1971), pp. 311-31. O'Brien's memoirs, *Forth the Banners Go*, were edited by E. McLysaght (Dublin, 1969).

57 E. Larkin, *James Larkin*, p. 262.

58 David Thornley, 'The Development of the Irish Labour Movement', in *Christus Rex* (1964), xviii, 16.

59 R. Roberts, op. cit., reckons affiliated membership at 92,000 in 1929; Professor Larkin, whose estimate of contributions I follow in the text, places membership even lower – at 85,000 by 1929 (*James Larkin*, p. 286 n).

60 M. Manning, *Irish Political Parties*, p. 71.

61 D. Nevin, 'Industry and Labour', in K. B. Nowlan and T. Desmond Williams (ed.), *Ireland in the War Years and After*, p. 95; for the difficulties of obtaining accurate figures see D. O'Mahony, 'Industrial Relations in Ireland: the Background', Economic and Social Research Institute Paper, no. 19 (May 1964).

62 Cited in D. Nevin, op. cit., p. 98.

63 Ibid., pp. 98-104.

64 R. Roberts, op. cit., p. 95.

65 Ibid., p. 95. The total number of trade unionists in the Republic in 1958 was estimated at 291,000 (D. O'Mahony, op. cit., p. 9).

66 R. P. Mortished, 'The Industrial Relations Act, 1946', in *Public Administration in Ireland*, iii.

67 See the estimate in D. O'Mahony, *The Irish Economy*, p. 70; see also the table in the same author's article, 'Industrial Relations in Ireland: the Background', p. 9.

68 D. W. Bleakley, 'The Northern Ireland Trade Union Movement', in *JSSISI* (1953-4), xix, 159-69; R. J. Lawrence, *The Government of Northern Ireland* (Oxford, 1965), p. 30.

69 D. P. Barritt and C. F. Carter, *The Northern Ireland Problem* (London, 1962), p. 142.

70 Tony Gray, *The Irish Answer*, p. 235; P. Blanshard, *The Irish and Catholic Power* (London, 1954), pp. 89-90.

71 Cited in D. Connery, *The Irish*, p. 138. See also the illuminating essay, 'Dublin's Archbishop', in D. Fennell (ed.), *The Changing Face of Catholic Ireland* (London, 1968), pp. 109-20.

72 The best evidence for the continued vitality of the reform movement is in the periodicals – chiefly *Christus Rex*, *The Furrow* and the Jesuit quarterly, *Studies*. See also the penetrating essay by S. Mac-

Reamoinn, 'The Religious Position', in O. Dudley Edwards (ed.), *Conor Cruise O'Brien Introduces Ireland*, pp. 61-70. For more pessimistic appraisals, see Sean O'Faoláin, *The Irish* (revised ed., London, 1969), and a very angry but curiously appealing book by Michael Sheehy, *Is Ireland Dying?* (London, 1968).

73 *Second Programme for Economic Expansion*, Part I (P. 7239), 1963, pp. 43-4; D. Connery, *The Irish*, p. 39.

Part IV, B

1. GROWING PAINS OF DEVOLUTION (pp. 695-705)

1 See especially the speech of Charles Curtis Craig, brother of Sir James Craig on 29 March 1920 in Hansard, H.C. debates, 5th series, vol. cxxvii, cols. 189-90.

2 *Correspondence between His Majesty's Government and the Prime Minister of Northern Ireland Relating to the Proposals for an Irish Settlement* (Cmd. 1561), 1921.

3 The best brief account of the Special Powers Act is by F. H. Newark, 'The Law and the Constitution', in Thomas Wilson (ed.), *Ulster Under Home Rule* (London, 1955), pp. 46-51.

4 R. J. Lawrence, *The Government of Northern Ireland: Public Finance and Public Services, 1921-1964* (Oxford, 1965).

5 N. Mansergh, *The Government of Northern Ireland* (London, 1936), pp. 166-7.

6 Cited in R. J. Lawrence, op. cit., p. 45; for the figures cited in the text, see pp. 41-3 of his book.

7 *Final Report of the Northern Ireland Special Arbitration Committee* (Cmd. 2073), 1925.

8 R. J. Lawrence, *The Government of Northern Ireland*, p. 61. Chapter iii of his book is an excellent guide to the financial intricacies of devolution. See also N. Mansergh, *The Government of Northern Ireland*, chap. x and T. Wilson (ed.), *Ulster Under Home Rule*, chap. vi.

2. THE DEPRESSION YEARS (pp. 706-14)

1 K. S. Isles and N. Cuthbert, 'Ulster's Economic Structure', in T. Wilson (ed.), *Ulster Under Home Rule*, pp. 96-7. See also *Report of Emigration Commission*, p. 3, for the earlier figures of the population of the six counties; the same Report suggests an annual average emigration of about 5,000 for 1926-37, which would give a total nearer 50,000.

2 L. O Nualláin, 'A Comparison of the Economic Position and Trend in Eire and Northern Ireland', in *JSSISI* (1942-7), xvii, pp. 504-40.

3 K. S. Isles and N. Cuthbert, *An Economic Survey of Northern Ireland* (Belfast, 1957), pp. 58, 515-16.

4 K. S. Isles, 'Northern Ireland: An Economic Survey', in T. W. Moody (ed.), *Ulster Since 1800* (London, 1954), p. 113; Isles and Cuthbert, *An Economic Survey of Northern Ireland*, p. 53.

5 L. O Nualláin, op. cit; even in 1945 eighty per cent of Northern Ireland farms did not exceed fifty acres (Isles and Cuthbert, *An Economic Survey of Northern Ireland*, p. 55).

6 K. S. Isles and N. Cuthbert, 'Economic Policy', in T. Wilson (ed.), *Ulster Under Home Rule*, p. 143. See also L. P. F. Smith, 'Recent Developments in Northern Irish Agriculture', in *JSSISI* (1947-52), xviii, pp. 143-60.

7 N. Mansergh, *The Government of Northern Ireland*, pp. 202-3. Annuities dating from the post-1920 period were also collected by the local government, but were set off by an equivalent deduction from the province's share of the reserved taxes; see also F. S. L. Lyons, 'The Twentieth Century', in T. W. Moody (ed.), *Ulster Since 1800*, II (London, 1957), p. 55.

8 Isles and Cuthbert, in *Ulster Under Home Rule*, pp. 138-40; L. P. F. Smith, op. cit., emphasises the element of compulsion in the pre-war marketing legislation of Northern Ireland. For figures of output see the articles by L. O Nualláin and L. P. F. Smith already cited; also Table ix (XVI) in Isles and Cuthbert, *An Economic Survey of Northern Ireland*, p. 291. The latter authorities reckon that the index number of the value of agricultural produce in the pre-war years (1936-7 to 1938-9) was forty-one compared with one hundred for 1945-6. Calculating pre-war *net* output at 1945-6 prices, they estimate the value to have been £31.3 million.

9 *Report of the Agricultural Enquiry Committee* (N.I., Cmd. 249, 1947), p. 212.

10 Isles and Cuthbert, *An Economic Survey of Northern Ireland*, (p. 227).

11 Ibid., p. 13.

12 K. S. Isles in *Ulster Under Home Rule*, pp. 116-17; see also the annual percentages and numbers of unemployment in Isles and Cuthbert, *An Economic Survey of Northern Ireland*, pp. 566, 577.

13 W. Black, 'Industrial Change in the Twentieth Century', in J. C. Beckett and R. E. Glasscock (ed.), *Belfast: The Origin and Growth of an Industrial City*, pp. 161-2.

14 Isles and Cuthbert in *Ulster Under Home Rule*, pp. 144-5.

15 Isles and Cuthbert, *An Economic Survey of Northern Ireland*, Table 28, pp. 606-7. Dr Black, in his essay on industrial change in Belfast in the twentieth century, gives the figures for service industries in Belfast alone as rising from 80,000 in 1926 to 100,000 in 1937. Sources are not given, but the dates suggest he is using the broader categories of the censuses of population; it is very possible that the whole total is greater than the number of insured people in the industries. For his estimate see J. C. Beckett and R. E. Glasscock (ed.), *Belfast: The Origin and Growth of an Industrial City*, pp. 163-4.

16 R. J. Lawrence, *The Government of Northern Ireland*, pp. 147-9.

17 Ibid., pp. 149-51. Figures in the text refer to 1924-39; in 1919-23, local authorities built 1,657 out of 2,155.

18 Ibid., chap. vii for a brief penetrating account of the state of public health in the province.

19 The rate of relief was doubled as a result.

20 R. J. Lawrence, op. cit., chap. ix, for the poor law in the six counties. See also J. W. Boyle, 'Industrial Conditions in the Twentieth Century', in

Ulster Since 1800, II, p. 133; J. J. Campbell, 'Between the Wars', in
Belfast: The Origin and Growth of an Industrial City, pp. 150-1.
21 R. J. Lawrence, op. cit., p. 38.

3. THE POLITICS OF SIEGE (pp. 715-27)

1 J. L. McCracken, 'Northern Ireland, 1921-66', in T. W. Moody and F. X.
Martin (ed.), *The Course of Irish History* (Cork, 1967), p. 315.
2 N. S. Mansergh, *The Government of Northern Ireland*, p. 230.
3 D. P. Barritt and C. F. Carter, *The Northern Ireland Problem* (London,
1962), p. 42.
4 St J. Ervine, *Craigavon: Ulsterman*, p. 516.
5 The whole subject has been exhaustively documented in a hitherto
unpublished doctoral thesis (Queen's University, Belfast) by S. Elliott,
'The Electoral System in Northern Ireland since 1920'.
6 J. L. McCracken, 'The Political Scene in Northern Ireland, 1926-37',
in F. MacManus (ed.), *The Years of the Great Test, 1926-39*, p. 155.
7 R. J. Lawrence, *The Government of Northern Ireland*, p. 65 and n. 1.
8 D. P. Barritt and C. F. Carter, *The Northern Ireland Problem*, p. 43.
9 J. M. Mogey, 'Ulster's Six Counties', in T. Wilson (ed.), *Ulster Under
Home Rule*, p. 9.
10 R. J. Lawrence, op. cit., p. 30.
11 K. S. Isles and N. Cuthbert, *An Economic Survey of Northern Ireland*,
pp. 211, 571.
12 The educational controversy can best be followed in D. P. Barritt
and C. F. Carter, *The Northern Ireland Problem*, chap. v, and R. J.
Lawrence, *The Government of Northern Ireland*, chap. vi. See also D.
Kennedy, 'Catholics in Northern Ireland, 1926-39', in F. MacManus (ed.),
The Years of the Great Test, pp. 140-2; and M. Wallace, *Northern
Ireland: 50 years of Self-Government* (Newton Abbott, 1971), pp. 102-7.
13 *Belfast Newsletter*, 13 July 1933. Lord Craigavon himself declared the
following year: 'We are a Protestant parliament and a Protestant
state . . .' (cited by J. J. Campbell in 'Between the Wars', in J. C.
Beckett and R. E. Glasscock (ed.), *Belfast: The Origin and Growth of an
Industrial City*, p. 152).
14 D. Kennedy, op. cit., p. 143.
15 Ibid., pp. 146-7; but see the criticisms by F. Newark in T. Wilson (ed.),
Ulster Under Home Rule, pp. 48-9 and note.
16 J. J. Campbell, op. cit., pp. 155-6.
17 D. Kennedy, op. cit., p. 146.
18 Cited in D. P. Barritt and C. F. Carter, *The Northern Ireland Problem*,
p. 45.

4. WAR AS A CATALYST (pp. 728-37)

1 For the statistics, which are strangely incomplete, see J. W. Blake,
Northern Ireland in the Second World War (Belfast, 1956), pp. 534-5.
2 A tribute to J. M. Andrews read out in the Northern Ireland House of
Commons (cited by R. J. Lawrence, *The Government of Northern
Ireland*, p. 64).

3 See Cyril Falls, 'Northern Ireland and the Defence of the British Isles',
  in *Ulster Under Home Rule*, chap. iv; also J. W. Blake, *Northern Ireland
  in the Second World War*, chaps. vii, viii and ix.
4 J. W. Blake, op. cit., pp. 232-3.
5 Ibid., pp. 238-9.
6 Cited in Lawrence, op. cit., p. 67.
7 J. W. Blake, op. cit., pp. 233-4.
8 For shipping figures see Blake, op. cit., Appendix II; aircraft production
  is dealt with in chap. ix of the same work and more briefly by Cyril
  Falls in *Ulster Under Home Rule*, pp. 87-8.
9 J. W. Blake, op. cit., p. 395.
10 Ibid., pp. 383-94.
11 Ibid., pp. 418-26.
12 K. S. Isles and N. Cuthbert, 'Economic Policy', in *Ulster Under Home
   Rule*, p. 141; see also the table on p. 291 of the authors' *An Economic
   Survey of Northern Ireland*.
13 J. W. Blake, op. cit., pp. 555-6, 413-18.
14 Ibid., p. 558.
15 Ibid., p. 410.
16 L. P. F. Smith, 'Recent Developments in Northern Irish Agriculture', in
   JSSISI (1947-52), xviii, p. 149.
17 J. W. Blake, op. cit., p. 432.
18 K. S. Isles, 'Economic Survey' in *Ulster Since 1800*, p. 118. According to
   the calculations of Isles and Cuthbert the money wage index for
   Northern Ireland showed a rise of one hundred per cent between
   1939 and 1948 compared with seventy-five per cent in Britain (*Ulster
   Under Home Rule*, p. 107).
19 J. W. Blake, op. cit., p. 434.
20 R. J. Lawrence, *The Government of Northern Ireland*, p. 70. This assurance was not made public until 1945, but a similar statement was read
   out in the Northern Ireland House of Commons in November 1943.

5. THE POLITICS OF WELFARE (pp. 738-59)

1 R. J. Lawrence, *The Government of Northern Ireland*, p. 88. Most of
  what has been said above is based on the extremely illuminating
  account of these matters in chap. v of Dr Lawrence's book.
2 *Financial Times*, 29 Aug. 1969, cited in P. Riddell, *Fire over Ulster*
  (London, 1970), pp. 185-6.
3 G. FitzGerald, *Towards a New Ireland*, pp. 161-66, 181-7.
4 R. J. Lawrence, op. cit., chap. vii. Even this, however, could not be
  carried through without controversy, for the leading Catholic hospital,
  the Mater, found itself, as a voluntary hospital outside the Health
  Service, ineligible for certain State grants. The resulting argument has
  continued in one form or another almost to the present day. (M.
  Wallace, *Northern Ireland*, pp. 112-16.)
5 Ibid., chap. viii; for the early beginnings of the Housing Trust see
  Ulster Year Book, 1950, pp. 233-4. Up to the early fifties, it has been
  suggested, the Northern Ireland government tended to stint somewhat on its domestic expenditure because of its obsession with the
  imperial contribution, but this could hardly be said to hold true of

the sixties (see K. S. Isles and N. Cuthbert in *Ulster Under Home Rule*, pp. 163-4). By September 1968 the total of new houses built since 1944 stood at 161,518 (*Disturbances in Ireland: Report of the Commission Appointed by the Governor of Northern Ireland*, Sept. 1969 (Cmd. 532), pp. 56-8), hereafter cited as *Cameron Commission: Report*).

6 Purchases by the British Ministry of Food at uniform prices were gradually modified after the war, but Northern Ireland farmers received, apart from the general subsidies, a special payment to offset their old bugbear, the transport differential.

7 K. S. Isles and N. Cuthbert, *An Economic Survey of Northern Ireland*, pp. 295, 297; also *Economic Development in Northern Ireland* (Cmd. 479), 1964 (reprinted 1967), p. 120; *Ulster Year Book, 1966-68*, p. 153.

8 K. S. Isles and N. Cuthbert, 'Economic Policy', in T. Wilson (ed.), *Ulster Under Home Rule*, p. 143.

9 T. P. Coogan, *Ireland Since the Rising*, pp. 294-5.

10 The relevant documents are *Belfast Regional Survey and Plan: Recommendations and Conclusions* (Cmd. 465), 1963; and *Economic Development in Northern Ireland* (Cmd. 479), 1965. For a convenient summary of the problem, see M. Wallace, *Northern Ireland*, chap. 5.

11 *Northern Ireland Development Programme, 1970-75*.

12 For the armed raids on Northern Ireland, see T. P. Coogan, *The I.R.A.*, chap. xiv; also D. P. Barritt and C. F. Carter, *The Northern Ireland Problem*, pp. 129-37; and J. Bowyer Bell, *The Secret Army* (London, 1970).

13 For economic discrimination see especially Barritt and Carter, op. cit., chap. vi, and for Catholics in higher education, chap. v of the same work. A survey of the Northern Ireland school population for 1963-4 (T. P. Coogan, op. cit., p. 301) suggests that the number of Catholics going to a university was 1,006 compared with 3,765 Protestants. This would give a Catholic proportion of about twenty-seven per cent. Most of these, no doubt, would have gone to Queen's University, but some may have gone to universities in the south.

14 The Londonderry situation is described in Coogan, op. cit., pp. 382-5 and in Barritt and Carter, op. cit., pp. 120-4; see also *Cameron Commission: Report*, pp. 57-9.

15 *Cameron Commission: Report*, p. 57.

16 Barritt and Carter, op. cit., pp. 120-4.

6. THE CONTINUING CRISIS (pp. 760-80)

1 See especially the 'key-note' speech he delivered at Pottinger in November 1962 when Minister of Finance. It is printed in T. O'Neill, *Ulster at the Crossroads* (London, 1969), pp. 32-40.

2 R. Rose, *Governing Without Consensus* (London, 1971), p. 213. Of the Catholics questioned only 14 per cent favoured union with the rest of Ireland, but it is probable that most of the other abolitionists who were vague about what they would put in the place of the border favoured reunification. To this it is perhaps worth adding that in March 1972 (on the very eve of direct rule) a *Sunday Telegraph* survey indicated that 82 per cent of Catholics asked and 66 per cent of Protestants asked were prepared to accept proposals which guaranteed Northern Ireland's existing link with Britain but also deliberately kept open the

possibility of future Irish reunification (*Sunday Telegraph*, 19 Mar. 1972).

3 Statement of Rory Brady; cited in *Sunday Times* 'Insight', *Ulster* (London, 1972, hereafter cited as *Sunday Times* 'Insight', *Ulster*), p. 21.

4 For the background to these events, see M. Wallace, *Drums and Guns: Revolution in Ulster* (London, 1970), pp. 89-98.

5 See chap. 4 of *Disturbances in Northern Ireland: Report of the Commission Appointed by the Governor of Northern Ireland* (Cmd. 532), Sept. 1969 (hereafter cited as *Cameron Commission: Report*. This careful inquiry, though criticised by some of those who were criticised in it, still remains the most reliable account of the events between October 1968 and April 1969.

6 Ibid., p. 84-6.

7 Miss Devlin's autobiography, *The Price of My Soul* (London, 1969), is essential reading for this phase of the developing crisis.

8 *Cameron Commission: Report*, pp. 80-4 and p. 123, Appendix xii.

9 For these and other attempts to implement the reform programme, see *A Commentary by the Government of Northern Ireland to Accompany the Cameron Report* (Cmd. 534), Sept. 1969, especially pp. 6-11. For the leisurely history of the official proposals for local government reform before the disturbances, see *The Reshaping of Local Government: Statement of Aims* (Cmd. 517), Sept. 1967. The accelerated pace of change can be judged by comparing this with a second White Paper, *The Reshaping of Local Government Further Proposals* (Cmd. 530), July 1969. It should be noted, to avoid confusion, that the decision to adopt one man, one vote was initially a decision of the Unionist party; it was only announced as government policy the following month, May 1969, i.e. *after* Captain O'Neill had fallen from power.

10 Some of the key exchanges between the two men are given in A. Boyd, *Brian Faulkner* (Tralee, paperback ed., 1972), chap. 7. This is an embittered and polemical book, but the author has a keen, journalistic instinct for the relevant facts.

11 *A Commentary by the Government of Northern Ireland to Accompany the Cameron Report* (Cmd. 534), Sept. 1969.

12 *Report of the Advisory Committee on Police in Northern Ireland* (Cmd. 535), Oct. 1969.

13 See the evidence collected in *Sunday Times* 'Insight', *Ulster*, pp. 164-8.

14 For this account I have drawn heavily upon the only detailed analysis which has yet appeared, *Sunday Times* 'Insight', *Ulster*, chaps. 1, 5 and 11.

15 For these events, see *Sunday Times* 'Insight', *Ulster*, chap. 12; also C. Cruise O'Brien, *States of Ireland* (London, 1972), chap. 10, which includes his diary of the events of that summer.

16 *Sunday Times* 'Insight', *Ulster*, pp. 238-42.

17. The offer was to be repeated later in the year in the context of further possible change. See *The Future Development of the Parliament and Government of Northern Ireland* (Cmd. 560), Oct. 1971.

18 For the press conference at which the new party was launched in Belfast, see *Irish Times*, 22 Aug. 1970.

19 *Sunday Times* 'Insight', *Ulster*, pp. 256-9. For the apologia which this incident evoked from the S.D.L.P., see H. Kelly, *Hhow Stormont Fell*, pp. 51-55.

20 A. Boyd, *Brian Faulkner*, p. 92, citing figures published by the National

Council of Civil Liberties. Another estimate, somewhat less and for a shorter period, but still bad enough, is given in *Sunday Times* 'Insight', *Ulster*, p. 269.

21 *The Future Development of the Parliament and Government of Northern Ireland* (Cmd. 560), Oct. 1971.

22 *Report of the Tribunal Appointed to Inquire into the Events on Sunday, 30th January 1972, which Led to Loss of Life in Connection with the Procession in Londonderry on that day* (H.L. 101, H.C. 220), April 1972, p. 38.

23 *The Times*, 13 Mar. 1972, interview with Mr William Hull, leader of the Loyalist Association of Workers.

Select Bibliography

An exhaustive bibliography of Ireland in the last hundred and twenty years would require a volume to itself. What follows is an attempt to provide some guidance to the existing sources, and especially to the very recent publications, for the reader who wishes to penetrate further into the subject. I have not attempted to list unpublished material, but I have included the more important newspapers and periodicals, as well as a selection from the relevant official publications. The sections devoted to secondary works are not intended to give total coverage, though they do contain the titles of the principal books and articles used in the preparation of this history; certain items with an unusually wide range of reference have been repeated in more than one section where appropriate. Many studies primarily relating to Great Britain also have a bearing on Irish affairs, but these have generally been omitted, except where a particularly close connection exists.

All books cited in the bibliography may be assumed to have been published in London, unless otherwise stated. Paperback editions are indicated by an asterisk. The abbreviations used are the same as those listed at the beginning of the book.

I. GENERAL HISTORIES

*Beckett, J. C., A Short History of Ireland, 3rd ed., 1966.
*Beckett, J. C., The Making of Modern Ireland, 1603-1923, 1966; paperback edition, 1969.
*Curtis, E., A History of Ireland, 6th ed., 1950; paperback ed., 1961.
Dudley Edwards. R., A New History of Ireland, Dublin, 1972.
*Inglis, B., The Story of Ireland, 1956; paperback ed., 1965.
McCaffrey, L. J., The Irish Question, 1800-1922, Kentucky, 1968.
*MacDonagh, O., Ireland, Englewood Cliffs, New Jersey, 1968.
*Moody, T. W., and Martin, F. X. (ed.), The Course of Irish History, Cork, 1967.
Norman, E. R., A History of Modern Ireland, 1972.
O'Brien, Máire and Conor Cruise, A Concise History of Ireland, 1972.
White, T. de V., Ireland, 1968.

2. BIBLIOGRAPHIES

Carty, J., Bibliography of Irish History, 1870-1911, Dublin, 1940.
Carty, J., Bibliography of Irish History, 1911-21, Dublin, 1936.
Eager, A. R., A Guide to Irish Bibliographical Material, 1964.
Hayes, R. J. (ed.), Manuscript Sources for the History of Irish Civilisation, 11 vols., Boston (Mass.), 1966.

Johnston, Edith M., *Irish History: a Select Bibliography*, revised ed., 1972.
Moody, T. W. (ed.), *Irish Historiography, 1936-70*, Dublin, 1971.
Writings on Irish history, 1936-   . A bibliography of current publications, published annually in *Irish Historical Studies* since 1938.

3. OFFICIAL PUBLICATIONS

Belfast Regional Survey and Plan: Recommendations and Conclusions (Cmd. 451), Belfast, 1965.

Bunreacht na h Eireann (Constitution of Ireland), Dublin, 1937.

Census of Population (Ireland), especially 1841, 1851, 1901 and 1911.

Census of Population (Irish Free State and Republic), 1926, 1936, 1946, 1951, 1956, 1961, 1966.

Census of Population (Northern Ireland), 1926, 1937, 1951, 1961, 1966.

Child Health Services: Report of a Study Group appointed by the Minister for the Gaeltacht, Dublin, 1971.

Comhairle na Gaelige, Local Government and Development Institutions for Health, 1967 (Pr. 171).

Commission on Higher Education, 1960-67: I Presentation and summary of report [Pr. 9326], Dublin, 1967; II Report, 2 vols. [Pr. 9588], Dublin, 1967.

Commission on the Restoration of the Irish Language: Summary, in English, of the Final Report [Pr. 7256], Dublin, 1963. Also: *The Restoration of the Irish Language: Government White Paper* [Pr. 8061], Dublin, 1965.

Constitution of the Irish Free State, Dublin, 1922.

Dáil Eireann. Minutes of Proceedings of the First Parliament of the Republic of Ireland, 1919-21: Official Record, Dublin, 1921.

Dáil Eireann. Official Report: Debate on the Treaty Between Great Britain and Ireland Signed in London on 6 December 1921, Dublin, 1922.

Dáil Eireann. Official Report for the Periods 16-26 August 1921 and 28 February to 8 June 1922, Dublin, 1922.

Dáil Eireann. Parliamentary Debates: Official Report, Dublin, 1922-

Disturbances in Northern Ireland: Report of the [Cameron] Commission Appointed by the Governor of Northern Ireland [Cmd. 532], Belfast, 1969. Also: *A Commentary by the Government of Northern Ireland to Accompany the Cameron Report* [Cmd. 534), Belfast, 1969.

Economic Development, Dublin, 1958.

Economic Development in Northern Ireland [Cmd. 479], Belfast, reprinted 1967.

Investment in Education: Report of the Survey Team Appointed by the Minister for Education in October, 1962 [Pr. 8311], Dublin, 1967.

Northern Ireland Development Programme, 1970-75. Belfast, 1970.

Northern Ireland Development Programme, 1970-75: Government Statement (Cmd. 547), Belfast, 1970.

Private Sessions of Second Dáil, Dublin, n.d. [1972].

Regional Studies in Ireland (the Buchanan Report, Dublin, 1968).

Report of the Consultative Committee on the Health Services, 1968. (Pr. 154), Dublin, 1969.

Report of the Advisory Committee on Police in Northern Ireland [Cmd. 535], Belfast, 1969.

Report of the Commission of Inquiry into Banking, Currency and Credit
[P. No. 2628], Dublin, 1938.
Reports of the Commission on Emigration and Other Population Problems,
1948-1954 [Pr. 2541], Dublin, 1956.
Report of the Council of Education: the Curriculum of the Secondary
School [Pr. 5996] Dublin, 1960-1961.
Report of the Boundary Commission, 1925, with introduction by G. J.
Hand, Shannon, Ireland, 1969.
Report of the Enquiry into Allegations against the Security Forces of
Physical Brutality in Northern Ireland, arising out of events on the 9th
August, 1971 (Cmd. 4823), 1971.
Report of the Joint Working Party on the Economy of Northern Ireland
[Cmd. 1835], 1962.
Report of the Royal Commission on the Rebellion in Ireland [Cmd. 8279],
H.C. 1916, xi, 171.
Report of the Select Committee on Industries (Ireland), H.C., 1884-5, ix.
Report of the Tribunal appointed to inquire into the events on Sunday,
30th January, 1972, which led to loss of life in connection with the
procession in Londonderry on that day, 1972.
Return of Evictions Known to the Constabulary in Each Year, 1849 to
1880, H.C. 1888, lxxvii, 725.
Reshaping of Local Government: Further Proposals (Cmd. 530), Belfast,
1969.
Review of 1971 and Outlook for 1972 (Pr. 2357), Dublin, 1972.
Sáorstát Eireann: Official Handbook, Dublin, 1932.
Seanad Eireann. Parliamentary Debates: Official Report. Dublin, 1922.
Second Programme for Economic Expansion, Parts I and II (Pr. 7239 and
Pr. 7670), Dublin, 1963-4. Also: Progress report for 1964 [Pr. 8244];
Progress report for 1965 [Pr. 8703]; Review of Progress, 1964-7 [Pr. 9949].
The Reshaping of Local Government: Further Proposals [Cmd. 530], Belfast,
1969.
Ulster Year Book, 1966-1968, Belfast, 1967.
Violence and Civil Disturbances in Northern Ireland in 1969 (Cmd. 566),
Belfast, 1972.

4. BIOGRAPHICAL AND OTHER WORKS OF REFERENCE

Crone, J. S., A Concise Dictionary of Irish Biography, Dublin, 2nd ed.,
1937.
Dictionary of American Biography, New York, 1928-37.
Dictionary of National Biography, 1908-9. Later volumes, of which the
most recent appeared in 1960, bring the dictionary as far as 1950.
Dod's Parliamentary Companion, 1852.
Thom's Irish Almanac and Official Directory, Dublin, 1844-
Who's Who, 1870-.
Who Was Who (1897-1916), 1920.
Who Was Who (1916-1928), 1929.

5. NEWSPAPERS AND PERIODICALS

An Claideamh Soluis.
Annual Register
Belfast Newsletter.
Belfast Telegraph.
Cork Examiner.
Freeman's Journal.
Irish Independent.
Irish Press.
Irish Times.
Irish Worker.
Leader.
Nation.
Round Table.
Sinn Féin.
Times.
United Ireland.
United Irishman.
Worker's Republic.

6. POLITICAL DEVELOPMENTS TO 1922

Béaslaí, P., *Michael Collins and the Making of a New Ireland*, 2 vols., Dublin, 1926.

Beaverbrook, Lord, *The Decline and Fall of Lloyd George*, 1963.

* Bennett, R., *The Black and Tans*, 1959; paperback ed., 1961.

* Blake, R., *Disraeli*, 1965; paperback ed., 1969.

Blythe, E., 'Birth Pangs of a Nation', *Irish Times*, 19 and 20 Nov. 1968.

Bourke, M., *John O'Leary*, Tralee, 1967.

* Bourke, M., *The O'Rahilly*, Tralee, 1967.

Boyce, D. G., *Englishmen and Irish Troubles*, 1972.

* Boyd, A., *Holy War in Belfast*, Tralee, 1969.

Boyle, J. W. 'The Belfast Protestant Association and the Independent Orange Order', in *IHS.*, xiii (Sept., 1962).

Boyle, J. W., (ed.), *Leaders and Workers*, Cork, n.d.

Boyle, J. W., 'Belfast and the Origins of Northern Ireland', in Beckett, J. C., and Glasscock, R. E. (ed.), *Belfast: The Origin and Growth of an Industrial City*, 1967.

Boyle, J. W., 'Connolly, the Citizens Army and the Rising', in Nowlan, K. B. (ed.), *The Making of 1916*, Dublin, 1969.

Brennan, R., *Allegiance*, Dublin, 1950.

* Bromage, M. C., *De Valera and the March of a Nation*, 1956; paperback ed., 1967.

Brown, T. N., *Irish-American Nationalism*, Philadelphia and New York, 1966.

Buckland, P. J., 'The Southern Irish Unionists and British Politics', in *IHS*, xii (Mar. 1961).

Buckland, P. J., *Irish Unionism*, 1 : *The Anglo-Irish and the New Ireland, 1885-1922* (Dublin and London, 1972).

Butt, I., *Home Government for Ireland*, Dublin, 1870.

Byrne, J. J., 'AE and Sir Horace Plunkett', in C. Cruise O'Brien (ed.), *The Shaping of Modern Ireland*, 1960.

* Caulfield, M., *The Easter Rebellion*, 1964; paperback ed., 1965.

Chavasse, M., *Terence MacSwiney*, Dublin and London, 1961.

Clarkson, J. D., *Labour and Nationalism in Ireland*, New York, 1925.

* Collins, M., *The Path to Freedom*, Dublin, 1922: paperback ed., Cork, 1968.

Colum, P., *Arthur Griffith*, Dublin, 1959.

* Comerford, M., *The First Dáil*, Dublin, 1971.

Connolly, J., *Socialism and Nationalism*. Introduction and notes by D. Ryan, Dublin, 1948.

Connolly, J., *Labour and Easter Week*. Introduction by William O'Brien, Dublin, 1949.

Connolly, J., *The Worker's Republic*. Introduction by W. McMullen, Dublin, 1951.

Corfe, T., *The Phoenix Park Murders*, 1968.

Coxhead, E., *Daughters of Erin*, 1965.

Curry, C. E., *The Casement Diaries and the Findlay Affair*, Munich, 1922.

Curtis, L. P., *Coercion and Conciliation in Ireland, 1880-92*, Princeton and London, 1963.

Curtis, L. P., *Anglo-Saxons and Celts*, New York, 1967.

Davis, Thomas, *Essays and Poems*, with a centenary memoir, Dublin, 1945.

Davitt, M., *The Fall of Feudalism in Ireland*, London and New York, 1904.

Devoy, John, *Recollections of an Irish Rebel*, New York, 1929.

Digby, M., *Horace Plunkett: An Anglo-American Irishman*, Oxford, 1949.

Dudley Edwards, O., and Pyle, F. (ed.), *1916: The Easter Rising*, 1968.

Dudley Edwards, O., 'Ireland', in Dudley Edwards, O., Evans, G., Rhys, J., and MacDiarmid, H., *Celtic Nationalism*, 1968.

Dudley Edwards, O. (ed.), *Conor Cruise O'Brien Introduces Ireland*, 1969.

Dudley Edwards, R., and Williams, T. Desmond (ed.), *The Great Famine*, Dublin, 1956.

Duggan, G. C., 'The Royal Irish Constabulary', in Dudley Edwards, O., and Pyle, F. (ed.), *1916: The Easter Rising*, pp. 91-9.

Ervine, St J., *Craigavon*, 1949.

Fanning, J. R., 'The Unionist Party and Ireland, 1906-10', in *IHS*, xv (Sept. 1966).

* Farrell, B., *The Founding of Dáil Eireann*, Dublin and London, 1971.

Fergusson, Sir J., *The Curragh Incident*, 1963.

FitzGerald, D., *Memoirs*, 1969.

Fogarty, L., *James Fintan Lalor: Patriot and Political Essayist, 1807-49*, Dublin and London, 1918.

Forester, M., *Michael Collins: The Lost Leader*, 1971.

Gallagher, F., *The Anglo-Irish Treaty*, 1965.

Gavan Duffy, Sir Charles, *The Legend of North and South*, 1886.

* Gleeson, J. *Bloody Sunday*, 1962; paperback ed., 1963.

Greaves, C. D., *The Life and Times of James Connolly*, 1961.

Greaves, C. D., *Liam Mellows and the Irish Revolution*, 1971.

Green, E. R. R., 'The Beginnings of Fenianism', and 'Charles Joseph Kickham and John O'Leary', both in Moody, T. W. (ed.), *The Fenian Movement*, Cork, 1968.

Greene, D., 'Michael Cusack and the Rise of the GAA', in O'Brien, Cruise, C. (ed.), *The Shaping of Modern Ireland*, 1960.
Griffith, Arthur, *The Resurrection of Hungary*, 3rd ed., Dublin, 1918.
Gwynn, D. R., *The Irish Free State, 1922-27*, 1928.
Gwynn, D. R., *The Life and Death of Roger Casement*, 1931.
Gwynn, D. R., *The Life of John Redmond*, 1932.
Gwynn, D. R., *Eamon de Valera*, 1933.
Gwynn, D. R., *The History of Partition, 1912-25*, 1950.
Hamer, D. A., *John Morley: Liberal Intellectual in Politics*, London, 1968.
Hamer, D. A., 'The Irish Question and Liberal Politics, 1886-1894', in *The Historical Journal*, xii, 3, (1969).
Hammond, J. L., *Gladstone and the Irish Nation*, 1938; new impression, 1964.
Harrison, H., *Parnell Vindicated*, 1931.
Hawkins, R., 'Dublin Castle and the Royal Irish Constabulary, 1916-1922', in Williams, T. Desmond, *The Irish Struggle, 1916-1926*, 1966.
Hayes-McCoy, G. A., 'A Military History of the 1916 Rising', in Nowlan, K. B. (ed.), *The Making of 1916*, Dublin 1969.
Henry, R. M., *The Evolution of Sinn Féin*, Dublin, 1920.
Hepburn, A. C., 'The Ancient Order of Hibernians in Irish Politics, 1905-14', in *Cithara*, x, No. 2 (St Bonaventure University, May 1971).
Hepburn, A. C., 'The Irish Council Bill and the fall of Sir Anthony MacDonnell in 1906-7', in *IHS*, xvii (Sept. 1971).
Hobson, B., *Ireland To-day and To-morrow, Tralee*, 1968.
Holt, E., *Portrait in Arms: The Irish Troubles, 1916-23*, 1960.
Horgan, J. J., *Parnell to Pearse*, Dublin, 1948.
Howard, C. H. D., 'The Parnell Manifesto of 21 November, 1885 and the Schools Question', in *EHR*, lxii (Jan. 1947).
Howard, C. H. D., (ed.), 'Joseph Chamberlain, W. H. O'Shea, and Parnell, 1884, 1891-2', in *IHS*, xiii (Mar. 1962).
Hurst, M., *Parnell and Irish Nationalism*, 1968.
Hyde, H. M., *Carson*, 1953.
Jenkins, R., *Asquith*, 1964.
Jones, T., *Whitehall Diary*, vol. iii, *Ireland, 1918-1925*, edited by K. Middlemass, 1971.
Kee, R., *The Green Flag*, 1972.
Laffan, M., 'The unification of Sinn Féin in 1917', in *IHS*, xvii (Mar. 1971).
Larkin, E., 'The Roman Catholic Hierarchy and the Fall of Parnell', in *Victorian Studies*, iv (June 1961).
Larkin, E., *James Larkin, Irish Labour Leader, 1876-1947*, 1965.
Larkin, E., 'Launching the Counter-attack: Part ii of the Roman Catholic Hierarchy and the Destruction of Parnell', in *Review of Politics*, xxviii (July 1966).
Le Roux, L. N., *Patrick H. Pearse*, trans. D. Ryan, Dublin, 1932.
Longford, Earl of, and O'Neill, T. P., *Eamon de Valera*, 1970.
Lucas, R., *Colonel Saunderson, M.P.: A Memoir*, 1908.
Lynch, D., *The IRB and the 1916 Rising*, ed. F. O'Donoghue, Cork, 1957.
Lyons, F. S. L., 'The Irish Unionist Party and the Devolution Crisis of 1904-5', in *IHS*, vi (Mar. 1948).
Lyons, F. S. L., *The Irish Parliamentary Party, 1890-1910*, 1951.
Lyons, F. S. L., *The Fall of Parnell, 1890-91*, 1960.

Lyons, F. S. L., *Parnell*, Dundalk (for Dublin Historical Association), 1963.

Lyons, F. S. L., 'The Passing of the Irish Parliamentary Party, 1916-18', in Williams, T. Desmond (ed.), *The Irish Struggle, 1916-1926*, 1966.

Lyons, F. S. L., 'Dillon, Redmond and the Irish Home Rulers', in Martin, F. X. (ed.), *Leaders and Men of the Easter Rising: Dublin 1916*, 1967.

Lyons, F. S. L., *John Dillon: A Biography*, 1968.

Lyons, F. S. L., 'Decline and Fall of the Nationalist Party', in Dudley Edwards, O., and Pyle, F., *1916: The Easter Rising*, 1968.

Lyons, F. S. L., 'The Two Faces of Home Rule', in Nowlan, K. B. (ed.), *The Making of 1916*, Dublin, 1969.

* Macardle, D., *The Irish Republic*, 1937; American edition, New York, 1965; paperback ed., 1968.

Macardle, D., 'Hyde, D. P. Moran and Irish Ireland', in Martin, F. X. (ed.), *Leaders and Men of the Easter Rising: Dublin, 1916*, 1967.

Macartney, D., 'The Church and Fenianism', in *University Review*, iv (Winter, 1967).

Macartney, D., 'Gaelic Ideological Origins of 1916', in Dudley Edwards, O., and Pyle, F., (ed.), *1916: The Easter Rising*, 1968.

Macartney, D., 'The Sinn Féin Movement', in Nowlan, K. B. (ed.), *The Making of 1916*, Dublin, 1969.

McCaffrey, L. J., 'Home Rule and the General Election of 1874', in *IHS*, ix (Sept. 1954).

McCaffrey, L. J., 'Irish Federalism in the 1870s: A Study in Conservative Nationalism', in *Transactions of the American Philosophical Society* (Philadelphia, 1962).

McCaffrey, L. A., *Daniel O'Connell and the Repeal Year*, Kentucky, 1966.

McClelland, V. A., *Cardinal Manning, His Public Life and Influence, 1865-92*, 1962.

McColl, R., *Roger Casement*, 1956.

McCready, H. W., 'Home Rule and the Liberal Party, 1890-1910', in *IHS* xiii (Sept. 1963).

MacDonagh, D., 'Plunkett and MacDonagh', in Martin, F. X. (ed.), *Leaders and Men of the Easter Rising: Dublin, 1916*, 1967.

McDowell, R. B., 'Edward Carson', in Cruise O'Brien, C. (ed.), *The Shaping of Modern Ireland*, 1960.

McDowell, R. B., *Alice Stopford Greene: A Passionate Historian*, Dublin, 1967.

McDowell, R. B., *The Irish Convention, 1917-18*, 1970.

Mac Giolla Choille, B. (ed.), *Intelligence Notes, 1913-16*, Dublin, 1966.

McHugh, R., 'Casement and German Help', in Martin, F. X. (ed.), *Leaders and Men of the Easter Rising: Dublin, 1916*, 1967.

McHugh, R., 'The Catholic Church and the Rising', in Dudley Edwards, O., and Pyle, F. (ed.), *1916: The Easter Rising*, 1968.

Mackey, H. O., *The Life and Times of Roger Casement*, Dublin, 1954.

Macintyre, A., *The Liberator: Daniel O'Connell and the Irish Party, 1830-1847*, 1965.

Mansergh, N. S., *The Irish Question, 1840-1921*, 1965, first published as *Ireland in the Age of Reform and Revolution*, 1940.

Mansergh, N. S., 'Ireland and the British Commonwealth of Nations: The Dominion Settlement', in Williams, T. Desmond, *The Irish Struggle, 1916-1926*, 1966.

Mansergh, N. S., 'John Redmond', in Cruise O'Brien, C. (ed.), *The Shaping of Modern Ireland*, 1960.

Marreco, A., *The Rebel Countess*, 1967.

Martin, F. X. (ed.), 'Eoin MacNeill on the 1916 Rising', in *IHS*, xii (Mar. 1961).

* Martin, F. X. (ed.), *The Irish Volunteers, 1913-1915*, Dublin, 1963.

Martin, F. X. (ed.), *The Howth Gun-running, 1914*, Dublin, 1964.

Martin, F. X. (ed.), *1916 and University College, Dublin*, Dublin, 1966.

Martin, F. X., 'The Origins of the Irish Rising of 1916', in Williams, T. Desmond (ed.), *The Irish Struggle, 1916-1926*, 1966.

Martin, F. X. (ed.), *Leaders and Men of the Easter Rising: Dublin 1916*, 1967.

Martin, F. X., '1916 – Myth, Fact and Mystery', in *Studia Hibernica* (Dublin, 1967).

Martin, F. X., 'The 1916 Rising – A *Coup d'Etat* or a "Bloody Protest"?' in *Studia Hibernica* (Dublin, 1968).

Moloney, W., *The Forged Casement Diaries*, Dublin, 1936.

Monteith, R., *Casement's Last Adventure*, Dublin, 1953.

Moody, T. W., 'The New Departure in Irish Politics', 1878-79', in Cronne, H. A., Moody, T. W., and Quinn, D. B. (ed.), *Essays in Honour of James Eadie Todd*, 1949.

* Moody, T. W., and Beckett, J. C. (ed.), *Ulster Since 1800*. 2 series. (1) A political and economic survey, 1955; (2) A social survey, 1957.

Moody, T. W., 'Parnell and the Galway Election of 1886', in *IHS*, ix (March 1955).

Moody, T. W., 'Thomas Davis and the Irish Nation', in *Hermathena*, cii (1966).

* Moody, T. W. (ed.), *The Fenian Movement*, Cork, 1968.

Mowat, C. L., *Britain Between the Wars, 1918-1940*, 1955.

Mowat, C. L., 'The Irish Question in British Politics, 1916-1922', in Williams, T. Desmond, *The Irish Struggle, 1916-1926*, 1966.

* Neeson, E., *The Civil War in Ireland, 1922-1923*, Cork, 1967; paperback ed., Cork, 1969.

Neeson, E., *The Life and Death of Michael Collins*, Cork, 1968.

Nevin, D., 'The Irish Citizen Army', in Dudley Edwards, O., and Pyle, F., *1916: The Easter Rising*, 1968.

Nicolson, Sir Harold, *King George V*, 1952.

Nowlan, K. B., *The Politics of Repeal, 1841-50*, 1965.

Nowlan, K. B., 'Dáil Eireann and the Army: Unity and Division, 1919-1921', in Williams, T. Desmond, *The Irish Struggle, 1916-1926*, 1966.

Nowlan, K. B., 'Tom Clarke, MacDermott and the IRB', in Martin, F. X., *Leaders and Men of the Rising: Dublin 1916*, 1967.

Nowlan, K. B. (ed.), *The Making of 1916*, Dublin, 1969.

* O'Brien, C. Cruise (ed.), *The Shaping of Modern Ireland*, 1960; paperback ed., 1970.

O'Brien, C. Cruise, *Parnell and His Party, 1880-90*, Oxford, 1957; corrected impression, 1964.

O'Brien, C. Cruise, 'The Embers of Easter', in Dudley Edwards, O., and Pyle, F., *1916: The Easter Rising*, 1968.

O'Brien, R. B., *The Life of Charles Stewart Parnell, 1846-1891*, 2 vols., 1898.

O'Brien, W., *An Olive Branch in Ireland*, 1910.

O'Brien, W. and Ryan, D. (ed.), *Devoy's Post Bag*, 2 vols., Dublin, 1948 and 1953.

O Broin, L., *Dublin Castle and the 1916 Rising*, Dublin, 1966.
O Broin, L., *Charles Gavan Duffy*, Dublin, 1967.
O Broin, L., *The Chief Secretary: Augustine Birrell in Ireland*, 1969.
O Broin, L., *Fenian Fever*, 1971.
* O'Connor, F., *The Big Fellow*, Dublin, revised ed., 1965; paperback ed., 1969.
O'Doherty, K., *Assignment – America*, New York, 1957.
* O'Donnell, P., *The Gates Flew Open*, 1932; paperback ed., Cork, 1965.
O'Donoghue, F., *No Other Law*, 1954.
O'Donaghue, F., *Tomás Mac Curtain*, 1958.
O'Donoghue, F., 'Plans for the 1916 Rising', in *University Review*, iii (1962).
O'Donoghue, F., 'Ceannt, Devoy, O'Rahilly and the Military Plan', in Martin, F. X., *Leaders and Men: Dublin 1916*, 1967.
O'Faoláin, S., *Constance Marciewicz*, 1934; paperback ed., 1968.
O'Farrell, P., *Ireland's English Question*, 1971.
O'Hegarty, P. S., *The Victory of Sinn Féin*, Dublin, 1924.
O'Hegarty, P. S., *A History of Ireland Under the Union, 1801-1922*, 1952.
O'Leary, John, *Recollections of Fenians and Fenianism*, 2 vols., 1896.
O Luing, S., *Art O Griofa*, Dublin, 1953.
O Luing, S., 'Arthur Griffith and Sinn Féin', in Martin, F. X., *Leaders and Men: Dublin, 1916*, 1967.
* O'Malley, E., *Army Without Banners*, 1936 (as *On Another Man's Wound*); in paperback under present title, 1967.
O'Shannon, C. (ed.), *Fifty Years of Liberty Hall*, Dublin, 1959.
O'Shea, K., *Charles Stewart Parnell: His Love-story and Political Life*, 2 vols. (1st ed.)., 1914.
* O Tuathaigh, G., *Ireland Before the Famine, 1798-1848*, Dublin and London, 1972.
Pakenham, F. (Lord Longford), *Peace by Ordeal*, 1935.
Pakenham, F., 'The Treaty Negotiations', in Williams, T. Desmond, *The Irish Struggle, 1916-1926*, 1966.
Palmer, N. D., *The Irish Land League Crisis*, New Haven, 1940.
Parmiter, G. de C., *Roger Casement*, 1936.
Paul-Dubois, L., *Contemporary Ireland*. Translated by T. M. Kettle, 1908.
Pearse, P. H., *Political Writings and Speeches*, Dublin, 1922.
Phillips, W. A., *The Revolution in Ireland, 1906-1923*, 2nd ed., 1926.
Plunkett, Sir Horace, *Ireland in the New Century*, 1904.
Ryan, A. P., *Mutiny at the Curragh*, 1956.
Ryan, D., *The Phoenix Flame: A Study of Fenianism and John Devoy*, 1937.
Ryan, D., *The Rising: The Complete Story of Easter Week*, Dublin, 3rd ed., 1957.
Ryan, D., 'Sinn Féin Policy and Practice', in Williams, T. Desmond, *The Irish Struggle, 1916-1926*, 1966.
Ryan, D., *The Fenian Chief*, Dublin, 1967.
* Ryan, D., 'James Stephens and Thomas Clark Luby', and 'John O'Mahony', in Moody, T. W. (ed.), *The Fenian Movement*, 1968.
Savage, D. C., 'The Origins of the Ulster Unionist Party, 1885-6', in *IHS*, xii (Mar. 1961).
Senior, H., *Orangeism in Ireland and Great Britain, 1795-1836*, 1966.
Shaw, F., 'The Canon of Irish History – a Challenge', in *Studies*, xli (summer 1972).
Sheehy-Skeffington, F., *Michael Davitt: Revolutionary, Agitator and Labour*

Leader, 1908; reprinted 1967.

Sheehy-Skeffington, O. S., 'Francis Sheehy-Skeffington', in Dudley Edwards, O., and Pyle, F. (ed.), *1916: The Dublin Rising*, 1968.

Singleton-Gates, P., and Girodias, M. (ed.), *The Black Diaries*, Paris, 1959.

Snoddy, O., *Comhghuai Uitne na Reabhtoide, 1913-1916* (Dublin, 1966).

Snoddy, O., 'The Midland Volunteer Force, 1913', in *Journal of the Old Athlone Society* (1968).

Steele, E. D., 'Ireland and the Empire in the 1860s: Imperial precedents for Gladstone's first Irish Land Act', in *The Historical Journal*, xi, 1 (1968).

Steele, E. D., 'J. S. Mill and the Irish Question: The Principles of Political Economy, 1848-1865', in *The Historical Journal*, xiii, 2 (1970).

Steele, E. D., 'J. S. Mill and the Irish Question: Reform and the Integrity of the Empire, 1865-1870', in *The Historical Journal*, xiii, 3 (1970).

Steele, E. D., 'Gladstone and Ireland' in *Irish Historical Studies*, xviii (Mar. 1970).

Stewart, A. T. Q., *The Ulster Crisis*, 1967.

Stewart, A. T. Q., 'Craig and the Ulster Volunteer Force', in Martin, F. X. (ed.), *Leaders and Men of the Easter Rising: 1916*, 1967.

Strauss, E., *Irish Nationalism and British Democracy*, 1957.

Sullivan, A. M., *New Ireland*, 2 vols., 1877.

Tansill, C. C., *America and the Fight for Irish Freedom, 1886-1922*, New York, 1957.

* Taylor, R., *Michael Collins*, 1958; paperback ed., 1961.

Taylor, R., *Assassination*, 1961.

Thornley, D. A., *Isaac Butt and Home Rule*, 1964.

Thornley, D. A., 'Patrick Pearse – The Evolution of a Republican', in Martin, F. X. (ed.), *Leaders and Men of the Easter Rising: Dublin, 1916*, 1967.

Thornley, D. A., 'Patrick Pearse and the Pearse Family', in *Studies*, xl (autumn-winter, 1971).

Travers, C. J., 'Seán Mac Diarmada, 1883-1916', in *Breifne* (1966).

Van Voris, J., *Constance de Markiewicz in the Service of Ireland*, Amherst (Mass.), 1967.

Wall, M., 'Partition: The Ulster Question, 1916-1926', in Williams, T. Desmond (ed.), *The Irish Struggle, 1916-1926*, 1966.

Wall, M., 'The Background to the Rising, from 1914 until the Issue of the Countermanding Order on Easter Saturday 1916', and 'The Plans and the Countermand: The Country and Dublin', in Nowlan, K. B. (ed.), *The Making of 1916*, Dublin, 1969.

Ward, A. J., 'Frewen's Anglo-American Campaign for Federalism, 1910-21', in *IHS*, xv (Mar. 1967).

Ward, A. J., 'America and the Irish Problem, 1899-1921', in *IHS*, xvi (Mar. 1968).

Ward, A. J., *Ireland and Anglo-American Relations, 1899-1921*, 1969.

White, T. de V., *The Road of Excess*, Dublin, Dublin [1946].

White, T. de V., 'Arthur Griffith', in O'Brien, C. Cruise (ed.), *The Shaping of Modern Ireland*, 1960.

White, T. de V., 'Mahaffy, the Anglo-Irish Ascendancy and the Vice-Regal Lodge', in Martin, F. X. (ed.), *Leaders and Men of the Easter Rising: Dublin, 1916*, 1967.

White, T. de V., *Kevin O'Higgins*, 1948; paperback ed., Tralee, 1967.

Whyte, J. H., *The Independent Irish Party, 1850-59*, Oxford, 1958.
Whyte, J. H., *The Tenant League and Irish Politics in the Eighteen-Fifties*, Dundalk, 1966.
Whyte, J. H., 'Political Problems, 1850-1860', in Corish, P. J. (ed.), *A History of Irish Catholicism*, Dublin, 1967.
Whyte, J. H., 'Revolution and Religion', in Martin, F. X., *Leaders and Men of the Easter Rising: Dublin 1916*, 1967.
* Younger, C., *Ireland's Civil War*, 1968; paperback ed., 1970.

7. POLITICAL DEVELOPMENTS SINCE 1922

A. From Free State to Republic

Aiken, F., *Speeches at the United Nations*, Dublin, 1958 to 1963.
* Bell, J. Bowyer, *The Secret Army*, 1970.
* Bromage, M. C., *De Valera and the March of a Nation*, 1956; paperback ed., 1967.
* Cohen, A., *The Irish Political Elite*, Dublin and London, 1972.
Coogan, T. P., *The I.R.A.*, 1970.
Coogan, T. P., *Ireland Since the Rising*, 1966.
Costello, J. A., *Ireland in International Affairs*, Dublin, n.d.
Dudley Edwards, O. (ed.), *Conor Cruise O'Brien Introduces Ireland*, 1969.
* Farrell, B., *Chairman or Chief?*, Dublin and London, 1972.
FitzGerald, G., *Towards a New Ireland*, 1972.
Gray, T., *Ireland's Answer*, 1966.
Gwynn, D. R., *The Irish Free State, 1922-7*, 1928.
Gwynn, D. R., *The History of Partition, 1912-1925*, Dublin, 1950.
Hancock, W. K., *Survey of British Commonwealth Affairs*, vol. i, Problems of Nationality, 1918-1936, London, 1937.
Harkness, D. W., *The Restless Dominion*, 1969.
Harrison, H., *Ireland and the British Empire*, 1937.
Harrison, H., *The Neutrality of Ireland*, 1941.
Hayes-McCoy, G. A., 'Irish Defence Policy, 1938-51', in Nowlan, K. B., and Williams, T. Desmond (ed.), *Ireland in the War Years and After, 1939-51*, 1969.
Hogan, V. P., *The Neutrality of Ireland in World War II*, Michigan, 1953.
Larkin, E., *James Larkin, Irish Labour Leader, 1876-1947*, 1965.
Longford, Earl of, and O'Neill, T. P., *Eamon de Valera*, 1970.
* Lyons, F. S. L., 'The Minority Problem in the 26 Counties', in MacManus, F. (ed.), *The Years of the Great Test, 1926-39*, Cork, 1967.
Lyons, F. S. L., 'The Years of Readjustment, 1945-51', in Nowlan, K. B., and Williams, T. Desmond (ed.), *Ireland in the War Years and After, 1939-51*, 1969.
McCracken, J. L., *Representative Government in Ireland, 1919-48*, 1958.
McInerney, M., 'Mr John A. Costello Remembers', part 4, in *Irish Times*, 7 Sept. 1967.
McInerney, M., 'Noel Browne: Church and State', in *University Review*, v (Summer, 1968).
* MacManus, F. (ed.), *The Years of the Great Test, 1926-39*, Cork, 1967.
Manning, M., *The Blueshirts*, Dublin and London, 1970.

* Manning, M., *Irish Political Parties*, Dublin and London, 1972.
Mansergh, N. S., *The Irish Free State: Its Government and Politics*, 1934.
Mansergh, N. S., *Survey of British Commonwealth Affairs: Problems of Imperial Policy*, 1931-39, 1952.
Mansergh, N. S. (ed.), *Documents and Speeches on British Commonwealth Affairs*, 1931-52, 1953.
Mansergh, N. S., 'Ireland and the British Commonwealth of Nations', in Williams, T. Desmond (ed.), *The Irish Struggle*, 1916-1926, 1966.
Mansergh, N. S., 'Ireland: External Relations 1926-1939', in MacManus, F. (ed.), *The Years of the Great Test*, 1926-39, Cork, 1967
Mansergh, N. S., 'Irish Foreign Policy, 1945-51', in Nowlan, K. B., and Williams, T. Desmond (ed.), *Ireland in the War Years and After*, 1939-51, 1969.
Mitchell, A., 'William O'Brien, 1881-1968, and the Irish Labour movement', in *Studies*, xl (autumn-winter, 1971).
Moss, W., *Political Parties in the Irish Free State*, Harvard, 1933.
Murphy, J. A., 'The Irish Party System, 1938-51', in Nowlan, K. B., and Williams, T. Desmond (ed.), *Ireland in the War Years and After*, 1939-51, 1969.
Nevin, D., 'Labour and the Political Revolution', in MacManus, F. (ed.), *The Years of the Great Test*, 1926-39, Cork, 1967.
Nowlan, K. B., 'President Cosgrave's Last Administration', in MacManus, F. (ed.), *The Years of the Great Test*, 1926-39, Cork, 1967.
* O'Brien, C. Cruise, *To Katanga and Back*, 1962; paperback ed., 1965.
O'Brien, C. Cruise, 'Ireland in International Affairs', in Dudley Edwards, O. (ed.), *Conor Cruise O'Brien Introduces Ireland*, 1969.
O'Brien, C. Cruise, *States of Ireland*, 1972.
O'Brien, William, *Forth the Banners Go*, edited by E. McLysaght, Dublin, 1969.
* O'Callaghan, S., *The Easter Lily*, 1956; paperback ed., 1967.
O'Sullivan, D., *The Irish Free State and its Senate*, 1940.
Pyne, P., 'The third Sinn Féin party, 1923-26', in *Economic and Social Review*, i (1969-70).
Shearman, H., *Anglo-Irish Relations*, 1948.
Stephan, E., *Spies in Ireland*, 1963.
Thornley, D., 'The Blueshirts', in MacManus, F. (ed.), *The Years of the Great Test*, 1926-39, Cork, 1967.
Viney, M., and Dudley Edwards, O., 'Parties and Power', in Dudley Edwards, O. (ed.), *Conor Cruise O'Brien Introduces Ireland*, 1969.
Wheare, K. C., *The Statute of Westminster*, 4th ed., 1949.
* White, T. de V., *Kevin O'Higgins*, 1948; paperback ed., 1967.
Williams, T. Desmond, 'De Valera in Power', in MacManus, F. (ed.), *The Years of the Great Test*, 1926-39, Cork, 1967.
Williams, T. Desmond (ed.), *The Irish Struggle*, 1916-1926, 1966.

B. Northern Ireland Under Home Rule

Armour, W. S., *Armour of Ballymoney*, 1934.
Barritt, D. P., and Carter, C. F., *The Northern Ireland Problem*, 1962.
Beckett, J. C., and Glasscock, R. E. (ed.), *Belfast: The Origin and Growth of*

An Industrial City, 1967.

Blake, J. W., *Northern Ireland in the Second World War*, Belfast, 1956.

* Boyd, A., *Holy War in Belfast*, Tralee, 1969.

* Boyd, A., *Brian Faulkner and the Crisis of Ulster Unionism*, Tralee, 1972.

* de Paor, L., *Divided Ulster*, 1970.

* Devlin, B., *The Price of My Soul*, 1969; paperback ed., 1969.

Dudley Edwards, O., *The Sins of our Fathers*, Dublin and London, 1970.

* Egan, B., and McCormack, V., *Burntollet*, 1969.

Elliot, R. S. P., and Hickie, J., *Ulster: a Case Study in Conflict*, 1971.

Ervine, St J., *Craigavon: Ulsterman*, 1949.

Falls, C., 'Northern Ireland and the Defence of the British Isles', in Wilson, T. (ed.), *Ulster Under Home Rule*, 1955.

Gwynn, D. R., *The History of Partition, 1912-1925*, Dublin, 1950.

Hastings, M., *Ulster 1969*, 1970.

* Heslinga, M. W., *The Irish Border as a Cultural Divide*, Assen, Neths., 1971.

Hyde, H. M., *Carson*, 1953.

* Kelly, H., *How Stormont Fell*, Dublin and London, 1972.

* Kennedy, D., 'Catholics in Northern Ireland, 1926-39', in MacManus, F. (ed.), *The Years of the Great Test, 1926-39*, Cork, 1967.

Kennedy, D., 'Ulster During the War and After', in Nowlan, K. B., and Williams, T. Desmond, *Ireland in the War ·Years and After, 1939-51*, 1969.

Lawrence, R. J., *The Government of Northern Ireland: Public Finance and Public Services, 1921-1964*, Oxford, 1965.

* Lyons, F. S. L., 'The Twentieth Century', in Moody, T. W., and Beckett, J. C. (ed.), *Ulster Since 1800*, second series, 1957.

* McCracken, J. L., 'Northern Ireland, 1921-66', in Moody, T. W., and Martin, F. X. (ed.), *The Course of Irish History*, Cork, 1967.

* McCracken, J. L., 'The Political Scene in Northern Ireland, 1926-57', in MacManus, F. (ed.), *The Years of the Great Test, 1926-39*, Cork, 1967.

McDowell, R. B., *The Irish Convention, 1917-18*, 1970.

Mansergh, N. S., *The Government of Northern Ireland*, 1936.

Mogey,, J. M., 'Ulster's Six Counties', in Wilson, T. (ed.), *Ulster Under Home Rule*, 1955.

* Moody, T. W., and Beckett, J. C. (ed.), *Ulster Since 1800*, 2 series; (1) a political and economic survey, 1955; (2) a social survey, 1957.

Newark, F. H., 'The Law and the Constitution', in Wilson, T. (ed.), *Ulster Under Home Rule*, 1955.

O'Neill, T., *Ulster at the Crossroads*, 1969.

Riddell, P., *Fire Over Ulster*, 1970.

Rose, R., *Governing Without Consensus*, 1971.

Rose, R., 'Ulster Politics: a Select Bibliography of Political Discord', in *Political Studies*, xx (June 1972).

Shearman, H., *Not an Inch: A Study of Northern Ireland and Lord Craigavon*, 1942.

* *Sunday Times* 'Insight Team', *Ulster*, 1972.

* Target, G. W., *Unholy Smoke*, 1969.

* *The Ulster Debate: Report of a Study Group of the Institute for the Study of Conflict*: papers by J. C. Beckett, Sir F. Catherwood, Lord Chalfont, G. FitzGerald, F. S. L. Lyons, R. Moss, 1972.

Wall, M., 'Partition: The Ulster Question, 1916-1926', in Williams, T. Desmond (ed.), *The Irish Struggle, 1916-1926*, 1966.

Wallace, M., *Drums and Guns: Revolution in Ulster*, 1970.
Wallace, M., *Northern Ireland: 50 Years of Self Government*, Newton
  Abbott, 1971.

8. GOVERNMENT AND LAW

Akenson, D. H., *The Irish Education Experiment: The National System of
  Education in the Nineteenth Century*, 1969.
Auchmuty, J. J., *Sir Thomas Wyse, 1791-1862: The Life and Career of an
  Educator and Diplomat*, 1939.
Auchmuty, J. J., *Irish Education, A Historical Survey*, 1937.
Balfour, G., *The Educational Systems of Great Britain and Ireland*, 1898.
Barrington, D., 'The Irish Constitution' in *Irish Monthly*, vols. 80, 81 and
  82 (1951-3).
Barritt, D. P., and Carter, C. F., *The Northern Ireland Problem*, 1962.
Bunreacht na h Eireann: Constitution of Ireland, Dublin, 1937.
Chubb, F. B., 'Vocational Representation and the Irish Senate', in *Political
  Studies*, ii (1954).
Chubb, B. (ed.), *A Source Book of Irish Government*, Dublin, 1964.
Chubb, B., *The Constitution of Ireland*, 1966.
Chubb, B., *The Government: An Introduction to the Cabinet System in
  Ireland*, 2nd (revised) ed., Dublin, 1968.
Chubb, B., *The Government and Politics of Ireland*, Stanford and London,
  1970.
Collins, J., *Local Government*, 2nd ed. by Roche, D., Dublin, 1963.
Costello, D., 'The Natural Law and the Constitution', in *Studies*, lv (1956).
Delany, V. T. H., 'The Constitution of Ireland, its origins and develop-
  ment', in *University of Toronto Law Journal*, xii (1957).
Delany, V. T. H., 'Fundamental Liberties in the Constitution of Ireland,'
  in *University of Malaya Law Review*, ii (1960).
Delany, V. T. H., *Christopher Palles*, Dublin, 1960.
Delany, V. T. H., *The Administration of Justice in Ireland*, 2nd ed.,
  revised by Grogan, V., Dublin, 1965.
Digby, M., *Horace Plunkett: An Anglo-American Irishman*, Oxford, 1949.
Farley, J., *Social Insurance and Social Assistance in Ireland*, Dublin, 1964.
Farrell, B., 'Dáil Deputies: the "1969 Generation" ', in *Economic and
  Social Review*, ii, No. 3 (1971).
Finlay, I., *The Civil Service*, Dublin, 1966.
FitzGerald, G., *State-Sponsored Bodies*, 2nd (revised) ed., Dublin, 1963.
FitzGerald, G., *Planning in Ireland*, Dublin and London, 1968.
Garvin, T., 'Continuity and Change in Irish Electoral Politics, 1923-1969',
  in *Economic and Social Review*, iii, No. 3 (1972).
Grogan, V., 'The Constitution and the Natural Law', in *Christus Rex*, viii
  (1954).
Grogan, V., 'Towards the New Constitution', in MacManus, F. (ed.), *The
  Years of the Great Test, 1926-39*, Cork, 1967.
Hensey, B., *The Health Services of Ireland*, Dublin, 1959.
Hoctor, D., *The Department: a History of the Department of Agriculture*,
  Dublin, 1971.
Hughes, J. L. J., 'The Chief Secretaries in Ireland', in *IHS*, viii (1952-3).
Kaim-Caudle, R., 'Social Security in Ireland and in Western Europe',
  Economic and Social Research Institute Paper, No. 20, Dublin, 1964.
Kaim-Caudle, R., *Social Policy in the Irish Republic*, 1967.

Kelly, J. M., *Fundamental Rights in the Irish Law and Constitution*, Dublin, 1961; second edition, Dublin, 1967.

Kelly, W. B., *Intermediate and University Education in Ireland*, London and Dublin, 1872.

Kohn, L., *The Constitution of the Irish Free State*, 1932.

Lawrence, R. J., *The Government of Northern Ireland: Public Finance and Public Services, 1921-1964*, Oxford, 1965.

McCracken, J. L., *Representative Government in Ireland: A Study of Dáil Eireann, 1919-48*, 1958.

McDowell, R. B., 'The Irish Executive in the Nineteenth Century', in *IHS*, ix (Mar. 1955).

McDowell, R. B., *The Irish Administration, 1801-1914*, 1964.

McElligott, T. J., *Education in Ireland*, Dublin, 1966.

McGrath, F., *Newman's University: Idea and Reality*, Dublin, 1951.

Mansergh, N. S., *The Irish Free State: Its Government and Politics*, 1934.

Mansergh, N. S., *The Government of Northern Ireland*, 1936.

Micks, W. L., *An Account of the Congested Districts Board of Ireland, 1891-1923*, Dublin, 1925.

Moody, T. W., 'The Irish University Question of the Nineteenth Century' in *History*, xliii (1958).

Moody, T. W., and Beckett, J. C., *Queen's Belfast, 1845-1949: The History of a University*, 2 vols., 1959.

O'Sullivan, D., *The Irish Free State and its Senate*, 1940.

A Page of Irish History. By the Jesuit Fathers, Dublin, 1930.

Rice, V., 'Education in Ireland', in Dudley Edwards, O. (ed.), *Conor Cruise O'Brien Introduces Ireland*, 1969.

Sáorstát Eireann: Irish Free State Official Handbook, Dublin, 1932.

Smyth, J. C., *The Houses of the Oireachtas*, 2nd (revised) ed., Dublin, 1964.

Sullivan, K., *Joyce Among the Jesuits*, New York and London, 1957.

Tierney, M. (ed.), *Struggle with Fortune: A Miscellany for the Centenary of the Catholic University of Ireland, 1854-1954*, Dublin, n.d.

9. THE ECONOMY

Armstrong, D. L., 'Social and Economic Conditions in the Belfast Linen Industry, 1850-1900', in *IHS*, vii (Sept. 1951), 263-7.

Barrington, T., 'A Review of Irish Agricultural Prices', in *JSSISI*, xv, (1926-7).

Beckett, J. C., and Glasscock, R. E. (ed.), *Belfast: Origin and Growth of An Industrial City*, 1967.

Black, R. D. C., 'The Progress of Industrialization, 1850-1920', in Moody, T. W., and Beckett, J. C. (ed.), *Ulster Since 1800*, first series, 1954.

Black, R. D. C., 'Sir James Pirrie', in O'Brien, C. Cruise (ed.), *The Shaping of Modern Ireland*, 1960.

Black, R. D. C., *Economic Thought and the Irish Question, 1817-1870*, Cambridge, 1960.

Black, W., 'Industrial Change in the Twentieth Century', in Beckett, J. C., and Glasscock, R. E. (ed.), *Belfast: Origin and Growth of an Industrial City*, 1967.

Bleakley, D., 'Industrial Conditions in the Nineteenth Century', in Moody,

T. W., and Beckett, J. C. (ed.), *Ulster Since 1800*, second series, 1957.

Bleakley, D. W., 'The Northern Ireland Trade Union Movement', in *JSSISI*, xix (1953-4).

Bourke, P. M. A., 'The Extent of the Potato Crop in Ireland at the Time of the Famine', in *JSSISI*, xix (1955-6).

Bourke, P. M. A., 'Uncertainties in the Statistics of Farm Size in Ireland, 1841-1851', in *JSSISI*, xx (1959-60).

Bourke, P. M. A., 'The Agricultural Statistics of the 1841 Census of Ireland: A Critical Review', in *Economic History Review*, 2nd series, xviii (1965).

* Boyd, A., *The Rise of the Irish Trade Unions, 1729-1970*, Tralee, 1972.

Boyle, J. W., 'Le développement du mouvement ouvrier irlandais de 1800 à 1907', in *Le Mouvement Social*, No. 52 (juillet-sept. 1965).

Boyle, J. W., 'Industrial Conditions in the Twentieth Century', in Moody, T. W., and Beckett, J. C. (ed.), *Ulster Since 1800*, second series, 1957.

Boyle, J. W. (ed.), *Leaders and Workers*, Cork, 1965.

Burn, W. L., 'Free Trade in Land: An Aspect of the Irish Question', in *Transactions of the Royal Historical Society*, 4th series, xxxi (1949).

Campbell, J. J., 'Between the Wars', in Beckett, J. C., and Glasscock, R. E. (ed.), *Belfast: Origin and Growth of an Industrial City*, 1967.

Clarkson, J. D., *Labour and Nationalism in Ireland*, New York, 1925.

Coe, W. E., *The Engineering Industry of the North of Ireland*, 1969.

Connell, K. H., *The Population of Ireland, 1756-1845*, Oxford, 1950.

Connell, K. H., 'Marriage in Ireland after the Famine: The Diffusion of the Match', in *JSSISI*, xix (1955-6).

Connell, K. H., *Irish Peasant Society*, 1968.

Connell, K. H., 'Peasant Marriage in Ireland: Its Structure and Development Since the Famine', in *Econ. Hist. Rev.*, 2nd series, xiv (1961-2).

Connolly, J., *Labour in Ireland*, new edition, with an introduction by O'Shannon, C., Dublin, 1960.

Coyne, W. P. (ed.), *Ireland: Industrial and Agricultural*, 1st ed., Dublin, 1901.

Cousens, S., 'Emigration and Demographic Change in Ireland, 1851-61' in *Econ. Hist. Rev.*, second series, xiv (1961-2).

Crotty, R. D., *Irish Agricultural Production: Its Volume and Structure*, Cork, 1966.

Cullen, L. M., 'Irish History Without the Potato', in *Past and Present*, No. 40 (July, 1968).

Cullen, L. M., *An Economic History of Ireland since 1660*, 1972.

* Cullen, L. M. (ed.), *The Formation of the Irish Economy*, Cork, 1969.

Cullen, L. M., *Life in Ireland*, 1968.

Drake, M., 'Marriage and Population Growth in Ireland, in *Econ. Hist. Rev.*, second series, xvi (1963).

Drake, M., 'The Irish Demographic Crisis of 1740-41', in Moody, T. W. (ed.), *Historical Studies*, vi (1968).

Dudley Edwards, R., and Williams, T. Desmond (ed.), *The Great Famine*, Dublin, 1956.

Fetter, F. (ed.), *The Irish Pound, 1797-1826*, 1955.

FitzGerald, G., *State-sponsored Bodies*, 2nd (revised) ed., Dublin, 1963.

FitzGerald, G., *Planning in Ireland*, Dublin and London, 1968.

Freeman, T. W., *Pre-famine Ireland: A Study in Historical Geography*, 1957.

Geary, R. C., 'Irish Economic Development Since the Treaty', in *Studies*, xl (Dec. 1951).

Goldstrom, J. M., 'The Industrialisation of the North-East', in Cullen, L. M. (ed.), *The Formation of the Irish Economy*, Cork, 1969.

Greaves, C. G., *The Life and Times of James Connolly*, 1961.

Green, E. R. R., *The Lagan Valley*, 1800-1850, 1949.

Green, E. R. R., 'Agriculture', in Dudley Edwards, O., and Williams, T. Desmond (ed.), *The Great Famine*, Dublin, 1956.

Green, E. R. R., 'Early Industrial Belfast', in Beckett, J. C., and Glasscock, R. E. (ed.), *Belfast: The Origin and Growth of an Industrial City*, 1967.

Green, E. R. R., 'Industrial Decline in the Nineteenth Century', in Cullen, L. M. (ed.), *The Formation of the Irish Economy*, Cork, 1969.

Grimshaw, T., 'A Statistical Survey of Ireland from 1840 to 1888', in *JSSISI*, ix (1889).

Hancock, W. K., *Survey of British Commonwealth Affairs, 1918-1939*, vol. 1, 1937.

* Healy, J., *The Death of an Irish Town*, 2nd ed., Cork, 1968.

Isles, K. S., 'Northern Ireland: An Economic Survey', in Moody, T. W., and Beckett, J. C. (ed.), *Ulster Since 1800*, first series, 1954.

Isles, K. S., and Cuthbert, N., 'Ulster's Economic Structure', in Wilson, T. (ed.), *Ulster Under Home Rule*, 1955.

Isles, K. S., and Cuthbert, N., *An Economic Survey of Northern Ireland*, Belfast, 1957.

Johnston, J., *Irish Agriculture in Transition*, Dublin, 1951.

Jones, E., *A Social Geography of Belfast*, 1960.

Larkin, E., *James Larkin, Irish Labour Leader, 1876-1947*, 1961.

Larkin, E., 'Economic Growth, Capital Investment and the Roman Catholic Church in Nineteenth Century Ireland', in *American Historical Review*, lxxii (Apr. 1967).

Lawrence, R. J., *The Government of Northern Ireland: Public Finance and Public Services, 1921-1964*, Oxford, 1965.

Lee, J., 'The Construction Costs of Early Irish Railways', in *Business History*, ix (1967).

Lee, J., 'The Provision of Capital for Early Irish Railways', in *IHS*, xvi (Mar. 1968).

Lee, J., 'Capital in the Irish Economy', and 'The Railways in the Irish Economy', both in Cullen, L. M. (ed.), *The Formation of the Irish Economy*, Cork, 1969.

Lee, J., 'Irish Agriculture', review article in *The Agricultural History Review*, xvii, part 1 (1969).

Lynch, P., and Vaizey, J., *Guinness's Brewery in the Irish Economy, 1759-1876*, Cambridge, 1966.

Lynch, P., 'The Social Revolution That Never Was', in Williams, T. Desmond (ed.), *The Irish Struggle. 1916-1926*, 1966.

Lynch, P., *The Irish Economy Since the War, 1946-51'*, in Nowlan, K. B., and Williams, T. Desmond (ed.), *Ireland in the War Years and After, 1939-51*, 1969.

Lynch, P., 'The Economic Scene', in Dudley Edwards, O. (ed.), *Conor Cruise O'Brien Introduces Ireland*, 1969.

Lynch, S. J., 'Land Purchase in Ireland,' in *JSSISI*, xlii (1912).

Lyons, F. S. L., 'The Economic Ideas of Parnell', in Roberts, M. (ed.), *Historical Studies*, ii (1959).

MacDonagh, O., 'Emigration During the Famine', in Dudley Edwards, R., and Williams, T. Desmond (ed.), *The Great Famine*, Dublin, 1956.

Matheson, R. E., 'The Housing of the People of Ireland During 1841-1901', in *JSSISI*, xi (1904).

Meenan, J., 'From Free Trade to Self-sufficiency', in MacManus, F. (ed.), *The Years of the Great Test, 1926-39*, Cork, 1967.

Meenan, J., 'The Irish Economy During the War', in Nowlan, K. B., and Williams, T. Desmond (ed.), *Ireland in the War Years and After, 1939-51*, 1969.

Meenan, J., *The Irish Economy since 1922*, Liverpool, 1970.

Milne, K., *A History of the Royal Bank of Ireland*, Dublin, 1964.

Mortished, R. J. P., 'The Industrial Relations Act, 1946', in *Public Administration in Ireland*, iii.

Munikanon, U., *The Use of State-sponsored Bodies in the Exploitation of the Natural Resources of Ireland, Unpublished Thesis*, Dublin, n.d.

Nevin, D., 'Labour and the Political Revolution', in MacManus, F., (ed.), *The Years of the Great Test, 1929-39*, Cork, 1967.

Nevin, D., 'Industry and Labour', in Nowlan, K. B., and Williams, T. Desmond (ed.), *Ireland in the War Years and After, 1939-51*, 1969.

Nevin, E., *Wages in Ireland, 1946-62*. Paper No. 12 of the Economic and Social Research Institute, Dublin, 1963.

Nowlan, K. B., and Williams, T. Desmond (ed.), *Ireland in the War Years and After, 1939-51*, 1969.

O'Brien, G., *Economic History of Ireland from the Union to the Famine*, 1921.

O'Brien, G., 'Industries', in *Sáorstát Eireann: Official Handbook*, Dublin, 1932.

O'Brien, J. A. (ed.), *The Vanishing Irish*, 2nd impression, 1955.

O'Carroll, B. M., and Attwood, E. A., *The Structure of the Food Industry in Ireland*, Economic Research Series, No. 4, An Foras Taluntais (August, 1962).

O'Donovan, J., *The Economic History of Live-stock in Ireland*, Cork, 1940.

Oldham, C. H., 'Economics of Industrial Revival in Ireland', in *JSSISI*, xii (1909).

Oldham, C. H., 'The History of Belfast Shipbuilding', in *JSSISI*, xii (1909).

Oldham, C. H., 'Changes in Irish Exports During Twelve Years', and 'Changes in Irish Exports', both in *JSSISI*, xiii (1919).

O'Mahony, D., *Industrial Relations in Ireland: The Background*, Paper No. 19 of the Economic and Social Research Institute, Dublin, 1963.

O'Mahony, D., *The Irish Economy*, 2nd ed., Cork, 1967.

O Núalláin, L., 'A Comparison of the Economic Position and Trend in Eire and Northern Ireland', in *JSSISI*, xvii (1942-7).

Pomfret, J. E., *The Struggle for Land in Ireland, 1800-1923*, Princeton, 1930.

Rebbeck, D., *The History of Iron Shipbuilding on the Queen's Island up to July, 1874*, unpublished doctoral thesis, Belfast, 1954.

Riordan, E. J., *Modern Irish Trade and Industry*, 1920.

Roberts, R., 'Trade Union Organisation in Ireland', in *JSSISI*, xx (1958-9).

Robinson, H. W., *A History of Accountants in Ireland*, Dublin, 1964.

Ross, M., *Personal Incomes by County, 1965*, Paper No. 49 of the Economic and Social Research Institute, Dublin, 1969.

Ryan, W. J. L., 'Measurement of Tariff Levels for Ireland', in *JSSISI*, xviii (1948-9).

Salaman, R. N., *The History and Social Influence of the Potato*, Cambridge, 1969.

Sáorstát Eireann: Official Handbook of the Irish Free State, Dublin, 1932.

Schrier, A., *Ireland and the American Emigration, 1850-1900*, Minneapolis, 1958.

Semmels, A. W., 'The External Commerce of Ireland', in *JSSISI*, xii (1909).

Shearman, H., 'State-aided Land Purchase Under the Disestablishment Act of 1869', in *IHS*, iv (Mar. 1944).

Smith, L. P. F., 'Recent Developments in Northern Irish Agriculture', in *JSSISI*, xviii (1947-52).

Solow, B., *The Land Question and the Irish Economy, 1870-1903*, Cambridge, Mass., and London, 1972.

Synnott, N. J., 'Housing of the Rural Population in Ireland', in *JSSISI*, ix (1904).

Thornley, D., 'The Development of the Irish Labour Movement', in *Christus Rex*, xviii (1964).

10. RELIGION AND THE CHURCHES

Akenson, D. H., *The Irish Education Experiment*, 1969.

Akenson, D. H., *The Church of Ireland: Ecclesiastical Reform and Revolution, 1800-1885*, New Haven and London, 1971.

Barkley, J. M., *A Short History of the Presbyterian Church in Ireland*, 1959.

Barritt, D. P., and Carter, C. F., *The Northern Ireland Problem*, Oxford, 1962.

Beckett, J. C., 'Ulster Protestantism', in Moody, T. W. and Beckett, J. C. (ed.), *Ulster Since 1800*, second series, 1957.

Beckett, J. C., 'Gladstone, Queen Victoria and the Disestablishment of the Irish Church, 1868-9', in *IHS*, xiii (Mar. 1962).

Bell, P. M. H., *Disestablishment in Ireland and Wales*, 1967.

Blanshard, J., *The Church in Contemporary Ireland*, Dublin, 1963.

Blanshard, P., *The Irish and Catholic Power*, London, 1964.

Connell, K. H., *Irish Peasant Society*, 1968.

Connery, D., *The Irish*, 1968.

Corish, P. (ed.), *A History of Irish Catholicism*, Dublin, 1967.

Corish, P., 'Political Problems, 1860-1878', in *A History of Irish Catholicism*, vol. 5, fascicule 3, Dublin, 1967.

* Corkery, J., 'Ecclesiastical Learning', in Corish, P. J. (ed.), *A History of Irish Catholicism*, vol. v, fascicule 9, Dublin, 1970.

Costello, N., *John McHale, Archbishop of Tuam*, Dublin, 1939.

* Cunningham, T. P., 'Church reorganization', in Corish, P. J. (ed.), *A History of Irish Catholicism*, vol. v, fascicule 7, Dublin, 1970.

Dudley Edwards, R., 'Church and State in Modern Ireland', in Nowlan, K. B., and Williams, T. Desmond (ed.), *Ireland in the War Years and After, 1939-51*, 1969.

Fennell, D., *The Changing Face of Catholic Ireland*, 1968.

Fitzpatrick, J. D., *Edmund Rice, Founder and First Superior General of* the Brothers of the Christian Schools of Ireland, Dublin, 1945.

Hurley, M. (ed.), Irish Anglicanism, 1869-1969. Dublin, 1970.

Johnston, T. J., Robinson, J. L., and Jackson, R. W., A History of the Church of Ireland, Dublin, 1953.

Kennedy, D., 'The Catholic Church', in Moody, T. W., and Beckett, J. C. (ed.), Ulster Since 1800, second series, 1957.

Kennedy, D., 'Catholics in Northern Ireland', in MacManus, F. (ed.), The Years of the Great Test, 1926-39, Cork, 1967.

* Kennedy, T. P., 'Church Building', in Corish, P. J. (ed.), A History of Irish Catholicism, vol. v, fascicule 8, Dublin, 1970.

Larkin, E., 'Church and State in Ireland in the Nineteenth Century', in Church History, xxxi (Sept. 1962).

Larkin, E., 'Economic Growth, Capital Investment and the Roman Catholic Church in Nineteenth Century Ireland', in American Historical Review, lxxii (Apr. 1967).

Latimer, W. T., A History of the Irish Presbyterians, 2nd ed., Belfast, 1902.

McCarthy, M. J. F., Priests and People in Ireland, Dublin, 1902.

Macartney, D., 'The Church and the Fenians', in University Review, iv (Winter, 1967).

McClelland, V. A., Cardinal Manning, His Public Life and Influence, 1865-92, 1962.

McGrath, F., Newman's University: Idea and Reality, 1951.

McHugh, R., 'The Catholic Church and the Rising', in Dudley Edwards, O., and Pyle, F. (ed.), 1916: The Dublin Rising, 1968.

McKevitt, P., 'Epilogue: Modern Ireland', in Corish, P. J. (ed.), A History of Irish Catholicism, vol. v, fascicule 10, Dublin, 1970.

MacRéamoinn, S., 'The Religious Position', in Dudley Edwards, O. (ed.), Conor Cruise O'Brien Introduces Ireland, 1969.

MacSuibhne, P., Paul Cullen and His Contemporaries, vol. iii, Naas, 1965.

Moody, T. W., and Beckett, J. C., Ulster Since 1800: A Social Survey History of a University, 2 vols, 1959.

Norman, E. R., The Catholic Church and Ireland in the Eighteen Sixties, Dundalk, 1965.

Norman, E. R., The Catholic Church and Ireland in the Age of Rebellion, 1859-1873, 1965.

* O'Faoláin, S., The Irish, revised paperback ed., 1969.

O'Riordan, M., Catholicity and Progress in Ireland, Dublin, 1906.

Phillips, W. A. (ed.), History of the Church of Ireland from the Earliest Times to the Present Day, vol. iii, 1933.

Plunkett, Sir H., Ireland in the New Century, 1904.

Seaver, G., John Allen FitzGerald Gregg, Archbishop, Dublin, 1963.

Senior, H., Orangeism in Ireland and Britain, 1795-1836, 1966.

* Shearman, H., How the Church of Ireland was Disestablished, Dublin, 1970.

Sheehy, M., Is Ireland Dying? 1968.

Viney, M., The Five Per Cent, Dublin, 1965.

Walsh, P. J., William J. Walsh, Archbishop of Dublin, Cork and Dublin, 1928.

Whyte, J. H., 'Political Problems, 1850-1860', in Corish, P. J. (ed.), A History of Irish Catholicism, vol. iii, fascicule 2, Dublin, 1967.

Whyte, J. H., '1916 – Revolution and Religion', in Martin, F. X. (ed.), Leaders and Men of the Easter Rising: Dublin 1916, 1967.

Whyte, J. H., *Church and State in Modern Ireland, 1923-1970*, Dublin and London, 1971.

II. SOCIETY AND CULTURE

Adams, M., *Censorship: The Irish Experience*, Dublin, 1968.
Arensberg, C., and Kimball, S. T., *Family and Community in Ireland*, 2nd York, 1937; reprinted, Gloucester, Mass., 1959.
Arensberg, C., and Kimball, S. T., *Family and Community in Ireland*, 2nd ed., Cambridge, Mass., 1968.
Atkinson, N., *Irish Education*, Dublin, 1969.
Beckett, J. C., and Glasscock, R. E. (ed.), *Belfast: The Origin and Growth of an Industrial City*, 1967.
Bell, S. H. (ed.), *The Arts in Ulster*, 1951.
Boyd, E. (ed.), *Standish O'Grady: Selected Essays*, Dublin, 1918.
Boyd, E., *Appreciations and Depreciations*, Dublin, 1918.
Boyd, E., *Ireland's Literary Renaissance*, new and revised ed., 1922; reprinted, Dublin, 1968.
Collis, M., *Somerville and Ross: A Biography*, 1967.
Colum, M., *Life and the Dream*, revised ed., Dublin, 1966.
Connell, K. H., *Irish Peasant Society*, Oxford, 1968.
Connery, D. S., *The Irish*, 1968.
* Corkery, D., *Synge and Anglo-Irish Literature*, paperback ed., Cork, 1966.
Coxhead, E., *Lady Gregory*, 1961.
Craig, M. J., *Dublin, 1660-1860*, Dublin and London, 1952.
Cullen, L. M., *Life in Ireland*, 1968.
Curran, C. P., *James Joyce Remembered*, 1968.
Curtis, L. P., *Anglo-Saxons and Celts*, New York, 1968.
Curtis, L. P., *Apes and Angels*, Washington and London, 1972.
Dillon, M., 'Douglas Hyde', in O'Brien, C. Cruise (ed.), *The Shaping of Modern Ireland*, 1960.
* Donoghue, D., *Yeats*, 1971.
Dudley Edwards, O. (ed.), *Conor Cruise O'Brien Introduces Ireland*, 1969.
Eglinton, J., *Irish Literary Portraits*, 1935.
Eglinton, J., *A Memoir of AE*, 1937.
Elliott, R., *Art and Ireland*, Dublin, n.d.
* Ellis-Fermor, U., *The Irish Dramatic Movement*, 2nd ed., 1954; paperback ed., 1967.
* Ellmann, R., *Yeats: The Man and the Masks*, 1949; paperback ed., 1961.
* Ellmann, R., *The Identity of Yeats*, 1954; paperback ed., 1964.
Ellmann, R., *James Joyce*, New York, 1959.
Ellmann, R., *Ulysses by the Liffey*, 1972.
Evans, E. E., *Irish Heritage*, 1942.
Evans, E. E., *Irish Folkways*, 1957.
Fay, G., *The Abbey Theatre, Cradle of Genius*, 1957.
Freeman, T. W., *Pre-famine Ireland: A Study in Historical Geography*, 1957.
Freeman, T. W., *Ireland: A General and Regional Geography*, 3rd ed., 1965.
* Gogarty, O. St J., *As I was Going Down Sackville Street*, 1937; paperback ed., 1954.

Greene, D., 'Michael Cusack and the Rise of the GAA', in O'Brien, C. Cruise (ed.), *The Shaping of Modern Ireland*, 1960.

* Greene, D. H., and Stephens, E. M., *J. M. Synge, 1871-1909*, New York, 1959; paperback ed., New York, 1961.

Gregory, Lady A. (ed.), *Ideals in Ireland*, 1901.

Gregory, Lady A., *Our Irish Theatre*, 1914.

Gregory, Lady A., *Hugh Lane's Life and Achievement*, 1921.

Gwynn, D. R., *Edward Martyn and the Irish Revival*, 1930.

Harvey, J., *Dublin, A Study in Environment*, 1949.

* Henn, T. R., *The Lonely Tower*, 1950; paperback ed., 1965.

Hone, J. M., *The Life of George Moore*, 1936.

* Hone, J. M., *W. B. Yeats, 1865-1939*, 1942; 2nd ed., 1962; paperback ed., 1965.

Howarth, H., *The Irish Writers: Literature under Parnell's Star*, 1958.

Humphreys, A. J., *New Dubliners: Urbanization and the Irish Family*, 1966.

Hyde, D., 'The Necessity for De-Anglicising Ireland', in Gavan Duffy, Sir G., Sigerson, G., and Hyde, D., *The Revival of Irish Literature*, 1894.

Hyde, D., *A Literary History of Ireland from the Earliest Times to the Present Day*, 1899; new ed., 1968.

Jackson, J. A., *The Irish in Britain*, 1963.

* Jeffares, A. N., *W. B. Yeats: Man and Poet*, 1949; paperback ed., 1962.

Jeffares, A. N., and Cross, K. G. W. (ed.), *In Excited Reverie*, London and New York, 1965.

Jones, E., *A Social Geography of Belfast*, 1960.

* Kaim-Caudle, P., *Social Policy in the Irish Republic*, 1967.

Loftus, R. J., *Nationalism in Modern Anglo-Irish Poetry*, Madison and Milwaukee, 1964.

Lyons, F. S. L., 'George Moore and Edward Martyn,' in *Hermathena*, xcviii (1964).

Macartney, D., 'D. P. Moran and Irish Ireland', in Martin, F. X. (ed.), *Leaders and Men of the Easter Rising: 1916*, 1967.

MacDonagh, T., *Literature in Ireland*, Dublin, 1916.

McElligott, T., *Education in Ireland*, Dublin, 1966.

McGrath, F., *Newman's University*, Dublin, 1951.

* McGrath, F., 'The University Question', in Corish, P. J. (ed.), *A History of Irish Catholicism*, vol. v, fascicule 6, Dublin, 1970.

MacManus, F., Imaginative Literature and the Revolution', in Williams, T. Desmond (ed.), *The Irish Struggle, 1916-1926*, 1966.

* MacManus, F., 'The Literature of the Period', in MacManus, F. (ed.), *The Years of the Great Test, 1926-39*, Cork, 1967.

MacNiece, L., *Collected Poems, 1925-1948*, 1949.

Malone, A. E., *Irish Drama*, 1929; reprinted New York, 1965.

Martin, A., 'Literature and Society, 1938-51', in Nowlan, K. B., and Williams, T. Desmond (ed.), *Ireland in the War Years and After, 1939-51*, 1969.

Meenan, J. (ed.), *Centenary History of the Literary and Historical Society of University College, Dublin, 1855-1955*, Tralee, n.d.

Mogey, J. M., *Rural Life in Northern Ireland*, 1950.

Moody, T. W., and Beckett, J C., *Queen's University, 1845-1949: The* (second series), 1957.

Moore, G., *Hail and Farewell*, Ebury ed., 1937.

Moran, D. P., *The Philosophy of Irish Ireland*, Dublin, 1905.
* Murphy, I., 'Primary Education', in Corish, P. J. (ed.), *A History of Irish Catholicism*, vol. v, fascicule 6, Dublin, 1970.
O'Brien, C. Cruise, 'Passion and Cunning', in Jeffares, A. N., and Cross, K. G. W. (ed.), *In Excited Reverie*, 1965.
*O'Connor, F., *An Only Child*, 1961; paperback ed., 1965.
* O'Casey, S., *Autobiographies*, 1939-54; combined paperback ed. (2 vols.), 1963.
O Catháin, S., 'Education', in *Studies*, xl (Dec. 1951).
O Catháin, S., 'Education in the New Ireland', in MacManus, F. (ed.) *The Years of the Great Test, 1926-39*, Cork, 1967.
O Cúiv, B., 'Education and Language', in Williams, T. Desmond (ed.), *The Irish Struggle, 1916-1926*, 1966.
O Cúiv, B. (ed.), *A View of the Irish Language*, Dublin, 1969.
O'Driscoll, R. (ed.), *Theatre and Nationalism in 20th Century Ireland*, 1971.
* O Faoláin, S., *The Irish*, 1948; revised paperback ed., 1969.
O'Farrell, S., 'The Changing Pattern of Irish Life', in *Studies* (Dec. 1951), xl.
O Suilleabháin, S. V., 'Secondary Education', in Corish, P. J. (ed.), *A History of Irish Catholicism*, vol. v, fascicule 6, Dublin, 1970.
O'Sulleahháin, S., *A Handbook of Irish Folklore*, Dublin, 1942.
O'Sullivan, D., *Irish Folk Music and Song*, Dublin, 1952.
O'Sullivan, T. F., *The Story of the GAA*, Dublin, 1916.
Plunkett, Sir H., *Ireland In the New Century*, 1904.
Praeger, R. Lloyd, *The Way That I Went*, Dublin, 1937.
Pritchett, V. S., *Dublin*, 1967.
Robinson, L. (ed.), *Lady Gregory's Journal, 1916-1930*, 1946.
Robinson, L., *Ireland's Abbey Theatre*, 1951.
Skelton, R., *The Writings of J. M. Synge*, 1971.
Stanford, W. B., and McDowell, R. B., *Mahaffy*, 1971.
Strickland, W. G., *A Dictionary of Irish Artists*, Dublin, 1913.
Synge, J. M., *Plays, Poems and Prose*, Everyman ed., 1941.
Thompson, W. I., *The Imagination of an Insurrection: Dublin, Easter 1916*, New York, 1967.
Tierney, M. (ed.), *Struggle with Fortune*, Dublin, n.d. [1954].
Ussher, A., *The Face and Mind of Ireland*, 1949.
Wade, A. (ed.), *Letters of W. B. Yeats*, 1954.
White, T. de V., *The Story of the Royal Dublin Society*, Tralee, 1955.
White, T. de V., *Ireland*, 1968.
White, T. de V., *The Anglo-Irish*, 1972.
Yeats, W. B., *Collected Poems*, 1952.
Yeats, W. B., *Autobiographies*, 1955.
Yeats, W. B., *Essays and Introductions*, 1961.
Zimmermann, G. D., *Songs of Irish Rebellion*, Dublin, 1967.

Index

Britain, Wolfe Tone's attitude to, 15, 28; and the Famine, 16-17, 42-3; Irish emigration to, 16, 38, 44-5, 123, 164, 622, 624, 685, 707, 732; and support for Church of Ireland, 17; and Catholic emancipation, 19, 72; and relations with the Vatican, 20-1; and disestablishment of Church of Ireland, 20-2, 142-8; and Irish industrial development, 55-60, 65, 67, 70, 583; and repression in Ireland, 30-1, 191-2, 217, 413, 415, 425-6; as market for Irish agriculture, 34, 37, 40, 43-4, 49, 56-7, 70, 526, 600, 611-14, 620-2, 623-4, 631-2; and administrative system for Ireland, 71-6, 480-2, 484; and Irish health policy, 76-9; and Land Commission, 80; and Board of Works, 81; and Irish education, 81-98, 224, 655; and growth in Irish incomes, 98-103; and 'Young Ireland', 104, 107, 109-13; and Chartism, 107; and Tenant League, 116-22; and Fenian movement, 127, 132, 134-7, 141-3; and 'Manchester Martyrs', 137; and Clerkenwell prison explosion (1867), 137, 142; and Home Government Association, 149-51; and Home Rule League, 152-8; and general election (1874), 152-5; and Land League, 169-74; and Kilmainham 'treaty', 175-6, 181; and Phoenix Park murders, 176, 192, 290; and Irish National League, 178-80; and general election (1885), 179-83, 287-8, 291; and Home Rule Bill (1886), 184-8, 196; and 'Plan of Campaign', 189-94; and trade union movement, 192, 271-2, 279, 283-4, 673, 677-8, 679-81, 720, 749; and Parnell's downfall, 195-203; and Home Rule Bill (1893), 202, 294; and Balfour's reforms, 204-7; and 'constructive Unionism', 207-23, 298-9; and Boer War, 248, 260; and general election (1906), 264, 296; and Liberal reforms (1906-9), 264-7; and constitutional crisis (1909-11), 266-9, 287, 297; and Home Rule Bill (1912), 301-10; and IRB, 315-18; and Ulster Volunteers, 321-3, 326-7; and Irish Volunteers, 322-3, 326; and Roger Casement, 324-6, 339-41, 352, 364, 377-8, 382; and First World War, 329, 339, 350, 359, 361-3, 376, 385, 392-3; and Easter Rising (1916), 351, 353, 359, 363-7, 372-82; and by-elections (1917), 383; and Convention in Ireland (1917-18), 386, 393; and East Cavan by-election (1918), 394-6; and 'German plot', 395-6; and general election (1918), 396-8, 400; and Declaration of Independence (1919), 401, 408; and Paris Peace Conference (1919), 401, 404; and suppression of Dáil Éireann (1919), 406; and War of Independence (1919-21), 408-13, 415-29; and Government of Ireland Act (1920), 413-14, 424-6, 451; and treaty negotiations

(1921), 427-38, 490; and Treaty of 1921, 438-49, 458-9, 471-2, 487, 511-23; and Provisional Government (1922), 451-3, 455-8, 460-1; and assassination of Wilson, 459-60; and Constitution of 1922, 471-2, 474, 478, 481-2, 536; and 'Treaty ports', 487, 522, 553-4, 705, 726; and Boundary Commission, 490-3; and 'Ultimate Financial Agreement' (1926), 495; and National League, 497; and Oath of Allegiance, 499, 506-7, 511-14, 526-7; and Commonwealth, 504-6, 563, 565-70; and Statute of Westminster, 509-10, 515-17; and Agreements of 1938, 522, 553-4; and land annuities, 526, 611-12, 614; and IRA bombings (1939), 534; and League of Nations, 550, 552, 553-4; and Second World War, 553-8, 589, 728-39; and Ireland Act (1949), 568, 738; and British Nationality Act (1948), 569; and Council of Europe, 591; and NATO, 591-2, 598; and Common Market, 597-8; and Irish social security system, 660, 661, 668, 670; and censorship, 686; and Northern Ireland, 695-8, 700-9, 713, 715-18, 725-39, 751-2, 767, 770n, 772-80
British Import Duties Act (1932), 612
British Liberation Society, 143
British Nationality Act (1948), 569
Brooke, Sir Basil, 725, 735-6, 748
Brookeborough, Lord see Brooke, Sir Basil
Browne, Dr Noel, social radicalism of, 560, 586; and connection with Clann na Poblachta, 560-1, 563; as Minister of Health, 563, 572, 576-9, 659n, 663, 683; and repeal of External Relations Act, 567n; and general election (1954), 580, 586; as member of Labour Party, 586
Broy, Eamonn, 529
Broy Harriers, the, 529, 530, 532
Brugha, Cathal, and Easter Rising (1916), 388, 462; and Sinn Féin, 391; and Irish Volunteers, 392, 395, 397, 410, 451; at first session of Dáil Éireann (1919), 400, 402, 404; at second session of Dáil Éireann (1919), 406; and IRA, 410, 411, 419; and War of Independence, 410-11, 419; his hostility to Collins, 411, 430-1; his attitude towards treaty negotiations (1921), 429-30, 430-1, 435, 438; and Treaty of 1921, 438-40; in Civil War, 462; mentioned, 428, 457, 636
Bruree, 384
Brussels Pact (1948), 591
Bryan, Colonel D., 416n
Buachalla, Domhnall Ua see Buckley
Buchanan Report, 642
Buckland, P. J., 292n
Buckley, D., 514, 518
Bunting, Major R., 764
Burke, Edmund, 488
Burke, T. H., 176
Burke, J. A., 485

855

Commonwealth [contd]
Imperial Conference (1930), 509; and Statute of Westminster, 509-10; Fine Gael's attitude to, 530, 531, 563; Clann na Poblachta's attitude to, 563, 565; secession of Ireland from, 566-70; tariff agreements within, 611-12; mentioned, 526, 549, 599, 676, 725

Commonwealth Conference (1948), 568-9

communications, and introduction of steamships, 57, 65, 101; and development of the railways, 58-9, 81, 101, 201-2; and expansion of the road system, 61, 206; and Board of Works, 81; and Coras Iompair Eireann, 618; in Northern Ireland, 705, 736, 744; mentioned, 52

communism, 502, 527-8, 591, 593, 595, 596, 674, 676n, 726; see also Marxism

Communist Party of Ireland, 502

Compton, Sir Edmund, 776n

Confederate Clubs, 124-6, 128

Congested Districts Board, 80, 101, 205-6, 211, 216, 218, 571, 606

Congo, the, 324, 415, 595, 596-7

Congress of Irish Trade Unions see trade union movement

Connaught, Protestant population of, 23; Tenant Protection societies in, 114; agricultural depression in, 165; IRB activities in, 318; unemployment in, 672; television in, 392n

Connell, Professor K. H., 20n-1n, 35n, 39n-40n, 52n

Connemara, 571

Connolly, James (critic), 242

Connolly, James (Labour leader), as socialist theoretician, 27-8, 273-6, 280-1, 285, 343-5, 372, 472, 502, 525, 675; influenced by Mitchel, 111; influenced by Lalor, 111; early life of, 273, 276; and Dublin Socialist Society, 273; and Irish Socialist Republican Party, 273-4; his part in the Easter Rising, 275, 280, 339, 342-8, 353-5, 366-70, 371, 374, 377; his work with Irish Transport and General Workers Union, 280, 283, 284, 286; and Irish Citizen Army, 285, 322n, 343, 346, 355; Pearse influenced by, 333, 343; and Proclamation of Independence, 342, 344-5, 370, 371, 376; and IRB, 347; and partition, 749; mentioned, 242, 401, 467, 533, 673, 676, 684, 721

Connolly, Nora see O'Brien, Nora Connolly

Conservative Party, and general election (1852), 117, 118; and general election (1858), 121; led by Disraeli, 141-2, 154-5; and disestablishment of Church of Ireland, 148; and Home Government Association, 148-50; and general election (1874), 152; and general election (1885), 180-3, 287-8; and Ashbourne Act, 181; and Home Rule Bill (1886), 187-8; and general election

(1892), 202; and growth of land purchase, 233; and general election (1906), 264; and constitutional crisis (1909-11), 266-8; and imperialism, 290; and devolution crisis (1904-5), 294-5; led by Bonar Law, 301; and Home Rule Bill (1912), 301-11; and treaty negotiations (1921), 433-4; and Northern Ireland, 697, 739, 761, 772, 778

Constitution (Amendment No. 17) Act (1931), 503

Constitution of the Irish Free State Act (1922), 471-3, 512-13

Constitution of 1922, 471-9, 481, 484-5, 498, 501, 511-19, 536, 542-7, 577, 637

Constitution of 1937, 518-22, 528, 536, 537-50, 577, 687, 689

Control of Manufactures Acts (1932-4) see industry

Conway, Cardinal, 548

Cooper, Major Bryan, 500

Cooper, Ivan, 763, 765, 775

co-operative societies, 101, 208-10, 215-16, 234

Cope, Alfred, 424

Coras an Trachtala, 573

Coras Iompair Eireann see communications

Coras na Poblachta, 560

Corish, Brendan, 580, 586

Cork, trade in, 55; population growth in, 62; education in, 86, 87, 88, 94, 96-8, 106, 124, 266, 651, 655, 656; Phoenix Society established in, 126; 1867 insurrection in, 136-7; and 'Plan of Campaign', 190; and Congested Districts Board, 206; co-operative societies in, 210; Celtic Literary Society established in, 247; O'Brien's stronghold in, 263, 267; trade union activities in, 272, 273, 278, 279; Irish Volunteers activities in, 353, 366; and Easter Rising (1916), 360, 364, 366, 377n; Collins's birth in, 387; murder of MacCurtain in, 413, 418; and War of Independence (1919-21), 413, 417, 419-20; and Civil War (1922), 464; local government in, 484; murder of Admiral Somerville in, 533; Milk Board in, 618; by-election in (1972), 588; and the Gaeltacht, 640n; welfare in, 661; housing in, 667n

Corydon, J. J., 136

Cosgrave, Liam, 580, 585, 593-4

Cosgrave, W. T., and Mansion House Committee, 390; and second session of Dáil Éireann (1919), 406, 407, 486; and Treaty of 1921, 439, 488-9, 509; member of Provisional Government (1922), 451; and Civil War, 466, 485, 488; and Constitution of 1922, 475, 478, 499; and Civic Guard, 480; leader of Cumann na nGaedheal, 484-5, 499-500; and general election (1923), 485; and Boundary Commission, 491, 492-3; concludes 'Ultimate Financial Agree-

ment' (1926), 495; and general election (June, 1927), 496, 497; and Electoral Amendment Act (1927), 499; calls general election (September, 1927), 499-501; defeated at general election (1932), 503-4, 510; and Statute of Westminster, 509; as leader of the opposition, 525-6; as Vice-President of United Ireland Party, 530; as President of United Ireland Party, 531; retirement of, 562; and the economy, 602, 607, 608, 609, 610; and censorship, 686; mentioned, 428, 512, 522-3, 528-9, 535, 676, 684
Costello, Declan, 585
Costello, John A., 562-8, 570-1, 572, 578, 579-81, 585, 750
Council of Action (1941), 679
Council of Agriculture, 213
Council of Civil Liberties see Northern Ireland
Council of Europe, 591, 598
Council of Ireland, 414, 424, 492-3, 695
The Countess Cathleen (Yeats), 238
County Management Act (1940) see local government
courts of law, 74-5, 408, 479-82, 512-13, 544, 588, 637, 698
Courts of Justice Act (1924), 481
Coventry, 534
Cowan, Captain Peadar, 564n
Cowper Commission, 188
Craig, Charles Curtis, 295n
Craig, Sir James, and Government of Ireland Act (1920), 424, 696; and general election (1921), 425; attitude of towards treaty negotiations (1921), 427, 433-8; on Boundary Commission, 434, 492, 715-16; and Special Powers Act (1922), 452; and Civil War, 454-5; achievement of, 705; views on proportional representation, 718; and general election (1938), 727, 728; and Second World War, 735; mentioned, 300-1, 309, 714, 719, 721, 725, 726, 741
Craig, William, 763, 764, 779
Craigavon, 747, 753
Craigavon, Lord see Craig, Sir James
Crawford, Major Frederick, 306, 308
Crawford, Robert Lindsay, 296, 297
Crawford, W. Sharman, 115
Crimes Act (1887), 189
Criminal Law Amendment Act (1935), 548
Croke, T. W., Archbishop of Cashel, 226
Cronin, Commandant E., 523, 531
Crozier, Brigadier-General E. F., 416, 419
Cullen, Cardinal Paul, on ultramontanism, 20-1; and higher education, 94-6; condemns Fenian movement, 129-32; on Church Act (1869), 146; mentioned, 119-20, 122
Cullen, Dr L. M., 35n, 38n, 56n
Cumann na mBann, 455n
Cumann na nGaedheal, 250-1, 255-6, 484-5, 493, 495-501, 503-4, 524, 527, 530

Cumann na Poblachta, 453, 455
Curragh, incident at, 308-9
Curran, C. P., 95
Currie, Austin, 762-3, 775
Curtis, Edmund, 693n
Curtis, Professor L. P., 222n
Cusack, Michael, 225-6

Dáil Éireann, First Dáil, 54, 400-8, 410, 421, 472, 635, 685, 777; Second Dáil, 426, 428-9, 451, 455, 457-8, 466-7, 534, 637; Treaty debates in, 436, 439-50, under Constitution of 1922, 473-9; MacNeill's resignation speech in, 491; under Constitution of 1937; 539-43; and repeal of External Relations Act, 564-8; and 'mother and child scheme', 574-9; mentioned, 486, 487, 488, 501, 513, 520, 523, 554, 586n, 592, 599, 611, 640, 654, 667, 679
Daily News, 415
Dairy Disposal Company, 618
Dalton, C. F., 489
Daly, Edward, 376-7
Daly, John, 255
Daly, P. T., 283, 318, 319
Davis, Thomas, 104-7, 112, 124, 126, 128, 133, 224, 228-9, 240-1, 243n, 248-9, 251, 442
Davitt, Michael, and position of wage-earners, 54; influenced by Lalor, 111, 163; early years of, 162-3; career as a nationalist, 163-7, 170, 171, 175, 178, 192, 197, 199, 200, 216, 270-1; and Wyndham Act (1903), 220
Déak, Franz, 251, 252
Declaration of Independence, by Dáil Éireann (1919), 400-1
'The de-Davisisation of Irish Literature' (Eglinton), 240
Defence of the Realm Act, 361
Democratic Programme of Dáil Éireann (1919), 54, 401-3, 472, 545, 588
Denieffe, Joseph, 125
Department of Agriculture and Technical Instruction, 31, 80, 86, 101, 213-16, 233, 264, 607
Derby, Edward Stanley, fourteenth Earl of, 117
Derby, Edward Stanley, seventeenth Earl of, 424
Derry, 353, 566, 588, 715, 727, 769; see Londonderry
Derry Apprentice Boys, 296
Derry Citizens Action Committee see Northern Ireland
Desart, Countess of, 474
Development Fund, 215
Devlin, Bernadette, M.P., 763, 770
Devlin, Joseph, 262, 277n, 296, 327, 394, 723-5
Devlin, Paddy, 775
Devoy, John, 122n, 134-5, 160-6, 318, 323, 334, 339, 340, 342, 350, 352, 395, 404, 421-2
Dickson, Thomas, 373

859

Dignan, Dr, Bishop of Clonfert, 575, 660n, 670-1

Dilke, Rt. Hon. Sir Charles, M.P., 180

Dillon, James, and creation of National Centre Party, 526; as Vice-President of United Ireland party, 530; and Second World War, 554n; and general election (1948), 561; as Minister of Agriculture, 562-3, 571, 580; and Health Act (1947), 576; as leader of Fine Gael, 585

Dillon, John, M.P., his opposition to Butt, 158, 168; and Land League, 169, 171-2, 174; organises 'Plan of Campaign', 188-93, 202-3; and Parnell's downfall, 198, 200; his hostility to Plunkett, 211, 212; and All-Ireland Committee, 212; and Wyndham Act, 220; on Sinn Féin movement, 257; and United Irish League, 261-2; and Irish Council Bill (1907), 265; and Budget crisis (1909), 267; and Home Rule Bill (1912), 309; and Irish Volunteers, 327; his relationship with Nathan, 362-3; on consequences of Easter Rising, 376-80, 381-2, 383; and Mansion House Conference (1918), 393-5; at East Cavan election (1918), 394-6; and general election (1918), 398; mentioned, 31, 110n, 176, 194n, 203, 222, 232, 271n

Dillon, John Blake, 104-5, 110

Dingle, 638

Disraeli, Benjamin, (later Earl of Beaconsfield), and Irish education, 96; his diagnosis of Irish question, 141, 142; and Home Rule movement, 154, 156

Dockers' Union see trade union movement

Document No. 2, 441-2, 443, 445n, 448-9, 512, 517

Doheny, Michael, 124, 125

Dolan, C. J., 257-8, 265

Donaghadee, 308

Donegal, county, education in, 88; and Congested Districts Board, 206; Unionists in, 294; and Boundary Commission (1925), 491; and Second World War, 556; emigration from, 622, 690; teachers' training colleges in, 638; and the Gaeltacht, 640n; mentioned, 147, 770

Doneraile, 210

Dowden, Edward, 223

Dowling, James, 396

Down, county, 62, 66, 300, 304, 360, 696, 712, 725

Downey, James, 778

Drake, Professor M., 39n

Drogheda, 190

Dublin, concentration of Protestant in, 23; housing in, 27, 546, 571, 667n; and Easter Rising (1916), 31, 339, 341-3, 349, 350-6, 357-8, 364-78, 381-2, 401; position of wage-earners in, 53, 54, 68-9; and expansion of communications, 58; as commercial centre; 59, 60; population growth in, 62, 101; ship building industry in, 66; manufacture of biscuits in, 67, 290n; liquor business in, 68, 253, 290n; appointment of stipendiary magistrates in, 75; and Dublin Metropolitan Police, 76; Model School established in, 85; education in, 85-7, 93-5, 97-8, 144, 225, 266, 647n, 651, 655-8; Tenant League formed in, 115; Catholic Defence Association formed in, 116; 1852 conferences in, 118; Cullen's career in, 119; Stephens's residence in, 126, 134; O'Leary's education in, 128; Lavelle's lectures in, 131; Devoy's imprisonment in, 134; 1867 insurrection in, 136-7; development of Home Rule movement in, 148-9, 154, 158, 165-6; and 1880 disturbances in, 170; Phoenix Park murders, 176; reaction to O'Shea divorce case in, 198-9; work of Department of Agriculture and Technical Instruction in, 213; co-operative movement headquarters situated in, 215; Land Conference (1902) held in, 218; Civil Service Academy set up in, 226; Society for the Preservation of the Irish Language founded in, 227; National Literary Society founded in, 228, 237; Dublin Hermetic Society founded in, 234; Synge's birth in, 236; Moore's and Joyce's departure from (1911), 245; Celtic Literary Society established in, 247; Oliver Bond Society established in, 247; Griffith's birth in, 248; agitation against visit of Edward VII to, 255; Dungannon Club established in, 255; United Irish League activities in, 265; trade unions and employers clash in, 271-2, 276-8, 281-6, 322, 333, 674-5, 679; Socialist Society established in, 273; Connolly's activities in, 297; Unionists in, 291, 299; Asquith's visit to, 304; Irish gun-running to, 310, 326-7; IRB activities in, 315, 316-17, 319-20, 341-2; and Irish Volunteers, 321n, 322-3, 324, 330-1, 341-2, 349, 364, 366-8, 387; Pearse's speeches in, 333, 387; effect of Easter rising upon, 359-80, 382; Dillon's residence in, 362; de Valera in, 388; Ashe's imprisonment in, 387; Collins's activities in, 388; and Mansion House Conference (1918), 394-5; Boland's activities in, 397; Barton's imprisonment in, 405; destruction of Customs House in, 408, 420, 427; 'Dáil Courts' in, 408; and War of Independence (1919-21), 412-13, 417-21, 423-4, 427; Smuts's visit to (1921), 426; and treaty negotiations (1921), 429-30, 432, 433, 435, 439, 441; and Irregulars seizure of buildings in (1922), 454-7, 461-2; during Civil War, 461-2, 486-7; and local government, 482, 484; and IRA mutiny (1924), 490; and assassination of O'Higgins, 498; IRA Phoenix Park raids in (1939), 534; during Second World War, 556, 589, 730; British embassy

Hume, John, 763, 765, 775
Hungary, 251-2, 593
Hunt Committee, *see* Northern Ireland
Hutcheson-Poe, Colonel, W. H., 218
Hyde, Douglas, 227-9, 235-6, 239n, 241, 336, 540, 635, 643; *see also Lovesongs of Connacht;* 'The Necessity of de-Anglicising Ireland'; *The Twisting of the Rope*
Hyland, W. J., 652n

The Idea of a·University (Newman), 94
Imperial Conference (1921), 505, 507, 510
Imperial Conference (1926), 508-9, 515, 516
Imperial Conference (1930), 509, 515
In the Shadow of the Glen (Synge), 241-4
Incorporated Society in Dublin for Promoting English Protestant Schools in Ireland, 82
Independent Labour Party, 202, 276, 279, 485
Independent Orange Order, 25n, 277n, 296, 297; *see also* Orange Order
Independent Republican Party, 497
Independent Television *see* television
India, 519, 549, 569
Industrial Advice and Enterprise Act (1964) *see* Northern Ireland
Industrial Advice and Enterprise Act (1967) *see* Northern Ireland
Industrial Alcohol Board, 618
Industrial Credit Company *see* industry
Industrial Development Authority *see* industry
Industrial Development (Encouragement of External Investment) Act (1958) *see* industry
Industrial Relations Act (1946) *see* trade union movement
Industrial Workers of the World, 280
Industries Development Acts (1945-53) *see* Northern Ireland
industry, nineteenth century developments in, 27, 54-70; linen, 27, 57, 60-4, 69, 101, 709-10, 731-2, 733, 748; shipbuilding, 27, 57, 64-7, 69, 101, 709-11, 731, 746n, 748; engineering, 27, 61, 64, 67, 101, 709-11, 731-2; and slow growth of trade union movement, 27-8, 270-2; concentrated in the north-east, 54-5, 60-2, 64-7, 101, 289-90, 715, 753; problems encountered by, 54-9; wool, 57, 64; cotton, 57, 63, 710, 731-2; brewing and distilling, 57, 67-8, 102, 290n, 601, 619; rope-making, 64, 710; biscuit manufacture, 67, 102, 290n, 601, 619; wage structures in, 68-9, 574, 620, 678, 735; building trade, 68, 69, 102, 270, 747; and Department of Agricultural and Technical Instruction, 80, 86; and Griffith's industrial policy, 253-7, 600, 610, 684-5; and First World War, 360-1; and Industrial Development Authority, 573; and

Whitaker Report, 583, 629; and export market, 599-602, 619, 620, 625, 748; and Tariff Commission, 610; and Anglo-Irish 'economic war', 611-14; and Control of Manufactures Act (1932-4), 615; and Industrial Credit Company, 615, 618; and Trade Loans (Guarantee) Amendment Act (1933), 615; state-sponsored bodies in, 616-19; and Second World War, 619, 622, 678, 730-2; in First Programme for Economic Expansion, 629-30; and Industrial Development (Encouragement of External Investment) Act (1958), 629; in Second Programme for Economic Expansion (1963-9), 631-2; and Third Programme for Economic Expansion, 633-4; in Northern Ireland, 702, 707, 709-11, 730-2, 745-8; mentioned, 559-60, 609
Inghinidhe na hEireann, 286
Inglis, Sir Robert, 94
Inniu, 643
Institute of Public Administration, 659
Intermediate Education Acts (1878, 1914, 1921) *see* education
Intermediate Education (Amendment) Act (1924) *see* education
Intoxicating Liquor Act (1927), 496
Investment in Education, 650n, 652
Invincibles, the, 176
Ireland, J. de Courcy, 352n
Ireland Act (1949), 568, 738
Ireland in the New Century (Plunkett), 209
Irish Agricultural Organisation Society *see* agriculture
Irish Amateur Athletic Association, 225, 226
Irish Archaeological Society, 225
Irish Association for Cultural, Economic and Social Relations *see* Northern Ireland
'Irish Brigade', 117, 118, 122
Irish Bulletin, 415
Irish Church Act (1869), 144-6, 148
Irish Church Temporalities Act (1833), 22
Irish Citizen Army *see* Citizen Army
Irish Confederation, 107, 109
Irish Congress of Trade Unions *see* trade union movement
Irish Convention (1917-18), 385-7, 393
Irish Council Bill (1907), 257-8, 264-5
Irish Education Act (1892) *see* education
Irish Federalism (Butt), 151
Irish Federation and Labour Union *see* trade union movement
Irish Felon, 111
Irish Free State, and ratification of Treaty, 439-50; and Civil War, 451-68, 485-9; and Constitution of 1922, 456-8, 466n-7n, 471-9, 501, 506-7, 512-13, 536, 542; Civil Service in, 479-80; police force in, 480-1; legal system in, 480-2, 514-17; local government in, 482-4; and general election (1923), 466n-7n, 485; law and order

Irish Free State [*contd*]
problem in, 486-90, 495-6, 498, 501-3, 523-4, 527-36; and Boundary Commission, 490-4; and land annuities question, 495, 511, 526, 611, 613-14; and general election (June 1927), 497-8; and Electoral Amendment Bill (1927), 498-9; and general election (September 1927), 500-1; and general election (1932), 503-4, 524-5; and the Commonwealth, 504-10, 516-22; and League of Nations, 507, 550-4; and removal of oath of allegiance, 511-14; and Constitution of 1937, 518-22, 536-50; trade union movement in, 524; economy of, 599-624

Irish Free State (Agreement) Act (1922), 507

Irish Free State (Constitution) Act (1922), 507

Irish Freedom, 258, 319, 328, 333, 362

Irish Homestead, 210

Irish Independent, 243, 263, 282, 352n, 375

Irish Labour Party *see* Labour Party, Irish

Irish language, and nineteenth century education, 86, 88, 91-2, 224-5; and twentieth century education, 88-9, 229, 331, 635-40, 645-6, 649, 651; Gaelic League and, 88, 227-30, 239; and Young Ireland, 112; and Phoenix Society, 126; Hyde's championship of, 227-9, 235, 241; and Society for the Preservation of the Irish language, 227; Moran's championship of, 230-3; Griffith's attitude towards, 249, 250; Pearse's work for, 330-3, 635; de Valera's attachment to, 384; and Constitution of 1937, 539; and Constitution of 1922, 637; in civil service, 637; and the Gaeltacht, 636, 638-43; and Language Freedom movement, 639n; and Irish-speaking population, 644-5; and television, 691; mentioned, 317, 682, 685

Irish Life Assurance Company, 618

Irish Literary Society, 228, 230, 237

Irish Literary Theatre, 238, 241-2

Irish Loyal and Patriotic Union, 291-2

Irish Nation League, 379n, 390, 391

Irish National Aid Association, 382, 388

Irish National Land League, 167-71, 174, 175-6, 200, 216, 217

Irish National League, 178, 188, 189, 261

Irish National Literary Society, 228, 237

Irish Neutrality League, 339

Irish Peasant, 239n, 258

Irish People, 128, 129, 131, 134

Irish Press, 503

Irish Protestant, 296

Irish Race Convention (1919), 404

Irish Reform Association, 220-2

Irish Republic, Wolfe Tone's vision of, 15, 28, 247; Fenians and, 28, 122-38; 142, 247; in 1916, 28, 111, 368-70;

Young Ireland and, 109, 110-11, 113; Sinn Féin and, 248-9, 250; advocated by Dungannon clubs, 255, 316, 324; Connolly's views on, 273-5, 281, 286, 343-4, 348n; development of, 315-20, 322, 329-58; Pearse's doctrine of, 330-9, 344-5, 348n, 570; revival of (after 1916), 381-99; declaration of (1919), 400-2; fight for (1919-21), 409-23; Civil War and, 440-68; and aftermath of Civil War, 494-8, 501-5, 523-4, 531-6, 683-4; achievement of, 559-70; pressures for in Northern Ireland, 716-17, 725, 751-3, 760-80

Irish Republican Army, and Dáil Éireann, 410-12, 425; and War of Independence (1919-21), 410-14, 416-21, 423, 427; and Treaty of 1921, 440, 450-1, 461, 489; and IRB, 440, 489; concerned in border incidents (1922), 452-3, 454, 457; in civil war (1922-3), 453, 461-7, 488, 532; and Army Convention (1922), 454; and activities of anti-Treaty Irregulars (1922-3), 454-6, 462-7, 485; Collins–de Valera 'pact' (1922) and, 457-8; involved in assassination of Wilson, 459-60; Army mutiny (1924) and, 488-90; and Army Convention (1925), 494; attacks on Civic Guard by (1926), 495-6; recruitment of, 502; 'executions' by (1931), 502-3; declared an illegal organisation (1931), 503; and general election (1932), 503, 523-4; and general election (1933), 527; and National Guard, 529; in conflict with Republican Congress, 532-3; declared an illegal organisation (1936), 533; and Spanish Civil War, 533; involved in bomb outrages (1939), 533-6, 556; during Second World War, 556-7; Sean McBride's connection with, 560, 580-1; and arms raids (1952), 580-1; and trade union movement, 676, 726; and 'offensive' against Northern Ireland (1956-62), 752, 761; and activities in Northern Ireland (1960s-70s), 587-8, 761, 768-73, 774-9; mentioned, 401, 582, 676n, 684, 716

Irish Republican Brotherhood, foundation of, 125; clerical opposition to, 126-7; enrolling of sodiers in, 134; Biggar's allegiance to, 156; expulsion of Biggar and Power from, 158, 160; linked with Clan na Gael, 161, 164, 318, 319; Davitt's allegiance to, 163; Yeats's connection with, 237, 242; Griffith and, 249n; Hobson's connection with, 255, 315-17, 328; McCullough's role in, 255, 315-17, 318; and Sinn Féin movement, 257, 258, 381, 388-9; and the Irish Volunteers, 309-10, 320, 322, 328, 330, 342, 346, 363, 364, 388, 392; MacDermott's connection with, 315, 316-17, 319, 343; and Dungannon clubs, 316; constitution of, 317-18; MacDonagh and, 331; and annual commemoration of Wolfe

Recess Committee, 211, 213
Redmond, John, M.P., supported by
  Parnellites, 202-3, 260; and All-Ireland
  Committee, 212; and Land Conference
  (1902), 218, 220, 263; D. P. Moran's
  comments on, 232; parliamentary
  talents of, 260-1; personality of, 260-1;
  and United Irish League, 260-2, 265;
  and general election (1900), 262;
  opposed by Healy, 263, 265-7; opposed
  by O'Brien, 263, 265-7; and Irish
  Council Bill (1907), 265; and budget
  crisis (1909), 267-8; and Parliament
  Act (1911), 269; and Irish Volunteers,
  286n, 309, 310, 327-8, 329-30, 341; and
  Home Rule Bill (1912), 302-4, 306-7,
  309-10; and First World War, 310, 329,
  361; and Government of Ireland Act
  (1914), 310-11, 379-80; and National
  Volunteers, 330, 349; and relationship
  with Nathan, 362; and Easter Rising
  (1916), 378-9; opposed by Sinn Féin,
  383, 386; and Irish Convention
  (1917-18), 385; mentioned, 30,
  258, 320, 333, 361, 393, 433, 489, 495,
  497
Redmond, Captain William, M.P., 499
Removal of Oath Act (1933), 513-14, 527,
  536
Renunciation Act (1783), 252
Representative Church Body, 144
Republican of Ireland Act (1948), 567
Republican Congress, 532-3
Restoration of Order in Ireland Act
  (1920), 417
The Resurrection of Hungary (Griffith),
  251-2, 257
Ribbon Societies, 262n
Ribbonism, 129
Rice, Sir Cecil Spring, 325
Rice, Rev. Edmund, 82
Rice, Mary Spring, 325
Rice, Vincent, 500
Richardson, Sir George, 305
The Riddle of the Sands (Childers), 325
Ring, 640n
Ritchie, John, 65
Ritchie, William, 65
roads see communications
Roberts, Field Marshal Earl, 305
Robinson, Sir Henry, 73
Robinson Seumas, 409
Rochdale, 115
Rolleston, T. W., 228, 237
Rome, 119, 120, 129-30, 529
Rooney, William, 229, 238, 248-9
Roosevelt, Franklin D., President, 555
Roscommon, county, 206, 227, 236, 382,
  389, 526
Rose, Professor Richard, 450n
Rosebery, Earl of, 264
Rosscarbery, 126
Rosse, Earl of, 91
Royal Free Schools, 90
Royal Irish Academy, 224, 225n
Royal Irish Constabulary, functions of,
  75-6, 409; and Easter Rising (1916),

349 364, 366, 375, 377n; and War of
  Independence (1919-21), 409-10, 412-
  13, 415-20; and Black and Tans,
  415-20, 452; Auxiliary Division of,
  416-20, 452; disbandment of, 452;
  payment of pensions to, 495, 611;
  mentioned, 480, 560, 699
Royal Ulster Constabulary see Northern
  Ireland
Rugby, Lord, 554-5, 567n
Russell (AE), 210, 215, 234-7, 245
Russell, George William see Russell (AE)
Russell, Lord John, 42
Russell, Sean, 450, 532, 534, 556-7
Russell, T. W., 215, 218, 296-7
Russia, 243 and see Soviet Union
Russo-Turkish War (1877), 158
'Ruthless Warfare' (Blythe), 397-8
Ryan, Dr Dermot, 690
Ryan, Desmond, 122n, 239n, 368, 388
Ryan, Frank, 556-7
Ryan, Dr James, 368, 584
Ryan, Dr Mark, 255
Ryan, W. P., 239, 240, 258

Sadleir, John, 117-19, 121
St Helen's, 162
Salisbury, Marquess of, and coercion, 31,
  181, 183; and Home Rule, 181-2, 187
Salvidge, Sir Archibald, 434
Sandycove, 324
Saoirse?, 644
Saor Eire, 502, 503, 532, 560
Saunderson, Colonel E. J., M.P., 211,
  212, 218, 291, 292, 296, 299
Sayers, Peig, 643
School Attendance Act (1926), 647
School Attendance Bill (1942), 544
Schwabe, G. C., 65
Scotland, in economic competition with
  Ireland, 61; and educational links with
  Ireland, 93; Irish emigration to, 123,
  732; and Irish Home Rule movement,
  150; and Ulster Loyalist Anti-Repeal
  Union, 292; IRB activities in, 318;
  mentioned, 65, 702, 739
Second International, 676
Second Economic Programme see Second
  Programme for Economic Expansion
Second Programme for Economic Expan-
  sion (1963), 631-3
Second World War, and Irish marriage-
  rate, 46; outbreak of, 535; and League
  of Nations, 552-3; emigration during,
  603, 622-3; and economic developments, 616-17, 619, 622-5, 628; and
  education, 655, 656; and welfare,
  659-63, 669, 670; and trade union
  movement, 678; and Northern Ireland,
  709, 713, 726, 728-38; mentioned,
  479-80, 549
Seely, Colonel J. E. B., 308
Sexton, James, 278
Shamrock, 225
Shannon Free Airport Development
  Company, 642

Shawe-Taylor, Captain John, 217-18, 219n, 233
Sheehy-Skeffington, Francis, 95, 373, 378, 382
Sigerson, Dr George, 228n; *see also Bards of the Gael and the Gall; Poets and Poetry of Munster*
The Singer (Pearse), 338
Sinn Féin, 257, 362
Sinn Féin League, 256
Sinn Féin movement, development of, 203, 256-9, 265; D. P. Moran's comments on, 231; Edward Martyn's allegiance to, 236; and hostility to Larkin, 279; Countess Markievicz's allegiance to, 286; and Dungannon clubs, 316; Sean MacDermott's work for, 316; O'Rahilly's work for, 320; Ceannt's membership of, 341n; opposes British Army recruitment, 360; and Easter Rising (1916), 375, 381, 388-9; and by-elections (1917), 383, 635; and Irish Convention (1917-18), 386-7; and Liberty League, 389-90; de Valera's election to presidency of, 391-2; and anti-conscription campaign (1918), 393-5, 398; and East Cavan by-election (1918), 394-6; Boland's work for, 397; and general election (1918), 398-400, 406, 724; and foundation of Dáil Éireann, 400-1, 405-8; and local elections (1920), 407; in War of Independence (1919-21), 409, 413, 414-15, 417, 418n, 424; and Government of Ireland Act (1920), 413; and Restoration of Order in Ireland Act (1920), 417; and general election (1921), 425, 724-5; and treaty negotiations (1921), 456; and Provisional Government (1922), 453; effect of Collins-de Valera 'pact' (1922) upon, 457-8; and general election (1923), 485, 486; O'Higgins's connection with, 486; de Valera's break with, 494-5; and general election (June 1927), 497; and general election (September 1927), 500; and general election (1957), 582; and I R A, 769, 772; and Common Market, 598; mentioned, 30, 229, 330, 375, 534, 751
The Sinn Féin Policy (Griffith), 256-7
Skelton, Dr O. D., 509
Skibbereen, 126
'Skirmishing Fund', 161
Sligo, county, 199, 206, 227, 236, 286, 500
Sloan, T. H., 296-7
Smith, Adam, 610
Smith, Erasmus, 90, 91
Smith, F. E. (later Earl of Birkenhead), 303, 430, 434, 437, 445
Smith-Barry, A. H., *see* Barrymore, Lord
Smuts, General Jan, 426, 505-6, 507-8
Smyllie, R. M., 500
Social and Democratic Labour party, 588, 775-6, 778, 780

Social Code (International Union of Social Studies), 545
Social Services Agreement (1949) *see* Northern Ireland
Social Welfare Act (1948), 663, 669
Social Welfare Act (1952), 663, 669
socialism, James Connolly and, 27-8, 273-7, 278-9, 285, 343-5, 371, 472, 502, 525, 675, 721; Catholic Church and, 127, 129, 525, 673; Pearse's attitude to, 333; and Saor Eire, 502; and welfare state, 739
Socialist Party of Ireland, 281
Society for Promoting the Education of the Poor in Ireland *see* Kildare Place Society
Society for the Preservation of the Irish Language, 227
Society of Friends, 547
Solemn League and Convenant, 305, 319
Soloheadbeg, 409
Some Experiences of an Irish R.M. (Somerville and Ross), 533
Somerville, Admiral, 533
Somerville, Edith, 75, 533; *see also Some Experiences of an Irish R.M.*
South Africa, 247, 260, 319 426, 444, 491, 504-8, 515, 518
South Dublin, Sir Horace Plunkett's constituency, 211, 215
'The Sovereign People' (Pearse), 344-5, 401
Soviet Union, 591, 592-3, 595, 674
Spain, 533, 553; *see also* Spanish Civil War
Spanish Civil War, 531, 533, 553 556n
Special Powers Act (1922), 452, 698-9, 761, 774
The Spectator, 415
Spencer, Earl, 264
Spender, Captain Wilfred, 305
Spindler, Karl, 350-2
Squad, the, 412-13
Stack, Austin, 411, 427-30, 439, 443, 462
Statute of Westminster (1931), 509-10, 515-17
Steed, Wickham, 415
Stephens, James, 123-9, 133-6
Stephenson, John, *see* MacStiofaín, Sean
Stewart, Delia, 157
Stokes, Whitley, 225
Stopford, Rev. E. A., 323
Strasbourg, 591
Suez crisis (1956), 593
Sullivan, Alexander Martin, 126-7, 134
Sunday Independent, 357, 365, 566-7
Supreme Court of Judicature Act (1877), 74n
Swanzy, District Inspector, 413
Sweetman, Gerald, 580, 583
Swift, Jonathan, 248, 253
syndicalism, 275, 280, 333
Syllabus of Errors, 129, 144
Synge, John Millington, 235-7, 241-5; *see also The Playboy of the Western World*